VIEW OF

OHIO,

'72

CHURCHES:

G. St. Bonifacius, Catholic. J. First Baptist.
H. St. Mary's, Catholic. K. Lutheran.
I. Methodist Episcopal. L. German M. E.

REFERENCES:

17. City Brewery, H. Plock.
18. Piqua Brewery, Schmidlapp & Bro.
19. Spring Street Brewery, Schneyer & Son.
20. J. F. Hummel's Marble Works.
21. John Graef's Wagon Shop.
22. John Reedy's Plow and Wagon Shop.
23. B. F. Jacob's Lumber Yard.
24. Planing Mill, Sash and Door Factory.
    I. J. Whitlock.

25. Planing Mill, Sash and Door Factory,
    A. A. McCandless.
26. Tress Hoop Factory, E. H. Butterfield.
27. Livery Stable, J. H. H. Spiker.
28. Carriage Factory, R. P. Spiker.
29. City Oil Mill, W. W. Wood.
30. Agricultural Machine Shop,
    O. Ferrall, Daniels & Co.
31. Conover's Opera House.

An Encyclopedia

of

Piqua, Ohio

James C. Oda

M.T. Publishing Company, Inc.
Evansville, Indiana
2007

The room décor is typical of a sitting room in 1900 Piqua.

M.T. Publishing Company, Inc.
P.O. Box 6802
Evansville, Indiana 47719-6802
www.mtpublishing.com

First Printing: December 2007
Second Printing: April 2008

This book is dedicated to my father, *Harry R. Oda* (1912-1995) who taught me to love history in all its many facets, forms and twists

Graphic Designer: Alena L. Kiefer

Library of Congress Control Number:
2007935664

ISBN: 978-1932439-83-0

Printed in the
United States of America

Table of Contents

This shows a Ladies' Day at the young men's summer campout in about 1905.

INTRODUCTION

The purpose of this book is to provide an overview of the history of Piqua, Ohio and the immediate territory surrounding the community. While as many topics as possible have been addressed, it is not practical to cover every aspect of a community's history.

The inspiration for this publication came from a Library local history project entitled, *Piqua and Miami County, A Primer of Community History* written by James Oda and Linda Grimes and published in 1991. The *Primer* material was the start of this book with additional material coming from area newspapers, archival collections in the Flesh Public Library and other record collections in the city and select microfilm materials.

It is certainly appropriate to take a moment to thank the many people that have helped make this project possible. The staff of the Local History Department of the Flesh Public Library has over the years compiled a great deal of information that has been very useful in producing the *Encyclopedia*. These wonderful staff people include Mary Scott, Barb Sanderson, Rachel Cron, Diedre Douglas, Sherry Furrow, Greg Herroon, Steve Greg-

gerson, LeAnn Werling, Gary Meek, Linda Zollinger, Thaleia Maher, Heather Zirkle, Amy Peters, Larry Fickenwirth, Megan Chapman, Barbara Lemmer, and Sharon Watson. Eleanor Thoma, a Local History Department volunteer, was responsible for organizing a number of very important archival collections used in the *Encyclopedia*. The Library secretary, Beth Hole has provided countless hours of typing, copying and editing. Gary Meek has done an outstanding job in preparing and scanning the photographs used in the book. He also was instrumental in the editing of this publication. Lorna Swisher, manager of the Mainstreet Piqua program, has been both encouraging and energetic in getting this book published. The members of the Piqua Bicentennial Committee have provided numerous topic suggestions as well as constructive criticism. Catherine Jane Bell Oda, my lovely wife, has been a source of inspiration and support through the many months of this project. She put up with not only the long hours this project took but also with the constant chattering of a local historian who thought each piece of Piqua's history should and must be discussed at great length.

James C. Oda

September 2007

View looking southwest on the 300 block of North Main Street in the late 1940's.

The students of the Madison Avenue School are shown in about 1903.

Almanac

Dairyman Blaine Statler is shown with his milk wagon prior to 1910.

The W.P. Orr Linseed Oil Company mill was located in the one hundred block of South Main Street next to the Miami & Erie Canal.

ALMANAC
INTRODUCTION

*T*he Almanac section of this work provides an alphabetically arranged selection of historical topics, events and individuals. Emphasis has been placed first on local Piqua topics, then Miami County, early Ohio and finally national topics. This section concentrates on areas where a limited amount of material has been published or when the primary or secondary sources are rare or difficult to use. This section was not intended to be used as a complete local history, nor was an emphasis placed on extensive historical interpretation. The format of the Almanac is that of a simple compilation. The section is by no means complete and suggestions for additional material will always be welcomed. The use of **bold** within the descriptive paragraphs indicates that more information is available elsewhere in the *Encyclopedia*.

ACCOUNTANTS, PUBLIC

Until after **World War I**, there were no publicly advertised public accountants in Piqua. In 1921 the Ideal Business School offered auditing, accounting systems, and income tax reports to local citizens. The following year J. P. Decker opened an accounting office in the Piqua National Bank building. Decker was one of the city's first advertised certified public accountant working in the public arena. He was followed by the P. R. Goering & Company managed by Robert J. Ashforth in 1923 and in 1930 by the Lybrand, Ross Bro. & Montgomery Co. managed by Ralph F. Gunter. SEE ALSO: Patron p. 259

ADENA CULTURE

During the prehistoric Woodland period, the Adena culture (500 B.C. to 1 A.D.) developed and flourished in the Ohio River Valley. The Adena built burial and effigy mounds. The best known effigy may be seen in Adams County (Serpent Mound). These people lived in small village sites consisting of ten or more circular houses (18 to 60 feet in diameter) surrounded by a wall 4 to 5 feet high. The Adena engaged in hunting, gathering, and maize agriculture. Individual artifacts included pottery, pipestone effigy pipes, copper beads, rings and sheets, mica sheets, engraved redstone tablets, side-notched projectile points, drilled gorgets, and bone needles and awls. The Adena Culture declined and was followed by the **Hopewell Culture**. SEE ALSO: Woodland Period.

AEROVENT FAN COMPANY

The firm began in 1926 as the Piqua Electric Service Company. One of its first products was the new "Airway" exhaust fan developed by Niels Lundgard. Two of the company's employees Lundgard, a designer and pattern maker and sales manager Martin Bauer took the fan production side of the business and created a new business, the Aerovent Fan Company in 1932. The new company moved to East Main Street in Shawnee and began producing fans with five employees. Aerovent moved its location to 700 East Ash in 1934. A future president of the company, Ray Loffer, joined Aerovent in 1937 as a shipping clerk. The company created an agricultural division in the early 1940's in Michigan. The firm continued to expanded with new factory and office space in the 1950's, additional factory space in 1964 (55,000 square feet) and 1970 (36,000 square feet). A new additional factory complex was completed in 1976 on Industrial Drive. During the 1960's and 1970's the firm was producing heavy industrial fans and crop dryers of all sizes and uses. Aerovent experienced several **strikes** in the 1970's and 1980's with the workers being represented by the International Association of Machinists & Aerospace Workers, AFL-CIO Lodge 2609. The firm had grown to over 325 employees by 1984. By the early 1990's, the firm had been sold to an overseas firm and renamed Asea Brown Bovieri (ABB) Aerovent Inc. The firm was sold again in 1993 to the Twin City Fan & Blower

The Aerovent Fan Company was located on West Ash Street in this 1940's picture.

The Booher Family Farm is shown in about 1900.

The cattle were grazing in the barn yard.

Above:
The hay wagon is shown with a mechanical rake loader attached.

Right:
The family gathered on the back step of the farm house for an amateur photography session.

Below:
A heavily loaded hay wagon needed two teams of horses.

Company of Minneapolis and the Piqua plant became known as TCF Aerovent. TCF made the **union** an offer that included pay and benefit reductions. When the union rejected the proposal, the firm closed down all local operations.

AFRICAN-AMERICAN

The African-American population in Piqua increased from one in 1820 to 499 in 1920. In 1880, the African-American population constituted 4.8% of the city's total population. This was the highest percentage reached between 1820 and 1920. The highest population figure was reached in 1910 with a total of 527. By 1900, Piqua's African-American population made up over 42% of the total county African-American population.

While escape routes from southern slavery did exist in Ohio, their number was greatly exaggerated by whites telling tall tales *after* the Civil War. In the Upper Miami Valley escaping slaves were aided mainly by the Quaker settlement at West Milton and by the African-American communities such as **Rossville**. An exception to this was the Wesleyan Methodist Church on the southeast corner of Ash and Downing Streets. Members in this church were active in the limited Underground Railroad activities through Piqua.

The city's first segregated African-American school was begun in 1854 at the Cyrene African Methodist Episcopal Church on the southeast corner of Ash and Downing Streets. The first teacher was Miss Amelia Clark who was selected by the African-American population of Piqua. She was followed by Elias Jones who was hired in 1855 at a total salary of sixty dollars for a three month term. The school was funded by the Piqua schools. However, the school session ran for only one to three months a year compared to the white schools that were in session for eight months a year. By 1862, the school had an attendance of fifty-five students under the direction of a part-time teacher. After the Civil War, it appears that African-American students were taught by separate teachers in a segregated classroom in an otherwise all white school. In 1872, the Piqua Board of education built a one room brick segregated school on northwest corner of Boone and College Streets. The Board of Education then formally segregated the schools with the following resolution.

Whereas in order to give the colored youth of the City of Piqua educational facilities equal to the whites, the Board has erected a good school house and has employed a teacher of demonstrated ability,...therefore resolve, that no colored children be hereafter admitted to the schools where the white children are taught without a special order of the board for that purpose.

Frank A Hardy was the teacher at the new Boone Street School. He had been hired in 1870. The African-American community did not desire a white teacher at the new school and advocated for the hiring of **Bugress R. Guy** as the school's teacher. Guy would take on the position in 1875 and remained the school teacher, principal and janitor until 1884. Guy was followed in 1884 by Mr. Molten. The school was closed in August of 1885 and its final twenty-five students integrated into the other Piqua ward schools. The school building was sold to J.C. Cruse in 1888 for use as a private residence.

African-American civil rights were championed in Ohio in 1867 when a statewide vote was taken on striking the word "white" from the Ohio constitution to allow full political rights to African-Americans. Miami County was one of only thirty-two counties (out of eighty-eight) to vote for the change. The total vote was 216,987 for and 255,340 against the change. Locally, the *Piqua Democrat* newspaper openly opposed African-American suffrage with the following July 1867 editorial.

"The negro, as a class in Ohio is inferior to the white race...Today the negro enjoys the benefit of every law in Ohio that a white man does, except to vote, sit on juries, and send their children into schools with white children...it is for the benefit of the negro as well as of the white man to let the white man do the voting."

African-American participation in local politics was extremely limited until the late 1870's and early 1880's. **Goodrich Giles** was the first African-American to run for seat on the Piqua City Council in 1885, 1886, and 1887. **W. N. Johnson** was the second African-American to run for office. He was a fifth ward candidate for council in 1893. The African-American political community was overwhelmingly Republican until the 1930's. The Independent Civic League (of Miami County) was formed on September 29, 1908. This organization was headed by James Pettiford and functioned as a non-partisan political organization for black citizens. At the same time African-Americans were trying to pursue political answers to racial issues, the Piqua police actively investigated a complaint (in 1909) that a "colored man was seen walking with a white women". George Lane, a Piqua barber would be one of the major supporters of the formation of the Miami County **NAACP**. At that same time, Mrs. Eva Smith became the first president of the Colored Women's Christian Temperance Union in June of 1921. This was the first city-wide African-American women's organization. It would not be until 1985, that **Charles Musco** would become the first African-American citizen to be elected to the City Commission.

The African-American community was active in segregated lodge groups including the Masons, Knights of Pythias, Odd Fellows and other groups. In February of 1896, A.W. Smith chaired an organizational meeting of a group known as the Keystone Club.

SEE ALSO: Baseball; Bowles, George S.; Civil Rights Movement; Civil War (List) – Colored Troops; Civil War; Clemens, Viola; Colored Men's Cooperative; Davis, Arthur; Dorsey, Godwin; Hanktown; Lodges and Organizations; Marshalltown; Ohio Federation for the Uplift Among Colored People; Randolph, John; Randolph Slaves; Rial, York; Rudd, Dorthea; Stoute, A.W.; Stoute-Harris Post, V.F.W.;Van Horne, Thomas; Wilson, Joseph P.; Piqua Colonization Society, Anti-Slavery Society; YMCA.

AGRICULTURE

Prehistoric peoples in the Miami Valley practiced maize (corn) agriculture as early as 2,500 years ago. Historic Indians continued the practice with women deciding when and where to plant crops as well as taking care of the fields. The first European-American settlers to plant crops in the Piqua area were the **Hilliard family**. The Hilliards planted a corn crop in the spring of 1797 on the flood plain of the East side of the Great Miami River. Early farms were small due to the intense labor needed to clear the trees from the potential fields. By the 1830's, corn and wheat had become the area's major crops, followed by rye, barley, and hay. By 1850 flax and tobacco had become major cash crops. SEE ALSO: Apples; Corn; Johnston, John; Linseed Oil; Market House; Pigs.

AIR CONDITIONING

The first air cooling system in Piqua was introduced by **Stanhope Boal** in the Bijou **Theater** at 122 West Ash Street. The system consisted of placing a fan behind a pan of ice and allowing the cool air to circulate around the building. Boal saw this system being used in a small New York City theater.

AIR TRANSPORTATION

The first recorded aerial event in Piqua was a hot air balloon ascent on June 18, 1828. Balloon ascents were popular in the nineteenth century, and Piqua witnessed several more balloon ascents including one from Fountain Park on June 29, 1882. After the invention of heavier than air flight in 1903, local interest turned to the airplane. In 1909 an Aeronautics Club was formed. By 1917, the **Hartzell Propeller Company** was producing walnut propellers for World War I planes. In 1923, Fred Charavay, Chief Engineer of Hartzell Propeller, designed a plane that won first place in air races at St. Louis and again in Dayton in 1924. In the early 1920's, C. E. Conover, a Main Street merchant, was advertising airplane coverings and upholstering. A flying club was organized in Piqua in January of 1940, known as the Wings of Piqua with Gerald Oliver as its first president. Other members of the new club included Ralph Blacke, Frederick Jean Charavay (aircraft designer with Hartzell Propeller Company), **Don Gentile** (P-51 Mustang fighter pilot in World War II, European Theater Ace), **Louis Ciriegio** (pilot in World War II, German POW), William Gibboney, Robert Smith, Raymond C. Fry Jr. (C-47 Transport pilot in World War II, killed over Burma in 1943), John W. Hardman (bomber pilot in World War II) and Harold Greenamyer. In the 1930's, the private Hall Airport was established by Acton Hall Jr. (Ohio Marble Company) with grass runways about a half mile long with a single small hanger. It was bounded by the Old Troy Pike on the west, Loy Road on the south and extended east to the Baltimore & Ohio Railroad. The **Lear Avia Company** moved to Piqua in 1941 and began manufacturing aircraft communication and direction finding equipment until 1946. Hartzell's took over an airport located on State Route 185 in 1957 and in 1967 expanded it to handle small business jets. In 1986, Hartzell TRW built the propellers for the Voyager aircraft that set the record for the first around the world un-refueled flight.

ALIEN REGISTRATION ACT

Congress passed the Alien Registration Act (aka Smith Act) on June 28, 1940 as part of a growing American fear of sabotage and espionage from the Axis powers of **World War II.** Registration in Piqua began at the Post Office on August 20, 1940 and ran through December 27, 1940. During that time, seventy non-United States citizens or "aliens" registered in Piqua. Nationally the total reached over 3.5 million people.

ALLEYS

The first alleys in Piqua were unofficial trails that followed the property lines behind homes. They were created to allow for access to the barns built at the rear of early structures. By the 1820's, alleys were a part of all the new plats being laid out in the village. The two blocks east and west of North Main Street originally had no alleys. Today many of these blocks still do not have alleys and where they have been put in they often intersect with building sites or property lines.

ALGONQUIAN LANGUAGE FAMILY

The Algonquian language family is a broad group of Indian languages divided into three groups, Central, Plains and Eastern. The Central Algonquian languages were spoken in the Great Lakes region. This area supported seven major languages within the Central Algonquian language family. They were the Ojibwa (including Chippewa, Ottawa, and Algonquian), Potawatomi, Menominee, Fox (including Saux and Kickapoo) **Miami**-Illinois, **Shawnee** and Cree languages. In a survey done west of the Mississippi River in 1965, only 300 to 400 people still spoke Shawnee as a native language, and the Miami-Illinois language was extinct.

ALUMINUM INDUSTRY

Aluminum first became commercially practical to produce in 1886 and the first cast aluminum products hit the market by 1891. In Piqua the first firm to specialize in aluminum castings was the Home Aluminum and Bronze Company established in 1922. Most of the firm's work revolved around castings for funeral coaches manufactured by the **Meteor Motor Car Company**, but the company did produce a small number of kitchen cooking containers. The company ceased production in 1964-65.

AMERICAN FOUR SQUARE STYLE ARCHITECTURE

The local variation of the American Four Square Style was popular from 1905 through 1925. These solid square houses were often built as mirror image doubles and used as rental properties or for members of the same family. This style was frequently covered in stucco, (the aluminum siding of the first two decades of the twentieth century). This style was often offered by the mail-order companies offering house plans such as the Sears Roebuck Company. This style has many of the following local architectural elements. This style has a low pitched hipped roof with one or more prominent central roof dormers. A relatively plain front porch extends across

The Piqua Airport off of State Route 185 used dirt and grass runways during it early years.

the entire front facade. This style usually has a fairly standard arrangement of four rooms on the first floor with a kitchen in the rear, a vestibule room in the front and an easily accessible living room to the side. This style had a central indoor bathroom on the second floor and separate bedrooms for parents and children. Interiors often featured oak woodwork and gas fireplaces surrounded by a mantle and decorative tiles. While stucco was popular, many of the local American Four Square homes were constructed with horizontal wood siding.

DOMESTIC EXAMPLES:
223 & 225 W. North, 1912
319 & 321 Boone Street, Louis Houses, 1905

AMERICAN LEGION

The American Legion was formed in Paris, France in 1919 by veterans of the American Expeditionary Force of **World War I.** In Piqua, the **Paul Schnell** Post No.184 was formed in October of 1919. The post was named for a Piqua native killed in action in France on June 22, 1918.

In 1935, Edward Bolden chaired the committee that organized the Frank Smith Williams Post No. 512 of the American Legion. The short-lived post met in the legion hall on the corner of Greene and Main Streets.

Prior to moving into their Colonial revival style home on Water Street, the legion meetings were held in a number of locations. These included the third floor of the former May's Opera House (Schine's Miami Theater) and the former Rathskeller Bar in the southeast basement room of the Favorite Hotel on the square from January 1944 through November of 1946. The Legion's Veteran's Memorial Home at 301 West Water Street was formally dedicated in November of 1946. At that same time the Legion added the name of a **World War II** Piqua marine killed in action, **John Westfall.** The Post became known as the Schnell-Westfall Post. Several auxiliary organizations were formed in 1927, the Miami County Voiture 420 and the Ladies' Auxiliary (an earlier auxiliary had disbanded).

SEE ALSO: Photographs p. 183; Patron p. 222.

The Veteran's Memorial Home of the American Legion was completed in 1946 on the southwest corner of Water and Downing Streets.

The American Pullmatch Company was located on Young Street in the old Favorite Stove factory.

AMERICAN PROTECTIVE LEAGUE

This was a **World War I** super-patriotic group dedicated to promoting the American war effort and opposing any Un-American activity. A part of their volunteer oath stated, "I solemnly swear … [to] promptly report all information of every kind and character and from whatever source derived, tending to prove hostile or disloyal acts or intentions on the part of any person whatsoever…". The League was formed in Chicago and informally came under the direction of the United States Department of Justice, Bureau of Investigation.

The local division of the League was established in 1917 and headed by industrialist and city councilman **William K. Leonard.** The local newspapers would credit Leonard and the League with orchestrating the arrest of local Socialist Mayor **Frank Hamilton** and five other local **Socialist** on charges of violating the U.S. Espionage Act.

AMERICAN PULLMATCH CORPORATION

This firm was incorporated in Delaware in 1936 with **William Boal Wood** (president) and Reinhard Mumm (vice president/general manager) as its chief officers. Mumm, a German national, held the production rights for the continuous strip pull matches. The firm organized their operations in a part of the former **Favorite Stove & Range Company** plant on the corner of Young and Weber Streets. The matches were sold in tight rolls of three hundred matches that were placed in seven to ten inch Bakelite (plastic) decorative dispensers. The firm used two automated machines from Switzerland to produce the matches. The firm ceased local production in 1939.

ANIMALS (MAMMALS)

The camp and village sites of the **prehistoric Adena** and **Hopewell** Peoples, and the later Native American Tribes, abound with the bones of the animals they hunted and killed. They include: elk, deer, bear, panther, wolf, beaver, muskrat, rabbit, wildcat, lynx, squirrel, fox, opossum, rat, woodchuck, otter, and skunk. Before 1749, buffalo were common and elk were seen until the late 1790's. Black bears were numerous before 1800 and as late as 1816. Henry Kerns of Miami County

was reported to have killed a bear whose quarters weighed four hundred pounds. By 1830, the panther had become quite scarce and by 1840 the wildcat population was down to a few widely scattered members. The wolf was still common up through the turn of the century, with the state offering a $4.50 bounty for each wolf scalp. The red and gray foxes, not nearly as numerous, can still be found ranging the river areas. The otter disappeared soon after the area was settled, due to the heavy trapping of the animals. As with most urban areas, the current animal population of the city is generally restricted to squirrels, an occasional raccoon, and the bane of backyard gardens, the rabbit.

ANTI-SALOON LEAGUE

The organization was formed in Oberlin, Ohio in September of 1893 as the Ohio Anti-Saloon League. It was organized nationally in Washington, D.C. in 1895. In 1962, the name was changed to the American Council on Alcohol Problems and continues to operate today under that name. The Piqua Anti-Saloon League was organized in the late 1890's.

ANTI-SLAVERY SOCIETY OF MIAMI COUNTY

Little is known about the Anti-Slavery Society in Miami County which was formed by white abolitionists. A meeting notice dated May 4, 1839 suggests that the group was formed in 1838 or early 1839. The group met in the Methodist Episcopal Church in Piqua. SEE ALSO: African-American

APARTMENTS

The first structure in Piqua built exclusively for individual and family apartments was the Colonial Saxony at 221 West Greene Street. This **Second Renaissance Revival Style** structure was built for **John Boyer** by **A. M. Fry** in 1903-1904 for a decidedly upscale clientele. Charles Vosler opened the Hazel-Marie Apartments (named for his wife) at 408 North Wayne Street in 1942-1943. Vosler had purchased the abandoned Knights of Columbus Hall in November of 1941 and turned the former Shipley home (1882 **Italianate Style**) and the newer 1920's lodge addition into sixteen new apartments. Both of these structures are currently (2007) still used as apartment buildings.

APPLES

One of the first apple orchards in the Piqua area was planted by Colonel **John Johnston** at his farm at Upper Piqua in the 1820's. Early pioneers were often reluctant to put the time and effort into orchard plantings since they took so long to develop. While John Chapman (Johnny Appleseed) was from nearby Urbana, it is unknown if he planted any trees in the Piqua area. As more and more apple trees were planted, apple products such as apple butter, applejack (alcohol), apple sauce and soft and hard cider became very common.. By the end of the nineteenth century apple trees were being sold and planted in the family backyards for their shade, beauty and as a source of apples for pies and snacks.

APPRENTICES

The practice of binding young children as apprentices came to America with the earliest European settlers. Children were legally bound to an individual to learn a trade. The earliest apprentice on record in Miami County was Jacob Lasner, age fourteen. In the summer of 1811, he was apprenticed to Martin Rouser to learn the "art, trade and mystery of tanning and currying leather". Jacob was bound to Mr. Rouser until he reached the age of twenty-one. It was stipulated that Jacob would be taught to read and write. During the 1820's and 1830's, the master held all authority and power over the apprentice. Many of the contracts included restrictions such as, "....he shall not play at cards, dice or any other unlawful games, he shall not haunt or frequent playhouses, taverns or ale houses except it be about his master's business, ...fornication he shall not commit, and matrimony he shall not contract...". SEE ALSO: Orr, William; Shoemakers; Tobacco.

ARCHAEOLOGY

Archaeology is the art and the science of investigating the past using the physical items and structures produced by former peoples and cultures. Many of these items and structures are found by excavating previously occupied sites. Archaeology is always done in a methodical and organized manner. Exact records, measurements and descriptions are made of every item and structure found. Excavating without keeping records is merely tomb robbing. An artifact out of context becomes meaningless. Some of the area's earliest amateur archaeologists were **John Rayner**, C.B. Jamison and Charles T. Wiltheiss all of whom excavated and recorded a number of prehistoric sites in northern Miami County.

ARCHAIC PERIOD

The Archaic Period covers a prehistoric time from 8,000 to 1,000 B. C. During this period, prehistoric man moved from a purely nomadic hunting group (**Paleo-Indian**) to the beginnings of civilization. The Archaic Period started the specialization of society, with the beginnings of medicine, magic, religion (mortuary ceremonialism), and stylized art (abstract thought).

ARCHITECTS

Early local builders were both designers and contractors. The community's first building styles were the relatively simple **Federal**, **Greek Revival**, and **Italianate** styles. Many houses were actually planned as the construction progressed. The first builders to also list themselves as architects were the Brielmaier Brothers in 1832. After the early 1890's, trained architects like Charles C. Barnett (1880's-1910's), Charles F. Bowdle (1905-1930's), Curtis A. Thompson (1890's), **Harry E. Whitlock** (c1891-c1907), and Harley Mowry (c1910's) designed many of the city's homes, factories, business' and churches. SEE ALSO: Architectural Styles; Russ, W. E.; Schenk and Williams; Yost, Joseph.

ARCHITECTURAL STYLES.

Identifying architectural styles and design elements is an inexact science at best. During the nineteenth and early twentieth centuries, local builders often borrowed bits and pieces of recognized national architectural styles. The builder then used locally available materials, traditional construction methods, and unique conditions to produce what often became distinct local style variations.

One feature in almost all of Piqua's Central Business District commercial structures is the two part commercial block building. These two to five story downtown structures are divided horizontally into two distinct usage zones. The first floor zones have very distinctive features and were used for retail shopping, banking, lobbies, or other open public activities. The upper

Architectural Styles

The Rundle House is a Prairie Style structure located at 620 Caldwell.

The Queen Anne Style Barber home at 324 West Greene Street was designed by J.W. Yost.

The French/Koon home at 615 North Wayne Street is an excellent example of a structure remodeled into a Georgian Revival Style house.

This stucco home at 223 West North Street was done in the popular American Four Square Style.

The Masonic Building on the southwest corner of Main and market Streets burned down and is currently a parking lot.

Vanishing Architecture

The Queen Anne Style Snyder house at 601 North Downing Street sat on the site of a blacksmith shop.

The Greene Street Methodist Episcopal Church was located on the southeast corner of Wayne and Greene Street. The location is currently a parking lot.

The Snyder house at 601 Downing Street lost all of its Queen Anne styling when it was stuccoed in the 1920's.

floor zones, with features that contrasted to those of the lower zone, were used as offices, studios, meeting halls, apartments, or other private or semi-private activities. The two part commercial block building contrasted to domestic architecture where the first and upper floors blended together. This type of two part downtown commercial construction is common throughout the United States from before the **Civil War** (1850) to after **World War II** (1950).

The architectural details and dates listed in these articles are specific to the Piqua area and do not necessarily reflect national trends or styles. The dates provided are only approximations and should be used only as rough guidelines. New archival and physical building research can and will increase and change the data base concerning architectural styles, building construction methods, and dates and periods of construction. The names of certain styles change as new national architectural historians combine or redefine styles. To add to this confusion, local styles often do not have all or even a majority of the architectural features that may be used to define a national or state style.

An important part of historic architecture is the realization that buildings do change. As use, styles, and prosperity changed, the buildings in Piqua changed to meet the new demands. Sometimes an earlier building was demolished and a new one, better suited to a new use or style, replaced it. Often a building was simply remodeled to fit a new use or to add "modern" architectural details. In downtown commercial structures, remodeling almost always occurred on the ground floor.

Change was common for domestic architecture. New styles, technology and social customs have a profound affect on the building of homes in Piqua. As homes are remodeled they often lose their uniqueness with regards to a single architectural style. Often these homes will be referred to as eclectic (not having a specific style) (example 111 Riverside Drive) or transitional (having the architectural elements of two different periods or styles) (example 510 North Wayne Street). Local homes were designed by builders until after last part of the nineteenth century. The builder would often use only bit and pieces of a "national" style to either keep costs down or to meet local tastes and conventions. Two national styles have no true Piqua examples. The best area Sullivanesque Style structure is the People's Federal Savings Bank, designed by Louis Sullivan in 1918 and located on the public square (101 East Court Street) in Sidney, Ohio. One of the best area examples of the Art Moderne Style is the former Hobart Brothers office on West Main Street in Troy, Ohio. SEE ALSO: American Four Square Style; Apartments; Architects; Art Deco Style; Bricks; Bungalow Style; Chateauesque Style; Chicago Commercial Style; Colonial Revival Style; Contemporary Style; Dutch Colonial Revival Style; Exotic Style; Federal Style; French Colonial/Norman Revival Style; Fry, A.M.; Gothic Revival Style; Greek Revival Style; Hartzell Propeller Company; High Victorian Italianate Style; Houses; Housing Developments; Inland Homes; Italianate Style; Jacobethan Style; Log Cabins; Manses; Mobile Homes; Post 1960 Style; Prairie Style; Prohibition Era Style; Quonset Type; Russ, W.E.; Schenk & Williams; Second Empire Style; Steel Houses; Queen Anne Style; Richardsonian Romanesque Style; Second Renaissance Revival Style; Tudor Style; War Cottage Type; Willow Cottage; Worker's Cottage Type; Yost, Joseph W.; Patron p. 227

ARTISTS

Some of Piqua's earliest artists included **William Best**, Mrs. Clark, Alfred Payne and Mrs. Thomas all of whom were active in Piqua prior to the Civil War. These artists rarely were able to make a living in Piqua off of fine art or portrait work. Best painted houses and signs as well as portraits to make a living

and Thomas taught art at the High School. One of the area's best known and most prolific nineteenth century artists was **Horace Rollins** of Springcreek Township.

ART DECO STYLE ARCHITECTURE

The local variation of the Art Deco Style was popular from 1920 through 1941. The Art Deco Style variation in Piqua was relatively subdued. The local and regional business owners did without most of the high style decorative elements of this style. During the 1920's and 1930's, the community was relatively conservative and very traditional and settled for the merest hint of decoration. There are some questions over the choice of light colored brick for commercial buildings during this era. While this type of brick was used for domestic structures on occasion, it was not common in commercial structures. The city helped change popular opinion by building a new Public **Market House** on North Downing in 1927-28 using the lighter colored bricks.

This style has many of the following local architectural elements. These commercial structures are built in a rectangular shape with one or two stories. The use of a light colored glazed brick (yellow-orange in color) was a common feature with this style. The storefronts had plate glass windows and recessed entrances (all the storefronts in this style have been massively remodeled). Usually there are brick and stone banding combined with the use of Carrara glass for the bulkheads. The openings in the facade are symmetrical casement or double hung sash with configurations such as eight vertical panes over one. This style commonly have flat brick patterns and designs made with bricks of contrasting colors and modestly decorated stone and brick parapets.

COMMERCIAL EXAMPLES:

326 North Main Street, Kresge-Jupiter Building/ **Chamber of Commerce**, 1931

413 North Main Street, M & M Café Building/Javawocky

ATLAS UNDERWEAR COMPANY

This company began in January of 1899 with the incorporation of the Piqua Underwear Company by M.G. Smith, Edgar A. Todd, and John M. Cahill (1857-1934). The firm opened a plant in the former **O'Ferrall** Agricultural Works on the corner of Downing and Riverside Drive to produce men and boys' union suits. The fledgling company was purchased in 1900 by **Leo M. Flesh**, **William P. Orr** and Edgar A. Todd and re-named the Atlas Underwear Company. The company grew rapidly and it built a new three story plant on the northwest corner of Downing and Rundle Streets (803 North Downing Street). The old factory, located directly to the north, was sold to the **Superior Underwear Company**. Business was good and Atlas sold its unionsuits to retail giants like Sears & Roebuck and Levi Strauss. Atlas added a fourth story to its plant in 1909 and a new four story addition in 1920. The firm also opened a branch in 1919-1920 in Urbana, Ohio to expand their labor pool. The company was active during both world wars producing underwear for the military. During the Great **Depression** the company began producing lighter cotton garments and briefs. The depression also saw a major **strike** hit the company in 1936 led by the United Textile Workers of America **union**. Flesh brought in a labor specialist Bill Wright to deal with the strike. In 1941, Atlas produced the first thermal underwear know as *Insulaire*. The company purchased the Allen-A Company of Wisconsin in 1941 to produce the new garment.

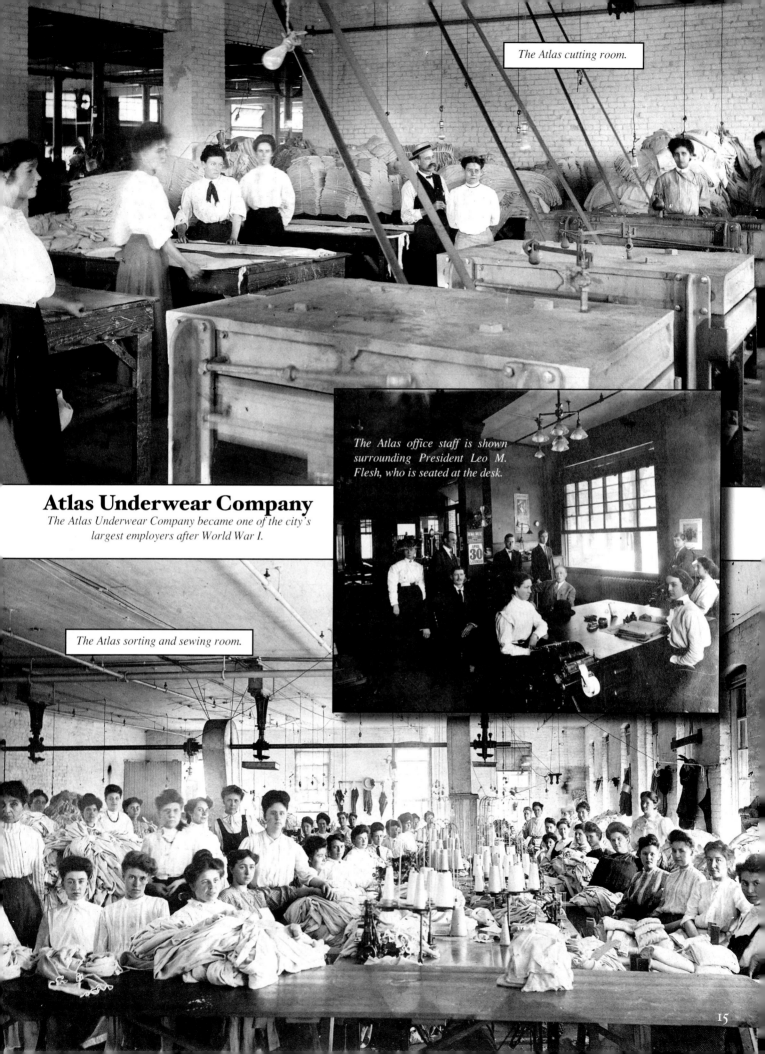

The Atlas cutting room.

Atlas Underwear Company

The Atlas Underwear Company became one of the city's largest employers after World War I.

The Atlas sorting and sewing room.

The Atlas office staff is shown surrounding President Leo M. Flesh, who is seated at the desk.

Leo M. Flesh served as president until 1928, when he became chairman of the board until his death in 1944. **Alfred Flesh** succeeded him as president until 1956 (then chairman of the board from 1956 to 1968) when Henry Flesh took over. In 1968, Karl Monson became president with Alexander Flesh as the executive vice president. Monson was followed by Robert J. Kine (c.1975) and Richard A. Smith (c.1976-c.1980).

Atlas acquired a number of other companies during its long history in Piqua. The Richmond Underwear Company of Indiana was founded in 1910 by Leo M. Flesh and merged with Atlas in 1915. The firm purchased the bankrupt **Imperial Underwear Company** of Piqua in 1926. Atlas took the assets and brand names of Imperial and with **Milton Erlanger** of the **B.V.D.** Company of Delaware created the Erlanger Knitting Company using the factory building on Water Street in Piqua. Alfred Flesh and Erlanger formed a holding company in December of 1929 to own and control Atlas, B.V.D. the Regatta Manufacturing Company Inc. of Baltimore (shipping for Regatta was out of the Water Street plant) and the quasi-independent B.V.D. Sales Corporations located in various states across the nation. In 1930, the B.V.D. Inc holding company purchased the **Piqua Hosiery Company**. A.L. Flesh made Atlas corporate secretary **Harvey Sims** the secretary/treasure of Piqua Hosiery. B.V.D. (Erlanger) and Atlas (Flesh) separated in September of 1933 with Flesh maintaining control of Piqua Hosiery and some of the B.V.D. Sales Corporations and Erlanger taking the Regatta Company, the Erlanger Knitting Company and the rest of the B.V.D. Sales Corporations.

The late 1960's and early 1970's were a major time of change for the firm. Monson instigated a new product line for Atlas in 1968 called *Ski Skins,* a type of full length underwear for skiers. Atlas became the largest supplier of ski underwear in the nation. The need for manufacturing space led Atlas to purchase the abandoned former **Superior Underwear Company** plant directly to the north in 1968. The following year saw the company add cotton turtle neck shirts and in the early 1970's a product called *Playskins* for tennis players. The company was also producing socks, sports shirts, swim suits, sweaters, pajamas, handkerchiefs, men's briefs and athletic undershirts. To better reflect their products Atlas Underwear became the Allen-A Company in 1971. The firm merged with Medalist Industries of Milwaukee in 1972 and changed their name to the Medalist Allen-A Company. Monson stayed with the company until c.1974-75. The firm's desperate need for additional storage and shipping space was met in 1980 with the erection of new 72,000 square foot distribution center at 8510 Industrial Drive. The firm marketed their products under private labels such as L.L. Bean, Lands End, J.C. Penney, and Eddie Bauer. As part of a marketing plan, the firm

was re-named Medalist Apparel. The firm became one of the industry's largest producers of premium thermal underwear in the United States. The firm also marketed and sold sweatbands, wristlets, tennis sweaters and men's baseball shirts. Medalist closed the city's last underwear company in 1993 and moved their operations to Sidney, Ohio. That operation closed down in 1995. The factory buildings in Piqua (both the former Atlas and Superior plants) were demolished in 1994 and the Heritage Green Park placed in that space. Lucy Fess was instrumental in getting the Medalist Corporation to donate the land to the city. SEE ALSO: Lists-Underwear; textile industry; YWCA

AUTOMOBILE DEALERS

The first **automobile** dealer was the Piqua Automobile Station located at 131 North Main Street. **Henry Bertling** and Ed Snyder began selling cars at this location in 1903. By 1911, there were 52 automobiles registered in Piqua, 35 in Troy, and 10 in Tipp City. The largest Piqua dealer was the Sherer-Bell Company with dealerships in Piqua, Troy, Dayton and Cincinnati. SEE ALSO: List-Automobile Dealers; Patron p. 223

AUTOMOBILES

William Lorimer purchased the city's first automobile in 1900. The first auto accident occurred in 1901. **Henry Bertling** and Ed Snyder opened the city's first auto garage and service station at 131 North Main Street in April of 1903. **Meteor Motor Car Company** was the first and only firm to manufacture automobiles in Piqua. (1913-1915). SEE ALSO: Driving Instruction; Gas Stations and Garages; Prohibition Era Style Architecture

BADMINTON

The game has its modern roots in the Indian game of Poona that was brought back to England by British Army officers in the 1870's. Its current name refers to the lawns where it was introduced, Badminton House, the home of the Duke of Beaufort in Gloucestershire, England. The first American club was created in 1878 in New York. The game revived during the Great **Depression**, in part, due to its popularity among the Hollywood movie stars such as Bette Davis, Ginger Rogers and Douglas Fairbanks.

Alfred French and John Ketchum held a badminton demonstration at the Piqua **YMCA**'s New Years Day Carnival in 1935. This may have been the first modern public badminton game in the city's history. The game's popularity grew and the YMCA held the city's first badminton tournament in March of 1936.

The Sanzenbacher Automobile Agency was located at 105 East Greene Street.

BANKS

Piqua's first bank was opened in 1847 as the Piqua Branch of the State Bank of Ohio. This branch later became the Piqua National Bank (1865-1985). Later banks included Citizens National Bank (1865-1963), Third National Bank (1887-1902), Piqua Savings Bank (1901-1930), Miami Citizens National Bank (1963-1985), Winters National Bank (1980-1983), Bank One (1984-present), Heritage National Bank (1985-1986), Citizens Heritage Bank (1986-1988), Fifth-Third Bank (1988-present). SEE ALSO: Dorsey, Godwin V.; Flesh, Henry; Orr Family; Scott, William; Patron pp. 234, 284

The Piqua National Bank building on the southeast corner of Wayne and Market Streets was erected in 1929 in the Neo-Classical Revival Style.

Right:
The Piqua High School basketball team of 1907-1908.

Below:
The Atlas Underwear Company sponsored a baseball team as part of the Industrial League in 1909.

BASEBALL

The city's first baseball team was organized in 1866 as the Sterling Club. They were followed by a local black team known as the Piqua Lincolns. Interest in the game waned in the early 1870's only to be revived again in the late 1870's. In 1878, the High School developed a baseball team known as the Athletes. In 1883, a stock company was organized, The Piqua Baseball Company. The company tried to raise money for uniforms, travel, and a playing field but it was only partially successful. Its only long term success was the establishment of a playing field on the south side of Ash Street (later the high school football field). In an attempt to control the game, a city ordinance was passed on January 19, 1884 prohibiting the playing of baseball on city streets and alleys. During this period, a few of the active Piqua teams included the Border Cities, Old Reliables, the Piqua Cadets, and the Piquas. During the first two decades of the twentieth century, several local semi-professional teams were established. A favorite playing field for these teams was Stein's Park in **Rossville**. The first was the Piqua Baseball Association formed in 1903 with fifty subscribers paying twenty-five dollars each. Charles F. Prince of Wheeling, West Virginia was chosen as the team's player/manager. Another semi-professional club was the Piqua Spots organized in 1912 under the management

of J.H. Jackson (president) and Edward Millheim (player/manager). The City Baseball League was organized in 1908 with six clubs consisting of bankers, lawyers, doctors, and three clubs of businessmen. SEE: Television; Parks.

BASKETBALL

This game was introduced in Piqua by the **YMCA** during the winter of 1893. The first team included the following players; Charles Jelleff, B. Blinn, H. D. Mitchell, Cloyd Smith, J. Hunter, and Walter Livingston. The first girl's high school team was organized in 1914-15. The game took a major step forward with the dedication of the Field House on West Ash Street on January 02, 1936. The largest basketball game crowd in the city's history to that time attended the opening game at the dedication.

BATH PARLORS

In the nineteenth century, bath parlors were relatively common until indoor plumbing in the 1880's and 1890's allowed each middle class residence to have its own individual bathroom. Early bath parlors were almost always associated with barber shops or hotels. After World War I, there was a renewed interest in the parlors, this time not for cleanliness but for good health. In 1922 Benjamin F. Harrison remodeled the former First Church of Christ, Scientist structure at 431 West High (southeast corner of High and Broadway) into the Harrison Bath Parlors (1922-1928). The parlors used the "Battle Creek Sanitarium Method" of electric, vapor, or sulphur cabinet baths. Harrison also offered salt glows, Turkish rubs and body shampoos. Other bath parlors in Piqua included: Nature's Vapored Mineral Health System at 320 West Water (c1928), Reynolds Bath Parlor, 317 West High (c1930-c1941), John F. Class Health System, 800 West North (c1930-c1935), John F. Class Vapo-Path Treatment, 523 North Wayne (c1936-1947), Dickerson Reducing Salon, 324 North Wayne (1946-1950), Miller's Vapor Mineral Baths, 523 North Wayne (c1948-c1968).

BATTLES

These are a few of the battles that have taken place in the Ohio country: Fallen Timbers (1794), Piqua (1780), Point Pleasant (1774), and Tippecanoe (1811). SEE ALSO: Clark, George Rogers; Delaware; Harrison, William Henry; Individual Battles; Miami; Shawnee.

BICYCLES

During the summer of 1881, the first high-wheel bicycles were cruising the streets of Piqua. The city's first organized group of riders was established in the early 1890's as the Piqua Cycle Club under the auspices of the **YMCA**. The club's objectives were to promote the recreational aspect of the high wheel cycle. E. L. Bennett served as the club's first president.

BLACKSMITHS

One of the community's first blacksmith shops was established by Joseph Defrees on the corner of Main and Sycamore Streets. The 1850 census listed 29 individual blacksmiths in Piqua. By 1890, there were seven active shops. The twentieth century began the decline for blacksmiths. In 1910, there were at least fifteen active blacksmiths listed. By 1920 the number had dropped to three. In 1950 John R. Redmond was the last full-time blacksmith to be listed in the Piqua city directories.

BORDER CITY

This was a nickname for the City of Piqua used in the nineteenth and early twentieth centuries. During the **War of 1812** in Ohio, Piqua was the northern most community that was free from Indian raids. Thus Piqua (or Washington as it was then known) was the "Border Town". In 1837, the Miami extension **canal** was opened from Piqua to Cincinnati. Piqua remained the northern terminus or border of the canal for five years. This was another reason to be known as the "Border Town". There is also some reference to "Border City" being used in a derogatory sense by the citizens of Troy during the court house wars. Troy was the county seat in the center of the county, and Piqua was up north on the fringes of the county, the "Border City". SEE ALSO: Court House Wars.

BOTTLE CAP MANUFACTURING

Paper bottle caps were cut and printed in Piqua for the large number of regional **dairies** and milk distributors. The first company to manufacture caps in the city was the Piqua Cap and Filler Company established in 1905. In 1940-41, the company sold out to the Smith-Lee Company before being closed in 1949-50. Other cap manufacturers included the Piqua Packer Company (1907-08), William Summers & Company (1908-1919), and the Ohio Bottling Cap Company (1924-1954-55). These highly specialized companies suffered as the number of locally owned milk distributors declined and as milk containers changed in style and construction. SEE ALSO: Milk Battlecap

BOTTLERS

The bottling and production of mineral and soda water in Piqua can be traced to the 1850's. Barnhart Pietz settled in Piqua in 1855 and began a bottling works on East Main Street in **Huntersville**. After Pietz's death in 1897, the mineral water and bottling plant was taken over by George Pfister. Pfister sold the company in 1894 to Ollie C. Klee who renamed it the Piqua Bottling Works. In 1916 **Fred** and Frank **Lange** purchased the works which two years earlier had moved to a new plant at 220 Spring Street. For roughly a year and a half Lange's continued

This late 1890's photograph shows the Reedy Blacksmith Shop on the west side of Main Street next to the river. The shop did side work in bicycle repair.

the Klee operations, adding "Orange Whistle" to the product line. In May of 1917, the Lange Brothers re-organized the firm as the Piqua Coca Cola Bottling Works. This firm remained active in Piqua until 1973. Other bottling works included Andrew Erb (1878-1890's), Favorite Bottling Works, Edward J. Granger (1897) and Nehi Bottling Company (1930-1932).

The "Coke Hall" began as the Strand Theater in 1915. It was remodeled by the Lange Brothers in 1937 to house Piqua's Coca Cola Bottling plant. The third floor was for lodge meetings (Odd Fellows), public meetings (Townsend Club), dances and many other community activities.

BOWLING

There is no record of the introduction of bowling in Piqua. The earliest mention of the game is on September 6, 1886 when the city council passed an ordinance suppressing ten pin bowling alleys. The first full-time bowling alley on record was the Atlantic Bowling Alley on the corner of Main and Water Streets established in 1898-99 by Chris Freyer. This was exclusively a man's sport and later alleys were often associated with billiard parlors, cigar stores and saloons. From about 1907 until the First World War, bowling was a very popular sport. It was also an elite sport as many of Piqua's civic and business leaders joined bowling teams at the **Piqua Club** (private men's club) and at the **YMCA** alleys (1908-1911). In 1908 the Piqua Bowling Association was formed as a part of the American Bowling Association. After **World War I**, the game's popularity declined and its participants changed. On February 3, 1926, the first women's bowling

The Centennial Lanes was a popular bowling spot in the late 1940's.

league in Piqua was established. By the 1930's and 1940's, industrial leagues had been formed. Later bowling establishments included Casey Bowling Alley (1939), Eagles Bowling Alleys (1930's-1960), Centennial Bowling Lanes (1948-1973), and the Brel-Aire Bowling Lanes (1959-present). Piqua's only bowling industry is Forrest Enterprises, Inc. (1955-present). It was founded by Forrest Roof to produce bowler's hand chalk. The company later expanded into foot spray, rosin, and hand conditioner for bowlers. SEE ALSO: Civil Rights Movement

BOXING

One of the most famous boxers to be connected with Piqua was **Luther McCarty**. On January 1, 1913, he became the "white heavyweight champion of the world" when he defeated Al Palzer, "the Iowa Giant". Five months later in a title bout in Calgary, Alberta, Canada against Arthur Pelkey, McCarty was knocked out during the first round. A half-hour later, at the age of twenty-one, Luther McCarty was dead. His funeral was held in Piqua, and he was buried in Forest Hill Cemetery.

During the 1930's and again in the 1950's, professional boxing matches were held in the National Guard Armory on East Ash Street. SEE ALSO: Dempsey, Jack; Theaters (Bijou).

BOY SCOUTS

The first unofficial local Boy Scout troop was organized in 1909 by the **YMCA.** The first scoutmaster was L. D. Roberts. These first twenty boys were to be trained as patrol leaders and then used to organize troops in the local churches. This first effort lasted only a few years before folding operations. The next Scout troop was part of the official national organization and was formed in 1911 under the leadership of YMCA physical director Christopher Kunz. But this troop also failed to last much past its original formation. In February of 1918, during the **First World War**, a new Piqua Boy Scout troop was organized and became the direct predecessor of today's scout troops. In 1943, Bennett Junior High school organized the first troop associated with a public school under the leadership of J.M. Kastner. The scoutmaster for the Bennett troop was J.J. Deisenroth. SEE ALSO: Girl Scouts

BREWERIES

The first brewery in Piqua was located on Piqua Island in the Miami River (just east of the North Main Street Bridge). It was established by John Suttle in 1835 and lasted until 1837. With an increasing number of German immigrants coming to the city, the number of breweries increased rapidly. Hartman Ploch established the City Brewery in 1835 on Spring Street. By 1859, part of Ploch's brewing operation had been moved to an area east of the Miami River and north of the Ash Street Bridge. Heinrich Schneider bought the brewery in 1881 and in 1902 his widow sold it to Carl H. Schnell. Schnell closed the brewery in 1909. John L. Schneyer established a brewery on the northeast corner of Spring and Water in the early 1850's. In 1898 Henry and Frank **Lange** bought the brewery and operated it until 1919 when it was changed to Lange Products Company, milk and dairy products distributors. Soon after the **Civil War**, William and Theodore Schmidlapp established the Piqua Brewery on the northeast corner of Spring and Water Streets. In 1881, Karl Kaiser purchased the brewery and moved it to Ash Street. The Ash Street brewery closed in 1895-96. County wide

Carl Kaiser's brewery was active in Piqua from 1881 through c. 1896.

This building on the northeast corner of Spring and Water Streets was the original home of the Lange Brewing Company

prohibition and finally national prohibition ended the brewing industry in Piqua. When national **prohibition** ended in 1933, Lange's resumed brewing until the death of Alex Lange in 1939. The plant then concentrated on ice production and dairy goods. In August of 1944, the dairy production was sold to Keller Sanders of Sanders **Dairy**. The plant and ice production was sold in 1945 to Walter Cunningham and Edison Steck the owners of the Polar Food Company. SEE ALSO: Industry; Prohibition.

BRICKS AND BRICK MASONS

In 1810, Colonel **John Johnston** brought brick mason John Keyt of New York to Upper Piqua to help build his new three story house. Johnston's house was the first brick structure in the area and Keyt was the community's first brick mason. Within the next few years, brick structures began going up in Piqua. The village's first brick structure was the "Seminary" a small one story building located on the public square and used as a school and a meeting room. In 1819, Doctor Daniel Ashton built Piqua's first brick home on the northwest corner of Main and Greene Streets. Doctor Ashton used part of the house as an office. From 1820 until 1833 the structure housed the Federal **Land Office**. During the 1820's, 1830's, and 1840's, large two story **Federal Style** brick homes were built by local residents Abel Brandon, Henry Kitchen, Byran Dayton, and **George Johnston**. Business for brick makers and brick masons was booming. Later nineteenth century building styles such as Greek Revival and Italianate continued the demand for larger and more elaborate brick homes. In the period from 1850 to 1900, active brick masons included Frank Geiger, James and David Keyt, William Hetherington, Samuel Redman, Howard Scudder, and William Betz. Brickyards from that period included those of Jacob Frichofer (1870's) and D. F. Frisch & Son (1880's). One of the largest brick laying jobs in Piqua was the **Hotel Plaza** in 1890. Eight hundred thousand bricks were produced for the four story structure and laid under the supervision of Joseph Geiger. SEE ALSO: Architecture; Industry; Patron p. 218

BRIDGES

Until 1820 the only way to reach Piqua from the east was to hope the water was low and then to ford the Great Miami River. The first bridge was built of wood and located near the present East Main Street bridge. The village added its second bridge in 1832 at the northern end of Main Street. The third bridge was erected in 1838 at the end of East Ash Street. By 1852 all three bridges had been covered with a roof and walls. The city's fourth bridge was erected in 1876-77 at Bridge Street and Statler Road. This was the city's first iron bridge. Piqua's first concrete bridge was the Lorimer (East Main Street) bridge dedicated in 1915. From the first bridge in 1820 until the Miami Conservancy Levees in 1921-22, the periodic **floodings** of the Great Miami River would cause the destruction of most of the city's bridges.

BROOM MAKERS

Pioneer families would usually make their own household brooms. But as the community grew, broom making became a specialty art. The first commercial broom manufacturer on record is John Page in 1853. He was followed by Joseph Sage (c1868-c1877), J. A. Edmonds (c1870-c1881), Alvin T. Gale (c1885-c1890's), Curtis & McCurdy (c1887-c1902), and the Ideal Broom and Brush Co. (Joseph McAtchett) (c1920). The last broom manufacturing company was established in 1897 by Henry C. Vosler as the Piqua Broom Factory. The firm was located at 1001 West Water and continued operations until 1932-33.

BUCHANAN, FORT

Fort Buchanan was erected on the site of Fort Rowdy (1793). A blockhouse, tower, and stockade, including a spring, was completed by May/June of 1812 near the site of Covington, Ohio by Captain George Buchanan and his Militia Company, 2nd Regiment, 5th Brigade, 1st Division, Ohio Militia. The fort was abandoned on or shortly after July 20, 1812. SEE ALSO: War of 1812.

The Ash Street Bridge looking east in the 1930's.

BUNGALOW STYLE ARCHITECTURE

The local variation of the Bungalow Style was popular from 1910 through 1930. Dr. Frame was one of the great local supporters of this style in Piqua, building a total of three Bungalow homes for his own use. These smaller houses had wide eves with rafter ends exposed and extended like brackets. The porches in this style are usually an integral part of the structure with extending roof lines and prominent supports or piers. The grander examples of this style had shingled and stucco side wall surfaces. In the west end of Piqua, this style often sported a single center front dormer sitting on a sweeping gable roof that covered a full-width inset porch. The Dormer Front Variation of the Bungalow Style blossomed as the electric street railway system at the turn of the century opened up the downtown area to the new building sites on the edge of the community.

These homes have many of the architectural elements found in the larger craftsman style structures. SEE ALSO: Interurbans

DOMESTIC EXAMPLES
512 North Downing, Dr. A.B. Frame House, 1915
320 North Downing, Dr. A.B. Frame House, 1917

B.V.D. COMPANY

This underwear company was founded by Bradley, Vorhees and Day in 1876 as a men's underwear company. This was the origin of the abbreviation and not the better known "Boy's [Better] ventilated drawers". By the twentieth century the company had changed ownership a number of times, but BVD's had become a common name for tighter fitting single drawers (instead of union suits). The firm was purchased by the Erlanger Brothers (Charles and Abraham) of Baltimore in 1908. In Piqua, the B.V.D. name had two specific connections. In December of 1929, a holding company was created, B.V.D. Inc. of Delaware, to control the B.V.D. Company, the **Atlas Underwear Company**, the Regatta Underwear Company of Baltimore, the Erlanger Knitting Mills Inc. of Piqua and various B.V.D. Sales Corporations (i.e.: B.V.D. Sales of Maryland, of New York, of Cuba, etc.). The holding company was in general controlled by **Alfred L. Flesh** of Piqua (president of the Atlas Underwear Company) and **Milton Erlanger** (president of the B.V.D. Company, a division of the Erlanger Mills). Flesh and Erlanger purchased the **Piqua Hosiery Company** in 1930. The two men split in 1933, with Flesh maintaining control of the Piqua Hosiery Company and a few of the B.V.D. Sales Corporations and Erlanger taking the B.V.D. Company, the Regatta Manufacturing Company and the rest of the B.V.D. Sales Corporations. Atlas would retain control of her B.V.D. sales corporations until 1950's.

The second B.V.D. connection to Piqua occurred when Sol Kittay & Associates of New York City purchased the **Superior** Company of Piqua in 1945. Kittay purchased the B.V.D. Company and most of its Sales Corporations in 1951 from the Erlanger Family and merged the company with Superior to form the B.V.D. Company Inc. The B.V.D. plant in Piqua closed down in December of 1967. Piqua's B.V.D. connection dropped at this time and the community's brief exposure with the brand name was ended. By the 1970's, B.V.D. had been acquired by Fruit of the Loom Inc.

CALIFORNIA GOLD RUSH

The *New York Herald* published a story on August 19, 1848 that gold had been discovered in California. Thousands of gold hunters flooded into the California area, and by the end of 1849 the territory contained over 100,000 people. A number of Piqua citizens traveled west to try and gain their fortunes. In 1849, William Johnston and T. J. Lawton organized a party of over one hundred men for the overland trek to California. Johnston and Lawton made money, not by panning for gold, but by selling the miners pots and pans for a very healthy profit. Joseph Walkup set up a retail establishment in California. He ran a grocery store in Placer County, as well as a small cattle ranch to supply his customers with fresh meat. Two other well known Piquads left Ohio to make their fortunes in the west, **Frank Hardy** in the spring of 1850, and **William P. Orr** in 1852. Both men stayed in California for roughly a year and a half before returning to Ohio. While several of the local adventurers did very well financially, none of them made the fortunes the gold fields had seemed to promise.

CAMP WAKONDA

Camping became part of the **YMCA** program in 1901 with the first boys' camp being located on Painters Creek south of Covington, Ohio. For the next twenty-five years, the camp moved to a number of sites including Evergreen Lake (ten miles north of Piqua) and the Stillwater River (near Covington). By 1919, the yearly camps were each called Camp Rundle after one of the local founding fathers of the YMCA. In 1924, the camp was held on the banks of Wise's pond in Shelby County. The camp consisted of old World War I army pyramidal tents erected over wooden platforms and a big dining tent. In 1926, **Allen G. Rundle** purchased land for the Piqua YMCA close to this site for a permanent camp. The 13.5 acres were part of the Lester Heaton farm adjoining Lackey's Pond off of Kuther Road in Shelby County. C.F. Bowdle designed the structures for the new camp consisting of a wooden dining lodge, a staff cabin and five tent houses. The site was named Camp Wakonda (Sioux for Great Spirit) and the first Y campers arrived in the summer of 1927. Later additions to the camp included a craft cabin (1929), a chapel in the woods (1931), a camp director's cottage (1941), Koester Lodge (1960) and a pool (1961). Over the years the camp has been used for scouting retreats, family reunions, and high school band camps. The Shelby County Health Department closed down the site as a residential camp in the 1970's. The YMCA sold the land and buildings to Piqua businessmen (Sanigard Company) Hershel Kyle and Meredith Shaffer in November of 1981 for use as a public camp ground. SEE ALSO: Civil Rights; YMCA.

CANALS

The first large scale canal project was begun in New York State by the Erie Canal Commission. This canal was built to connect Buffalo and Lake Erie with a direct water route to New

The one room wooden cabins were the standard housing for over-night campers at the YMCA's Camp Wakonda.

York City. Ohio's canals began with the formation of a canal commission on January 31, 1822. Three years later, construction was authorized for two canal systems along an eastern and western route. Work on the western route or Miami Canal began in July of 1825. The first canal boats reached Dayton from Cincinnati on January 25, 1829. After considerable political lobbying, the state agreed to the construction of the Miami Extension Canal from Dayton north to Lake Erie. One of the chief supporters of this extension was canal commissioner Colonel **John Johnston** of Piqua. Johnston served on the commission from 1825 until 1836 acting as one of the most vocal advocates for canal expansion. The canal extension cut directly through Johnston's farm north of Piqua.

Work began on the extension of the canal in the spring of 1833. Local canal contractors included Loring R. Brownell, N. Sumner, Jeremiah G. Furrow, Abel C. Furrow and William Johnston. Construction work reached Miami County in 1835, but the pace of building slowed down. Completing the canal bed and the ten locks located in the county took until June 20, 1837. The following day on June 21, Piqua's first canal boat, the "Emigrant" was launched. The town held a grand dedication of the canal on July 5, 1837. The principal speakers were **William Henry Harrison**, **John Johnston**, and Ohio Militia General **Joseph G. Young**.

Piqua remained the terminus of the canal until 1842, resulting in major industrial and population growth for the community. By June of 1845, the canal had been completed, creating a water route reaching from Cincinnati north to Toledo. The state officially named the route the Miami and Erie Canal in 1849. The canal was profitable until 1852 when revenues began to decline and competition from railroads began to increase.

The state leased the canal to a private investment company in 1861 for the sum of twenty thousand dollars a year for ten years. In 1871, the state renewed the lease but falling revenues caused the investment company to abandon control in 1877. The State Board of Public Works once again was in control of the canal.

In 1878, the Miami and Erie Canal Association was formed to help upgrade the canal. Headed by local Physician **G. V. Dorsey** and later by local banker **Henry Flesh**, the Association promoted the building of new canal boats and the general improvement of the canal. They also supported the Miami and Erie Transportation Company in their attempt to lay tracks and pull the canal boats by means of an electric "mule". Like many schemes before it, this attempt failed due to a lack of financial support. Traffic began dwindling to fewer than one or two boats a week.

By 1912 large areas of the canal had been either formally or informally abandoned. The last known

canal boat to travel through Piqua was the quarry boat the "De Camp Statler" in 1912. The flood of 1913 destroyed the canal's ability to function by washing out locks, aqueducts and embankments. The Miami **Conservancy District** began building flood protection levy banks on top of the canal in Piqua along Riverside Drive and South Main Street. The city filled in the last section of the canal from East Water Street north to the Miami River in the summer of 1926. By fall of 1926, the tracks of the Western Ohio Railway had been moved from Main Street to the old canal bed. A footnote to the history of the Miami and Erie Canal occurred in 1972 when the Ohio Historical Society reopened a section of the canal at the area of the Johnston Farm Site (**Piqua Historical Area** State Memorial). The Society currently (2007) runs the second "General Harrison," a replica of an 1840's era canal boat, on this restored area of the canal. SEE ALSO: Border City; Coopers; Ice Production; Randolph Slaves.

By 1910, most of the Piqua bridges over the canal had been switched to mechanical lift bridges such as this one on East High Street.

This postcard view of Lock Nine on the Miami & Erie Canal shows that canal was still a vital local transportation system during the early years of the twentieth century.

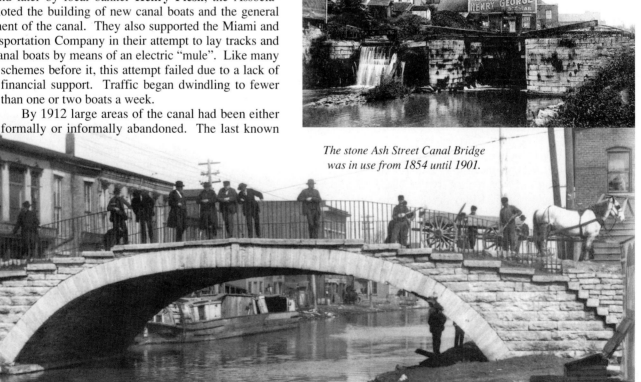

The stone Ash Street Canal Bridge was in use from 1854 until 1901.

CANDLEWOOD HILLS

This subdivision on Piqua's west end off of South Street was developed by **Mid-Continent Properties** in 1965 and continued through the early 1970's. SEE ALSO: Housing Develpments

CELEBRATIONS

CENTENNIAL OF THE DECLARATION OF INDEPENDENCE (1776-1876)

Held on the Fourth of July in 1876, this was one of the first large celebrations in the city. A parade was held with over one thousand teams of horses which attracted over fifteen thousand visitors to the city. Four large cartoons made by Amos Sawyer and J.F. Hummel hung across Main Street. The cartoons represented Piqua in 1776, Piqua in 1876, the Liberty Bell and an Indian Chief offering a peace pipe. A National Guard and G.A.R. (Civil War veterans) military encampment was held at Fountain Park. A full community dinner was held at the park which was followed by a speech by **Stephen Johnston**. During the afternoon games were played such as chasing the greased pig, wheel barrowing and sack races. The day ended with a formal dress parade by all the military units present followed by a mock military battle and fireworks.

Captain Don Gentile with Ohio Governor Frank Lausche in August of 1946 at Piqua's Sesquicentennial Celebration.

SESQUICENTENNIAL OF THE NORTHWEST TERRITORY (1788-1938)

This celebration was held in September of 1938. Some of the many events included a downtown parade, an historic pageant "Winding Waters" written by R.E. Perry, a Candlelight Promenade down Main Street when all the street lights were turned off and all the stores illuminated only with candles, a tour of area historic sites and a five hundred voice Orpheus Chorus performance directed by **C.M. Sims** and **Philip Gates**.

DON GENTILE DAY (1944)

This celebration was held on May 25, 1944 to honor Piqua native Captain **Don Gentile**, a World War II Ace. A parade featuring military units from Patterson Field, local bands and choirs, and students was held to honor Gentile, his wingman Captain Godfrey, and Lieutenant Martin Minnich (a Piqua native who served as a bomber pilot and was shot down over Europe and escaped across occupied France back to England). Ohio Lt. Governor Paul Herbert, Congressman Robert Jones and

a representative of the North American Aircraft Corp. (makers of Gentile's P-51 Mustang) were among the dignitaries present. The celebration was promoted as a war bond rally.

PIQUA SESQUICENTENNIAL (1796-1946)

Sponsored by the newly organized Piqua Chamber of Commerce, this celebration was held to boost local spirits and pride after the large plant closings (Lear, Robbins-Meyers) at the end of World War II. The coming of **Job Gard** to Piqua in 1796 was the rationale for the event. Activities during the celebration included an historic pageant "Through the Years" which was kicked off by the presentation of Miss Piqua (Antoinette Thoma) and Miss Ohio (Maxine Staley) with a full chorus directed by **C.M. Sims**, a fly-in at the Piqua airport with World War II ace **Don Gentile**, downtown window displays of both historic artifacts and new "Made in Piqua" materials, boat races on the Great Miami River, a live radio broadcast by WLW-Cincinnati from the Hotel Favorite and a closing celebration speech at the football stadium by Ohio Governor Frank Lausche.

The 1946 Piqua Sesquicentennial Celebration was promoted by contestants in the beauty pageant in this Step Lange photograph.

BICENTENNIAL OF THE UNITED STATES (1776-1976)

Piqua celebrated this event with a series of activities that spanned the entire year. The driving force behind this celebration was Bicentennial Committee chairman Lou Havenar. Bicentennial events included a huge parade in September, a wooden reconstruction of Fort Pickawillany on the public square, historic displays in downtown merchant windows, the publication of *Historic Piqua, An Architectural Survey* by the A.A.U.W., an antique fire equipment display, a postage stamp show, Christmas caroling, an oral history project, a *Bicentennial Souvenir Year Book* by the Piqua Moose Lodge #1067 and a local production of the Broadway musical *1776*. SEE ALSO: canals; Chautauqua

Captain Don Gentile was interviewed on WLW radio in a room at the Favorite Hotel (Plaza) during Don Gentle Day in 1944.

CHAMBER OF COMMERCE

The Citizens Association of Piqua, Ohio was organized in February of 1884 with Stephen Johnston as its first president. The Association was formed to promote industrial growth within the city. This group would develop into the Piqua Board of Trade which was responsible for bringing the **Favorite Stove and Range Company** and the **Cincinnati Corrugating Company** to Piqua in 1888-1889.

A short lived Chamber group was organized in 1914 to "generally foster, protect and advance the commercial, mercantile, educational, social and manufacturing interests of the City of Piqua, Ohio and its vicinity." This organization had disbanded by the First World War era.

The modern Chamber of Commerce traces its roots to the end of the Second World War. The initial meeting was held on February 01, 1944 and chaired by **Meteor Motor Car Company** leader **Armotte Boyer**. Those present began organizing for postwar Piqua development. Out of these early meetings, the Piqua Chamber of Commerce was formed on March 3, 1944. Boyer was elected as the new organization's first president. Two existing civic groups, the Piqua Civic Association headed by Joe Dine and the Piqua Business Association headed by Frank Albright agreed to merger with the new Chamber. The Chamber organized its committees around the following programs; service to existing industries, trade expansion, industrial development, transportation, legislation, civic affairs, public relations and aviation. By June of 1944, the Chamber had named William M. Cory of Alliance, Ohio as its first managing director. During its early years the Chamber promoted the creation of a City Park Board (August 1944) coupled with the passage of a Park levy (November 1944), promoted the creation of a **Piqua Historical Park** at the Johnston Farm, the sponsorship of a Piqua Air Show (September 1944), creation of a Veterans Service Center (January 1945) and sponsorship of the Piqua Sesquicentennial Celebration (1946). By June of 1946 the Chamber had grown to 830 members. SEE ALSO: Celebrations (Piqua Sesquicentennial); Order of George Award; Patron p. 261

CHARITIES

The earliest attempts at community aid and assistance were very selective in nature. In 1818, **Rachel Johnston** organized the Piqua Female Bible and Charitable Society to provide bibles and aid to the "worthy poor", particularly recent widows. This group soon began concentrating on bibles and aid to the needy was undertaken by various church groups for their own members.

The **Civil War** brought the next community relief organization. It was organized in 1861 as the Soldier's Aid Society to provide bandages for wounded soldiers. But as the war continued, the needs of the soldiers' families became apparent. The Society began providing the wives and children with food, fuel and cash.

The first wide-spread community aid program came about in 1885 with the formation of the Ladies Aid Society. This group was formed by twelve women representing the various churches in town. They began sewing clothing, collecting food and raising money for the city's less fortunate. A reorganization occurred in 1893 and the group began raising funds as the Associated Charities. By 1910, the Association allowed men to join and in 1920 hired their first staff person, Miss Harriet Fleming. During **World War I** (1918-1919), the Miami County National War Fund raised money for the homeless and starving in Europe and the United States.

The Great **Depression** hit the group very hard and they held their last public fund raiser in 1933. It did, however, continue under the auspices of the Piqua City Schools for use as a fund for children without shoes. [Associated Charities lost its individual identity and governing committee in 1988 when the organizational funds were placed under direct school control.] During **World War II**, fund raising was resumed in 1943 under the banner of the National War Fund of Miami County. The group funneled money to dozens of national and international groups. After World War II, the Piqua Community Welfare Federation was created by the Piqua Chamber of Commerce to raise funds for the **Salvation Army**, the **YWCA**, the **Boy Scouts**, the **Girl Scouts**, the Mental Health Association and the **YMCA**. The young organization joined the national group in 1949 becoming the Piqua Community Chest. A drastic drop in fund raising led to a final reorganization in 1958 which created the modern Piqua Area **United Fund** [Way] which in 2006 funded twenty-three agencies. SEE ALSO: Patron p. 273

CHASE, CAMP

This Civil War training camp was established on the outskirts of Columbus. Piqua units from the 11th Ohio Volunteer Infantry Regiment were mustered into service at this camp.

CHATEAUESQUE STYLE ARCHITECTURE

There is only one local variation of this style in the city, the mansion built for **Atlas Underwear Company** founder, **Leo M. Flesh** at 650 North Downing Street. The home was designed by Harvey Hiestand and constructed by Airhart M. Fry in 1907. Built with a matching carriage house, this home used a style that mimicked the classical mansions of France. With its steeply pitched hipped roof and massive dormers, this was the largest private home in the city at the time of its construction. The style encourages formal living styles and entertainment on the grand scale. The Flesh Family enhanced the home with a world class art collection that featured paintings by Millet, Carots, Reynolds, Whistler, Gainsborough, Constable, Stuart, Romney and Raeborn. Mr. Flesh also collected and displayed Faberge jeweled boxes and Napoleon I pieces. The home had the third floor servant's quarters tied to the rest of the house by a system of electric call bells.

The Leo M. Flesh home at 650 North Downing Street is the city's only Chateauesque Style home.

CHAUTAUQUA

The Piqua Chautauqua was the city's longest running community festival. The Piqua-Community Chautauqua Association held their first festival at Fountain Park from August 16 until August 25, 1912. The festival grew in popularity and after **World War I**, a permanent pavilion was built in the park (today known as the Hance Pavilion). Local and imported talent competed for the attention of Chautauqua goers. Local talent included the Piqua Drama League, the Piqua Band under **Phil Gates**, and the Elks Glee Club. International presentations were represented by groups such as the Star Russian Company (vocal group from the Soviet Union), the Ramos Mexican Orchestra and the Gypsy Troubadours. Speakers were a main draw for Chautauqua and included Billy Sunday, Lowell Thomas and numerous senators, governors, and other public figures. Camping was allowed in the park, but a 1917 program stated that "all tent holders will furnish their own electric light bulbs". The Association held their last Chautauqua in 1931. The American Legion Drum Corps took over for an additional two years, but could not make a go of the festival during the Depression. A small revival of Chautauqua was organized in 1975 and 1976 by Don Smith on the Piqua public square.

CHICAGO COMMERCIAL STYLE

The local variation of the Chicago Commercial Style was popular from 1905 through 1910. There are no local domestic examples of this style. The era of downtown department stores hit Piqua in 1896 with the construction of the three story Romanesque Style Benkert Building. The owner, George Benkert, had been strongly influenced by the **Richardsonian Romanesque Style** of the Hotel Plaza building located only a half a block to the north. The next two department stores built during the first decade of the twentieth century looked to a different influence in their construction. Edgar A. Todd and J.W. Brown each built their department store buildings with the new steel skeleton construction method and the highly popular Chicago Style windows. Both men had visited Chicago and were most likely influenced by the Chicago Commercial Style that was so popular there at the turn of the nineteenth century. This style with its large upper floor windows was well suited to the demands of a department store that would use all four floors for direct retail sales. Both men modified the Chicago Style to meet local needs for commercial decoration by using some of the classical features of the **Second Renaissance Revival Style** and/or locally common **Italianate** elements.

This style has many of the following local architectural elements. These stores were built in a rectangular shape abutted between shorter row buildings and they are the tallest building on the block. Built with a steel frame construction with a brick or stone facade, the upper floors contained central pivot windows topped by fixed transom windows. These upper facades are dominated by windows in either a horizontal or vertical orientation with pilasters or embedded columns flanking the windows. A decorated cornice or parapet was very common. The first floor storefronts contained deeply recessed entrances with plate glass display windows on each side and plate glass display windows oriented inward towards the recessed entrance way. The buildings had a free standing kiosk display area with plate glass windows in the center of the front recessed entrance way. A transom and fascia cover the entire top of the storefront and the steel beam piers on each side of the storefront are encased (hidden) by brick or stone.

In 1913, The Piqua Chautauqua Festival was held on the grounds of Fountain Park.

COMMERCIAL EXAMPLES
    405-407 North Main Street, Todd Building/Apple Tree Gallery, 1907
    322-324 North Main Street, J.W. Brown Building, 1908-09

CHILLICOTHE (VILLAGE)

Chillicothe was the name of one of the main divisions of the **Shawnee** tribe. This division occupied separate villages during most of the early history of the tribe. In Ohio, Chillicothe was located at the mouth of the Scioto River (c1760's), on the Little Miami River near Oldtown in Greene County (c1775), and on the Great Miami River near Piqua in Miami County (1780-1782). SEE ALSO: Huntersville, Ohio; Piqua (Village); Shawnee Indians.

CHINESE

In 1879, Sam Lee opened Piqua's first Chinese business establishment, a **laundry** in the 100 block of North Main Street. Lee had come to the United States from China in 1864. By the mid-1880's, at least a half a dozen Chinese families had moved to Piqua. The growing Chinese community in Piqua was short lived. By 1900, there were no Chinese laundries doing business in the Piqua area and most of the families had moved to larger cities..

CHRISTMAS TRADITIONS

CAROLING. An exact history of local caroling is very difficult to determine. During the early pioneer period singing was held indoors and many local churches discouraged public celebrations of Christmas. By the 1840's and 1850's, several **churches** (particularly the Episcopalian and Lutheran) established the custom of male singers gathering on the steps of the church to sing carols accompanied by brass instruments. After the Civil War and especially during the 1880's through World War I, private caroling parties were very popular. Mixed groups of men and women would walk around their own neighborhoods singing at individual homes before retiring to a single residence for food and hot beverages. After World War I, community caroling began under the leadership of the **YMCA** and **YWCA**. This caroling would take place on the public square on Christmas Eve or during the week of Christmas. Public caroling during the 1980's began again under the sponsorship of the Piqua Heritage Festival Committee and later under Mainstreet Piqua auspices.

This c. 1920's photograph shows Piqua's downtown Christmas decorations in the middle of Main Street at the public square.

CHRISTMAS TREE. During the Post-Civil War period in Piqua, the Christmas tree tradition gained in popularity with the growth of the **German** population. The idea of the holiday tree came from Germany, but those early trees were usually very small, table top size. They were an intimate, family size symbol. After 1900, larger trees became more popular. The first record of a community tree lists the YWCA as its sponsor. On December 14, 1919, the YWCA's welfare clubs worked together to place a community Christmas tree on the northwest corner of the public square next to the Rowan Memorial. The second tree was set up in the square in 1920. The tree was cut by Mayor A. W. DeWeese from a lot along South Main that was the site of the future Bennett Junior High School. It was decorated by both the YMCA and the YWCA. With a few lapses during the 1930's and 1940's, the tradition of a community Christmas tree on the public square has continued to this present day.

HOUSE DECORATION. The tradition of placing candles in the windows at Christmas was well established in the last half of the nineteenth century in Piqua. The candles originally were meant to represent the Star of Bethlehem. Later they were also used to signify that the family was at home and would welcome visitors. During the 1980's, the custom of decorating the home with candles in the windows (now electric candles) was revived at many houses in the historic district.

CHURCHES

The earliest European-American settlers worshiped in their homes, with simple non-denominational services. Bible readings and hymn singing dominated these early services. Itinerant preachers (some trained and some not) traveled through the area, and for room and board, preached to a gathering of neighbors, often standing on a tree stump in a recently cleared field. Church structures constructed of logs began appearing as the local population increased and people began worship in specific denominational groups.

The first local church to be organized was the Methodist Episcopal in 1807.

The first actual church structure was erected by the Methodist Episcopal congregation next to the **Johnston** Farm in 1815.

The first church structure to be built in Piqua was created in 1816 by the Associate Reformed Presbyterian Church.

The first church to use the **German** language for the church service was St. Paul's Lutheran in 1835.

The last church congregation to use the German language in a regular church service were the German Methodists in 1958.

The first African-American church in Piqua was the Cyrene A.M.E. established in 1853.

The first church to have a pipe **organ** was the Second Presbyterian Church.

The oldest church still standing in Piqua was built by the First Baptists in 1848 (215 West High). SEE ALSO: List-churches

The Park Avenue Baptist Church was built in 1885-1889. Note the wooden steeple in this 1940's photograph.

CINCINNATI CORRAGATING COMPANY/PIQUA ROLLER MILL

The Corrugating Company was established in 1879 in Cincinnati. It was moved to Piqua in 1888 by James Hicks (president) and Colonel **John G. Battelle** (secretary/general manager). The firm was attracted to Piqua by the availability of industrial sites, its strong railroad connections and the availability of natural gas. The firm made iron and steel roofing, doors and shutters and terne plate (high grade roofing and ceiling tin). Immediately

*This 1897 photograph of the Cincinnati Corrugating Company
shows the plant located between South Main and South Roosevelt Streets.*

after moving to Piqua, the company created the Piqua Rolling Mill Company with Battelle as president, **William P. Orr** as vice president and Hicks as secretary/treasurer. Both companies were located on the south end of Main Street on the west side. The firms received a big contract from the federal government in 1899 to furnish iron building materials for use in military barracks in Cuba. The contract was for over $57,000 and was the largest single order ever handled by a local firm up to that time. The firm averaged roughly three hundred regular workers during the 1890's. Both firms were merged into the American Sheet Steel & Tin Plate Company in April of 1900 with over twenty other steel companies under the presidency of Daniel Gray Reid (1858-1925) with Battelle serving as vice president. American Sheet & Tin Plate was merged with the United States Steel Corporation (owned by Carnegie and Morgan) in 1903. The local plant experienced several **strikes** over the issue of unionization in 1908 and 1909 as well as several closings due to work shortages. The workers were represented by the Amalgamated Association of Iron, Steel, & Tin Workers **Union** (this was the same national union that led the Homestead Strike at the Carnegie Steel Company). The plant was closed down in c.1909. SEE ALSO: McKinley, William

CINCINNATI, OHIO

The site for the first village was purchased from John C. Symmes in 1788. Matthias Denman, Robert Patterson, and John Filson laid out the village they called Losantiville. In 1789, the village became the capital of the Northwest Territory and was renamed Cincinnati by Governor Arthur St. Clair. SEE ALSO: Canals; Forts (Washington); Hilliard Family; Hutchins, Minabelle; Railroads; Symmes, John C.

CIRCUS

The railroads were a source of great entertainment when they brought the circus to town. The Pennsylvania **Railroad** freight yards on Wood Street west of Roosevelt were transformed into another world. Organized chaos would occur when the circus began unloading their wagons, tents and animal cages. The performers would cause another stir as they began exiting the train wearing strange and exotic costumes. Many of the circus' would plan for a grand parade down Main Street to promote attendance to the evening performances. Some of the biggest names in traveling shows came to Piqua, such as Buffalo Bill's Wild West Show, The Ringling Brothers Circus, The Barnum

and Bailey Circus and many more. The traveling shows stopped coming to the smaller towns such as Piqua by the late 1950's.

CITIZENS MILITARY TRAINING CORPS

This organization was created by the National Defense Act of 1920. It was created to offer voluntary military training to young men from the ages of sixteen through nineteen. Training took place during four week summer camps with instruction being provided by Regular Army personnel. The camps offered four levels of training beginning with basic training for new recruits to a final course that prepared the volunteer with the qualifications for a reserve officer commission. This organization opened a recruiting office in Piqua on June 26, 1923.

CITY COUNCIL

The State Legislature reincorporated the village of Piqua on March 9, 1835, and provided for the election of a mayor and four councilmen, one for each ward. An election was held on April 11 and William C. Dills, James M. Defrees, John Brown, and William H. Keyt became the community's first councilmen. After an 1843 reincorporation, a new ward and a new councilman were added to the village government. On March 19, 1850, the village was reincorporated as a city. After the election of April 6, 1850, Rankin Walkup from the fourth ward became the first councilman to serve as president of the council. In 1853 the council was increased to eight members. The council was increased again in 1885 to twelve members, in 1892 to fourteen members, and in 1894 decreased to ten. By 1903 the State of Ohio passed a new municipal code and the city council was trimmed to four ward councilmen and three councilmen at large. This system stayed in place until Piqua voted in a City Manager/City Commission form of government in 1929. The first election for the new commission was held on November 4, 1929. The following men became the city's first commissioners; **Charles B. Upton**, John French, Ben Wise, Logan Frazier and **Vernon Osborn**. SEE ALSO: Dorsey, Godwin; Flesh, Henry; Mayors; Orr, William; Socialists.

CITY MANAGERS

The Piqua City Charter, adopted on July 30, 1929 transferred the day to day operation and control of Piqua from the elected mayor to a city manager appointed by the elected city commission. Lester G. Whitney, the first city manger was appointed in 1930.
SEE ALSO: City Council; Mayors; List-City Managers

CIVIC HALL OF FAME, PIQUA

The Hall of Fame began in 1995 with the induction of three citizens. The Hall of Fame continues today (2007) with three inductees each year. SEE ALSO: List-Civic of Fame Inductees.

CIVIL RIGHTS MOVEMENT

This article deals primarily with the African-American experience in Piqua from the 1930's through the 1970's. The Northern Civil Rights movement was in some ways more difficult to organize than the southern movement that took place in the 1950's and 1960's. Northern racial prejudices and restrictions were often subtle and "understood" rather than the more overt Jim Crow laws or "whites only" signage. But segregation and racial injustice were very much alive in Ohio. The state had passed the Public Accommodations Law in 1884 to end discrimination but it was only sporadically enforced. Ohio strengthened this law in 1959 with a new civil rights law to eliminate discrimination in employment based on race, color, religion or ancestry. To enforce this new act, the Ohio Assembly created the Ohio Civil Rights Commission. **African-American** political power in Ohio took a huge jump forward with the 1967 election of Carl B. Stokes as mayor of Cleveland. Stokes was the first African-American to be elected mayor of a major American city.

SEGREGATION AND DISCRIMINATION. The African-American population of Piqua was set apart in variety of different ways in the first half of the twentieth century. A poor African-American or even an individual from the working class was refereed to as "colored". If an individual was considered prominent, influential or a veteran he or she was referred to as a negro. The nineteenth century custom of calling older African-Americans Uncle or Aunt had not died away. Employment was restricted for the most part to jobs such as domestic service, cleaning, elevator operators, janitors, day laborers (day to day jobs), junk yards, hauling and other menial tasks. One of the few exceptions to these restrictions was the employment of African-American barbers.

Services and entertainment in Piqua were segregated by race in such areas as restaurants, movie theaters, the **YMCA** and the **YWCA**. Restaurants and soda fountain and lunch counters would either completely deny service or would require African-Americans to purchase food and drinks at the back door to be consumed off premises on the sidewalks or curbs. The Piqua Schines **Theater** on Main Street restricted African-American seating to the rear three or four rows. The Miami Schines Theater (former May's Opera House) on North Wayne Street restricted African-American seating to the balcony.

The YMCA at first totally denied African-American membership. After World War I, membership activities were limited to segregated clubs such as the Alpha Sepia Hi-Y and segregated weeks for African-American boys and girls at **Camp Wakonda**. African-American boys were denied use of the indoor Y pool. The YWCA allowed African-American membership but maintained the standards of the day with segregated clubs such the Senior Triangle. The Coca-Cola Hall (Coke Hall) on the east side of the public square allowed African-American attendance only on "special nights". Youth activities such as Girl Scouts and Boy Scouts were segregated. High School sports such as **football** were usually racially mixed however individual indoor sports such as skating and bowling were usually denied to African-Americans prior to World War II. When the local skating rinks and **bowling** alleys were finally opened to all races in the late 1950's, African-Americans were denied shoe or skate rentals and had to bring their own equipment.

Organizations such as the **United Way**, **Red Cross**, **World War II** War Bond Drives and similar community groups subtly discouraged participation or segregated African-American volunteers into separate and often less important committees. There is no record of any African-American being elected or chosen to lead or chair these type of community groups until Elmer Harris was elected to head the United Way in the 1960's. Many veterans' groups prohibited African-American veterans from joining beginning with

the **American Legion** in 1919 which continued this unofficial ban until the beginning of the twenty-first century. African-American veterans from Piqua frequently joined the Covington American Legion. A segregated Veterans of Foreign Wars Post was formed in March of 1946.

Housing segregation was at times difficult to pin down in Piqua. A single segregated housing area located on the other side of a physical boundary (i.e.: river, railroad, street) did not exist in Piqua. African-American housing was segregated in small clusters scattered throughout the city. Some of these clusters included Rossville to the northwest and across the river, Bassett Avenue to the south, the west ends of Greene, Boone and North Streets at Washington Avenue, Camp Street on the west end, and Sycamore Street in the center of the city along the railroad. The city's oldest traditional African-American churches (Park Avenue Baptist and Cyrene A.M.E.) were located on the north and south boundaries of Piqua's early twentieth century elite housing area (Wayne, Downing, Caldwell Streets).

While segregated seating on city buses was a major part of the southern civil rights movement that did not appear to be an issue on the Dodge **Taxi** Company buses that ran in Piqua.

BREAKING SEGREGATION. The local chapter of the **N.A.A.C.P.** led the fight in Piqua to desegregate public institutions in the city during the first few years following the end of World War II (1945-1947).

One of the first of the post-war events (1945) was staged by about a dozen N.A.A.C.P. members (including Emerson Clemens, **Viola Clemens**, **Darrell Taylor**, Shirley Thomas, Albert Henderson, John Vosler and Rev. Howard Foston) at the lunch counter of the bus station located in the southeast corner of the Favorite **Hotel**

Viola and Emerson Clemens were two of Piqua's early Civil Rights leaders.

Mrs. Cass and Mrs. Taylor were the leaders of the first African-American girl scout troops.

on the public square. When these men and women attempted to sit down at the counter, they were told by the waitress that "coloreds were not served inside". When the lunch counter and bus station owner was told that the N.A.A.C.P. members refused to leave (one of the first sit-ins in the Miami Valley) he changed his policy on the spot and served everybody sitting at the counter. The Terry family that owned and ran the bus station would, in the ensuing years, support the N.A.A.C.P. This was highlighted in a later publicity photograph of the bus station that showed an N.A.A.C.P. fund raising poster prominently displayed. Prior to the sit-in, the local members of the N.A.A.C.P. had contacted Piqua attorney and former Ohio Speaker of the House **William McCulloch** for assistance if needed. McCulloch's office was located just across the public square from the bus station. Since the Terry family agreed to open their lunch counter to all races equally, McCulloch's aid was not needed. McCulloch would later serve as the Congressman from the local district and become the main sponsor for the landmark Civil Rights Act of 1964.

The second major battle for the N.A.A.C.P. was segregated seating in the city's theaters. Local members attended an evening show at the Piqua Schines Theater on Main Street and took seats throughout the theater refusing to sit in the rear three rows of designated segregated seating. It was primarily the same group that had staged the sit-in at the bus stop with the exception of Darrell Taylor. Mr. Taylor objected to theater attendance based on his own religious convictions. The Schines management refused to show the movie until the N.A.A.C.P. members returned to the "appropriate" seats in the rear. When they refused, it was reported that a white male, a veteran of World War II, stood up and allegedly said" If they're good enough to serve with me, they're good enough to watch a movie with me, now show the #&8@! movie". One of the African-American women attending this action remembers being shocked by his language but pleased by his actions. After additional delays, the movie was shown and segregated seating in both of Piqua's two movie houses ended.

Breaking the segregation barrier in youth activities took a little longer. It appears that the segregated High School Y Clubs such as the Alpha Sepia Hi-Y were disbanded in 1949-1950. In 1950, David Thomas (treasurer) and Shirley Thomas (secretary) served as High School senior class officers breaking another racial barrier. It would not be until 1958 the Clayton Freels would break the ban on African-Americans swimming in the indoor YMCA pool. After World War II, the concept of "special nights" for African-Americans diminished and vanished by the late 1950's in almost all local public and semi-public facilities. While public accommodations opened gradually for Piqua's African-American youth, other issues like the bias against inter-racial dancing or dating did not begin to diminish until the 1970's. SEE ALSO: African-American History; Rossville; Soute-Harris Post.

CIVIL WAR

HOME FRONT. At the beginning of the war, Piqua was a growing town of 4,600 with two railroad lines and a busy Miami-Erie Canal lock. With the first call to service, Piqua eagerly responded with Company K of the First Ohio Volunteer Infantry. While recruiting for new soldiers was never as easy as the first time, local volunteers kept Piqua's quotas filled and the city never had to rely on the draft.

The town was also very active politically with two local men serving in prominent positions. Democrat **John F. McKinney** served as the district's representative to Congress, while Republican **Godwin V. Dorsey** served as treasurer of the State of Ohio. Dorsey was one of the early organizers of the State's Union Party, a combination of **Republicans** and War-**Demo-**

crats. The Union Party held a mass rally on the public square on October 6, 1863. The speakers for the Union Party included Major General Ben F. Butler (a Democratic politician from Massachusetts), Major General John C. Fremont (Republican presidential candidate in 1856), Daniel S. Dickinson (former New York Democratic Senator), D. P. Morton (Governor of Indiana), David Todd (War-Democrat, current Governor of Ohio), William Dennison (Republican Ex-Governor of Ohio), and Godwin Volney Dorsey of Piqua (Republican Treasurer of Ohio). This was one of the largest political rallies held in the Upper Miami Valley during the entire Civil War.

As soldiers left to join the various Ohio Volunteer Infantry regiments, the women of Piqua organized the Soldier's Aid Society in 1861. The original purpose of the society was to furnish soldiers with bandages, knit stockings and mittens and meals for soldiers leaving or coming back on the trains. As the war lengthened, it became obvious that the families of soldiers also needed assistance. The Society and other community groups banded together to furnish food, fuel, and money to families in need. This was the first city-wide charity effort.

OHIO VOLUNTEER INFANTRY REGIMENTS.
FIRST REGIMENT. Company K of this regiment was raised in Piqua by Thomas J. Lawson on September 5, 1861. After sustaining significant losses in over two and a half years of combat, the regiment sent Major **Stephen C. Writer** (formerly with the Eighth Regiment) back to Piqua to recruit new members. In 1864, Major Writer opened a recruiting office over Scott's Store on Main Street. New recruits were offered four hundred dollar bounties (three hundred from the government and one hundred in local funds). The regiment was involved in the Battle of Shiloh, Stone River, Chickamauga, Lookout Mountain, Missionary Ridge, and Kennesaw Mountain.

EIGHTH REGIMENT. Company I of this cavalry regiment was raised in Piqua by the editor of the *Piqua Register*, Stephen C. Writer. The regiment was sworn in on September 23, 1861.

ELEVENTH REGIMENT. On April 18, 1861 Captain **Stephen Johnston** raised Piqua's first Civil War unit. It was mustered into three months service in Columbus on April 26, 1861 as Company F of the Eleventh Regiment. On the evening before the Company left for Columbus, a reception was held for the men at the Greene Street Church. A silk flag was presented to the company with the words "Piqua Invincibles" embroidered upon it. Almost all of the company re-enlisted for three years when their original enlistment ended in August. Company B was organized shortly after Company F by Captain Thomas L. P. Defrees. The regiment was involved in the Battle of Antietam, Chickamauga, Lookout Mountain, and Missionary Ridge.

NINETY-FOURTH REGIMENT. This regiment was organized at **Camp Piqua** on August 23 and 24, 1862 with Companies B, C, and D coming from Miami County, the rest from Clark, Darke, and Champaign counties. Combat losses forced Company C, the "Excelsior Company", to set up a recruiting office in the City Hall's council chamber in early August of 1864. Local officers included Captain Fred W. Walton, First Lieutenant James H. Petticrew, and Second Lieutenant **Frank A. Hardy**. The Ninety-Fourth Regiment participated in the following battles; Tate's Ferry, Stone River, Chickamauga, Lookout Mountain, Kennesaw Mountain, Missionary Ridge, Siege of Atlanta, and Bentonville.

ONE-HUNDRED TENTH REGIMENT. This regiment was organized at **Camp Piqua** on October 3, 1862 under the command of Colonel J. Warren Keifer of Springfield and Lieutenant Colonel William N. Foster, who resigned as Mayor of Piqua to accept this commission. **Lucius C. Cron**, a future Mayor of Huntersville, would serve as the regiment's principal musician

Civil War re-enactors were a common sight in the 1990's during the Piqua Heritage Festival.

Commodore Stephen C. Rowan is credited with firing the first naval shot of the Civil War.

Piqua In The Civic War

This Civil War tombstone at the Forest Hill Cemetery commemorates George Ewell who fought with the Twelfth United States Colored Infantry Regiment.

A Civil War Memorial in the Forest Hill Cemetery is surrounded by the graves of local men who fought for the Union in the Civil War.

L.C. Cron, was an active member of the G.A.R. Drum and Fife Corps. Cron made the drum shown and carried it during the Civil War.

(drummer). Captain William D. Alexander of Company A, set up a recruiting station in Piqua offering one hundred dollars bounty and one hundred sixty acres of land for signing up. Advertisements promised good pay, rations, arms, and equipment furnished, and free medical attendance. The regiment participated in the battles of Wilderness, Spotsylvania, Cold Harbor, Petersburg, and Appomattox. In 1868, the members of Company A were the first to hold a reunion. By 1871, the entire regiment was holding annual reunions. These gatherings lasted through the first decade of the twentieth century.

ONE-HUNDRED FORTY-SEVENTH REGIMENT. This regiment was organized on May 16, 1864 for one hundred days of service. A major portion of the regiment was made up of the Eighty-seventh Battalion, Ohio National Guard from Miami County. The unit spent most of its service time on guard duty in and around Washington, D.C.

UNITED STATES COLORED TROOPS. At the beginning of the Civil War, Ohio refused African-Americans the right to enlist or serve in the military. In January of 1863, John M. Langston and O.S.B. Wall began recruiting in Ohio for volunteers for Massachusetts' African-American regiments. At least a half a dozen men from Miami County signed up with the 54th Massachusetts Colored Regiment including Paul Crowder and Jesse Lockyear from Piqua. Ohio began its own **African-American** regiments in June of 1863. The African-American recruits did not receive any state or local enlistment bonuses. All of the officers for the new regiments were white veterans from the Ohio Volunteer Infantry units. Sergeant Ancil Marcellus Bowdle was one such individual from Piqua who was given a Cap-

tain's Commission to a command company of the 12th U.S.C.T. Other African-American regiments that contained Piqua men were the 4th, 5th (formerly 127th OVI), 12th, 23rd, 27th, 42nd,. Other units included the 124th United States Colored Troops and the 5th United States Colored Heavy Artillery. The 5th Regiment participated in the Siege of Petersburg, Virginia and battles at New Mareot Heights and Wilmington. The 27th Regiment was engaged in the Battles of Petersburg and the fall of Fort Fisher. SEE ALSO: Chase, Camp; Dennison, Camp; Fleming, David; Grant, Ulysses S.; Lincoln, Abraham; Mitchell, John; Moody, Granville; Music; Piqua, Camp; Rowan, Stephen; Streets; Lists-Civil War

COLLEGES AND BUSINESS SCHOOLS

The community's earliest known business school was the Piqua Commercial College, a branch of Grundry's College of Cincinnati, which existed for a short time in 1866. Other early short-lived business schools included: Moore's Piqua College (c1872-c1876), Aisre and Wright's Commercial Night School (1880), and Foley's Business Night School (1882). These early schools were run exclusively for young boys and concentrated on teaching bookkeeping skills. The Piqua Commercial College was organized by Charles E. Beck in 1889. The school was renamed Beck's Academy by 1905, and taught both men and women the basics of penmanship, bookkeeping, and shorthand. A second business school was established in 1905, the Ideal Business School with J. Albert Kirby as the first principal. Beck's and the Ideal combined in 1909 as the Ideal Business School on the third floor of the Piqua National Bank building on the northwest corner of Main Street and the public square. Chauncy and Theodore Lindley took over management of the school in 1913-14 maintaining control of it until the early 1920's. At this point local businessmen took over the school's operation with **Harvey E. Sims** (Secretary of the **Atlas Underwear Company**) as President, Warren Gravett (Cashier of the Citizens National Bank) as Vice President and William W. Edge (Secretary/ Treasurer of the

Edison State College is located on Looney Road east of Piqua. This 2005 photograph shows the inner courtyard.

Pioneer Pole Company) as Treasurer. The reorganized school offered courses in higher accounting, bookkeeping, cost accounting, shorthand, typewriting, and "comptometer". Classes were offered on a day or night basis and managed by Bert B. Baker. The school was sold in 1929 to the Joiner-Alvoid Business College Corporation of Columbus. The new ownership lasted only until 1931when the school was purchased by Herman Stayman of St. Paris. By 1937-38 the school had been renamed the Stayman's Ideal Business College and moved to rooms leased from the Congregational Christian Church on Broadway. The school closed in 1942.

The next school was organized by the **Lear-Avia Company** in 1943 as the Applied Engineering Trades School located at 226 West High Street. Lear's school was used to rapidly train new employees in electrical and mechanical assembly procedures and techniques.

Higher education reached Piqua in 1956 when Miami and Ohio State Universities began offering joint off-campus classes. In 1958, the Piqua Academic Center was established by Miami University and located in the Piqua High School on College Street. The center was taken over by Wright State University in 1968.

The Ohio Board of Regents chartered the Edison State General and Technical College on May 18, 1973 to serve Darke, Miami and Shelby Counties. The new school was the first general and technical college sponsored by the state under a new provision of the Ohio Revised Code. During the summer of 1973, the governor appointed a board of trustees. One of their first acts was the hiring of James E. Seitz as the college's first president. The first classes were held in the former Spring Street Elementary School on the northeast corner of East Ash and Spring Street. The offices were in the large former

James E. Seitz served as Edison State College's first president from 1973 to 1985.

clothes closets and in the former restroom areas of the basement, with the library on the stage of the second floor auditorium. The first instructors were from Wright State University, and the students paid their tuition and fees directly to Wright State. On September 23, 1974, the first classes using Edison's own full time faculty were held. During that first year, the school had five full-time faculty members and 491 students. The ground breaking ceremony for the new college building on Looney Road was held on May 24, 1975. At this ceremony the college graduated its first student, **Greg Simmons**. The college opened for classes on its new 130 acre campus designed by Sidney architects Freytag & Freytag on September 23, 1976. The college assumed the name Edison State Community College, in September of 1977. Since its formation, the college has had three presidents; Dr. James E. Seitz (1973-1985), Conrad W. Burchill (1985-1987) and Dr. Kenneth A. Yowell (1988 to present). The Advanced Technology Building was dedicated in 1998, the Conference and Student Center and gymnasium in 1994 and the Emerson Center and library in 2007. The college went from 309 students in 1973 to over 3,000 in 2006. SEE ALSO: Oda, Kathy.

COLONIAL REVIVAL STYLE ARCHITECTURE

The local variation of the Colonial Revival Style was popular from 1910 through the 1930's. These rectangular shaped homes used classical elements that tried to echo the popular image of American's Revolutionary War Period. Their simple lines were highlighted by classically decorated centered front entrances and symmetrical openings on the first and second floors.

DOMESTIC EXAMPLES
525 Caldwell, Robert Shannon House, 1915
726 Caldwell, Losh Harbaugh House, 1923
1220 Park Avenue, **William Boal Wood** House, 1929

COLORED MEN'S COOPERATIVE TRADE ASSOCIATION

The Colored Men's Cooperative Trade Association was established on September 25, 1867.as Piqua's first **African-American** business. The function of the association was "to buy and sell dry goods, groceries, and produce". The association formed a grocery store that lasted until c.1875. The original incorporators were John Collins, Arthur Horwell, Robert Anderson, P. B. Delaney, **Robert Smith**, Peter M. Bray, Joseph P. Wilson, William A. Fox, and Nelson Clark. SEE ALSO: African-American

COMMUNITIES, MIAMI COUNTY

The total number of communities in Miami County (past and present) is sixty-one. There were twenty communities located east of the Great Miami River and forty-one west of the river. SEE ALSO: Lists-Miami County Communities

CONGRESSMEN

The following United States Representatives lived in Piqua; **William McClean** (1823-1829), **John F. McKinney** (1863-1865) and (1871-1873), **Robert M. Murray** (1883-1885), and **William M. McColloch** (1949-1971).

CONSERVANCY DISTRICT

After the March 1913 **flood**, a Miami Valley Flood Prevention Association, representing five counties, was organized in Dayton. Arthur E. Morgan was hired to report on plans for future flood prevention. On December 19, 1913 and January 7, 1914, meetings were held in Piqua by the Association to explain the purpose behind the proposed conservancy flood control bill. Governor **James M. Cox** signed the Conservancy Act into law on February 17, 1914. Opposition to the formation of the Miami Conservancy District was strong in Miami, Logan, Shelby, and Greene Counties. In February of 1914, the Anti-Reservoir Committee of Miami County was formed to oppose what many felt was a flood protection program for Dayton which the northern counties were being forced to financially support. At the time, the resistance was compared to colonial opposition to the Stamp Act of 1765. The opposition continued, but on June 28, 1915 the Miami Conservancy District was formally established. Mass meetings were held in Piqua on April 8 and 13, 1916 to voice opposition to the district but attendance was very small. Finally a delegation of thirty Piqua leaders met with the Conservancy directors on April 17, 1916 and after a day long discussion agreed to support the flood control plan. In November of 1917, construction began on five retaining basins and dams (Lockington, Englewood, Taylorsville, Huffman, and Germantown), and nine major river improvements and embankments or river levees. In the Piqua area over 260,000 cubic yards were excavated from the Miami River channel and a protective levee bank was built on top of the defunct Miami and Erie Canal bed. The work in Piqua was supervised by Albert Schroeder and completed in December of 1922. The original work of the Conservancy was completed by April of 1923 at a total cost estimated at $30,850,000. SEE ALSO: Floods.

CONTEMPORARY STYLE ARCHITECTURE

The local variation of the Contemporary Style (American International) was popular in the early 1950's. This style features a flat roof with limited architectural detailing. These one story rectangular frame houses have a roughly centered stone or concrete story high decorative wall that projects at a right angle from the front of the facade. The front facade also usually contains a picture window with sidelight panes on both sides. This style is described on a national level in the McAlester *A Field Guide to American Houses*. The local example used for this style contains first floor and roof steel beams manufactured by the Truscon Steel Company of Youngstown, Ohio.
DOMESTIC EXAMPLE
1615 West High Street, Smith House, 1951-52

COOPERS

The first cooper, or barrel maker, in Piqua was Joseph Porquette who built a small shop in 1804 on what would become South Main Street. Porquette stayed in business until 1830 when Philip Ellis took over. It would not be until 1837, when the Miami Canal Extension reached Piqua, that the cooperage industry would take off. An informal census in 1825 listed four coopers in Piqua. By the time of the 1850 census (thirteen years after the coming of the canal), eighty-five men listed their occupations as coopers. Cooperage became the city's first major industrial expansion. Early prominent barrel makers included: **Frank A. Hardy** (1843-1850) Charles **Wood** (c.1853-c1870's), George and Peter Vogel (c1850-c1880), Reihard and John Stelzer (c.1868-1902), and Simon Shepard (c.1860's-c.1880's). The success of the cooperage industry rested on the need for the packing of produce to be shipped south to Cincinnati by canal. With the decline of the canal in the 1860's, came the decline of the barrel trade. The last functioning commercial barrel company in Piqua was the Piqua Cooperage Co. (later Elbert Cooperage). The business was established in c.1889 by Frank Elbert and closed by **Charles R. Elbert** in 1950-51. SEE ALSO: Canals; Industry; Wood, William Sr.

CORN

Native Americans identified corn as one of the Three Sisters (corn, squash and beans). Area tribes (Miami and Shawnee) planted the "Sisters" together in one plot. This Native American corn, known as maize, was originally a hybrid grass from the Peruvian Andes known as teosinte. The first European-American family to plant corn in the Piqua area was the Hilliards in 1797. They used the abandoned maize field of the Shawnee Tribe located on the flood plain on the east bank of the Great Miami River. Corn was used as food (corn meal), animal feed, molasses sugar, and for the production of corn whiskey. One the area's first industries, the **distilleries** were established to deal with surplus corn production.

COURT HOUSE WARS

The Court House Wars began in 1807 when the newly formed Miami County commissioners surveyed and platted out **Troy** as the new county seat. Piqua, or Washington as it was then called, was outraged. **Piqua** had been platted out in June of 1807 with a public square or commons already laid out and dedicated for the use of county buildings. Piqua argued that a new county seat was not needed since Piqua already existed. In 1839, the war erupted again when a new courthouse was needed. Two years earlier Piqua had become the terminus of the Miami Extension **Canal** and was growing at a rapid rate. Piqua's argument was that it was larger than Troy. A new courthouse in Troy was competed in 1841. It was eighty by fifty feet and two stories tall. Piqua built a new town hall to match the courthouse. It was forty by sixty feet and three stories tall.

The Piqua-Troy rivalry moved to transportation in 1851 when Piqua businessmen invested in the Louisville, Eaton and Sandusky **Railroad** with a route from Dayton to Piqua that by-passed Troy. The investors ran out of money in 1854 and the line was never built. Troy businessmen came back with an investment of their own, the Dayton and Michigan Railroad in 1851. On this route from Troy to Sidney, the route was surveyed so that it passed Piqua one mile to the east of the city.

The war heated up again in 1884 when the county commissioners decided the county needed a new courthouse. Piqua moved into high gear to try and convince a legislative committee that the county seat should be moved to Piqua. The committee was wined and dined in both communities. Local legends state the emphasis was on the wine, but whatever the reasons, the committee decided to leave Troy as the seat of county justice.

The new courthouse was designed by **J. W. Yost** and completed by January of 1888. The structure is topped by a statue of Lady Justice gazing south over Troy and Tipp City, but aiming her bustle towards Piqua. In 1890, Piqua made her final gesture with the erection of the **Plaza Hotel** designed by J. W. Yost. The hotel opened in October of 1891. It was 150 feet by 107 feet to the courthouse's 114 feet by 114 feet. This was Piqua's final response to the Piqua-Troy Court House Wars. SEE ALSO: Border City; Johnston, John.

CRON, KILLS COMPANY

The firm was established by **Andrew Jackson Cron** and **Robert B. Kills** in 1881. Both men lived in **Huntersville** and gained their woodworking skills at the **L.C. & W.L. Cron & Company** furniture plant. Other investors in the new company included grocer Samuel Zollinger and merchant tailor/banker **Henry Flesh**. The first plant was located in the former Rouzer Machine Shop on the north end of North Main Street. The firm produced tables, piesafes and cupboards. A small fire and the need to expand led the firm to construct a new factory on First

The Cron-Kills Company furniture plant shown in this 1940's picture was located on Third Street in Shawnee.

Street in Huntersville. Increasing markets made possible by Piqua's two railroad systems resulted in the rapid expansion of the plant and its work force. A major fire destroyed two-thirds of the Cron, Kills factory in November of 1892. But by 1894, the plant had been rebuilt and the firm's employment reached over 125 workers.

As the firm moved into the twentieth century, a number of changes occurred. The firm was incorporated as the Cron-Kills Inc. with Henry Flesh as president, Samuel Zollinger as vice president and Samuel M. Allison as secretary/treasurer. Both Cron and Kills retired from the firm. Cron died in 1905 and Kills in 1907. The firm continued to expand and by 1910 the plant covered twenty-five acres in five multi-storied buildings with over two hundred employees. Cron-Kills produced over thirty-two different styles of wardrobes in oak and mahogany, as well as tables, desks and dining room furniture. Flesh died in 1919 and **John P. Spiker**, an underwear manufacturer and banker took over as president and the firm expanded into living room, hall and bed room furniture.

The Great Depression of the 1930's hit the firm hard and employment dropped to about one hundred men. The firm went into receivership from 1934 through 1939 with a majority of the debt being held by **Leo M. Flesh** and the **Atlas Underwear Company**. **Harvey E. Sims**, the secretary/treasurer of Atlas Underwear Company, took over first as receiver and then as president of the company. He would hold this position until 1951. A **strike** led by the Carpenters and Joiners Union Local No. 1877 at the plant in 1936 led to the closing of the plant for over three months. Violence between the picketing workers and special police resulted in some minor injuries and several arrests.

The production of wooden office desks and filing cabinets for the United States Treasury Department during **World War II** led to a brief revival of the company. Incentives to get and keep employees during this period included group life, health and accident **insurance,** group hospitalization (Blue Cross) and fifty hour weeks with time-and-half overtime pay. By 1944, the firm had over three hundred employees.

After the war (1944-1945), Cron-Kills created a subsidiary company known as the Fore-Site Home Furnishing Company to create modern living room and dining room furniture. The firm struggled with the post-war conversation and the lack of government contracts. The company began specializing in wooden radio and television cabinets in the late 1940's with a continued employment of over two hundred workers. The firm was sold to the Dane Brothers Syndicate from Mystic, Connecticut in June of 1950. All plant and office functions had been closed down by July of 1951. SEE ALSO: Railroads.

CRON, L.C. & W. L. COMPANY

The first of the city's major furniture companies, this firm was established in 1868 by former **Civil War** "Drummer Boy" **Lucius Cowan Cron**. A year later Cron's first cousin **William L. Cron** joined the firm in 1869 followed by **John Schneyer** in 1870-71. By 1873, the firm had fifty employees and was producing drawing and dining room furniture, sideboards, hall stands, desks, beds and office furniture. The firm had a sidelight of selling curled hair or wool mattresses during the 1870's. The company had erected three buildings on five acres of ground in **Huntersville** by 1880. At its height in the early 1890's, the firm employed over 165 men and was shipping furniture across the nation. The financial crisis of 1893-94 hurt the company, and was the beginning of a thirty year decline. In 1905, William L. Cron had sold his interest in the company and W. H. Carroll had taken over as president. He was followed by W. D. Root, and by 1920 H. C. Jeffery had become president. Under Jeffery, the firm became known as The Cron

Company, and went into receivership in October of 1923. SEE ALSO: Cron, Kills Company.

DANCE HALL WAR

The State of Ohio passed a law in early 1924 that required dance halls to obtain a permit from the mayor or the police chief of a city in order to operate. Piqua followed suit on October 6, 1924 by passing an ordinance regulating public dance halls and public dancing in Piqua. The major sections of the ordinance prohibited any dances after 11:30 p.m. and prohibited any person under the age of eighteen from attending a public dance or taking public dance lessons without a parent or guardian present. In a talk to the local Lions Club, Police Chief Gehle stated that the new dance ordinance was as positive and moral as the prohibition laws. Not everyone agreed and the Dance Hall War began. A petition with over six hundred signatures requested the filing of a referendum in November of 1924 to remove the ordinance from the city's books. On December 26, 1924,

This 1949 photograph shows the Winter Garden on South Wayne. The Garden was a favorite dance spot and featured a number of nationally known Big Bands.

Judge Walter D. Jones issued a restraining order on the enforcement of the dance ordinance until its constitutionality could be determined. In response, Mayor William G. Crozier stated that he would not issue any dance permits required by the State of Ohio. No public New Year's Eve dances were held that year.

Kenneth Miller, manager of the Winter Gardens filed an injunction with Judge Jones to prohibit Mayor Crozier from closing down his establishment. The injunction was denied and there was no dancing in Piqua. A second petition was circulated and 1,100 people signed to show their support for the dance ordinance. In late January, 1925, Judge Jones ruled for the city ordinance, but by this time the city council had decided to compromise. A new and less restrictive ordinance was passed in February of 1925 that both the city and the dance hall owners felt was fair.

DELAWARE TRIBE

This tribe, part of the Eastern-Algonquian language family, originally occupied the Delaware River basin. They called themselves Lenape, or "real men". Pastimes included a game similar to football, a gambling game using reeds, and mutual delousing activities, including the eating of the lice. In 1751, they established settlements in eastern Ohio along the Muskingum River. Delaware divisions active in Ohio were known as the Wolf, the Turtle, and the Turkey. The Delaware had extensive dealings with Moravian Missionaries and many became Christians. The Munsee or Wolf division, held the closest ties to the Moravians. During the Revolutionary War the other two Delaware divisions sided with the British. The Delaware signed the **Treaty of Greenville** in 1795 and by 1800 most of the tribe had moved to the White River area in Indiana.

DEMOCRATIC PARTY

The national Democratic Party was organized between 1791 and 1794 under the tag of the Democratic-Republicans. The election of 1800 saw the party's presidential candidate Thomas Jefferson come to power. Until the Civil War Era, Miami County Democrats were opposed by various small parties, the best organized being the Whig Party. Locally, the first major Democratic showing came with the election of Piqua attorney John F. McKinney to the United States House of Representatives in 1863 and again in 1870. In 1882 Robert M. Murray, a local industrialist, was elected to Congress from the Third Ohio District. He was the last local Democrat to be elected to a national position. In Piqua, the Democratic Party in the nineteenth and early twentieth centuries was led by **Henry Flesh** and **Lucius C. Cron**. The Democrats held the office of Mayor in Piqua for twenty-five years between 1875 and 1929, maintaining control of the office completely between 1875-1889, 1897-1905, and 1910-1913. The **Republicans** dominated the office in the 1890's and the 1920's. SEE ALSO: Civil War (Home Front); Dorsey, Godwin; Mayors; McKinney, John; Murrary, R.M.; Newspapers; Parades; Presidents.

DENNISON, CAMP

A **Civil War** training camp established eighteen miles northeast of Cincinnati and named for Ohio Governor Dennison. Piqua units of the First Ohio Volunteer Infantry Regiment mustered in at this camp.

DENTISTS

Early dental work was usually performed by a physician if available or, if not, by a friendly neighbor. Regular dental work was often forced to wait until a traveling dentist set up a office in one of the local hotels for a few days. In the fall of 1832, Piqua's first permanent dentist set up his office. He ran an advertisement in the *Piqua Gazette* in December of 1832 as follows, "E. Taylor, new Surgeon Dentist, will set natural and artificial teeth in most cases without pain, ladies waited on at their residences if requested".

DEPRESSION ERA

The New York Stock Market crashed on October 29, 1929 and brought the United States economy down with it. Industrial production declined and unemployment climbed steadily. Locally during the first two years, over nine hundred jobs were lost with the closing of ten major industrial plants. The total value of Piqua's manufacturing production dropped from roughly $19,800,000 in 1929 to $12,370,000 in 1931. The total number of wage earners in the city dropped from 3,228 in 1929 to 2,386 in 1931, an almost 26% drop in employment. During the winter of 1932-1933, the city government was providing direct aid to over five hundred families (roughly 2,000 people). In January of 1936, the Piqua office of the national Re-Employment Service had listings for 1,636 men and 383 women seeking employment. Office manager Howard Collmorgan saw as many as 150 clients a day.

The election of Franklin Delano Roosevelt (FDR) in November of 1932 appeared to be a turning point for the nation. It was also a turning point for Piqua. Several local industries began experiencing a gradual growth. The **Wood Shovel and Tool Company** added one hundred twenty employees to keep up with the demand for shovels from the federal government's work programs. **Aerovent Fan Company** was organized in 1932 and the four major textile companies (Orr Felt, **Atlas**, **Piqua Hosiery**, and **Superior**) continued to add new employees until they were responsible for an estimated forty percent of the city's industrial work force. New companies were established during this era, such as the Piqua Emery Cutter and Foundry Company, which took over the defunct Hetherington Company. The city added to this growth with the building of the Piqua Municipal **Power Plant** which began operations in October of 1933.

Three of FDR's federal relief agencies had a major impact on the city. In 1933-34 the National Recovery Act (NRA) led to local retail and business codes. The retail code mandated a minimum wage of thirteen dollars a week for a maximum forty hour week. The various business codes were more exact. For example, twenty-seven barbershops in Piqua signed the NRA Barbers Code in June of 1934. They all agreed to be open Monday through Friday, 8:30-6:30, close at noon on Thursday, and stay open on Saturday from 8:30-9:00 p.m. Prices were set at thirty-five cents for a haircut and twenty cents for a shave. Most of the city's shops and retail establishments designed and signed similar local codes. The local leaders of the NRA organized one of the city's largest **parades** on Main Street on October 25, 1933.

The Civil Works Administration (CWA) provided unskilled labor jobs to area workers. Local projects included improvements to the Ohio State Fish Hatchery, repair and enclosure of the Piqua Hydraulic Canal on South College, cleaning and dredging out parts of the abandoned Miami and Erie **Canal,** removing the Dayton and Troy Electric Railway tracks from Main Street to the former canal bed and building display cases for the Schmidlapp **Museum**. The Public Works Administration (PWA) provided funds for other major local projects including $25,000 for the Roosevelt Park Field House, $42,700 for the Washington Township Consolidated School and a majority of the funding for the **Hydraulic** Canal drainage sewer on South College Street, the South Street School remodeling and addition and the Miami River dam. In 1940, a new WPA sewage disposal plant was completed south of the municipal power plant with a small brick building, underground sedimentation tanks, a primary treatment plant and a furnace to incinerate dried solids. From February of 1935 through August of 1937, August Moser lived in Piqua as the resident PWA project engineer for Upper Miami Valley region.

Union organization was very active during the mid 1930's. The Piqua Central Labor Union of the American Federation of Labor (AFL) reorganized its operation in August of 1933. It had only five local unions (down from seventeen in 1919), and under two hundred members. The union began intensive campaigning with machinists, meat cutters, textile workers, power engineers, and shovel workers. By June of 1934, the Central Labor Union had grown to nineteen local unions with roughly fifteen hundred members. During this period, the unions used their most potent weapon, the **strike**, at the plants of the **Val Decker** Meat Packing Company, Orr Felt and Blanket Company, **Cron, Kills Company, Piqua Handle** and the **Atlas Underwear Company**. Unions were not the only organizations actively seeking the support of workers during this period. The Miami County **Socialist Party** was reactivated in 1933 after an almost ten year absence. The party managed a brief surge of popular recognition before being swept away by the social activism of FDR and the Democratic Party. Another short-lived political organization was the Unemployed League. This group held open-air meetings during the summer of 1933, and claimed a local membership of about 860.

Other activities during the period included the curtailment of Associated **Charities** in April of 1933 due to a lack of funds. The **Red Cross** Chapter of Piqua became active again in 1934 to help supply food, shelter, and medical aid to those in need. Also during this period, Prohibition came to an end in December of 1933 allowing the reopening of bars and saloons in the city. The Depression Era closed with an upsurge in manufacturing as the United States began preparing itself for the conflict with Germany and Japan in **World War II**. SEE ALSO: Favorite Stove & Range Company; Miniature Golf

DILBONE MASSACRE

In Springcreek Township, along what is now State Route 36, Henry Dilbone, his wife, and four children had established a small family homestead. On August 18, 1813, the family was clearing a flax field when two Indians surprised the family at their work. Henry was shot and his wife was struck in the back of the neck with a tomahawk. None of the children were harmed. Henry lived long enough to tell the local militia leader Captain Dye that he had been shot by a local Indian known as Mingo George. Mingo George was later hunted down and killed by local militia volunteers. The Dilbones had known their killer and had had several arguments with him. This was not a case of an Indian uprising, but rather an individual crime that was punished with brutal and violent "frontier justice". SEE ALSO: War of 1812.

DISEASE

The earliest known epidemic to hit Piqua was the Cholera Epidemic of 1833. A sanitary meeting was called in the village on August 22 and each of the four wards was assigned six men to assist in preserving cleanliness which was believed to stop cholera. A local Board of Health was appointed at that time to stop the spread of the disease. The Board members included: Dr. Thomas Pierce (President of the Board), Demas Adams, Lucius Cone, and John W. Jordon. This would be the last Health Board in Piqua until state law mandated the establishment of City Board in 1889. The last major health crisis to hit Piqua was the Influenza Epidemic of 1918.

DISTILLERIES

The first **industry** to be established in Piqua was a distillery built by **John Manning** in 1805. It was located on the east bank of the Great Miami River. Turning corn into whiskey allowed local farmers to create a cash crop for badly needed supplies. **Corn** whiskey was also important as a local home cure for whatever ailed you. As the government caught up with the pioneer distilleries and taxes were levied on the product, local legal distilleries went out of business. The illegal distillery business came back strong during Prohibition of the 1920's and early 1930's. Illegal corn whiskey stills were active throughout Piqua and the Upper Miami Valley. The end of **prohibition** also saw the demise of "stills".

DOGS

A mayor's proclamation in July of 1834 ordered Piqua's Marshall to kill, destroy and bury every animal of the dog species that might be found running at large.

DRIVING INSTRUCTION

In 1936, the State of Ohio passed new legislation requiring all drivers to have driver's licenses. If a driver was an adult with at least one year of driving experience then a license would be issued. If the prospective driver was under age or with limited driving experience then a "driving test" would be required. The first driver's test in Piqua was held on November 11, 1936 at the Piqua Police Station. It was under the auspices of the Ohio State Highway Patrol. Of the six original individuals to apply for licenses, three failed to pass the test. It was probably only happenstance that on November 16, 1936, a new twenty mph speed limit was authorized by the Piqua City Commission for just over seventy-five percent of city streets. This was the beginning of formal driving instruction and driving schools.

DRUG STORES

Drug stores were one of the first types of specialized businesses in Piqua. In 1832, **Moses G. Mitchell** established the city's first drug store on the corner of Main and High Streets. It was identified with a wooden sign showing a golden mortar. In 1846 James Starett joined Mitchell as a partner. Mitchell retired in the summer of 1852 and Starett continued the business until c1856. For a short time in 1834, Dr. John P. Finley established a drug store in connection with his medical practice. Dr. Daniel Ashton came to Piqua with his family in 1834, and in 1835, followed the example of Doctor Finley by establishing a drug store on the northwest corner of Main and Greene Streets under the sign of the Good Samaritan. Dr. Ashton died in 1847 and the store was managed jointly by his widow and his son William B. Ashton. In 1865 the store was sold to L. G. Lecklider. William joined his brothers, Dr. A. S. Ashton and Daniel Ashton, to re-establish a family drug store at 417 North Main Street. The brothers continued in the drug business until 1920. Other early drug store owners included Drs. **O'Farrell & Dorsey** (1840's), Samuel Gordon (c1840's), D. L. Jordan (1840's), and I. S. Clark (1840's). SEE ALSO: Van Horner, Thomas.

DUBLIN HILL

This was a nickname for High Street Hill. The name refers to the significant Irish population that lived in the area in the last half of the nineteenth century.

DUTCH COLONIAL REVIVAL STYLE ARCHITECTURE

The local variation of the Dutch Colonial Revival Style was popular from 1910 through 1925. This domestic style features the distinctive gambrel roof with side gables on a rectangular frame. A number of mail-order catalogs, such as Sears Roebuck, featured this style.

DOMESTIC EXAMPLE   218 West Greene Street

EARTHQUAKES

From 1788 through 1976, thirty-six quakes were reported in the southwestern Ohio area. The earthquake prone district extends from the Bowling Green area south to Cincinnati. In 1937, an earthquake destroyed a school building in Anna, Ohio. The earliest major quake was in 1875 when tremors brought chimneys crashing down from as far north as Sidney and as far east as Urbana. During the past one hundred years, five major quakes have hit the Upper Miami Valley area.

EAST PIQUA

Traditionally this portion of the city is border by the old canal (between Main and Spring Streets) on the west and the

Great Miami River (the bend) on the north, south and east. The area contains a mixture of pre-**Civil War** era **Federal** and **Greek Revival** Style two story brick homes and fill-in structures of frame built between c.1880 and c.1915. East Piqua has also supported the Decker Meat Packing Company and the **Aerovent Fan Company** both located on the east edge along the river. Roosevelt Park on East Ash later became the site of the **football** stadium (Wertz Field) and the Field House (**basketball**). The Board of Education took over the old Decker plant. East Piqua contains the following streets; Spring, Harrison, Race, New, Manning (all north-south) and East North, East Greene, East Ash, East High, East Water (all east-west). SEE ALSO: Photographs p. 38

ELECTIONS

Early elections were generally an oral affair where the voter came to the poll, stated his name and then told the poll worker which candidates he wished to support. Obviously this system led to widespread voter intimidation and voter manipulation (the buying of votes). The first use of the secret ballot, also known as the Australian style ballot, in Piqua and Ohio was in the fall election of 1891. The ballot gave voters the option of voting for individual candidates or voting a "straight ticket" which meant voting for all of a party's candidates by simply marking the Party name or symbol. Voters were given a five minute deadline in which to fill out this new written ballot.

Nineteenth century elections were a time of intense entertainment in the city. The **Republicans** and the **Democrats** were best known for holding campaign **parades** and mass meetings. Local, state and national candidates and speakers would talk for hours on end to the gathered crowds. A politician who could not speak for at least two hours and be heard by those standing in the back was not considered as a truly viable candidate. SEE ALSO: Presidential visitors; individual political parties.

EMPLOYEE BENEFITS

Benefits for industrial employees were extremely limited in the nineteenth and early twentieth centuries. The prime source of benefits came from Odd Fellows Lodge (IOOF) membership which offered health and death insurance for a small fee. By **World War I** some local industries began offering in-house cafeterias, company grocery stores (**French Oil** and **Piqua Handle**) and company sponsored sports teams and bands (**Meteor Motor Car**). More substantial benefits came during the waning years of **World War II** when firms tried to keep employees when wages were frozen by the federal government. New benefits incentives included paid vacations, partially paid health insurance and child care services. Post war industrial strikes often included **union** demands for both wage and benefit increases.

EMPLOYMENT IN PIQUA (INDUSTRIAL)

By 1890, Piqua had become a booming industrial community with over sixty major industries employing over 1,300 men. The number of industries did not change significantly in the next one hundred or so years. The 1980 census listed 72 industrial companies in Piqua. The biggest difference is that industrial employment increased to 5,778. SEE ALSO: Labor and Unions, Servants/Domestics; Wages.

EXOTIC STYLE ARCHITECTURE

The local variations of the Exotic Style were popular from 1900 through 1930. This style includes homes built from a wide range of unusual materials and in strange shapes and sizes. The **Willow Cottage** was built in Rossville as a summer getaway and was constructed of bent willow branches. The Shack was a "party" house for A. Acton Hall and was built over a number of years. It featured bark slabs as shingling which resulted in the name "The Shack".

DOMESTIC EXAMPLES
Rossville, Willow Cottage, c. 1905
Hemm Road, "The Shack", A. Acton Hall Jr., 1929-30

FALLEN TIMBERS, BATTLE OF

This battle took place on August 20, 1794 near the site of the present day city of Maumee in Lucas County. General **Anthony Wayne** marched his army down the Maumee River Valley and met two thousand Indian warriors under the control of the **Shawnee** Chief **Blue Jacket**. In less than an hour the Indian forces had fled, breaking the back of Indian resistance in the Ohio country. Wayne's victory led to the signing of the **Treaty of Greenville** in 1795. .

FAMOUS VISITORS

Piqua enticed more than her share of famous visitors. **May's Opera House** was a draw, as well as Piqua's location half-way between Chicago and New York on the Pennsylvania Railroad line. A few of Piqua's better known visitors included: Helen Keller (n.d.), poet James Whitcomb Riley (1888), boxer **Jack Dempsey** (1919), **Henry Ford** (1918), athlete and actor **Johnny "Tarzan" Weismuller** (1924-1931), singer **Bing Crosby** (1963), black activist Frederick Douglas (1868), markswoman **Annie Oakley** (1896), and eight presidents of the United States. SEE ALSO: Plaza Hotel; Presidents.

FAVORITE STOVE AND RANGE COMPANY

In 1887, the Favorite Stove and Range Company moved to Piqua from Cincinnati. The new firm became the city's largest manufacturer. It was also the first new business to be brought to Piqua by the Board of Trade, a predecessor of the **Chamber of Commerce**. The company had a major impact on the community. Piqua became known as the "Favorite City" with several local firms also adopting Favorite as part of their name. The area west of the factory on South Street became known as Favorite Hill because houses were built on the hill for use by company employees.

The original firm was organized in 1848 by William C. Davis and known as the W. C. Davis Company. After the Civil War, the Cincinnati firm became known as the Great Western Stove Works. In 1872, **William King Boal** purchased a partial ownership in the firm. By 1880 he had taken over the firm, renaming it the Favorite Stove Co.

Boal visited Piqua during the first week of June of 1886. On June 25 of that year, he signed a contract with the city to bring the Favorite Stove and Range Company to Piqua. The new plant was located on eight acres of land bordered by Young, Weber, and South Streets and the Hydraulic Canal (now College

This pre-Civil War structure is one of the very few homes in the Piqua area to use limestone as its primary building material.

Italianate and Queen Anne Styles were often mixed to create highly decorated brick homes in this area.

The early twentieth century Queen Anne Style frame homes were often tucked in between the older brick homes.

Below:
The stone lintels identify this brick 1850's Greek Revival Style home.

East Piqua

*E*ast Piqua is located east of Spring Street in the bend of the Great Miami River. Architectural styles in the area range from the Federal Style of the 1830's to the late Queen Anne structures of the 1910's. Building materials range from locally made bricks to area limestone to milled framework and shingles.

Street). The firm began operations on February 23, 1887 with eight brick buildings and over two hundred sixty employees. By 1896 the company had expanded to over three hundred employees and was producing in excess of fifty thousand stoves each year. A **strike** hit the firm in 1919 with demands for a twenty-five percent increase in wages for common laborers. The strike lasted eleven days. The workers may have been represented by a **Socialist union** known as the Industrial Workers of the World (Wobblies).

W. K. Boal died on January 02, 1916 and was succeeded as president by his son, **William Stanhope Boal.** Boal was president until 1923 when he became Chairman of the Board of Directors. During the next five years, the company went through three presidents until William C. Katker took over in 1928. The Great **Depression** hit the company hard. With the death of Boal on December 17, 1933, the firm reorganized and, by 1935, had been liquidated. The Foster Stove Company of Ironton, Ohio (Lawrence County) purchased the patents, patterns, dies and trade marks for the Favorite Range products at the time of the liquidation. The Foster Stove Company's Favorite Gas Ranges were sold in Piqua in c.1937 by the Atlas Gas Store, 203 North Main Street. The store was operated by O.O. Millhouse, agent for the Atlas Fuel Gas System.

Katker took over what was left of the business, renaming it the Favorite Manufacturing Company. The new firm produced coal and wood heating stoves, furnaces, hollow ware, gas cooking stoves and parts for old Favorite Stove & Range Company items. Molding work for the new firm was handled by the Champion Foundry Company of Piqua. In 1937, Katker's company employed twenty-five moulders and iron workers at the Champion plant and a dozen or so assemblers at the Weber Street plant. After World War II, demand for Favorite products diminished and by 1958 the firm suspended operations. SEE ALSO: Lear Avia; Strikes.

FEDERAL STYLE ARCHITECTURE

The local variation of the federal style was popular from 1819 through 1841. This was the first true architectural style following the building of log cabins and clapboard homes in Piqua. It began locally with the construction of the Ashton home in 1819 on the northwest corner of Main and Ash Streets. These early structures were very plain, but in comparison to the simple log and clapboard buildings of the era they stood out as almost palatial. The layout of these Federal Style Variations reflected the need for fireplaces in every room as the main source of heating. The homes were constructed so that the fireplaces on each end and on both floors could utilize the same gable end chimneys. These homes also sat on the extreme front of their lot lines

This interior shot of the Favorite Stove and Range Company shows the pattern shop.

in order to leave plenty of room in the rear of the lots for frame summer **kitchens**, barns, outhouses, and sheds.

The local Federal Style can be identified in domestic architecture by some or all of the following elements. The houses were rectangular in shape containing two stories with symmetrical openings/bays (often five equally sized bays) facing the streetscape. The gable ends rarely contained window or door openings, though openings were often added at a later date. The plain brick facades were often painted and contained an average count of seven stretcher brick rows between each header brick row. The lintels were made up of header bricks and topped windows that may have used twelve over twelve double hung sash windows (no known examples of windows have survived). The windows were framed by functional shutters. A semielliptical door transom is a common element along with a chimney on each gable end The structures boasted a low pitched roof with side gables covered by over-lapping wooden shingles and plain/undecorated cornices and eaves. The roofing materials were often replaced in the last part of the nineteenth century with overlapping slate tiles. The Federal Style houses sit directly on the sidewalk and often have a two or three stone step staircase projected out onto the sidewalk.

DOMESTIC EXAMPLES:
628 North Main Street, **Henry Kitchen** House, 1822
615-617 North Main Street, Byram Dayton House, 1833
518-520 North Main Street, **George Johnston** House, 1835
501 Spring Street, William Dills House, 1841

It appears that most of the commercial versions of the local Federal Style were either very small one story **brick** structures or frame structures. There are no known examples of the commercial variation of this style left in Piqua.

FIRE DEPARTMENT

The earliest settlers protected Piqua from the threat of fire with loosely organized bucket brigades. The first volunteer fire company was organized in 1839 under the leadership of **Stephen Johnston**. The group was known as Reliance Fire Company No. 1. A steam pumper was purchased and fire fighting entered a new stage. Later volunteer companies included the Washington Fire Company (1856), and the Jefferson Fire Company (1858). The volunteer companies were reorganized in May of 1882, and placed under the direct control of the city. **Stephen Genslinger** was appointed as the community's first fire chief. The new department took over the defunct Spiker Wagon Factory at 313 North Wayne Street for its central fire house. Two substations were built to speed up the horse-drawn equipment's response to fires. The first was built in 1892 at 120 Garnsey Street and the second in 1909 at 835 Park Avenue. A new central station was erected in 1904-1905 at 219-221 West Water Street. Finally all three stations were consolidated as the department turned to motorized equipment in 1915-16, and a new station was completed at 229 West High in 1927. SEE ALSO: City Hall; List-Fire Chiefs.

This c. 1910 postcard shows the Central Fire Station on Water Street. The station would later be remodeled into the City Hall.

FLAGS

During the past two hundred and fifty years five different sovereign flags have flown over the Piqua area. In 1747, English traders flew the British Union Jack over the Miami Indian town of **Pickawillany**. When the French burned the village in 1752, they raised the French Fleur-De-Lis over the abandoned site. In 1792 Anthony Wayne established a supply fort near the future site of the **Piqua Historical Area**. Known as **Fort Piqua**, it was probable that the thirteen star American flag flew over the Fort. In 1901 the Ohio State flag was designed and within the next ten years or so was flown in Piqua. In 1964, Thelma Jeanne Martin designed the Piqua City Flag. It was produced and hung in the City Commission Chambers.

FLOODS

On Tuesday, March 25, 1913, the Great Miami River broke free of its banks and swept through Piqua, **Rossville**, and Shawnee. Unlike floods that had struck Piqua before, this one took its toll in human lives as well as property. Within three days, fourteen men, women, and children had been taken to the temporary morgue established in the print shop of W. F. Steiner at 424 North Main Street. Dozens more were simply listed as missing or locations unknown. At the end of three weeks, thirty-three bodies had been recovered. At the end of a month, thirty-eight fatalities had been recorded with another four names still unaccounted for.

The average age of the flood victims was approximately forty years old. But this is a bit misleading. Of the thirty-eight deaths listed in the *Leader Dispatch* by May 28, 1913, ten were over the age of sixty and nine were under the age of eight. Issac Kerns was the oldest at age eighty and Charles Kenneth Croner was the youngest at only thirteen months. Family tragedies were common. Jacob and Grace Millhouse, 118 First Street, lost three children: Hazel, age 8, Helen, age 6; and John M., age 3. George Heidle, 108 East Main Street, lost his wife Bertha, his son Paul, age 6, and his daughter, Pauline, fourteen months old.

There were many tragic stories associated with the flood and one of the saddest was told in the *Leader Dispatch* on April 29, 1913. The body of Mrs. Belle Spencer had just been recovered from the Miami River near Farrington. According to eye-witness accounts, Mrs. Spencer, her son Leon, and his wife had all been trapped by the flood waters in their residence on Home Avenue. Leon Spencer knocked a hole through to the roof, pushed his wife up onto the roof, and then climbed up himself. He then attempted to pull his mother up through the hole to what they thought was the safety of the roof. But the current pushed the house off of its foundations and Leon lost his grip. "Mrs. Spencer threw up her hands with a wild appeal for help and then sank. Mr. Spencer walked rapidly from the hole through which his mother had disappeared and went to his wife, huddled on the roof. She rose to meet him and laying off her raincoat enfolded her husband in her arms and both went down together."

The 1913 Flood was not the first flood to hit Piqua and the Miami Valley. The earliest flooding in this area after the arrival of the city's pioneer settlers was in April of 1805. During the next one hundred years, the Great Miami River would overflow its banks on nine separate occasions.

During the first fifty years of the nineteenth century, the river flooded only twice, in June 1835 and during the first part of 1847. The later flood was the worst to date with a recorded high of twenty-five inches. It was also the first flood to wash away the city's bridges. But the overall damage to the city was light and the river stayed within its bank for the next thirteen years.

The 1913 Flood flooded the intersection of High and Wayne Streets.

During 1859 and 1860, the city built a small levee along the west bank of the river at the head of Spring, Harrison, and Manning Streets. But, unfortunately, the levee was no match for the floods of the 1860's. The first flood of the decade hit in April of 1860 and punched through the levee at Harrison Street. Most of the eastern portion of the city was flooded. Within five years, two more floods hit Piqua with an overflow of seventeen inches in 1865, and almost twenty-two inches in 1866. The 1866 flood hit on September 19 and destroyed the **bridge** of the Columbus, Piqua, and Indiana **Railroad** Company.

This postcard view shows the devastation of the 1913 Flood and the corner of New and Greene Streets.

The city did not experience another flood for seventeen years, but the flood of February 2 and 3, 1883 hit hard with an overflow of thirty-nine inches. After this disaster, the city rebuilt the levee and extended it in both directions. For ten years the levee did its job and the river stayed within its banks.

The floods of the 1890's hit Piqua extremely hard. In 1893, the overflow reached almost twenty-one inches. On March 5, 1897, the flooding reached just over twenty-nine inches. Finally, on March 23, 1898, the largest flood to hit Piqua up to that time reached a high of over forty-one inches. The city east of Harrison Street, as well as Rossville and Huntersville, suffered major water damage. Residents were forced out of their homes and at least five industries closed due to damaged stock, machinery, and factory buildings. The west half of the iron truss bridge into **Huntersville** was swept away in the flooding. The area was cut off from direct access to the city.

Despite all the damage, the city did very little to improve its flood protection plan. The levee along the west bank of the river was repaired but not enlarged. So when the 1913 flood hit fifteen years later, the city was totally unprepared for the devastation it caused.

The levee and flood dams of the 1920's would prove their worth during the heavy rains and flooding in January of 1937. Local flooding was limited to Rush Creek overflowing in Rossville and basements being flooded on the south end of South Main Street. Massive damage was experienced in Cincinnati. SEE ALSO: Conservancy District.

FLORISTS

The first listing for a full-time florist was in 1878 for Chester W. Church who had a shop on Ash Street. Italianate and Queen Anne style homes of the period were often decorated with freshly cut flowers. Church was able to furnish his customers with a wider selection than could be found in most home gardens. He was followed by Max Schroeder (early 1880's) and Harry P. Smith (1884), and William Frisch (1894). In 1991, florists that had connections to either Smith or Frisch included Andy's Garden Florists, Gerlach the Florist, and Smith Greenhouse. SEE ALSO: Patron p.236

This 1920 photograph shows William Gerlach Jr., one of Piqua's early florists.

FLOUR MILLS

The first local flour or grist mill was built by John Manning on Water Street between Harrison and Manning Streets during the spring of 1804. This was the first flour mill north of Dayton. Two other early mills were erected, one by Enos Manning in 1821, and the other by John Johnston in 1834. When the Miami Extension **Canal** reached Piqua in 1837, the city's most enduring mill was established. Benjamin B. Beal opened the Merchant's Mill in October of 1837. It was located on the canal and used the Piqua's lock nine as a power source. From 1837 until 1884, the mill had at least twelve different owners before being sold to five Piqua businessmen who formed the Piqua Milling Company, Incorporated. The corporation had numerous partners, until by the late 1930's, Loren W. Pool and his two sons Benjamin and Allen gained complete control of the firm. The mill has been rebuilt twice since 1835 after fires burned it to the ground. The last structure was built in 1900, and active operations in the mill ended in 1990. SEE ALSO: Industry.

FOOD

From the earliest prehistoric hunting camp in 5,000 B.C. to the twenty-first century modern kitchen, food preparation has been an important part of the area's day to day life. The **Paleo-Indian** peoples hunted big game like mastodon, the bison and the giant sloth. The game was slaughtered at the kill site with cooking limited to meat thrown on to fire stones. Later prehistoric cultures such as the **Adena**, **Hopewell** and **Fort Ancient** peoples raised maize, squash and beans that they crushed into a paste using stone mortars and pestles. The **Shawnee** and **Miami** tribes, that came to the area in the 1700's, mixed hunting with maize agriculture and woodland gathering of nuts, berries and roots.

European-American settlers built log cabins in the very early part of the nineteenth century with crude stone fireplaces that served as both a heating and cooking source. By the 1820's, brick homes were built with larger fireplaces complete with baking ovens and cast iron cooking cauldrons. After the **Civil War**, cast iron cooking stoves heated with wood or coal became the preferred way to cook food. Meals became more complex with multiple courses and cakes and pies for desert. By 1887, cooking stoves were not only a convenience but also a source of family income. The **Favorite Stove and Range Company** moved Company moved to Piqua from Cincinnati and by the mid-1890's was producing fifty thousand stoves a year with an employee count of over five hundred. Local butchering also hit the big time in the mid-1890's when Val Decker Meat Packing Company was established. That firm went on to become one of the area's major producers of packaged meats.

As the community grew, buying food changed from a farmer's market on the public square to neighborhood groceries and meat markets. From the 1890's to the 1940's, food shopping was very localized and personalized. But as food became more and more prepackaged, new food marketing ideas were developed. The community's first "super market" was built in 1942 at 130 North Market Street by the Kroger **Grocery** & Baking Company chain from Cincinnati.

By 1915, food preparation at home had begun to change as gas stoves with their ability to maintain a constant temperature made cooking more precise and less labor intensive. It was no longer necessary to constantly monitor cooking and make temperature adjustments by banking the fire or by adding new wood or coal. Electric stoves became popular by the late 1930's along with other electric **kitchen** appliances such as the refrigerator, toasters and electric mixers. After Piqua built its own electric **power plant** in 1933, the city began using newspaper advertisements to promote the use of new and labor saving electric kitchen devices. By the last decades of the twentieth century, the microwave oven had become a kitchen necessity and food preparation was measured in minutes rather than in hours. Kitchen pans became easier to use and clean after Pleasant Hill, Ohio's own Ray J. Plunkett discovered Teflon as a slick covering for utensils while working for the DuPont Corporation.

The Tabler Groceries and Meats Market at 533 Park Avenue provided a home delivery service in c. 1910.

FOOTBALL

Piqua native **William Wilson Wood III** learned the American game of football while attending the Phillips Exeter Academy in New Hampshire. The game was already quite the rage among the Ivy League colleges and its expansion to the Midwest was confirmed with the creation of the Western Conference (later the Big Ten) in 1896. During his summer breaks in Piqua in 1896 and 1897, Wood taught the game to some of his local friends. In 1898-1899 the **YMCA**'s secretary C.W. Bassett coached a local team assisted by Edward H. Allen. It was during the era of the Y sponsorship that the Piqua-Troy football rivalry began. Piqua lost its first game to Troy 17 to 0 and then proceeded to lose its next four games. But practice makes perfect and the Piqua team beat Troy the next four times in a row. The rivalry cooled down and the teams would not play each other for another two years.

The rough nature of the early games caused the YMCA to stop sponsoring the team. But football was firmly established in Piqua and local players in 1900 formed a community team with C.C. Sank as manager and Mr. Crawford as coach. Sank managed Midway Park (near what is now the UVMC campus) and the early football games were often held on the park's grounds. Football at the turn of the century seemed to encourage violence. Few games ended without a fist fight between teams and between players and spectators. Uniforms were non-existent and equipment varied from player to player. To modern spectators, the game would look more like a soccer/rugby combination since kicking was encouraged and the forward pass prohibited. The early rules included three downs to go five yards and touchdowns being worth only two points while field goals got a whopping five points each. The 1900 team began the tradition of the

Piqua-Troy Thanksgiving Day game to end the season. This tradition would last until the end of World War II.

The next big change in local football was the creation of an official high school football team in 1901. Piqua joined a league that limited players to current high school students. The league consisted of Piqua, Troy, Sidney, Urbana, Bellefontaine, and Greenville. Piqua refused to play two of the league teams in 1901 when they continued to bring in non-high school ringers to play on their teams. The new high school team was led by captain Joseph Hagan (Class of 1902) but the team played without a coach. The home games were played in fields around the city but the favored spot was the old baseball field on East Ash Street. The new high school team left the community team with dwindling attendance and 1901 would be their last season.

The Piqua high school team competed under the name the Big Reds and had their best season in 1910 when they compiled a season record of 140 points to 0 points. By World War I, the team was known as the Red and Blues but they still did not have a permanent home.

In 1920, the Board of Education decided to purchase the abandoned field on East Ash Street as a new park for the schools. The site had been first used by the Piqua **Baseball** Company as a semi-pro baseball field in 1883 and was ideally suited for school activities. A community fund raiser was sponsored by the Piqua **Rotary Club**. By the early spring of 1920, the site held new

The score board at the Alexander Stadium is one of the largest high school score boards in the area.

Piqua Football

World War II flying ace, Don Gentile is shown during his High School football days.

The 1926 High School football team sits on the wooden bleachers of the Roosevelt Football Field on East Ash Street.

Below: The 1911 High School football team wore quilted shoulder pads sewn onto their football jerseys. The leather helmets that two of the boys in the front row are holding covered only the top of the head.

Football in 2006

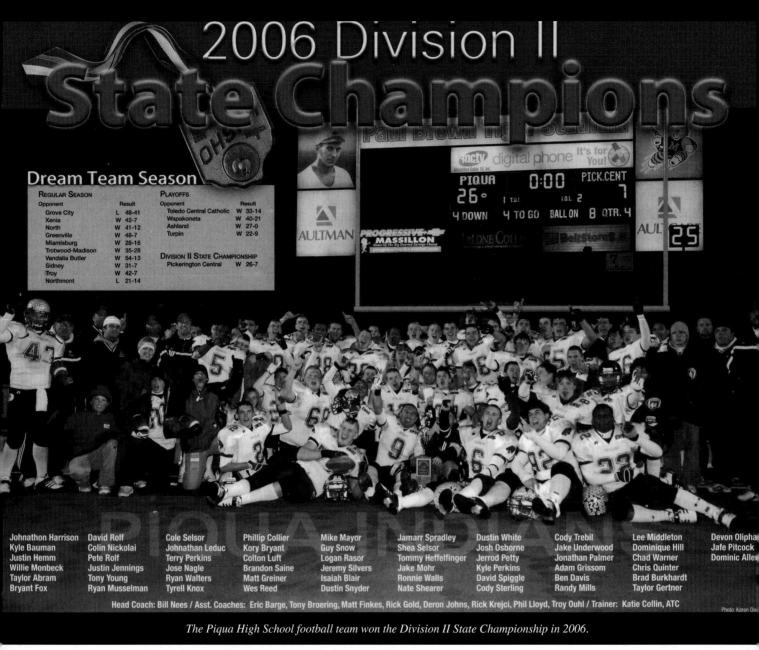

2006 Division II State Champions

Dream Team Season

REGULAR SEASON				PLAYOFFS		
Opponent		Result		Opponent		Result
Grove City	L	48-41		Toledo Central Catholic	W	33-14
Xenia	W	42-7		Wapakoneta	W	40-21
North	W	41-12		Ashland	W	27-0
Greenville	W	48-7		Turpin	W	22-9
Miamisburg	W	28-16				
Trotwood-Madison	W	35-28		**DIVISION II STATE CHAMPIONSHIP**		
Vandalia Butler	W	54-13		Pickerington Central	W	26-7
Sidney	W	31-7				
Troy	W	42-7				
Northmont	L	21-14				

Scoreboard: PIQUA 26 — PICK.CENT 7 — 0:00 — 4 DOWN — 4 TO GO — BALL ON 8 — QTR. 4

Johnathon Harrison	David Rolf	Cole Selsor	Phillip Collier	Mike Mayor	Jamarr Spradley	Dustin White	Cody Trebil	Lee Middleton	Devon Olipha
Kyle Bauman	Colin Nickolai	Johnathan Leduc	Kory Bryant	Guy Snow	Shea Selsor	Josh Osborne	Jake Underwood	Dominique Hill	Jafe Pitcock
Justin Hemm	Pete Rolf	Terry Perkins	Colton Luft	Logan Rasor	Tommy Heffelfinger	Jerrod Petty	Jonathan Palmer	Chad Warner	Dominic Allen
Willie Monbeck	Justin Jennings	Jose Nagle	Brandon Saine	Jeremy Silvers	Jake Mohr	Kyle Perkins	Adam Grissom	Chris Quinter	
Taylor Abram	Tony Young	Ryan Walters	Matt Greiner	Isaiah Blair	Ronnie Walls	David Spiggle	Ben Davis	Brad Burkhardt	
Bryant Fox	Ryan Musselman	Tyrell Knox	Wes Reed	Dustin Snyder	Nate Shearer	Cody Sterling	Randy Mills	Taylor Gertner	

Head Coach: Bill Nees / Asst. Coaches: Eric Barge, Tony Broering, Matt Finkes, Rick Gold, Deron Johns, Rick Krejci, Phil Lloyd, Troy Ouhl / Trainer: Katie Collin, ATC

Photo: Karen De

The Piqua High School football team won the Division II State Championship in 2006.

Football in 1930's

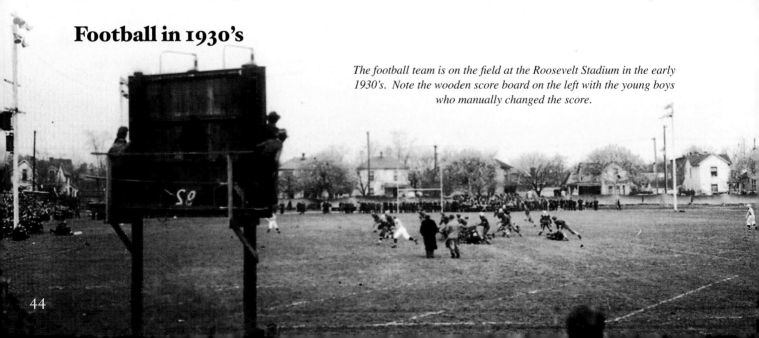

The football team is on the field at the Roosevelt Stadium in the early 1930's. Note the wooden score board on the left with the young boys who manually changed the score.

playground equipment, a tennis court, a track, and a graded football field. The area was formally dedicated on May 1, 1920 as Roosevelt Park in honor of former President **Teddy Roosevelt**. Roosevelt had visited Piqua during the Campaign of 1912. The home field advantage did not help the team in October of 1920 when they suffered their greatest loss in school history when a brutal Dayton Stivers team crushed Piqua 83 to 0. In 1928, at the suggestion of Richard Cron, the team became known as the Piqua Indians.

Dr. David Gallagher was formerly with the Chicago Bears.

Roosevelt **Park** was the scene for many community activities including the annual children's May Day Games. The **Don Gentile** Bond Rally, the Sesquicentennial Pageant, various religious crusades, band concerts and contests, and high school graduations. During the Great **Depression** and using federal WPA funds, the schools added a brick field house in 1935 and an outdoor concrete stadium seating in 1940. The field was renamed **George P. Wertz** Stadium to honor the city's premier football coach and athletic director. The last high school football game at Wertz Stadium was played on October 20, 2000. Located behind the High school off of Looney Road, the newest football stadium was dedicated in August of 2001. It was called as the Alexander Stadium (named in honor of Clifford R. and Joyce A. Alexander Jr.) and Purk Field (named in honor of Edward Purk).

Two Piqua High School football players, Craig Clemons (Piqua High School 1968), and David Gallagher (Piqua High School 1970) went on to play professional football with the Chicago Bears. The high school's winningest football coach was George P. Wertz with 163 wins, 65 losses, and 21 ties. Piqua won its first modern Ohio State Championship in 2006 under Coach Bill Nees. SEE ALSO: Lists-Athletic Hall of Fame; Lists-Schools-Football Coaches; Parades.

FORT ANCIENT CULTURE

During the Prehistoric Mississippian Period, the Fort Ancient Culture (900 A.D. to 1700 A.D.) developed in the Ohio River and Miami River valleys. The name was coined by William C. Mills in 1904. The Fort Ancient peoples built a few platform mounds for ceremonies, but not for burials. Their dead were buried underground in stone covered tombs. A majority of the information about the Fort Ancient Culture comes from their fortified village sites. The best known site is the "Sunwatch Village" in Dayton, Ohio. The villages could hold two to four hundred people in rectangular houses and larger community structures. The Fort Ancient Culture declined before Ohio's historic Indian groups entered the area in the early 1700's.

FORTS, OHIO

Military forts were first erected in the Ohio country in the last half of the eighteenth century. They were usually composed of earthen walls with wood palisades that enclosed log cabins, barns

and other structures. Active fort building eras included the 1790's and during the **War of 1812**. SEE ALSO: Lists-Forts, Ohio

FOURTH OF JULY

This was one of the earliest community celebrations. By the 1820's, the Fourth of July was celebrated with parades showing off local militia units in a parade led a Grand Marshall in a buggy. Outdoor meals were served at local hotels, followed by speeches and numerous toasts. By the 1880's, fireworks had become an important part of the celebration along with local baseball games. After **World War II,** the celebration was centered at Fountain Park with music, food booths, games and **baseball** followed by evening fireworks.

FRENCH COLONIAL/ NORMAN REVIVAL STYLE ARCHITECTURE

The local variation of the French Colonial/Norman Revival Style was popular from 1925 through 1930. This is strictly a domestic style and there are no commercial examples in Piqua. The best local example of this style was built by **Alfred F. Flesh** in 1928-1929 at 100 Orchard Road overlooking Echo Lake. The house was called "The Echoes" and was the first of a new development of upscale homes around Echo Lake and Orchard Road. By the 1950's, the structure was the home of *Piqua Daily Call* publisher Charles and Mabel F. **Ridenour**. During the Ridenour ownership, Gratton Conden, a brother-in-law stayed with the family. Conden was a national recognized artist. This style is easily recognizable with its central two story turret, steeply pitched hipped roof and front dormers.

DOMESTIC EXAMPLE

100 Orchard Road, Alfred Flesh House, 1928-1929

FRENCH AND INDIAN WAR

The Ohio country was the prize in this conflict between the French in Canada and the British on the eastern seaboard. The various Indian tribes were often caught in the middle and forced to choose one side or the other. This was lasted from 1754 until the signing of the Treaty of Paris in 1763. In 1756, this American war became part of the larger European conflict known as the Seven Years War. In the Ohio country, the conflict involved the destruction of the Indian village of **Pickawillany**, the campaigns of General Braddock and George Washington, and the conflicts over Fort Pitt. By 1760 the war in the west had ended, and the British occupied Canada and all the major French forts along the Great Lakes, including Fort Detroit. SEE ALSO: Celoron De Blainville; Washington, George.

FRENCH OIL MILL MACHINERY COMPANY

This firm (FOMMCO) was incorporated on May 25, 1900 by **Alfred W. French Sr.,** William Cook Rogers and Myron E. Barber in Piqua to manufacture French's patented linseed oil cake cutting machine. French had chosen Piqua for his new enterprise because of the city's heavy involvement in the linseed oil production industry. The new firm expanded rapidly and built its own factory at the West end of Ash Street in 1903. FOMMCO would develop world markets for its products and by 1919, French Oil products were in use in every continent except Antarctica. The firm expanded its products with introduction of hydraulic presses for molding steel, rubber and plastic. During **World War II** the firm produced hydraulic barrel straighteners for United States naval guns. After the war, FOMMCO moved heavily into solvent extraction equipment, creating the world's first desolventizer-toaster to improve animal feed in 1954. Continuing its quest for diversity, the firm sold its first hydraulic press for molding golf balls in 1965 to the Ben Hogan Golf Ball Company. In 1992, the FOMMCO designed and equipped the largest soybean preparation and extraction plant in China. Under the leadership of the A.W. French Sr.'s grandson, Daniel P. French, the firm celebrated its one hundredth anniversary in 2000. SEE ALSO: Patron p. 235

Alfred W. French Sr. was the founder and first president of the French Oil Mill Machinery Company in Piqua in 1900.

FUNERAL HOMES

The earliest undertakers in the community were the cabinet/**furniture** makers. Since they made the wooden coffins it was an easy stretch to become an undertaker when the bodies were viewed in the home and there was no embalming. During the 1840's, Robert Muchmore, a cabinet maker in the 600 block of Main Street advertised undertaking and the availability of the village's first hearse. Other undertakers/cabinet makers from the 1850's through the 1880's included Casper Brendel Sr. (1853-1898), Henry P. Dackey & John Compton (1870's), C. Elliott (1870's) and August Fritsch Sr. (1877-1898). Traditionally the furniture stores would store the coffins on an upper floor. The bereaved would view a selection of coffins sitting upright on their edges with open lids like a row of monuments. When embalm-

Jackson C. Cron (seated center) and his three sons ran one of the city's most successful funeral homes. L.C. Cron's portrait hangs on the wall behind them.

ing became the norm in the early twentieth century, it was almost always done in the home of the deceased usually in the parlor. The process involved the use of hand or foot powered embalming fluid pump with the body placed on a mesh cooling bed.

The **L.C. & W.L. Cron Furniture Company** was organized in 1868 and by the early 1870's had moved into retail furniture sales and undertaking on Main Street. By the early 1880's, the retail side had become W.L. Cron & Sons (William L., Hartley and Volney). L.C. Cron's son **Jackson Cron** left the firm and joined with Frank E. Campbell in 1888 to form their own furniture store and undertaking establishment in the Music Hall at 124 West Ash Street. Cron bought out his partner in 1893 and the following year he bought out W.L. Cron & Sons and moved into their store at 321 North Main Street. Cron went through several partners including Seth Zemer (c.1904-1905) and William P. Walker (1905-1919). After **World War I**, Cron dropped the retail furniture business and became a funeral home at 400 North Wayne Street. The custom of having funerals in the home was diminishing and the undertakers began creating parlor-like environments in their establishments or "funeral homes". Cron's sons joined him (Kenneth, John C. and Robert D.) and firm was incorporated in 1936 as J.C. Cron & Sons. Cron's moved to 608 West High Street in 1958. The last years of the funeral home began in 1974 when S. Howard Cheney joined the firm and the name became Cron-Cheney Funeral Homes Inc. and the firm moved to new location at 1760 West High Street in 1979. Clifford Stocker joined the firm at that time and it became Cron-Cheney-Stocker. Stocker would close the Piqua facility in 1982.

When Frank Campbell and Cron split in 1893, Campbell established his own furniture store and undertaking business at 410 North Main Street (the former Fritsch location). Campbell went through several partners Adam Bowers (1898-1902), Besanceney (1902), M.D. Sperry (1903-c.1910) and Robert Jackson (c.1914-1920). James D. Finfrock joined the firm in 1920 and it became Campbell and Finfrock. Finfrock took over the undertaking portion of the firm in c.1923 and established his own funeral home which was active until 1952. Its last location was at 628 North Main Street.

Walker Wagner and Bernard Groven Sr., both former employees of L.C. & W.L. Cron Furniture, established a furniture store and undertaking business in the Music Hall on West Ash Street in 1898. Wagner left the firm in 1915 to establish his own funeral home at 128 West Ash Street. The new firm advertised ambulance service and motor or horse drawn hearses. After World War I, Walker moved to 407 West High Street and remained active at this location until the early 1950's. Groven partnered with Edward McDowell and move the undertaking business to the southwest corner of Ash and Wayne Streets. By 1918, the firm had become Groven & Company and his sons Bernard Jr. and Harold B. would join the business. By 1956-1957, Louis W. Melcher had taken over the business at 646 West High Street. Jerry Sowers joined the firm in 1984 and he became a partner in 1986. The firm continues in operation today as the Melcher-Sowers Funeral Home at the same High Street location.

Owen Conley and Boniface F. Brendel opened a furniture and undertaking business in c.1897. Within a year, Conley was out on his own as an undertaker at 132 North Main and then at 125 North Main. After the death of Conley in c.1903, his wife Callie L. Conley took over the business. Until 1910, Mrs. Conley had several partners including Leo Wammes and Boniface Brendel. After 1910, she continued alone at 125 N. Main until World War I when she moved to 532 South Main. In 1920,, she moved the firm to 323-325 East Ash Street where it continued under her ownership until c.1948.

Harry Mulvihill and Leo W. Wammes, undertakers were active in Piqua at four different locations from 1904 until World War I.

In c.1936 Cylde W. Madison established the Madison Home for Funerals at 507 West High Street and by 1939 he had partnered with Ferman L. Krabill. After his death in 1945, his wife Lucile Trowbridge Madison Kiefer Jessup continued the business through 1979.

Thomas J. Jamieson Sr. was an embalmer at Groven's from 1929 through 1940. He left in 1940 to establish his firm at 512 North Main. In 1941 he moved to 333 West High and after World War II, his son Thomas Jamieson Jr. joined the firm. In 1970, Mr. Jamieson Sr. retired and by 1976 Michael Yannucci joined the company. He became a partner in 1986 and firm continues today as the Jamieson and Yannucci Funeral Home.

During the twentieth century, High Street was the center of the funeral business in Piqua, with five major funeral homes being located at one time or another on this street. In 2007, the city's last two funeral homes are both located on West High Street.

SEE ALSO: Furniture Manucturing; Rudd, Dorothera; Patron pp. 246, 252

FURNITURE MANUFACTURING

As Piqua grew, the demand for household furniture also grew. This led to one of the community's earliest industries, cabinet making. Among these early cabinet makers were Joseph Caldwell (1820-1821), Joseph Bennett and his son William P. Bennett (c.1820-c.1880's), F.P. Tinkman (1830-1831), Cone [Cron] and Shannon (1834), Benjamin Matthews (1836), Walkup & McClure (1837) and R.F. Cole (1839). One of the first of these cabinet makers to specialize was Robert Arheart (1826-1829) who made Windsor chairs on North Main Street. This is far from a complete list since cabinet makers were often part time and combined their craft with other activities such as undertaking (made the wooden coffins), saw mills and farming.

Robert Muchmore was a furniture maker and undertaker from the late 1830's through about 1880. His small factory was located in the 600 block of North Main Street where he sold furniture on both the wholesale and retail plan. Muchmore would be one of the first cabinet makers to make the move from single and unique hand crafted pieces to a more mass produced product line. Another early furniture manufacturer was the Helpman & Company which operated for a short time from 1869 through the early

1870's. Many of the community's cabinet makers worked for the Helpman Company including A. Helpman, David E. Helpman (Troy), J.M. Evans, August Fritsch and Samuel Bowman.

The city's biggest furniture firms would be created by the Cron Family. The **L.C. & W.L. Cron [Furniture] Company** was begun in 1868 by **Lucuis C. Cron**. The **Cron, Kills Company** would open in 1881 under the leadership of Andrew Jackson Cron. The Cron, Kills plant would be the last of the local furniture companies, closing its doors in 1951. Both companies built their factories in **Huntersville** (later the Shawnee part of Piqua).

August Fritsch's sons would form their own furniture factory. in the mid-1870's as the Central Furniture Room, later known as the Fritsch Brothers (John, Charles, William and August Jr.). By the late 1880's, their factory was located at 636 West Water Street. The firm merged with the Parker & Gano Company under the name Fritsch-Parker Furniture Company. The new firm specialized in extension tables until its closing in c.1907.

The Bowman, Brendel Furniture Company was active in the 1880's until its plant on North Wayne Street burned down in February of 1890. **William Hinsch** was a cabinet maker in the early 1880's, the son of a planning mill operator. He partnered with Thomas L. Waggoner to establish the W.L. Hinsch & Company, makers of specialty furniture. Hinsch was active in business until his death in 1919. His sons **Louis L. and Charles L. Hinsch** would establish the Art Plate Manufacturing Company in c.1941 to manufacture chrome furniture at 900 South Downing Street. The firm was relatively inactive during World War II, but started up again after the war until the early-1950's.

One of the true specialty companies opened in 1890 as the Piqua Lumber Company with **William P. Orr** as president. By c.1892-93, they had turned to furniture manufacturing as the Piqua School Furniture Company with Orr still as president and a plant on the west side of Washington Avenue near High Street. The firm made "Columbia" school desks with a folding seat and a built-in ink well. A major fire in 1903 set the company back and it was sold in c.1904-05 to the American School Seating Company. The plant had been inactive from 1906 to 1907 when it was sold to the Sprague-Smith Company of Chicago. The new firm produced china cabinets and dining room furniture until the plant was closed down in c.1912.

In 1906, the Piqua Furniture Company was established by Joel W. Flesh, Horace E. Whitlock, Charles E. Miller, and John Young with a plant opposite the Wood Shovel & Tool Company on South Avenue (South Roosevelt). The company built extension and library tables. The firm was purchased by George Klanke in c.1913 and became the Klanke Furniture Company specializing in kitchen tables. The firm closed down by **World War I**. SEE ALSO: Funeral Homes.

GARBAGE

During most of the nineteenth century garbage and trash removal was considered an individual problem. Trash however was not much of a problem. Paper was burned, and glass bottles more often than not were simply tossed under the back porch. Garbage was a different matter. Until the 1880's, it was routinely tossed out into the alley or a side street. Roaming **pigs** made short work of these leftovers. Families with larger homes often kept pig pens exclusively for this purpose. This changed in 1888 with two city ordinances. The first ordinance was

The workers at the Piqua School Furniture Company factory are shown here in c.1898.

promoted by the Piqua Board of Health and banned the throwing of garbage into city streets or alleys. During that same period, the city council outlawed hog pens within the city limits or the practice of letting them roam free. This created a question about what could be done with garbage within the city. In April of 1889, the Board of Health discussed the possibility of some type of organized garbage removal. In May, the Board recommended to the city council the building of garbage carts and the beginning of regular garbage collection. The concept of collecting other people's garbage seemed so ridiculous that the council literally laughed the idea away. The Board of Health continued to promote the idea and in June of 1890 the city council authorized the first citywide garbage collection system. Sherman Robbins was then appointed by the Board of Health to serve as the city's first sanitary policeman charged with collecting garbage. In 1951, the city began the more systematic collection of garbage by organizing pickup on specific days for each section of the city.

GAS

The first artificial gas plant was built at 622 Spring Street in 1855 by the Piqua Gas Light and Coke Company (1855-1911). The firm held a city contract for street lighting from 1856 until 1889. The first local exploration for natural gas began in March of 1886 with the organization of the Piqua Natural Gas and Oil Company. The first well was drilled to a depth of 1,350 feet near the corner of South Wayne and Clark Streets, but nothing was found. Subsequent drilling on the East Main Street hill found small oil and gas deposits, but never in marketable quantities. During 1886 and 1887, the oil and gas craze hit Piqua and wells were drilled in Fountain Park and on farms north and northeast of town with no practical results. One of these local groups was the Piqua Natural Gas & Oil Company. They hit natural gas deposits in Piqua in March of 1886 with a well at four hundred feet but the gas deposit turned out to be very small. In 1888, natural gas was piped into the city by the Mercer Gas and Fuel Company from wells around Lima, Findley, and Mercer County. The firm later became the Miami Valley Gas and Fuel Company, then the Ohio Fuel Gas Company before finally being absorbed by the Dayton Power and Light Company in 1928. SEE ALSO: Street Lights.

GAS STATIONS
AND GARAGES

In 1900, automobiles were almost unknown in Miami County, but three years later a new business was established to take care of the city's growing **automobile** population. This first garage was established in April of 1903 by **Henry Bertling** and Ed. Snyder. It was located at 131 North Main (a former bowling alley) under the name of the Piqua Automobile Station. The station took care of automotive repairs, storage and selling of gasoline in cans. In 1905-06 the garage began selling the Oakland automobile on a special order basis. A second garage and auto dealership was established by Simon E. Amman in March of 1909. The new firm known as the Miami Automobile Company sold Buicks and repaired automobiles in the garage of Ed Meinders at 121 West Water Street. Meinders' started as a bicycle repair shop and moved into auto repair by 1909. Ohio State registration records in 1911 show only 124 automobiles in Miami County with fifty-four in Piqua. But during the following years, the automobile's popularity grew by leaps and bounds. During the **World War I** Era (1917-1920), over 4 dozen automobile dealers were established. The 1920 City Directory listed twelve garages, one automobile laundry and seven tire dealers. By 1926, ten gasoline and service stations were operating in Piqua. SEE ALSO: List-Automobile Dealers; Meteor Motor Car Co.

GAY HISTORY

The earliest openly gay cocktail lounge in Piqua was known as the Water Main and was located on the northwest corner of Main and Water Streets. The bar was opened and operated from 1974-75 through 1986-87 by Frederick J. Worley, the owner of the Off Broadway Beauty Salon. The bar was identified by a sign featuring a poodle urinating on a fire hydrant.

One of the best known gay socializing areas in the 1980's and 1990's was the Roadside Park on State Route 66, directly across from the Piqua Water Plant.

In 2005, St. Paul's Church left the United Church of Christ denomination for the Evangelical and Reformed denomination over, among other things, the issue of homosexuality.

GEORGIAN REVIVAL STYLE
ARCHITECTURE

The local variation of the Georgian Revival style was popular from 1895 through 1925. This classical and symmetrical style was in reaction to the earlier and more flamboyant **Queen Anne Style**. Rectangular in shape, these two story brick homes were considered very up scale and can usually be found slid into the empty lots or on the site of demolished homes of the older neighborhoods. The largest and grandest example of this style is the **John Spiker's** 1921 home on North Wayne Street. Spiker's mansion was the last of the large homes to be built in the **Caldwell National Register District**. After this period the grand homes in Piqua were built to the west on the top of the Park Avenue Hill. The grand front facade of the Spike home faced Wayne Street, while the rear of the structure, with its second story porch, overlooked a formal garden sloping down to Downing Street and a view of the **Leo M. Flesh's Chateauesque Style** mansion. Spiker and Flesh owned rival underwear companies that were located next to each other while their homes looked across the street from one another. Flesh was a **Republican** and president of the Citizens National Bank. Spiker was a **Democrat** and a director of the rival Piqua National Bank.

This style has many of the following local architectural elements. Oversized classical elements such as keystone lintels and prominent balustrades, classical entrances with sidelights and prominent decorated chimneys are common with this style. SEE ALSO: Textile Manufacturing

DOMESTIC EXAMPLES
518 North Downing Street, Irvin House, c. 1910
700 North Wayne Street, **John Spiker** House, 1921

The Spiker Mansion at 700 North Wayne Street was built by A.M. Fry in 1921 in the Georgian Revival Style.

48

GERMANS

One of the largest immigrant groups to settle in Piqua came from the German states of Western Europe. By 1870, an estimated six percent of the city's population had come directly from Germany. Many of the German families settled in the southern end of Piqua. They brought with them their own religious beliefs and established the following German speaking churches: St. Paul's Evangelical Protestant (1835), St. Boniface Catholic (1855), German Methodist (1867), and the Zion Reformed (1873). The immigrants brought new technical skills with them particularly in the field of **brewing**. Breweries by Ploch, Schneider, Schnell, Schmidlapp, and Lange were all located in the city. The German community also had its own **newspapers**, German language classes in the high school, and formed groups like the German American Alliance in 1907. The anti-German hysteria of **World War I** banned the teaching of German in the school system. SEE ALSO: Christmas Traditions; Immigration; Lodges and Organizations.

The St. Boniface Parochial School was built in 1890 by A.M. Fry on the southwest corner of South Downing and Wood Streets.

GIRL SCOUTS

The first troop in Piqua was organized in 1925 at the Presbyterian Church. The first troop leader or captain was Eleanor Jamieson Reck. The troop contained over 120 girls but it lasted only about three years. A new scout troop was organized in 1940 at the Presbyterian Church and shortly there after a brownie troop was formed. In 1941, two troops were organized at St. Paul's and modern scouting became an active part of Piqua's youth development. The Piqua Girl Scout Association was granted a charter in 1944. Camp Happy Haven was opened in 1948 on the old Patterson Farm. SEE ALSO: Boy Scouts; Civil Rights Movement.

GLACIERS

Ohio experienced a number of glaciers. The earliest known glacier that covered this area was the Nebraskan Glacier in circa 950,000 years before the present time (B.P.). This was followed by other glaciers that covered Ohio, the Kansan Glacier (c.700,00 B.P.), the Illinoian Glacier (c.300,000 B.P.) and the Wisconsin Glacier (c.100,000 B.P.). This last glacier slowly receded from Ohio leaving behind literally hundreds of feet of glacier debris or till. This till would fill-in the valley of the prehistoric Teays River which had at one time been wider than the entire State of Ohio. In the Miami Valley, the glacier left a mile-wide river that would become the **Great Miami River**. The climate in Ohio remained cold with a tundra-like flora and fauna. By 8,000 B.C., forests and grasslands had developed and were supporting big

game such as the mastodon, the mammoth and the giant bison. The large game animals brought the first settlers to the area, the nomadic **Paleo-Indian** Peoples.

The Piqua Country Club, shown here in the 1940's, led to the demise of the Piqua Club in the 1930's.

GOLF

Piqua's earliest golf course was developed west of the city in 1896 in Kelly's Grove near Rush Creek. Local legend states that **William King Boal** was talked into setting up the small course at the Grove. When Boal, a novice golfer, took his first swing he hit the ball into the cup. He declared that the game was too easy. This "easy course" would gradually develop into today's Piqua Country Club. A community golf course on the flood plain of the Great Miami River north of the Main Street Bridge was created by the Piqua Federated Women's Club several years prior to World War I. One of the ironies of this new course was that women were not allowed to play golf there. Golf became a high School sport when the first team was organized in 1927. The Echo Hills Municipal Golf Course was opened in west of the city on Echo Lake Drive in 1949 as part of the post-war community development plan. SEE ALSO: Miniature Golf

GOTHIC REVIVAL STYLE ARCHITECTURE

The local variation of the domestic Gothic Revival Style was popular from 1850 though the 1880's. These brick houses are rectangular in shape with two stories and a steeply pitched hipped roof. The style often contains a central roof gable on the front facade and at last one pointed-arch windows usually located on the second floor.

DOMESTIC EXAMPLES
827 Caldwell, James Raisbeck House, 1851
905 Covington Avenue,
John F. McKinney House, 1870

The Echo Hills Golf Course had a small pro shop just behind the first tee.

GOVERNORS, OHIO

No area citizens have ever been elected as Governor of the State of Ohio. However, two local citizens have been candidates for the office. In 1877, **Stephen Johnston** ran for Governor under the Ohio Independent State Ticket (**Greenback Party**). **Frank Hamilton** was the other local gubernatorial candidate running under the **Socialist Party** of America Banner in 1920. SEE ALSO: Cox, James M.; Harding, Warren G.; Hayes, Rutherford B.; May's Opera House; Piqua, Council of.

GRAND ARMY OF THE REPUBLIC

This was the Civil War veterans' organization for union soldiers and sailors. The national group was organized in the late 1860's. Piqua veterans established the Alexander Post in 1881 and the Mitchell Post shortly there after. The two posts merged as the Alexander-Mitchell Post in 1897. The Women's Relief Corps was created in 1888 and a Sons of Veterans was formed in 1886. The G.A.R. was very active politically generally supporting national Republican candidates. This was one of the very few veterans' organizations that was not segregated. African-American members could and did join the local G.A.R. and were buried together with white soldiers in the Civil War burial lot at Forest Hill Cemetery.

GREAT MIAMI RIVER

It was formed after the Wisconsin **Glacier** receded in about 12,500 years ago leaving a mile-wide river valley through the Piqua area. This river was known by the French as the R*iviere a la Roche*. During the early years of the nineteenth century, flat boats used the river to float down to Cincinnati and the Ohio River. But the rough nature of river bed and its shallow water never let the Great Miami River become a true navigable river. The closest the river became to a major transportation route is during the last half of the nineteenth century when it provided water for the Miami & Erie **Canal** located along its west bank.

The Grand Army of the Republic lodge encouraged and assisted in reunions such as this gathering of Civil War veterans from Company G of the 110th Ohio Volunteer Infantry Regiment.

GREEK REVIVAL ARCHITECTURE

The local variation of the Greek Revival Style was popular from 1837 to c.1860. This was the dominant pre-**Civil War** style variation in Piqua. With the coming of the Miami and Erie Canal in 1837, the community experienced an economic boom which was reflected architecturally in the local variation of the Greek Revival Style home. **Canal** lock construction also created the need for cut quarry stone (usually limestone) and the stone masons to do the cutting. Local builders began using the newly available limestone blocks as lintels over the windows instead of brick. The ease of canal boat travel allowed the shipping of glass from Cincinnati and buildings of this era boasted larger window panes as a result. Local **brick** masons and brick works began producing a brick with a harder exterior that did not need the protection of paint. The main entrance doors were often solid wood, but the sidelights were a deep red colored glass that allowed the occupants to see out without being seen. This style often featured two story frame side porches that allowed the women of the house to sit freely outside, but by being on the second floor, their actions were not considered too brazen or unseemly.

These homes maintained the same general shape and lot location as the earlier Federal Style variation. Fireplaces and free standing iron stoves both played a role in the heating of these homes. Increased prosperity was indicated by additional architectural decorations and stylings. This style of home was located primarily in the areas one to two blocks to the east and west of Main Street. Several of the Greek Revival Style variation homes doubled as small shops or doctor's offices featuring prominent second entrances.

This style had many of the following local architectural elements. The houses are rectangular in shape with two stories containing symmetrical openings/bays (often three equally spaced bays). The gable end faces either the street or the side and contains either a full or broken triangular pediment. Pilasters are a common feature and extend from the facade about one brick deep topped by a capital. The unpainted brick facade contains an average count of seven stretcher brick rows between each header brick row. A wide limestone band called a water table decorates the home roughly three feet above the ground. Plain limestone lintels that are slightly larger than the window opening top the six over six double hung sash windows framed by functional shutters. A recessed entrance contains a door framed by sidelights and a transom. The front entrance is framed by engaged pillars and a simple entablature. The cornices are decorated with dentils and freize-band windows. A low pitched roof was covered by over-lapping wooden shingles (this roofing material was often replaced in the last part of the nineteenth century with over-lapping slate tiles). The houses sit back from the sidewalk roughly six to eight feet.

DOMESTIC EXAMPLES

400 North Wayne Street, William Kirk House, 1842 (remodeled with most detailing removed)

514-516 North Main Street, Joseph Sage House, 1846 (house and shop)

502 North Wayne Street, Samuel Davis House, 1847

325 Riverside Drive, John Butler House, 1847

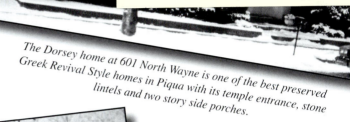

This home on the southwest corner of Ash and Wayne Streets was later remodeled into a lodge hall, a funeral parlor and then offices.

Hemmerts House

The Dorsey home at 601 North Wayne is one of the best preserved Greek Revival Style homes in Piqua with its temple entrance, stone lintels and two story side porches.

Greek Revival Architectural Style

Above: In the 1890's, this home was part of one the city's upscale residential areas on Sycamore Street.

Right: This home at 438 Adams Street was very wide but originally only one room deep.

603 North Wayne Street, **Godwin V. Dorsey** House, 1850
718 North Wayne Street, David Keyt House, 1850
516 North Wayne Street, Amos Sawyer House, 1852

The Greek Revival Style also had a local commercial variation. The canal brought new business, industries, and settlers to Piqua. During this period stores selling specialized products (i.e.: hardware, groceries, bakeries, merchant tailors) began replacing the older general stores. New two and three story brick buildings with two to four bays began to dominate the streetscape on Main. The older frame and log structures were demolished and store buildings began butting up next to each other forming solid rows of buildings.

The abutting walls can be classified in three ways. The first was that each structure had its own side wall that simply rested against the wall of its neighbor with no spacing in between. The next method was when a newer building made use of an older building's already existing wall. The two buildings would then simply share a wall, known as a common or party wall. This is demonstrated in numerous land deeds where, for example, five inches of wall is deeded over to building owner. The last and most common method used, allows for each of the abutted buildings to have its own wall. However, a space is left between the two walls which was filled with stone, brick, and earthen rubble. This last method not only created strong supports for each structure, it also created a "fire wall" to slow down or stop the spread of fire between the buildings. In all three of these methods the gable end walls were often extended above the roof line to act as an additional fire break.

These new row buildings were particularly prominent on the lots on the east side of Main Street which also faced the canal. Lot prices climbed and empty spaces vanished. Many of the shops in this period boasted of main entrances facing both Main and the canal. These rear canal facades featured first floor zones with floor to ceiling side folding doors (with a double tier of three to four windows each) that allowed the entire first floor to open up to receive freight deliveries. Often a boom was attached to the second floor wall that allowed goods to be lifted off the canal boats and set directly into the rear of the shops. These landing areas behind the shops were paved with limestone slabs that provided solid footing and support for the transfer of heavy wooden crates and barrels.

While the canal side of many of these commercial structures had exterior paving, the Main Street sides did not. The solution to the dirt sidewalk/street (for both the front and rear) was the placement of a limestone band or step that extended the entire width of the facade. This protected the store's interiors from excessive amounts of dirt, water and animal by-products flowing directly onto the floor. These ground bands acted as built-in street curbs. Today's higher streets and sidewalks have covered all but the upper portion of the stones. Also later remodelings of the main entrances have often cut the stones into two or more smaller segments. However the stone bands have often survived in the rear of the buildings since the alley and any associated sidewalks are at a lower elevation and remodelings have not been as drastic in the back.

Almost all of these canal era structures were built with the retail trade in mind. Upper floors were reserved as residences in the smaller structures and offices and meeting halls in the larger ones. But the ground floor was almost uniformly constructed to attract pedestrian or slow moving horse drawn traffic. Windows and doors dominated the first floor facades with only narrow support piers breaking the facade. The windows were flush with the dirt street/sidewalk to allow easy visibility by shoppers. The doors recessed only a couple of feet to allow an airlock ef-

fect for screen and storm doors. The interior display of goods for sale was the most prominent decorative feature of the first floor facades. Exterior signs were small and relatively plain. These early signs rarely extended the entire width of the building. Architectural detailing was minimal to maintain the focus on the window displays. Windows were also large to provide the maximum amount of natural light into the otherwise windowless interior of the retail space. Goods for sale were also prominently stacked, leaned or hung in front of and on the front of retail shops during most of the nineteenth and early twentieth centuries. Most shop owners did not expect the pedestrian shoppers to be able to see much in the way of building details.

Without exception, the first floor facades of these Greek Revival Commercial Style Variations have been remodeled to reflect changing commercial needs. From the 1880's through the 1920's, almost all of the original first floor facades were removed and usually replaced with plate glass windows and deeply recessed main doorways. As automobiles in the 1920's started replacing foot and horse drawn vehicles, signs grew larger and more dominant as a way to attract the faster vehicular traffic.

The Commercial Greek Revival Style had many of the following local architectural elements. The stores are rectangular in shape and are usually a part of a row of abutted buildings two or three stories in height. The height of each individual story is shorter than the later commercial story heights. The upper floors have symmetrical openings/bays (ranging from two to four bays) facing the streetscape. The original first floor Main Street facade was capped by an undecorated, building-width cornice supported by four to seven narrow support piers. The remodeled first floor Main Street facades usually have the building width cornice removed or covered over by an awning or a sign (late nineteenth and early twentieth century remodeling). The original first floor Main Street facades used single hung windows with twelve to sixteen panes between the piers and supported on the bottom by modestly decorated wooden bulkheads. The remodeled first floor Main Street facades removed the multi-paned windows and often replaced them with plate glass windows, the support piers were removed leaving only two on single shop facades and one between each shop on multiple shop facades. The wooden bulkheads were usually retained. The original Main Street facades used a centered and recessed (one to three feet) main entrance with narrow double doors often topped by single central glass panels and upper and lower wooden panels topped by a three or four pane glass transom. A remodeled Main Street facade removed the double front door and often replaced it with a single wide door with a single large plate glass window topped by a single panel transom. The remodeled entrance way was often enlarged and recessed back roughly four to six feet in a triangular pattern with the truncated point at the door. A Main Street facade often contained a secondary entrance on one side with a slightly recessed plain and undecorated door. A limestone band (four to six inches high) is often found at the original ground level on both the front and rear facades (remodeling often results in covering up the band). The upper floors of the Main Street facade are plain with unpainted stone lintels extending past the windows on both sides (remodeling often resulted in painting the lintel). These upper floor Main Street facades feature six over six (panes) double hung sash windows (remodeling in the late nineteenth century often resulted in two over two double hung sash windows). The cornice, under the slightly protruding eaves, is painted wood without decoration. The first floor rear or canal facade is capped by a building width limestone cornice supported by large, undecorated limestone piers. The first floor canal facade featured ten to twelve foot high folding doors with windows (currently all the folding doors have been removed or massively remodeled). These folding doors facilitated removing merchandise from the canal boats and moving it into the building. The upper floor canal facade is plain with unpainted stone lintels copying the style of the front facade. The rear facade contains six over six double hung sash windows (often survive to the present). The gently pitched roof is constructed with an off center ridgepole so that the roof drains to the east and west (on Main Street). The gable ends often abut other buildings and are not visible. The early shingling was over-lapping wooden shingles which were usually replaced in the 1890's by sheet tin and steel roofing produced locally by the **Cincinnati Corrugating Company**. The building of taller commercial structures on either or both sides of these building often resulted in constructing higher pitched roofs.

COMMERCIAL EXAMPLES
415 North Main Street, Matthew Caldwell Building/Pat & Bob's Lamp, c.1838
419-427 North Main, Canal Era Building/Little House, c. 1840's (one or two buildings)
501-503 North Main Street, Harbaugh Building/Modern Shoe Repair, c.1850 (rare dentil work under eaves)
116-118 North Main Street, Stewart Building/Illusions, c.1851 (almost all architectural details have been covered over)
313-315 North Main Street, Canal Era Building/Bijou/ Zenders, c.1850's
513-515 North Main Street, Canal Era Building/Piqua Automotive Supply, c.1850's (almost all architectural details have been covered over)
523 North Main Street, Canal Era Building/Question Mark, c.1850's (almost all architectural details have been covered over)

GREENBACK PARTY

Formally known as the National Independent Party or the Greenback-Labor Party, this political party held its first national convention in Indianapolis in 1876. The party was a populist coalition of farmers and working men. In 1877, the Greenback or Ohio Independent state ticket included gubernatorial candidate **Stephen Johnston** of Piqua. Johnston garnered just over three percent of the state-wide vote. In Piqua, he received 3.36% of the vote. In 1884, **Benjamin F. Butler**, presidential candidate on the People's Labor Greenback Party ticket, made a campaign stop in Piqua. SEE ALSO: Presidents.

GREENE VILLE, FORT

This was the largest Fort in the Ohio area. It was erected by General Wayne in the fall of 1793 at the future site of **Greenville** in Darke County and named after Revolutionary War General Nathanael Greene. It was bordered by the Greenville and Mud Creeks, and was configured in a rough fifty acre rectangle about 1,800 feet by 900 feet with ten foot high palisades. It was the site of the **Treaty of Greenville** in 1795, and the remains of the Fort were used in 1814 for the **Second Treaty of Greenville**. The Fort was abandoned in 1796 and dismantled by local settlers. SEE ALSO: Greenville, Treaty of; Greenville, Second Treaty of; Wayne, Anthony.

GREENVILLE, SECOND TREATY OF

This treaty was signed at Greenville on July 22, 1814 by the **Wyandot, Delaware, Shawnee, Ottawa, Seneca, Miami, Po-**

Stephen Johnston was the Greenback Party candidate for Governor of Ohio in 1871.

tawatomi, and Kickapoo tribes. The chief commissioners were General **William Henry Harrison** and Lewis Cass, Governor of Michigan Territory. They were assisted by Indian Agent **Colonel John Johnston**. The tribes agreed to give their allegiance to the United States during the war against the British.

GREENVILLE, TREATY OF

This treaty was signed on August 3, 1795. It was the direct result of General **Anthony Wayne**'s victory over the Indians at the Battle of **Fallen Timbers** in August of 1794. Twelve tribes signed the treaty; **Wyandot, Delaware, Shawnee, Ottawa**, Chippewa, **Potawatomi, Miami**, Gel River, Wea, Kickapoo, Piankeshaw, and Kaskaskia. Anthony Wayne signed for the Federal Government and was assisted by **William Henry Harrison**, General Lewis, and interpreter **William Wells**. The Treaty opened up the southern two thirds and the northeastern portion of the future State of Ohio for white settlement. The treaty also ended all hostilities, exchanged all prisoners, provided for annual delivery of goods to the various tribes, denied settlement of white persons on Indian lands, and licensed trade with the various tribes. SEE ALSO: Black Hoof; Little Turtle.

GROCERY STORES

The first store to specialize in groceries in Piqua was owned by **David Hunter** in 1834. The first modern supermarket was built in 1942 by the Kroger Company at 130 North Main Street. Prior to this first supermarket, Kroger's had operated five separate neighborhood stores in Piqua. In 1941, there were a total of fifty-eight groceries in the city. By 1990 that number had dropped to seven. SEE ALSO: Food. Patron p. 283

HALLOWEEN

The Piqua **Kiwanis Club** organized the first Piqua Halloween parade and costume contest in 1956. The parade went down Main Street turning onto the public square and ending at the YMCA for costume judging. As of 2007 the parade was still being held.

HANKTOWN, OHIO

This small community was located on State Route 571 between South Rangeline Road and South Shiloh Road in Union Township. The **African-American** community was settled between 1847 and 1850 by the manumitted slaves of John **Randolph**. The former slaves were aided in their early settlement period by the Society of Friends located in Union Township. In 1894, the community contained a church/school and several houses.

HARTZELL INDUSTRIES

The firm traces its roots back to the **Greenville, Ohio** saw mill established in 1875 by John T. Hartzell. The mill specialized in hardwoods for wagon construction. His son **George Washington Hartzell** purchased the company and moved it to Piqua in 1900. The new firm was known locally as the American Wagon Stock & Walnut Manufacturing Company located on the east side of South Avenue (South Roosevelt) on the abandoned Piqua Wagon Works site. G.W. Hartzell had been active in the Piqua area for since 1899 working with H.P Bailey of Lockington in the production of Black Walnut lumber. Bailey became the firm's first plant superintendent. The saw mill concentrated on walnut lumber and soon developed a strong European market. In 1914-5, the firm purchased land on Clark Avenue and built a plant to produce walnut veneer primarily for the furniture industry. However, the **First World War** started an embargo and European markets were abruptly closed.

Looking for new markets, the company in 1915 added wooden gunstocks for British and later American rifles used in World War I. This is also the era when the firm became commonly known as the George W. Hartzell Company. Hartzell's a started producing another major war product in 1917, the wooden airplane propeller. George Hartzell lived in Oakwood near Orville Wright's home. Wright suggested that Hartzell begin producing propellers from walnut for the Dayton Wright Airplane Company. The first **Hartzell propellers** were individually crafted using draw knives. By September of 1917, Hartzell's had purchased the two story brick factory on Washington Avenue formerly used by the Sprague-Smith Company to make school desks. The company was soon producing walnut Liberty propellers for the government (army and navy). The firm also briefly made steering wheels for United States Army trucks.

After the war, Hartzell's began to diversify producing civilian automobile steering wheels, automobile battery cases (plant on West Water Street), wooden Victrola cabinets and in 1927 propeller-type fans. Directly after the war was over, Hartzell's designed and built several

This interior view of the Hartzell Propeller Company on Washington Avenue shows the early hand shaping required for each propeller.

bi-planes, the Hartzell FC-20, which won air races in St. Louis. The company's chief engineer Fred Charavay was responsible for most of the aircraft design. However this was just a short experiment for Hartzell's and aircraft construction never really took off. The company was incorporated in December of 1928 as Hartzell Industries Inc. With the death of G.W. Hartzell in 1933, his son **Robert Norris Hartzell** took over as president. The innovations of the company continued with the development of "Hartzite" a plastic material first used in cooling tower fans (1940 on) and the creation of a process for gluing wood to metal for the production of gliders (1942). Fan production became a big part of Hartzell's business and a separate plant was constructed in 1940 and greatly enlarged in 1950.

The firm enlarged its scope of operations and by the early 1950's had new facilities and/or warehouses in Iowa, West Virginia and Canada. The firm organized the Hartzell Hydraulic Products Company in Piqua in 1961 to produce automated machinery for saw mills and veneer plants. The company purchased Decatur Industries of Indiana who produced specialty walnut items such as pipe racks, trophies and gift items. In 1975, the firm added the American Woodcrafters Division to produce furniture kits originally sold through the mail. During the 1970's, Hartzell's added a fan plant in Indiana, and veneer plants in Arkansas and North Carolina. The propeller division was sold to TRW of Cleveland in 1981. In 1998, George W. Hartzell stepped down as president and was replaced by Michael Bardo as president and CEO of Hartzell Industries. Thomas Hartzell stepped down in 1998 as president of Hartzell Fan Inc. to be replaced by Richard Wallace. The Hartzell brothers are the sons of Robert N. Hartzell who died in 1968. By 2007, the firm employed 310 men and women, 195 working in Piqua. SEE ALSO: Hartzell Propeller Company; Patron p. 240

HARTZELL PROPELLER COMPANY

Robert N. Hartzell was responsible for the creation of this division of the George W. Hartzell Company in 1917. Propellers were produced for both the Army and Navy during **World War I**. Hartzell Propeller furnished propellers for Curtis (JN.4 Jenny), Dayton-Wright (Liberty engine powered DH-4), and Loening planes among others. With the end of the war, government contracts ended and the firm began looking for new uses for propellers including building their own airplanes, propellers for rigid airships (USS Shenandoah in 1924) and introducing propeller blades into cooling fans. The Washington Avenue plant struggled to keep its skilled workers, but gradually civilian aircraft began to make a common back. Hartzell's produced props for WACO planes in Troy (1924-1930) and by the end of the 1930's was producing props for navy planes. During the **Second World War,** material shortages led the company to produce its first composite blade propellers using Hartzite plastic (patented in 1939), a material invented by the firm. After World War II, David Biermann, an expert in propeller re-

Dick Grimes is shown standing next to a Hartzell propeller.

search, joined the firm. Biermann led the Hartzell research team in the development of the all metal controllable pitch propellers in 1948. A practical move for the company was the purchase of the Piqua Airport in 1957. A new 4,000 foot runway was added in 1967.

Hartzell's moved heavily into the light aircraft market with constant speed, full-feathering propellers. An addition was made to the Washington Avenue plant in 1959. When the founder and company president Robert N. Hartzell died in 1968, the firm was led in turn by Thomas Hartzell, David J. Biermann, Richard Grimes and James Hartzell. One of the firm's new products was a composite propeller, lighter than aluminum and suitable for larger commuter planes. Increased sales volume in the 1970's led to production space becoming extremely cramped. The firm purchased the former Champion Paper factory at 1800 Covington Avenue and moved part of their operations there in 1979. Hartzell Propeller with approximately $25 million in annual sales was sold to TRW of Cleveland with roughly $5 billion in annual sales. Arthur R. Disbrow became the divisional manager for TRW Hartzell Propeller. One of the modern day highlights of the company was the production of the custom built constant speed, variable pitch propellers for the experimental aircraft the Voyager in 1986. Dick Rutan and Jeana Yeager flew this plane on the first non-stop non-refueled flight around the world. The division was sold to the Horsbaugh & Scott Company and James Brown in 1987. Disbrow was named president of Hartzell Propeller, a position he would hold until 1997. James Brown Jr. of Cleveland, a former naval aviator, bought out his partners in 1988 and Hartzell's became a privately held corporation. The company began the manufacture of a new dual acting propeller, the company had previously only made single action props. This new product allowed the company to market to larger airplanes such as the German Dornier 328, the first to use this new propeller. Another product innovation was the six-blade aluminum hub propeller. With well over 250 different blade designs, Hartzell offered more styles and types of propellers than any other company in the world. The main factory was expanded and remodeled in 1996. The strikingly modern office/factory complex features free-flow, curved clerestory windows and was designed by Lorenz & Williams of Dayton. After Dis-

brow's retirement in 1997, James Brown III and Joseph Brown became co-presidents of the firm. The firm created the Charter Aerospace Partners Inc. in 2004 as a holding company for Hartzell Propeller and two additional California based companies, Electrofilm Manufacturing (Valencia) and the Industrial Tube Corp. (Parris). As of late 2006, the firm had in excess of three hundred employees. SEE ALSO: Hartzell Industries; Patron p. 241

HIGH SCHOOL, PUBLIC

On October 11, 1853 the citizens of Piqua voted on the question of whether to establish a Piqua Union School system. The vote was 289 and 13 against the new system. Two weeks later, a six-man Board of Education was elected. J. D. Holtzerman (merchant), William Humphreville (contractor), **Godwin V. Dorsey** (physician), **William Wood** (cooper), **William Scott** (banker), J. T. Janvier (politician). By the end of 1853, the city had also passed a levy enabling the Board of Education to build a new school. Land was purchased from Matthew Caldwell in December of 1854. It was located on the west edge of the city on the newly laid out College Street. Plans for the school were drawn up by William Humphreville and John Rayner, Sr. Work began on the school in 1855 under the supervision of Rayner. The building was completed in the fall of 1856 at a total cost of just over thirty-three thousand dollars. The first school was torn down in 1884 and replaced by a newer and larger structure. The second school was torn down in 1911 to make way for the third high school, completed in 1912. The fourth and present high school was built east of Looney Road and formally dedicated in 1981. The third high school was taken over for a few years as office space for the Board of Education. The College Street building became senior housing by the turn of the twenty-first century. SEE ALSO: List-Schools; Piquonians

HIGH VICTORIAN ITALIANATE ARCHITECTURE

This style was popular with commercial structures in the 1890's. The domestic **Queen Anne Style** led to an increasing number of decorative elements, particularly at the parapet and cornice. This style is the commercial variation of the domestic Queen Anne Style. The strong and massive design elements of this local style variation showed a definite confidence and enthusiasm in doing business in the downtown. Unfortunately many of these elements have been lost to neglect, remodeling, or fire. Their location on the tops of buildings has made their maintenance difficult and their destruction fairly common.

This style has many of the following local architectural elements. The stores are rectangular in shape and usually form part of a row of abutted buildings This style almost always has at least three stories. The upper floor openings are often built with rounded arches on the second floor and squared-off elongated windows on the third with two over two double hung sash windows. Large inset stone keystone lintels over arched windows were common. A decorative stone belt course was used on the upper floors under a decorated cornice of corbeled brick. The style differs from the domestic Empress Anne (massive Queen Ann type) by the use of a highly decorated parapet that rises four to six feet above the roof line. This parapet is constructed using a light-weight wooden frame covered by tin to provide the illusion of massive decorations at the roof line without the need for heavy building support. The parapet decorative elements often include brackets, dentils, finials, or rectangular pediments. The year of the buildings construction or remodeling and the name of the building owner are commonly placed on the parapet.

COMMERCIAL EXAMPLES

204 North Main, Paul's Bar, 1891

HOME GUARD

The first home guard unit in Piqua was established during the **Civil War**. Company E, Third Regiment, Ohio Militia was organized in September of 1863. The original muster under the command of Captain A. G. Conover, was held on the vacant lots located on the northwest corner of Broadway and Camp Streets. The unit was known as the "Border City Guards". It was disbanded soon after the end of the war.

During the **First World War**, the local Ohio National Guard Company was called-up for active duty. The federal government authorized replacements with the passage of the Home Guard Act of June 14, 1917. In Piqua, former Captain James F. Hubbard promoted the formation of a home guard unit under the auspices of the Piqua Branch, National Council of Defense. After the election of **Socialist Party** candidate **Frank B. Hamilton** as Piqua's mayor in November of 1917, the home guard unit refused to be sworn-in. The unit members stated that they would not serve under a Socialist administration. As a result of the refusal, no official home guard company was established in Piqua during World War I.

On October 5, 1940, Piqua's artillery batteries of the Ohio National Guard were activated into federal service. Locally they were replaced by Company L, Third Battalion, First Regiment, Ohio State Guard. The company was organized in 1941 and commanded by Captain **George P. Wertz**. He was assisted by First Lieutenant Richard Bemus and Second Lieutenant **William M. McCulloch**. Congress authorized the State Guards in 1940 and disbanded them in 1947.

The State Legislature re-established the State Guard under the name Ohio Defense Corps (ODC). Captain George P. Wertz and First Lieutenant Joseph Terry organized Company C, 42nd Battalion in Piqua in 1947. The unit was first issued double barrel shotguns, and later Enfield rifles, then M-l rifles. Annual training was held at Camp Perry, Ohio. The Company disbanded in late 1948.

In the 1980's, the ODC was re-organized by the state and became the Ohio Military Reserve (OMR). Company B, 12th Military Police (MP) Battalion, First Infantry Brigade. OMR was organized in Piqua in January of 1986 under the command of Captain Max McDaniel of Troy. The unit was reorganized in 1988 and became Headquarters and Headquarters Company, 12th MP Battalion, First MP Brigade, OMR. The unit was commanded by Major McDaniel, then by Major James C. Oda and finally by Captain Daniel Ferguson. In 1992, the HHC was transferred to Dayton and replaced in Piqua by the 122nd Support Company commanded by Captain Michael Ashcraft. The Support Company was disbanded by the mid-1990's. SEE ALSO: Militia and National Guard.

HOPEWELL CULTURE

During the prehistoric **Woodland Period**, the Hopewell Culture (100 B.C. to 300 A.D.) developed in the Ohio River Valley from Marietta to the Indiana border and as far north as Columbus. The name comes from mounds excavated in 1920 on the farm of M.C. Hopewell in Ross County, Ohio. The Hopewell Culture followed the Adena Culture and continued their tradition of earthworks. The Hopewell peoples built geometric earthworks and mound groups. The mounds covered charnel houses (houses of the dead), one stacked on top of another. Hopewell artifacts indicate a wide and complex series of trading networks.

The artifacts include: intricate platform pipes, mica sheets (from the Carolinas), obsidian spear points (from Mexico), and sharks teeth (from the coastal regions). The Hopewell Culture declined and was followed by minor transitional or intrusive cultures during the late Woodland Period. SEE ALSO: Adena Culture.

HOSPITAL

In May of 1904, Mrs. Julia Ball Thayer offered to the city of Piqua a hospital in memory of her brother DeLoss C. Ball, a local linseed oil manufacturer. In June of 1904, a hospital board was appointed with **W. P. Orr** as its first president (1904-1912). Mrs. Thayer's gift to the city was formally dedicated on Thanksgiving Day, November 30, 1905. The Ball Memorial Hospital was constructed on the site of a former city cemetery on Park Avenue and built by **A. M. Fry** at a cost of eighteen thousand dollars. An additional four thousand was spent on equipment. This first hospital contained a male ward (five beds), female ward (five beds), thirteen private beds, a consultation room, operating room, and a laboratory. Miss Mary Melville was appointed as the hospital's first superintendent. Dr. George Upton established an out patient department (free clinic) at the hospital in 1935. Major additions and remodeling occurred in 1927 (east wing), 1938 (maternity north wing), 1941 (third floor), 1959, 1969 (original facade demolished) and 1983 (support services wing).

In 1986, the Piqua Memorial Medical Center merged with Dettmer and Stouder Memorial Hospitals to form the Upper Valley Medical Center (UVMC). The Hospital on Park Avenue was closed when the UVMC opened a new facility midway between Piqua and Troy on 25-A in 1998 on the 100 plus acre campus of the former Dettmer Hospital. As of 2007, the former Park Avenue Hospital Building is vacant.

UVMC broke ground for its new 220,000 square foot facility in May of 1996. The building was designed by NBBJ architects of Columbus and constructed by the Turner Construction Company. The new hospital's grand opening was held in July of 1998 and it contained 128 inpatient beds. UVMC supports four outpatient facilities in Miami County; the Hyatt Center in Tipp City, the Outpatient Care Center/North in Piqua (on Looney Road on the east side of I-75), the Outpatient Care Center/South in Troy and the Stanfield Place in Troy. The hospital also runs two long-term care facilities, the Koester Pavilion on the UVMC campus and SpringMeade in Tipp City. SEE ALSO: Nurses; Physicians; Patron p. 286

The Ball Memorial Hospital was originally constructed in 1905. This postcard shows the Nurse's Home on the far left, the 1927 addition on the right and the additional of a third floor in the center in 1941.

HOTELS AND MOTELS

The first local tavern was established in 1807 by Alexander Ewing. It was a log structure located halfway between Water and Sycamore Street. The first full fledged hotel was a two story frame building erected prior to 1820 on the northeast corner of

56

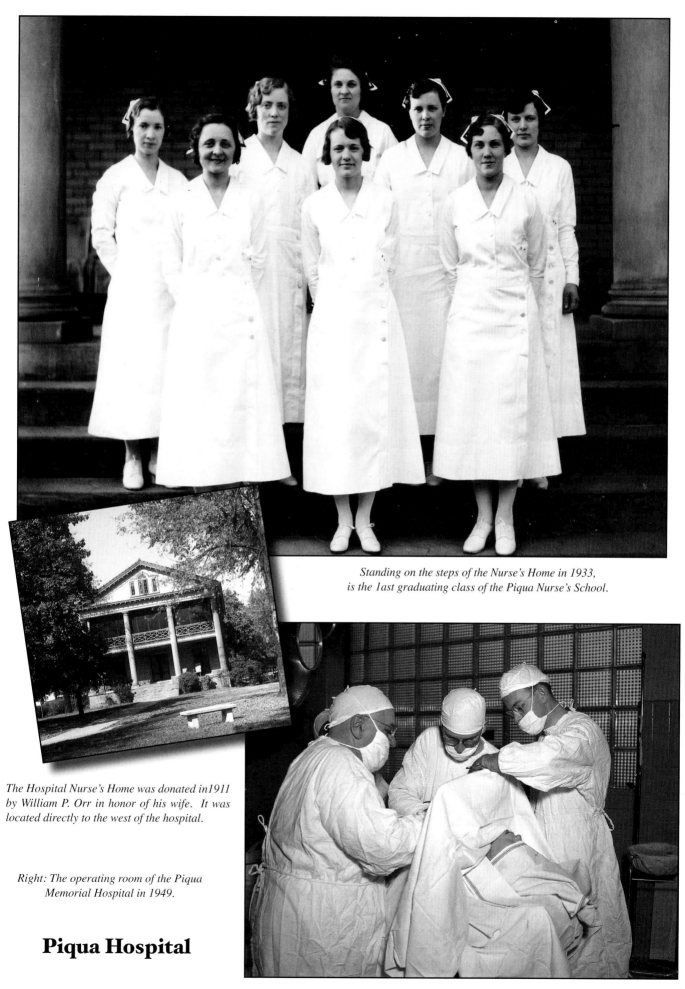

*Standing on the steps of the Nurse's Home in 1933,
is the 1ast graduating class of the Piqua Nurse's School.*

*The Hospital Nurse's Home was donated in1911
by William P. Orr in honor of his wife. It was
located directly to the west of the hospital.*

*Right: The operating room of the Piqua
Memorial Hospital in 1949.*

Piqua Hospital

Main and Water Streets by James Tamplin. Tamplin's Piqua Hotel advertised rates in 1821 of $1.50 a room per week, 37-1/2 cents per night for a horse, 18-3/4 cents for a meal and 6-1/4 cents for a half pint of whiskey. From 1820 until 1961, Tamplin's original structure was remodeled three times, owned or managed by over thirty different people, and operated under ten different names.

The next major hotel was Union Hall built in 1820 by James Bennett as a house of entertainment, a tavern and a business location on the southwest corner of Main and Ash Streets. In 1849, the original structure was replaced by a seventy-room hotel on the same site. The newly erected hotel was named the City Hotel and run by Loring R. Brownell with seven employees. The hotel was remodeled in 1877 with outdoor bathrooms connected to the building. Eighteen different proprietors followed Brownell from 1849 until the hotel closed in 1895.

Perry Tuttle opened the last of the major early hotels in 1840. Tuttle's Miami House was located on the northwest corner of Main and North Streets. The hotel was known for its ballroom which featured a blue ceiling decorated with stars. The Miami House became a gathering place for the contractors, engineers, and commissioners who were pushing the Miami Extension Canal northward. The hotel went through at least eight owners after Tuttle before closing down in 1908-9. The last major hotel to be built was the **Plaza Hotel** in 1890-91.

Other pre-Civil War Piqua hotels include: Cold Springs Hotel (1830's), Leavell's Inn (1831), Columbian Inn (1830's), Abby Tavern (1830's), Hale Tavern (1836), Exchange Hotel (1837-1881), Wither's Hotel (1839), Swartz's Tavern (1840's), Eagle Hotel (1850-1853), Naterman Tavern (1850), William Tell House (1859), Farmer's Hotel (1860), Washington House (1860).

With the increase in automobiles after World War II, hotels in the cities began to give way to rural motels. The first motel in the Piqua area was located north of Piqua at 8468 North County Road 25-A. It was known as the Motel Piqua.

HOUSE NUMBERS

In May of 1887, a city ordinance was passed providing for the re-numbering of houses within the city limits. Even numbers would be placed on the north side of east-west streets and the west side of north-south streets. For the city's main north-south streets, a division was made at the railroad tracks. Prior to this ordinance, only structures on the main streets were given numbers. This old system started at the Miami River and numbered each structure beginning with number one on the west side of the street. The city was forced into renumbering the city by **post office** regulations which required cities wanting free home delivery to have complete street numbering systems.

HOUSES

Piqua's first **brick** house was built by Dr. Daniel Ashton in 1819 on the northwest corner of Main and Greene. The first **steel house** in Piqua was built in 1936 at 518 Vine Street. The first prefabricated houses manufactured in Piqua were built by **Inland Homes** in 1952. SEE ALSO: Architecture; Housing Developments; Log Cabins

HOUSING DEVELOPMENTS

After the **Second World War**, the restrictions on building supplies were lifted and housing developments began to grow in Piqua. The west end of town saw the creation of subdivisions such as **Landon Park** off of Covington Avenue in 1955, Dr. William H. Trosel's Marymont development off of Park

Avenue in 1953-54, and Sidney Philbrook's Flo-Gene Company's Highland Acres in 1953-54. The early 1960's saw the creation of the Meadowlawn Subdivision, Margene Manor, Bellaire Park, Sunset Gardens and Mar-Wood Estates. One of the community's biggest developments on the far west end of town off of South Street was **Candlewood** which was begun in 1965 and continued through the early 1970's. Another major development in the late sixties and early seventies was Park Ridge off of Sunset. This subdivision picked up steam again 1980's and early 1990's. The late 1980's saw the creation of Eagles Nest on the northeast corner of Piqua off of Sunset. On the far west edge of town off of High Street, the Deerfield Subdivision was created by Craycon Homes in the early 1990's. SEE Also: Inland Homes; Mid-Continent Properties; Patron p. 227

HUNTERSVILLE, OHIO

This village was located in Springcreek Township directly east of the Great Miami River and the city of Piqua. The village was laid out in January of 1838 for **David Hunter**. It was incorporated in 1848 and annexed by Piqua in 1893. **L. C. Cron** served as Mayor of the village from 1875 until 1891. The village fire department was organized in 1879 and a fire station built on East Main Street. Huntersville School on Staunton Street was built in 1889 with Lafayette Westfall as its first principal. The village's two biggest industries were the **L. C. & W. L. Cron Furniture Company** and the **Cron, Kills Furniture Company**. Before any white settlers had come to Miami County, the location of Huntersville had been the site of the **Shawnee** village of Chillicothe (or Lower Piqua) from 1780 until 1782. It was from this brief Indian occupation that the village acquired the nickname of Shawnee. After its absorption by Piqua, the village was known as East Piqua (often confused with the East Piqua east of Spring Street). SEE ALSO: Bottlers; Hilliard Family.

HYDRAULIC CANAL

One of the major undertakings of the last half of the nineteenth century in Piqua was the building of the hydraulic canal. In 1865, the first meetings were held to discuss the concept. The first supporters of this plan were **Godwin V. Dorsey, A. G. Conover**, and **John O'Farrell**. In December of 1865, a charter was granted to these men who had formed a joint stock company known as the Piqua Hydraulic Company. Dorsey was elected the company's first president on February 26, 1866. But the project was more costly than the originators had anticipated. In 1872, the City of Piqua bought out the stock company and continued the work to bring both a source of power and a reliable supply of water to the community. A city waterworks board was set up to control this new project. The formal opening of the hydraulic canal took place on June 16, 1876. The hydraulic canal ran from the Miami and Erie Canal at Lockington to Piqua following a route from Swift Run back to the cemetery and Fountain Park to Water Street, then to College Street and finally east to South Main Street and the canal. The canal today is only open from High Street north to Swift Run off State Route 66. As a source of hydraulic power, the canal was only a limited success with only four or five firms taking advantage of this power source. But as a water supply, it provided Piqua with its first public water system under pressure. SEE ALSO: Johnston, Stephen.

ICE PRODUCTION

During the nineteenth century, large blocks of ice were cut from the Miami River and area lakes and ponds. The ice was packed in sawdust and stored in specially constructed and insulated sheds.

Cold winters meant ice all summer long, mild winters caused small ice harvests with ice becoming scarce by August. During the first part of the nineteen hundreds, families cut their own ice or bought it from freelance ice cutters. Until the 1870's, there were no organized ice companies in the city. During that time period a **canal** boat captain, George Hager, was bringing ice down to Piqua from Toledo and the Great Lakes area. Hager saw the need for a local organization to harvest ice in Piqua. In 1879, Hager joined with William and George Roeser and Thomas Ginn to establish the Piqua Ice Company. The firm harvested ice first from the Miami River and then from the Miami and Erie Canal turn around basin located between the river and Broadway. Finally the company moved its operation to Echo Lake where they built an ice storage house. This facility stayed in operation until it burned down in 1917. By 1907, the Piqua Ice Company was servicing Piqua customers with nine horse drawn wagons, delivering ice door to door. The age of naturally harvested ice came to an end in 1909 when the Peckman Coal and Ice Company built an artificial ice plant in Shawnee, located two blocks from the river between Ohio and East Main Streets. The Piqua Ice Company sold the new artificial ice for Peckham until 1911. In that year, Piqua Ice Company incorporated and bought out the Peckham plant. The firm continued operations until the 1990's at 240 East Main under the name of the Piqua Fish and Ice Company, Inc. SEE ALSO: Refrigerators

IMMIGRATION TO PIQUA AND MIAMI COUNTY

1870 (Miami County)

Place of Birth	Immigrants	% of Total Population
Germany	1,537	4.69%
Ireland	580	1.77%
England	188	0.57%
Switzerland	34	0.10%
Canada	49	0.15%
France	84	0.26%

1900 (Miami County)

Place of Birth	Immigrants	% of Total Population
Germany	1,237	2.87%
Ireland	228	0.53%
England	164	0.38%
Switzerland	25	0.06%
Canada	86	0.20%
France	34	0.08%

TOTAL FOREIGN BORN POPULATION IN PIQUA

Year	Foreign Born	% of Total Population
1870	1,127	18.90%
1880	872	14.46%
1890	1,065	11.71%
1900	901	07.40%
1920	581	04.00%

SEE ALSO: Population; Migration.

IMPERIAL UNDERWEAR COMPANY

The firm was begun in 1902 as the Stuart-Brown Underwear Company to produce men's unionsuits. The company became the Stuart-Hance company in 1910. The Imperial Underwear Company was incorporated in February of 1909 in Columbus, but was purchased in April of 1909 by Allen D. Hance (1862-1919) and Charles Stuart and in 1913 merged with the Stuart-Hance Company. Imperial Underwear went bankrupt in June of 1922 and was sold to Frank and Clint Campbell. **Alfred Flesh**

The Imperial Underwear Company used classical Greek art to promote their union suits in the pre-World War I era.

of the **Atlas Underwear Company** purchased the company in 1926. In partnership with **Milton Erlanger**, president of the **B.V.D.** Company, Flesh created the Erlanger Knitting Mills Inc. in June of 1928. The new firm used the former Imperial plant on the southeast corner of Wayne and Water Streets as well as the Imperial trade names. The Great Depression hit the mill hard and the Piqua plant closed down in September of 1933. SEE ALSO: List-Underwear Companies.

INCOME TAX

The city commission placed a city income tax on the ballot in November of 1966. The tax was fixed at seven-tenths of one percent. The measure was passed and went into effect January 1, 1967.

INDUSTRY

The industrial growth of Piqua can be divided into five different periods.

PIONEER PERIOD. During this period (1800-1840), industry was very small and oriented toward agriculture and the land. Local industries included grist mills, **sawmills**, **distilleries**, **flour mills**, carding mills, flaxseed/**linseed oil** mills, and tanning mills. Industries were individually or family owned and concentrated on selling their product locally (usually within a five to ten mile radius). The owners constituted a major part of the work force with only a limited amount of technology to assist them. Examples of these pioneer industries include: the **John Manning** Grist Mill in 1804, the Manning Distillery in 1805, the Montgomery Tanning Yard in 1809, and the Wiley Sawmill in 1815.

FIRST GROWTH PERIOD. This period (1840-1880) continued the concept of small individual or family owned industries. Agriculture was still the prime orientation, but a growing consumer population created markets for coopers, foundries, breweries, furniture manufacturers, carriage and cigar makers. The market for local industries expanded to cover the entire state with the addition of the Miami and Erie **Canal** (1837), the east-west route of the Columbus, Piqua, and Indiana **Railroad** (1851), and the north-south route of the Dayton and Michigan Railroad (1854). The owner still worked in the factory, but his work force had increased to an average of ten to fifteen men. Technology was still relatively limited, but new skills were added to the work pool by **German** immigrants (**brewing**), former east coast settlers (carriage makers and foundry workers), and southern workers (cigar making).

CORPORATION AND CONSOLIDATION PERIOD. This period (1880-1920) was a major growth time for local industry. It was also a period of diversity, with the production of underwear and knitwear (**Piqua Hosiery, Atlas, Superior**), **linseed oil (Orr, Daniels, Wood,** and **Leonard**), **patent medicine** (Dr. Bosanko, **Rundle**), **furniture** (Cron, **Cron-Kills, Hinsch**), meat packing (**Decker's**), and printing (*Der Correspondent*, McGee Brothers). This was the beginning of corporate ownership (usually limited or closed corporations). New firms coming to Piqua were incorporated entities such as the **Favorite Stove and Range Company** (1888), **Cincinnati Corrugating Company** (1889), **Hartzell Company** (1900), Orr Felt and Blanket Company (1900), **French Oil Mill Machinery Company** (1900), and the **Wood Shovel and Tool Company** (1902). Locally produced products were marketed across the nation. For example, the Favorite Stove and Range Company in the mid-1890's was shipping over fifty thousand stoves a year to all areas of the United States. Increased production meant larger work forces with plants employing anywhere from fifty to six hundred men, women, and children. The owner now rarely worked in the plant, which led to the division of management from labor. Without the close ties of owner and workers, the beginnings of unionization occurred. In 1886, a **Knights of Labor** organization was formed in Piqua. National **union**s followed in the 1890's, with organizations such as Stove Mounters' and Cigar Workers' Unions. Technology increased in local plants with new ideas in iron molding and mass assembly; and the new power sources such as steam, natural gas, and electricity. Marketing skills increased with the introduction of salesmen and coordinated advertising and promotional ideas. National conglomerates began buying up and consolidating local industries. The local linseed oil industry was dismantled by the American Linseed Oil Company and the National Linseed Oil Company. The Cincinnati Corrugating Company was purchased by The American Sheet Steel and Tin Company (later United States Steel), and closed down. Piqua Strawboard Company was sold to The American Strawboard Company who dismantled the plants and moved them to more central locations. The buyouts brought huge amounts of investment capital to Piqua, and the loss of jobs was reduced by the introduction of new local industry.

MODERN DIVERSITY PERIOD. This period (1920-1945) was a time of diverse manufacturers with a wide variety of products and production capabilities. Hartzell Industries manufactured products as varied as propellers and steering wheels, and from veneer products to ventilator fans. That diversity was matched by the **Meteor Motor Car Company** which produced automobiles, hearses, records, phonographs, and speed boats. The **Second World War** brought **Lear Avia** and Robbins and Myers Companies to Piqua. They manufactured aircraft instrumentation and bomb sights. The industry of this period was often owned by large public or semi-public corporations. This was also the beginning of significant out of town ownership. With the increased size of many of these firms, their markets had increased to an international level. While the Favorite Stove and Range Company had sold some of their products in Europe and the Far East, the first major international marketing effort was made by the **French Oil Mill Machinery Company** in China in the 1930's. The labor forces for these firms were varied both in composition (men and women), and in their union or non-union affiliations. The American Federation of Labor (AF of L) began a major union recruitment effort in the 1930's that led to several major **strikes** (Decker's, Atlas, and Orr Felt). This period saw little improvement in industrial technology or marketing methods. Transportation moved from total dependence on the railroad for long distance hauling to the creation of industry owned trucking fleets.

POST WAR PERIOD. During this last period (1945-2000), industrial size varied but the trend towards product diversity continued. New firms included: Piqua Engineering (electrical parts), Burks Pumps, Evenflo (juvenile furniture), Miami Industries (steel tubing), Crayex (plastic films), and Champion Paper. Ownership varied from out of town corporations to small local corporations. A number of small or home owned, companies became very active during this period. The focus on national and international markets continued with local sales being almost nonexistent. The work forces were still a mixture of union and non-union workers, but union labor appeared to be in a decline. Technology played a large part in post-war industrial development. The following industries have depended on new high tech advances during this period; Crayex (**plastic** films), Action Mold (plastic molds), Duer Plastics (thermoplastics), EDM (electrical discharge machine), Burks (centrifugal sump pumps), Ledex (remote control systems), Medalist (flame retardant underwear), and Hartzell Propeller (high tech propeller design).

LOCAL INDUSTRY TRIVIA.
The first local industry was John Manning's grist mill in 1804.
Local Piqua **linseed oil** firms in the 1890's combined to become the second largest producers of linseed oil in the United States behind Philadelphia in the 1890's.
The largest industry brought to Piqua in the nineteenth century was the **Favorite Stove and Range Company** in 1888-89.
The local industry in continuous operation for the longest period was the **Piqua Milling Company,** which operated under various owners from 1837 until 1990.
Two of the community's most diverse industries were the **Meteor Motor Car Company** which produced automobiles, ambulances, hearses, speed boats, records, phonographs, cargo plane doors, trailers, and the **Hartzell Industries** which produced hardwood veneer, wooden furniture, airplane propellers, fans, steering wheels, battery boxes, and hydraulics.
The city's largest industrial field was the textile/underwear companies of the 1920's. They included **Atlas, Superior, Piqua Hosiery, Imperial** and Orr Felt. These industries were also the largest employers of women in the city.
The first major industry to use electrically powered machinery was the **French Oil Mill Machinery Company**.
The last known local industry to use the canal system to transport their goods was the Statler Stone Quarry.
SEE ALSO: Air Transportation; Depression Era; Employment; Inland Homes; Japanese; Korean War; Marble Works; Plastics; Pottery; Radio; Tanning; Telephone Equipment Manufacturing; Textile Manufacturing; Time; Tobacco; Toys; Wages; Young Women's Christian Association (YWCA); individual companies by name. SEE ALSO: Patron p. 260

Atlas Underwear Company

Hartzell Fan Company

Aerovent Fan Company

Val Decker Meat Packing Company

Industry in 1966

Miami Industries

INLAND HOMES

This company was incorporated on July 27, 1952 by two Toledo, Ohio men, **Eugene "Gene" R. Kurtz** (president) and Roger Thyer (executive vice president). Both men had been part of the management of the Thyer Manufacturing Company of Toledo, a producer of prefabricated homes. Inland Homes set up shop in the former **Favorite Stove** factory on the corner of College and Weber Streets. Production of prefabricated homes began in the fall of 1952 with about thirty-five employees. A one story plant with 45,000 square feet was constructed in 1955-1956 at 1950 Covington Avenue. By 1955, the firm employed over two hundred men and women. During the mid-1960's, the firm had additional production facilities in Hanover, Pennsylvania, Clinton, Iowa and Cedartown, Georgia. The company established the **Landin Park** Corporation to build one story prefabricated homes in Piqua south of West Covington Avenue. After Kurtz's death in 1964, the firm was taken over by a former Inland Homes vice president John J. Flynn. Thyer moved to **Mid-Continent Properties** (builders of **Candlewood Hills** in Piqua) as vice president. In 1966 the firm became known as IHC and got out of the direct home building business. The Piqua plant continued to manufacture prefabricated homes as a division of the Inland Systems Inc. a Springfield Corporation. In 1974, M.K. Miller, president of Inland Homes, closed the plant citing a decline in the housing market and high local wages. He stated that some members of the Miami Valley Carpenters District Council (the local workers' union) made as much as $4.50 an hour. Miller also stated that the firm was building a new prefabricated home plant in Oklahoma where labor rates were lower.

INSURANCE

The first record of insurance sales came in 1839 with the organization of the Independent Order of Odd Fellows. This lodge, like many early fraternal organizations, sold life, accident, and health coverage to its working class members. For most working men, this was the only way they could protect themselves and their families from the loss of income caused by death, illness, or accident. National insurance companies, such as Aetna and Hartford, had local agents in Piqua by the late 1840's. These agents concentrated on fire and life insurance for business and property owners. The number of insurance firms increased dramatically after the **Civil War**. In 1870, four local agents represented sixteen national or regional insurance companies. None of the early agents sold insurance as a full time occupation. The most common occupations that combined with insurance sales were retail businessmen, attorneys, and real estate agents. By the 1880's, several full time local insurance agencies had been formed. One of the first of these agencies was the Henry C. Grafflin and Company established in 1880. Grafflin and partner John E. Mendenhall sold a mixture of fire, life, and health/accident insurance. Grafflin retired from the firm in 1895, and Mendenhall took in John Ben Wilkinson as a partner. Wilkinson took over the firm in 1918-19 and the agency stayed in the Wilkinson family until 1957 when it was acquired by the Stelzer and Reed Agency. Stelzer and Reed have continued to the present (2007) under the name Reed-Mote-Staley Insurance Company.

Group insurance was first introduced on a mass scale by industries during **World War II**. The shortage of skilled workers led firms to offer incentives such as group life and hospitalization (Blue Cross) insurance to their employees.

SEE ALSO: Cron-Kills Company; Lodges and Organizations; Patron p. 257, 275

INTERURBANS

Local interurban service had its origins in the establishment of the Piqua Electric Street Railway Company in 1889. The firm was reorganized in 1893, and became the Miami Valley Railway Company. The new organization built an electric railway from Piqua to Troy which began operations in August of 1893. To increase business, the company opened up Midway Park in 1894 halfway between Piqua and Troy. The railway's tracks were leased by the Dayton and Troy Electric Railway Company in 1902. The new line would later open a passenger station at 333 North Main, a freight station at 110 S. Wayne and car barn at the southwest corner of South and Blaine Streets. The Dayton and Troy line continued in operation in Piqua until it was replaced on February 1, 1930 by the Dayton and Troy bus line under the name The Piqua Transit Company. The bus line was taken over by the Dodge Transportation Company in 1931 and ran successfully until the early 1960's.

The second interurban line to Piqua was established in 1901 as the Dayton, Covington, and Piqua Traction Company. The company owned Overlook Park near West Milton and used the large dance hall, baseball field and boating and bathing facilities to draw customers to the line. The Dayton, Covington and Piqua ran from 1903 until 1926, when the Dayton and Western Bus Line took over the route.

The third interurban line in Piqua was the Western Ohio Railway which began its connection with Piqua on April 1, 1903. On this date, car number thirteen left Piqua for the first trip north to Sidney. By 1905, the Western Ohio had expanded its route all the way north to Toledo. Travel time on the Western Ohio in 1906, from Piqua to Sidney, was twenty-six minutes and cost twenty-five cents one way and forty-five cents round trip. The Western Ohio tracks were removed from Main Street in 1926 and re-laid on the former bed of the Miami and Erie Canal. The company shared its passenger station with the Dayton and Troy route and built a freight station on Riverside Drive near Broadway. The last trip of the Western Ohio left Piqua on January 16, 1932.

Two other interurban lines were franchised for operations to Piqua, the Columbus, Mechanicsburg, Urbana and Piqua Traction Company in 1902, and the Springfield, Troy and Piqua Traction Company in 1915. Neither company reached Piqua with an active route. SEE ALSO: Parks; Street Railway; Strikes.

The Piqua City Bus Line shown in this 1949 photograph took over from the electric street car line in 1930.

ITALIANATE STYLE ARCHITECTURE

The local variation of the Italianate Style was popular from 1860 through 1885. **Railroad** transportation first reached downtown Piqua in 1856 with the coming of the Columbus, Piqua

The O'Ferrall home on the southwest corner of Main and North Streets was built in the Italianate Style with a mansard roof added later on to make it a Second Empire Style home.

and Indiana Railroad. The Dayton and Michigan Railroad line ran about a mile east of the town in 1854. As a crossroads for north-south and east-west lines the Piqua economy took another leap forward. The construction of the iron rails led to an expansion of the iron foundry industry. This resulted in higher quality and lower priced cast iron lintels and building piers. Another technological innovation, the free standing stove, led to more efficient heating which impacted on the height of ceilings. As easily heated rooms became taller, the windows for these rooms became taller or elongated. New Italianate homes became squarer with a variety of interior room shapes. The need to build a room to match a chimney was no longer necessary.

These larger brick homes set further back on their lots than the earlier **Federal** and **Greek Revival Style** structures. As the community expanded west of Main Street, the lot sizes grew larger and it became more common to buy more than one lot to accommodate the larger homes. As the prosperity of this type of home owner grew, so did his use of the horse and buggy. The Italianate homes usually were paired with two story frame stables/barns. The earlier horse sheds became full fledged structures that incorporated storage for feed, hay, straw, buggies, as well as accommodations for two or three horses.

This style may have some or all of these elements: a square shape with two stories, usually with symmetrical openings/bays (often three to five bays), often have a projecting, two story bay windows, a plain/unpainted brick facade, arched or curved decorative cast iron lintels (the lintel often surrounded the upper portion of the window sash on three sides and projecting down an average of six to twelve inches past the top of window sash), elongated windows often with two over two double hung sash windows and upper panes had curved tops, an elaborate door enframement with decorated side pillars supporting flat or arched or triangular pediments, single or double front doors with large glass panes that replaced earlier sidelights, cornices decorated with single or paired brackets and often with dentils, a hipped roof often with a flat truncated top and a cast iron "window's walk" balustrade at the top.

DOMESTIC EXAMPLES
523 North Wayne Street, Daniels House, 1868
519 North Wayne Street, Johnston-Purcell House, c1876

The Italianate Style also had a local commercial variation. Railroads, the canal (beginning to decline in use), and toll roads had made Piqua a center for commerce and industry. The community's population increased by over thirty percent and the downtown grew in size and complexity. The one and two hundred blocks of Main Street experienced major building growth at

this time. The agricultural market on the public square became a central focal point for surrounding communities and farms. This added traffic led to an increase and enlargement of hotels and to the establishment of numerous livery stables. Rural visitors now had a place to house both their families and their horses. Rail freight traffic allowed merchants to make frequent offerings of new and fashionable merchandise. Increased sales and an increase in the size of the inventory resulted in the need for new and larger commercial buildings. By 1860, the commercial core of Main Street was bounded on the north by industrial buildings and residences in the 600 block. The southern boundary was the railroad tracks and the industrial buildings in the 100 block of South Main.

Older Greek Revival Style commercial buildings were demolished in the 300, 400, and 500 blocks of Main Street. The gaps in the 100 and 200 block were filled in, leaving an almost unbroken brick streetscape on the east side of Main Street from North Street south to Sycamore Street (railroad). The new Italianate structures used the heating technology of the free standing stove, placing the stove's pipes partially inside the walls for the entire length of the building. The ceilings of these buildings average ten to twelve feet high with elongated windows to match. This changed the general roof line of Main Street by erecting structures whose average story height was three to five feet higher than the Greek Revival Style commercial buildings. A two story Italianate commercial building often was the same height or higher than a three story Greek Revival commercial building. These larger structures added more architectural elements to their upper stories to provide a stronger visual appeal. Decorative cast iron lintels were usually painted in multicolors to contrast with the plain brick facade. The cornices under the extended eaves were highlighted with brackets that drew the eye upward. Lodges, churches, and political groups used these upper floors as meeting halls, frequently painting small signs on the upper windows to advertise their occupancy. The rents from these halls helped pay the construction and maintenance costs for the larger buildings. Use of the halls also helped build customer traffic downtown and increased retail sales on the first floors.

The **Friedlich** family (merchant tailors) built the first and largest (three stories with nine bays) of the Italianate Commercial Style Variations in 1860. It set the standard for multi-store first floor use, second floor storage, office and occasional retail use, and third floor lodge hall use. The Civil War (1861-1865) brought commercial building to a stand still until the late 1860's and early 1870's. In the 1870's, the Citizens National Bank and the Conover's Opera House were erected and the Piqua **Hotel** and the City Hotel were massively rebuilt. These large structures anchored the building growth of the downtown during this period

Demolition for twentieth century structures has leveled many of the Commercial Italianate buildings. All of the commercial Italianate structures have been removed from the 400 block of North Main Street where they were once a very prominent feature of the east side streetscape.

The Commercial Italiante style has many of the following local architectural elements. The stores are rectangular in shape as part of a row of abutted buildings with two or three stories. The average height of the individual stories is taller than the earlier **Greek Revival** Commercial Style structures. The first floor facade maintains most of the same elements of the earlier Greek Revival Commercial Style. The first floor facade is capped by a decorated (often cast iron) building-width cornice usually with paired brackets placed periodically along its length (the brackets have almost all been removed during remodeling efforts). The first floor support columns are often cast iron and highly decorated, painted with multiple colors. A first floor secondary entrance may be found on one side of the store front with a slightly recessed plain and undecorated wooden panel door. The upper floor facades have elongated two over two or six over six double hung sash windows often with the upper panes containing curved tops. Over the windows are arched or curved decorative cast iron lintels often surrounding the upper portion of the window sash on three sides and projected down an average of six to twelve inches past the top of the window sash. The top floor windows are usually situated directly under the cornice with only limited separation. The plain and unpainted brick facades use the decorated lintels and cornices for color and contrast. Corner buildings are occasionally decorated with stone quoins. Under the wide projecting eaves, the cornice is decorated with symmetrically placed brackets with dentils placed beneath the brackets. In the later buildings, decorated and jagged edged lintel boards replaced the use of brackets. Hipped roofs were prominent on corner structures and gently pitched roofs with off center ridgepoles are common on row structure buildings. The rear facades often maintained the undecorated **Greek Revival** style facade with plain stone lintels and undecorated cornices.

COMMERCIAL EXAMPLES
312-316 North Main, Commercial Block/Barclay's, 1860 (south end removed in 1898)
108 North Main Street, c.1870's
112 North Main Street, c.1870's
529-531 North Main Street, Foreman Block/Quality Quick Printing, c.1870's
527 North Main Street, Rundle Building/IAM Appliance, 1887
523 North Main Street, **Gerlach** Bakery Building, c.1871
323 North Main Street, **Dorsey** Building/Susie's Big Dipper, c.1868

JACOBETHAN STYLE ARCHITECTURE

The local variation of the Jacobethan Style (combination of the English Jacobin and Elizabethan) was popular from 1905 through 1910. There were no local domestic versions built in this style. The closest homes to this style were done in what is known as the Tudor Style.

The first local version of the Jacobethan Style was built in 1907 as the private **Piqua Men's Club** located on the northeast corner of North Wayne and West Greene Streets. The three story structure originally housed a bowling alley and barbershop in the basement, billiards and card rooms on the first floor, dining areas on the second floor, and a ball room and custodial apartments on the third floor. The building had a prominent second entrance off of North Wayne Street which led directly to the second floor dinning areas. This was to allow women to skip the embarrassment of watching men play cards and billiards in public. The building was remodeled and occupied by the Flesh Public Library in 1931 following the demise of the Piqua Club. The distinctive red tile roof was removed from the building in 1974. An architecturally compatible addition was erected on the east side of the library in 1977-1978.

The second Jacobethan Style structure was built about 1910 for the **George H. Rundle** Company as an office and manufacturing facility. Located on North Downing Street, in a quiet residential neighborhood, the building fit in with its one story brick facade, massive curved windows and central projecting entrance topped by a Flemish gable and very modest castellations.

This style has many of the following local architectural elements. The structures often had an irregular shape (although the Rundle building is rectangular to fit into a relatively narrow lot). Projecting one or two story bays are common. The brick structures often had upper floor decorative half-timbering filled in with painted stucco or a stone belt courses. A central front entrance with double doors and decorative surrounds were the norm for this style. SEE ALSO; Tudor Style

COMMERCIAL EXAMPLES
124 West Greene Street, Piqua Men's Club/Flesh Public **Library**, 1907
419 Caldwell, George H. Rundle Company, 1910.

JAILS

The first official community jail was added to the first floor of the **Town Hall** in 1847. The cells were built of wood, and according to newspaper reports not very secure. A number of prisoners were able to either break through the bars or move them apart sufficiently to squeeze between them. In 1863, new iron cells replaced the wooden ones in the Town Hall. In 1890, the city built a new single story concrete jail house. It was located behind the Wayne Street Fire Station in the center of the block bounded by Main, Wayne, Ash and High Streets. The structure cost over sixteen hundred dollars and contained five new self-contained iron cells. When the city offices were moved to the current City Hall on Water Street in 1928, a jail was added to the first floor rear portion of the building. During the 1960's, a new **police department** building was erected east of the city building and the concrete block community jail cell was located in this structure. By the 1990's the Piqua police stopped using the local facility and transported all prisoners to a facility in Troy.

JANITORS

Some of the earliest full time janitors on record worked for the Piqua Board of Education after the Civil War era. It was not uncommon for the janitor and his family to live in the basement of the school building they maintained. In the 1850's, the average janitor's salary was one hundred fifty dollars a year.

JAPANESE

Piqua's first Japanese retail business, The Nippon Food Store, was established at 441 East Ash Street in 1989 by Mrs. Mako Dorsey and Nikki Bray, both natives of Japan. Piqua's first Japanese industry, Piqua Technologies, Incorporated, was established by the Kyoshin Shoji and Taiyo Packing Companies as a joint venture to produce parts for the automotive, electronics, and office equipment industries. The industry began operations during the summer of 1988 and continues to the present (2007).

JEWISH

Almost all of Piqua's early Jewish citizens were immigrants from southern Germany. Many of them came to the United States during the big German immigrant wave of the 1840's and 1850's. Among the most prominent of these immigrants were the Friedlich, Flesh, LeBolt, Urbansky, and Newhoff families. Many of these families organized merchant tailor stores. In 1858, the Anshe Emeth congregation was formed. They met above a number of different clothing stores on Main Street. A permanent temple was built 1925 at 320 Caldwell with the help of the **Flesh** family. Other early Jewish leaders included David Louis (grocer), Abraham Wendel (jeweler), Henry **Flesh** (banker), and H. S. Sternberger (mattress manufacturer). SEE ALSO: Churches.

The Anshe Emeth temple was built in 1925 at 320 Caldwell.

JOSSE'S HILL

Located on the original Versailles Pike (later Echo Lake Drive) at the north edge of the city, the hill was named after the early farmers of this area, the Josse Family.

JUNIOR CHAMBER OF COMMERCE

The "Piqua JC's" was first organized as an auxiliary to the Chamber of Commerce on March 23, 1939. The JC's were primarily young men in their twenties who participated in a number of community activities. The group was active until through the early 1980's.

KITCHENS

Pioneer kitchens were located at the main fire hearth of the house. They usually consisted of a large cast iron kettle that could be swung by a hook over the fire. The kitchen and dining area were one room. With the advent of cooking stoves using wood and later coal and gas, kitchens became separate rooms with built-in cabinets and counters to store utensils and foods stuffs and space to prepare the meals. The family usually still ate in the kitchen, but as the houses grew larger, a separate dining area for more formal meals became more and more common. During much of the nineteenth century, larger homes almost always had "summer kitchens" to the rear of the house which were porch-like areas with screens that allowed cooling air into the hot cooking areas. The cooking stoves were dismantled, cleaned and then move from the kitchen to the summer cooking area. By the early twentieth century, most kitchens had running water with a pump to a household well. As the city expanded water and sewer lines, modern day sinks were added along with ice boxes (later refrigerators), electric stoves and other electrical appliances. SEE ALSO: Federal and Greek Revival Styles; Power plants

KIWANIS CLUB

On December 12, 1935, Dr. S.C. Phibrook, Walter Lape and attorney Cromer attended a meeting of the Covington Kiwanis to determine if a local community service club of this type could be formed. Seven days later, on December 19, 1935, a group of Piqua men met at Retter's Tea Room at 212 West High Street to form a Piqua Kiwanis Club. The local club was formally sponsored by the Covington club. Walter E. Lape was elected as the temporary club president with H.J. Miller as secretary. The club's first formal weekly meeting was held on January 22, 1936 with twenty-eight charter members. Walter Lape was elected as the first permanent president. The Piqua Kiwanis Club was formally chartered in 1936. In 1951, the club organized Piqua's first **Halloween** Parade and costume contest. The club began sponsoring the upkeep of Kiwanis **Park** on the corner of North and Walker Streets in 1982. The park was the site of the demolished North Street Elementary School. As of 2007, the parade/contest was still being held.

The Club sponsors a Key Club for students in the Piqua schools. SEE ALSO: Patron p. 269

KU KLUX KLAN (KKK)

The original Klan developed in the south after the Civil War as a means of harassing and intimidating recently freed slaves. The modern Klan traces its history to the popularity of Thomas Dixon's book *The Klansman* which was the basis for D.W. Griffith's epic movie *The Birth of A Nation*. William Simmons, a Methodist minister in Atlanta organized a Klan "dedicated to defending White Protestant America against blacks, aliens, [Catholics] and dissenters [**Socialists**]. The Klan of the teens and 1920's was strongest in Indiana and Ohio.

The Klan held a big parade in Piqua on Saturday evening, November 03, 1923. Several thousand men and women gathered to watch the six to seven hundred white robed marchers go down Main Street led by a band and a drum corps. The entire Piqua police force was out in force to handle the crowds. The *Piqua Daily Call* stated that most of the Klansmen did not wear their white masks but that the Piqua Klan members did hide their faces. The marchers represented the Klan from Miami, Darke and Auglaize counties. The Klan finished their day by marching out the Piqua-Urbana Pike (U.S. Route 36) to Looney Road and on to the Schultz farm for speeches and fireworks. Local tradition talks about the top of the East Main Street hill as being a popular spot for Klan meetings and cross burnings.

Sporadic Klan appearances occurred in Piqua after World War II, however they usually only consisted of a few men passing out the predictable hate literature. In 1999, a handful of Klan members handed out pamphlets on Water Street in front of the City Building. The Piqua Council of Churches sponsored a prayer/hymn meeting at the pavilion in Fountain Park to voice public opposition to the racism and hatred of the Klan's ideology. SEE ALSO: NAACP

KNIGHTS OF COLUMBUS

The Piqua Council No. 1094, Knights of Columbus was founded in 1906 by men from St. Mary's Catholic Parish. The Piqua Council flourished until the Great **Depression** of the 1930's and was revived after the **Second World War.**

KNIGHTS OF LABOR

The Success Assembly No. 5417 of the Knights of Labor was organized in Piqua in February of 1886. The Knights of Labor was first organized nationally in 1874 and established in Ohio the following year. This was a politically oriented group of skilled workers from all the major industrial crafts. Locally the Knights sponsored moderation in drinking (alcohol was outlawed at meetings), the sale of reasonably priced life insurance (begun in August of 1887), and the improvement of wages and working conditions through political action. In the local April election of 1886, Knight of Labor candidates Walter Lacey (58% vote in third ward), Abram Chryst (unopposed in second ward), Ed Roegner (51% in fourth ward, 1 year term), and **Jacob W. Nigh** (52% in fourth ward, 2 year term), were all elected as Piqua City Councilman. The Knights held four of twelve council seats. Nigh, as one of the city's first labor candidate ran against **Goodrich Giles**, the city's first black candidate. Working as an independent carpenter gave Nigh the freedom to become the 1886 candidate for Congress under the independent (Labor) ticket. He came in third in Miami County, gathering eight percent of the county's vote. In Piqua, Nigh did much better gathering 27.2 percent of the city's vote. While he did not carry any of the city's six wards, he did beat Republicans in three wards, and the Democrats in one. The Democratic candidate for Congress was Piqua citizen and former congressman Robert M. Murray. In 1887, a Miami County convention was held for the Union Labor Party, the political arm of the Knights of Labor. Piqua candidates were Abe Chryst for Congressman, Walter Lacy for County Treasurer, and Ed Lowenstine for County Coroner. The labor candidates received over twelve percent of Piqua's vote coming in third out of four candidates. The following year, the **Republican Party** made a big push for labor votes with the slogan "Protection to American Labor – Fair wages for a fair day's work". The lure worked and the local Union Labor Party, along with the Knights of Labor went into decline in Miami County. SEE ALSO: Democrats; Murray, Robert M.; Socialists; Union.

KOREAN WAR

The Korean War began in June of 1950 with an invasion of South Korea by North Korean military forces. United States forces joined with United Nations troops to stop this invasion. The Ohio National Guard was activated on January 25, 1952. Locally Battery C, 136th Field Artillery, went on active duty for one year at Camp Polk, Louisiana. Numerous individuals from Piqua served in Korea. The first local citizen to be killed in action was Private First Class Herbert E. Tamplin, Jr. on July 25, 1950. Several local firms contributed to the war efforts. The most direct effort was made by the Sefton Fibre Company (established in 1951) which produced fiber cylinder containers for 90mm and 120mm artillery shells. SEE ALSO: Militia (Battery C, 136 Field Artillery)

LABOR DAY

The first attempts to organize a special celebration for working men occurred in New York City in 1882. The Labor Day movement picked up steam when dozens of cities held Labor Day celebrations on the first Monday of September in the 1880's. Various states passed legislation officially sanctioning the day with Ohio joining the crowd in 1890. National recognition of Labor Day would be passed by Congress in 1894. Piqua held one of its very first Labor Day parades in September of 1890. The forty-five minute parade featured wagons and carriages representing dozens of Piqua factories and businesses. The parade went down Main Street with decorated wagons, two enormous flags carried flat, three bands and over twelve hundred marching workers, many of whom carried canes and were dressed in their "Sunday best". SEE ALSO: Unions

LAND OFFICE

The Federal Land Office was opened in Piqua in 1820 on the northwest corner of Main and Greene Streets. Colonel **Thomas B. Van Horne** was appointed as register for northwest Ohio for this office in 1820, and served as the land agent until 1837.

The office remained in Piqua until 1833 when it was moved to Wapakoneta, and in 1836 to Lima. The local office's biggest transactions occurred in the 1820's and 1830's with the sale of the **canal** lands and the former **Shawnee Reservation** lands near Wapakoneta. The State Land Office was also located in Piqua during the late 1820's and early 1830's. J. G. Young was in charge of the State Office.

LANDIN PARK

This Piqua subdivision was developed beginning in 1955 by the **Inland Homes** Corporation. The **housing development** was located between West Covington Avenue and South Street on the west edge of the city. The development created the avenues of Brentwood, Pinewood, Glenwood and the non-connected extension of Edge Street. During the first five years of the subdivision over 100 one story frame and brick-faced homes were built using Inland Homes' prefabricated plans and materials. This was the first wide spread use of picture windows in Piqua. The development housed the first childhood homes of Piqua's growing baby-boomer generation. By 1962, the area contained over one 140 occupied homes.

LAUNDRIES

During most of the nineteenth century washing the family clothes was a tiresome and arduous task. If a family could afford it, a laundress was hired to come into the home and help with this job. It was not until after the **Civil War** that the laundry industry was established in Piqua to fill the needs of families who could not afford a private laundress, but still needed help with the cleaning. The early laundry industry in Piqua was dominated by **Chinese** immigrants. The first Chinese laundry was established by Sam Lee on May 1, 1879 on Main Street. Little is known about Lee, and his laundry establishment lasted only until 1882-83. The next laundry on record was established in the mid-1880's by Lew Chung. The firm was located at 117 East Water Street and operated under the name of the Piqua Steam Laundry. Chung was born in China in 1870's. A few years later, he moved to Piqua and established the business with Hong Lee. Chung continued the laundry until 1900 when it was purchased by Frank and Henry E. Butsch, Jr. and James Fisher. The laundry was closed down after 1911. Other early laundries included the White Laundry (c1887-c1890), Perfection Steam Laundry (c1888-c1890), Metropolitan Laundry (1890-1898), Conway's Laundry (1898-1930's).

LAWYERS

Early attorneys at law passed their Ohio State Bar exams by studying under practicing attorneys. Formal attendance at a law school did not become common until after the 1870's. In nineteenth century Piqua, an attorney could rarely make a living solely from the practice of law. Many attorneys turned to politics on the state and national level. Another common source of income for attorneys after the **Civil War** was selling **insurance** and functioning as collection agencies. Pre-Civil War attorneys were also very active in the Ohio State Militia. Lawyers during this period were general practitioners of the law, specialization did not generally appear until after **World War I**. In 1820, there was one attorney for every 320 local citizens. By 1990 the ration had changed to one attorney for every 1,000 citizens. One the city's oldest local law firms in 2007 is the firm of McCulloch, Felger, Fite and Gutmann. By the 1990's, local attorneys representing large non-Piqua law corporations were becoming common. SEE ALSO: Johnston, Stephen and William; Jones, Matthew and Walter; Mayors; McCulloch, William M.; McKinney, John F. and Samuel S..; McLean, William; Mott, Gordon; Representatives, State of Ohio; Senators, State of Ohio; Young, Joseph and Robert; Patron p. 249

LEAR AVIA CO.

The Lear Wuerful Company was incorporated in Chicago in 1930. It became the Lear Development Co., Inc. in 1931, and eight years later moved to Vandalia under the name Lear-Avia. By March of 1941, the firm had moved to the southwest corner of Young and Weber Streets in Piqua, into a portion of the former Favorite Stove and Range Company plant. The company began manufacturing electro-mechanical aviation equipment, direction finding radio accessories (Lear-O-Scope), communication equipment, and instrumentation for aircraft landings. During **World War II**, the plant became a prime contractor for the United States Army Air Corps. The firm furnished nearly all of the work for two other war industries, Piqua Engineering Company on East Ash Street and the McLaughlin Company on West High Street. In 1943, the firm instituted the community's first formalized industrial training department under the direction of Joseph Hosley. In 1946, the Piqua plant was dismantled and moved to other Lear facilities. By 1953, Lear's last warehouse operation in Piqua was closed down. SEE ALSO: Air Transportation; Colleges and Business Schools; Lear, William; Radio; Television.

The Richardson Romanesque facade on the Schmidlapp Free School Library at 509 North Main Street was designed by J.W. Yost.

This 1940's photograph shows the Lear Avia office in Piqua, originally built for the Favorite Stove & Range Company on Young and Weber Streets

LIBRARIES

The earliest known local public library was the Piqua Reading Room at the corner of Main and Greene Streets established in 1876 by the **Women's Christian Temperance Union.** This was taken over by the **Young Men's Christian Association** in 1877 and continued for approximately three years. In 1879, a short-lived People's Library Association was formed. The **Grand Army of the Republic** (Union Civil War veterans) tried to open a public reading room in their lodge hall in the 1880's, but the effort failed after only two months. In 1889, **Jacob G. Schmidlapp** donated his family's **grocery** and homestead at 509 N. Main to the Piqua Board of Education for use as a Free School (and public) Library. The store front was remodeled into a **Richardsonian Romanesque** facade of red Michigan sandstone using the designs of architect J.W. Yost. John Anderson was the contractor for the project and was issued city building permits in February of 1890. The Schmidlapp Free School Library formally opened on October 18, 1890. The library was under the control of a Library Committee, a sub-committee of the Piqua Board of Education. The

first Committee consisted of **R. M. Murray** (chairman), John E. Anderson, School Superintendent **C.W. Bennett**, and Leopold Kiefer (citizen member). The Piqua Board of education hired Sue E. Hetherington in 1890 as the first librarian at a salary of $25.00 a month. The library's first books were selected from lists provide by Board of Education members. Bertha Carson became the library's second employee when she was hired in 1893 at a salary of seventy-five cents per afternoon and evening. The library building was expanded in 1898 (designed by architect C.A. Thompson) by taking over the retail space to the north. The library moved into the former **Piqua Club**, 124 West Greene, donated to the library by **Leo M. Flesh**, in 1931. The name of the library was changed to the Flesh Public Library. The library is moving to the former **Plaza Hotel** on the public square in 2008.

This 1950's photograph shows a patron using the Library's card catalog to find a book. The card catalog was replaced by a computer system in 1996.

LINSEED OIL

The production of linseed oil from flax seeds began as early as 1816 in Piqua, when John Mc-Corkle built the first linseed oil mill on the west side of the Great Miami River. But it was not until after 1870 that large scale linseed oil production began. William P. Orr, William Kendall and Louis Leonard purchased the Delos C. Ball (1855-1870) Linseed Oil Mill in 1870. This small start would eventually lead to Piqua's place as the second largest producer in the United States (Philadelphia was the largest). Later mills included: the **Wood**, Farrington Company (1874-1896); Orr, Leonard and Daniels Company (1877-1887); **W. P. Orr** Linseed Oil Company (National Linseed Company (1887-1902); and Leonard and Daniels Company (American Linseed Oil Company) (1887-1902). By 1902 nationwide linseed oil trusts had purchased all of the local mills and closed them down. SEE ALSO: Industry; French Oil Mill Machinery.

The Orr Linseed Oil Mill was located at the intersection of Main and Sycamore Streets just to the west of the Miami & Erie Canal. This c.1895 photograph shows the decorative railway gate tender's hut just to the front of the plant.

LIVERY STABLES

During Piqua's Pioneer Period (1807-1830's), most local citizens took care of their own horses, and visitors stabled their horses in the barns of the community's first inns and taverns. This was the beginning of the livery business. The livery stable grew out of the specialized need or demand for the care of visitor's horses. When the **railroads** came along in the 1850's, visitors arrived in the city without any means of travel within the city. The liveries began expanding from just boarding horses, to renting horses and carriages. As the community's population grew, so did the expense and trouble of caring for one's own animals. The liveries began long-term boarding of horses and taking care of individual tack and equipment. With growing railroad traffic, the need for moving large groups of people and their luggage was answered by the various liveries developing hack lines and general hauling services. These two services would evolve in the twentieth century into **taxi** lines and moving companies.

One of the first men in Piqua to establish a full-time livery stable was Hiram Brooks. He came to Piqua in 1840 and almost immediately established a livery stable. The stable was a major success and Brooks stayed in the livery business until 1897. John H. H. Spiker was another early liveryman, opening a stable behind the City Hotel on Ash Street in 1859. Spiker stayed in the livery business until 1895. In 1882 the city's last major livery was opened by W. F. Robbins and J. B. Moore. This livery would eventually be housed in a three story frame structure on the northeast corner of the public square. At its height in the 1890's, the livery was under the sole ownership of the Robbins family. During this period, the stable could handle seventy-five horses at once and had on hand twenty-five carriages for rent. The stables burnt to the ground in 1912 and the family built new quarters on Harrison Street. By 1920, the city's last livery had been turned into an auto garage. SEE ALSO: Giles, Goodrich

LODGES AND ORGANIZATIONS

Early men's lodges were usually formed as fraternal, ethnic, civil, social, or patriotic groups. Many of the fraternal organizations sold death, accident and illness (medical) **insurance** to their members. For most working men, this was the only way they could obtain any type of protection for their families. The Odd Fellows Lodge was the first to offer insurance of any type in Piqua. SEE ALSO: Parades; Piqua Club.

LOG CABINS

The first log cabin in Piqua was built by Job Gard in 1797 on what is now Harrison Street. The area's early log cabins (single pen type) were rectangular, one room, one or one-and-a-half story affairs with a hard packed earthen floor, a crude stone fireplace at one gable end and constructed of hand hewn, square notched logs. A ladder or narrow stairway allowed access to what was often a loft rather than a full half story upper room. Log houses followed with multiple rooms and often with a half or even full second story. SEE ALSO: Architecture; Houses

LORAMIE'S POST

Peter Loramie, a French-Canadian trader, established a trading post at the mouth of Loramie Creek in 1769 (Shelby County). It was destroyed by a detachment of General **George Rogers Clark**'s army in November of 1782

MANSE

The official residence of a minister or priest was known as a manse, church house, parsonage, vicarage or rectory. When these homes were built or extensively remodeled by the church, a separate entrance for the minister was usually built on the side of the house. From the 1890's through the World War I period, these special entrances were mark by a brick parapet with castle-like squares and spaces that formed a battlement above the door.

EXAMPLE   312 West Greene Street, St. Paul's manse

MARBLE WORKS

Early marble works such as Ludlow and Underhill (c1837) concentrated on the production of simple rectangular cemetery markers with rounded tops. Later companies began expanding into carved figures and highly decorative tombstones. Companies after the Civil War include: Hathaway (c1862-c1870), Ebenez Benson (c1865-1879), McKee and Son (1879-c1905),

John F. Hummel (1871-1885), Miami Granite and Marble Co. (1887-c1911), Piqua Granite and Marble Company (1882 to present). SEE ALSO: Industry; Patron p. 266

MARKET HOUSE

The first market house was built on the east side of the public square in 1818. This small frame structure was the center of the community's produce and meat market for twenty-six years. The market house gave area farmers an outlet for surplus produce that could be turned into hard cash. For the community, the market house provided a source of fresh groceries at reasonable prices. Both groups also used the market house area as a place for trading of goods and the latest gossip. When the Town Hall was built, the structure included meat stalls on the first floor and an area for produce outside on the square. This arrangement lasted only six years when the city fathers decided that city business and market business were not mutually compatible. A one-and-a-half story brick market house was built in 1850 on the public square west of Main Street. Stalls inside the market house were reserved for butchers and outdoor stands were set up north of the market house for gardeners and produce dealers. With the new market house came the city's first marketmaster, T. H. Anderson. He was charged with the normal running of the market, with making sure that the sellers' weights and measures were accurate and that open air produce and meats were sold only in the confines of the market house area. In 1882, the market house was torn down since meat was being sold almost exclusively in neighborhood meat stores. The open air produce market continued on the square. After 1889, it was held on Wednesday and Saturday from 5:00 a.m. to 8:00 p.m. during the period of April to October. Selling permits during the last decades of the nineteenth century cost ten cents a week for farmers and fifty cents a week for any other individual. A third market house was erected in 1927-28 at 101 North Downing. The new indoor market struggled through the Great **Depression** and **World War II** before being turned into the City Garage in 1943. At its demise only nine stands were in regular use. SEE ALSO: Food; Town Hall.

The City Market House was located in the 100 block on the east side of North Downing Street.

MARSHALLTOWN, OHIO

This small **African-American** community was located in the southern half of section thirty-five and bounded by Pemberton, West Horseshoe, South Shiloh, and Fenner Roads, in Newton Township. It was settled around 1847 by the families of Simon Gillard, Stephen Gillard, F. Hill, and N. Phillips. These four men and their families were part of a group of slaves manumitted by the will of John **Randolph** of Virginia. The location was chosen due to the proximity of a Society of Friends Church that had offered the former slaves aid. In 1911 the Miami County Atlas showed four houses located at the site.

MAY DAY

In the late 1880's in Europe, May first became Labor Day, a time to celebrate the cause and triumphs of the labor movement. The United States decided on September 1 as the official Labor Day (1894) and the first of May in America was informally dedicated to children. During the 1930's in Piqua, May Day became a student celebration. The May Day celebrations were curtailed during **World War II**, but picked up again in the late 1940's and early 1950's.

MAYORS

Prior to 1835, the village of Piqua was headed by the president of the trustees. When the community was reincorporated in 1835, mayors were elected for one year terms. Piqua became a city in 1850 and continued the office of Mayor as the chief administrator of the city. When the city voted in the city commission-city manager form of government in 1930, the Mayor ceased to be the chief administrator and was elected directly by the city commission for two year terms. All the city commissioners, including the Mayor, were also required to run for office on a non-partisan ticket. The city charter was changed in 1978 to allow for the city-wide election of mayors. Under the 1930 charter, Mayors must be city commissioners prior their election as Mayor or elected as a commissioner at the same time as being elected Mayor. If a Mayor resigns or no eligible Mayor is elected then the position may be filled by a vote of the city commission from among its own members. SEE ALSO: Lists-Mayors

MAY'S OPERA HOUSE

The Opera House was located at 207-209 North Wayne Street. It was built in 1902-1903 for **Charles H. May** by local contractor **Airhart M. Fry**, and designed by Chicago Architect George O. Gransey. The grand opening of May's was held on February 17, 1903, with Master of Ceremonies General **William P. Orr** and Ex-Governor of Ohio Asa S. Bushnell. The opening day performance was a play entitled "A Country Kid". May's supported the forty piece Piqua Symphony Orchestra directed by W. E. Simpkinson. In 1906, the theater hosted its first vaudeville performance. Two years later a "Cameraphone" (talking and singing pictures) production was held. The theater workers at May's were organized as the Theatrical Mechanics, Local Number 61 **union** (c1910). Many famous entertainers and politicians appeared at May's including **W. J. Bryan**, **W. G. Harding**, Houdini, J. P. Sousa, Tyrone Power and Otis Skinner. In 1912, May's Motion Pictures were being advertised with an admission of five and ten cents a show. In 1919-1920, the theater was sold to the Piqua Amusement Company. By 1932, the structure had been sold to Schines Enterprises and remodeled into the Schines Miami (Motion Picture) Theater. The theater closed in 1953, and the building was torn down in June of 1958. SEE ALSO: Motion Picture Theater; Theaters.

May's Opera House is shown in c.1910 at its North Wayne Street location.

This c.1910 view of the interior of May's Opera shows the two balconies available to patrons.

MEDAL OF HONOR

David Urbansky was awarded the medal during the Civil War. **Wilson Vance** also earned his medal during the Civil War. Sergeant **Stanislaus Roy** was awarded the medal in 1878 for his exploits during the Indian Wars. **William Pitsenbarger** was awarded the medal for heroism during the Vietnam Conflict.

MERMAID

Piqua's first mermaid on record was Kimberly Coyne Cox, a 1980 graduate of Piqua High School. Ms. Cox worked as a finned swimmer at Weeki Wachee Springs in Florida.

METEOR MOTOR CAR COMPANY

This company was incorporated in May of 1913 by **Maurice Wolfe** in Shelbyville, Indiana. In December of that same year, the company re-incorporated under Ohio law and moved to Piqua. The first local factory was located on Washington Avenue at Greene Street (formerly the Spraque-Smith School **Furniture** Company plant). Wolfe began the production of luxury automobiles at this site. In 1915, Meteor moved to the northwest corner of Spring and High Streets (formerly the **Union Underwear Com-**

This post-World War II photograph by Step Lange shows the production line of the Meteor Motor Car Company.

pany plant) and began producing a combination funeral coach-ambulance. The vehicles sold for $1,750, which was over one thousand dollars less than other manufacturers. According to one source, the Meteor Motor Car Company model was to funeral coaches what the Ford Model T was to passenger cars. In 1916, the company began producing two different models of the industry's first twelve-cylinder funeral coach.

In 1919, Meteor took over the Jones Recording Laboratories of New York City and began the production of records. This was to complement their production of **phonographs** begun in 1916. This enterprise supported its own retail outlet at 212 West High Street. Meteor continued in the record industry until about 1923. By 1919, the company built a new plant on the south side of Clark Avenue at South Downing.

By the 1920's, Wolfe sponsored a number of benefit programs for his over two hundred non-union employees. Some of the benefits included a free nurse and physician at the plant, reduced health and life **insurance**, and support for a company band, baseball, and basketball teams. Wolfe also founded a chain of low price filling stations in the Miami Valley. For a short time (1929 to c1932), the firm manufactured high quality wooden speed boats. After Wolfe's death in 1935, the company concentrated on hearses and ambulances under the management of A. H. Boyer and later **Charles B. Upton**. The Wayne Works Incorporated (bus manufacturers) of Richmond, Indiana leased the Meteor works in 1953, and in January of 1954 purchased the company outright. Wayne Works purchased the A. J. Miller Co. (funeral coach manufacturers) of Bellefontaine, Ohio on March 19, 1956 and moved the firm to Piqua. The first Miller-Meteor funeral coaches were marketed in 1950. The Wayne Corporation closed down the plant on October 31, 1979. SEE ALSO: Hinsch; Music; Radio.

MEXICAN BORDER CONFLICT

On March 9, 1916, Mexican Revolutionary, General Pancho Villa, crossed the United States-Mexican border leading fifteen hundred men. On this raid into New Mexico, seventeen American citizens were killed. President Woodrow Wilson ordered a military mobilization along the Mexican border on May 9, 1916. Brigadier General John J. Pershing was given command of the American troops. The War Emergency Act activated National Guard troops on June 24, 1916. In July of 1916, Piqua's Company C, Third Regiment, Ohio National Guard (ONG), commanded by Captain James Freshour, was ordered to report to Columbus, Ohio. The company joined other Ohio National Guard units and was shipped to the Texas-Mexican border in September of 1916. Company C was stationed at Fort Bliss, Texas, from September 1916 until March of 1917. They engaged in guard duty and training, but no combat duty in Mexico. The company was shipped back to Columbus for guard duty in March. On April 4, 1917, Congress declared war on Germany, and in July, Company C was merged into active federal service during **World War I**. SEE ALSO: Militia and National Guard.

MEXICAN WAR

The United States declared war on Mexico on May 13, 1846, and authorized the recruitment of fifty thousand soldiers. A rally on the public square in Piqua was held soon after this declaration. A local company of soldiers was raised by Gordon F. Mott. The volunteers took the canal down to Camp Washington in Cincinnati to enlist, but the company as a whole was rejected. **Frank Hardy** and seven other Piqua volunteers signed up as privates with Company I and were attached to the Third Regiment. All three of Ohio's volunteer regiments were shipped to Mexico by steam boat down the Mississippi River, and served as train guards and on garrison duty. The men were mustered out on June 20, 1847.

In another phase of the war, United States Army Captain **Abraham R. Johnston** of Piqua was attached to the Army of the West commanded by Brigadier General Stephen Watts Kearney. He served as Kearney's aide-de-camp and was present on the march from Kansas, the occupation of Santa Fe (August 18, 1846), and the march to California. During the march west, Johnston met Kit Carson, who served as a guide for the army. At San Pascual, General Kearney defeated the California troops under General Andres Pico, who had attempted to take control of California. Johnston was killed during this battle and became Piqua's only known casualty of the war. Another Piqua citizen, **Stephen C. Rowan**, served in the United States Navy during the war. On July 29, 1846 Rowan led a detachment of Marines from the Navy Sloop "Cyane", and attacked and held San Diego for a short time. In January of 1847, Rowan was present when General Kearney occupied Los Angeles. SEE ALSO: Johnston Family (Abraham); Rowan, Stephen.

MIAMI COUNTY

The county was created on January 16, 1807, by the Ohio State Legislature from the northern section of Montgomery County. It was formally established on April 1, 1807 (the twenty-second county to be organized in Ohio). It originally stretched north to the Greenville Treaty line and west to Indiana. Darke County was separated from the western Miami County lands in 1809. The county was extended in 1812 to take in all the area north to the Michigan border. In 1819, Shelby County was formed from Miami County giving the county its present northern boundary. Miami County is named for the **Miami Indians** who inhabited the area in the 1740's and 1750's. The county's current size is listed at 404.25 square miles with a population of 98,868 (2000). The county has twelve townships and twelve incorporated municipalities. SEE ALSO: Communities; Population; Townships.

MIAMI COUNTY BOATING COMPANY

The firm was organized in June of 1881 to promote recreational use of the **Hydraulic** Canal. They built a boathouse at the west end of Ash Street on the upper level of the Hydraulic. The company provided canoes and row boats for entertainment and romantic interludes.

MIAMI COUNTY FAIR

The first county fair was first held in 1846 by the Miami County Agricultural Society. In 1881, Piqua requested that the annual fair be held alternately at Troy and at Piqua. The request was turned down.

MIAMI INDIANS

This tribe was part of the central Algonquian language family and originated in Illinois and Indiana. One of the divisions or bands of The Miami Tribe were known as the Twightwee (Cry of the Crane). By the mid 1700's, the Miamis were divided into three bands led by LePied Froid, Trepicon and LaDemoiselle. In 1747, Chief LaDemoiselle (**Old Britain**) led his band into Ohio to escape the influence of the French. The village of **Pickawillany** was established with the help of English traders at the fork of the Great Miami River and Loramie Creek. The village was attacked and destroyed in 1752 and the LaDemoiselle band was dispersed. The Miami actively fought against white settlement in Ohio country. The Miamis signed the **Treaty of Greenville** in 1795 and the **Second Treaty of Greenville** in 1814. SEE ALSO: Little Turtle.

MIAMI VALLEY STEEL

This firm was founded in 1983, by four men one of whom was Brian Williamson. The first factory was on East Main Street and consisted of a used steel splitter. A new facility was built on Fox Drive, which with additions, totals roughly 315,000 square feet. As a steel service center, the firm cuts steel into a variety of lengths and forms. The company takes forty to fifty thousand pound steel coils and custom cuts them for their customers. An estimated 2007 output is about 180,000 tons of steel with 150 employees.

MID-CONTINENT PROPERTIES

This **housing development** firm was established by Peter R. Thompson in 1962. Thompson came to Piqua to work with **Inland Homes** Corporation from 1958 through 1961. Another member of the Inland Homes management team, Roger Thyer joined the company as a vice president. The firm developed the Candlewood Hills subdivision on the west edge of Piqua off of South Street in 1965. The firm specialized in brick homes in the thirty to forty-five thousand dollar range. Thompson's company built over 636 homes in Piqua from 1962 through 1977. It built other subdivisions including Troy's King's Chapel off of West Main in 1976, and housing developments in Sidney and Xenia. During its height in the mid-1970's, the firm was one of the largest builders of single family homes in Ohio. Well over three thousand homes were constructed by Mid-Continent from 1962 through the early 1980's. The firm closed in 1985-86. SEE ALSO: Candlewood Hills.

MILITIA AND NATIONAL GUARD

1803-1844 Era. When Ohio became a state in 1803, a militia was organized with Return J. Meigs appointed as its first colonel. Miami County was organized in 1807 and the first local militia units followed shortly after. Early officers of the county's militia units included General Munger, Colonel Alexander Ewing, and Major John McCorkle. The militia members elected their own company grade officers who in turn elected the field grade officers.

During the **War of 1812**, four local militia companies were raised. After the war, the state reorganized the militia into five basic command levels; Divisions, Brigades (one per county), Regiments, Battalions and Companies. During the 1820's, Miami County was part of the Second Brigade, Tenth Division. The Second Brigade's first commander was Major General **Robert Young** of Piqua. The Brigade contained three rifle regiments and a total of seven companies.

An 1837 muster roll for the brigade listed 16 officers and 234 men, 12 swords, 208 rifles, 54 powder horns and pouches, 3 drums, and 3 fifes. During this period, training musters consisted of two days of close order drill and target shooting. Two new Piqua companies were formed in the late 1830's, Brownel's Union Cavalry Troop (Piqua Grays) in 1837 and Adams' Piqua Light Infantry Company (Piqua Blues) in 1838. In 1840, Captain Adams' company formed part of an honor guard for the Whig presidential candidate William Henry Harrison during his campaign stop in Dayton. The regular musters gained such a reputation for drunken brawling that the state legislature disbanded the entire Ohio Militia in 1844.

1850-1864 Era. The Ohio Militia was reinstated in 1851. Shortly after this the Piqua Light Guard Company was organized with thirty-four men under the leadership of Captain Robert F. Levering. The unit was nicknamed the "Piqua Rough and Ready Grays". The company was part of the Second Brigade (Miami County), Second Division (Miami, Darke and Shelby Counties). At the beginning of the **Civil War**, the company disbanded and returned their equipment to the state. During the war, a number of companies and two full regiments of Ohio Volunteer Infantry (OVI) were raised in and around Piqua.

1875-1896 Era. The memories of the carnage of the Civil War put a damper on militia enlistments. In 1875, the state reorganized the militia into the Ohio National Guard. In that same year, two new local units were established. The Piqua Light Guard was organized in August of 1875 under the command of Captain J. O. Neer. No further information has been found on this company. The second was organized by Captain **Leopold Kiefer** as Company D, Third Infantry Regiment, Ohio National Guard. Locally the company was known as the "Kiefer Guards". Company D served its five year commitment and disbanded in 1880.

A third unit, Company F, Third Regiment, was organized in 1876 under the leadership of Captain Harry Gear. It was known as the "Wikoff Centennial Guards". The unit was named after the Adjutant General of Ohio and the 1876 Centennial Celebration. Company F was reorganized in 1881 as "Wikoff Guards", again in 1886 as Piqua Light Guards and, finally, in 1891, as Company E, Third Regiment. During its twenty years of service, the unit was called up four times. The first call-up came in 1877 when the unit helped put down the Baltimore and Ohio Railroad strike in Columbus. Between 1879 and 1884, the company was sent to Newark, Wheeling, and Cincinnati (March 1884) to restore civil order during rioting. The company was disbanded in May of 1896. The last commander of the forty-four man unit was First Lieutenant James Frank Hubbard.

1903-1917 Era. During the period from 1896 until 1903, the city was without a National Guard unit. During the **Spanish-American War**, twenty Piqua men joined Company A, Third Regiment of Covington and were activated into federal service.

In the summer of 1903, Captain James F. Hubbard moved Company C, Third Infantry Regiment, Ohio National Guard, from Gettysburg to Piqua. The recently organized company was armed with Krag Jorgesson rifles and the officers with swords.

This is the earliest existing exterior photograph ever taken in Piqua. This is a view of the west side of the four hundred block of North Main Street showing the Piqua Light Guard on parade in 1854 taken by A.H. Rice.

The unit was called-up in March of 1904 for guard duty in Springfield during race riots in that community. The company was called-up again for local guard duty during the 1913 flood.

By 1915, Captain James G. Freshour had taken command of the company. The unit was activated in June of 1916 and by September, Company C was on active duty on the United States-Mexican border (**Mexican Border Conflict**) at Fort Bliss, Texas. The unit left the Mexican border and were re-organized as part of the 148th Infantry Regiment, 37th Division. The unit served in France during **World War I.**

1920-1946 Era. After the end of World War I, the entire Ohio National Guard was reorganized. In Piqua, F Troop, First Ohio Cavalry was organized in 1920 under the command of Lieutenant Alfred P. Reck. The troop was reorganized on January 1, 1922, as Battery E, 2nd Battalion, 135th Field Artillery Regiment, 37th Division, Ohio National Guard, under the command of Captain Caleb Worley Orr. The new unit drilled at the former Robbins Livery Barn at 239 Harrison Street. The Battery was sent to Marion, Ohio, in 1923 for guard duty during the funeral of President **Warren G. Harding**. The Battery was called out again in April of 1930 to assist in recovering bodies after the Ohio State Penitentiary fire.

The Battery took over the newly built National Guard Armory at 623 Ash Street on April 6, 1931. The two story brick structure contained stables for thirty horses, storage rooms for the gun carriages, a main drill hall with a packed earthen floor as well as offices, restrooms, and assembly hall, storage rooms and classrooms. The Battery was motorized in 1934 with the arrival of six, one-and-a-quarter ton Dodge trucks and two Chevrolet station wagons.

On June 1, 1937, the unit was reorganized as Battery C, 2nd Battalion, 136th Field Artillery under the command of Captain Wilbert A. Lewis. At the same time, the Headquarters and Headquarters Battery of the 2nd Battalion, 136th Field Artillery, moved to Piqua under the commands of Major Caleb W. Orr and Captain George W. Nicholas.

On October 15, 1940, all members of the 2nd Battalion, 136th Field Artillery, 37th Division were activated by the federal government for one year's training (later extended to eighteen months) prior to **World War II**. The two Piqua units left at 6:15 a.m. on October 23, 1940, for Camp Shelby, Mississippi, under the command of Lieutenant Colonel Caleb W. Orr. On December 8, 1941, Congress declared war on Japan and, three days later, on Germany and Italy. The 37th Division was shipped to the Fiji Islands in May of 1942.

1946-1952 Era. During January of 1947 the Ohio National Guard began the reactivation process for Battery C, 136th Field Artillery, 37th Division in Piqua. The unit took control of the armory on East Ash Street and began normal training operations.

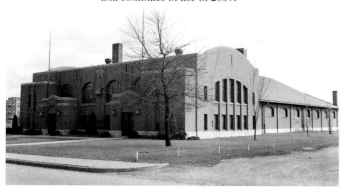

The Ohio National Guard Armory was built in 1931 and continues in use in 2007.

Drills were held weekly with an annual fifteen day field training exercise. Annual training was held at Camp Perry, Ohio in 1947, and later at Camp Atterbury, Indiana and Camp McCoy, Wisconsin.

The **Korean War** began in June of 1950, but the 37th Division was not put on alert until September of 1951. Battery C was inducted into federal service on January 15, 1952 and sent to Camp Polk, Louisiana for training. In 1952, the Battery was under the command of First Lieutenant Virgil Alexander of Sidney. The Battery remained at Camp Polk until January of 1954 but, by that time, most of the Piqua men had been rotated out of the unit.

1953-1980 Era. The Battery was reorganized in Piqua during the spring of 1954 under the command of Captain Chuck Staley. By 1957, Battery C was joined at the armory by Battery D, 180th AAA Gun Battery. The two units were reorganized in 1959 as Battery B, 2nd Howitzer Battalion, 136th Artillery (former Battery C) and Battery D, 1st Gun Battalion, 174th Artillery, 371st Air Defense Artillery Group. Reorganized again in 1963, Battery B became Battery C, 2nd Howitzer Battalion, 136th Artillery, and Battery D. became Battery B, 1st Howitzer Battalion, 134th Artillery. By 1968, Battery B had been transferred out of Piqua.

During the 1968 Dayton race riots, Battery C was called-up to aid in restoring order. The Battery sent sixty-five men to the Ohio State University campus in Columbus on April 30, 1970, to help quell the anti-war student demonstrations. Also during the early 1970's, the unit was called upon to restore order on the Ohio Turnpike during a trucker's strike.

1980 -2007 Era. In the 1980's the 1487th Transportation Company moved from Covington to the Piqua Armory. In the fall of 1990, the transportation company was activated into federal service during the **Persian Gulf War**. The company was sent to Camp McCoy, Wisconsin, for training and, in January of 1991, shipped to Saudi Arabia.

During the Second Gulf War, Battery C was sent to Great Britain for ten months in 2004 to guard Air Force installations there and the 1487th was sent to Iraq returning in 2006.

In September of 2006, Battery C was reorganized into Bravo Battery, 134th Field Artillery. The unit change was part of the Ohio National Guard's downsizing. The unit also reconfigured its weaponry moving away from the M109 self-propelled (tracked) howitzer with its 100 pound shells to the M119 towed howitzer with its thirty pound shells. The new artillery piece is lighter and can be lifted by helicopters or parachuted to a site. Bravo battery remained the same size with between eighty and one hundred men.

SEE ALSO: Citizens Military Training Corps; Home Guard; Lawyers; Nicaragua Incursion; Persian Gulf War; Philippine Revolution; Roads; Vietnam War.

MILK BOTTLE CAP COMPANIES

Beginning about 1900, milk bottles became a popular way to deliver milk to customers. This led directly to the creation of flat printed bottle caps for the re-usable milk bottles. One of the earliest milk cap companies in Piqua was the Piqua Cap & Filler Company established in 1905 by William Freshour, F.L. Schmidlapp and Christopher Loeffler. The firm sold out to the Smith-Lee Company in 1940-41 which closed down in c.1949-1950. Other milk cap firms included the Piqua Packing Company (1907 – 1908), the William Summers & Company (1908 – 1919) and the Ohio Bottling Cap Company (1924 – c. 1955). SEE ALSO: Bottle Cap; List-Dairies

MILLINERS

The millinery shop was the most successful of all the early women's business ventures. Shops for the sale of women's hats were also the very first type of women's business ventures on record. In 1856, the first Piqua listing in a state business directory of local milliners included: Mrs. Margaret Irvin, Mrs. E. Castle, Mrs. A. E. Espy, and Mrs. L. Moore. These types of shops really came into their own in Piqua during the 1870's and 1880's with the creation of the large establishments of Mrs. Sarah Aspinall, Mrs. A. Larger, and Miss Charlotte Orr. These women built up substantial businesses that competed successfully with any retail shop downtown. Mrs. Larger went on to become a major landowner in the city, and built her own business structure at 320 North Main Street in 1888. SEE ALSO: Women.

MINIATURE GOLF

Miniature golf started out in the early 1900's as a shrunken version of regular golf known as "garden golf" on real grass without borders. The 1920's saw the addition of rails or "bumpers" and artificial surfaces. Garnet Carter patented the game in 1927 under the name "Tom Thumb Golf". The first course was built at Carter's hotel on Lookout Mountain in Tennessee. This rapidly became a chain of courses manufactured by the Fairyland Manufacturing Company. By 1934, this firm had sold over three thousand courses across the nation. The game declined nationally with the coming of **World War II** but in came back with a bang in 1953 when Don Clayton established Putt-Putt Golf ®.

The miniature golf craze first hit Piqua in the 1930's. Two courses were established in 1930, Buchanan's Indoor Country Club located on the public square, and the Green-o-Links Golf Course off Covington Avenue. On August 19, 1930, the world record for the longest continuous playing of the miniature golf was set at the Green-o-Links course. Miniature golf returned briefly in the 1960's and 1970's with a course located just west of the cemetery. SEE ALSO: Golf.

MISSISSIPPIAN PERIOD

The Mississippian Period covers a prehistoric time from 1000 A.D. until 1650 A. D. During this period, prehistoric man in the Miami Valley developed the **Fort Ancient Culture** (900 A.D. until 1700 A. D.). This is the last prehistoric period in the Ohio Valley and is followed by the period of Historic Indians.

MOBILE HOMES AND PARKS

Travel trailers became popular across the nation in the 1920's, as automobile owners towed tents on wooden platforms behind them on trips around the country. These mobile tents evolved into hard sided trailers. Mobile homes grew out of the travel trailers in 1956 when ten foot wide trailers were introduced as semi-permanent homes. During the next two decades, these trailers became known as manufactured homes with the single wide (ten to sixteen feet) becoming the standard mobile home. These mobile homes were set on permanent foundations with sanitary and utility hookups. Double wides were added (they had to be shipped in two pieces) with widths of over twenty feet in the 1970's.

After **World War II**, mobile home parks sprang up on the outskirts of Piqua. One of the first of these parks was the Treon Trailer Camp created by Lewis W. Treon in circa 1943-1944 and located just north of the Piqua city limits on State Route 66. Treon's camp was located on the site of his earlier Modern Victory Village. A 1943 advertisement for the village promoted modern defense cabins with insulation and ventilation for rent, "ideal for the small family". The village also offered a laundry room as well as modern toilet and shower rooms. Trailer space was also available next to the cabins. After the war Treon removed most of the village cabins to make more room for mobile homes. By 1951, the trailer camp was taken over by accountant H. Lester Routson and renamed the Na-Bor-Hood Trailer Court. Other mobile home parks are located on South Main Street and Garbry Road (early 1970's).

MONTGOMERY COUNTY

This county was formed from part of Hamilton County on May 1, 1803. It is named for Revolutionary War hero General Richard Montgomery. **Miami County** was formed from the northern part of this county in 1807.

MOTION PICTURE THEATERS

The first motion picture theater in Piqua opened on July 9, 1906 at 205 North Main. The theater was known as the Star and was operated by the Van Amusement Company. Admission was five cents. By 1909, the theater was under the management of Herbert Johnson. When it closed down in 1915-16 control had passed to J. M. Newman. Other early motion picture **theaters** included the Pastime (c1906-c1908), Dream (c1908), Zig's (1908-1912), Princess (1909-1918), Favorite (1912-1932), and the Strand (1915-c1919). Two former live performance theaters turned to motion picture after **World War I**, the Bijou (1919-1934) and **May's Opera House** (1918-1953). May's had been the location for the city's first "Cameraphone" talking and singing pictures in 1908. The Piqua Amusement Company was incorporated in 1916 by Harry W. Kress and by 1919, controlled May's, the Strand, the Princess, and the Bijou theaters. He ran them all as motion picture theaters. In 1928, the Ohio Theater was built at 430 North Main for Collins and Fulton of

The 36-Drive In on U.S. Route 36 west of Piqua was built in 1947.

In c.1914, the Favorite Theater on the northeast corner of Main Street and the Public Square was offering five cent admission to the movie the Village Pest.

Lancaster, Ohio. In 1932, Schine's Enterprise purchased both the Ohio (renamed Schine's Piqua) and May's (renamed Schine's Miami) theaters. The Miami was closed in 1953 and the Piqua (later renamed the Piqua Twin Cinemas) was closed in 1990. Other theaters include the 36-Drive In which opened west of Piqua on U.S. Route 36 in 1947 and closed in the 1990's, and the Cinema Six which was opened in 1988 by Cinemark Theatres in the Miami Valley Center Mall. SEE ALSO: Civil Rights Movement.

MUSIC

Music has always been an important part of Piqua's heritage from early pioneer sing-a-longs to the modern uniformed high school marching band. Pioneer entertainment often consisted of individual families singing familiar patriotic songs and well known hymns. The first secular group known to have organized was the Piqua [Brass] Band in 1840 by, among others, **Augustine Thoma**. During the Civil War, local musicians joined regimental bands. Best known in that period was drummer **Lucius C. Cron**, who became the chief musician for the 110th Ohio Volunteer Infantry Regiment. During the 1870's, the Piqua Amateur Minstrel Company was formed by Ed Wilbur, Harvey Redman, and J. W. Norris to tour around the Midwest. During the 1880's, groups such as Oblinger's Cornet Band and J. F. Hummel and Sons (German band) gave free concerts on the public square. The 1880's saw the formation of numerous military style uniformed bands such as the Piqua Military Band led by F. C. Shafer, and the Knights of Pythias Regimental Band led by Frank Priest. In the first part of the twentieth century (pre-**World War I**), the Western Ohio Music Festival (1911), the Piqua City Band, and Parlett's Band were organized. The Elks Band was organized in 1933 and in the 1960's became the Piqua Civic Band. A few of the early better known Piqua musicians include: **Bill Manning** (minstrel singer in 1870's), William Edwards Simpkinson (violinist, director of May's Symphony Orchestra, pre-World War I), **Henry Ward Beecher Barnes** (high school music teacher,

*High School music director Henry Barnes presented a combined band,
orchestra and chorus concert at May's Opera House in 1905.*

The Elk's Band is shown here in the former Chautauqua Pavilion (Hance) in Fountain Park.

Robert M. Hance Jr. was superb musician and director of the Piqua Civic Band.

church choral director, church music composer, organizer of Western Ohio Music Festival, and founder of Pi-Qua-City Publishing Company, all from 1900-1916), **Philip Gates** (high school music director, school song composer, 1920's-1950's), Harold Greenamyer (orchestra leader 1920-1940's), the **Mills Brothers** (nationally recognized singing group 1930's-1980's), and **Robert Hance** (cornetist, director Civic Elks Band 1940-1980's). SEE ALSO: May's Opera House; Meteor Motor Car Company; Theaters.

NAMES

In 1887, a school enumeration (census) was taken of all Piqua unmarried youth from the age of six to twenty one. The most common girls' names in order of popularity were Mary, Annie, Kate, and Lizzie. For boys' it was William, John, Charles, and Frank.

NATIONAL ASSOCIATION FOR THE ADVANCEMENT OF COLORED PEOPLE (NAACP)

On a national level, the NAACP was organized in 1909 in New York City in response to the extreme violence of a race riot in Springfield, Illinois in 1908. In the early 1920's, a local chapter of the NAACP was formed in Piqua. One of the earliest presidents was C.H. Bray. On November 01, 1921, a mass meeting was held at the Park Avenue Baptist Church to "convince

candidates that we as voters are not being sold out". An advertisement for the event stated that "This will be the largest colored political meeting ever held in Miami County". The local chapter appeared to decline in the mid-1920's. Possibly because of the flare-up of potential violence created by the **KKK** cross burnings and parades in Piqua in 1923. A local chapter of the NAACP was revived in the summer of 1942. **Darrel Taylor** was the first president of the local group and along with Samuel H. Mitchell, Rev. H. B. Brightman, Maude Woodson, Pearl Strange, Louise Taylor, Emerson Clemens, Rev. Howard D. Foston, **Viola Clemens**, among many others, began promoting African-American civil rights in Piqua. The organization sponsored a sit-in at the bus station lunch counter and at the Piqua Schines **Motion Picture Theater**. Louise Taylor served as the advisor to the group's Youth Council from 1943 to the late 1940's. By 1945, the NAACP was meeting in its own hall in the Masonic Building on the southwest corner of Main and Market Streets. Civil Rights activities slowed down in the late 1940's and early 1950's. By the early 1980's, the local NAACP was part of the Ohio Tri-County NAACP (Logan, Miami, Shelby counties) headquartered in Sidney. SEE ALSO: African-American; Civil Rights.

NATIVE AMERICAN POPULATION

In the Great Lakes area in 1768, it is estimated that there were approximately 3,500 **Delaware**, 2,000 \Kickapoo, 4,000 **Miami**, 1,000 **Ottawa** (northwest Ohio), 3,000 **Potawatomi**, 1,800 **Shawnee**, and 1,000 **Wyandot**. By 1830, within the State of Ohio, the combined population of the Wyandot, Shawnee, Seneca, and Delaware tribes had shrunk to less than 2,000.

NATIVE AMERICAN TRIBES (OHIO)

The following tribes were all active in the Ohio country; **Delaware, Miami, Ottawa, Potawatomi, Seneca** (Mingo), **Shawnee,** Tuscarora, and **Wyandot**. SEE ALSO: Agriculture; Algonquian Language; Reservations; Roads; Native American Villages

NATIVE AMERICAN VILLAGES

This is only a brief list and does not attempt to name the hundreds of historic Indian villages established in the Ohio country. The following villages were established between approximately 1740 and 1830; Captain Pipe's Town (**Delaware**), Chillicothe (**Shawnee**), Cranetown/Tarhe (**Wyandot**), Girty's Town (Shawnee), Grapeville Town (Delaware), Grenadier Squaw's Town (Shawnee), Killbuck's Town (Delaware), Lewistown (Shawnee and **Seneca**), Licktown/**Piqua/Chillicothe** (Shawnee), Meskeman (**Ottawa**), Mequakake (Shawnee), Mingo Town (Seneca), Mohickon John's Town (Delaware), Newcomerstown (Delaware), Oquanoxa (Ottawa), **Pickawillany (Miami), Piqua**

(Shawnee), Roche de Boeuf (Ottawa), Sandusky (Wyandot), Seneca Town (Seneca), Tushquegan (Ottawa), Upper Sandusky (Wyandot), Wakatomica (Shawnee), Wapakoneta (Shawnee), White-Eyes Village (Delaware), and Wolf Rapids (Ottawa).

NEO-CLASSICAL REVIVAL STYLE ARCHITECTURE

The local variation of the Neo-Classical Revival style was popular from 1910 through 1930. This style was not used locally for domestic structures. The Piqua version of this style reflects a strong sense of dignity, prosperity, and security. The institutions that built structures in this style wanted to project those qualities. Banks and the Post Office in the decades surrounding the **First World War** were viewed locally as society's bastions of progressive stability. The towering columns and pillars of stone and blocks of marble reflected the glory of the ancient world as interpreted through the American Dream. This style was used to prove to the outside visitor that Piqua was a community of strength and vitality.

The **Post Office** first brought the style to Piqua in 1914 as part of a standard floor plan for federal buildings used to serve communities of a certain size and prosperity. Citizens National **Bank** & Trust Company located on the northeast corner of Ash and Main streets followed suit. Citizens demolished their 1880's structure and built a Neo-Classical structure on the same site in 1920.

The community's other bank, the Piqua National Bank & Trust Company purchased the southwest corner of the public square (opposite the Post Office) and demolished the older two story frame and brick commercial buildings located there. In 1928-1929, just before the start of the Great **Depression,** a new Neo-Classical bank building was erected. Piqua National followed the practice of the Post Office by placing professional offices on the second floor. The bank also followed the interior plan of the Post Office by created a first floor with a one-and-a-half story open interior space clad in stone and marble.

This style has many of the following local architectural elements. The buildings are constructed in a rectangular shape with two-and-a-half stories and a strong sense of symmetry. The facades are graced by classical stone columns or pilasters and can have a full portico. The facades consist of stone and marble with massive architectural elements with limited detailing that show a simplicity in design. There are enlarged windows with single pains of glass all topped by an unadorned roof line.

COMMERCIAL EXAMPLES

220 North Wayne Street, Post Office, 1914
401-403 North Main Street, Citizens National Bank, 1920
123 Market Street, Piqua National Bank/Fifth Third, 1928-29

The interior of the Piqua National Bank shows it massive classical detailing. This photograph is looking north showing the front entrance.

The Citizens National Bank on the northeast corner of Ash and Main Streets was built in the Neo-Classical Revival Style in 1920.

NEWSPAPERS

Beginning in 1820 when The *Piqua Gazette* was the first newspaper to be published in Miami County, newspapers have challenged the status quo. Newspapers in the nineteenth and early twentieth centuries were very partisan in nature and made no attempt to "balance" their news delivery. Editor/publishers strongly endorsed or condemned national, state and local political candidates and issues. Early letters to the editors were often anonymous or signed using pseudonyms. Politics were taken so seriously in the local media in the nineteenth century that the death of a local Republican would not be listed in the Democratic newspapers and vice versa.

The Piqua Daily Call, with its 1940's era presses shown here, was the county's largest paper during the World War II era.

Local Newspaper Trivia

The first community newspaper was the weekly *Piqua Gazette* first published by **William R. Barrington** on July 6, 1820.

The first daily paper in Piqua was the *Miami Valley News* printed in 1869.

The first **German** language paper was the *Evangelfsche Relfgfoese Zeitschrift* published in 1837 by **Lebright L. Hinsch**. The last German language newspaper was the *Die Miami Post* published by August Bartel who closed down the press in 1919

The first Republican newspaper was the *Piqua Journal* published in 1860.

The first Democratic newspaper was the *Western Courier & Piqua Enquirer* printed in 1833.

The first and last **Socialist Party** newspaper was the *Piqua Searchlight* published in 1910.

The first newspaper to promote the cause of **Temperance** was the *Miami Helmet* published in 1874. The last newspaper dedicated fully to temperance was the *Business Men's Appeal* in 1912.

The *Lilliputian* was the smallest newspaper in the city in 1870.

The *Piqua Daily Call* has the longest continuous run in the city, starting in 1884 and continuing to the present (2007).

During the 1913 **flood**, the *Piqua Daily Call* ran an emergency newspaper reduced in size

The largest number of local newspapers in a single year was eleven in 1883.

The first horse racing paper was the *Daily Bulletin* published in 1875.

The first newspaper dedicated to art news was the *Art Loan* printed in 1886.

The first newspaper to champion the cause of veterans was the *Miami Observer* printed in c.1888.

The first known local newspaper dedicated to fraternal news was the *Pythian News* printed in c.1888.

SEE ALSO: Lists-newspapers; Patron p. 265

NICARAGUA INCURSION

On May 10, 1926, the United States Marines landed in Nicaragua to help quell a revolution. Marine Lieutenant **Kenneth W. Benner**, a Piqua High School graduate (class of 1921), was part of that invasion force. After the revolt was put down, Benner was made the Military Chief of Police of the city of Manaqua in Nicaragua. By 1928-9, Benner had been transferred to the naval radio station in Haiti.

NORTHWEST ORDINANCE

This ordinance was drafted by Nathan Drake and passed by the United States Articles of Confederation Congress on July 13, 1787. The ordinance became the foundation for the American Territorial System. It allowed for three stages of government based on population with progressive amounts of popular participation. It also contained an Articles of Compact Bill of Rights that provided for religious liberty, trial by jury, the sanctity of contracts, promotion of public education, the prohibition of slavery, and mandated good faith toward Indian lands and properties.

NUCLEAR POWER PLANT

In 1953, the Director of Piqua utilities, John Gallagher began promoting the idea of a nuclear facility in Piqua. On July 6, 1959 construction began on the reactor under the auspices of the Atomic Energy Commission (AEC). The AEC approved the operation of the reactor and in June of 1962 the contractor, Atomics International, turned the plant over to the city of Piqua. By October of 1963, the reactor was producing steam to power the city's 11,400 kilowatt

Piqua's nuclear power plant was located east of the Great Miami River and became operational in 1963.

generators. Piqua had earned its nickname, the "Atomic City". In 1963, the Piqua reactor was one of six in the United States producing power. It was unique in two ways. It was the only municipally owned reactor in the world, and it was the only one cooled and moderated with an organic hydrocarbon liquid. The reactor's structure was a seventy-three foot high silver cylinder that was sunk fifty-three feet into its limestone base. It was built at a cost of twenty-eight million dollars. A number of the plants early employees learned about nuclear power while serving in the United States Navy on nuclear powered vessels (submarines). January of 1966 saw the reactor closed down for repairs and it was never reactivated. On June 20, 1968 the plant was finally and officially closed down. In 2007, the concrete shell is used by the city as a storage facility. SEE ALSO: Power Plants.

NURSES

Nurses through much of the nineteenth century in Piqua were considered on the same level as domestic servants. Little or no training was required and service was limited to helping invalids with their personal body needs. The closest occupation to nursing at this time was mid-wifery. By the 1890's, trained nurses were available in Piqua for professional home care.

Piqua's nuclear reactor vessel was brought into Piqua by rail.

In 1908, the Memorial Hospital Nurse's Training School opened in Piqua. The two year program was under the direction of Superintendent Miss E. L. Hatfield. Miss Lillian Robinson of Cincinnati was the first nurse to graduate from this school on May 26, 1910. In October of 1911, the Francis Meilly Orr Nurse's Home (located west of the hospital) was dedicated. The three story structure was designed by W. E. Russ of Dayton and constructed by A. M. Fry. The nurses' training school was closed in 1933. SEE ALSO: Photographs p. 57.

OHIO FEDERATION FOR THE UPLIFT AMONG COLORED PEOPLE

This organization was founded in Columbus in July of 1917 at a conference of nearly seven hundred individual men and women, black and white who gathered to discuss the issues of black migration into Ohio from the South. J. Walter Wills of Cleveland served as the group's first President. Shortly after the Columbus meeting, a district meeting was held in July of 1917 in Fountain Park, in Piqua. Local arrangements were made by Rev. W.T. Noris and Rev. C.M. Hogans. Both white and African-American speakers addressed the gathering. One of the speakers was retired Piqua School Superintendent Dr. C.W. Bennett, who spoke in his role as the secretary of the Freedom Aid Society of the Methodist Episcopal Church. In Miami County, both Piqua and Troy had established local chapters by the spring of 1918. The group's primary concerns revolved around health, housing, soldiers, welfare, education and employment. SEE ALSO: African-American.

OLYMPICS

Piqua has several claims to Olympic fame. In 1976, Augie Hirt was a member of the United States Olympic Racewalk Team. Hirt finished twenty-seventh in the fifty kilometer race. He has held the American records for the fifty mile and 75K and 100K racewalks. Another local Olympic hopeful was Tim Winans, who qualified for the Olympic Swimming Trials in 1984. **Kristen King** was "number nineteen" on the women's ice hockey team in the 2006 Winter Olympics. The team won the bronze medal.

Olympic Hockey Team medalist Kristen King is shown in this 2006 photograph standing next to the uniform she used as a child.

OPTICIANS

During the years before the Civil War, jewelry stores would carry a number of lenses of different strengths and the customer would pick out the spectacles that would best help him or her to see. The Thoma Jewelry Store, established in 1838, was the first store to advertise spectacles (in the 1870's). The city's first permanent optician was Dr. Albin Louis Thoma, grandson of the founder of the Thoma Jewelry Store. Dr. Thoma graduated from the New York Optometry Institute and returned to Piqua to practice. In 1908, Dr. Thoma organized the Piqua Lodge No. 1 of the Noble Order of Ku Ku, the first lodge of its kind in the nation for jewelers and opticians. The first listing for an optician not connected with a jewelry store was for Henry Max in 1902. He was followed by Seth C. Philbrook in 1908.

ORGANS, CHURCH

The Second Presbyterian Church on North Wayne Street was the first local church to install a pipe organ. The Carnegie Foundation donated several pipe organs to local churches including St. John's Lutheran Church on Wood Street.

ORDER OF GEORGE AWARD

This award was begun by the Piqua **Chamber of Commerce** in 1968 to honor a civic person of the year. The award's criteria revolved around community service and dedication to the needs of others. The name comes for the phrase, "Let George do it". This phrase meant that an individual citizen just did not have the time or inclination to help the community and anyway that the mythical "George" would get it done. The award was then created to recognize the "Georges" that actual got things done in Piqua. It was often referred to as "the highest award bestowed in Piqua". SEE ALSO: List-Order of George Recipients

OTTAWA TRIBE

This tribe was part of the southeastern Ojibwa language family and originated in the Upper Great Lakes area. In Ohio, Ottawa villages were concentrated along the Maumee River and western tip of Lake Erie during the 1750's. One of the greatest of the Ottawa leaders was Pontiac (1760's). After signing the **Treaty of Greenville** in 1795, and other treaties in 1807 and 1817, the Ottawas lived on reservation lands in the northwest part of the state including Wolf Rapids, Roche De Boeuf (1807-1831), Blanchard's Ford, Oquanoxa's Village (1817-1831), Tuckquegan (1807-1833), and Meskemau's Village (1817-1833). Most of the Ottawas migrated out of Ohio after being forced to relinquish their lands in 1831-1833.

PALEO-INDIAN PERIOD

The Paleo-Indian Period covers a prehistoric time from 10,000 B.C. to 6,000 B.C. During this period, prehistoric man survived through big game hunting by small, extended family groups. This period is best known for the two basic spear points that were used. The Clovis Point with it short fluted side was used from approximately 10,000 B.C. to 8,000 B.C. The Folsom Point with its much longer fluting was used from 8,000 B.C. to 6,000 B.C. SEE ALSO: Food.

PARADES

The history of parades in Piqua is almost as old as the community itself. In the 1820's, the Fourth of July parades were a major village event. Three to four musicians, the local ministers,

Circus parades were very popular in Piqua. This c.1920's one is shown in the 300 block of Main Street.

and almost the entire population participated. In 1837, a major parade and celebration was held to mark the opening of the canal and to welcome the speaker of the day, General William Henry Harrison. Nineteenth century political torch-light parades were very important. Every presidential election generated hundreds of marchers, wagons, banners, bands, and fife and drum corps. Circus parades were also very popular. The earliest one on record was in 1833. It was a traveling menagerie with caged lions, zebras, and camels that were pulled down Main Street by teams of decorated horses. Lodge conventions became another good reason for parades. Groups such as the Order of Red Men, Order of the Elks, and Knights of Pythias all maintained marching color guard units and bands.

During both **World War I** and **World War II**, bond rallies and parades were staged to drum up support and funding for the effort. During the twentieth century, specialty parades were held for various occasions such as the Great **Depression's** NRA Booster parade, and the Fire Parade of the 1970's. Since the turn of the twentieth century, major parades have been held for the many **celebrations** including the Fall Festival (1908), the Sesquicentennial of the Northwest Territory (1938), the Sesquicentennial of Piqua (1946), the Bicentennial of the United States (1976) and the Bicentennial of Piqua (2007). Since the 1960's, smaller parades have been held for Memorial Day, home football games, Christmas season, and **Halloween** (begun by the **Kiwanis Club** in 1951). SEE ALSO: Fourth of July; Presidents.

PARKING METERS

Parking meters were first put into operation in the downtown area of Piqua in October of 1947. The tandem style of meter was placed into operation c.1960.

PARKS

DOWNS PARK. This park was laid out in the center of the public square by Captain Downs, the Superintendent of the City Streets in 1891.

FOUNTAIN PARK. In August of 1874, thirty Piqua businessmen organized the Western Ohio Fair Association. This organization was the result of another in a long line of disagreements with the county seat in Troy. An agricultural had begun in Piqua in 1841, and was to rotate between the two communities on a yearly basis. But, by the late 1840's, the fair had become

permanently located in Troy. With the expanding population base in Piqua, the city leaders decided that the community needed its own fair. The Western Ohio Fair Association was the answer. Land was leased from Samuel S. and John F. McKinney on the west end of town. A one-mile race track was laid out, along with a grandstand, dwelling for a caretaker and stables. The first fair was held in October of 1874. The second fair in 1875 was much bigger, with horse races and numerous agricultural and craft displays and athletic contests. The next two years saw a diminishing attendance and a shrinking of events until only the horse races were held. By January of 1878, the Association had dissolved and the land was sold at a sheriff's auction. There were several changes in the ownership of the land and, sometime during this period, the area acquired the name, Fountain Park. In February of 1885, the park was purchased by the Fountain Park Company, headed by Judge William C. Johnston. This investment company was unable to develop the park, and in 1887, it was sold to the Piqua Improvement Company. Part of the park was offered to the city in 1888, but other obligations forced the city to turn down the purchase. About 1907, the Fortnightly Club of Piqua took an interest in Fountain Park. This was eventually taken up by the City Federation of Women's Clubs (CFWC) and the city purchased the area for use as a city park. The CFWC raised funds for improvements that included a wading pond, playground apparatus, a dancing pavilion, and a bandstand. The city's landscaping efforts included the creation of natural ponds, fountains, and walkways. The current Hance Pavilion was erected in the early 1920's for use by the **Chautauqua** Festival.

ROOSEVELT PARK. This park was located on the south side of East Ash Street and was previously used as a **baseball** field. In 1920, the site was purchased by the Board of Education. The Piqua **Rotary Club** raised funds to improve the site with playground equipment, tennis courts, a track, and a graded field. On May 1, 1920, the park was formally dedicated and named after former President Theodore Roosevelt. In 1935, an eighteen hundred seat field house was built, followed in 1940 by an outdoor stadium. The park was discontinued in favor of a **football** stadium.

MIDWAY PARK. The Miami Valley Electric Railway Company opened this park on June 14, 1894 in an attempt to increase business on its new Piqua to Troy electric interurban line. It was located on twelve acres of land leased from S. K. Statler in the northeast corner of Concord Township. The original park contained a dance hall and the twelve-hundred seat Midway Park Opera House. In August of that first year, the baseball field was inaugurated by an exhibition game played by the Cincinnati Red Stockings. By 1896, the park had been expanded to twenty-five acres. In the fall of 1896, the first regional high school football game, a contest between Troy and Sidney, was played at the park. The park expanded in 1898 with a bowling alley, a quarter mile bicycle track, croquet and tennis courts, as well as popularly promoted boxing matches. Boating and bathing were encouraged when a local stream was dammed to form an artificial lake. The park continued to grow and, in 1900, added a merry-go-round, a shooting gallery, a roller coaster, and a number of small summer cottages. The interurban line was leased to the Dayton and Troy Railway line in 1902. Within two years the park was sold to an outside amusement company. During the summer of 1906, the

The "band plays on" during the 1946 Sesquicentennial Parade

This 1971 Knights of Columbus float was featured in the downtown Christmas Parade.

Piqua Parades

The Campbell Furniture Company float, featuring a "Tom Thumb Wedding," was used in about 1910.

They were not just "horsing around" in the 1966 United Fund Parade.

Lock Nine Park is located on Water Street at the dead end of Spring Street.

park was dismantled and the area reverted to Statler farmland.

STEIN'S PARK. This park was located in **Rossville** east of County Road 25-A on four acres of land owned by Charles J. Stein. Stein built a baseball park on the site prior to 1910. In the summer of 1915, an airdome was erected for outdoor movies and live entertainment, but this lasted less than a year. The park continued to host amateur and semi-pro baseball under Stein's administration until 1933-34, when it became the Kiefer's Athletic Park. Kiefer's maintained the park until 1948-49.

MOTE PARK. The City of Piqua organized this park in 1947-48. It is located between South and Summit Streets, east of Gordon Street. The park was named after **Raymond Mote**, long time track coach and high school physical education teacher. The Mote Park Community Center was opened in July of 1953, providing space for the Piqua Players community theater, family reunions, wedding receptions, offices for the City's Park Department, training area for the Piqua Dog Club, as well as countless other reunions, get-togethers and parties. The park also contains baseball fields and tennis courts.

PITSENBARGER SPORTS COMPLEX. In 1969, Victory Heights Park was formally renamed Eisenhower Park in honor of its origins as a World War II emergency housing project. During the next twenty years the sixty-five acre park was developed and enhanced. Baseball fields, soccer fields, tennis courts, a football field, and horseshoe pits were added. Much of the work on the baseball fields was accomplished by the Piqua Youth Baseball and Softball Association. In 1984, a local committee was formed to promote a new city pool at Eisenhower Park. The S.P.L.A.S.H. (Support Piqua's Long Awaited Swimming Hole) Committee helped pass a levy in the November 1984 election. The Piqua Municipal Pool was formally dedicated on May 24, 1986. The Park was renamed **Pitsenbarger** honor of the hero of the Vietnam Conflict.

HOLLOW PARK. The city purchased this privately owned park and **swimming pool** in 1974, but was forced to close the pool in 1977 because it did not conform to county health codes. The pool area was filled in during 1988, and the entire forty acre site became a picnic area. The area was formally rededicated as a city park in 1992.

GARBRY'S BIG WOODS SANCTUARY. The Sanctuary is part of the 260 acre Big Woods Reserve located east of Piqua on Statler Road. Half of the park was donated by J. Scott Garbry in 1981 and the rest was purchased by the Miami County Park District. The park contains the largest stand of upland woodland in this area. It was opened to the public on October 5, 1982.

KIWANIS PARK. This park is located on the lot formally occupied by the North Street Elementary School on the northeast corner of North and Walker Streets. This children's park area

was developed in 1982 by the Piqua **Kiwanis Club**.

DAS PARK. This park is located on the lot previously occupied by the Park Avenue Elementary School on the northeast corner of Park Avenue and Broadway. It was donated to the City of Piqua by Dr. and Mrs. Ramen Das in 1988 in memory of their daughter, Ann, for use as a small children's play area.

LOCK NINE PARK. This park was established south of Water Street at the southern terminus of Spring Street. The park contains the remains of Lock Nine on the Miami & Erie Canal. It was dedicated in 1998.

FRENCH PARK. It was created in 2001 on land donated by the **French Oil Mill Machinery Company** and the French Family and located at corner of West Water and Steel Streets.

It is an access point and small picnic area for the city bike path located at the crossroads of the paths east-west and north south routes.

LINEAR PARK. This is a loop of paved biking/walking trails that go through the center of Piqua on the abandoned east-west Pennsylvania railroad tracks, along the banks of the hydraulic canal and along the banks of the Great Miami River. It was completed in phases during the first decade of the twenty-first century. The first part of the path (5.5 miles) was dedicated in 2001. The path totaled over thirteen miles, with a new addition to be added in 2008 as a southern extension from Lock Nine Park to the city limits along the Great Miami River.

ROWAN PARK. It is located at the west end of the Shawnee Bridge at the V of East Main and First Streets. The small park contains the monument dedicated to Piqua's Admiral **Rowan.**

GOODRICH GILES PARK. This is located on South Main Street, south of the Municipal Power Plant. It was dedicated to Piqua African-American citizens in the 1990's.

SEE ALSO: Depression; Interurban.

PATENT MEDICINE

Patent medicines were an important part of American daily life in the nineteenth and early twentieth centuries. Piqua businessmen began producing their own brands of these medical cure-alls by the mid-1870's. The earliest known patent medicine manufacturers in Piqua were George Wall on Downing Street and William Dobie on Greene Street. Both of these men operated small shops out of their homes. Patent medicines in Piqua and across the nation offered cures for just about every ill imaginable, from coughs and colds to rheumatism and frostbite. Most of these cures were not legally patented and the term patent medicine was used to define unusual or unique medicines. These early "cures" usually had two things in common, a secret formula of herbs and minerals and a high alcoholic content. After several or more sips of some of these concoctions you might not have been cured of your affliction, but you certainly did not care as much.

Piqua moved into the patent medicine business in a big way when E. C. DeWeese began manufacturing a new patent medicine under the name of Dr. Bosanko Medicine Company in 1878. His products included Dr. Bosanko's Pile Remedy, Dr. Gunn's Improved Liver Pills and Dr. Bosanko's Cough and Lung Syrup. DeWeese moved his firm to Philadelphia in 1890. But Piqua was not left without a local "cure for what ails you". **George Henry Rundle Sr.** had filled the gap with his own brand of curative, Porter's Pain King.

Born in New York, Rundle grew up in Connecticut before moving to Lima, Ohio in 1871 at the age of twenty-four. He went to work for Lima, Ohio druggist Mr. Porter who had created a formula for Porter's Pain King. Rundle met and married Fletcher, Ohio native Amanda Hance in 1874. He took an opportunity for advancement when Mr. Porter retired in 1875. He purchased his former employer's formula for Porter's Pain King.

The George H. Rundle Company built this office/laboratory at 419 Caldwell in 1916

Moving to Fletcher, Rundle drove throughout Miami County in a horse-drawn medicine wagon. His sales methods were relatively unique. He offered his customers a free bottle of Pain King. On his next trip through the neighborhood, Rundle would stop again and ask if they wished to purchase the bottle. If they did, he had created a loyal customer. If they did not, he would take the partially used bottle back, refill it and offer it to his next customer. Rundle's early advertisements stated that drinking Porter's Pain King could cure coughs, headaches, mouth cankers, liver complaints, colic, dysentery and fevers. Using Porter's externally could alleviate burns, boils, sprains, bruises, cuts, swelling of the joints, frostbite and rheumatism.

Rundle's business methods slowly began to increase sales. By the mid-1880's, it became apparent that Rundle's growing family and growing business needed a new home. Rundle moved both his firm and his family to Piqua in the spring of 1886. With his brother-in-law Allen D. Hance, Rundle setup a new laboratory and shipping facility in a frame warehouse in the 200 block of West Water Street. The next year (1887) saw the firm moving to a newly constructed three story brick office and laboratory/ manufacturing plant at 527 North Main Street. The firm installed one of the city's earliest hydraulic elevators in their new office and plant. By 1890, the firm had twenty salesmen driving horse-drawn medicine wagons throughout the Miami Valley. The firm formally incorporated in February of 1897 under the name of the George H. Rundle Company. Rundle expanded again in 1906 with the creation of a new firm in Windsor, Canada to distribute Porter's Pain King across the border. The company added new products that included salves, laxatives and aspirin.

Rundle was an active and vocal promoter of **Prohibition** around the county. Though he died in 1917, three years before Prohibition became the law of the land, his active stance on the matter helped promote Ohio's ratification of the Eighteenth Amendment which prohibited the sale, manufacture or transportation of alcoholic products. One consequence of Prohibition that Rundle most likely did not foresee was that his own formula for Porter's Pain King would be banned in 1920 for containing too high an alcoholic content. The firm adapted to the new circumstances by promoting Porter's Pain King as a salve or liniment. The strong and distinctive odor of the new liniment wrinkled the noses of thousands of local and area residents for several generations to come.

After George Rundle Sr.'s death, the company stayed under family control, first with his son **Allen G. Rundle** (Piqua High School Class of 1898), then with his son-in-law Logan A. Frazier, and finally with his grandson George H. Rundle Jr. The firm prospered through most of the twentieth century. New and larger offices and laboratories were constructed in 1916 at 419 Caldwell.

By 1969-1970, the Rundle family had moved to Florida and the Piqua plant closed its doors. But that is not the end of the story. William E. Roecker, treasurer of the George H. Rundle Company during its final decades, followed the example of the firm's founder. As Rundle had purchased the Porter's Pain King formula and started his own business, Roecker did the same thing. He bought the Rundle formula and moved the business to Covington, Ohio under the name Porter's Products. The firm continues today (2007) to distribute the famous liniment around the country.

Other companies that operated during the last quarter of the nineteenth century in Piqua included the Jewel Medicine Company, the Imperial Golden Oil Company, the Oliver Elliott Company and the Daniel Rumple Company.

PERSIAN GULF WARS

The first of these Middle Eastern crisis' began with Iraq's invasion of Kuwait on August 2, 1990. President George Bush sent active duty troops to Saudi Arabia in response to this invasion. In the fall of 1990, select Reserve and National Guard troops were activated to reinforce the U. S. troops already in the Persian Gulf area as part of Operation Desert Shield. On January 17, 1991, American and allied forces attacked Iraq in Operation Desert Storm.

In Miami County, the 1487th Transportation Company (Ohio National Guard) in Piqua, the 656th Transportation Company (U.S. Army Reserves) in Troy, and the 641 Quartermaster Detachment (water purification) (Ohio National Guard) in Covington were activated into full-time federal service. The two transportation units were shipped to Fort McCoy, Wisconsin for additional training before being sent to Saudi Arabia in January of 1991. The 641st Detachment was sent directly to the Gulf area.

Several local organizations gathered recreational and personal items to send to troops serving in Desert Shield and later Desert Storm operations. On January 16, 1991, a candlelight "Prayers for Peace" vigil was held at the Ohio National Guard Armory on East Ash Street, sponsored by the ONG Family Support Group. Orange ribbons were worn or tied to posts and fences as signs of support to the troops in the Gulf.

The Second Gulf War began after the 9/11 destruction in New York and Washington, D.C. During the Afganistan and Iraq Wars, a number of local individuals served on active duty in these conflicts. Battery C, Ohio National Guard served for ten months in Great Britain in 2004 serving as a security force at an Air Force base. The 1487th Transportation Company served a tour of active duty in Iraq in 2006. Piqua's first casualty in the War in Iraq, Samuel Frederick Pearson (PHS Class of 1998) was killed in October 2007. SEE ALSO: Militia and National Guard.

PHILIPPINE REVOLUTION

On December 10, 1898, the Philippine Islands were ceded to the United States from Spain. This was a direct result of the American victory in the Spanish-American War. From 1898 until 1901, Filipino revolutionary forces fought against the United States occupation of the islands. Two Piqua men, serving in the regular United States Army units, fought in the Philippine Revolution. Second Lieutenant Charles W. Bowdle wrote several letters home about his experiences in the conflict. The letters were published in the local newspapers. Corporal Edgar F. Wallace was also in the Philippines, serving with Company H, 17th Infantry Regiment. Both men served during the period 1900-1901.

PHONOGRAPH

The first phonograph was exhibited in Piqua at the City Hall in 1889. The **Meteor Motor Car Company** briefly manufactured phonographs from 1916 until c.1923.

PHOTOGRAPHERS

The earliest photographers in Piqua were known as daguerreotype artists. In 1850, A. McDonald and Isaac Davis were the first such artists to be listed in Piqua. Charles A. Gale (1868-1891), and John R. Thorne (1869-1910), were two post Civil War photographers who established galleries in Piqua. Other nineteenth century photographers were; A. H. Rice (c.1859-1868), Robert Burdge (c.1868-c.1872), Edward W. Matthews (c.1885-1909), H. Mein (1886-c1889), and John M. Lloyd (1899-1915). One of the most successful of all early Piqua photographers was **Ethan E. Huntzinger** (1907-1943). Huntzinger was responsible for a large number of picture postcards that document the history of Piqua from 1908 to about 1914. During the early 1930's, Huntzinger moved his operation to 803 Covington Avenue where he established the Huntzinger School Photo Service. This new firm used a specially built camera that took individual student pictures that could be printed with the rest of the school class on a single photographic sheet. By 1936, Huntzinger and his agents had taken individual/group pictures at over 743 schools in fourteen states. The firm was sold in 1946 to William R. Webber, who continued operations until 1950.

PHYSICIANS

When Colonel **John Johnston** settled near Piqua in 1812, his knowledge of wounds, cuts, and breaks was the closest the village had to a doctor. Henry Chappese came to Piqua in 1815 and was the first local physician with any formal training. He was followed in 1819 by the twenty year old Dr. **John O'Farrell**. The O'Farrell family would furnish Piqua with two more generations of doctors. John Jr. began practicing medicine in 1842, and his son, Robert M. began in the 1880's. During the 1820's, local physicians advertised their services. One advertisement promised to "pull teeth, cure piles, correct eyesight, and mend broken bones". Until after the **Civil War**, all physicians' offices were in their homes, with minor surgeries being done there. If the patient could not, or would not, be moved, the surgery was done in the patient's home. Prior to 1883, medicine in Piqua was purely the domain of men. In 1883 Dr. **Belle C. Buchanan [Evans]** broke the barrier when she opened an office on Park Avenue and a dispensary on the southeast corner of the public square. SEE ALSO: Dorsey, Godwin V.; Drug Stores; Hospital.

PICKAWILLANY

This Miami village was established in 1747 at the fork of Loramie Creek and the Great Miami River. **Old Britain,** also known as La Demoiselle, Chief of the Piankeshaw (aka Twightwee) Sept or Band of the **Miami** Nation moved his band to this site to remove them from the influence of the French at Fort Miami on the Maumee River. With the help of English traders (among them Thomas Burney and **George Croghan**), a village and trading post was constructed. In 1749, **Celoron de Blainville** visited the site to try and persuade Old Britain to return to the area around Fort Miami. He gave eight belts of wampum as gifts but the Miami did not return to the French fort. By 1751, over four hundred families lived at the site from various tribes. Pickawillany became the largest settlement west of the Allegheny Mountains and south of the Great Lakes with members of the Miami, Weas, Mascoutens, Piankashaws and Kickapoo tribes living there. The French learned about a plan of the Illinois, Wea, Piankashaw, **Miami, Delaware, Shawnee** and the Iroquois Five Nations to hold a council at La Demoiselle's village some time in 1752. To stop what might have become an alliance against them, the French sent Charles Langdale and a body of Indians loyal to the French to attack and burn Pickawillany to the ground. On June 21, 1752 Langdale succeeded in destroying Pickawillany and its English trading houses. The only English traders to escape were Thomas Burney and Andrew McBryea. During its five years of existence, Pickawillany was mentioned in the journals of Celoron, **Gist**, and **Trent**. SEE ALSO: Callender; Montour.

PIGS

This animal was very important in early pioneer life on both the farms and in the village. Pigs were relatively easy to raise and would eat almost anything. In Piqua, pigs were used as a primitive sanitary collection service. Free ranging pigs would traveling the streets and alleys eating the garbage put out by local residents. This worked fairly well until the growing pig population became a problem in the 1830's and loose pigs were banned within the village. With the coming of the Miami & Erie Canal in 1837, pork became a major product for shipment to Cincinnati. Mound Street, a one block east-west Street between Main and Wayne Streets, was known as Pork Alley for the pork slaughter houses located there. Pigs from the surrounding farms were regularly herded down Main Street to the slaughter houses. Young boys with long sticks were used to direct these pig herds and thus the legends of the Piqua Pig Boys began. Actually there were no legends since this was a very dirty and difficult job that most boys were very reluctant to do and which nobody glamorized. The pig drives generally ended by the **Civil War**. At the end of the nineteenth century (1891), the city Health Department closed down most of the city's domestic pig pens in thickly settled neighborhoods. In the last part of the nineteenth century, the city's largest pork producer was the J.W. Shipley Company. At the end of the hog season in January of 1887, the firm had slaughtered over twelve hundred hogs.

PIQUA, OHIO

This community is located at the junctions of U.S. Route 36, State Route 66, State Route 185, County Road 25-A, and Interstate 75 in Washington and Springcreek Townships. The area was first settled west of the **Great Miami River** by **Job Gard** in 1796 and east of the river by the Hilliard family. The village was laid out on June 24, 1807, by surveyor **Armstrong Brandon** for **John Manning** and **Matthew Caldwell**, and named Washington. In 1816, the village returned to the traditional name of Piqua. Piqua (or Pique) was the name of a division or clan of the **Shawnee** Indians, who occupied the site from 1780 until 1782. The village was incorporated in 1823 and reincorporated as a city in 1850. The community absorbed the village of **Huntersville** in 1893 and **Riverside** in circa 1920. In 2000, the city's population was 20,865 with approximately 7,800 separate households. In 2000, the city's size was approximately 7.2 square miles with a Main Street elevation of 875 feet. The city's geographic location (intersection of Main and Ash Streets) is latitude north 40 degrees 08 minuets 59.7 seconds and longitude east 84 degrees 14 minuets 21.8 seconds. There are two other Piqua's in the United States; Piqua, Kentucky and Piqua (Woodson County), Kansas. SEE ALSO: Border City; Hilliard Family; Population; Public Square; Roads; Streets.

Piqua Physicians

*Dr. Joseph Buasman is shown in this
1962 photograph.*

*Dr. G.V. Dorsey was one of the city's
most active pre-Civil War physicians.*

*Dr. John Beachler Jr. and Dr. John Beachler Sr., shown here in 1949,
represented over seventy-five years of medical practice.*

PIQUA, BATTLE OF

In 1780, the **Shawnee** village of Piqua was located on the Mad River near present day Springfield, Ohio. General **George Rogers Clark** led an army of roughly one thousand Kentucky militia men on an expedition into Ohio in an attempt to stop British influenced Indian attacks against Kentucky. This was also in response to Captain Bird's attacks on Fort Laurens in 1779. The Shawnee village was the home of Chief **Black Hoof**, who resisted Clark's attack. Also present at Piqua was **Simon Girty** who led a force of mixed Miami, Mingo, and Delaware Indians. Black Hoof was defeated and the village and its surrounding corn fields were destroyed. The Shawnee fled to the Great Miami River and established the village of **Upper Piqua**. SEE ALSO: Piqua, Indian Village.

PIQUA-CALDWELL NATIONAL REGISTER HISTORICAL DISTRICT

Work to establish the city's first National Register District began in February of 1978 with the formation of a Historical Inventory Committee chaired by James Oda. During the summer of 1978, Richard K. Reed, working with the committee, inventoried three hundred of Piqua's historical structures. In February of 1983, the Piqua Historic Preservation Committee was formed, and in March, Connie Porcher began work on the National Register nomination form. The district is bounded on the east by Main Street, on the west by Caldwell, on the south by High Street, and on the north by Park, Camp, Rundle Streets, and Riverside Drive. This area contains over two hundred structures with a variety of styles and functions dating from 1822 to the 1920's. The district was accepted by the State in 1984 and by the National Park Service, Department of the Interior in 1985.

PIQUA, CAMP

Fort Sumter fell on April 14, 1861, and the **Civil War** began. A year later the Adjutant General of Ohio established Camp Piqua by Special Orders No. 659, dated July, 1862. The camp was established for the formation and early training of the 94th Regiment of the Ohio Volunteer Infantry. Ten companies were raised with companies B, C, and D coming from Miami County. The rest came from Clarke, Greene, and Darke counties for a total of 1,010 men. A one hundred dollar bounty was paid to all those who enlisted. Fifty dollars was paid out before the troops left the camp. Twenty-five dollars was given in advance, thirteen dollars as an advance on the first month's pay, ten dollars was given by the City of Piqua, and two dollars from various townships. The regiment drew arms and equipment on August 27, but no canteens or uniforms were available. The next day the 94th Regiment boarded the Dayton and Michigan **Railroad** for Cincinnati. After arriving in the "Queen City", uniforms were finally issued. On August 30, the unit marched south to Lexington, Kentucky. The following day after completing a road march, the regiment was ambushed by Confederate forces. The 94th suffered two causalities and four wounded only three days after leaving Camp Piqua.

In September, Camp Piqua was being used to recruit members for the 110th Regiment from Miami, Clarke, and Darke Counties. Company A came almost exclusively from Piqua. Colonel M. G. Mitchell of Piqua assumed command of Camp Piqua, and Colonel J. W. Keifer took command of the 110th Regiment. Piqua Mayor **William N. Foster** resigned his position with the city to sign on as Keifer's second-in-command. The regiment was formally mustered into service on October 3, 1862. The 110th left Camp Piqua for western Virginia on October 19, 1862, and the Camp was closed down permanently.

PIQUA CLUB

During the fall of 1901, a group of local business and industrial leaders met to form a new civic organization. The Piqua Club was formally established on December 1, 1901 and met at 510 North Wayne Street. **William P. Orr** was elected as the club's first president, a position he would hold until his death in 1912. Another long term officer was J. Ben Wilkinson who held the office of Secretary/Treasurer from roughly 1905 until World War I. The organization worked to improve the community's economic stability and growth by bringing in new business and industry. The club prospered and on January of 1907, work began on a new club house on the northeast corner of Wayne and Greene Streets. The structure was built by local contractor **A. M. Fry** using the **Jacobethan Revival style** designed by the Dayton firm of **Schenk and Williams**. At its grand opening on January 21, 1908, the new Piqua Club became the city's largest structure dedicated to a social or civic group. The building contained two **bowling** alleys, a "ratskeller", lounge, dining room, kitchen, billiard and card rooms, private dining rooms, and a banquet/dancing facility on the third floor. The club continued as an active organization through the 1920's with the following men serving as president: J. H. Young, Abraham Kahn, Frank C. Davies, and J. H. Clark. The city-oriented Piqua Club declined in the later 1920's as the idea of a Country Club expanded. In December of 1930, the Piqua Club building was purchased by **Leo M. Flesh,** who donated it to the public library. The former club was rededicated in 1931 as the Flesh Public **Library**. The library moved to the former **Plaza Hotel** in 2008.

PIQUA COLONIZATION SOCIETY

The Piqua Colonization Society was established by local white citizens in 1826 as a local chapter of the American Colonization Society. The objective of the society was to send freed slaves back to Africa (Liberia). **Robert Young**, an attorney, was the first president of the society and Dr. Isaac Henderschott the first secretary. The organization faded away by the late1830's. SEE ALSO: African-American

PIQUA, COUNCIL OF

Two months after the United States had declared war on Great Britain, beginning the **War of 1812**, a major council was held at Piqua. On August 15, 1812, three commissioners appointed by President James Madison met with delegates from the **Shawnee, Miami, Wyandot, Delaware, Seneca**, and other tribes. The commissioners were three of Ohio's highest elected officials, Return J. Meigs (Governor of Ohio), Thomas Worthington (Ohio's Senator and future Governor), Jeremiah Morrow (U. S. Representative from Ohio, and future Governor). Also present were Major General **William Henry Harrison**, and Federal Indian Agent Colonel **John Johnston**. The chief spokesmen for the gathered tribes were Chief **Little Turtle** of the Miamis, and Chief **Black Hoof** of the Shawnees. The council was held on the farm owned by Colonel Johnston. As a result of the council, the gathered tribes agreed to stay neutral during the war. From 1812 through 1814, an estimated four to six thousand Indians stayed at Johnston's Farm, keeping them away from the influence of the English. SEE ALSO: Greenville, Second Treaty of.

This Tudor Style Rundle home was located on the northwest corner of Downing and Ash Streets.

Piqua Caldwell National Register Historic District

Below: The Orr Family stable was constructed in the Second Empire Style and located on the east side of North Downing Street between Greene and North Streets.

Right: This view of North Wayne Street shows off Piqua's World War I era Ohio National Guard unit. Behind the Guard unit are located two of the historic district's Greek Revival Style homes.

Left: The Colonial Saxony apartment complex at 221 West Greene Street was built in the grand Second Renaissance Revival Style of architecture.

PIQUA GAZETTE

The *Piqua Gazette* was the first **newspaper** printed north of Dayton in the Miami Valley. The publisher/editor/printer was **William R. Barrington** from Philadelphia. He brought a press to Piqua and established the newspaper on the northeast corner of Main and Greene Street. The first issue was available to local citizens on July 06, 1820. Barrington moved his entire operations to a small addition to his home in 1825 located on the east side of Main Street, north of North Street. During 1826-1827, Jeremiah A. Dooley ran the paper, but Barrington took back control in 1827. Barrington again backed away from the all consuming job and sold his newspaper to Dooley on June 23, 1829. Dooley sold the paper to Dr. J.B. Gregory in September of 1834 who let the publication of the paper lapse shortly thereafter. See Also: List-newspapers

PIQUA, FORT

This fort was built by elements of General **Anthony Wayne**'s army as a supply depot in 1793. It was located on the Great Miami River on the future site of **John Johnston**'s Farm (Piqua Historical Area). It was garrisoned by troops under the command of Captain J. N. Vischer. The fort was abandoned in 1795. Logs from the fort were used by **Job Gard** in 1796 to build a log cabin on what would become the corner of Harrison and Water Streets in the city of Piqua.

PIQUA HANDLE AND MANUFACTURING COMPANY

R. M. Murray, H. C. Nellis, H. H. Bassett and W. C. Gray established this company in May of 1882 in a small factory building on Riverside Drive between Main and Wayne Streets. Murray was elected the firm's first president. He continued until 1888 when Frank Chance took over and moved the plant to the northwest corner of High and Lincoln Streets. During the first part of 1892, William C. Rogers came to Piqua and established the W. C. Rogers Manufacturing Company which produced push button door bells and wooden door knobs. In September of that year, Rogers' company and the Piqua Handle Company merged with Chance continuing as president and Rogers taking over as vice-president. By 1900, Rogers had taken over as president and the firm was manufacturing handles for farm tools, miscellaneous wooden products, and selling coal and scrap wood on the side. During **World War I**, the firm held a contract with the Federal government to produce over a half million tent poles and shovel handles. After the war, the company joined with the **French Oil Mill Machinery Company** to form the French Oil and Piqua Handle Employees Store (1920-c1929), on the southeast corner of West Greene and Washington Streets. During the 1920's, Rogers purchased the Munsing Wooden Ware Company (Michigan) and the Chapman-Sargent Company (Georgia). In 1934, the three firms merged to form the Piqua Munsing Wood Products Company with Rogers as the chairman of the board. In 1936-1937, a lockout followed by a **strike** by **Union** Local No. 18787 of the A.F. of L. In c.1938-39 the company went into bankruptcy and was acquired by the Cliffs Iron Company of Cleveland and permanently closed down. The factory itself was sold to the French Oil Mill Machinery Company in November of 1940.

PIQUA HISTORICAL AREA

In the 1940's, Piqua Mayor **Joseph A. Thoma, Sr.** was one of the first local citizens to promote the idea of a state park at the site of Colonel **John Johnston**'s homestead. In the 1950's,

This early twentieth century photograph of the Colonel John Johnston home shows the "Mother's Addition" that was demolished during the historic restoration of the site.

Leonard Hill became an active promoter of the Johnston Farm Park idea. A committee was formed in 1962 to promote a state park at this site. It was chaired by Glen Thompson, editor of the *Dayton Journal-Herald*. Committee members included **Charles B. Upton** (General Manager of **French Oil Mill Manufacturing Company**) and **Robert M. Hance** (Piqua **City Manager**). The 174 acre property was purchased in 1964 with restoration work beginning in 1966. Del Harder of Columbus served as consulting engineer, and John Carpenter as contractor. The Piqua Historical Area was formally dedicated on September 3, 1972. The site is located at the corner of Hardin Road and State Route 66, and contains the restored home, outbuildings, and the barn of Colonel Johnston. There is also a restored section of the Miami and Erie Canal with an operating canal boat, and an Indian Museum. Clinton Hosher served as site manager from 1972-1986, followed by Victoria Tabor Branson (1986-1993), John Nielson c.1993- 1997, and Andy Hite (1997-present (2007). Hite would be the first manager to live off site. SEE ALSO: Patron p. 268

PIQUA HISTORICAL MUSEUM

The Piqua Historical Museum traces its history back to 1877 when James Carson donated display cases to the High School for use in a small "cabinet style" museum. From 1877 through 1912, the High School exhibits continued to grow until they contained a wide array of specimens such as; stuffed coyotes, military swords, archaeological artifacts, and sea shells.

In 1912, the museum material was moved to 509-511 North Main Street, the home of the Schmidlapp Free School Library. The display cases were set up on the second floor of the library and the area was opened for public view. By 1924, the museum displays were not in good condition and part of the collection was packed away.

The library moved out of the Schmidlapp building in November, 1931, leaving the museum materials behind. During the early years of the Great **Depression** little was done with the material until 1933-34 when Fletcher Moffett volunteered to reorganize the museum and serve as its first curator. Assistance for the museum came from the WPA (a federal New Deal agency) for the building of display cases and from the City Federation of Women's Clubs who furnished volunteers for Saturday afternoon public hours. In 1935, George Kiefer Sr. joined the museum's volunteer staff. The museum was active until 1944 when Moffett resigned as curator and moved from Piqua. During **World War II**, the museum had to share quarters with the United States Office of Price Administration and the Rationing Board. The displays were relocated to out-of-the-way corners and again partially packed away.

In 1946, the Board of Education moved into 509-511 North Main. What remained of the museum was boxed and put into storage. It was during this storage period that some of the museum's collections were lost or stolen.

The materials subsequently were moved to Spring Street School, then to the Flesh Public **Library** and, finally, to the City Building on Water Street. **Leonard Hill** and **Joseph Thoma, Sr**. began promoting the idea of a local museum in the mid 1950's. Nothing was accomplished, however, until 1972 when the Board of Education vacated its offices in the Schmidlapp Building. Once again, this building became a museum, this time under the guidance of the Board of Education and a volunteer Board of Trustees. Operation of the Piqua Historical Museum was transferred to the Flesh Public **Library** in 1989. After the opening of the public library in the former **Hotel Plaza** site on the public square in 2008, the museum's collections were moved from Main Street to High Street and exhibited throughout the library.

PIQUA HISTORICAL SOCIETY

The first local historical society was organized in 1889, and continued to function for about ten years. The Society was re-established in 1912, but died out during **World War I**. A third society was organized in the early 1930's under the name Piqua Historical and Archeological Society. It was active until **World War II**. In 1976, the Piqua Historical Society was incorporated. The Society added a part-time executive director in 1986 and was re-incorporated in 1988. By the late 1990's the Society was dormant. A move was made in 2007-2008 to re-activate the Society.

PIQUA HOSIERY COMPANY

In July of 1886, it was publicly announced that a new knitting mill would be established in Piqua. By October, the Piqua Hosiery Company had been formed and local contractors Brotherton and Scudder had completed a two story frame factory on the west side of Spring Street between Ash and High Streets. The first officers were **C. L. Wood** (President), C. A. Kitts (Vice-President/Plant Manager), Clarence Langdon (Treasurer), J. O. Neer (Secretary), and as directors H. C. Nellis, Samuel Gross, and A. J. Roe. The firm opened in November with twenty-four female employees working at twenty three machines. By December, employment had risen to sixty-seven. In the middle of January, 1887, the total was up to seventy-five and by the end of the month it was over ninety. The total company salaries by that time had risen to almost nine hundred dollars a week. The firm had begun producing the nation's first "commercially practical drop seat union suit" in the 1890's. In 1896, the firm was making ladies' jersey underwear, combination suits, and equestrian tights.

Like many of Piqua's underwear companies, Piqua Hosiery grew by taking over other companies. Hosiery took over the S.H. Halsted & Company of Cincinnati, Ohio in 1888 and the Jackson Underwear Company of Indiana in 1894 and moving both firms to Piqua. The final acquisition was the Monarch Underwear Company of Bowling Green, Ohio in 1917.

In 1912, a new three-story brick and concrete factory was built on the southwest corner of Ash and Spring Streets. Man-agement had changed by 1900 with **W. K. Leonard** as President and Frank M. Shipley as Plant Manager. By this time the company was advertising Piqua as "the quality union suit city of the world". Hosiery began using the brand name P.Q.A. in c.1909. During the 1930's, Frank Shipley became President. And **A. L. Flesh** (President of the **Atlas Underwear Company**) had became a dominant stockholder in B.V.D. The **B.V.D.** holding company took over Hosiery Piqua Hosiery Company as a division of B.V.D. The firm began featuring knit swimwear and sweaters for B.V.D. The company used Olympic medal medalist **Johnny Weismuller** (future movie star playing Tarzan) to promote their new band of men's swim wear.

The company began the production of B.V.D. swimming suits for women under the name *La Bourrasque (The Squall)* in 1935. The style had originally been created in the 1930's in California by MABS of Hollywood and promoted by movie star Jean Harlow. The new suits were made of cellophane and an elastic material known as Lastex yarn. [Lastex was trademarked by the Dunlap Company in 1931 and consisted of a rubber core wrapped in cotton or silk.] Hosiery also produced knit sweater coats for men during this period. B.V.D. split away in 1933, and Alfred Flesh became the managing director of Piqua Hosiery of which he owned a twenty-five percent share. The firm suffered a series of very bad years from 1935 on and Flesh closed down the plant in July of 1940. In the summer of 1941,the factory buildings were sold to the Robbins and Meyers Company of Springfield.

PIQUA HUMANE SOCIETY

The first society was organized in 1890 and lasted for several years. On March 8, 1904, a new society was organized and a constitution was adopted. William Sniff was elected President, C.C. Barnett was First Vice President, and Miss Martha E. Weddell Second Vice President. This was one of the first modern civic organizations to be formed jointly by men and women. The second group was also relatively short lived and future societies were organized on a county level.

PIQUA, NATIVE AMERICAN VILLAGE

Piqua (or Bi-co-we-tha) was the name of one of the main divisions of the **Shawnee**. The divisions' occupied separate villages during most of the early history of the tribe. Piqua has been located at Pechoquealin on the Delaware River in Pennsylvania (1694-1728), Piqua or Lick Town on Scioto River in Pickaway County (1758-1776), on the Mad River in Clarke County (1776-1780), and on the **Great Miami River** in Miami County (1780-1782). There were two settlements on the Great Miami River, **Upper Piqua**, near the present Piqua Historical Area (Johnston's Farm), and Lower Piqua or **Chillicothe** on the flood plain south and east of the bend of the Great Miami River. Today Lower Piqua is known as Shawnee. The following are variations on the Piqua name: Bi-co-we-tha, Paquea, Pecawa, Pecuvwesi, Pechoquealin, Pekowev, Pekuegi, Pequea, Pequenan, Pickawa, Pickaway, Pickawee, Pickawes, Picoweu, Picque, and Pikoweu. SEE ALSO: Clark, George Rogers; Piqua, Battle of.

PIQUA STEEL COMPANY

The firm was established in 1933, during the Great **Depression**. One of their early jobs was salvaging the rails from the Piqua's street electric railway. The firm changed its name to PSC Crane and Rigging Company when they stopped steel supply and fabrication. In 2006, the firm was run by Earl Severs III and his two sons Randy and Jim. The firm employs between 75 and 100 men and women. SEE ALSO: Patron p. 272

PIQUAD

This is the term used to refer to those individuals living in Piqua, Ohio. The word was apparently printed for the first time in the *Miami Helmet* and *Piqua Daily Call* newspapers in the 1880's.

PIQUONIAN

In the fall of 1909, a group of Piqua High School students and their faculty advisor met to discuss the production of a school publication. At first it was to be called the *Pickawillian* or the *Twightewee*, but saner heads prevailed and the first issue came out as the *Piquonian*. Originally, the *Piquonian* came out four times a year, at Thanksgiving, Christmas, in the spring, and finally a senior issue with photographs of the faculty, organizations, and students. The quarterly issues continued until the early 1960's. They contained fictional stories, sports columns, alumni columns, and reviews of school events. In 1974, color photographs were first used. By 1976, color photographs were taken of each graduating senior.

PLASTICS

The EDM Corporation was one of the city's first major companies to become part of the plastic industry. The firm was established in 1960 to make molds for plastics products in the automotive industry. The Blue Magic of Ohio, Incorporated was the next local industry to move into plastics. Blue Magic was the first household-cleaner manufacturer to also produce its own plastic bottles. Other early plastics firms in Piqua include Crayex Corporation established in 1972 to manufacture plastic film for shrink wrapping, and the Action Mold and Tool Company (1976). SEE ALSO: Industry

PLAZA HOTEL

On May 3, 1890, the heirs of John M. Brown sold the building and lot on the northwest side of the public square to **William P. Orr** and **Samuel K. Statler** for twenty-four thousand dollars. Orr and Statler brought in Columbus architect **Joseph W. Yost** to design a hotel in the **Richardsonian Romanesque Style**. Yost was best known in Miami County for designing the Miami County Courthouse in **Troy**. The new structure would use over 800,000 bricks and contain five stories and a basement with a 115 foot high corner tower, one-hundred guest rooms, and a grand two-story high dining room on the fourth floor. The final cost of the structure was roughly $125,000. In April, **hotel** operations were leased to Norman C. Johnston of Grand Rapids, Michigan. The grand opening was held on October 22, 1891. In 1914, **Stanhope Boal** bought out S. K. Statler and changed the name to the Hotel Favorite. In 1946, the Packard Hotel chain purchased the hotel and changed the name to the Hotel Fort Piqua. By the late 1980's, the hotel operations were closed down by owner William Supinger. The hotel was purchased in the 1990's and donated to the Piqua Improvement Corporation for private development. The City of Piqua and the public **library** joined together and began renovating the structure in 2007-2008 for use as a Library with a community center on the fourth floor. SEE ALSO: American Legion; Bricks and Brick Masons; Bryan, William; McKinley, William; Plumbing; Prohibition; Taft, William; Whitlock, Isaac and Horace.

PLUMBING

The city's first indoor plumbing came with the construction of the **Plaza Hotel** in 1891. The hotel had too many rooms for outhouses to be constructed, so the city agreed to dig a sanitary sewer line from the hotel to the Great Miami River south of town. The hotel's first indoor bathrooms were located in the basement.

POLICE DEPARTMENT

The formation of Miami County and Washington Township in 1807 brought with it the first organized "police" protection. In that year, two township constables were elected. These constables would be Piqua's only protection until the village was re-incorporated in 1835. Under this reorganization, a village marshal was elected. The first marshal was Robert Shannon. The marshal served alone and special deputies were sworn in during times of great need. One of the city's earliest major crimes changed this arrangement. On May 18, 1868, Doctor W. P. Hall and wife were the victims of a murder attempt. The city was so outraged that by May 30, 1868 the council had passed an ordinance authorizing six night policemen. This new organization

The Cigar and Candy Counter in the Favorite Hotel (Plaza) was run by Ernest Wegley and Joseph Connema from the 1920's through 1980.

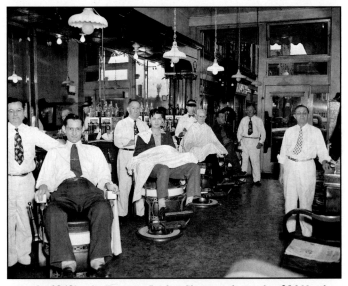

In the 1940's, the Favorite Barber Shop was located at 306 North Main in the northeast corner of the Favorite Hotel (Plaza Hotel).

A worker was cutting through one of the stone walls in the basement.

Many of the stone and brick walls were retained as seen in this photograph of the basement looking out of a hole in the sidewalk immediately in front of the main entrance.

Hotel Restoration

Work began on the grand restoration of the Plaza Hotel (Orr-Statler Block) on the public square in 2007 as the new home of the Piqua library in 2008.

Small earth movers were lowered into the basement to help remove the demolition debris.

Construction workers are seen working on the window framing in the turret room on the second floor.

Library staff members Gary Meek and Sharon Watson photographed the reopened space on the fourth floor formerly used as the main dining room.

was under the supervision of the mayor and a two-man police board. The first policemen hired by the city were: J. S. Blood, Patrick Fitzgerald, J. W. Manson, Elza Julian, Adam Conover, and Frank A. Hardy. The men received approximately two dollars a night. This first force was rapidly reduced and by 1870 only two men remained on the payroll. It was not until 1900 that the police force again reached the level of six full time officers. In 1903, the new state mandated municipal code created a newly organized police department headed by a full time police chief. After completing a competitive test, former semi-pro wrestler and bartender, **Frank Gehle**, was appointed Chief of Police. Gehle served as head of the department until 1936. The department was a male domain until March 7, 1990 when Dawn Blake was hired as its first female officer. SEE ALSO: Jails, List-Police Chiefs; Patron p. 291

POPULATION

Year	Piqua	Troy	Miami County
1820	350	293	8,851
1830	488	504	12,807
1840	1,480	1,351	19,688
1850	3,277	1,956	24,999
1860	4,616	2,643	29,959
1870	5,967	3,005	32,740
1880	6,031	3,803	36,158
1890	9,090	4,494	39,754
1900	12,172	5,881	43,105
1910	13,388	6,122	45,047
1920	15,044	7,260	48,428
1930	16,009	8,675	51,301
1940	16,049	9,697	52,632
1950	17,447	10,661	61,309
1960	19,219	13,685	72,901
1970	20,741	17,186	84,342
1980	20,150	18,838	89,463
1990	20,612	19,478	93,182
2000	20,738	22,183	98,868

SEE ALSO: African-American; Employment; Immigration, Migration

POST-1960 MODERN STYLE ARCHITECTURE

This local variation of the Post-1960 Modern Style was popular from 1960 through 1990. This is strictly a local style name with no direct ties to national styles. This style uses a light colored brick with a variety of widow and door openings. The structures are almost always two stories in height with flat or gently sloping roofs.

COMMERCIAL EXAMPLES

300 West High Street, Border City Savings & Loan, **YMCA** Center

223 West High Street, YMCA,

418 North Wayne Street, **YWCA**

100 Block East Ash Street, Citizens Bank Trust office

417 North Wayne Street, Continental Beauty School

POST OFFICE

The first post office in Piqua (1811) was located on the west side of Main Street, south of Water Street, and operated by Postmaster **Armstrong Brandon**. By 1836, mail arrived daily by four-horse post carriages. Persons receiving mail would look for their names in the *Piqua Gazette* and would then pay the postmaster the postage due on each letter. After the **Civil War**, the sender began paying for the mailing of letters, and this led to free home delivery.

In February of 1887, Piqua Postmaster J. R. Thorne met with the city council to begin planning for free mail delivery within the city. One of the prime federal postal requirements stated that mail delivery could only be instituted in a community where the **streets** were properly identified and each building plainly numbered. The city moved quickly to comply with these requirements. Henry Becker, a local sign painter, was contracted to paint and erect signs for all of Piqua's fifty-one streets. On May 16, the council passed an ordinance for the numbering of all buildings (**house numbers**) within the city limits. Piqua's current numbering system dates from this ordinance. The Cincinnati, Hamilton and Dayton Railroad tracks on Sycamore Street became the boundary for north and south Piqua, and Main Street served as the east-west line. All numbers on the north and west sides of the streets were designated even, and south and east sides odd. For the first time, the blocks were broken up into units of one-hundred instead of the former, rather haphazard, method of continuous numbering beginning at the river and moving south. The city engineer took charge of the physical numbering of buildings, and charged each owner twenty cents for a set of three numbers.

On Friday morning, July 1, free mail delivery began in Piqua with three new mail carriers, David Legg, Frank D. McKinney, and John Daly. Louis Simon served as a substitute. These first mailmen wore grey suits and matching caps. On Main Street, the mail was delivered three times a day, and on all other streets twice a day, with the carriers leaving the Post Office at 7:00 a.m. and 4:00 p.m. The now familiar corner mail boxes were also put up in 1887 in twenty locations throughout the city. Like delivery, Main Street received extra attention with collections, with the Main Street boxes emptied four times a day and all other boxes twice a day.

The *Miami Helmet* published the statistics for the first three months of operation of the new system. From July 1 through September 30, the three Piqua mail carriers delivered 67,719 letters, post cards, and newspapers, and collected 60,360 pieces. This averaged out to just over 540 pieces of mail for each carrier every day, six days a week. Each carrier also delivered more than 124 newspapers each day.

Rural free delivery (R.F.D.) would not begin until October 3, 1898. The current **Neo-Classical Style** Post Office building was completed in 1914 at a cost of about $200,000. SEE ALSO: Zip Codes.

POTAWATOMI TRIBE

The Potawatomi are part of the Algonquian language family and originated in southern Michigan and northern Indiana. The Potawatomi settled in parts of northwestern Ohio. They signed the Treaty of Fort Harmar in 1789 and the **Treaty of Greenville** in 1795. During the War of 1812, the tribe was caught between the British and the Americans and was forced to choose sides. A majority of the Potawatomi sided with the British. After the war, the tribe agreed to all the white demands. In fact, from 1803 until 1867 in Ohio and Oklahoma, the Potawatomi signed or participated in fifty-two treaties.. SEE ALSO: Johnston, Stephen.

POTTERY

The city's first professional potter was David J. Jorden, who began operations in 1836. His kilns were located on South Main Street, near the corner of Miami Street. Other early potters included Benjamin Riffle, John Ewell, John Bapp, and Xavier Oweger.

POWER PLANTS

The community's first electric power plant was incorporated in 1883 as The Edison Electric Illuminating Company of Piqua, Ohio. The plant was built by the Ohio Edison Electric Installation Company of Cincinnati (incorporated in 1883) and began operations on April 30, 1884 at 8:00 P.M. There were over fifty lights (ten candle power each) at eight locations on that first night. The first private home with electric lights turned on that same night was the home of Harvey Clark at 628 North Main street. The plant was located at 118 East Water Street and used a hundred horsepower steam engine fueled by coal to run two bipolar "Y" direct current dynamos. The plant could send power no further than two miles and operated only from sundown to sunup. Piqua was the second or third electric power plant in Ohio. Tiffin had the first operating plant in January of 1884 and Middletown may have beat Piqua by several weeks in opening their plant. When the Tiffin plant opened it was the third electrical power plant in the nation. The city's first arc lights were introduced in the clothing store of A.W. Loewi on the northwest corner of Main Street and the public square in 1889.

The Piqua Electric Light and Power Company took over the old Edison plant in 1889 and added an alternating current dynamo for street lamps and to furnish power to the **street electric railway** system. In the early 1890's, 110 volt service was begun. A new plant was erected at 113-123 West Sycamore in 1899-1900. Piqua Electric was sold to the Miami Light Heat, and Power Company (later became Dayton Power and Light Company) in 1903. The new company finished the Piqua Electric plan for hot water lines for local homes and businesses. In 1911, the company was furnishing plans for home lighting installation and electric signs for businesses, as well as selling electric household appliances.

In 1931, the Citizens and Taxpayers League was formed by Harry Croner and **Maurice Wolfe** to promote the building of a city light and power plant. The city passed the idea at the November 3, 1931 election by a margin of two to one. The new plant cost a total of $854,000 and began operations in October of 1933 with two 4,000 kilowatt turbines. By the end of the year, the plant was serving 3,432 of an estimated 5,000 local customers. The city began promoting the use of electricity and electrical appliances, totting the cheap city electrical rates. Appliance store manager Homer Monroe advertised in 1935 that his home at 309 Spring Street had the first all electric kitchen in the city with an electric range, mixer, dish washer, refrigerator, toaster, percolator and waffle iron. Additions were made to the plant in 1939, 1948, 1952, and 1961. Three main substations were constructed in 1957.

The Pioneer Rural Electric Cooperative was incorporated in 1936 to provide electricity to the Miami County's rural areas. The Co-op received its power from the Piqua power plant.

In 1959, work began on the construction of a Piqua **nuclear power** facility. The nuclear plant began producing steam in 1963, but was closed down only three years later. SEE ALSO: Street Lights.

The generator room in the Piqua Municipal Power Plant.

PRAIRIE STYLE ARCHITECTURE

The only example of a local variation of the Prairie Style was built in 1913. This style was begun by architect Frank Lloyd Wright. Low horizontal lines and asymmetrical openings are typical of this style. Extended eves over earth tone bricks and stucco with prominent wall banding and narrow vertical windows help give this style its very distinctive look. Piqua's example of this style was designed by architect Harry Williams from the Dayton firm **Schenk & Williams**. The prime contractor for the house was Piqua builder **Airhart M. Fry**.

DOMESTIC EXAMPLE

620 Caldwell, **Allen G. Rundle** House, 1914

PREHISTORIC PERIODS AND CULTURES IN OHIO

PALEO-INDIAN PERIOD 10,000 B.C.. to..6,000 B.C.
    Clovis Period .... 10,000 B.C.. to..8,000 B.C.
    Folsom Period .... 8,000 B.C.. to..6,000 B.C.
ARCHAIC PERIOD............ 8,000 B.C.. to..1,000 B.C.
    Early Period...................... 8,000 B.C.. to..6,000 B.C.
    Middle Period.................. 6,000 B.C.. to..4,000 B.C.
    Late Period .... 4,000 B.C.. to..1,000 B. C.
WOODLAND PERIOD .... 1,000 B.C.. to..1,000 B.C.
    Early Period...................... 1,000 B.C.. to......100 B.C.
    This period was dominated by the **Adena Culture.**
    Middle Period..................... 100 B. C.. to.... 300 A. D.
    This period was dominated by the **Hopewell Culture**.
    Late Period ....300 A. D.. to..... 900 A.D.
    This period saw the growth of the Intrusive-Transitional Culture.
MISSISSIPPIAN PERIOD ....900 A. D.. to.........contact (1600-1700)
    This period was dominated by the **Fort Ancient Culture**.

PRESIDENTS

The following presidents or presidential candidates visited Piqua between 1812 and 2004. The Presidential Campaign of 1912 was the most active time of candidate visitation in the city's history. The dates after each name refer to the year(s) during which that individual visited Piqua. The individuals listed below include those who were actively campaigning and those who were visiting either before or after their own political campaigns.

William Henry Harrison (Whig Party)   1812, 1837, 1840
John C. Fremont (**Republican Party**)   1863
Abraham Lincoln (Republican Party) (Funeral Train) 1865
Rutherford B. Hayes (Republican Party)   1883, 1892
Grover Cleveland (Democratic Party)   1887
Thomas A. Hendricks (Vice President) (Democratic Party)   1884
Benjamin F. Butler (People's Labor **Greenback Party**)1884
Benjamin Harrison (Republican Party)   1889
William McKinley, Jr. (Republican Party)   1891, 1892
William Jennings Bryan (Democratic/Populist Party)   1896, 1915, 1919
Eugene V. Debs (Socialist Party)   1910
Theodore Roosevelt (Republican/Bull Moose Party)   1912
William H. Taft (Republican Party)   1912
Thomas Woodrow Wilson (Democratic Party) (Campaign train)   1912
Warren G. Harding (Republican Party)   1910, 1912
James M. Cox (Democratic Party)   1912, 1920
Harry Truman (Democratic Party) (Campaign train)   1948
Ronald W. Reagan (Republican Party) (Campaign train)1984
Robert Dole (Republican Party)   1996
George W. Bush (Republican Party) (Campaign bus)   2004
    SEE ALSO: Elections; Parades; Politics.

PRINTERS & PRINTING

Early **newspapers** beginning with the *Piqua Gazette* also served as the community's first job printers. These early presses were hand powered with handset type. Late twentieth century Piqua printers included Miami Printery at 216 West High Street, Quality Quick Printing at 531 North Main Street and Eagle Printing located at 318 North Wayne Street established in 1986 by the De Laet Family. The invention of photo copiers (after **World War II**) and computerized desktop publishing (1990's) changed the world of printing making it more diverse and more accessible.

Teddy Roosevelt, gave a campaign talk at the Plaza Hotel in 1912.

Right:
The Strand Theater on the east side of the public square is decorated for the 1920 presidential campaign of Warren G. Harding.

PROHIBITION

The City Council of Piqua passed an ordinance on June 23, 1874 that prohibited the selling or giving away of alcoholic beverages on the Sabbath Day. The ordinance also prohibited saloons or taverns from being open or having any lights burning on Sundays. This was the first local legal ban on the sale of alcohol. A second law, passed in December of 1874, attempted to ban the consumption of alcohol at any establishment where it was sold. This law was weakly enforced and generally ignored. The city expanded its control of drinking with an 1883 ordinance that punished public drunkenness or persons in a "state of intoxication" with a fifteen dollar fine. In February of 1894, the city passed a second "Sunday Ordinance" to reinforce the 1874 law.

After the turn of the twentieth century, the State of Ohio passed the Rose Law that allowed counties to decide whether to be "dry" or "wet". In 1908, Miami County first voted itself dry. The county would swing back and forth several more times until 1920, with the last dry spell coming as a temporary national prohibition during World War I. In 1908, **brewer** Carl Schnell, stated that if he could not sell his beer in his own hometown then he would not sell it at all. Schnell went to his brewery on the banks of the Great Miami River and lined his beer casks up along the river. One by one he broke open the great casks, spilling the beer into the river. Local legend says that the men standing on the East Ash Street bridge to watch this event, openly wept at the terrible sight. Twelve years later, the city's last brewer, the Lange Brewing Company, turned to milk bottling and distribution.

On December 18, 1917, the Eighteenth Amendment to the United States Constitution was passed by Congress. After ratification by the states, the amendment became the law of the land on January 16, 1920, beginning National Prohibition. The city waited four years after national prohibition (1920) before passing an anti-liquor ordinance on March 17, 1924. The ordinance outlawed liquor in any form with the single exception of the use of alcohol for medical purpose by the hospital. One of the major problems of national prohibition was the lack of money for effective enforcement, either at the national or local level. Piqua had its share of bathtub gin and speakeasies during prohibition. Locally they were called "joints". The most common way people by-passed prohibition was by the production of "home brew" or beer. At almost any corner grocery it was possible to legally buy hops, malt extract, and yeast that went into the making of bitter beer. Illegal liquor arrests were most often made for operating stills used to create corn whiskey often fortified with Jamaica Ginger (Jake). The biggest bust for transporting liquor in Piqua occurred in 1927 when a Chevy Coupe was pulled over by police and found to contain over sixty gallons of corn whiskey.

With Franklin D. Roosevelt's election to the presidency, prohibition lost its national support. By the spring of 1933, 3.2% beer was approved for legal consumption. Lange's Brewery reopened in June of 1933, but national competition forced its closing after only a short run. The city's first new bar "Der Rathskeller" opened on July 29, 1933, in the basement of the Favorite Hotel, with live music, sandwiches, and beer. The eighteenth amendment was formally repealed in December of 1933, ending the "Great Experiment". State regulation came about with the establishment of state controlled liquor stores. Piqua's first "State Store" opened early in 1934.

Piqua police arrest records do show a decline in intoxication arrests during the early years of prohibition. Just prior to prohibition in 1919, the total number intoxication arrests for the year were listed at 126. That number dropped to 44 in 1920. But in the following years the number grew steadily, 63 arrests in 1923, 91 arrests in 1926, 165 arrests in 1930 and 168 arrests in 1933.

With the end of prohibition, intoxication arrests climbed rapidly with 214 arrests in 1935, 229 arrests in 1941 and a peak number of 376 arrests in 1946. The 1950's saw a decline in arrests with 308 arrests in 1950, 229 arrests in 1955 and 210 arrests in 1959.

SEE ALSO: Anti-Saloon League; Bryan, William J.; Depression; Prohibition Party; Temperance; Nation, Carrie.

PROHIBITION ERA STYLE ARCHITECTURE

This style name is purely a local designation used to identify a commercial style that was popular in Piqua in 1920 through 1933. There is no domestic version of this style.

The use of the **automobile** became a major factor in both new downtown construction and the remodeling of older structures beginning in the 1920's. The faster pace of mechanized vehicles changed the way potential shoppers viewed shops and the services and goods they offered. Horse and buggy riders could view small commercial signs with ease, automobile, interurban, and bus travelers could not. As a result commercial signs grew in size and in the amount of information they provided. These larger signs obscured portions of buildings that were never meant to be covered.

Storefronts were remodeled to create larger heavily illuminated window display areas to attract customers who would only have a quick glimpse of the offered goods. New structures were often streamlined, with only limited architectural detailing. Fanciful facades gave way to reflective baked porcelain-enameled steel panels (remodeled storefront at 204 North Main Street) or decorations framed by neon lights and signs or structural elements surrounded by small light bulbs.

Traffic and parking became a problem in the downtown area. Speeds of twenty to thirty miles an hour down Main Street led to the installation of stop signs in 1924. Painted on the street, the new stop signs were only marginally effective. The **Miami County Automobile Club** donated the first traffic lights on Main Street in 1927 to help control the increasing traffic flow in the downtown area. Parking of horse and wagons along the city streets had been relatively easy. The city solved one of the only horse-era problems by passing an ordinance that prohibited promiscuous horse hitching (hitching a mare in heat in close proximity to a stallion) in the downtown area. Automobile parking was not as easily solved. Numerous changes in the parking patterns on the public square were tried with only limited success. With the filling-in of the old Miami & Erie **Canal** bed in 1926, off-street parking became available for the first time in the community's history.

Public transportation in the form of the city street car line, the three interurban lines, and beginning in 1930, the City Transit Bus Line competed with the automobile in moving shoppers in and out of the downtown area. It would not be until the 1960's that the automobile would be the sole source of transportation in the city.

The Prohibition Era Style of commercial structure ignored architectural detail in favor of strong and prominent brick facades that would stand out among the more highly decorated buildings surrounding them. Like the speakeasies in Piqua during this period, this style of buildings sported functional, almost plain exteriors that covered a much more exciting interior.

This style has many of the following local architectural elements. The stores are built in a rectangular shape, usually as part of a row of abutted buildings with two or three stories. These structures often used dark brick on a plain façade with a stone banding between floors. The upper floors often have a rectangular decorative pattern in the brick with the corners of the rectangle highlighted by pieces of stone. At the ground floor storefronts, simple plate glass widows rest on undecorated bulkheads that flank a recessed central entrance. There are a variety of window sizes and groupings, however all openings in each story are symmetrical, often with one over one double hung sash windows. There are subdued parapets capped by stone and a flat roof or very gentle pitched roof.

COMMERCIAL EXAMPLES
409 North Main Street, Angle Hardware Building, c.1920's
333 North Main Street, Traction Line Office/Knobby's, 1928

PROHIBITION PARTY

The national Prohibition Party was organized in Chicago in 1869 and became one of the nation's most enduring third parties. However, it was not very effective at electing people to local, state or national office. The Ohio ballot in 1884 presented John P. St. John as the Prohibition Party candidate for president. Piqua was not supportive of St. John giving him only 21 votes out of the 1632 cast. Even the prohibitionist paper, the *Miami Helmet* would not support the Prohibition Party, stating that the **Republican Party** could and would do more for the prohibition cause than a third party ever could.

A local political prohibition movement looked for other political solutions and formed the Prohibition Home Protection Party of Miami and Darke Counties in February of 1884. This was a rival party to the Prohibition Party. The short lived Protection Party (nationally 1881-1884) was supported by the **W.C.T.U.**

In 1888, George E. Lee of Piqua was elected to the State Party's Central Committee. Through the 1880's and 1890's, the Miami County Prohibition Party faithful continued to field county and city slates. However, none of the Prohibition candidates were ever elected.

PROSTITUTION

Prior to the **Civil War**, prostitution did not appear to be much of an issue in Piqua. But after 1880, with the establishment of **Nellie Foster**'s Geneva Hotel on Chestnut (South Roosevelt), prostitution flourished. Foster's operation was close to the railroad and was known to bring in traveling men. Foster's house became the center of a flourishing Red Light District in Piqua until about 1913-1914. Other centers of this illegal activity included the Joseph and Sarah Harris saloon in Rossville. The police raided the saloon a number of times in 1906 and charged the owners with "decoying underage girls to a house of ill fame". Police records often show prostitution and intoxication or the possession of illegal still arrests tied together, but rarely was prostitution tied to an illegal gambling. Some of the communities low end hotels were often the scene of numerous police raids. During the 1930's, the Wayne Hotel at 115 1/2 North Wayne Street was viewed by the police as a house of ill fame. During the 1940's, Hazel Wilson spearheaded a new Red Light District on East Street.

PUBLIC SQUARE

On June 29, 1807, **Armstrong Brandon** began surveying and plotting one hundred and one lots for the new village of Washington (Piqua). Brandon also laid out a public square on land donated by John Manning. The area was given with the stipulation that the Miami County government buildings would be erected there. The county commission decided instead to establish a county seat at **Troy** and from 1807 until 1834, the public square at Piqua was used as a commons for the village. In 1834, the Manning heirs attempted to reclaim the land, stating that the purpose of the square had never been fulfilled. The Ohio Supreme Court decided against this claim and Piqua retained its public square. A few of the major structures on the square included: the Town Hall (1844), Conover's Opera House (1872), **Plaza Hotel** (1891), and the two Piqua National Banks (1898) (1929). The square has been the site for speeches by **William Jennings Bryan, Theodore Roosevelt, William Howard Taft, William McKinley**, John Glenn, and **Don Gentile**. The square has been a popular place for musical entertainment for groups like orchestras, bands, Christmas carolers, medicine shows, and organ grinders.

QUEBEC ACT

This act, which was passed by the British parliament in 1774, extended the boundaries of the Province of Quebec in British Canada south to the Ohio River and west of the Mississippi River. While there were no permanent settlements in the Upper Miami Valley at this time, the area was officially part of Quebec, Canada.

QUEEN ANNE STYLE ARCHITECTURE

The local variation of the Queen Anne Style was popular from 1885 through about 1910. During the mid-1880's and early 1890's, the Piqua Board of Trade began actively soliciting new industries to move to Piqua. The Board's two biggest successes were the luring of the **Favorite Stove and Range Company** and the **Cincinnati Corrugating Company** to Piqua. These two firms alone added over eight hundred new jobs to Piqua. During this same period local entrepreneurs established The Piqua Rolling Mill Company, The **Cron-Kills Furniture Company**, The Orr **Linseed Oil** Company, and other smaller firms. Piqua's economy was booming and new homes reflected this prosperity.

The new Queen Anne Style homes reflected a changing artistic and cultural pattern. The older **Federal, Greek Revival,** and **Italianate** styles appeared too symmetrical and with their plain brick facades, a bit too staid. The late nineteenth century home owners wanted something colorful and architecturally varied. The Queen Anne Style provided for a variety of roof pitches, wall textures and/or materials (i.e.: wood and brick used together), and window sizes and locations. This style provided different wall textures and architectural elements painted in a variety of different colors. Turrets, towers, and extended bays offered the home owner of this period a large number of nooks and crannies. Perfect for the Victorian Age's mania for collecting and displaying everything from clay pots and souvenir bowls to sea shells and drift wood.

The reintroduction of significant exterior porch areas (not popular since the two story side porches of the 1840's and 1850's) met the need of the new social custom of strolling. A formal visit to a neighbor's home involved a great deal of strict social protocol. However a couple strolling down the street could casually visit a neighbor or friend if they were found sitting outside on their new porches. Strolling became so important in society that one of the most frequent building activities of the era was the construction of new porches or verandas. One of the earliest of homes built with the distinctive Queen Anne cutout corners was erected for Ellis Baxter at 508 Caldwell in 1883.

From the 1930's through the 1950's, the Queen Anne Style was viewed as cluttered and over done. Most of the brightly colored areas were painted white and much of the architectural detail was often removed.

This 1946 aerial shot shows the hotel and the square looking towards the north-west.

By the 1960's, the angled parking plan had been instigated as shown in this 1967 photograph of the west side of the square.

Piqua Public Square

Bus traffic was a major issue in the square as shown in this 1946 photograph of the west side of the square at Main and High Streets.

This shot shows the southwest corner of Market and Main Streets in 1948.

*The Barber House on West Greene Street was
designed by J.W. Yost in c.1890 in the Queen Anne Style.*

The Queen Anne Style has many of the following local architectural elements. The houses are asymmetrical in shape and contain two to two-and-a-half stories. Most of the openings are asymmetrical with groupings of window and door openings of different sizes and shapes combined with projecting bays, towers, turrets and/or cut-out corners. The wall textures are varied with wooden shingling topping lower walls or differing wood slatting (direction, shape, configuration) and/or differing brick patterns. The architectural details and shingling were painted in contrasting colors to highlight the details. The window lintels are of a variety of styles and materials. The windows themselves are of differing shapes and sizes and groupings. The use of colored glass, one over one double-hung sash windows, special small multi-paned windows, casement windows, small curved glass attic windows, and round windows are commonly found on houses of this style. Porches are often decorated with spindle-work. Recessed or flush doorways with simple surrounds and doors with carved detailings were popular. The gables are usually decorated with shingles or spindling. Brick homes in this style often use enlarged versions of earlier architectural details such as keystones, dentils and highly decorated stone lintels. The roof pitches are variety with the gabled ends highly decorated. Decorative slate roofing was very common. Queen Anne Style brick houses of unusual size with oversized architectural elements are sometimes referred to as being of the Empress Anne Style.

DOMESTIC EXAMPLES
626 Caldwell, Francis Gray House, 1886
613 Caldwell, Curtis House, 1889
324 West Greene Street, Barber House, c.1890
520 North Wayne Street, **C.W. Orr** House, 1891
528 North Downing Street, John Vallery House, 1899
718 North Wayne Street, **J.W. Brown**/Gutmann, 1902
417 Caldwell, Simon House, c.1908

The Queen Anne Style also has a local commercial variation. The booming economy only slowly changed the downtown area during this period. The population had doubled from 1880 to 1900 and the retail and professional trade in the downtown was growing. However the limited number of commercial lots in the downtown did not allow new construction to grow as rapidly as was needed. With only a few exceptions new buildings meant the demolition of older structures.

During the 1880's the downtown also suffered from the southern and western growth of the city. As housing developed further and further away, it became increasingly difficult for people to reach the downtown to do their daily shopping.

The growth of the neighborhood grocery and meat market was a partial solution to the problem. But these new food outlets were viewed as direct competition to downtown stores. Local businessmen addressed the problem with the construction of the Piqua Electric Street Railway in 1889. The new street car line helped bring the growing community back to its traditional daily shopping center on Main Street. The neighborhood markets continued to flourish and the downtown shops reacted by becoming specialty markets selling what at the time was referred to as "fancy groceries".

Prosperous businessmen and professionals such as A.C. Wilson (druggist) and Dr. Parker invested in the downtown by erecting multi-story brick structures to lure new businesses into the downtown area. This also allowed current business owners to continue with the downtown "shop shuffle". This was when a successful business moved into a bigger shop vacated by a more successful business which had in turn built or moved into even larger accommodations. During the twenty or thirty year life span of a downtown business, the average shop owner would move three to four times. Investment properties and the Piqua "shop shuffle" kept the downtown active and vital.

The Commercial Queen Anne Style has many of the following local architectural features. A store in this style is rectangular in shape (usually is part of a row of abutted buildings) of two or three stories with the individual story being a little higher than the earlier Commercial Italianate Style structure. The commercial structures usually held at least two ground level stores with the first floor storefronts featuring large plate glass windows supported by four to seven decorated cast-iron columns originally painted in contrasting colors. Signs were often painted on the windows while the main store sign was located above the storefront and stretched over half the structure. The entrances are recessed one to three feet with a single wide door containing a central plate glass panel which was topped by a single pane transom window for additional natural light and ventilation. Usually small pane glass transoms extended the entire width of the first floor façade. The secondary entrance to the upper floors was located on one side of the storefront and slightly recessed with a decorated or carved wooden panel door. The upper floor decorative brick sandstone work featured horizontal banding and indentations combined with cast stone insets. The upper floor openings are symmetrically spaced with one over one or two over two double hung sash windows. The upper floor often has a central window or windows of a different size or pattern, from the rest of the windows. The decorative brick, stone, or cast iron lintels (one or a combination of these materials) usually decorated the façade. A decorated cornice is common using corbeled brick tied to enlarged brackets and dentils. The roof is usually sloping or flat. The rear facades often maintain the undecorated Greek Revival style facade with plain stone lintels and undecorated cornices. The upper interior floors were often built with specific renters in mind (such as building in skylights for photographic studios). SEE ALSO: High Victorian Italianate

COMMERCIAL EXAMPLES
418-420 North Main Street, Parker Building, 1891
317-319 North Main Street, Wilson Building, 1887
318-320 North Main Street, **Daniel**-Larger Building, 1888

QUONSET TYPE BUILDING

Locally, this type of building was popular from 1943 through the 1950's. The style was originally used for military structures but it rapidly became popular for utilitarian civilian uses. It was almost exclusively used for commercial structures and storage facilities. This is a prefabricated, steel rib frame, semi-cylindrical building type that was fast to put up on a pre-poured concrete foundation and floor. The large Quonset structure feature wooden frame rectangular fronts with doors and large commercial windows that were added after the building was erected.

COMMERCIAL EXAMPLES
8928 State Route 66
9071 State Route 66
308 East Ash Street

RADIO

The first radio waves crossed the Atlantic in 1901 using equipment invented by Italian physicist Guglielmo Marconi. The first public broadcast in the United States was in 1906. The first wireless receiving system in Piqua was installed in May of 1916 by Thoma and Sons Jewelers. This early radio receiver would bring in official Arlington time signals from the east coast as well as national and international news. KDKA of Pittsburgh became the first regular broadcasting station in the United States in November of 1920. In March of 1922, Powell Crosley, Jr. went on the air with WLW-Radio in Cincinnati. With a regional station now on the air, the first wireless radios were sold in Piqua.

Meteor Motor Car Company announced on March 27, 1922 that the firm would begin manufacturing radios. This would be a very limited venture for the company. By 1926, at least three retail establishments were selling radio equipment. E. C. Scott, an optometrist and jewelry store owner, was the first merchant to specialize in radios when he formed the Scott Radio Company (126 West High) in 1927-28. From 1941 until 1945 **Lear-Avia Company** manufactured radios and radio direction finding equipment for airplanes.

The next major step in local radio history occurred on December 7, 1947. On this date, WPTW went on the air. The call letters "PTW" stand for Piqua, Troy, and West Milton. The new 250 watt station located at 1625 Covington Avenue was owned and operated by the Miami County Broadcasting Company, Incorporated. **Richard E. Hunt** of Troy served as the first President and General Manager. In 1951, the station expanded to include a remote studio at 604 S. Broadway in Greenville. C. Oscar Baker purchased a half interest in the company in 1959. The firm was reorganized as WPTW Broadcasting Station, Incorporated with Baker as President and General Manager, and soon after added an FM station (1960). The station served Miami, Darke, and Shelby Counties. With Baker's death in 1974, Hunt resumed full ownership, and in 1976 he appointed Joanna Hill as one of the area's first woman station managers. In 1985, WPTW added stereo broadcasting and boosted their power to 50,000 watts. On January 1, 1987, the station went to twenty four hour programming. In 1989, the station expanded their market into Dayton with the establishment of WCLR Radio FM, while continuing WPTW as a local AM station. A disastrous fire swept through the Covington Avenue station in 1990. The station was rebuilt and in 1993 the station changes its format from "Clear 95" became "KOOL 95" under the management of Dave Dexter. The station was purchased from Hunt and Dexter in 1997 by Xenia Broadcasting. The station would be sold again in 2003 to Frontier Broadcasting. In 2006, the format changed to conservative syndicated talk shows and live local sports broadcasting. SEE ALSO: Hutchins, Minabelle.

The live WPTW broadcast of the "Our Lives Show" in 1948.

In 1951, Minabelle Hutchins began broadcasting her show "Your Best Bet" on WPTW Radio in Piqua.

RAILROADS

A public meeting was held on February 5, 1836 to discuss a transportation route from Fort Wayne, Indiana to Piqua. Two options were presented to the group. The first was to build a toll road, the second to construct a railroad. The group pushed for a railroad and, in March of 1836, the state legislature passed a bill authorizing the incorporation of the Fort Wayne and Piqua Rail Road Company. The new company was never able to raise the capital to lay the iron track or build the horse-drawn coaches.

When the steam locomotive reached Ohio in 1837, it revolutionized the railroad industry. In 1849, the following local men helped form a stock company known as the Columbus, Piqua and Indiana Railroad: Moses G. Mitchell (merchant), John P. Williamson (druggist), **John Reed Hilliard** (contractor), and Rankin Walkup (architect). The firm's charter was drafted by local attorney **Stephen Johnston**. The townships of Washington, Newberry, Springcreek, and Brown subscribed for a total of eighty thousand dollars worth of the new railroad stock. The City of Piqua, in May of 1851, authorized the railroad company to lay their track on the north side of Sycamore Street. Construction began in Columbus and, by 1856, the route reached Piqua. Local work was under the supervision of engineer **A. G. Conover**. The route terminated in Piqua from 1856 until 1858-59, when it was completed as far as Union City, and then Indianapolis. During this period a roundhouse was built on Sycamore Street west of Roosevelt, and a bridge was erected over College Street. The roundhouse operations were transferred to Bradford in 1864. The railroad turned to east coast financiers in the late 1850's and local financial control ended. The name was change to the Pittsburgh, Cincinnati and St. Louis Railroad by the 1860's. During this change, the line acquired the nickname of the "Panhandle Route". A frame depot was erected in the 1870's on the northwest corner of Wayne and Sycamore Streets. The Railroad's name changed again in 1884, becoming the Chicago, St. Louis and Pittsburgh Railroad (C.St.L.&P). During the 1880's, this route had ten passenger trains stopping in Piqua daily (five going east and five west). During this same time, twenty to thirty freight trains a day would also pass through the city. In 1890, a consolidation of routes resulted in the railroad being renamed the Pittsburgh, Chicago, Cincinnati, and St. Louis Railroad. The panhandle route was taken over by the Pennsylvania lines, Indianapolis Division, in 1891.

The Pennsylvania line initiated two major improvements in Piqua. The first was the construction by immigrant Italian laborer of the twenty-two foot high concrete and earth elevation with double tracks in 1912-13. This was followed in 1914 by the opening of the area's largest passenger station at 110 North Wayne Street. The two story brick station was roughly seventy-five feet by seventy-five feet in size, and connected to the elevated tracks by a covered concrete walkway. Rail traffic reached a peak during World War II, but began gradually to decline during the next forty years.

The passenger station was closed in 1960, and by 1968 the railroad had been reorganized into the Penn Central Transportation Company. The federal government established the ConRail Corporation in 1976, which absorbed all of Penn Central's traffic through Piqua. ConRail abandoned the local tracks in 1983 and began removing them in 1985. The City of Piqua purchased the elevated right-of-way in 1986, and beginning in 1991 started demolishing the elevation.

The second major railroad line for Piqua was the Dayton and Michigan Railroad Company. In 1851, the original line survey for this north-south railroad passed directly through Piqua. A second survey pushed the line one mile east of the city. The line was in operation from Piqua to Dayton by December of 1854. After the Civil War, the line was leased to the Cincinnati, Hamilton and Dayton Railroad (C.H. & D.). The line was running six passenger trains a day by the 1880's, three north and three south.

During 1881, local businessmen joined with the Dayton and Michigan Railroad Company to incorporate the Piqua and Troy

Railroad (P. & T.). For six years the P. & T. remained a paper railroad. Construction did not begin until the summer of 1887, with the last spike being driven on September 30, 1887, by D. C. Statler and Ed Farrington. The line began running four trips daily between the two communities on October 4, 1887. The C.H. & D. had taken over direct control of the route by 1889. The track for this route was removed in the early 1990's.

The Baltimore and Ohio Railroad (B.&O.) absorbed the C.H.&D. in July of 1917. The last "official" steam locomotive, Engine 51 pulling a mail train, came past Piqua in October of 1956. After this date almost all the trains on the B & O were pulled by diesel locomotives. The B & O maintained local control of the line until the early to mid-1960's when it was purchased by the Chesapeake and Ohio Railroad to become the Chesapeake and Ohio, Baltimore and Ohio Railroad. In 1973, the Chessie System, Incorporated, was formed to run the combined lines. Finally in the 1980's, CSX (a holding company) was formed by the merger of the Chessie System and the Seaboard Coast Line. Currently (2007), CSX runs the only railroad line through Piqua. The former B.&O. buildings in the community are all gone. The station east of town was demolished in the early 1960's and the signal tower on Garbry Road 1990.

Three other railroad lines were proposed for the Piqua area, but none of them ever became operational. The city granted the Louisville, Eaton and Sandusky Railroad a right-of-way north of Broadway in 1853. A route was cleared and graded through the city in 1854 and 1855, but the line ran out of money and was never completed. The Dayton, Piqua and Toledo Railroad persuaded the Washington Township trustees to financially support their proposed line in 1872, but the company failed before the

The switch tower was located at the junction of Piqua's two railroad systems just west of the city.

The Pennsylvania Railroad was one of the major transportation systems connecting the city to the rest of the nation. A train is shown here crossing the iron truss bridge over the Great Miami River prior to 1910.

The Pennsylvania Freight Station as shown in this 1960's photograph was located on North Downing Street.

This 1940's interior photograph of the Pennsylvania Railroad Station shows the main ticket counter.

The railroad freight station on Downing Street was one of the busiest areas of the city during the first half of the twentieth century.

township could raise their contribution. The last route proposed for Piqua was an extension of the Lake Erie and Western Railroad. Calvin S. Brice, president of the line, stated that the St. Mary's-Minster Branch would be extended south to Piqua. The extension was never begun.

Miami County had another major railroad line, the Indiana Bloomington and Western, which reached Troy in 1882. The northeast and southwest line changed hands in 1890 to become the Cleveland, Cincinnati, Chicago and St. Louis Railroad, better known as the "Big Four Line". This route passed through the Miami County townships of Union, Monroe, Concord, Staunton, Elizabeth, and Bethel. In 1914, the Big Four Line consolidated with several other lines to become part of the New York Central Railroad Company. In 1968, the line merged with the Pennsylvania Railroad to become the Penn Central Transportation Company which, in 1976, became the ConRail Corporation. During the 1980's, the tracks were abandoned.

At the beginning of the twentieth century (1900), railroad traffic was growing but railroad building was ending. With the exception of a few minor side tracks, new railroad construction virtually ended in Miami County by 1900. A state report for 1900 credits Miami County with a total of 157.73 miles of railroad track. By 1991, a large portion of the railroad tracks in the county had been removed. Only the approximately forty miles of CSX line remains functional in the county in 2007.

The Pennsylvania Railroad Passenger Station was located on North Wayne Street. It was the area's largest passenger station and served the city from 1914 until 1960.

RANDOLPH SLAVES

John Randolph of Roanoke, Virginia, died on May 24, 1833. In his will, he designated that all of his three hundred slaves be set free. The Randolph family contested the will, and it was not until 1837 that the slaves were formally manumitted (freed). Eight thousand dollars from the estate was given to the former slaves to enable them to purchase land in Ohio. Judge William Leigh administered the estate. He purchased thirty-six hundred acres of land in Mercer County next to the black community of Carthagena. When the Randolph Slaves arrived by canal boat at New Bremen, Ohio in 1846, they were not permitted to disembark. Many local white settlers feared that the addition of three hundred black settlers to Carthagena would allow the black community to dominate the county. The freed blacks returned south along the canal to settle in scattered small communities in Shelby, Miami, and Montgomery counties. One of the major settlements was east of Piqua at **Rossville**. Other settlements in Miami County included **Hanktown** and **Marshalltown**. SEE ALSO: African-American

RED CROSS

WORLD WAR I. On April 6, 1917, the United States declared war on Germany and formally entered the World War. Two months later, on June 15, 1917, an organizational meeting was held for the Piqua Chapter of the American Red Cross. James L. Black chaired the first meeting which, was held in the Greene Street M.E. Church on Wayne and Greene Streets. J. Ben Wilkinson, an insurance agent, was elected the Chapter's first formal chairman. A board with forty-seven members was also selected. The first chapter board was made up of a wide range of people from the mayor to the chairman of the Ministerial Association, and from the president of the Central Labor Union Council to the president of the Miami County Humane Society. The Chapter's activities included: the production of surgical cotton bandages, knitting sweaters, stocking caps, socks, mufflers, and the "French caps" for American soldiers or Doughboys serving in France. Locally oriented activities included aid to dependent families of soldiers, local disaster work, furnishing public nurses, and feeding soldiers passing through the city at the Pennsylvania Station on North Wayne Street. Chapter funding came in part from Piqua's share of the Miami County War Chest drives and from private fund raising. The Chapter's chief fund raisers were **Leo M. Flesh** (President of **Atlas Underwear Company**), **John P. Spiker** (President of **Superior Underwear Company**), and Allen D. Hance (President of **Imperial Under-**

wear Company). After the war, Red Cross work slowed down and significant activities did not resume until the **Depression** Era of the 1930's.

WORLD WAR II. In 1940, the Chapter reorganized with a larger board and expanded responsibilities for Springcreek, Washington, Brown and Newberry Townships. John C. Cron chaired the expanded Chapter with Mrs. Pauline E. Tafel serving as executive secretary. After Pearl Harbor (December 7, 1941) and the American entry into World War II, the Piqua Chapter added a surgical dressing unit, a camp and hospital project, and a blood donor service (March 1943). By the end of the war in 1945, the Piqua Chapter offered over nineteen different services. From 1942 until 1945, over two thousand local citizens served over 175,000 volunteer hours in various Red Cross services. The canteen committee served in excess of eight thousand lunches for departing draftee and returning veterans. A POW club was organized to help the families of prisoners. In a repetition of World War I, local committees knitted sweaters, socks, gloves, mufflers, caps, and blankets for "GI's" overseas. From September of 1942 until April of 1945, the local chapter produced 1,333,000 surgical dressings and collected forty-seven hundred pints of blood. The disaster committee fed, housed, and transported victims of the Pennsylvania Railroad troop train derailment on May 21, 1945 in which one soldier was killed and seventy-four injured. The Camp and Hospital Committee set up and furnished day rooms at Patterson and Wright Fields. During this period, the Piqua Chapter continued its local activities, including first aid training, furnishing nurse's aids, and training in home nursing and nutrition.

The Piqua Chapter of the American Red Cross received a free agency automobile from the Sherer-Bell Agency in front of the Chapter office on the northeast corner of Downing and Greene Streets.

POST WAR. The Piqua Chapter continued after the war with new courses and activities such as water safety, CPR training, boating safety, and baby sitting training. The Chapter became a United Way agency in 1958. In December of 1987, James C. Oda chaired the Piqua Chapter's last meeting. On January 1, 1988, the Piqua Chapter and the Miami County (Troy) Chapter merged to become the Miami County, Ohio Chapter, American Red Cross. In 2002, the chapter merged with the Shelby County Red Cross Chapter to become the American Red Cross of the Northern Miami Valley.

RENTAL HOUSING

In 2000, the United States census listed 8,875 housing units in Piqua. Of that total, 5,603 units were built prior to 1960. With 63% of Piqua's homes being over forty years old, that helps explain why 33% of all Piqua homes (3,001) were rental properties. Many of the nineteenth century and early twentieth century homes were simply too big to serve the smaller families of the later twentieth century. World War II's rent freezes and housing shortages led to many of the larger homes (six to nine plus rooms) being divided up into apartments and duplexes. Rents of between $400 and $650 a month were charged by a vast majority of the property owners in 2000.

REPRESENTATIVES, STATE OF OHIO

Piqua has sent a number of representatives to Columbus over the years. **William McCulloch** was the only one to serve as Speaker of the House. **Ted Gray Jr.** holds the record for the longest service for a representative originally from Piqua.

SEE ALSO: Lists-Representatives, State of Ohio; Politics; Senators, State of Ohio.

REPUBLICAN PARTY

On July 13, 1854, politicians from the **Whig Party**, Democratic Party, Free Soil Party, and the Know-Nothing Secret Society met in Columbus to organize political resistance to the passage of the Kansas-Nebraska Act passed by Congress. The group had many names including the Fusion Party, the Anti-Nebraska Party, and the People's party, but by July of 1855, it had become known as the Republican Party of Ohio. The party's first showing at the polls in 1854 had a decided effect on Piqua. The Anti-Nebraska candidate for the Fourth Congressional District (which included Miami County) Matthias H. Nichols soundly defeated his **Democratic Party** opponent **G. Volney Dorsey** of Piqua by a vote of 10,307 to 4,377. The party showed its power in the election of November 1855 with their gubernatorial candidate, Samuel P. Chase, capturing the governor's seat. 1855 was also the first year the Republicans elected a Piqua man to state office with **Alexander G. Conover** being selected as a member of the Ohio Board of Public Works.

The party was successful in Piqua in the 1856 presidential election when the Republican candidate John C. Fremont, received 601 votes to 391 votes for Democrat James Buchanan. In the 1856 Fourth District's congressional race, Republican incumbent M. H. Nichols once again faced off against Piqua Democrat G. V. Dorsey. The results were the same as the 1854 election, however Dorsey lost this time by only 245 votes (9,417 to 9,172). The spoiler in this election was American Party candidate Phillip Beeman who garnered 369 votes. In the 1860 election, Piqua once again voted Republican, with 636 votes for **Abraham Lincoln** and 423 votes for Democratic candidate, Stephen Douglas. At the beginning of the **Civil War**, Ohio Republicans joined with War Democrats to form a Union Party Convention on September 9, 1861. One of the main speakers at this convention was the prominent Ohio Democrat Dr. Godwin Volney Dorsey from Piqua. He would remain a dominant figure in the party running under the Union ticket banner for the office of **Treasurer of the State of Ohio**. Dorsey was elected in 1861 by a higher majority than any other state official. At the 1863 state convention, Dorsey was renominated as the candidate for State Treasurer. He was the only state official nominated unanimously without any opposition. Dorsey was reelected in 1863 by over 95,000 votes. During the war, Dorsey was a member of the Ohio Republican Central and Executive Committees along with Piqua newspaperman **David M. Fleming** (Central Committee). Dorsey served as the chairman of the Republican Executive Committee in 1864-1865. At the National Republican Union Convention in Baltimore in June of 1864, Dorsey served on the Convention's Credentials Committee. During the 1864 presidential campaign, Lincoln ran on the Union ticket and won Piqua's vote, 694 votes to 435 for the Democratic candidate, George McClelland. Piqua continued its strong presence on the state level in 1865 when local minister and Civil War veteran **Reverend Granville Moody** opened the state convention with prayer. Michael G. Mitchell of Piqua joined the state central committee in 1865. After the early 1870's, Piqua's influence on the state level began to wane with no further local citizens active on that level until the 1890's. This was partially the result of redistricting when Miami County became tied to Montgomery County in its Congressional District. This allowed Dayton to dominate the state political offices and committees. Piqua newspaperman **John W. Morris** took Piqua back to state Republican politics in 1889 with his appointment to the State Convention's permanent organization committee and his election to the state central committee in 1895. Morris was the campaign manager for state senator **McPherson Brown** from Piqua who held office from 1894 through 1897.

The Republican Party was however firmly entrenched in the City of Piqua. From 1870 until World War I, the local Republican Party formed an election club every four years to work for Republican presidential candidates. The clubs, with names such as the Lincoln Club, and the Blaine and Logan Club (1884), organized ward clubs, drill teams, drum corps, glee clubs, and parade committees. The local Republican Clubs also brought in big names to give speeches supporting state and local candidates. Speakers included: **Rutherford B. Hayes**, **William McKinley, Jr.**, **William Howard Taft**, and **Warren G. Harding**.

Local Republican politics concentrated on the mayor's office, the city council, the county commissioners and county offices. From 1880 until his death in 1912, the most influential Republican in Piqua was **William P. Orr**, who served for many years as President of the Lincoln Club and chairman of the Miami County Republican Committee. Orr also vied with Democrat **Henry Flesh** for control of the city council as council president. From 1875 until 1900, Orr was President for fifteen years and Flesh for seven years. The two parties also jockeyed back and forth trying to control the mayor's office. From 1875 until 1929, the Republicans elected eight mayors for a total of eighteen years, compared to six democratic mayors serving a total of twenty-five years. During the last two decades of the nineteenth century, Piqua was fairly evenly split between the Republicans, who dominated the western and northern wards, and the Democrats, who did the same in the eastern and southern wards. In the twentieth century, the party was dominated by **William McCulloch** from 1932 until 1973. McCulloch served as Ohio's Speaker of the House before moving on to the United States House of Representatives. SEE ALSO: Brush, Emmett; Newspapers; Parades; President.

RESERVATIONS, NATIVE AMERICAN (OHIO)

By 1820, Ohio contained the following Indian Reservations; Lewistown, Wapakoneta, Wyandot (Upper Sandusky), Ottawa, Big Spring, Seneca of Sandusky, and Ottawa on the Maumee River. These areas were all north of the 1795 **Greenville Treaty** line. The reservations were established by several treaties in 1817 and 1818. Most of the reservations were abandoned between 1829 and 1836 in response to the Federal Indian Removal Act of 1830. The Wyandot was the last tribe to leave their Ohio reservations. They concluded a treaty with Colonel **John Johnston** in 1842 and moved to a reservation west of the Mississippi River. SEE ALSO: Greenville, Treaty of; Individual Indian Tribes; St. Mary's, Treaty of; Wapakoneta.

REVOLUTIONARY WAR (1775-1783)

The Revolution's impact on Ohio was relatively limited. The forts that dominated Ohio's destiny were evenly split with Fort Pitt (Pennsylvania) in American hands and Fort Detroit (Michigan) in British hands. Both sides tried to influence the various Indian tribes in Ohio, with the British being the most successful. Major activities in the Ohio country during the period included: **George Rogers Clark**'s campaign against the Indians, the building of Fort Laurens, and the massacre of the Moravian Indians. The Peace of Paris in 1783 ended the war and gave the new United States legal claim to the Ohio Country. SEE ALSO: Bird, Henry; Boone, Daniel; Boyer, Lewis; Cornstalk; Darke County; Girty, Simon; Montgomery County; Piqua, Battle of; Shelby County

RICHARDSONIAN ROMANESQUE STYLE ARCHITECTURE (1890-1895)

The local variation of the Richarsonian Romanesque Style was popular from 1890 through 1895. There were no domestic examples of this style built in Piqua only commercial ones. This style was introduced into the city by Columbus architect **Joseph W. Yost**. In 1889, his local designs included the First Presbyterian Church (Ash and Caldwell), the Schmidlapp Free School **Library** (509 North Main), the Scott-Slauson building (Ash and Wayne), and the North Street School. The following year Yost designed Piqua's largest structure, the **Hotel Plaza** on the public square. Yost is also known for his designs for the Miami County Courthouse in **Troy** in 1885.

His buildings feature rough-faced massive stone walls decorated with intricate carvings of animals, ivy vines, and human faces. On most of his Piqua structures, Yost used stone carver James Whyte to decorate the facades. Community folklore tells of Whyte looking down from his scaffolding and selecting local pedestrians to use as his models. But judging from the number of cherub faces carved into the buildings by Whyte, it is highly unlikely that Piqua's citizenry served as his patterns.

The Hotel Plaza became the centerpiece for the downtown area. Its size dominated the square and its style created a renaissance for commercial and public building in Piqua for the next thirty years. The hotel not only served as a home for weary travelers but also as a major retail center with its upscale multiple storefronts.

Richardsonian Romansque Style has many of the following local architectural elements. The structures were roughly rectangular in shape with two to five stories. The front facades feature rough-faced squared stone work covering a basic brick structure. Massive and wide rounded stone work arches top the recessed windows. These windows have a variety of sizes and groupings and usually contain only one pane of glass per sash. The use of large stained glass windows is very common. There are often fixed transoms over the ground floor windows. Strong cornices and parapet elements sometimes include small curved attic windows. Stone or decorated metal screen bulkheads support the first floor plate glass windows. Rounded and recessed entrances were prominently highlighted by stone pillars or columns. The interior spaces were often supported by solid cast iron beams and pillars.

COMMERCIAL EXAMPLES

509-511 North Main Street, Schmidlapp Library/Museum, 1890

110-122 West High Street, Hotel Plaza, 1891

212-214 North Main Street, Benkert Department Store, Unity Bank, 1896 (not designed by Yost)

RIVERSIDE, OHIO

This unincorporated subdivision was located on Miami County Road 25-A just south of Hemm Road in Washington Township. It was laid out prior to 1911 and absorbed by the City of Piqua sometime shortly after **World War I**.

ROADS

Early Indian trails followed the west bank of the **Great Miami River** for a north-south travel route. The current location of Main Street in Piqua served as a short cut in that trail, cutting out the east bend of the river. Later military expeditions into the Ohio country also used this route, known as the Detroit Trail (**George Rogers Clark** and **Anthony Wayne**). The first official roads were established in the area after Miami County was formed in 1807. The first new roads to Piqua came in 1808-09 with the building of the Piqua to Fort Loramie Road (northern route), Piqua to Fort Loramie Road (northwestern route, now State Route 66), Piqua to Troy Road (now County Road 25A south), and the Piqua to Urbana Road (now United State Route 36). These early county roads were dirt and gravel with a few cordwood sections. In 1813-14, the county divided the various townships into road districts. Washington Township was divided into seven districts, each with its own paid supervisor. Road taxes in 1821 were used for road construction and repair. The taxes were based on the number of horses, oxen, and wagons owned by each taxpayer.

The Piqua-Urbana Road was rerouted in 1822. The village of Piqua petitioned the state legislature to straighten the road to make a direct connection with Ash Street. The former route is now known as Garbry Road, which connects with East Main Street.

During the 1830's, toll road companies were privately organized and chartered by the state. Tolls during the early years were set by the State Legislature. Foot passengers were charged three cents, a horse and rider six and one quarter cents, cattle, one cent each, sheep and hogs a half cent each. There was to be no charge for travelers going to and from public worship, funeral processions, **militia** going to or from training, and children going to or from school. The toll roads were a vast improvement over the county roads, since they used crushed stone over a smoothed road bed. A few of the toll roads to Piqua included: the St. Paris, Elizabethtown [Lena], Fletcher, Piqua, and Covington Turnpike (1839), the Dayton, Charlestown, and Piqua Turnpike (1846), and the Piqua and St. Mary's Turnpike (1850). The Piqua and St. Mary's Turnpike eventually came under the control of Stephen Widney. In 1889 Widney sold the turn-pike to the Miami County Commissioners. This was the last private turnpike in the county.

In 1914, the first concrete road in the county was constructed from Piqua to Troy (now County Road 25A South). The Interstate Highway Act was passed by Congress in 1956 allowing for federal funding of vast new highway system. Piqua was connected to this super highway with the completion of the road section from Farrington to U.S. Route 36. This section was formally dedicated on July 31, 1958 as part of Super Route 25. The route was completed in the 1960's and renamed Interstate 75. The route it replaced, formerly known as the Dixie Highway, was officially renamed County Road 25-A in July of 1962. Currently (2007), there are approximately 867 miles of surface roads in Miami County. SEE ALSO: Streets.

ROLLER SKATING

In 1885, the indoor roller skating craze hit Piqua. The city's first rink was opened on January 24, 1885, on the southeast side of the public square under Conover's Opera House. Two months later, the Ideal Rink was built on the southeast corner of High and Downing Streets. The rink was 172 feet long and 54 feet wide and reached a height of 18 feet. It would seat seven hundred people to watch six hundred skaters, and contained a bandstand. Not everyone, however, favored skating. In a local newspaper, a Dayton physician is quoted as stating "Roller Skating is the most harmful sport that our young people can indulge in.....". The nineteenth century skating craze faded out and, by January of 1887, the Ideal Rink was leased to the National Guard as a drill site. In the twentieth century, roller skating again became popular prior to **World War II**. In 1939, Alfred L. Maher opened Skateland at the site of a former National Guard Armory at 238 Race Street and 239 Harrison Street. The rink burned down in 1983-84. One of the largest rinks in the Miami Valley was built in 1952-53 as the Piqua Roller Rink at 4845 West Route 36. In 2007, the rink is known as the 36 Skate Club. SEE ALSO: Militia and National Guard

ROSSVILLE, OHIO

This is a small, unincorporated village in Springcreek Township on the Great Miami River directly north of Piqua. The village is split by County Road 25-A North. It was laid out on March 20, 1841, by William Knowles. It was named after Elizah Ross who had operated a small **sawmill** and carding mill on the site. On some maps it is recorded as the Knowles Addition. In 1847, the manumitted slaves of John Randolph purchased lots in Rossville and built several two and four-room frame houses there. In 1866, the African Cemetery was established at the edge of the community. Rossville contained the Second Baptist Church (c1860's-1880's) and a school (1873-1922). In 1978, Mrs. Helen Gilmore and Mrs. Scott established the Rossville-Springcreek Historical Society to promote and preserve the area's African-American. In 2007, Mrs. Gilmore still keeps local African-American heritage alive in her museum in Rossville. SEE ALSO: African-American ; Randolph Slaves.

ROTARY CLUB

Rotary was organized by Paul Harris in Chicago in 1905. The club was originally oriented to large urban areas and Ohio clubs were organized in Cincinnati (1910), Toledo (1912), Dayton (1912) and Springfield (1914). Piqua was the first club to break the small town barrier in 1915.

The local club would go on to sponsor clubs in Troy (1918), Sidney (1928), Urbana (1938) and West Milton (1945). The Piqua club's first president was **William K. Leonard**, the driving force behind the club's organization. The club held its first regular meeting on Tuesday, October 13, 1914. The Tuesday meeting tradition continues to the present (2007). Piqua Rotary was chartered by the national organization on January 01, 1915 as the 135th Rotary Club in the nation. The Club has met in seven different locations during its existence, the **Piqua Club**, the **Plaza**/Favorite Hotel, **Chamber of Commerce** on the southwest corner of Wayne and Water Streets, the Old **YMCA**, the New YMCA, the Elks and the Piqua Country Club. SEE ALSO: Patron p. 271

ROWAN MEMORIAL

Jacob G. Schmidlapp of Cincinnati presented a cannon and a granite memorial to Piqua in honor of Vice Admiral **Stephen**

The Rowan Memorial Cannon (1909) is shown in this postcard view of the Favorite Hotel (Plaza) (1891), the public square and the Piqua National Bank building (1898).

Clegg Rowan, who had lived in Piqua from 1818 until 1825. The monument was dedicated on October 13, 1909, with a large parade and a speech by Ohio Governor Harman. It was located in a small park on the northwest corner of the public square. In response to the need for additional downtown parking, the city moved the cannon, cannonballs, and monument to the east end of the Shawnee Bridge. In 1942, during **World War II**, the cannon and cannonballs were donated by the city to one of the local scrap drives. By 2006, a replica of the cannon was placed on the granite base.

ROWDY, FORT

This fort was established by elements of General **Anthony Wayne**'s army in 1792. It was located at the mouth of the Greenville Creek on the Stillwater River at the future site of Covington, Miami County. The log blockhouse was used for supplies until 1795. A second block-house was built on this site in 1812 and named **Fort Buchanan**.

RUBBER

On May 16, 1898, **William K. Leonard** of Piqua discovered a process for producing a rubber substitute from corn oil, sulpher, and paraffin. The process was patented on December 13, 1898. It is unknown if Leonard ever produced rubber in the Piqua area.

ST. MARYS, TREATIES OF

In 1818, a series of treaties were negotiated at Fort Barbee by Lewis Cass, Governor of the Michigan Territory, with the **Wyandots, Delawares, Miamis, Senecas, Ottawas**, and **Shawnees**. Cass was assisted by Indian Agents **Colonel John Johnston**, B. F. Stickney, and Interpreter Francis Duchouquet (Piqua). The first treaty, signed on September 17, granted **reservations** at Upper Sandusky (55,680 acres) to the Wyandots, at Big Spring (16,000 acres) to the Wyandots, at Wapakoneta (12,800 acres) to the Shawnee and Seneca, and at Sandusky River (10,000 acres) to the Seneca. A second treaty, signed on October 3, granted to the Delawares $13,312.25 for claims which were to be paid by agents at Fort Wayne and Piqua. A third treaty, signed on October 6, granted small tracts of land to individual members of the Miami tribe and promised annual payment of $15,000 in silver to the tribe, in addition to building a gristmill, sawmill, and supporting a blacksmith and a gunsmith.

SALES TAX

On January 27, 1935 at 12:01 AM, all local merchants were required to start collecting the state's new three percent sales tax. The merchants used pre-purchased "Tax Stamps" to record each sale.

SALOONS

By the 1870's in Ohio, there was one saloon for approximately every thirty adult men. Native born women often saw the saloon as a moral threat to "home and hearth". But many of the German immigrants saw the saloons/beer gardens as family gathering areas. Late nineteenth and early twentieth century saloons offered their customers cheap food such as sandwiches, soups, oysters and other inexpensive delicacies. In letters protesting the **temperance** movement in the 1870's, local **brewers** and saloon owners stated that saloons offered the highest form of brotherhood. The temperance movement did not seem to have a profound effect on the popularity of saloons in Piqua. Prior to the beginning of the **W.C.T.U.** in Piqua in 1874, there were approximately nineteen saloons (1870). Twenty years later in 1890, the number of local saloons had grown to forty.

SALVATION ARMY

The Salvation Army was founded by William Booth in London in 1865 and adopted the name Salvation Army in 1878. A year later, in 1879, the Army started in Philadelphia and by 1885 had spread to Ohio. Piqua's connection to the Army began in June of 1886 when a letter in the *Miami Helmet* suggested that the Army rent the empty Ideal Skating Rink in Piqua for their mission meetings. The Rink would instead be rented to the local unit of the Ohio National Guard in January of 1887. Piqua's start came from the success of Sidney's first Army meetings in January of 1887. Sidney's outreach hit the city in April of 1887. A facility was rented on the southeast corner of Main and Greene at the Border Hall. Captain and Mrs. Hinton, assisted by Cadet Clark of Sidney took charge of the new facility. Open air meetings and marches were held every evening with an indoor meeting held at 8:00 PM. On Sundays, meetings were held out of doors at 7:00 AM, 10:00 AM, 2:30 PM, 7:00 PM and indoors at 8:00 PM. The notice to the Salvation Army's *War Cry* was that the Piqua Corps had "Opened ground, large crowds, devil defeated. Hallelujah!" The local *Miami Helmet* reported that a group of thirty or so men and boys regularly disrupted meetings and marches with mocking and yelling. The Army's presence this first time was rather short lived with the Piqua Corps shutting down in July of 1887. The Army tried to establish a corps in Piqua several times with limited success starting in 1901 with Ensign Ward and Lt. McDonald (closed in 1902), with Captain and Mrs. Pond in 1905 (closed in 1911), briefly during **World War I** and finally in 1923 with Commandant and Mrs. C.E. Smith with their operations being headquartered at 507 North Main and by 1928 at 538 South Main Street. The Salvation Army moved to 129 South Wayne in 1933 and a new citadel was built at this site in 1953-1954. The Salvation Army is currently (2007) an active church and social service agency (headed by a community Advisory Board) in Piqua. The Army is one of the United Way's original service organizations. SEE ALSO: Militia and National Guard

SAWMILLS

This early **industry** was responsible for the demise of the **log cabin**. The local sawmills made the production of lumber and shingles a vital part of the village of Piqua's architectural growth. The first known local sawmill was begun by Samuel Wiley prior to 1815 near the mouth of Rush Creek on the east

Bing's, located at the southeast corner of Young and Weber Streets and shown in this 1978 photograph, has been a family tavern for several generations.

Saloons In Piqua

The interior of the Schnell Saloon in about 1905 shows the traditional polished bar and decorative posters.

The lads stopped to have a beer in the rear garden area.

The J.G. Schnell Saloon, was a German beer hall located at 117 Market Street.

bank of the Great Miami River (later site of Rossville). Other early local sawmill owners prior to 1830 included: William and John Wiley, John and Willard Manning, Robert Hars, Robert Aldrich, William Berry, Abram Miller and John and Abner Keyt.

SCHENK AND WILLIAMS

This Dayton architectural firm was responsible for the design of the **Piqua Club** (1907), the **Prairie Style** Rundle House at 620 Caldwell (Harry Williams) and the remodeled **City Hall** Building (1927).

SCHOOLS

Piqua's first school was a small log structure, erected in 1808 on South Main Street at Wood Street. The second school in Piqua was built in 1809 on the northeast corner of Main and High Streets. It was built of logs, thirty feet by twenty feet, chinked with clay. There were two windows covered by greased paper or "foolscap". One wall of the school was taken up by a stone fireplace. The students were seated on a row of writing benches formed into a U-shape, open to the fireplace. Discipline was extremely harsh, with some students being hung by their thumbs and flogged for breaking the strict rules of the school. Educational methods enforced rote memorization, and discussions or original thinking were discouraged. In 1817, a third school was built on the southwest corner of the public square. It was a brick structure, thirty feet by thirty feet, built by public subscription. It burned to the ground in 1831.

All of Piqua's first three schools were semi-private, with each student paying a fee based on a sliding scale that depended on the number of courses taken. In 1834, an advertisement for the private or "select school" known as H. D. Woodworth's English School, listed the following courses: reading, spelling, writing, arithmetic, English grammar, geography, history, natural philosophy, chemistry and composition. The average cost for the twelve week course was four dollars per student. Select schools were taught in the academy, local churches, and private homes. Early private school **teachers** included: John Vaile, James H. Anderson, Nathan Dow, Ardivan Rogers, George Parker, Robert McMurdy, Jonathan Fairbanks, and Mrs. Nancy. A. Evans. In 1854, Mary T. Bunyan opened the first select school strictly for young **women**. It was located on Spring Street, and lasted until 1858.

The city built three public elementary school buildings in 1845. They were located on Caldwell (Northwest House), Wayne (South House), and Harrison Streets (East House), each standing two stories tall with dimensions of forty by twenty-eight feet. These schools were run by a Board of Managers (the Managers dissolved in 1854).

The next major step for public schools in Piqua was the establishment of a Union School System with a high school. This had become allowable by an Ohio law passed in February of 1849. The question was put to a vote on October 11, 1853 and passed by a margin of 289 to 13. With the system approved, a Board of Education was elected on October 29, 1853. The board consisted of Dr. **Godwin V. Dorsey**, **William W. Wood**, J. D. Holtzerman, William T. Humphreville, William Scott and J. T.

Janvier. The Board met for the first time on November 5, 1853 in Janvier's offices, and elected G. V. Dorsey President. The first re-election for new board of education members was held in October of 1855. There were no formal candidates or even ballots, each citizen just came to the city hall and wrote down a name of an individual that they favored. The top four names were elected (G.V. Dorsey and W.W. Wood for three year terms and W. J. Lawton and M.H. Jones for two year terms). The central part of the Union School System was the building of a high school, and by October 1856, that had been accomplished. The new school was located on College Street on two plus acres of land purchased from Matthew Caldwell. Construction was completed for just over $34,000. A. G. Chambers served as the high school's principal, as well as school superintendent, for an annual salary of eleven hundred dollars.

The high school curriculum included: English grammar, composition, music, geometry, trigonometry, algebra, philosophy, biology, elocution, Greek, Latin, French, and German, as well as daily Bible readings. The sexes were strictly segregated and communication between boys and girls was forbidden. Smoking had become a problem in the schools in the 1880's and the school board banned students "from using or having in their possession cigarettes, cigars, tobacco or pipes either in the building or on the grounds".

North Street Elementary school was designed by J.W. Yost and erected in 1889.

The second high school was designed by architect W.R. Brown and constructed in 562 days in 1884-85 for $44,488.00. At the request of School Superintendent **Bennett**, pneumatic tubes were installed to connect his office with all of the class rooms. The grand opening of the new high school was held on November 16, 1885.

The late 1880's and early 1890's was another big school building boom period. North Street School was designed by architect **J.W. Yost** and built by local contractors Brotherton and Scudder. The school was completed in 1889. **Jacob G. Schmidlapp** gave his family's grocery on Main Street to the schools and paid for it to be remodeled into a school library in 1890. South Street School (designed by J.W. Yost of Columbus) was built in 1890 and Spring Street School (designed by J.W. Brown of Cincinnati) in 1894. The Huntersville School was absorbed by the Piqua City schools at the same time the city annexed the village in 1893. The members of the **Huntersville** Special School District's last board of education were **Andrew J. Cron** (president), James Hilliard, William Graham, Thomas Mitchell, Lovell Brown and board clerk J.W. Ely.

From 1912 until 1914, the third high school was under construction. This three story school continued in use until 1981. The 1920's were another active period for the schools. Piqua instigated a Junior High School program with the construction of Bennett and Wilder Junior High schools in 1925. In the mid-1920's, Mary Mitchell was the first and only teacher of the Crippled Children's School. This was an active part of the school system until 1936. During the 1927-1928 school year, Laura Churchill started a School for the Deaf. The schools also began a religious education course in 1927 to "provide character based on Biblical principals". The thirties saw an increase in professionalization of teachers. In 1911, only eleven Piqua teachers had college degrees. By 1936, the local schools supported forty-five teachers with bachelor de-

The Romanesque St. Boniface Elementary School located on South Downing Street dominated the German Catholic south end.

1890's
Piqua Schools

Piqua went through a school building spurt during the decade of the 1890's.

St. Mary's School served as both an elementary and high school building.

The high tower of South Street School allowed the school bell to be heard for blocks.

Spring Street School was built on the east end of town to replace a decaying and cramped home that had been turned into a school.

grees and eleven with masters. The Piqua city schools also adopted a free textbook plan beginning with the elementary students in 1931 and ending with high schools seniors in 1938.

The first school constructed after **World War II**, was the new Favorite Hill School on South Street designed by Walker, Norwich & Templin of Dayton, Ohio at a cost of $402,000 in 1949. The mid-1950's also saw the construction of new schools at Staunton Street, High Street and Nicklin Avenue. The fourth high school was completed off Looney Road and County Road 25-A in 1981. A new junior high school building was constructed next to the high school in 1999.

School Firsts

1865	The school's first language teacher (German) was hired.
1866	The school's first piano was purchased for the high school.
1880	Telephones were first used to connect the city's schools.
1880	The first single seat student desks were installed.
1882	The school's first music teacher, Professor E.D. Morgan was hired.
1887	The first business course (bookkeeping) was taught in the schools by Mr. Foley.
1888	The first school science laboratory was organized on the third floor of the high school.
1888	The school's used natural gas for heating for the first time, a change from individual wood and coal stoves.
1890	Dr. **C.W. Bennett**, Superintendent of schools established the community's first "Normal School" for the instruction of future school teachers.
1891	Schools adopted Standard Time (established by the railroads) for the first time instead of Sun Time for schools openings and closings.
1910	The first High School annual, the *Piquonian* was issued.
1918	For the first time, prejudice and violence were directed against the schools for teaching the German language during World War I.
1922	Mary Mitchell began teaching the city's first classes for physically handicapped children. The classes were held in the High School auditorium off of West Ash Street
1935	Teachers were given their first days off with pay, five days of absence that could not be accumulated from year to year.
1941	Teacher's salaries are paid in twelve month rather than in ten month installments for the first time.
1946	For the first time, all newly hired teachers were required to have four year degrees.
1946	For the first time, the Board of Education presented a salary schedule that did not separate salaries by gender.
1946	The Piqua Education Association was first organized.

SEE ALSO: African-American; Colleges and Business Schools; High School; Lear Avia; Library; List-Schools; List-Principals; List-Superintendents; Roads; Patron p. 285; Piquonion.

SECOND EMPIRE STYLE ARCHITECTURE

The local variation of the Second Empire Style was popular from 1865 through 1890. By the end of the **Civil War**, local industrialists wanted a way to show off their new found wealth and prominence. This style provided a grand structure at a relatively low cost. Earlier **Greek Revival** and **Italianate Style** homes were purchased and mansard roofs with decorative slate tiles added to make a new third story. Mansard roofs have steep vertical sides with prominent dormers that provide sufficient head room to make a full story of usable space for the remodeled homes. In some of the Second Empire Style homes, the added space was used for dances floors and in others they housed the servants' quarters. Many of these Second Empire homes retained the window and door characteristics of the earlier styles. The mansard roof is the distinguishing element of this style.

Commercial structures in the 1880's and 1890's used the mansard roof to added grandeur to the front façade as well as a third or fourth story storage space or lodge hall. None of the grand commercial mansard roofed structures on Main Street have survived. During the 1970's and 1980's several commercial structures were remodeled using a protruding pseudo-mansard roof (often with a shingle façade) to cover the upper floors.

DOMESTIC EXAMPLES
700 Caldwell, Charles C. Barnett, 1868
502 Caldwell, Samuel Zollinger House, 1884
600 Caldwell, **Charles L. Wood** House, 1890

SECOND RENAISSANCE REVIVAL STYLE ARCHITECTURE

The local variation of the Second Renaissance Style was popular from 1898 through 1910. The building of the **Plaza Hotel** (in the **Richardsonian Romanesque Style**) in 1891, led Piqua into a large building explosion during the next thirty years. The Second Renaissance Revival Style was well suited to the three to five story buildings being constructed. By the mid-1890's, the highly decorated and unsymmetrical buildings of the **Queen Anne** and **Victorian Italianate** variations were going out of style. Classical styles and symmetry became the new desirable architectural forms. However, enough of the Victorian need for variety was still in vogue to produce classical forms that changed from floor to floor. The use of differing window sizes, lintels, brick and stone work kept each story zone symmetrical within itself but different from those zones above and below it.

The first building in Piqua constructed in this style was the Old Piqua National **Bank** on the northwest corner of Main Street and the **Public Square** (310-312 North Main Street). To make room for the 1898 structure, the southern third of the 1860 Commercial Block (Barclay's) was demolished. The new bank used the ground floor, while various tenants, including the Ideal **Business College**, used the upper floors. Constructed for bank use, the original first floor of this building contained a deeply recessed arched Main Street entrance. A projecting entrance on the south side of the building encouraged use by those attending the agricultural market on the public square.

The first domestic structure in this style was built for **John Boyer** in 1903 and was known as the Colonial Saxony **Apartments**. This structure was the first building constructed specifically as an upscale apartment building. The basement level contained areas for laundry and servants living quarters. The three story building with its projecting bays contains one of the signature items of the Second Renaissance Revival home, a massive front porch. These porches or verandas had groupings of pillars or columns (or even a mixture of columns and pillars) that supported massive looking pediments and balustrade balconies.

The feel or look of great weight in these porches is misleading. They were constructed with wood framing covered in painted tin to simulate carved stone. Porches and verandas in this style were added to a number of larger Italianate (example Orr House, 515 North Downing) and Queen Anne (example Gray House, 626 Caldwell) style homes. There were no single family homes built in the city in this style.

The commercial-retail variation of the Second Renaissance Revival Style (three to five stories) often used single shop storefronts with large plate glass windows. These stores were the first constructed to emphasize the use of the upper floors as primary retail selling space. This type of structure was also the first to use the electrical elevators. The Orr-Flesh Building on the corner of Ash and Main Streets was the sole exception to this upper floor retailing trend. The Orr-Flesh Building used the first floor for retail space, but the upper four floors were constructed for office and professional space. This was the first true office building in the city.

This style has many of the following local architectural elements. The commercial buildings in this style are square or rectangular in shape with three to five stories showing vertical variations with three or four bays. There is also a horizontal variation with three stories with ten bays as typified in the Buntin-Young Building (406-416 North Main Street). Usually the first floor storefronts had large plate glass display windows separated by narrow cast iron decorated columns with the windows resting on simple bulkheads. These first floor display windows often had retractable awnings located directly above them and small, multi-paned transoms immediately above the awning rods. The first floor signs were narrow and usually contained only the name and store number and often used gilded projecting wooden letters and numbers. The signs were usually located above both the awning and transom windows. Often the facades had rusticated stone work and contrasting brick work with stone quoins around the windows. Each story zone is unique in its configurations of windows, brick and stone work, lintels and differing story heights. However, each story zone is symmetrical within itself in terms of bay openings and spacing of architectural details. It is common to see earlier classical decorative elements used on a larger scale (dentils, keystones, belt courses). The openings are often one over one double hung sash windows or casement windows with transom windows. It is common to find stone or brick belt course between floors and rounded arch sash windows contrasting with rectangular windows. The balustrades were large with prominent parapets and protected from view the very gently sloping roofs.

EXAMPLES

310-312 North Main Street, Old Piqua National Bank/Joe Thoma's, 1898

400-404 North Main Street, Orr-Flesh Building, 1903

221 West Greene Street, Colonial Saxony Apartments, 1903

406-416 North Main Street, Buntin-Young Building, 1903 (vertical variation, with multiple store fronts)

SENATORS, UNITED STATES

No United States Senator has ever lived in Piqua, however Ohio State senators have been elected from Piqua. . SEE: Brown, McPherson; Gray, Theodore; List- Senators, State of Ohio; Representatives, State of Ohio.

SENECA TRIBE

The Seneca were the largest of the Iroquois Tribes and the western most of the Iroquois Confederation (six nations). By 1750, several bands of Seneca had moved into the Ohio country.

These bands were called Mingo by the **Delaware** and **Shawnee** Indians. In the 1760's, the Seneca established a village on the Ohio River near Steubenville, and, by 1800, had moved to the Scioto and Sandusky River region. Several Seneca bands settled with the Shawnee at Lewistown. The Seneca signed the **Second Treaty of Greenville** in 1814. SEE ALSO: Greenville.

SERVANTS AND DOMESTICS

From the 1850's through the end of the **Second World War**, domestic servants were common in middle and upper class households in Piqua. The census returns during the nineteenth century list live-in servants under various descriptions including domestics, housekeepers, coachmen, nurses, butlers, cooks, seamstresses, stewards and matrons. Domestic employment was dominated by women from the age of seventeen to twenty-two, from second-generation rural immigrant families. The 1860 census for Piqua listed 145 domestics. By the 1900 census this number had increased to 230. The increasing number of jobs opening for women in Piqua led to the gradual decline of domestic work in the city. SEE ALSO: Nurses; Textiles; Women.

SHAWNEE TRIBE

The Shawnee are part of the **Algonquian language** family and probably originated from southern Ohio. The Shawnee were a very fragmented people, and from 1700 until the 1860's were located in diverse locations from Georgia to Pennsylvania, and from Ohio-Indiana to Kansas-Oklahoma. The Shawnee tribe was organized into Divisions, the best known being the Pekowi and the Gawikia (Chillicothe). After 1700, the Shawnee were pushed steadily west across Pennsylvania, Ohio, and Indiana. The Shawnee signed the **Treaty of Greenville** in 1795, attended the **Council of Piqua** in 1812, **Second Treaty of Greenville** in 1814, and the **Treaty of St. Mary's** in 1818. In 1831, the Shawnee **reservations** at Wapakoneta, Hog Creek and Lewistown were sold and the Shawnee of Ohio forced to move to Kansas. SEE ALSO: Black Hoof; Blue Jacket; Chillicothe; Cornstalk; Huntersville, Ohio; Piqua; Tecumseh; Wapakoneta.

SHOEMAKERS

During the earliest years of settlement, pioneers made their own shoes, usually a type of moccasin made from deer skin. As the village of Piqua grew, there was a need for what were called "Sabbath shoes". Good shoes and boots for church were expensive and were shipped north from Dayton and Cincinnati. Women and children would walk barefoot to church and, when in sight of the church building, stop to put on their shoes. This saved wear and tear on costly shoe leather.

The first known cobbler, or shoemaker, in Piqua was Nathaniel Whitcomb in 1805. The most prominent early cobbler was Byram Dayton who came to Piqua in 1814. Business accounts of Colonel **John Johnston** recorded Dayton as the family boot and shoe maker in the 1820's. Dayton built a two story brick home and shop at 615-617 North Main Street. His business prospered and newspaper advertisements showed that he was often looking for both apprentice and journeymen shoemakers. Other shoemakers in the 1820's and 1830's were Merrick Martin, Sam Gibson, J. W. Horton, James Clark, and Sam Jacobs.

SHOPPING CENTERS & MALLS

The increased usage of the automobile during the 1950's changed local shopping patterns from downtown shopping to shopping malls and centers oriented towards the automobile. Several shopping centers or strips with huge parking areas to the front were constructed on the west side of Piqua in the early 1960's. In 1969, construction began on the city's first enclosed mall, the Piqua East Mall. This mall was demolished in c.2004. In 1988, the community's second enclosed mall, the Miami Valley Centre, opened for business. SEE ALSO: Patron p. 255

SIDEWALKS

Piqua first mandated prepared sidewalks in public areas in 1856. The materials that were to be used for the new sidewalks included brick, crushed rock, stone and wooden planking.

SOCIALISTS

The Socialist Party of America was formed nationally in 1902 by **Eugene V. Debs.** He would lead the party and become the perennial Socialist presidential candidate until the 1920's when Norman Thomas took on this mantle. The Piqua Socialist Party was organized in about 1906 and ran its first slate of candidates in the 1907 city election. Among the first Socialist candidates were **Addison Bell** for Mayor, Edgar Williams for President of the City Council, and Mrs. Mary Johnson for a seat on the Board of Education. The party drew its strength from factory workers and union members, particularly those employed by the American Sheet, Tin and Plate Company (formerly the **Cincinnati Corrugating Company**), and the **Favorite Stove and Range Company**. The party's political platform in 1907 included: public ownership of utilities, an eight hour day, a two dollar minimum wage for city employees, maintaining public playgrounds, free school textbooks for students, higher salaries for public school teachers, a lower number of students per class, and free school lunches for the needy. The Socialist ticket in 1907 received roughly of five percent of the total vote. The exceptions were the second ward voters who cast twenty-four percent of their votes for Socialist candidates and Mrs. Johnson who received fifteen percent of the city-wide vote. Mrs. Johnson received 940 votes to become the leading Socialist candidate. Despite this encouraging note, none of the Socialist candidates won on their first time out. For the next ten years, the Socialists continued to field candidates at every election with continued negative results.

In 1917 the Socialists were not very optimistic about the party's chances. Voting totals had dwindled since the high vote total in 1912. The party fielded a full city and township ticket in 1917, but it was one of the most inexperienced groups the party had run since 1907. Of the seven candidates for city offices, only two had any campaign experience. At the head of the Socialist ticket was **Frank B. Hamilton** for Mayor. He was opposed by John M. Lloyd (**Republican**), **John V. Daganhardt (Democrat)**, and **J. Harrison Smith** (Independent). This was the first election since the United States had entered World War I, and enthusiasm was high. The campaign started out slowly but gradually heated up. The Republican candidate for mayor was accused of losing city records during his tenure as clerk of the city council. These charges were never proved. Smith, the Independent candidate, became ill and discontinued active campaigning. The Socialist took most of the heat. Henry Kress refused to rent **May's Opera House** to the Socialists because they refused to sign a rental agreement that included a pledge not to criticize the federal government. The party moved their meetings to the public square. James M. Cox, the Democratic Governor of Ohio, in a speech made in Piqua stated that the Socialists were guilty of treasonable utterances. The *Piqua Leader Dispatch*, the local Democratic newspaper, said

that the Socialists were un-American, unpatriotic pro-German, and that a "vote for Socialism is a vote for the Kaiser". Despite the city's **World War I** bias', Hamilton was elected Piqua's first and only Socialist Mayor. He won thirty-two percent of the vote with a plurality of seventy-six votes over Republican candidate Lloyd. Hamilton led two other party members to election as city council members.

1918 and 1919 were not good years for the Socialists. In the city government, most of the party's proposals were defeated by the Republican majority and Hamilton's vetoes were frequently over-ruled. On a more personal level, a major catastrophe hit the party. On October 17, 1918, federal marshals came to Piqua and arrested six Socialist party members; Mayor Hamilton, City Safety Director Herman Grunnert (appointed to the position by Hamilton), City Councilman Louis Neff, and three other party regulars. The men were handcuffed and taken to Dayton on the Dayton and Troy Interurban Line. They were charged in Federal Court with sedition and seditious utterances which violated Section III of the Espionage Act of 1917. The charges revolved around statements the men were supposed to have made in the hearing of their non-Socialist accusers. Statements such as, "Don't buy any Liberty Bonds" and "Let the guys who got money buy them" were entered into evidence against the Socialists. A local newspaper editorial stated, "Now pro-Germanism, treason, and disloyalty can no longer exist". The legal system was not so positive. On December 24, 1918, the Federal Grand Jury in Cincinnati dropped all charges against the six men. The United States District Attorney stated that the case simply did not warrant prosecution.

Ignoring these set backs, the Socialists ran a full city ticket in 1919, with Hamilton running for re-election as mayor. The opposition was almost overwhelming as the Republican and Democratic parties joined forces to create the Non-Partisan Citizens Party. The new organization chose former Independent candidate J. Harrison Smith to oppose Hamilton. Other Non-Partisan candidates included bankers, industrialists, and labor/union leaders. The Non-Partisan ticket began the campaign on a patriotic note stating that the "American flag is the vital issue of the hour". This referred to the Socialist habit of carrying both the American flag and the Socialist red banner in their parades. The campaign soon moved to lower ground with the Non-Partisan campaign asking "If you were heavily armed and a reptilian monster was about to strike to death your innocent child, would you stand idly by?", and local editorials reporting that "in one Bolshevik den of iniquity [referring to Socialist Party headquarters] where Red leaders meet, their vile mouths, when not vomiting riot and revolution, automatically become fountains of filth and sewers of profanity". The November 1919 election gave Smith and the Non-Partisan party a plurality of 951 votes or fifty-seven percent of the vote. Hamilton was defeated, but Louis H. Neff was re-elected to his Second Ward seat on the council. Neff was prohibited from taking his seat through a legal technicality and the Socialists never again held power in Piqua. The party continued with Hamilton and Neff appearing on the State Socialist ticket for Governor and Auditor in 1920. The local party would run its last political ticket under the Socialist name in 1923. The only other appearance of the Socialists came about in 1932 when a reorganized party ran a county slate under the Independent banner. Many of the Socialist programs such as the eight-hour day, higher salaries for teachers, and public ownership of utilities, free school lunches for the needy would be implemented by political organizations that would never acknowledge the Socialists beginnings of these ideas. SEE ALSO: American Protective League; Militia and National Guard; Newspapers; Presidents; Sharts, Joseph.

SPANISH-AMERICAN WAR

The war with Spain over Cuba officially began on April 21, 1898. Two days later President **McKinley** called for 120,000 volunteers. Ohio organized three volunteer infantry regiments to fight in what was called "This Splendid Little War". Company A, Third Regiment, from Covington was organized and called-up in April, and Company K, Third Regiment, from Piqua followed in June of 1898. The Piqua unit, commanded by Captain **McPherson Brown** and First Sergeant Charles W. Bowdle, left Piqua in June of 1898 for Columbus and then to Florida in July to join the rest of the regiment camped near Tampa. In the early fall, the Third Regiment moved to a camp near Huntsville, Alabama. The regiment was mustered out of service in October of 1898. One of the regimental surgeons was local physician James E. Shellenberger.

On the home front, the Sons of Veterans Lodge organized Company I of First Regiment of Ohio National Guard (Home Guard). **William P. Orr** and Dr. James E. Shellenberger of Piqua were appointed by Ohio Governor Asa Bushnell to serve on the Ohio National Guard staff. Orr became Quartermaster General of Ohio and Shellenberger his assistant. The war ended in August of 1898. Several men enlisted in the regular army for service in the Philippines. Edgar F. Wallace received a back injury in the **Philippine Revolution** that would lead to his death in 1904. The local Spanish-American War veterans organized and named their unit in honor of Wallace, the Edgar F. Wallace Camp No. 12, United Spanish War Veterans. SEE ALSO: Home Guard; Lodges and Organizations; Militia and National Guard.

SPRINGCREEK TOWNSHIP

This township was created on June 18, 1814 and named for a creek fed by a natural spring. The township contains 16,085 acres or 28.3 square miles. It is the smallest of Miami County's twelve townships in terms of total size. Four settlements have been established in the township: **Huntersville** (1838), Jordan, **Piqua**, and **Rossville** (1841). In 2000, the township's population was 1,826.

STAUNTON, OHIO

This community is located at the junction of Staunton Road and State Route 202 in Staunton Township. The site was first settled in 1798 when five families, under the leadership of John Knoop, erected a blockhouse there under the name Dutch Station. The village was formally laid out on August 23, 1806, for John Smith. At that time the area was still part of Montgomery County. When Miami County was formed in 1807, Staunton was designated as the first county seat. In 1894, the unincorporated village contained thirteen major structures.

STEEL HOUSES

The first steel house in Piqua was built by contractor/owner Charles H. Vosler at 518 Vine Street in 1936. Known as "Steelox", this fabricated steel home was produced by Steel Building Inc., a subsidiary of American Rolling Mills Company (Armco) of Middletown, Ohio. The local representative for the Steel Building Company was Robert P. Campbell, who serviced Miami and Shelby counties for the firm. The one story, five room homes were marketed as termite resistant, vermin proof, long life with a reduced upkeep and fireproof walls. Vosler would live in his "Steelox" home for almost twenty years.

The second steel home at 1253 West High Street was constructed by the Lustron Corporation of Columbus, Ohio in 1948.

This 1948 steel Lustron Home is located at 1253 West High Street.

The Lustron Corporation built approximately 2,498 homes after the end of **World War II** from 1948 to 1950. The Piqua home is a one story side gable structure with a front façade comprised of steel panels with a baked porcelain coating blue-gray in color (fourteen panels wide and four panels high). The door is set back on the side and the front façade supports two widows each with three paneled sidelights.

The Hobart Welded Steel House Company, a subsidiary of Hobart Brothers of Troy, Ohio built prefabricated welded steel homes from 1937-1941. There are no known Hobart homes in Piqua. SEE ALSO: Architecture

STOUTE-HARRIS POST #6816, VETERANS OF FOREIGN WARS

Most local veterans organizations were racially segregated and African-American veterans were forced to form their own groups. The Stoute-Harris Post was organized in March of 1946 by African-American World War II veterans. The first officers of the post included Marion W. Clemmons (commander), James Ross Sr. (vice commander), Frederick Bowles (Jr. vice commander), Elmer Harris (quartermaster), Napoleon Williams (judge advocate), Ogden French (surgeon), James Davis (trustee), Merchant Page (trustee), and Homer Rial (trustee). The post was named for two African-American veterans, Sergeant **Alex Stoute** (killed during the D-Day invasion at Normandy) and Master Sergeant **William M. Harris** (killed in Italy). Other early members included Charles Dorsey, Edward Evans, Robert Smith, Pat Jones, William Smith, Hal Reaves, Holman Sawyer, James Taylor, Charlie Parker, Jesse Parker, Dave Clemens, Jesse Olden and Hal Reaves. SEE ALSO: Civil Rights Movement.

STREET LIGHTS

The Piqua Gas, Light and Coke Company was organized in 1855, and built a plant at the end of Spring Street. In August of that year, the company erected twelve artificial gas street lights on prominent street corners. By 1856, this number had increased to eighty-nine lights and by 1889, the number reached 133. For the next thirty-three years the city street lights were manually lit every evening and extinguished the following morning. Piqua Gas Company's five year contract came up for renewal in 1889 and for the first time, the contract was challenged. The new electric **power plant**, the Edison Electric Light Company of Piqua promised more lights at a better price, so the city awarded the contract to the Edison Company. During the fall of 1889, forty miles of copper wire was strung to 206 regular lights and five arc lights. In December the lights were turned on and the city streets, according to one source, were "turned from night into day".

STREET RAILWAY

S. T. Dunham of New York was granted a one year franchise by the city council in August of 1888 to lay out a street railway. Dunham failed to make the deadline and three local businessmen took over the franchise, F. C. Davies, A. M. Orr, and **L. M. Flesh**. These men incorporated as the Piqua Electric Street Railway Company on August 8, 1889. A. M. Orr was elected the company's first president. The route was laid out to run the complete length of Main Street (north and south), up South Street to the top of the hill, along Washington Avenue to the cemetery and, finally, an Ash to College Street. The entire route (not including side tracks) was 20,785 feet long. The track was the standard gauge Johnston flat rail. The last spike on the route was driven in by Davies at 10:00 A.M. on December 5, 1889 on South Street hill. On December 30 the cars arrived. They were twenty-two feet long with sixteen feet of interior space. The exteriors were painted yellow and orange on the top and brown and white on the bottom. Using the Sprague System of electrical power supported by eight dynamos, the street railway in Piqua made its maiden voyage on January 3, 1890. SEE ALSO: Interurbans.

STREETS

Piqua's ten original streets were laid out in 1807 by **Armstrong Brandon**. They were Ash (named for a species of tree), Downing (named for a street in London), Greene (named for General Nathaniel Greene), Harrison (named for General **William Henry Harrison**), High (origin unknown), Main (named as the central and most important street), Spring (named for a group of springs located near the river at its south end), Sycamore (named for a species of tree growing near the river at its east end), Water (named for its proximity to the river) and Wayne (named for General **Anthony Wayne**).

The first streets were simply scraped dirt paths, full of ruts and mud holes. The first brick street paving occurred on High Street when Hotel Plaza was completed in 1891. Main Street would not be improved with brick paving until 1895. As the size of Piqua increased, the need for standardized street signs became apparent. In 1907, blue enameled metal signs with white letters were attached to buildings at most of the city's intersections. With the beginning of heavier automobile traffic, the city passed an ordinance in 1924 creating five stop signs at designated intersections. These first stop signs were painted on the street at the intersections of Ash and Main, Roosevelt and High, Union and Main, South and Main, and Broadway and High. The first traffic lights were put into operation in 1927 after the Miami County Auto Club purchased three signal lights and donated them to the city. In 1990, Piqua contained approximately eighty-two miles of paved streets.

STREET TRIVIA.
PRESIDENTIAL STREETS: Adams, Cleveland, Ford, Garfield, Grant, Harrison, Jackson, Lincoln, Madison, McKinley, Roosevelt, Washington, Wilson.
LONGEST NORTH-SOUTH STREET: Main Street.
LONGEST EAST-WEST STREET: High Street.
STREET GOING THE MOST DIRECTIONS: West Parkway Drive, North Parkway Drive, East Parkway Drive.

CIVIL WAR STREETS: Grant, Lee, Lincoln, Sheridan, Sherman.
STREET WITH SHORTEST NAME: Y.
STREETS OF HIGHER EDUCATION: College, Harvard, Yale.
WET STREETS: Brook, Brush Creek, Lake, Lakewood, Mote, Riverside, Spring, Springbrook, Water.
BOYS' STREETS: Alexander, Bryan, Leonard, Peters, RonAire, Scott.
GIRLS' STREETS: Ann, Beverly, Carol, Colleen, Janet, Jean, Margene, Patricia, Sharon, Sherry, Virginia.
MEASURED STREETS: Broadway, High, Long, Short, Upway.
DIRECTIONAL STREETS: North, South, East, Westview.
WOODY STREETS: Ash, Buckeye, Cedarbrook, Cherry, Elm, Elmwood, Forest, Maple Maplewood, Mulberry, Orchard, Pinewood, Sherwood, Sycamore, Walnut, Woodlawn, Woodbridge.
VANISHED STREETS: Bellas (now Grant), Canal (along the canal), Cathcart (now Linden), Cemetery Alley (now Park Avenue), Charles (now Elm), Cheever (now Armory Drive), Chestnut (now Roosevelt) Cron (now Third), Fountain (now Steele Avenue), Harding (now Harrison), Hicks (now Wilson Avenue), Langdon (now Fourth), LaSalle (now Hancock), Linn (now Lindsey), Locust (now Robinson Avenue), Mill Alley (now under river levy on east bank), Neer (now Fifth), Pork Alley (now Mound), Sherman Avenue (now Nicklin), Smithman (now abandoned, south of Fifth), South Avenue (now south part of Roosevelt), Sternberger Avenue (now abandoned, south of Fifth), Stillwater Pike (now Sunset Drive), Texas (now Park Avenue), Union (now eastern part of Wood Street), Urbana Pike (now eastern part of Ash Street), Versailles Pike (now Echo Lake Drive), Welcou (now Miami), and Wolcott (from Wayne to Downing now part of Miami). SEE ALSO: Public Square; Roads; Dublin Hill; Josse's Hill.

STRIKES

The earliest record of an organized local strike occurred on June 30, 1886, when the cigar maker's working in the shop of John Lang (118 North Main) walked off the job. The workers were represented by the Cigar Makers' International Union. The strikers demanded an advance in pay of one dollar per one thousand cigars produced. The Union stated that the workers averaged only six dollars a week. The outcome of the strike is unknown.

This c.1900 photograph shows some of the workers at the Favorite Stove & Range Company.

An example of another early strike was the 1917 strike by the Interurban Brotherhood of Trainmen against the Dayton, Covington, and Piqua Traction Company. The trainmen demanded an increased wage from twenty-five to thirty-two cents an hour.

The cupola men, yard men, milling department, sandblast men, gas department, and common laborers of **Favorite Stove and Range Company** went out on strike in 1919 demanding a twenty-five percent wage increase for common laborers.

The trainmen on the Dayton and Troy Electric Railway went on strike for six days in 1919 asking for a wage increase. The **Union** stated that the average worker received nineteen dollars for a sixty-three hour, seven day week.

290 employees of the Val Decker Meat Packing Company walked out on strike on April 18, 1934 led by union organizer Robert Call. The workers demanded a minimum wage of forty-five cents an hour for women and fifty cents an hour for men.

An Orr Felt & Blanket Company strike was the result of the company closing down the plant in September of 1934. The Textile Workers of America, Local No. 2251, led by Samuel Kendall, stated that the company was using a lockout to try and break-up the union. Federal mediators from the Labor Board failed to bring the employees and employers together. The strike ended on October 13, 1934 with the union not officially recognized and the mill not being designated as a closed shop. However the workers were given the right of collective bargaining and seniority rights were recognized when promotions were made.

A **Cron-Kills** strike in January-February of 1936 led to a pitched battle between special police and strikers on Union Street on February 13, 1936. Three policemen and several strikers were injured. Two strikers were arrested.

Wood Shovel & Tool Company workers went out on strike from January to April of 1946. United Auto Workers, CIO, Local No. 827 led over 300 men for an 107 day strike over wages. The union heavily picketed the plant and at first did not allow anyone to enter the factory or office. The strike ended when the union agreed to a twelve cents an hour increase.

The United Textile Workers of America led a strike against the **Atlas Underwear Company** in the fall of 1936. SEE ALSO: Aerovent Fan Company; Depression Era; Piqua Handle; Tobacco.

SUNNYSIDE, OHIO

This unincorporated subdivision was located between Hemm Road and Manier Street, east of Gordon Street in Washington Township. The subdivision was laid out prior to 1911 and absorbed by the city of Piqua after **World War I.**

SUPERIOR UNDERWEAR COMPANY

This firm was established in 1898 by **John Spiker** on the second floor of a blacksmith shop on the corner of Broadway and Water Streets. James L. Black of Bowling Green, Ohio became one of the investors and the firm moved to Bowling Green in 1900. Late in 1905, Superior purchased the old factory buildings of the **Atlas Underwear Company** on the corner of Riverside Drive and Downing Street. The firm moved back to Piqua in 1906 and by 1909 had completed a new five story plant on the same site to produce union suits. The company grew rapidly and James Black established a subsidiary company known as the Superior Athletic Underwear Company in 1911. The main company expanded with plants in Tipp City (1913-1930) and Bradford (1920). The firm was now producing knit underwear, bathing suits, sweaters and pajamas.

The Superior Underwear Company plant stood on the corner of Riverside Drive and Downing Street. The plant was next to the interurban tracks and the Miami & Erie Canal.

The Great **Depression** hit Superior hard and the company tried to rebound with new products. In 1933 the firm produced *Les-on* and *Short-eez* boxer style shorts as a reaction to bulky union suits. The Coopers Company of Vermont (later Jockey International) produced the first commercial men's briefs with an elastic band in 1934-35. Superior came out with its own version of the brief known as *Gan-dee pants* (named after the brief garment wrap used by Mahatma Gandhi). Superior advertising said it was "A French style short that fits snug". During World War II, the company produced silk parachutes for the military. During the war, the company reorganized as the Superior Inc. and shortly afterwards C. H. Loeffler took over as president with C. Foster Stickler as corporate secretary and general manager. John P. Spiker died in 1946.

The Superior Underwear Company promoted their union suits in this c.1910 advertising postcard.

The company was purchased in March of 1946 by Sol Kittay & Associates of New York City. Kittay sent Dimitri Nicholas to Piqua to serve as the corporate vice president and plant manager. The stock company was reorganized in 1951 as the Onyx Superior Mills Inc. and Kittay purchased the **B.V.D.** name and franchise. The local plant became the B.V.D. Company Inc. The company created some very new and innovative marketing tactics. The clear plastic polybag was introduced to allow customers to actual see the briefs and t-shirts as they were displayed on eye-catching store fixtures. The company began marketing fashion or colored underwear in the 1960's. One of the enduring B.V.D. slogans was "Next to myself, I like B.V.D. best". The local plant was closed down in 1968 and the factory was purchase by the Atlas Underwear Company. B.V.D. would be purchased by Fruit of the Loom Inc. in 1976. SEE ALSO: List-Underwear; Textiles

SWIMMING POOLS

Early swimming took place in the Miami River, the canal, and hydraulic, and other local ponds and streams. The first known attempt to control swimming took place in 1887 when the city council passed an ordinance stating that "swimming with or without suits" is forbidden within the corporation limits before 10:00 P.M. The first organized swimming pool was built in 1894 by the **YMCA**. This was also the community's first and only indoor pool. New YMCA pools were built in 1962 and 1977. Prior to 1907, Phillips' Natatorium was opened to the public. This board and frame aboveground pool was located next to Swift Run and north of the current water works plant on State Route 66. The pool offered covered bleacher seats for women to watch various swimming events. No mixed swimming was permitted at this pool. Lange's swimming pool was opened by George F. and Alex M. **Lange** in June of 1923. The pool was located on the south side of East Water Street at the end of Spring Street. The pool operated from 1923 until 1939-40, and its biggest claims to fame were the two appearances of **Johnny Weissmuller**, Olympic medal winner and later the star of many Tarzan movies.

The Hollow swimming pool almost became a city dump. The city council visited the site located just east of the Miami River and north of the current U. S. Route 36 in 1914. The city was unable to convince owner Will Unkerman that his land, then known as Shinny Hollow was a desirable dump site. In 1930, Walter A. "Arch" McKinney built the Shinny Hollow Amusement Park on the twelve acre site. It included a pool and a forty-eight foot square, two story stone bath house and road house that housed lockers, a dance floor, and a restaurant/lunchroom. In the fall of 1930, the park was taken over by Leon F. Koester and he renamed it The Hollow. The pool was enlarged to three hundred feet, with cement walls and a sand bottom. The deep end went to a depth of nine feet and contained diving boards and swings. A "kiddie pool", seventy-five feet square and two feet deep was added. The pool was managed by Koester's son-in-law, Wiles Kellen. The main pool was filled with artesian well water at a rate of two hundred gallons a minute. In 1936, twenty acres of picnic grounds were added to the site and a sixty-foot toboggan slide. The following year the pool was cut down to a three hundred foot square with a concrete bottom covered by sand with a capacity of two million gallons of water. By the end of the decade, the Hollow had grown to include thirty acres of picnic grounds. The pool had grown with the toboggan slide increased to eighty feet and the addition of two diving boards. In 1974, the city of Piqua purchased the entire site. County and State health regulations forced the city to close the pool in March of 1977 due to an inadequate filtration system.

These men were swimming in the Great Miami River south of Piqua since nude swimming had been banned in Piqua in 1887.

The Hollow was located west of the Great Miami River and was a popular with local swimmers from 1930 through 1976.

The Piqua Country Club added a concrete adult pool (twenty-five by seventy-five feet), as well as a children's wading pool in the summer of 1936. The next pool in Piqua was not opened until August 14, 1958. Tecumseh Woods, Inc. built a private membership pool on sixteen acres of wooded land at 1103 Lenox Drive. The original two-hundred members built a twenty-five meter pool with a diving platform and bathhouse at a cost of $55,000. Tennis courts were added to the pool complex in 1973. In 2007 the pool was still in active use.

The Piqua Municipal Pool resulted from the activities and promotion of the Chamber of Commerce's Piqua Manufacturers Association and the citizen's S.P.L.A.S.H. Committee, headed by Michael Yannucci. The $845,000 complex opened in Eisenhower Park off South Street on May 24, 1986. The pool's first manager was Richard C. Feightner. The 1986 season ended with an average daily attendance of 584. Fees for that first season included season tickets for families at sixty-five dollars, single adult at forty-five dollars, and students at thirty dollars. Daily tickets were available at two dollars for adults and a dollar and a half for students. The pool was open from noon to 9:00 P.M. and had a minimum of three lifeguards on duty at all times. SEE ALSO: Parks.

TANNING

The tanning of animal hides was a skill common to most pioneer homesteads. The uses for tanned hide were varied, including shoes, clothing, caps, rugs, blankets, window and door coverings and harnesses. It was not until the village of Piqua began to grow that tanning became an industry outside of the home. The first recorded commercial tanner was Joseph Montgomery in 1809. His tanning yard was located along the west bank of the Miami River on what would become the 400 block of South Main Street. The yard's location was due to the need for water for the tanning process. Because of the smell, the yard also needed to be outside of town. Montgomery was succeeded by his sons William and Robert, and then Martin Simpson in 1831. After the Miami and Erie Canal cut through the property in 1839, Thomas J. Wiley took over the yard. The Wiley family continued the tanning business well into the twentieth century. Other tanners in the 1820's and 1830's included, William Johnston, McClure and Jenkinson, James Carson, John Brown, William Jones, and M. Haethan. By the 1850's many of these men had moved from tanning to the more profitable business of harness and saddle making. SEE ALSO: Industry.

TAXI CABS

One of the earliest automobile taxi companies was established by a former livery stable (W.F. Robbins & Company) employee, Harry Hance. His firm was established with three

The Dodge Taxi Company vehicles parked outside the Favorite Hotel (Plaza) in the 1940's.

automobiles in 1917 and known as the Hance Taxi Company located at 111 East Water Street. He moved to 329 North Main in 1919, but the firm closed down shortly after that. Hance's competition was intense for a small town. The Yellow Bonnet Taxi Line at 109 East Greene was created by Carl F. Sexauer in 1918. It stayed in business until 1923-24 moving people and baggage. 1918 also saw the creation of a new firm by J. Edward Stengel. He started in the spring of 1918 with the Favorite Taxi Company at 215 Spring Street. By the summer of 1918, the name had changed to the Good Taxi and Baggage Service and finally it went out of business in 1919 under the name the Best Taxi and Transfer Company.

During the 1920's and 1930's, at least eight taxi firms were established: Buick Taxi & Transfer Line (c.1923), Williams Taxi (c.1923-c.1930), Red Top Cap Company of Lima (1924-July 1935), George Lett Taxi (c.1926), Dodge Taxi Company (c.1926-1960) City Cab Company (c.1928), Piqua City Cab (c.1931-1934), Yellow Cab Company (c.1937-1938).

With all this competition, some of the companies tried to specialize their services. In the early 1920's, Clifford L. Burch and his Buick Taxi & Transfer Line had their office above May's Opera House. He specialized in long trips, funerals and weddings and offered the option of open or closed cars.

The People's Corner at the northwest corner of South Wayne and Wood Streets was the headquarters for the Calland Cab Company.

The Dodge Taxi Company would dominate the taxi industry until the mid 1970's. The firm operated out of the Union Bus Terminal at 110 West High Street in the Hotel Building. Later cab companies included the Calland Cab Company (c.1947-c.1948), Piqua Cab Company (c.1954), the Dodge Taxi Company (1960-1974) run by Harold Sheets, the Courtesy Cab Company (1975-1977) by William and Betty Roeser at 410 South Wayne Street, the Jacque's Taxi Service (1977-c.1978) and the Piqua Taxi Service established in 1980 by Robert J. Reddell, president of RJ Industries at 8970 Looney Road. Piqua Taxi held a contract with the City of Piqua for community taxi services.

TEACHERS

The first paid teacher in Piqua was Isaac Henderschott, who began his local career as a young man in 1808-09. He taught in a private **school** at the corner of South Main and Wood Street. Like most local occupations prior to the **Civil War**, teaching was the total domain of men.

Mrs. **Nancy A. Evans** broke the male monopoly in the public school system in 1830. Within twenty years the education field had completely turned around, with men becoming a distinct minority. The glaring exception to this was the position of high school principal, which was dominated by men. In fact, during the first 122 years of the Piqua City School System, there was only one women who has served as high school principal, **Mary E. Hall** (1877-1905). Katherine Davisson became the second in 1977.

In 1856, there were three male and seventeen female teachers in the Piqua system. The teacher's salaries were as follows; the male wage averaged at $50.00 a month, the female wage at $21.92 a month and the **African-American** wage at $20.00 a month. Twenty years later, wages for teachers, while not high, did compare favorably to other occupations for women. The Ohio Bureau of Labor reported that the average wage for women teachers in Miami County in 1879 was thirty-four dollars a month for elementary teachers and ninety dollars a month for high school teachers. Male teachers were listed with monthly salaries of fifty-three dollars for elementary, and ninety-six dollars for high school. As a comparison, an average monthly wage for women in a woolen mill in 1879 was $17.32. The factory worker would have worked on an average a sixty-hour week compared to the teacher's forty hours. The state report for 1905 showed a moderate increase for elementary teachers ($49.17 a month) and a decrease for high school teachers ($73.60 a month). Cadet teachers in 1905 were listed as being paid only a token salary of twenty dollars a month. By 1913, the *Piqua Leader-Dispatch* reported significant advances for teachers. High school teachers earned eighty-eight to one hundred dollars a month. Elementary school **principals** were paid between sixty-six to one hundred dollars a month, while elementary teachers received from forty-seven to seventy-five dollars a month. The pay increases were significant and the differences between the salaries of male and female teachers had narrowed significantly.

However, the major gain for teachers came in 1913 with the addition of a school pension. It was relatively small, but it was a start. After thirty years of teaching within the Piqua system, a teacher could expect a pension ranging from three hundred-fifty to four hundred dollars a year, or an average of thirty-one dollars a month. In 1913, teaching moved from being merely a job to a career.

Working conditions improved gradually over the years from the dark and badly heated and ventilated ward school of the 1860's to the light and airy schools built from 1889 through 1912. The 1891 South Street School was the first school building to eliminate teachers' platforms. This put the teacher's desk on the same level as the students. Qualifications for teaching included a high school diploma, a high moral character, and the ability to pass a standard state teaching examination. These examinations covered topics as diverse as history, geology, botany, astronomy, arithmetic, elocution, and teaching methods. Based on the scores received, teachers were awarded teaching certificates for one, two, three, and five year intervals. Every summer, county-wide schools were held to help teachers master new skills and improve old ones.

The Great **Depression** was tough on teachers, they went without raises from 1932 to 1937. With a four year degree, first year elementary schools teachers in 1933 made $1,000 a year. First year male high school teachers made $1,300 a year and

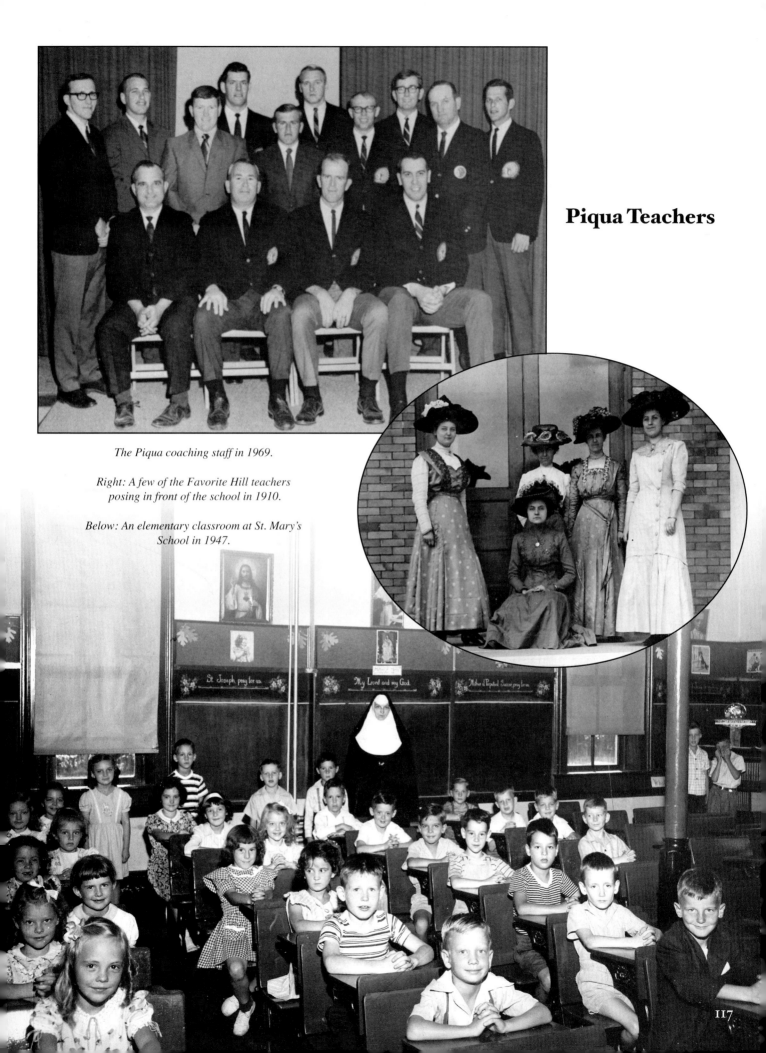

Piqua Teachers

The Piqua coaching staff in 1969.

Right: A few of the Favorite Hill teachers posing in front of the school in 1910.

Below: An elementary classroom at St. Mary's School in 1947.

117

women made one hundred dollars less at $1,200 a year. After seven years in the system, male high school teachers made $1,900 a year and women made four hundred dollars less at $1,500 a year. In June of 1941, the Board of Education laid out a new set of rules for teachers that included: no inefficient or immoral teacher shall be continued, no women who has changed from single to a married status shall be continued and no teacher shall use his or her position to teach lessons that are subversive. SEE ALSO: List-Principals; Schools; Wages.

TELEGRAPH

The first long distance telegraph in the United States was established in 1844 on the east coast. Six years later, Dayton, Troy, and Piqua had been connected by telegraph wires. In 1860, the Western Union Telegraph Company took over the existing lines and established an active office in Piqua until 1983. From 1894 until 1943, the Postal Telegraph and Cable Company also maintained an active office in the city.

TELEPHONE

Alexander Graham Bell succeeded in developing the first practical telephone in 1876. Four years later on March 20, 1880, Bell Telephone Company of Dayton announced its intention to install a telephone system in Piqua. By August the new system had almost fifty subscribers. C. E. Machir, manager of the local office of the Western Union Telegraph Company, was appointed manager of the new system. In November, the first switchboard was installed and the system moved to a full twenty four hour a day operation. The switchboard was located on the second floor of the Piqua National Bank building on the northwest corner of Main and the public square. Piqua and Troy systems were tied together in January of 1881.

The Ohio Bell Telephone Company's switch board was located on North Wayne Street in the 1940's.

Later in 1881, the exchange was moved into larger quarters on the third floor of the Scott building on the northwest corner of Main and Ash Streets. Nat Johnson became the manager of the system in its new location. Johnson hired his wife to be the first full-time "telephoner", or operator. By March of 1883, 103 telephone subscribers were listed in what was known as the Central Telephone System.

A rival telephone system, the Piqua Home Telephone Company, was organized in February of 1889 by local investors **Stanhope Boal**, W. A. Snyder, **Henry Flesh**, William Sniff, **S. K. Statler**, M. G. Smith, and **Leo M. Flesh**. The company was incorporated in May of 1899 with a capital of $75,000. The

systems operated side by side until July of 1919, when the Union Telephone Company took over the operations of the Home Telephone Company.

The Ohio Bell Telephone Company was formed in 1921 and began operations locally at 311 North Wayne (built by Central Telephone in 1918-19). By this time, the local system used thirty-five operators for 2,200 Piqua subscribers, plus exchanges for Lena and Fletcher. Soon after **World War II**, a major labor dispute between the Ohio Federation of Telephone Workers and Ohio Bell Telephone Company led to a **strike** which shut down phone service for almost a month from April to May of 1947. The local exchange built a new and enlarged building at 122 West High and moved in 1952. The Piqua system changed to a direct dial system on May 4, 1958, using the "PR3" prefix. The prefix was changed to 773 in 1961. Ohio Bell was separated from A.T. & T. on January 1, 1984, to become part of the Ameritech Company. SEE ALSO: Lorimer, George W.

TELEVISION

The first demonstration of electronically transmitted moving pictures occurred in England in 1926. By 1941 regular broadcasting began in the United States. **Lear-Avia** of Piqua began manufacturing television parts from 1946-47. Dayton's WHIO-TV (Channel 7) came on the air in 1947, and the Miami Valley had its first television station.

The Thoma and Sons Jewelry Store sold the city's first televisions in 1948.

In 1948, Thoma and Sons (Jewelry Store) at 321 North Main became the community's first commercial outlet for television receivers. Robert Sprinkle, a former Lear-Avia electrical engineer and a Thoma family son-in-law, began selling, installing, and repairing Piqua's first televisions. The sets were displayed in the store's windows. Every time a Cincinnati **baseball** game was televised crowds would gather in front of the window for the unusual treat of watching, as well as listening, to a game in progress. In March of 1949, Jasper (Jack) Wagner opened the city's first shop dealing exclusively with televisions, Favorite Hill TV at 1213 South Street. When the business closed in 2007 it was the oldest continuing television shop in the entire area.

In 1964, the City of Piqua passed an ordinance granting Valley Antenna Systems, Inc. a franchise to conduct a community antenna television (CATV) system. Valley Antenna Systems, Inc. was organized and headed by C. Oscar Baker, which he jointly managed with WPTW-Radio. In 1984, Centel Cable Television Company of Ohio, part of Warner Cable Communications, took over the Piqua CATV franchise.

Video stores became part of the city's business landscape in the 1980's. The first stores were locally owned and operated. By the late 1990's national chains such as Blockbusters, Hollywood Video and Family Video began to dominate the market. SEE ALSO: Radio.

TEMPERANCE

The first local group to organize against excessive drinking was the male oriented Piqua Temperance Society on July 4, 1831. This early organization did not try to prohibit liquor, only to "temper" its use. Its major focus was to convince men to drink beer or soft cider instead of hard liquor. The Temperance Society lasted for about five years and succeeded in gathering several hundred temperance pledges. In 1846, Piqua Division, No. 19 of the Sons of Temperance was organized in Piqua. The following year, the Mount Olive Division, No. 301, Sons of Temperance was established in the city. These groups had only limited success and, by the beginning of the **Civil War**, interest in temperance had waned.

It revived on February 18, 1874, with the Women's Crusade. **Women** marched and sang (several rousing verses of *A Rock of Ages*) and prayed in front of the city's saloons as snow fell on the muddy streets. During the following weeks and months the Crusade continued visiting local saloons. At the bar located within the City Hotel, the local bartender countered the women's actions by declaring, "I must take a bath" and then proceeded to remove his clothing. The women abruptly ceased their singing and praying and left the saloon. Other saloon keepers attempted to stop the women by throwing buckets of dirty cleaning water at them. The Crusade also began trying to influence the passage of legal restrictions. The women presented a petition to the city council requesting the passage of an ordinance restricting the selling of beer at the same location in which it was consumed. The ordinance was passed in December of 1874 by a vote of six to two (The **Republicans** generally favored temperance and the **Democrats** generally opposed it). The Crusade celebrated this legal victory but within six months the ordinance was generally ignored. In January of 1875, saloon owner Charles Roser brought charges against fifteen Crusaders for trespassing. The charges were brought in front of the Washington Township Justice of the Peace and the defendants included three ministers and two minister's wives. After a two day jury trial the defendants were declared not guilty with the jury stating that the Crusaders had only used the public sidewalks and had not trespassed on saloon property. After the trespassing charges, direct picketing of saloons tapered off and the Crusading women changed tactics. Two women would target a specific saloon and then, seated on camp stools, would proceed to take down the names of those men seen entering the saloon. The saloon owners countered this by setting out beer barrels in the street and passing out free glasses of beer to passersby. The active street work of the Crusade gradually diminished but organized temperance work did not end.

The Crusade led to the formation of a local chapter of the **Women's Christian Temperance Society** (W.C.T.U.). Another strong temperance group came into being when, in August of 1874, **Isaac Morris** established the city's first temperance **newspaper,** the *Miami Helmet*. The *Miami Helmet* dutifully recorded the activities of the Crusade and helped promote their cause.

The nationally inspired Murphy Movement held a meeting in Piqua at the First Presbyterian Church in April of 1877. At the first meeting 160 men signed the abstinence pledge and by the end of the week that number had grown to over one thousand pledges. The leader of the movement, **Francis Murphy** spoke in Piqua in October of 1877.

The Presbyterians, Methodists, Baptist and United Brethren churches in Piqua were very active in promoting and encouraging temperance in the late nineteenth century

The last major temperance organization was the male dominated Piqua National Temperance Union, established in May of 1877. In July of 1883, a Young W.C.T.U. was organized. In the 1890's, the anti-liquor organizations moved from temperance to **prohibition**. SEE ALSO: African-American; Lodges and Organizations; Nation, Carrie

TENNIS

Two tennis enthusiasts are responsible for making the sport popular in Piqua, **Allen Rundle** and **YMCA** executive secretary Harry Martin. The two men organized the Miami County Tennis Association in c.1910. Rundle was also responsible for the construction of courts on the grounds of the Ball Memorial **Hospital** on Park Avenue during that same time.

The Piqua Tennis Club was organized in May of 1933 with Dr. A.B. Carson as its first president. The club sponsored the construction/improvement of courts on the east bank of the Great Miami River just north of Bridge Street in 1933. Tennis courts had also been constructed to the south of the YMCA and the Hall Courts across from the quarries in Shawnee. The 1932 Piqua city directory listed the YMCA tennis courts at 701 North Main.

TEXTILE MANUFACTURING

In 1848, the Young and Yager Company began producing jean and flannel material, blankets and knitwear. The firm also operated a wool carding mill, a **saw mill** and a **flour mill**. After several major changes in ownership including the Gray, **O'Ferrall** & Company that produced doeskin and yarn (1869-1876); the W.C Gray & Company/Piqua Knitting Works that produced men's seamless woolen and cotton hosiery (c.1876-1878), the F. Gray Company/Piqua Woolen Mills that produced papermaker's felts (1878-1881) and the F. Gray Company Inc. that produced felts and industrial felt jackets(1881-1901) the firm went bankrupt in 1900 and was taken over by **William P. Orr**. The company became known as the Orr Felt and Blanket Company and produced papermaker's felts and blankets. In 1901, Orr Felt was producing blankets for the Pullman Sleeper Company (sleeping cars on railroads). During **World War I** the company made olive drab blankets for the army and in **World War II** it was blue blankets for the navy. The company stayed in the Orr family for most of the first half of the twentieth century. In 1964, it was purchased by Dimitri Nicholas, the former general manager of the **BVD** Company in Piqua. The Nicholas family continues to own the firm today (2007) as the Orr Felt Company.

The next big step in the city's textile history comes with the formation of the **Piqua Hosiery Company** (1886-1941). This firm made history with the production of the first commercially practical drop seat union suit in the early 1890's. Other early woolen mills included William Gibson (c.1850), Joseph Aspinall (c.1859-c.1860), Harriet Brown Woolen Factory (c.1868), [Thomas] Parkinson & Walker Knitting Works (c.1875) and the Piqua Fabric Company (1894-1896).

The number of underwear manufacturers would increase dramatically over the next thirty years, providing a new job market for **women**. The introduction of major industrial employment for women gave many families the opportunity to earn two or three incomes for the very first time. Another outcome of the underwear industry was the formation of the **YWCA** as a recreational outlet for women factory workers. SEE ALSO:

Atlas Underwear Company; Imperial Underwear Company; Lists-Underwear Companies; Superior Underwear Company; Union Underwear Company; Wages

.

THEATERS

The community's first theater with a formal stage was on the second floor of Union Hall on the southwest corner of Main and Ash Streets. The structure was built in 1820 and was Piqua's only theater for thirty years. In 1850, Zollinger and Clark built a three story brick structure on the southeast corner of Main and Greene Streets. The building was known as Border Hall. The third story contained a sloping floor for the audience and a full stage with gas footlights and scenery for **theater** productions. Early mid-west traveling shows appeared in this theater.

In 1872, **A. G. Conover** built Conover's Opera House on the southeast corner of the public square. It was a four-story brick structure with the theater occupying the top two floors. Conover's contained a full stage, a balcony and private boxes. Seating prices were; orchestra and first circle chairs seventy-five cents, balcony seats fifty cents, with private boxes going for four and five dollars. A reserved seat was twenty-five cents extra. The theater burned down in 1892.

In 1890, **Cron** and Sternberger remodeled the interior and changed the facade of the former First Presbyterian Church on the southeast corner of Ash and Wayne Streets. The structure was renamed the Music Hall with the theater located on the second floor. In the mid-1890's, Charles C. Sank took over the management of the Hall renaming it the Piqua Opera House. The structure was gutted by fire in 1903.

In February of 1903, the city's single largest theater, **May's Opera House** on Wayne Street was opened to the public.

In March of 1906, W. M. Ormsbee leased the store room at 122 West Ash and contracted O. W. Richardson to remodel the structure into a family vaudeville theater. The Bijou Family Theater was formally opened on May 7, 1906. In 1907, **Stanhope Boal**, the owner of the building, installed the city's first commercial **air conditioning** system in the theater. The Bijou presented a wide variety of acts including small theatrical productions, circus, exotic dancing (bare feet), boxing matches, and cowboy acts. One of its most unusual acts was held in September of 1912 when the theater featured Najah Toxico. She was advertised as a "Barefoot Indian Dancing Sensation". Toxico was actually a female impersonator wearing a wig and other female enhancements. Also in 1912, the Bijou began showing motion pictures for the first time. Live entertainment was not presented at the Bijou after the theater was taken over by the Piqua Amusement Company in 1919.

COMMUNITY THEATER. Local theatrics in Piqua date back to the Thespian Association of Piqua established in 1829. Numerous small acting troupes were organized and sponsored by local churches, lodges, clubs, and fraternal organizations. In July of 1924, the Piqua Community Players Club was organized, but it lasted only a few years. Twenty-five years later in November of 1950, Piqua's recreational director helped organize the Piqua Players as a community theater organization. Jack Wilson served as the group's first president. Piqua Players received a permanent home with the opening of Mote Park Community Center in July of 1953. The group is still active to the present day (2007). SEE ALSO: Motion Picture Theaters.

TIME

Piqua meetings in the 1820's and 1830's were often announced as being held at early or late candle lighting (meaning after dusk). By the 1880's, the city's time was controlled by local industries. The whistles sounded at 6:00 A.M. to begin the day, and at 6:00 P.M. to end it. During this period, standard time was determined by the railroad depot clocks. In 1920, discussions raged about Piqua and Dayton being on "separate times". Daylight Savings Time was finally introduced to the city with the passage of Piqua Ordinance No. 218 by the City Council on April 21, 1924. Daylight Savings went into effect at midnight on Sunday, May 21, 1924. The city returned to Central Standard Time on September 28, 1924. During **World War II**, "War Time" went into effect for the first time at 2:00 A.M. February 9, 1942, moving clocks ahead one hour. This ended another conflict between Piqua and Dayton about the two cities having "different" times. SEE ALSO: Schools.

TIPPECANOE, BATTLE OF

Tippecanoe was a **Potawatomi** village on the west bank of the Wabash River (Tippecanoe County, Indiana). In 1808, it became the headquarters for **Tecumseh** and his brother, the Prophet, and was known as Prophetstown. The gathering of Indians supported by the British was deemed a serious threat by Indiana Territorial Governor **William Henry Harrison**, who led an army of 900 troops which attacked and destroyed the village on November 7, 1811. Tecumseh was not present during that battle and the Indians were led to their defeat by the Prophet. Harrison used this victory as part of his slogan in the presidential campaign of 1840 "Tippecanoe and Tyler, Too".

TOBACCO

During Piqua's first three or four decades, rolled tobacco was a rare luxury item which was imported from Cincinnati. Tobacco use was usually limited to chewing tobacco. This was a very popular recreation. So popular, in fact, that an anonymous letter was published in the *Piqua Courier* on July 18, 1835 complaining about its use. The letter complained that too many men "were using to excess the notorious and obnoxious Indian weed and throwing their quids by the mouthful on the floor where they, the members of the church (Methodist), commonly kneel in time of prayer". By the 1850's, chewing tobacco had given way to the smoking of cigars. In 1856, William Schroerluke opened a cigar store where he manufactured his own brand on the second floor. His four sons kept the business going until about 1905. Two of Schroerluke's apprentices, John Laug (c1870 – c1897), and Joseph DeFrees (c1869-c1871), established their own cigar manufacturing shops. The largest producer of cigars in Piqua was **Leopold Kiefer**. In 1869-70, he opened a cigar store and factory which lasted until early1890's. At its height in the early 1880's, Kiefer's "Havana Cigar Factory" employed between thirty and forty women. SEE ALSO: Agriculture; Labor and Unions; Strikes.

TORNADO (CYCLONE)

A tornado hit Piqua on May 02, 1887 and destroyed several roofs.

TOURIST CAMPS

These camps became very popular in the 1920's as America turned to the automobile for its method of vacation travel. A camp was established near Piqua off of the Dixie Highway (25-A North) in the early 1920's. After **World War II**, the Woodland Camp operated 4.5 miles north of Piqua on 25-A. This camp offered heated cabins, hot and cold showers, trailer accommodations and steak and chops for tourists. SEE ALSO: Mobile Homes

TOWN HALL

From 1822 until 1844 Piqua's elected officials met in private homes, public halls, hotels, schools, and even, on occasion, in local taverns. A committee of village council members was formed on May 2, 1843, to ascertain the costs of building a council house. They reported that a two-story brick structure (using seventy thousand bricks) forty feet by sixty feet with a cupola, would cost thirteen hundred dollars. At this time, the Odd Fellows Lodge No. 8 proposed to council to build a third story on the new City Hall to be paid for by the lodge. The Council agreed to a twenty year lease in return for nine hundred dollars for the construction of the addition. The council also granted Washington Township a ninety-nine year lease on the use of one of the lower meeting rooms in return for a three hundred dollar lump sum payment. The building contract was awarded to **John Reed Hilliard**, who was assisted by Rankin Walkup, James Hardesty, Samuel Redman, Jim Godall, and John **Rayner**, Sr. The completed structure cost a total of thirty-three hundred dollars and contained market stalls, a fire engine house, a council chamber, township offices, **lodge** hall, and a public meeting hall. Fees for the public hall were set at fifty cents for regular use, and an additional twelve and a half cents for a fire in the fireplace, and thirty-seven and a half cents if lights were desired. The council met for the first time in the new structure on March 3, 1845 under the leadership of Mayor David Jordan. The new building was located on the public square on the east side of Main Street, with East High Street deadending at the rear of the building. In 1852, pigeons had become such a major problem that the council suspended the ordinance against shooting firearms in the city so that Mayor William Elliott could shoot pigeons off the roof of the building. The structure was remodeled and expanded (mansard roof) in 1886 to meet the needs of the growing city government. By the first few decades of the twentieth century, the building was beginning to deteriorate. After the council moved its offices to the former fire station on West Water Street in 1927, the one hundred seventeen year old Town Hall was demolished on May 7, 1928. A new Municipal Government Complex was completed on Water Street in 2001. SEE ALSO: Jails; Weather Flags.

The three story tall brick Town Hall was built in 1845 on the east side of Main Street in the middle of High Street and torn down in 1928.

Piqua's Municipal Complex on the southwest corner of Water and Wayne Streets was completed in 2001.

TOWNSEND CLUB

The Townsend Movement was created in 1933 by Dr. Francis Townsend, a semi-retired physician from California. The Townsend plan was for the government to give all workers over the age of sixty, two hundred dollars a month for an agreement to retire from active employment. In return for this income, the recipient was required to spend the entire two hundred dollars before the end of the month. Dr. Townsend felt that this would help end the Great **Depression** by pulling surplus workers out of the labor pool and provide an economic stimulus to the struggling economy. Clubs supporting this plan sprang up around the nation including one in Piqua. President Roosevelt's Social Security Plan generally ended the popularity of the Townsend Plan.

TOWNSHIPS, MIAMI COUNTY

In 1807, Bethel, Concord, Elizabeth, Union and **Washington** were the first townships to be established. Between 1810 and 1819 portions of these original five townships were split off to form new townships. Staunton would be the last township to be formed in the county in 1819.

TOWNSHIP TRIVIA

Six townships are located east of the river and six west.

Union is the largest township containing 48.0 square miles.

Springcreek is the smallest township with only 26.3 square miles.

In 2000, Concord had the largest population with 27,335 and Brown the smallest with 1,554.

The first township to be settled by European-Americans was Washington Township by **Job Gard** in 1796-1797. (An argument could also be made for the settlement of Colonial English traders at **Pickawillany** in 1747-1752).

Washington Township (not including Piqua) had the oldest population in 2000 with a median age of 46.4 and Concord had the youngest at 36.4.

SEE ALSO: List-Miami County Communities; List-Townships.

TOYS

Pioneer toys were usually handmade items constructed of wood, corncobs, rags, or straw. With the coming of the canal in 1837, and the railroads in the 1850's, handmade toys were gradually replaced by manufactured toys shipped from Dayton and Cincinnati.

Piqua's first local toy manufacturer was Richard Grosvenor, who established the Tykie Toy Company (1941-1951). The firm was named after the Grosvenor's baby son Michael, whose nickname was Tyke. The Tykie Toy Company produced baby toys and rattles made of "catalin plastic" and marketed under such names as "Baby Bunny", "Tom-Tom Rattles", and "Eppy Elephant". The second local toy manufacturer was the Warren-Kennedy Company, established in the spring of 1946 to produce

The Tykie Toy plant was located in the one hundred block of East Greene Street.

toy guns. The company was sold in December of 1946 and became the Keal-Kennedy Company. The local plant closed in 1948-49. The last local toy producer, the Piqua Products Company, a division of the All Metal Products Company, came to Piqua in 1950 and built a plant at 1800 West Covington Avenue. The firm produced plastic, metal, and die cast toys and marketed them under the name Wyandotte Toys. **John E. Scarbourgh** served as the firm's Executive Vice President and General Manager. Piqua Products Company closed down its production facilities in 1959-60.

On the commercial level, most general stores carried toys during the nineteenth and twentieth centuries. Other common local sources for toys included hardware stores, corner groceries, and department stores. The first retail store dedicated completely to the sale of toys was the Orr Toy and Novelty Shop (1946-1983), located in the two hundred block of North Main Street. The first wholesale toy operation was begun by the Piqua General Supply Company in 1948.

TREASURER, STATE OF OHIO

In 1861, **Godwin V. Dorsey** was elected State Treasurer under the Union Party banner. He was re-elected in 1862. Dorsey promoted the granting of enlistment bonuses to African-American soldiers during the **Civil War**. At the end of his second term, Dorsey was accused of misuse of funds. After a lengthy investigation, Dorsey was acquitted of all charges.

TREATIES

Following is a list of treaties that impacted on Ohio and later the Miami Valley: Fort Stanwix (1784), Fort McIntosh (1785), Fort Finney (1786), Fort Harmar (1789), **Greenville** (1795), Fort Industry (1805), Detroit (1807), **Second Greenville** (1814), Maumee Rapids (1817), **St. Mary's** (1818), Lewistown (1831), and Upper Sandusky (1842).

TROY, OHIO

This city is the county seat of **Miami County**, and is located at the junctions of Interstate 75, State Route 41, 55, 718, and County Road 25A in Concord and Staunton Townships. It was laid out for the newly formed county government on December 16, 1807, and named after the classical city in Homer's "Iliad". The community was connected to the rest of the state by the Miami and Erie **Canal**, the New York Central ("Big Four" **Railroad)** and the Cincinnati, Hamilton and Dayton Railroad. The

current Miami County Courthouse building in Troy was designed by **J. W. Yost** and occupied in January of 1888. The village was first incorporated in 1813. Troy's population in 2000 was 22,183. SEE ALSO: Football; Population; Roads; Telephone; Courthouse Wars.

TUDOR STYLE ARCHITECTURE

The local variation of the Tudor Style was popular from 1905 through 1910. **George Rundle,** manufacturer of a **patent medicine** known as Porter's Pain King, built the community's first Tudor Style home and stable in 1907. The stable alone was larger than over fifty percent of the homes in Piqua at that time. This was era prior to federal income tax when personal wealth was displayed through richly decorated homes located on prominent street corners within the community. These homes were constructed to house large families and two or three live-in servants (usually in attic rooms). There are no Tudor Style commercial structures in Piqua.

This style has many of the following local architectural elements. These homes are rectangular in shape with a multi-gable front and a projecting wing. There are usually two-and-a-half stories tall. The first floor is often brick with prominent windows and multi-paned window transoms. A prominent porch is common with double brick column supports. The second floor has a broad decorative half-timbering filled in with painted stucco and windows surrounded by half-timbering. The windows are a variety of types including six over one double hung sash and small multi-paned casement windows. The roof maintains a variety of pitches. The commercial examples of this style in Piqua are usually part of a subtype known as the **Jacobethan Style**.
DOMESTIC EXAMPLES
400 North Downing Street, Rundle House, 1907

UNIONS

The first known local labor organization was incorporated on April 8, 1861, as the McClarn Working Mens' Institute of Piqua. The nature and purpose of this organization is unknown. The **Knights of Labor** organized a local group in 1886. By 1899, Piqua workers had established over twenty trade union locals. The first major **Labor Day** celebration in Piqua featured a parade in 1890. In the late 1890's, the Junior Order of United American Mechanics was organized as a fraternal working man's organization opposed to foreign workers and merchants. The American Federation of Labor organized a local Piqua Trade and Labor Council about 1906. The council came out against the Industrial Workers of the World (IWW) or the Wobblies in 1919. The IWW was a radical group of **socialists**. The central Labor Union of Piqua, American Federation of Labor organized fourteen new unions in 1934. The Great **Depression** in the 1930's was a period of heavy unionization and **strikes** in Piqua. SEE ALSO: Employee Benefits; Employment; Greenback Party; List-Unions; Lodges and Organizations; Telephone.

UNION UNDERWEAR COMPANY

This firm was established in 1894 by **John L. Boyer** and moved into the former printing plant on the northwest corner of Spring and High Streets. The company produced ribbed union-suits for men and women. Their key product was the *Piqua Perfection* suit that was patented on August 31, 1897. By about 1905, Union had over one hundred employees in both Piqua and

This building on the northwest corner of Spring and High Streets was used by the Union Underwear Company.

Greenville, Ohio. The firm moved all of their operations to Greenville 1917 due to a shortage and strong competition for **women** workers in Piqua

UNITED WAY (FUND)

After World War II, the Piqua Community Welfare Federation was created by the Piqua **Chamber of Commerce** to raise funds for the **Salvation Army**, the **YWCA,** the **Boy Scouts**, the **Girl Scouts**, the Mental Health Association and the **YMCA**. The new group held the first purely local **charity** fund drive since 1933, in May of 1947. The young organization joined the national group in 1949 becoming the Piqua Community Chest. From 1952 to 1957, the Community Chest did not reach its goal and this, combined with local industries requesting consolidated funding drives, led to a final reorganization in 1958 which created the modern Piqua Area United Fund. At this time the Cancer Society, the Campfire Girls and the **Red Cross** were added to the funded agencies. By 2007, the United Way funded twenty-three agencies. United Way executive (secretaries) directors included Cleo Groven (c.1951-1953), Irene Ditmer (1952-1974), Joanne Harman (c.1975-c.1977), Doris Perry (c. 1977-c.1992), Cheryl Stiefel-Francis (c.1992-2000), Lisa Whitaker (2000-2006), Alesia Barnhizer (2006-2007) and Ginny Koon (2007-present). SEE ALSO: Civil War (Soldier's Aid Society).

The 1965 United Fund Campaign parade featured this YMCA Swim Team float along the 400 block of Main Street looking northeast.

UPPER PIQUA, OHIO

This settlement was located near the junction of State Route 66 and Hardin Road in Washington Township. It was first established as a **Shawnee** settlement, and after they abandoned it, Colonel **John Johnston**'s family established a residence there in 1812.

VICTORY HEIGHTS

During the first years of **World War II**, Congress passed the Lanham Act that provided for the construction of housing for war workers and families of military personnel. In Ohio, thirty-two housing projects were built, two in Miami County. In Piqua, housing project OH-33161 was begun in 1943 under the auspices of the Federal Public Housing Administration. Seven residential courts were laid out and named after military leaders; Kelly, Doolittle, Eisenhower, MacArthur, Nimitz, Stillwell, and Wainwright. But Victory Heights became more than just a collection of frame and concrete block buildings. A number of Victory Heights organizations were formed. They included the Resident Council of Victory Heights, the Victory Heights Community Church, a Victory Heights Boy Scout troop sponsored by the American Legion, and the Victory Heights Elementary School classroom staffed by teachers from Favorite Hill School. After the war, Congress passed the Housing Act of 1950 that allowed local governments to take over the federal housing projects. On April 1, 1953, Piqua City Manager **Robert Hance** paid one dollar to the Federal Housing Authority allowing the city to take over the Victory Heights project. The city managed the area as low-income housing until 1966-67, when the last residents left the site. The closed buildings were gradually torn down and work began in the 1970's to turn the former Victory Heights project into the Eisenhower Community Park.

Victory Heights began in 1943 to provide emergency housing for war workers and the families of soldiers. It was located on the west edge of the city off of McKinley Avenue.

VIETNAM WAR

Active United States military involvement in Vietnam began in 1955. Large scale military operations started with the deployment of the entire First Cavalry Division (Airmobile) in 1965. The war was brought home on April 11, 1966 with the death of **William H. Pitsenbarger**. A graduate of Piqua Central High School in 1962, he joined the Air Force in December of 1963. He was killed in action in Vietnam while attempting to rescue men wounded during a ground fire fight. For his heroism, Pitsenbarger became the first Air Force enlisted man to be awarded the Air Force Cross. In 2000, Pitsenbarger was awarded the **Medal of Honor**. He was the first of eleven men from Piqua to die in Vietnam.

William J. Baugh, a 1952 Piqua Central graduate, was shot down over North Vietnam on January 21, 1967. Major Baugh became a Vietnamese Prisoner of War from 1967 until 1973.

Medal of Honor winner William Pitsenbarger is shown at the Bien Hoa Air Base in South Vietnam in c.1966.

Upon his release, a welcome celebration was held in Piqua on March 25, 1973 as a "Vietnam Service Recognition Day".

On the home front, the National Draft Lottery inaugurated on December 1, 1969, affected thousands of eighteen and nineteen-year-old men in Miami County as they received their draft call-up numbers. From 1965 until 1973, hundreds of men were drafted from Miami County. There are no figures available that state how many of these men actually served in Vietnam. Locally, Battery C, 136th Field Artillery, Ohio National Guard was called to active duty for a short time to help quell anti-war student riots at the Ohio State University campus. For this duty, the guardsmen were issued M-1 rifles with bayonets and tear gas. Support for the war was shown locally with the "Letters for Life" campaign in 1970. This operation sent letters to Prisoners of War and was coordinated at a headquarters located at 333 North Main. In March of 1971, Jim DeWeese of Piqua accompanied over 100,000 of these letters to Paris where, as part of a delegation, he attempted to deliver them to the Hanoi Peace Delegation. The letters were refused.

Interest in Vietnam veteran's concerns was revived in 1989 when the William Pitsenbarger Chapter of Miami County, Vietnam Veterans of America was chartered. SEE ALSO: Militia and National Guard.

WAGES

The following figures were the average weekly industrial wages in Miami County from 1860 until 1985.

1860	$ 6.91	(women $ 2.99)
1870	$ 7.26	(women $ 3.67)
1900	$ 9.00	(women $ 4.55)
1920	$20.00	(women $20.00)
1943	$48.00	
1964	$119.05	
1985	$185.14	

SEE ALSO: Employee Benefits; Employment; Labor and Unions; Strikes; Teachers

WAPAKONETA

This Shawnee village was named for a chief whose name meant White Jacket. The village was located near the present city of Wapakoneta in Auglaize County. First settled in 1795 after the **Treaty of Greenville**, it became the principal village of the **Shawnee** Tribe. The Shawnee were removed from the area by treaty in 1831 and the land was sold to European-Americans. The village became the site for the Federal **Land Office** when it was moved from Piqua in 1833. SEE ALSO: Johnston, George.

WAR COTTAGE TYPE ARCHITECTURE

This is strictly a local type or style name and does not directly correspond to any national style name. The War Cottage Type of home was popular in Piqua in 1943-1944. The homes were built to meet the housing shortage existing in the city during **World War II.** They were built by the Modern Construction Company (Fred and John Walters) of Cincinnati and sold by local realtor Joe Dine. Many of these war cottages can be found on Brice and Manier Streets and Clark Avenue. These type of homes are one story, side gabled, rectangular structures made of concrete block with brick facing. The original floor plan called for two bedrooms, a living room, a kitchen and a dinette. The front façade features a central doorway covered by a frame porch supported by a short brick wall. There are two almost square one-over-one double hung sash windows flanking the front. A raised foundation allows for a front entry into a basement level garage. The homes have no decorative wood or brick trim. Later remodelings have often removed or changed the front porch area and closed or modified the basement garage entry. The Modern Construction Company also built a number of plain two story brick duplex houses in the same areas (example 723 Brice).

DOMESTIC EXAMPLES
725 Brice Street, built in 1944
722 Brice Street, built in 1944
815 Clark Avenue, built in c.1943-1944

WAR OF 1812

President James Madison declared war on Great Britain on June 18, 1812. In Miami County, the threat of British backed Indian tribes had already been felt. Captain George Buchanan (West Milton) raised a company of fifty-two men to serve in the state militia from May 5 to August 13, 1812. Buchanan's junior officers were Lieutenant James C. Caldwell (Piqua) and Ensign Gardner Bobo (Springcreek Township). The company was run by five sergeants in charge of forty-five privates. Three other Miami County militia companies were also recruited. Captain Reuben Westfall raised thirty-five men who served from October 24 to November 13, 1812. Lieutenant Gardner Bobo commanded a company of twenty-seven men from September, 1812 until March, 1813. Captain Charles Hilliard raised the county's largest company, with a total of fifty-nine officers and enlisted men. SEE ALSO: Border City; Dilbone Massacre; Greenville, Second Treaty of; Harrison, William H.; Johnston, John; Militia and National Guard; Piqua, Council of; Potawatomi; Van Horne, Thomas; Wayne, Fort.

WASHINGTON TOWNSHIP

This township was created on July 21, 1807, and named for President **George Washington** and the village of Washington. The original township included the present-day townships of Brown, Newberry, Springcreek, and Washington, as well as most of Darke and Shelby counties and parts of Mercer and Auglaize counties. By 1814, the township had been reduced to its present size of 18,647 acres or 29 square miles. Five settlements have been established in the Township: Farrington, Peterson, **Piqua,** Riverside, and **Upper Piqua**. In the 1990's, Washington successfully petitioned the county to re-draw its boundaries and exclude the City of Piqua. That left Piqua as the only community in Miami County not to be located in a township. In 2000, the Township's total population was 1,803 with a median age of 46.4. SEE ALSO: List-Townships; Miami County; Piqua; Town Hall.

WAYNE, FORT

The first of several French (later British) forts on this site was established (Fort St. Phillippe renamed Fort Miami) in c1680. The fort was located at the site of the present day city of Fort Wayne in Indiana. General **Anthony Wayne** erected a fort at this site in 1794. During the next two decades, the fort served as military and Indian trading post. It weathered a siege by British and Indian forces during the **War of 1812**. In 1815-16, a new and larger fort was built adjoining the old fort. The post was abandoned in 1819, and the last structure torn down in 1852. During the years 1802-1811, **John Johnston** served as the factor and later as Indian Agent at Fort Wayne.

WEATHER

The average winter weather in the nineteenth century was considerably colder than it is today. It was not unusual to have sub-freezing temperatures in late April. The winter of 1851-52 was one of the most severe on record, with January temperatures regularly dipping from 15 to 20 degrees below zero. In 1885, the temperatures for all of March stayed at or below zero. In the twentieth century, 1950 and 1978 are best known for their winter blizzards. In 1950 over 14-1/2 inches of snow fell in a twenty-four hour period. The blizzard of January 26, 1978 had seventy mph winds mixed with snow that created six to ten foot drifts. 1988 is best known as the year of the drought, as rainfall fell far below its yearly average. SEE ALSO: Floods.

WEATHER FLAGS

On May 27, 1886, the City of Piqua began receiving weather information on a daily basis from the Signal Office of the War Department in Washington, D.C. The city broadcast each day's weather forecast by hanging a flag from the **town hall** on the public square.

There were six white flags in all, each with a different symbol. There were three flags with red symbols; a sun (higher temperatures), a moon (lower temperatures), and a star (constant or same temperatures). The same symbols were also in blue; a sun (rain or snow), a moon (clear or fair), and a star (local rain or snow). The flags could also be flown in combinations. The local newspaper stated that the first twenty-four predictions had been fairly accurate. The War Department discontinued the service on March 1, 1887 as a method of saving money.

WEST POINT MILITARY ACADEMY

The first woman from Piqua to attend the military academy was Diane Birman, appointed in 1980. During her four years at the "Point", she became captain of the "Rabble Rousers" cheerleaders. SEE ALSO: Johnston, Abraham.

WHIG PARTY

The National Whig Party was formed in the 1820's to oppose the presidency of Andrew Jackson. In Piqua, the most prominent members of the Whig Party were **William McLean** and **John Johnston**. McLean, a local attorney, was elected in 1823 to the United States House of Representatives. He served until 1829. Johnston, while holding no elective office, was a major supporter of the party. In 1840, he attended the National Whig Convention in Pennsylvania to work for the nomination of his friend, **William Henry Harrison**. By the early 1850's, the party began breaking up. In 1854, party members joined with other groups in Ohio to form the Fusion Party. By 1855, this group was known as the **Republican Party**.

WHITE HOUSE

Pumps constructed by the Enpo-Cornell Company of Piqua were used in the White House (Washington, D.C.) to keep water out of the basement.

WILLOW COTTAGE

This small structure was a one story cottage located in Rossville. It was made of woven willow saplings. The cottage was destroyed in the Great **Flood** of 1913. SEE ALSO: Exotic Architecture.

The Willow Cottage was located in Rossville and used as a summer cottage.

WOMEN

The role of women in small rural American communities during the nineteenth and early twentieth centuries was varied and often confusing. The ideal woman was viewed in often conflicting terms. She was placed on a pedestal to be honored, protected, and cherished while, at the same time, accorded a second class status. Women were viewed as inferiors in physical strength, mental acuteness and emotional stability. This dual view was promoted not only by men, but also by the women themselves. Social pressure prevented women from easily entering the work force, but all too often economic pressure made it a necessity. The home was viewed as the place for women, but if they must work, occupations were as limited as their perceived abilities.

Like occupations, only certain social causes were deemed appropriate for the women. These perceptions of women limited and shaped the role they played in their local communities.

EARLY PERIOD. During Piqua's pioneer period from 1800 until 1820, women held a relatively equal status with men. Division of labor was based upon the work load, not on the proper roles of men and women. Pioneer women cleared the fields, chopped down trees, and helped plant the crops. Children past the infant stage were a joint responsibility simply because they were usually in the fields or woods with their parents. While cooking and cleaning chores were often done by women, it was not unusual to find men assisting with these tasks. The pioneer period was a time of survival, and the luxury of assigned sexual roles simply did not occur.

By 1820 Piqua had grown into a small village with shops, small industries, churches, a school, and a newspaper. Women's roles in the community began to change. The division of labor began to be more pronounced and more narrowly defined. Women vanished almost completely from the community work force and became the sole worker in the home. Cooking, cleaning, and childrearing were thought to be the only appropriate work for women. As small industries grew, they became bastions of the male world. The only outlet for women outside the house became the church and, in certain very limited circumstances, small millinery or dress shops operated out of the home.

It was the church that expanded the role of women in community related activities. The destitute or those in ill health were seen as the responsibility of the women of the church. It was this role that first brought women out of the home. The first group to organize outside of confines of single church was the Piqua Female Bible Society, formed in 1818. This group not only supplied Bibles to people in the community, but also provided information on those families that were in need of financial, as well as spiritual, aid. The Piqua Female Bible Society would continue in operation until 1969 providing a unique continuity to women's activities in Piqua.

By the beginning of the Civil War, Piqua had grown into a city of second-class size with a broad economic base supported by small locally owned industries, and a growing commercial and trading district. Over a dozen churches and numerous social and fraternal organizations created a complex and diverse social structure. Women's roles were usually limited to a very small circle of activities which included; church work, teaching; clerking in women's shops or departments, domestic service, dressmaking, and any work oriented towards the home.

WORK FORCE. Women in the work force were restricted by social customs and job availability to a relatively narrowly defined number of jobs. The jobs were uniformly low paying, with a correspondingly low social image. Any paying job for a women was viewed as somehow slightly less than morally sound. A majority of the occupations open to women demanded little in the way of training or background. These attitudes and limitations were promoted by both men and women. Middle and upper class women who did not have to work often criticized and ridiculed those who did. Working women in the last half of the nineteenth and first part of the twentieth centuries lived in a world that only grudgingly accepted their right to work.

SUFFRAGE. On April 24, 1894, the Ohio Legislature passed a resolution allowing any woman twenty-one years of age and a United States citizen to vote for members of local boards of education. This resolution also allowed women to run for membership on these boards. The law went into effect in the spring of 1895. The women of Piqua held their first public political convention on Monday, March 11, 1895. Mr. H. G. Hall called the meeting to order and presided until Mrs. William S. Wertz was chosen as chairman, and Mrs. Frances E. Purcell as secretary. This convention was more in the way of an informational session rather than a political convention. The women present decided to establish a voting school and agreed to call a second meeting to choose a woman candidate for the school board.

An interesting question was raised at this first meeting when it was asked how many women intended to vote at the upcoming election. Only two-thirds of the approximately seventy women present stated that they would actually vote. The implication of this informal poll was that an amazing number of local women were either against, or indifferent to woman's suffrage, although the actual vote totals would disagree.

As shown in this c.1905 photograph, women made up the largest percentage of employees at the Atlas Underwear Company.

The second meeting of local women voters was held March 14, 1895. Attendance increased by one-third to just over one hundred women. Mrs. Wertz again chaired the meeting and asked the women present how they stood on setting up an Independent Women's ticket. The *Miami Helmet* quoted two women at length. Mrs. Frances J. Bowdle stated that she did not believe that the time had come for them to put up an Independent ticket and that if they did, they would only meet defeat, and that it would be better for them to try their strength first, as they had no backing whatever. Mrs. Dora C. Zollinger stated that she was not in favor of an Independent ticket but that she was in favor of a woman candidate. The idea of an Independent ticket was voted down and the proposed voting school was held.

The week before the election, the *Miami Helmet* stated in an editorial "We have no objection and have not had for years. If women want to vote and will exercise their privilege, as fully, as earnestly and even as carefully as men do, they have our hearty assent and support". City elections were held on April 1, 1895, and even though there were no women candidates, an estimated three thousand women turned out to vote. Out of an estimated city population of ten thousand, this is an amazing figure.

Twelve years after gaining partial suffrage, two women ran for membership of the Piqua City School Board. Mary Small Johnson, a Piqua native, ran for the position on the Socialist ticket. Her qualifications included active participation in politics and two years as a teacher in the city schools. The other woman candidate was Mrs. **Frances Meilly Orr**, who ran on the Republican ticket. These two women were joined by only three other women in the entire state as school board candidates. Three men were also running for the two available School Board seats. Mrs. Orr came in second to become the city's first woman School Board member. During her two year term she was an energetic and positive leader.

The question of state-wide suffrage was presented on the Ohio ballot in 1914 and again in 1917, and defeated on both occasions. In Miami County the suffrage question was voted down in 1914 by a margin of over twelve percent. Three years later that same negative margin had dropped to nine percent. The national suffrage question was presented as the Nineteenth Amendment to the Constitution, and was ratified nationally on August 18, 1920. Women across the nation voted for national candidates for the first time on November 2, 1920.

In Piqua, women voters rapidly moved into the political arena. The month of October, 1920 saw the creation of both a Harding Woman's Club (Republican) and a Piqua Women's Democratic Club. Women were becoming involved in politics. In 1923, Mary Johnson, a Socialist, became the first woman to run for city office (city auditor). In 1991, Lucy Fess was the forst woman to be elected to serve on the city commission and as Mayor. SEE ALSO: Basketball; Bowling; Civil War; Employment; Humane Society; Johnston, Rachel; List-Unions; Milliners; Nation, Carrie; Parks; Physicians; Piqua Hosiery Company; Police Department; Radio; Servants/Domestics; Schools; Teachers; Telephones; Temperance; United Fund; West Point; Women's Christian Temperance Union; World War II; YWCA.

WOMEN'S CHRISTIAN TEMPERANCE UNION

The national W.C.T.U. was formed in Cleveland in 1874. The Piqua Chapter was formed on February 18, 1874 during the first Crusade meeting. It was known as the Women's Temperance Prayer League. Nancy A. Wallace was elected as the group's first president. The WCTU's local goals were summed up in a letter to the *Miami Helmet* on December 12, 1874, "Be practical. Use the means to succeed. Enforce the law. We need

no better law, nor more law than we have…" The Piqua WCTU held a Victory Service at the Presbyterian Church on January 21, 1920 to celebrate national prohibition which had begun on Friday, January 16, 1920 at midnight. The WCTU would continue until the 1960's in Piqua. SEE ALSO: Temperance; Women.

WOOD SHOVEL AND TOOL COMPANY

The firm was established in 1902 by **Harley K. Wood** and his son **William W. Wood III.** The firm began producing shovels in 1903 but a fire in that same year shut down the plant. It was rebuilt and gradually expanded until the firm would cover over 150,000 square feet of production space in Piqua. The firm would be known as the "Tiffany of the shovel industry" for the high quality of its product. To maintain a steady supply of handles, Wood Shovel purchased thousands of acres of ash timberlands. **World War I** would be a big boost to the company as they began producing entrenching tools for the United States Army. During the Great **Depression** the firm was able to expand through the production of shovels for New Deal federal programs like the WPA and the PWA. Wood Shovel returned to the production of entrenching tools for the Army during World War II. The company produced over two million shovels on contract with the government. A massive **strike** hit Wood Shovel in 1946, when the U.A.W. Local 827 struck for higher wages. The strike lasted 107 days. In 1952, Wood Shovel purchased the

The classical lines of the Wood Shovel & Tool Company office was typical of the pride the Wood family took in the company.

assets of the Iwan Brothers Company of South Bend, Indiana. The firm's production equipment was moved to Piqua, where Wood Shovel began making hand earth Augers, diggers, floor scrappers, sidewalk cleaners and snow shovels. At its peak in the 1950's and 1960's, before it was purchased by outside interests, the firm employed over five hundred employees in plants or warehouses in Wapakoneta, Ohio (Bryant Manufacturing Company); Rock Falls, Illinois; White Mills, Pennsylvania; Reno, Nevada and Phoenica, New York. During the 1960's, Wood Shovel was making over 2,000 types and grades of forks, hoes, rakes, shovels, cultivators, augers, wheelbarrows, a line of garden tools and baseball bats. The Piqua plant used almost exclusively Armco-made steel and aluminum. Bissell Inc. purchased Wood Shovel in January of 1966 when the company was garnering roughly $6.5 million in sales every year. Wood Shovel was considered one of the "Big Four" in the garden tool industry. E.D. Marvin continued as the Piqua company's general manager. Bissell Inc. leased Wood Shovel to the Union Fork & Hoe Company effective in January of 1966. The local plant was

The Wood Shovel and Tool Company handle department in c.1914-15.

DOMESTIC EXAMPLES
204 East Main Street
451 Riverside Drive

WORLD WAR I

HOME FRONT. World War I began in Europe in 1914 and the United States entered that war in 1917. Politically, Piqua was undergoing drastic changes in 1917. **Frank Hamilton** was elected as the city's first **Socialist** mayor. The community's National Guard unit was on active duty on the Mexican border and later, as part of the 37th Infantry Division, would be sent to Europe (summer 1918). Community involvement in the war effort included the formation of the Piqua Chapter of the American **Red Cross**, holding liberty bond rallies, raising victory gardens, and participation in the first national military draft since the **Civil War**. Anti-**German** feeling was manifest in Piqua on April 25, 1918 by the public burning of German language textbooks stolen from the high school. Piqua industry geared up for war production. The **Wood Shovel and Tool Company** produced over a million and a quarter entrenching shovels for the Army. **Atlas Underwear Company** knit and assembled over one and a half million suits of long underwear for the military. Six thousand stoves were shipped out of the **Favorite Stove and Range Company** plant for military cantonments (camps) and hospitals in the United States and overseas. Tent poles for Army pup tents were produced by the **Piqua Handle and Manufacturing Company** with production figures exceeding 350,000. The Orr Felt and Blanket Company reported producing one hundred thousand wool army blankets. The **Hartzell Companies** contributed to the war effort by manufacturing walnut gun stocks and airplane propellers.

MILITARY. Company C, of the Third Infantry Regiment, Ohio National Guard of Piqua was called up for active service along the **Mexican border** in 1916-17. On August 14, 1917, they were stationed at Camp Sherman in Ohio for training. The Company was reorganized and became part of the 148th Infantry, 37th Infantry Division. The entire 37th Division was shipped south to Camp Sheridan near Montgomery, Alabama, for additional training. From Sheridan, the 37th Division was sent to Camp Lee near Petersburg, Virginia. After another period of training, the 37th boarded the U.S.S. *Susquehanna* in June of 1918 and sailed for France. They arrived at Brest, France on July 5 and, after several weeks, were sent to the Alsace-Lorraine area. On August 4, 1918, the division was given the responsibility for about fifteen kilometers of the front known as the Baccarat sector. In September, the division was moved to an area near Verdun and participated in the Meuse-Argonne Campaign, which succeeded in breaking through a portion of the Germans' Hindenburg line. During this campaign, the division moved to the St. Mihiel sector where they suffered through several gas attacks. On October 18, 1918, the 37th moved to Belgium near Ypres, and was placed under the command of the French Army. On October 31, the division advanced across no-man's land and, by November 3, had secured the area between the Lys and Escault (Scheldt) Rivers. The division sustained over sixteen hundred casualties. The Division's final conflict was on November 10, 1918, under the command of the 34th French Army Corps. The 37th re-crossed the Escault River and established secured positions. This was one of the last conflicts of the war, since the German Armistice was signed the next day on November 11, 1918. In all the units of the United States Army, forty-one men

down to an employment of about 115 men. In 1970, the firm dropped the "Wood" name and became Uniwood Division of the Union Fork & Hoe Company. Local activities continued to decline until early 1974 when all activities ceased. During the various buyouts and leases of Wood Shovel, the Retiree Pension Funds were liquidated and many long time Piqua employees lost their hard earned retirement funding.

WOODLAND PERIOD

The Woodland Period covers a prehistoric time from 1,000 B.C. to 1,000 A. D. During this period, prehistoric man in the Miami Valley developed two major cultural groups. The **Adena Culture** developed about 1,000 B.C. and lasted until about 1 A.D.

The **Hopewell Culture** developed about 100 B.C. and lasted until about 300 A.D. During the late Woodland Period (300 A.D. to 1,000 A.D.), a transitional period occurred that included and intrusive culture that briefly used early Adena and Hopewell sites and structures.

WORKER'S COTTAGE TYPE ARCHITECTURE

This is strictly a local type or style name and does not directly correspond to any national style name. The Worker's Cottage Style was popular in Piqua from the 1870's through the 1890's. These houses are found throughout all the older portions of the city. However, there are concentrations of this style on East Main Street, East North Street and New Street. These homes are small one-and-a-half story brick structures with an original layout of one or two rooms on the first floor and several bedrooms in the upper half story. The structures have a plain central doorway flanked by one window on each side on the front facing gable end. The half story has a single plain window in the center above the doorway. The cottages have little or no architectural decorations however they are very well constructed. A number of these homes on East Main Street survived being completely covered by the **flood** waters of 1913.

from Miami County died as a result of direct military action, wounds or disease, seventeen of these men were from Piqua. SEE ALSO: American Protective League; Boy Scouts; Debs, Eugene V.; Home Guard; Militia and National Guard; Parades.

WORLD WAR II

HOME FRONT. On December 7, 1941, the Japanese attacked the major American naval base at Pearl Harbor in Honolulu. The following day Congress responded to President Roosevelt's request and declared was against Japan. Three days later war was declared against Germany and Italy. Communities across the nation began preparing for war. Piqua was not totally unprepared for the conflict. The local Ohio National Guard Unit, Battery C, 136th Field Artillery, had been activated on August 27, 1940, and sent to Camp Shelby, Mississippi for training with the 37th Division.

President Roosevelt signed the Selective Training and Service Act (Burke-Wadsworth Act) on September 16, 1940. The Miami County Selective Service Board No. 1 (draft board) was organized in October of 1940 in Piqua under the leadership of Emmett P. Brush. The draft act required that all men from the ages of twenty-one to thirty-five register for the draft on October 16, 1940. In Piqua, registration took place from 7:00AM through 9:00 PM using the regular precinct voting locations. The draft registration took an average of fifteen minutes to complete and was the first of six steps which included: the October 16 registration, the Washington lottery which determined the order of call, the interrogation which was an eight page questionnaire sent out to all those individuals whose numbers were called, the deferment determined by the review of the draft board questionnaires and included verifying items such as working in an industry vital to national defense or having dependents, the physical examination, and

During World War II, military volunteers and inductees left for Cincinnati on the Baltimore & Ohio Railroad.

finally the enlistment for active duty. Miami County Board No. 1 covered Piqua and Washington, Springcreek, Brown and Newberry townships. Board No. 1 registered 3,731 men. The national registration total was estimated at over seventeen million. James Gray of 716 Young Street received the local board's draft number one. The National Draft Lottery began on October 29, 1940. The first man in Piqua to have his peacetime conscription number drawn (#102) was William "Bill" Edward Burnett, a Piqua High School graduate with the Class of 1934. He was an employee of the **Atlas Underwear Company**. The Northern Miami County Board sent its first two Piqua inductees, Edmond McCarthy and Curtis Smith, to Fort Hayes in Columbus on November 26, 1940. From that date until August of 1945, Board No. 1 would induct 2,723 men from northern Miami County into the Army and Navy. The draft was segregated with separate draft lists and quotas for white and African-American draftees. Ohio's first draft call was used to bring the 37th Infantry Division up to full strength.

By the beginning of 1942, the community was becoming fully involved in war. On January 2, 1942, alien residents of Piqua were ordered to turn in all shortwave radios, firearms, and cameras in their possession. Two individuals came forward and surrendered one gun and three cameras.

A Piqua Civilian Defense Corps first met on December 12, 1941 was formally organized on January 27, 1942, with Ken Symons as Commander. A week later, J. R. Kippart was appointed as the Corps' Chief Air Raid Warden. Each ward in the city was then organized with its own air raid captain and team of air wardens and fire watchers. Symons and Kippart organized the state's first complete blackout test in Piqua on June 5, 1942. Sirens and factory whistles were blown, blackout curtains closed, traffic halted, and the streets cleared of pedestrians. The Corps continued its effort with the establishment of an Emergency Hospital at the vacant Orr home on the northeast corner of Greene and Downing Streets. In September of 1942, Piqua became only the second city in Ohio to establish a Civilian Defense Corps short wave **radio** communications network (WLIK). The Corps received its "uniforms" in March of 1943 consisting of helmets (surplus World War I flat helmets), arm bands and gas masks. The Citizens War Services branch of the Civilian Defense Corps was headed by Frank Z. McColloch. The War Services group led many of the city's scrap drives under the leadership of Salvage Section chairman Melvin Baker. The numerous scrap drives collected metal, rubber, and anything else needed for the war effort. A 1942 campaign slogan stated "Get in the Scrap – Lick the Nazis and the Jap". Another slogan advised "Conserve the rubber in your girdles and help win the War". Enthusiasm for these drives was so high that some people donated their automobiles, and the city donated the cannon from the Rowan Memorial. While not tied directly to the scrap drives, local citizens even donated their dogs in the 1943 "Dogs for Defense" drive which trained and used dogs for patrolling military defense installations, Rationing was common during the war. The Piqua Rationing Board, chaired by Robert Patterson, was established in April of 1942. Ration stamps were required for wool, gasoline, sugar, shoes, and meat.

Housing became a major issue during the war. With new war industries spring up, housing for workers became scarce. New construction was severely limited with standard building materials very difficult to obtain. Even though rents were frozen at pre-war rates, many families split their homes into upstairs and downstairs units to take advantage of the massive need for housing. The Modern Construction Company did build a series of small brick and concrete two bed room bungalows in Piqua in 1943 and 1944. They were one of the very few private construction firms building new homes in the city. One of the unfortunate effects of the shortage of housing materials was the increasingly common practice of re-siding older homes. During the war a new product known as "Glatex" was marketed in Piqua. It was a flexible siding material made of a mixture of asbestos fibers and Portland cement and sold as a fireproofing siding for wooden structures.

The War was a boom time for local industries and completely ended the economic problems of the Depression. Two new major industries came to Piqua to engage in war work in 1941. The **Lear-Avia Company** took over the offices of the former Favorite **Stove**

Don Gentile

Captain Gentile is being decorated by
General Dwight D. Eisenhower.

In this early photograph, Don
Gentile is shown as a teenager
with his first love, an Aero Sport
biplane.

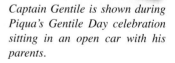

Captain Gentile is shown during
Piqua's Gentile Day celebration
sitting in an open car with his
parents.

The Gentile markers were placed
at the entrances to Piqua after
Major Gentile's tragic jet fighter
accident

Captain Gentile and fellow Ace Captain Johnny Godfrey are shown in front
of a P-51 fighter.

This 1942 photograph shows Piqua's volunteer Red Cross canteen workers.

and Range Company and began producing aircraft instrumentation and directional finding gear. Robbins and Myers Company of Springfield occupied the vacant Piqua Hosiery Company plant and produced small electrical motors for Norden bomb sights. The company was the first Piqua firm to be awarded the Army-Navy "E" award for outstanding production of war material. The "E" flag would fly over the plant for the rest of the war. But not all of the city's industrial work picture was as rosy. In April of 1943, a full page advertisement in the *Piqua Daily Call* showed a drawing of an American soldier with the caption, "They are counting on every man and women in vital industry in Piqua to speed the day of victory! Absence makes the war grow longer! 12% absenteeism from war work, which is the humiliating record of our town". The following is a partial listing of other local industries involved in war production: the **Hartzell Propeller Company** made wooden and metal propellers for the Army Air Corps and the Navy; the Orr Felt and Blanket Company made blankets and sleeping bag liners for the Army and Navy; the **Meteor Motor Car Company** produced doors for the C-46 cargo plane and trailer units for the Army Signal Corps; the **Wood Shovel and**

Tool Company manufactured entrenching tools for the military; The **French Oil Mill Machinery Company** produced machines used to straightened naval gun barrels that warped after heavy use; Jackson Tube Company made parts for Navy landing crafts, Val Decker Packing Company shipped almost half of its meat products to the military; **Cron-Kills** made desks and filing cabinets for the government, **Atlas Underwear Company** made long underwear for the Army, the **Superior Underwear Company** made silk parachutes for the Army Air Corps, and war Piqua workers in Troy and Dayton. Local employment levels increased rapidly during the war. In three separate surveys of employees at Piqua's sixteen largest plants, employment went from 2,238 in January of 1941 to 3,238 in January of 1942 to 3,960 in May of 1942. "Essential War Work" was the key to this surge with 69% of the workers being engaged in war work in January of 1942 jumping to 81% by May of that same year. Another indicator of the strength of the economic surge during World War II was the level of wages. In Miami County, wages paid out in 1935 topped $154,000. By 1945, the county wage total had reached over $267,000.

During the war, the Piqua **Red Cross** Chapter offered nineteen separate services, including a surgical dressing unit, camp and hospital project, canteen corps, home nursing, home services, motor corps, Junior Red Cross and, in March of 1943, a blood donor service. During the war, the Chapter was headed by John C. Cron, President and Mrs. Pauline R. Tafel, Executive Secretary. Over two thousand local citizens served over 175,000 volunteer hours in various Red Cross services. The canteen served eight thousand lunches for men entering the service and returning veterans. Other activities included the formation of a POW Club for families of prisoners, the production of over 1,333,000 surgical dressings, and the collection of forty-seven hundred pints of blood. The local disaster committee assisted soldiers when a Pennsylvania Railroad troop train crashed over the elevated tracks near Roosevelt Avenue in Piqua. Over four hundred returning veterans were fed and housed, and seventy-four men were treated for injuries.

The U.S.O. was active in Piqua. The local branch advertised in 1944 for young women ages eighteen to thirty to serve as dance hostesses for U.S.O. dances held in the Elks ballroom on Ash and Wayne Streets. Hostess selections were based upon age, health, neatness, reputation and references. The local U.S.O. also helped out with events at Wright and Patterson Fields in Dayton.

During World War II the Rowan Memorial cannon and cannon balls were donated to the metal scrap drives.

The fighting also hit Piqua as hundreds of its men and women left home to join the armed services. In February of 1942, when twenty to forty-five year old men were required to register for the draft, 1,254 men from Piqua signed up. By July of 1942, six hundred men from northern Miami County had joined the armed services. The city's first brush with the tragedy of war came when Private Harry Lorimer of Piqua was listed as missing in action at Pearl Harbor. The city would eventually lose sixty-nine men to death while serving in the military. The community's best known hero was Captain **Don Gentile**, a flying ace in the European campaign. Piqua's highest ranking soldier was Major General **Lester J. Whitlock**, who served on General Douglas MacArthur's staff in the Pacific and later in occupied Japan. SEE ALSO: Alien Registration Act; Celebrations (Don Gentile Day); Ei-

World War II War Bond Drives were an important part of the war's home front activities as shown in this 1945 photograph of Citizens National Bank employees.

sert, Leo; Ellerman, Alexander; Gentile, Don; Graef, Robert; Harris, William; Hemm, John; Hydeman, Earl; Militia and National Guard; Mobile Homes; Parades; Red Cross; Rowan Memorial; Ruffner, Elbert; Sherwood, James; Stoute, Alex; Stoute-Harris Post, V.F.W.; Taylor, Jean; Time; United Fund; Victory Heights; War Cottage; Whitlock, Lester.

WYANDOT TRIBE

This tribe was part of the Iroquoian language family and originally occupied an area of Upper New York State. By the late 1600's, the tribe had moved into the Upper Great Lakes area where they were identified by the French as the Tionontati (Petun) Hurons or, simply, as the Hurons. A Wyandot village was established at Detroit in 1702-04 and continued for almost fifty years. In 1738, a Wyandot village was established at Sandusky, Ohio, and from 1745 until 1748, Pennsylvania traders set up a blockhouse at this location. Another village was established at Upper Sandusky, Ohio. This village was attacked by William Crawford in June of 1782. The Wyandots signed the Treaty of Fort Harmar in 1789, **Treaty of Greenville** in 1794, **Second Treaty of Greenville** in 1814, Treaty of Rapids of Maumee in 1817, and the **Treaty of St. Mary's** in 1818. By the terms of these last two treaties, the Wyandots occupied **reservations** at Upper Sandusky, Big Springs, and one west of the Sandusky River until 1832 and 1842. SEE ALSO: Johnston, John.

YOUNG MEN'S CHRISTIAN ASSOCIATION (YMCA)

Reverend H. L. Badger presided over the founding meeting of the YMCA in March of 1877. The new organization elected Joseph D. Sawyer as President and established a reading room on the northwest corner of Main and Greene Streets. This first group had a charter membership of 123, and continued meeting through January of 1881. The YMCA was abandoned for over ten years until December of 1891, when a reorganization took place under the leadership of newly elected President **George H. Rundle**. From 1892 to 1894 a new YMCA building was erected on the southeast corner of High and Downing Streets. The building included an auditorium, reading room, gym, and the city's first indoor swimming pool. The building went through numerous remodelings and additions before being torn down in 1962 to make way for the current YMCA building, which was dedicated in November of 1963. A major addition was completed in 1977 to incorporate a new gym and pool.

One of the first African-American young men from Piqua to represent the YMCA was Thomas Clayton who served in France in 1919 as a YMCA secretary.

SEE ALSO: Badminton; Basketball; Bicycles; Bowling; Boy Scouts; Civil Rights.

YOUNG WOMEN'S CHRISTIAN ASSOCIATION (YWCA)

Miss Elizabeth Hughes, the Field secretary of the National YWCA, visited Piqua on January 4, 1909. She met with local citizens interested in forming a Piqua YWCA. Local enthusiasm for this new idea was rather lukewarm and it lacked any widespread local support. But in 1915, Mrs. A. Acton Hall, President of the City Federation of Women's Clubs, began once again promoting the idea of a local YWCA. This time the idea had a warm reception

This photograph shows the original 1894
YMCA building with the later 1930's additions.

and from 1915 until 1917, over one thousand dollars was raised for a YWCA. **World War I** interrupted fund raising activities, but, in 1918 a six thousand dollar bequest from the estate of Robert Patterson got the campaign rolling again. A general rally was held on February 24, 1919, oriented towards women working in the city's textile mills. This led to an organizational meeting held at the *Piqua Daily Call* building at 316 North Wayne Street. Miss **Lucy Patterson** was elected the YWCA's first president, and Miss Alice M. Bartlett of Maine was hired as the first General Secretary. On May 1, 1919, an open house was held in the new YWCA headquarters on North Wayne. By October of 1919, over thirteen hundred women had enrolled as YWCA members. One of the most active groups in the early YWCA was the Blue Triangle Welfare Club, which had five divisions: Fiwelco (First Welfare Club) composed of women from the **Superior Underwear Company**; Twightwee, with women from the **Atlas Underwear Company**; Hiticlu (High Times Club), from the Orr Felt and Blanket Company; **Pickawillany**, from the **Piqua Hosiery Company**; and Swastika Smiles, from the **Imperial Underwear Company**. The Piqua YWCA became a member of the National YWCA on November 23, 1919. SEE ALSO: Christmas Traditions; Civil Rights; Textile Manufacturing; Women; Patron p. 289

This 1930's photograph shows the first permanent home of the YWCA on North Wayne Street.

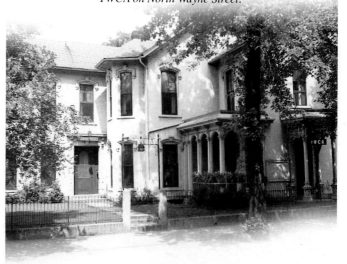

ZIP CODE

Zone Improvement Program (ZIP) codes were introduced on July 1, 1963. Piqua was given the zip code 45356. SEE ALSO: Post Office.

Young Men's Christian Association

The 1894 YMCA building on the southeast corner of High and Downing Streets showing the 1909 addition in the rear.

This 1908 postcard shows how popular bicycles were to the patrons of the YMCA.

This 1977 postcard shows the 1963 YMCA building.

Romance was assured if you kissed your date in the shadow of two trees that had grown together, better known as a "Wedded Tree"

She is dressed to the nines, only waiting for her beau to appear.

Biographies

This proper Victorian gentlemen took his rest in his favorite hammock.

Biographies

Introduction

This section covers the biographies of men and women that have had either a direct or indirect impact on the community of Piqua. Also included are short sketches of individuals who have visited the area or in some way had an impact without visiting. The material does not purport to be a complete genealogy but rather a small review of the individual's connection with Piqua. The individuals selected offer only a small portion of the many men and women that have made Piqua and the nation a better place in which to live. The biographies offered here are an attempt to provide a mixture of races, genders, ethnicities, occupations and accomplishments. The list is far from complete and as such can only offer a brief glimpse into the lives of people that have made Piqua a unique community. The symbol * is used after the name to indicate those individuals that had some impact on the community but were only in Piqua or the vicinity for a brief period of time. The use of **bold** within the biography paragraphs indicates that additional information can be found in within the *Encyclopedia*.

Melville W. Alexander (1909- 1972)

He was born in Piqua and is best known for organizing the Ohio Thoroughbred Breeders and Owners Association. For a time, he was the owner of the Polo barns located north of Piqua.

Bertha Anderson (1987 - 1971)

She was born in Piqua and was the author of several nationally known children's historical fiction books including *Tinker Tim and the Witches* (1951) and *Eric Duffy, American* (1955). Anderson's book on Tinker Tim was picked as a Weekly Reader Book Club edition in 1953 and it won the Ohioana Award in 1954.

Clara Anderson (c.1850's - 19__)

She served as one of Piqua's first African-American public school teachers in the 1870's. She was born in Ohio, the daughter of Robert E. and Mary Ann Anderson.

George Artman (1914 – 2004)

Artman was the son of Ervin Artman and graduated from Piqua High School in 1932. In 1938, he graduated from the United State Military Academy at West Point. One of his first assignments was with the 65th Infantry at Fort Buchanan, San Juan, Puerto Rico. He was sent to Europe in 1943 and commanded the 58th Armored Infantry Battalion, 8th Armored Division. By 1945, he had attained the rank of Lt. Colonel. He would retire with the rank of Colonel. For gallantry in action in Germany in 1945 he received the Silver Star.

Daniel Ashton (1783-1846)

Ashton was a pioneer physician and druggist in Piqua. He built the community's first brick home on the northwest corner of Main & Greene Streets in c. 1819. He married Olivia Ashton (1779 – 1863). His son Daniel was also a local physician.

Henry Ward Beecher Barnes (1873- 19__)

He was born in Holmes County, Ohio and came to Piqua as the High School music teacher. He also served as the choir director for the Episcopal and First Presbyterian churches. Barnes organized the Western Ohio Music Festival (1911) in Piqua and created a music publishing house known as the Pi-Qua-City Publishing Company. As a composer, he is best remembered for his church choral works. He left Piqua in 1916 for a position at St. Mark's Episcopal Church in San Antonio, Texas. During World War I he served in the military overseas. After the war he worked in Chicago, Florida and several other locations.

William R. Barrington (1796 – 1844)

Barrington was born in Philadelphia, the son of Irish immigrant Henry Barrington (1771-1839). His mother was Catherine Robinson, possibly a relative of Colonel John Johnston's wife, Rachel Robinson. Barrington married Jane Robb (c.1800-1859) and moved to Piqua in 1819-1820. The couple would have ten children between 1819 and 1842. In 1820, Barrington brought the first printing press into the Upper Miami Valley and began publishing the *Piqua Gazette*. This was the first local **newspaper** in the area. Barrington stayed with the *Gazette* from 1820 through 1826 and from 1827 to 1829. He purchased the *Western Courier and Piqua Enquirer* in 1836 and retained ownership until 1840. As an editor, publisher and reporter, Barrington became very involved in early Piqua activities including service as a local militia captain, a founding parish member and clerk of St. James Episcopal Church (Colonel Johnston was another founding member), a township school board clerk and as village mayor (1843-44). By the mid-1820's, Barrington's father Henry had moved to Piqua, setting up a jewelry store in 1829.

August Bartel (1862 – 1935)

Bartel was born in Piqua the son of German immigrants Adam and Mary Hergenham Bartel. At the age of seventeen he went to work for the German language **newspaper**, the *Der Piqua Correspondent*. He purchased the paper in 1894 and changed the name to the *Die Miami Post*. Anti-German bias during World War I led to the gradual demise of the newspaper in 1919. However Bartel continued as a job printer until his death in 1935.

Clarence J. Bartel (1892 – 1942)

Bartel was born in Piqua, the son of Aloysius and Antonia Bartel. He was an overseas veteran of **World War I**. He was appointed Piqua Postmaster in 1934 and served until his death.

Bartel also served as the president of the Home Aluminum and Bronze Company.

John Gordon Battelle (1845 – 1918)

He was born in Clarksburg, West Virginia the son of Methodist minister Rev. Gordon B. Battelle. He was active in the manufacturing of iron in Wheeling, West Virginia and later in Tennessee. He came to Piqua in 1889 with James Hicks to manage the **Cincinnati Corrugating Company** (secretary/treasurer) and the Piqua Rolling Mills (president).

William C. Beachler (1919-20__)

Beachler was the brother of Dr. John Beachler and graduated from Piqua High School in 1937. He joined the United States Army in 1941 and attended Officer Candidate School. By 1942 he had been promoted to the rank of Captain. With the 6th Division on Luzon in the Philippine Islands, Beachler was awarded the Silver Star for gallantry in action. He retired with the rank of Colonel.

Addison Bell (18__ - 19__)

Bell was the first local **Socialist** to run for the office of Mayor in 1907. He was also the president of the Iron, Tin and Steel **Union** Local No. 194 at the **Cincinnati Corrugating Company**.

Harry L. Bell (1892 - 1965)

Bell was born near Winchester, Ohio and moved to Piqua in 1921 after serving in **World War I**. He established the Sherer-Bell Auto Agency in Piqua. Bell purchased the Queen City Chevrolet Company in downtown Cincinnati in February of 1938. The following year he took over the Winders Motor Chevrolet Sales Company in Columbus. Bell acquired other Midwest agencies including one in Chicago to become one of the largest Chevrolet dealerships in the world. In 1939, Bell had gross sales of over three million dollars. Bell was an active local philanthropist providing funds for everything from band uniforms to hospital emergency equipment. He was responsible for the rebirth of the Piqua Community Chest in the late 1950's.

Kenneth W. Benner (c.1904 – 19__)

Brenner was the son of Walter Benner and graduated from Piqua High School in 1922. He was a graduate of the United States Naval Academy and began a life-long career in the United States Marine Corps. He participated in the 1926 **Nicaragua Invasion** and later he was stationed in Haiti. In July of 1940, he was sent to Midway Island to survey anti-aircraft defenses and then returned to Hawaii where he helped to defend Pearl Harbor on December 7, 1941 against the Japanese attack at the beginning of **World War II.** He was active in the assault on Guadalcanal in August of 1942 where he was awarded the Purple Heart. As a colonel, he served on the staff of General Vandegrift commander of the First Marine Division.

Charles W. Bennett (1840 - 1922)

He was born and raised in Miami County and served in the Civil War. In 1874 he was appointed as Piqua's Superintendent of Schools serving until 1907. During his tenure, the second high school was built in 1885 and the Schmidlapp Free School **Library** opened in 1890. He was elected president of the Ohio State Teacher's Association. He served as the secretary (c.1921) of the Ohio Freedman Aid Society of the Methodist Episcopal Church. An author, a civic leader, and pioneer educator, Bennett was recognized in Piqua with the naming of the Bennett Junior High School.

Louisa Timmons Bennett (1841 - 1883)

She moved to Piqua with her husband School Superintendent **C.W. Bennett** in 1874. She was the first women to receive a Masters of Music degree from Ohio Wesleyan College. Bennett was active in the Piqua Female Bible Society and the W.C.T.U.

Henry Bertling (c.1861 - 1944)

He opened the first automobile garage in the city 1903 with Ed Snyder. He also established the first auto dealership in 1903 known as the Piqua **Automobile** Station.

William Best (17__ - 1849)

An English immigrant, he came to Piqua in the 1830's and became one of the city's first commercial artists specializing in portraits. He was one of the founding members of Piqua's Wesleyan Methodist Church. In 1835, Best advertised his availability to paint portraits, signs or houses.

Jacob Bettman (1856 – 1935)

Bettman was born in Cincinnati and lived most of his life there. His connection to Piqua began in 1883, when he became a major investor in the **Favorite Stove & Range Company**. He moved to Piqua in 1887 and served as the firm's secretary-treasurer until 1912. He returned to Piqua in 1934 as chairman of the board of the firm and helped with its liquidation that same year. He died in his suite at the Favorite Hotel in Piqua.

Herbert Seeley Bigelow (1870 – 1951) *

Bigelow was born in Hamilton County, Ohio and became well known in Ohio for his stands against imperialism and war. He was one of the founders of the Cincinnati Anti-Imperialist League in the late 1890's. He was a Congregationalist minister and socialist and was one of the leading lights of the Social Gospel Movement. He served in the Ohio House (1913), Cincinnati Council (1936) and as a U.S. congressman (1937). He spoke to Piqua **Socialists** on the public square in October of 1917. He criticized the management of the May's Opera House for banning the Socialist from meeting in their facility. May's manager Harry W. Kress criticized the Socialist's for their anti-war passivism.

Henry Bird (17__ - 18__) *

Captain Henry Bird of the King's 8th Foot Regiment (stationed in Canada 1768 to 1785) led an Indian and British attack on the American Fort Laurens in February of 1779. The attack ended when Bird's forces ran out of food. In 1780, Bird left Fort Detroit in an offensive move against the Americans. This major raid was in retaliation for Clark's attack against the Ohio Indians in 1778-79. Bird's forces moved through the Miami Valley on their way to attack Kentucky settlements. After destroying two fortified settlements, Bird ordered a retreat back to Detroit taking with him over three hundred prisoners.. The ability of the British to raid Kentucky, led to Clark's expedition that pushed the Shawnee tribes from the future site of Springfield to the future site of Piqua.

Black Hoof (1740 – 1831) *

Black Hoof was a chief of the **Shawnee** tribe also known as Catahecassa. He was an active and successful opponent of European-American settlement west of the Allegheny Mountains. He was present at British General Braddock's defeat (1755), at the Battle of Point Pleasant (1774), the Battle of Piqua (Clark County in 1780) and at the defeats of General Harmar (1790) and General St. Clair (1791). He made his peace with European-American settlement and signed the two Treaties of Greenville in 1795 and 1814 and the Treaty of St. Mary's in 1818. With Chief **Little Turtle**, he was an advocate for Native American neutrality at the **Council of Piqua** held at Johnston Farm in 1812. Black Hoof died on the Shawnee Reservation at Wapakoneta.

Blue Jacket (c1750-c1810) *

A **Shawnee** chief, also known as Weyapiersenwah, led the Native American forces against General Wayne at the Battle of Fallen Timbers in 1794. He signed the Treaty of Greenville in 1794, the Treaty of Fort Industry in 1805, and the Second Treaty of Greenville in 1814. SEE ALSO: Battle of Fallen Timbers, Girty, Simon; Shawnee Indians; Treaty of Greenville.

William King Boal (1831 – 1916)

Boal was born in Pennsylvania, the son of a Scottish immigrant James Boal. He moved to Cincinnati from Kentucky in 1863 and establish a grocery/commission merchant business. In 1872 he purchased the W.C. Davis Company (Great Western Stove Works). He changed the name in 1888 to the **Favorite Stove & Range Company** and moved the firm to Piqua. By the mid-1890's, the firm was producing fifty thousand stoves a year and was the city's single largest employer. Boal was a life-long **Democrat** who split with the party in 1896 over the silver-gold issue. He became an active supporter of presidential candidate William McKinley and the gold standard. In 1855, he married Miss Eliza Naomi Von Bibber.

This is an oil painting of Stanhope Boal.

William Stanhope Boal (1856 - 1933)

Boal was born in Kentucky, the son of William and Naomi Van Bibbler Boal. By 1880 he was working as a traveling salesman for his father's stove company. When the company reorganized and moved to Piqua, Boal became the manager of the sales department. By 1900, Boal had been promoted to Vice President and after the death of his father in 1916, he was elected President of the firm. In 1925, he was elected Chairman of the

Board, a position he held until his death on December 17, 1933. When the firm moved to Piqua in 1889, Boal became one of the community's most active citizens. He purchased and remodeled the **Plaza Hotel** (Favorite Hotel) in 1914. He served as the first Exalted Rule of the Piqua Elks Lodge, was one of the founders of the Piqua Country Club, created the Boal Colonial Inn next to the golf course and was one of the founders of the Home **Telephone** Company. Boal introduced the first commercial **air conditioning** system in Piqua in the Bijou **Theater** on Ash Street in 1907.

Father Joseph Pierre de Bonnecamps (1707 – 1790) *

Bonnecamps was a Jesuit priest that served as a chaplain with Celeron's expedition down the Ohio River in 1749. He visited **Pickawillany** and **Old Britain** with **Celeron** and wrote a journal about the entire expedition. Father Bonnecamps was the first Catholic priest to visit the Upper Miami Valley. SEE ALSO: Celeron, Old Britain, Pickawillany.

Daniel Boone (1735-1820) *

Pioneer, settler, explorer, Indian scout Daniel Boone is a legend in American history. In 1782, Boone led a company of Kentucky militiamen up from Kentucky into the Ohio country. The expedition was under the overall command of General **George Rogers Clark**. The army marched up the Miami Valley, and on November 10, 1782, the **Shawnee** villages at Piqua were destroyed. Piqua's other connection to Boone was through Colonel **John Johnston** who met Boone in Kentucky in 1794. Johnston also served as a pallbearer when Boone's body was returned to Kentucky from Missouri.

Henry Bouquet (1719-1765) *

A Swiss soldier of fortune, Henry Bouquet was hired by the British to help pacify the Ohio Valley. In 1764, he led a British expedition into Ohio from Fort Pitt. Bouquet persuaded the Ohio tribes to sign a treaty promising to support the British and end raids against white settlements. SEE ALSO: Groghan, George.

C.W. Bowdle (18__ - 1863)

He was a pioneer local blacksmith and machinist in Piqua, establishing the Bowdle Machine Shop. He was politically active serving on the Piqua city council in the 1830's and 1840's and as council president from 1856 until his death in 1863.

George S. Bowles (c.1865-19__)

Bowles was born in Piqua and became very active in the **African-American** fraternal life of the community. In the 1880's, he served as the Worshipful Master of the Masonic Union Lodge No. 18. Bowles was one of the original organizers of the Colored Knights of Pythias in 1892. He was a barber by profession and worked in partnership with **Albert Pressly** in the 1880's.

Armotte Harvey Boyer (1887 – 1960)

He was born in Piqua, the son of John Lee and Ida Harvey Boyer. He attended the Piqua High School and graduated from the Culver Military Academy in 1907. Boyer then went to work for his father at the **Union Underwear Company**. He served as the assistant to the president (Maurice Wolfe) of the **Meteor Motor Car Company** from 1920 until Wolfe's death in 1935. By 1930, he had become the secretary-treasurer of the corporation and president of the Meteor Phonograph Company. He was president of the firm from 1935 until the late 1940's. Boyer served as vice president of the Champion Cutter & Fixture Company (roll paper cutters) from the 1920's until after World War II. Boyer was the president and general manager of the Union Finance Company from the 1920's through the 1950's. SEE ALSO: Meteor Motor Car Company

John Lee Boyer (c.1850's -19__)

He was born in Clermont County near Cincinnati. He began his business career in 1874 with the John Schillito Company, a major retail clothing establishment. He moved to Piqua and established the **Union Underwear Company** in 1891. He was very active in the community serving as a director of the Piqua Savings **Bank** and the Piqua Home **Telephone** Company. In 1903-4, he contracted with **A.M. Fry** to build the Colonial Saxony Building on West Greene Street, one of the community's first apartment buildings. SEE ALSO: Apartments; Union Underwear Company

Lewis Boyer (1755 – 1843)

Boyer served during the **Revolutionary War** as a Second Lieutenant in General George Washington's Dragoons. This unit served as Washington's military bodyguard. He died in Miami County and is buried in a small cemetery just over the boundary line in Shelby County.

William M. Boyer (1854 – 1937)

He was born in Mifflinburg, Pennsylvania, the son of Samuel and Catherine Miller Boyer. He first came to Piqua in 1882 to work as a miller at the Eagle Mills on Water Street. He stayed only a year before returning to DeGraff, Ohio. Boyer returned to Piqua in 1896 and bought a controlling interest in the Piqua Milling Company with L.E. Chamberlain. He served as president of the firm and during the next forty years purchased grain elevators on South Main and at Farrington south of Piqua as well as gasoline stations on East Ash Street and Farrington. He was an active member of Greene Street Methodist Episcopal Church and served as a director of the Citizens National **Bank**.

Alfred Brady (c.1910 – 1937)*

Brady was a national criminal and head of the Brady gang in the 1930's. After Dillinger's death, he became the FBI's "Public Enemy Number One". He was known for his use of heavy gunfire and the killing of innocent civilians. Brady and his gang robbed the Piqua Swisher-Fulmer Market on March 21, 1936. Twenty-one year old Edward Lindsay walked in on the crime and was shot to death by Brady. While hiding out in Bangor, Maine, Brady was killed in a gun battle with police and FBI men in October of 1937.

Armstrong Brandon (1770 - 1827)

One of the early pioneer settlers in the Piqua, he was the community's first surveyor and civil engineer. In June of 1807, he surveyed out 101 lots for land owners **John Manning** and **Matthew Caldwell**. This became the village of Washington (**Piqua**). Brandon remained in the new village and in 1811 became the first postmaster, serving until 1816.

By 1818, Brandon had moved to Indiana where he published a newspaper.

Richard Brandriff (1803 - 1887)

He was born in New Jersey and moved to Ohio with his family as a young boy. At the age of eighteen he became an itinerant Methodist minister riding the circuit in south central Ohio. In 1862, he moved to Piqua and opened a drug store on Main Street. He developed the formula for what would become the nationally known "Cook's delight" baking soda. Rev. Brandriff was an active abolitionist and later a leader in the **temperance** movement.

Robert Lee Brandt (19__ - 1943)

He served as an officer and by 1943 commander of Battery C, 136th Field Artillery, **Ohio National Guard** stationed in Piqua. Brant was activated with the unit in 1940 just prior to World War II and went to Camp Shelby with the 37th Infantry Division, ONG. He was promoted to captain and transferred to the 174th Field Artillery Regiment. He died in an automobile accident on his way to his new assignment at Fort Sill, Oklahoma. He was Piqua's first military service casualty of **World War II**.

John Wyant Brown (c.1849 -1937)

He was born in Athens, Ohio, the son of Henry and Elizabeth Hyde Brown. He moved form Akron to Piqua in 1883 and started a dry goods store that would become the J.W. Brown Department Store. By 1909, the Brown Store would be the largest department store between Dayton and Toledo. Brown was a major investor in Piqua industry serving as vice president of the Miami Light, Heat & Power Company and the French Oil Mill Machinery Company and as a director of the Piqua Handle Manufacturing Company, the Piqua National Bank and the Piqua Savings Bank. He was married in 1888 to Nettie Brooks.

McPherson Brown (1860 – 19__)

Brown was born in Pittsburg, Pennsylvania, the son of John Brown Jr.. He came to Piqua in 1889 with the Cincinnati Corrugating Works as an expert sheet-iron roller. He then moved to the insurance field where he became the general manager of the Loyal Mutual Insurance Company of Piqua from 1893 through 1899. He became a director of the Hubbard Grain Company and the Piqua Building and Loan Association. He was a strong **Republican** elected in 1893 and 1895 to the office of **State Senator** for the Twelfth Senatorial District. In May of 1898, he organized Company K, Third Infantry regiment, **Ohio National Guard** and was elected its captain. In July of 1898 the company was sent south but the **Spanish-American War** ended before the company was sent to Cuba.

Emmett Parker Brush Jr. (1917 – 1989)

He was born in Springcreek Township, the son of Emmett P. and Mary B. Widney Brush Sr. He graduated from Piqua High School with the class of 1934. He served in the United States Army Air Corps during **World War II.** He served as a Ohio Fire Marshall and in 1958 was appointed as Piqua's postmaster. Active in Republican politics he served as chairman of both the Miami County Central and Executive Committees.

William Jennings Bryan
(1860-1925) *

Nicknamed the "Great Commoner", Bryan ran for president under the Populist and **Democratic** Party banners. He was also an ardent supporter of temperance and prohibition. During his presidential campaign against McKinley, Bryan spoke in Piqua on October 19, 1896. His speech on the public square was well attended but he did not gain any significant support, losing Piqua by over two hundred votes. In the 1900 presidential election, he failed to carry the city by 131 votes and in 1908, he failed by only forty-eight votes. Bryan visited Piqua twice again in the years following his presidential campaigns. On October 23, 1915, he spoke at May's Opera House to promote state-wide **prohibition.** Four years later, on October 28, 1919, Bryan spoke at the First Presbyterian Church, this time promoting national prohibition. Bryan died in 1925 as one of the nation's most respected senior statesman. SEE ALSO: Prince, William J.

Belle C. Buchanan
SEE EVANS

William Insco Buchanan
(1852 –1909)

He was born in Miami County and moved to Piqua in 1876. He served as the U.S. Ambassador to Argentina and as the first U.S. Minister to the Republic of Panama. In 1901 he served as the Director General of the Pan-American Exposition in Buffalo, New York.

George W. Bush
(1946 - present) *

After a speech at a **Republican** Party rally on the public square in Troy in 2004, Bush's campaign bus traveled down Main Street in Piqua. Bush spoke to the crowds through a loud speaker system on the bus. The bus slowed but never stopped on its way north to Sidney. On April 19, 2007, Bush spoke at the Tippecanoe High School and left immediately afterwards on Air Force One.

William T. Busser
(c.1840's – c.1930's)

He began in the confectioners trade in 1862 in Urbana and moved to Piqua in 1892 to establish the W.T. Busser Store at 320 North Main Street. The store continued in business until the late 1940's. being run by Celia Busser Howell

Benjamin Franklin Butler
(1818-1893) *

During the **Civil War**, General Butler was the commander of the occupation troops in New Orleans. His harsh treatment of the civilian population led to the nickname "The Beast of New Orleans". During the war Butler visited Piqua on October 6, 1863, to participate in a Union Party rally on the public square. General Butler was a presidential candidate in the 1884 election, running under the People's Labor Greenback Party and the Anti-Monopoly Party banners. On November 3, 1884, he passed through Piqua on a special campaign railroad car on his way to the west. The train slowed only long enough for Butler to wave as the train passed Main Street. There is no record of Butler's vote in Piqua, but on a countywide basis, he received fourteen votes, or 0.15% of the total popular vote.

Matthew Caldwell Sr.
(1757-1810)

Caldwell was born in Ireland and immigrated to the United States shortly after the Revolutionary War. He brought his family into the untamed forests of the Upper Miami Valley in 1804 and cleared land for a small family farm. With a vision of future growth, he joined with John Manning in 1807 and laid out lots along the Great Miami River for the new village of Washington. Caldwell's original land was bordered by the current streets of Camp, Wayne, and South. Caldwell and his family helped the new community grow into the city of **Piqua.** Caldwell Street was named for this pioneer settler. He was inducted into the Piqua Civic Hall of Fame in 2004.

Matthew Caldwell Jr.
(17__ - 1864)

Caldwell was born in Kentucky and moved to what would become Piqua with his parents in 1804. He was an early farmer and developer of his family land. He actively farmed much of the land west of Downing Street and after his marriage to Harriet Kemper, built a brick home on what is now the northeast corner of Ash and Caldwell Streets. He was responsible for platting out large sections of pre-Civil War Piqua. He served as the treasurer of Washington Township from 1825 through 1829.

Robert Callender (17__ - 17__)*

Callender was a Pennsylvania trader, tavern owner and soldier. In January-February of 1751, he accompanied other traders including George Croghan and Christopher Gist to the Miami village of **Pickawillany**.

James Carson (18__ - 1877)

Carson was a tanner, politician and amateur scientist. He served on the Piqua town council in 1843-1844 and the city council 1863-1866. He was a Washington Township trustee in 1868-1869. He served as a member of the Piqua Board of Education from 1860 to 1867 and as president of the Board 1867 to 1877. He was an avid traveler and was known for his geological specimen collection which was donated to the city schools after his death. Captain Carson served as the last commanding officer of the Piqua Blues Light Infantry Company in the 1840's. He was married to Mary E. Carson who died in 1903.

Piere-Joseph Celoron,
Sieur de Blainville (1693 - 1759)*

This French explorer/soldier and future commandant of Detroit (1752-1754) was sent down the Ohio River with 250 men in 1749 by the Governor of New France. The journey was chronicled by his chaplain, Father **Joseph Pierre de Bonnecamps**. The objective of the expedition was to claim the area for France and keepout the English/Colonial traders. Celoron planted leaden plates at the mouth of each important tributary of the Ohio River. The last plate was buried at the mouth of the Great Miami River. Celoron's expedition traveled north up the river to **Pickawillany.**

Celeron met with the Miami Chief **Old Britain** in September of 1749. He urged the Chief to return to the French post in modern day Indiana and abandon Pickawillany. Celeron was unable to influence the Indians to abandon either Pickawillany or the English allies. Celeron returned to Montreal recommending that French merchants either lower their prices when trading with the Indians or that the military be used to forcibly remove all English/Colonial traders. SEE ALSO: Pickawillany, Bonnecamps

Louis Ciriegio (c.1919 - ____)

He was the son of Julius and Caroline Sciaccitano Ciriegio and graduated from Piqua High School in 1937. He worked as reporter and later as an employee of the Val Decker Packing Company. He entered the United States Army in 1941. Ciriegio earned his wings and commission in February of 1944. He had flown thirty bombing missions over Germany when he was shot down in December of 1944. He was a German prisoner of war until his liberation in May of 1945.

George Rogers Clark (1752-1818)*

Trained as a surveyor, Clark took an early interest in the west, particularly Kentucky. At the beginning of the American Revolution, Clark raised and trained militia units to fight the British and the Indians who occupied large sections of land in the west. In 1780, he led troops into the future State of Ohio and destroyed several Shawnee villages. In November of 1782, General Clark led approximately one thousand militiamen north from Kentucky up the Great Miami River. Other leaders in this army included Colonel Robert Patterson, Colonel **Daniel Boone** and Captain **Simon Kenton**. On November 10, 1782, the Shawnee village of Chillicothe or Lower **Piqua** (located on the east bank of the Great Miami River) was attacked and destroyed by Clark's men. The **Shawnee** at Upper Piqua (located near the present site of the Piqua Historical Area) fled before Clark could attack. The army camped on the site of Lower Piqua and sent a detachment of 150 men up north along the river to destroy the trading post of Frenchmen Peter **Loramie** on Loramie's Creek. SEE ALSO: Girty, Simon; Piqua, Battle of; Roads.

Viola Ruth Bowdry Clemens (1908 – 2004)

Clemons was born in London, Ohio, went to school in Mechanicsburg, Ohio and moved to Piqua in 1925 with her husband Emerson. Her first job was as a seamstress at the Piqua Memorial Hospital. Clemens took Red Cross nurses' training during World War II and volunteered hundreds of hours at the Piqua Memorial Hospital. During the 1940's, she was an active member of the local chapter of the **N.A.A.C.P.** She participated in several sit-ins that helped end segregation in restaurants and movie theaters in the city. She began a catering business in Piqua in 1951 that stayed active until 1983. Clemens was the first **African-American** member of the Piqua Altrusa, a local women's professional group. She served on the board of directors of the YWCA, a leader with the Negro Girl Reserves and treasurer of the Miami County Republican Women's Club. She was awarded the Chamber of Commerce's **Order of George Award** in 2001.

Grover Cleveland (1837-1908) *

The presidential campaign of 1884 was a hotly contested battle between Cleveland, the **Democratic** candidate, and James G. Blaine as **Republican** contender. Piqua voted Democratic by a margin of 51.35% to 48.65%. The national election was very close with Cleveland receiving 48.5% of the vote, and Blaine 48.25%. As our 22nd president, Cleveland passed through Piqua on the Chicago, St. Louis and Pittsburgh Railroad on October 1, 1887. The train did not stop and the President did not appear at the window or on the rear train platform. The voters of Piqua ignored this slight and in the 1888 election, Cleveland carried Piqua with 51.96% of the popular vote to 48.04%. When Cleveland ran for president again in 1892, he carried Piqua by a margin of only 21 votes out of the 2,456 votes cast. Cleveland died on June 24, 1908. SEE ALSO: Hendricks, Thomas A.

Alexander G. Conover (1819 – 1876)

Conover was born in Dayton but moved to Piqua in his twenties. He was a civil engineer and served as Piqua's city engineer in the 1850's and 1860's. He worked on the **Miami & Erie Canal** route north of Piqua, the Piqua **Hydraulic Canal**, the Columbus, Piqua & Indiana **Railroad** and built Conover's Opera House in 1872. He also served as a lieutenant in the a local **militia** unit known as the Piqua Grays. He was the first local citizen to be elected to a state office under the Republican Party banner, with his election to the Ohio Board of Public Works in 1855. He served one two year term on the Board.

Cornstalk (c.1720-1777)*

Cornstalk was a Chief of the **Shawnee** tribe who led the Native American forces at the Battle of Point Pleasant in 1774. He signed a treaty with Lord Dunmore in 1774. He was taken hostage at Point Pleasant (West Virginia) by European-American settlers and subsequently murdered.

James Middleton Cox (1870-1957) *

Cox was well known locally for his ownership of the *Dayton Daily News*. He was also a prominent **Democratic** politician serving as Ohio's governor in 1913-15, 1917-19, and 1919-21. As a gubernatorial candidate, Cox visited Piqua on May 16, 1912. His visit may well have helped his election, as he won the local vote with a margin of 43.6% of the vote over three other candidates. Cox visited the city again during his presidential campaign against Harding on October 14, 1920. A large crowd gathered on the public square to hear the governor speak on world peace and the League of Nations. Cox lost the election, receiving only 38.1% of the vote in Miami County and 34.1% on a national level. James M. Cox died at his home in Dayton, Ohio on July 15, 1957. SEE ALSO: Harding, Warren G.

Crane – SEE TARHE.

George Croghan (c1720-1782)*

Croghan was a native of Ireland, immigrating to Cumberland County, Pennsylvania in 1741. By 1746, he was actively engaged in the Indian trade in the Ohio country. In 1748, he established a trading house at Logstown and later one at **Pickawillany**. In the 1750's, Croghan served as a representative of the Governor of Pennsylvania to the Indians of the Ohio county. He journeyed to Pickawillany in 1751 with Christopher Gist and Robert Callender. Croghan negotiated a treaty at Pickawillany with the Miami and representatives of the Delaware, **Shawnee** and Ottawa tribes. The Pennsylvania traders were represented at the negotiations by Croghan, **Gist**, Callender, and Thomas T. K. Kinton. The Pennsylvania Assembly later rejected the treaty as too costly. By 1753 Croghan was a major land owner in Huntington County, Pennsylvania and maintained an active Indian trade in partnership with William Trent. He was commissioned a Captain of militia and served in the defense of western Pennsylvania during the Indian uprisings in the 1750's. In 1754, he served with George Washington in the Fort Necessity Campaign. In 1755, he served with General Braddock's soldier scouts. In 1763, he served the British under Sir William Johnson as Deputy for Indian Affairs. During Pontiac's Rebellion in 1763, he accompanied Colonel Bouquet in his campaign against the Ohio tribes. A year later, Croghan negotiated a peace treaty with Pontiac in the Illinois country. By the 1770's, Croghan was bankrupt and living in Pittsburgh. He died in obscurity in Philadelphia. SEE ALSO: Bouquet, Henry; Callender, Robert; Gist, Christopher; Pickawillany.

Andrew Jackson Cron (1855 - 1905)

Cron was born in Huntersville, the son of **Nicholas** (1810-1887) and Nancy Wood **Cron** (1814-1876) and the younger brother of **Lucius C. Cron**. He worked for his brother at the **L.C. & W.L. Cron Furniture Company** before founding his own furniture company in 1881 with Robert Kills known as the **Cron-Kills Company**. Cron served fourteen terms on the **Huntersville** Village Council from 1879 through 1893. He was also the president of the Fifth Special School District [Huntersville] being instrumental in the passage of the 1889 levy campaign for a new Huntersville School on Staunton Street and served as the Board of Education president in 1889. From 1887 through 1892, Cron served as the village fire chief. After Huntersville was absorbed by Piqua, Cron was elected to three terms on the Piqua City Council (1893-1898). He married Almeda Noland in 1873 and they had ten children.

Jackson Clifford Cron (1869 - 1952)

He was born in Piqua (Huntersville), the son of **Lucius C.** and Margaret Ginn **Cron**. He left high school to work for his father in the **L.C. & W.L. Cron Furniture Company**. He partnered briefly with Frank C. Campbell in the retail furniture business before establishing the J.C. Cron & Son furniture store in 1888. Cron was granted Ohio State Embalming License 8B (the B meant he had not attended a formal embalming school) in about 1903. In 1919, the Cron store had established a **funeral home** at 400 North Wayne Street. Cron would be joined by his sons Kenneth L., John C. and Robert D. in the funeral business. He married Stella Irene Denman in 1898.

Lucius Cohen "Coney" Cron (1836 - 1926)

Cron was born in a log cabin on Water Street in Piqua the son of **Nicholas** (1810-1887) and Nancy **Cron** (1814-1876). At age eighteen (1854) was apprenticed to a local cabinet maker. In 1860, he had established a cabinet shop as a junior partner with S. Alware. In 1862, he became "a drummer boy" in the **Civil War** for the 110th Ohio Regiment, making his own inlaid wooden drum. He was mustered out of the unit in 1865 as the regiment's chief musician. Cron founded the **L.C. & W.L.**

Cron Company in 1868, which became one of the largest of its kind in the entire area. The company's plant was built just east of his father's home in Huntersville at 218 East Main Street. He remained as the firm's president until 1905. He was also one of the founders of the **Democratic** Publishing Company, president of the Third Building & Loan and the Piqua Natural Gas and Oil Company. Cron served as the Democratic Mayor of the Village of **Huntersville** (Shawnee) from 1867 to 1891. He moved west of the river in 1898 (moved into the **W. K. Boal** home on the ridge of the Park Avenue hill over looking the **Hydraulic Canal**) and in that same year was elected to the Piqua City Council. During 1900 to 1901 he served as president of the council and from 1906 to 1909 as Piqua's **Mayor**. During the years from 1910 to 1915, Cron served as a Washington Township Justice of the Peace, trustee and treasurer. He was very active with the G.A.R. Drum & Fife Corps. Cron married Margaret "Maggie" Ginn (1838-1873) in 1859 and after her death married Marcella Edwards (1848-1931) in 1874. His children were Maggie (1866), Charles L. (1867), Jackson C. (1869), Florence and Clarence (1883).

Nicholas Cron (1810 – 1887)

He was born in Franklin County, Ohio and moved to Springcreek Township with his parents Jacob (1775-1837) and Mary Davis Cron in 1813. His parents had moved to Ohio from New Jersey in 1808. By trade, Nicholas was a carpenter/turner and in 1831 he married Nancy Wood (born c. 1814). They setup housekeeping in a log cabin on Water Street. By 1840, the couple had moved into a frame home on East Main Streets in Huntersville on land they had purchased from David Hunter in 1834. He was the brother of John, Henry and Harvey Cron. His children were Mary (c.1831), **Lucius C.** (1836), Sarah (c.1840), Henry (c.1845), William R. (c.1849) and **Andrew Jackson** (1852).

William L. Cron (1826 - 1907)

Cron was born in Springcreek Township the son of John (1803-1888) and Matilda Tucker Cron (1804-1867) (John had four wives 1824, 1872, 1873, 1877) and the grandson of Jacob (1755-1837) and Mary Davis Cron. Jacob Cron moved to Ohio in 1808 and Springcreek Township in 1813. William Cron served as an apprentice to a cabinet maker in 1845. During the Civil War he served as a First Lieutenant in Company A, 110th Ohio Volunteer Infantry Regiment that was raised at **Camp Piqua**. After the war, he was one of the founders of the **L.C. & W.L. Cron Furniture Company**. Cron sold his interest in the furniture plant in 1905. He would also establish a retail furniture store on Main Street that would be later taken over by **Jackson C. Cron**. His first wife was Annis B. Day (1852) and his second wife was Mary F. Frost (1857).

Harry E. Croner (1881 – 1972)

He was born in Piqua the son of Charles E. and Louisa Weidner Croner and graduated from Piqua High School. He worked at Magee Brothers Printing Company from 1905 to 1943. In 1929, he was one of the major supporters and promoters of the **City Commission-City Manager** form of government. During the early years of **World War II** he served as chairman of the Piqua Civilian Defense Council. He was a commissioner at large on the Piqua City Commission and became the mayor of Piqua in 1940. He resigned from the commission and as mayor in 1943 when he was appointed as Piqua's postmaster. He served as postmaster until 1958.

Harry Lillis "Bing" Crosby (1903 - 1977) *

Singer and movie star, Bing Crosby with his wife Kathryn Grant and their daughter Mary Francis, flew in a private plane to Piqua. They stayed with the Wood family at their mansion on Park Avenue (Arrowston). Crosby attended mass at St. Mary's Catholic Church and sat in the rear balcony.

John Vinton Daganhardt (1881 – 19__)

Daganhardt was born on a farm near Piqua, the son of a German immigrant. He graduated from the Piqua High School in 1902 and then graduated from Ohio State University. Shortly after graduation he began practicing law in Piqua. He served as a Justice of the Peace in Washington Township. He was a published poet and was best known for the poem *There's an Old Home in Ohio* which was set to music and sold on a national level. He also served as president of the Cosmopolitan Club.

John W. Daniels (c.1857 – 1931)

Daniels was born and educated in Piqua before becoming one of the partners of the Orr, Leonard & Company, a **linseed** processing company in 1879. With his father-in-law, Lewis Leonard, Daniels would be very active in local linseed manufacturing. In 1901, he became a director with the American Linseed Oil Company. The following year, Daniels became one of the founding partners of what would become the Archer-Daniels-Midland Company out of Minneapolis. A-D-M Inc. is one of the world's largest agribusinesses, with over five hundred processing plants in the United States. In 1890, Daniels was one of the founding members of the Citizens Library Committee that helped furnish the Schmidlapp Free School **Library**.

Thomas L. Daniels (1828 – 1873)

Daniels was born in Hamilton County and moved to Piqua in the 1850's. As an early local manufacturer, he joined with his father-in-law, **Dr. John O'Ferrall** in organizing the Piqua Agricultural Works (farm machinery), F. Gray, O'Ferrall & Company (woolen manufacturing) and the O'Ferrall & Daniels Company (flour mill). He served on the city council from 1863 through 1867, the last four years as council president. He also served as Piqua city treasurer from 1871 until his death.

Thomas Leonard Daniels (1892 – 1977)

Daniels was born in Piqua and graduated from Yale in 1914. After serving in **World War I**, he entered the United States Foreign Service in 1921 serving until 1929. At that time he joined the Archer-Daniels-Midland Company of Minneapolis as assistant treasurer. Moving through the corporate ranks, in 1947 he became the giant corporation's third president. A-D-M is one of the world's largest agribusinesses operating over five hundred processing plants in the United States.

Arthur Davis (c. 1806- 18__)

Davis was the first **African-American** on record to live within the city's boundaries. The 1820 census shows a fourteen year old Davis living with Charles Murray as a servant or laborer.

Arthur N. Davis (18__- 19__)

An American dentist, Davis moved to Germany to become the personal dentist to Kaiser Wilhelm II of Germany in 1905. Davis later wrote a book about his experiences at the German court. Davis had a brief practice in Piqua.

Robert M. Davis (1923 - 1990)

He grew up in Troy, but moved to Piqua and joined the staff of the Citizens National **Bank**, an institution he would serve for thirty-four years, retiring as the Chairman of the Board. As a banker, he actively promoted the economic growth of Piqua by encouraging and supporting the creation of new and vital local industries. As a community leader he was a driving force in

Robert M. Davis (1923-1990)

the expansion of the **YMCA**, the Piqua Memorial Hospital, the United Fund, and the Chamber of Commerce. He was inducted into the **Piqua Civic Hall of Fame** in 2006.

Eugene Victor Debs (1855-1926) *

Debs was the founder and long time leader of the **Socialist Party** of America (SPA), established in 1898. He was the SPA candidate for president in 1900, 1904, 1908, 1912, and 1920. By 1906-7, a local Piqua **Socialist Party** had been organized. Debs visited the local organization on September 17, 1910 and held a rally on the public square. Debs' highest vote total in Piqua came in the 1912 election when he received 8.06% of the total popular vote. During World War I, while giving a speech in Akron, Ohio, Debs was arrested by federal agents and charged with violating the 1917 Espionage Act. The socialist Mayor of Piqua, Frank Hamilton, was with Debs on the speakers' platform when the arrest took place. Debs was released from prison in 1921 on the orders of President Harding. Debs died in his home in Illinois on October 20, 1926.

Valentine Decker (1847 - 1937)

A German immigrant born in Baden, Decker came to the United States at the age of twenty-one in 1868 as a journeyman sausage maker. He went to work as a butcher for his uncle in Troy for ten dollars a month. Shortly after his marriage to Johanna Schaeffer in 1873, he established a retail butcher's shop at 512 West High Street in Piqua. He built his own slaughter house in 1887 on east end of East Ash Street next to the Great Miami River. In 1898, he established the Val Decker Packing Company. Decker greatly enlarged the packing plant 1903 and got out of the retail side of the meat business. Decker had four sons that joined him in the meat packing business, Louis F., George H., Carl F. (died 1916), Walter J., and William J. Decker remained active in the management of the plant until ill health forced his retirement in 1936. SEE ALSO: Patron p. 229

Walter O. Decker (1898-1970)

Decker was born in Piqua, but was not directly related to the Decker meat packing family. However, at age eighteen he joined the Val Decker Meat Packing Company as the firm's first and, at that time, only office employee. Through hard work and a keen business sense he became president of the company in 1960.

John Dougherty Defrees
(1810 – 18__)

He was born in Sparta, Tennessee and moved to Piqua with his family in 1818. From age 14 to 17 he was apprenticed to **William Barrington**, the owner and editor of the *Piqua Gazette*. Leaving Piqua in the late 1820's, he worked as a journeyman printer in Xenia, Cincinnati, Louisville and Lebanon. In Lebanon he read law under Thomas Corwin. With his brother Joseph H. Defrees, he established a newspaper in South Bend, Indiana from 1831 to 1833. He served in the Indiana legislature and in 1845 purchased the *Indiana State Journal* in Indianapolis. In 1861, he was appointed the first Superintendent of Public Printing in Washington, D.C. until he was removed by President Andrew Johnson. The United States Senate overrode his dismissal and appointed him back to the same position with the title Congressional Printer, a position he held until 1869.

Jack Dempsey (1895-1983) *

Dempsey won the heavy-weight boxing championship in 1919. On July 6 of that year, he stopped in Piqua for gasoline. SEE ALSO: Boxing.

George Craig Dietrich
(1874 – 1944)

George C. Dietrich (1874-1944)

He was born in Coopersville, Ohio the son of Henry and Mary Craig Dietrich. He was a graduate of the Ohio State University. Dietrich came to Piqua in 1909 to serve as the **Superintendent of Schools**. He would hold that position for thirty-five years until his retirement in 1944. During his leadership the school system built a new high school and two new junior high school buildings. He led the **schools** through the economic crisis of the **Great Depression** and the upheavals of the **Second World War**. Dietrich was very active in the community serving as president of the Associated **Charities**, the Flesh Public **Library** Board of Trustees and the Piqua Rotary Club. He also served as the executive director (1924-1944) of the Central Ohio Teachers' Association, a trustee of the **YMCA** for twenty years and one of the organizers of the Piqua Historical Society in 1912.

Henry Thornton Dietrich
(1903 – 1966)

Dietrich was of born in Sandusky, Ohio the son of George and Louise Dietrich and graduated from Piqua High School in 1922. He graduated from the United States Naval Academy in 1926. He served as a naval pilot on three U.S. aircraft carriers, the *Lexington*, the *Langley* and the *Yorktown* prior to **World War II**. During the war he commanded the Naval Air Stations in Bermuda (1941-1943) and Dallas, Texas (1944-1945). After the war he spent the majority of his time in Washington, D.C., retiring from the navy after thirty years of service in 1956 with the rank of captain.

Irene Ditmer (1905 - 1991)

She was the daughter of Clyde and Clara Shepard Snavely Ditmer. She was appointed as the executive secretary of the Pi-

qua Community Chest (later the United Way) in August of 1952 and retired in 1974. She also served as president of the **YWCA** board and as a staff member with the Miami County Mental Health Association. SEE ALSO: Charities

Godwin Volney Dorsey
(1812 – 1885)

Dorsey was born in Oxford, Ohio, the son of James Maxwell and Martha Dorsey. He attended school in Oxford and studied under Professor McGuffey, the author of the *McGuffey Readers*. Dorsey received his Bachelors degree from Miami University and in 1836, his medical degree from the Medical College of Ohio. In that same year he came to Piqua and joined in partnership with Doctor John **O'Ferrall**, Sr. He left the partnership in 1842 and set up his own office in the basement of his residence at 618 North Wayne Street. Dorsey took an increasingly active role in his profession serving as one of the early presidents of the Miami County Medical Society. In 1851, he served as the chairman of the Committee of Surgery for the Ohio State Medical Society. Dorsey formed a partnership with Doctor V. D. Brownell that lasted from 1853 until 1862. At that time, his active practice was taken over by Doctor Brownell and Dorsey's son-in-law, Doctor C. S. Parker.

Dorsey's political life began in the 1840's as he became an active member of the **Democratic Party.** In 1848, Dorsey attended the National Democratic Convention in Baltimore as a working member of the Committee on Resolutions which drafted one of the earliest national anti-slavery political platforms. Dorsey also served as a presidential elector for the Democratic candidate, General Lewis Cass of Michigan. (Cass was a long time acquaintance of Colonel **John Johnston**). In 1849, Dorsey was elected as a Senatorial District (Miami, Shelby, Darke Counties) Delegate to the Ohio Constitutional Convention. He served with distinction during the 1850-51 sessions and repeated this performance twenty-three years later during the 1873 Ohio Constitutional Convention. Dorsey ran for Congress on the Democratic ticket in 1854 and 1856, and for Ohio State Auditor in 1856. He was defeated by the **Republican Party** candidates on all three occasions. During the election of 1860, Dorsey supported Democrat Stephen Douglas against Abraham Lincoln. After the start of the **Civil War** in 1861, Dorsey was one of the first Ohio politicians to advocate the joining of the Republicans and those Democrats who supported the War into a single, new Union Party. As a candidate for the Union Party for the office of **Ohio State Treasurer**, Dorsey was elected in 1861 and again in 1863. During the war years, Dorsey advocated aid for the families of **African-American** soldiers serving in the Army or Navy. During this same period, he also served as the Chairman of the Ohio Republican Executive Committee. In 1864 he attended the National Republican Convention as a delegate pledged to President **Lincoln.** Dorsey's last major political activity occurred in 1869 when he served as a member of the Electoral College pledged to U.S. Grant and Schuyler Colfax.

On a local level, Dorsey was elected to Piqua's first Board of Education in 1853 and served as its president until 1861. He would be re-elected to the board in 1877 and again serve as president until his resignation in 1884. As a businessman, Dorsey was one of the founders and the first President of the Piqua **Hydraulic** Company from 1866 until 1868. In 1867 Dorsey purchased the Citizens National **Bank** and served as President until 1885. He also held interest in a stone quarry, the Dorsey **Linseed Oil** Company, and a number of downtown business structures. Dorsey was also active in civic affairs including the City Council (1868-1870), President of the **Miami and Erie Canal** Association, and Trustee of Miami University. He produced a number of literary works including translations of Horace's Greek Tragedies and Medieval Latin hymns, and a "History of Piqua and Washington Township" for *The History of Miami County, Ohio* (1880). Dorsey's home was built in the 1850's and still stands today at the northeast corner of Wayne and North Streets. It is one of the best examples in the city of the **Greek Revival Style**. He was married to Laura Pamela Morrow Dorsey (1811-1884). He was inducted into the **Piqua Civic Hall of Fame** in 2002.

Leo C. Eisert (1908 – 1945)

He was the son of John Eisert and was a graduate of St. Boniface School in Piqua. He joined the United States Marine Corps in December of 1943 and was shipped overseas in November of 1944. Private First Class Eisert was killed in action at Iwo Jima in March of 1945. He was survived by his wife Alvera and his two children Eddie Lee and Gloria.

Frank Elbert (1866 -1935)

Elbert was one of city's last independent **coopers** or barrel makers. He established his cooperage in the city in 1888.

Alexander H. Ellerman III (c.1920 – 1944)

He was born in Piqua, the son of Alexander H. and Roxana B. Ellerman. He graduated from Piqua High School in 1938 then attended Ohio University. Ellerman joined the United States Army Air Force and was assigned to the 8th Air Force as a flying fortress bomber co-pilot. In December of 1943, his flying fortress, the "My Darling" crashed into the North Sea but he was rescued by a British naval minesweeper. In March of 1944, on a bombing raid over Berlin his plane was shot down and Second Lieutenant Ellerman was killed.

Milton Erlanger (1888 – 19__) *

He was born in Baltimore, Ohio and graduated from John Hopkins University in 1907 at age nineteen. He joined the family business, the Erlanger Mills the owners of **B.V.D.** He followed his brother Sidney as president of the Mills in 1951. The Erlanger family sold B.V.D. to Sol Kittary who began producing them at the **Superior Underwear** Company in Piqua. Erlanger had an earlier connection with Piqua when he partnered with the **Flesh** family to produce garments under the **Imperial Underwear Company** label.

Belle C. Buchanan Evans (1854 – 19__)

She was born and graduated from High School in Piqua. She served as the first female physician in Piqua in the 1880's, an era when medicine was almost completely dominated by men. She received her medical degree from Pulte Medical College in 1883 as a homoeopathic physician. She began practice in Piqua in 1883, specializing in the diseases of women and children. She set up a dispensary on the public square for the care of those in need. Dr. Buchanan returned to Cincinnati to receive a second degree from the Women's Medical College in 1894.

Nancy A. Evans (c.1800 - 18__)

Evans became the first woman to teach in Piqua's public **school** system in 1830. She continued to teach in the public elementary schools until 1873-1874.

John P. Finley (18__ - 1883)

He was one of the early **teachers** in Piqua. Finley taught in a private school located on what is now South Main and Wood Streets.

Joseph A. Flatz (1842 – 1912)

Flatz was the founder of the Piqua Granite and Marble Company in 1882. By 1906, he was partnered with two other major marble workers, Hauk and Eby. Flatz and his wife Susan are buried at Forest Hill Cemetery. Their grave markers, a granite stele topped by a round ball with two separate carved balls, highlights the best in the monument arts.

David M. Fleming (1827 – 1898)

Fleming was born in Eaton, Ohio the son of Levi Fleming and moved to Piqua in 1849 and helped established the **Democratic newspaper** the *Piqua Enquirer* where he served as editor. In 1860, he broke away from the Democrats over the slavery issue. He bought out the paper's other stockholders and changed the paper into the **Republican** *Piqua Journal*. His newspaper carried the banner slogan "Devoted to politics, literature, agriculture and the true interests of mankind". In 1886, Fleming established the *Piqua Daily Dispatch* which he published jointly with the weekly *Journal*. Fleming was an active publisher and editor in Piqua until his death in 1898. Fleming served on the Ohio Republican Union Party's Central Committee in 1862-1863. He also was a delegate to the Baltimore Republican National Convention of 1864. He served as chairman of the Miami County Republican Central Committee for a number of years.

Henry Flesh (1837-1919)

Flesh was born and educated in the German Kingdom of Bavaria. In 1852, at the age of fifteen, he came to the United States, settling in Dayton, Ohio. In 1856 he moved to **Troy** and two years later to Piqua. Flesh went to work for the Moses Friedlich Clothing Store as a salesman and bookkeeper. In 1862 he married Caroline Friedlich, the boss's daughter, and went into business for himself as a merchant tailor (later as Flesh and Prugh, then Flesh and Louis). Flesh was elected cashier of Citizens National **Bank** in 1878 and upon the death of **William P. Orr** in 1912 become president. He was followed in this position by his son Leo M. Flesh (1919-1944) and his grandson Alfred L. (1945-1956). Flesh's business activities were numerous. He was an organizer and served as President of the **Cron-Kills Furniture Co.**, the Covington Citizens National Bank, the Loyal Mutual Accident Association, and the Piqua Savings Bank. Flesh served as an officer or director of the Border City Savings and Loan Co., the **Dorsey Linseed** Oil Company, the Dr. Bosanko **[Patent] Medicine** Company, the Piqua and Troy Branch Railroad, and the Miami Valley Railway Co. He was elected numerous times to the city council as a **Democrat** and off and on from 1870 until 1903, he was president of the city council. Flesh served as President of the Ohio Bankers Association and the **Miami and Erie Canal** Association. He was an organizer and officer of the Humane Society (1890), the Piqua Boards of Trade, and the Ball Memorial **Hospital**. With William P. Orr, he was one of the co-owners of the Orr-Flesh Building on the northwest corner of Main and Ash Streets. Flesh's last home in Piqua, built in 1897-1898, was located on the northwest corner of North and Wayne Streets. Henry and

Caroline Flesh were survived by two sons Leo M. and Joel W. He was inducted into the Piqua **Civic Hall of Fame** in 2001. SEE ALSO: Interurbans; Railroads; Telephones.

Leo Moses Flesh (1863 - 1944)

He was born in Piqua, the son of Henry and Caroline Flesh. Flesh was the founder and president of the **Atlas Underwear Company** from 1900 to 1928. He served as the firm's chairman of the board from 1928 to his death in 1944. He followed his father as president of the Citizens National **Bank** from 1919 until 1944. Flesh built one of the city's largest mansions in 1907 in the **Chateauesque Style.** He was a major classical art collector with works by Gainsborough, Whistler and Constable displayed in his home. He also collected jeweled Faberge snuff boxes. He served as a director or officer of the **Cron, Kills Company**, the Orr Felt & Blanket Company, the Piqua Savings Bank and the Piqua Home **Telephone** Company. Flesh donated the funds to build the **Jewish** Temple on Caldwell in 1925 in honor of his father. Flesh also purchased the former Piqua Club at 124 West Greene Street and donated it to the **library** for use as a new facility (Flesh Public Library).

Alfred Louis Flesh (1890 – 1971)

He was born in Piqua, the son of Leo M. and Gertrude S. Flesh. He then followed his father into the family business and served as the president of the **Atlas Underwear Company** (1928-1956) and a major stockholder of the **B.V.D. Company.** He served as Atlas' chairman of the board from 1956 until 1968. Flesh also followed his father as president of the Citizens National **Bank** from 1945 until 1956. He was married twice, his first wife being Marion Buford Alexander (1920). His second wife, Patricia Cunningham (1937), worked for the B.V.D. Company and held a number of patents for women's swimwear.

Martha (Anna) Sanborne Hamilton Flick (c.1861 – 1937)

Flick was born in Piqua, the daughter of Harvey and Jane Hamilton. She became a reporter for some of the nation's largest newspapers in Philadelphia, Chicago, San Francisco and Washington, D.C. While working as the society editor of the *Washington Post*, she was one of the founders of the American Pen-Women's Club (later known as the National League of American Pen Women) in June of 1897. The group was formed in reaction to the all male Press Club. The organization currently (2007) promotes Letters, Art and Music from its headquarters in the nation's capital. By 1900, she was living in Oklahoma with her husband George Flick.

Henry Ford (1863 – 1947)*

Henry Ford, president of the Ford Motor Car Company, stopped in Piqua on May 2, 1918, to see his old friend H. C. Waite, Vice President of the Elgin Tractor Company Inc. of Piqua.

Nellie Wolf Foster (1851 - 1914)

Foster was born in Union, Ohio and moved to Piqua with her family in 1863. She was known as Piqua's premier "madam" in an era when women had very few career choices. Foster contested one of her arrests for operating a "house of ill fame" all the way up to the Ohio Supreme Court. She was very active in the community relief efforts during the 1913 Flood. SEE ALSO: Prostitution

William N. Foster (c.1821 - 1873)

Foster served as Mayor of Piqua 1857-1863. He resigned his office in February 1863 to become the Lt. Colonel of the 110th Ohio Volunteer Infantry Regiment. He resigned his command in late 1863. Prior to his **Civil War** service, Foster had served as the Washington Township clerk 1856-1862, the Washington Township Justice of the Peace 1859-1863 and a Volunteer Fire Warden in the city's second ward in 1855.

John Franz (18__ - 1892)

He was one of the area's early law enforcement officers. He served as the Washington Township constable from 1868 to 1871 and again from 1875 to 1885. Franz served as the Piqua city marshal from 1868 to 1871. He served as one of four policemen for the city from 1871 to 1877. During his second tenure as city marshal, from 1877 to 1885, Franz was the only law enforcement agent in the city or township

Alfred Willard French Sr. (1862 - 1925)

French was born in Connecticut, the son of Henry and Mary Willard French and graduated from M.I.T. in 1889. He stayed at the college for several years after graduation to teach mathematics. In 1899, he patented an improved cake trimming machine for use in the **linseed oil** industry. The next year he founded the French Oil Mill Machinery Company in Piqua. French received over fifty different patents before his life was cut short by a tragic automobile accident. He was inducted into the **Piqua Civic Hall of Fame** in 2006.

Alfred W. French Jr. (1903-1992)

French was born in Piqua, the son of Alfred and Grace Albers French Sr. He was a graduate of M.I.T in 1926 and came to work full time at the French Oil Mill Machinery Company. In 1938, he received the first (for mechanical screw improvements) of over twenty patents. He took over as president of the firm in 1962 and chairman of the board in 1979.

Aaron Friedlich (1821-1889)

Friedlich was born in Germany and immigrated to Cincinnati and then to Piqua in 1846. He partnered with Leopold Block to form Friedlich & Block, clothiers and merchant tailors. He went out on his own and by 1861 he built the Commercial Block on the northwest corner of Main Street and the Public Square to house his growing business. Active in the community, Friedlich served for a number of years on the Piqua Board of Education. Emanuel joined his father in the family business from 1883 to 1886 before joining a wholesale clothing firm in Rochester, New York. The Friedlich store was taken over by Aaron's son-in-law, A.W. Loewi of Cleveland. Loewi operated the store form 1888 until 1897.

Moses Friedlich (1812-1892)

Friedlich was born in Bavaria, Germany and immigrated to New York City in 1834. He began moving west, first to Pennsylvania and then to Piqua in 1849. He established a small merchant tailor's shop in two hundred block of Main Street. His clothing store prospered and for a short time in the 1860's his son Jacob M. joined the family business. His daughter Caroline married Henry Flesh who would set up his own merchant tailor's shop in 1862.

Airhart Marion Fry Sr. (1860 – 1939)

Fry was born in Montgomery County and came to Piqua in 1890 as an independent carpenter and contractor. During his almost five decades in Piqua, Fry literally changed the physical appearance of the city. He was responsible for the construction of commercial structures such as the Benkert Store (1899), the Orr-Flesh Building (1903) and the J.W. Brown Store (1908) all located on Main Street. His community buildings included St. Boniface School (1890), the YMCA (1892), May's Opera House (1903), the Ball Memorial Hospital (1905), the Piqua Club (1907), YMCA Bowling Alley (1908) and the City Market House (c.1929). He built a number of churches including the First Reformed, United Presbyterian, Greene Street Methodist Episcopal and Grace Methodist Episcopal and numerous industrial plants for companies as diverse as the Atlas Underwear Company, the French Oil Mill Machinery Company and the Orr Felt and Blanket Company. Private homes built by Fry included the **Henry Flesh** home (600 North Wayne in 1898), the J. W. Brown home (718 North Wayne in 1902), the **Leo M. Flesh** home (650 North Downing in 1907), the George Rundle home (400 North Downing in 1908), the Allen G. Rundle home (620 Caldwell in 1914) and the **John Spiker** home (700 North Wayne in 1921). His skill and dedication to the building trade created a new standard for construction in the city. His son by his second wife, A.M. Fry Jr. continued the family tradition of building construction. Fry Sr. was inducted into the **Piqua Civic Hall of Fame** in 1999.

John Scott Garbry (1902 – 1990)

Garbry was born on a farm in Springcreek Township, beginning his life-long interest in agricultural management and environmental conservation. He was honored for these activities by the State of Ohio in 1963 and inducted into the Ohio Conservation Hall of Fame in 1986. Garbry's promotion of historical preservation was highlighted by his service to the **Piqua Historical Museum** and the creation of the Garbry Museum. His philanthropic endeavors included the donation of Garbry Big Woods to the Miami County Park District and the donation of the site of the Willowbrook Land Laboratory to the JVS. He was inducted into the **Piqua Civic Hall of Fame** in 1996.

Job Gard (17__ - 1829)

Gard served as a wagon driver in **Anthony Wayne**'s army in the Ohio country during 1793-1794. Liking the land he saw while marching through the future site of Miami County, he returned during the winter of 1796-1797. He tore down the abandoned supply fort at Upper Piqua and built a log cabin on what is now the corner of Harrison and Water Streets. Gard sold his improved plot of land to pioneer settler John Manning in 1799 and left the Miami Valley area.

Samuel B. Garvey (18__ - 1883)

He served as Washington Township constable from 1850 to 1864. In Piqua, he served as both city marshal and marketmaster from 1851 to 1855. Garvey was elected Piqua mayor in 1867 and continuing serving until 1875.

Philip P. Gates (1894 – 1983)

Gates moved to Piqua in 1917 to become the director of music at the high school, a position he would hold until August of 1944. He changed the face of music in Piqua by reorganizing the high school marching band, creating a boys glee club, composing the Piqua High School Alma Mater, organizing and directing the Elks Band (Piqua Civic Band) and creating and directing several local church choirs. Regionally he was known for sponsoring one of the area's first band festivals in the 1930's. He was inducted into the **Piqua Civic Hall of Fame** in 2003.

Frank Gehle (1869 - 1939)

Gehle had a varied and exciting background. He owned a saloon, worked as a bartender, spent a stint as a semipro wrestler and worked as a gym boxing instructor with future president Teddy Roosevelt as one of his students. During some economic downtimes he had been a hobo and a circus roustabout. In 1903, under the newly adopted Municipal Code, he became the city's first modern police chief, serving until 1936. As Chief, he introduced the automobile, the motorcycle (1910), automatic weapons, a modern jail facility and a fingerprint identification system. His thirty-three year career included protecting the city from the looting that followed the 1913 **Flood**, labor violence, prohibition violations, robberies, assaults and murders.

Stephen Genslinger (1831 - 1885)

He was born in Germany and immigrated to Ohio. He served on the city council from 1872 to 1874. The all volunteer Reliance Fire Company reorganized in 1876 as a hose company with Genslinger as its captain. The Piqua City Fire Department was re-organized in 1882 with Genslinger as the new chief with a pay rate of $180.00 a year. He was one of the founders of the Spiker Wagon Company.

Dominick Salvatore "Don" Gentile (1920 – 1951)

Gentile was born in 1920 in Piqua, the son of Italian immigrants Pasquale and Josephine Gentile. As a teenager, Gentile was interested in flying and began "barnstorming" while still in high school. When **World War II** began, he joined the Royal Canadian Air Force. He shot down his first German plane flying a Spitfire as part of the Eagle Squadron while serving in England. When the United States Air Force arrived in England, Gentile transferred to the American Forces, eventually becoming commander of the 336th Squadron. He flew

A teenage Don Gentile with his first airplane.

a Mustang Fighter and was credited with destroying twenty-six German planes. During his time in England, he flew 182 combat missions. He was known as the "Messerschmitt Killer", "Captain Courageous" (by President Roosevelt) and "a one man Air Force" (by General Eisenhower after Gentile had shot down German flying ace Major Kirk von Meyer). Gentile received fourteen American and seven foreign military decorations for bravery. He came out of the war with the rank of Captain in 1946. He worked for a time with the Globe Aircraft Company out of Fort Worth, Texas. Gentile joined the Ohio National Guard Fighter Squadron out of Dayton in 1947 with the rank of Major. He would go back to active duty and began military study at the University of Maryland. He was killed in January of 1951 when a T-33 Jet Trainer he was piloting crashed in a Maryland field. He was survived by his wife Isabella Masdea. A statue on the public square in Piqua was dedicated to Gentile on July 6, 1986. Gentile was inducted into the National Aviation Hall of Fame in 1995 and the **Piqua Civic Hall of Fame** in 1996.

Frederick Page Geyer (c.1892 – 19__)

Born in Piqua, he graduated from the Piqua High School with the Class of 1910. In 1915, he joined the **Ohio National Guard** obtaining the rank of sergeant. He served as a lieutenant in the United States Army in France during **World War I.** From 1919 to 1920, Lieutenant Geyer was a member of the 34th Infantry Regiment and participated in the Allied invasion of Russia (Siberia). He served most of his time in and around Valdivostok guarding mines and the railroads against Bolshevik forces. Returning to San Francisco in 1920, Geyer resigned his commission and reentered civilian life.

William Gerlach (c.1840's – 1922)

He served in the Civil War and in 1868 established a bakery at 525 North Main Street. He ran the bakery until his death in 1922 when he was followed in the business by his son Rudolph Gerlach. The younger Gerlach retired in 1947, selling the bakery to Lewis H. Grunnert who had worked as a baker at Gerlach's from 1922 until 1927.

Goodrich Giles (1845 – 1927)

Giles was born a slave on a Virginia plantation of John Randolph on December 29, 1845, the son of Archie and Sarah Giles. The Randolph slaves were manumitted under the terms of Randolph's will. Archie Giles came to Piqua in 1846 and his wife Sarah joined him in c.1850. Goodrich Giles stayed in the Richmond, Virginia area and fought with the Confederacy in the Civil War. He came to Piqua in c.1865. Both of his parents died in 1875. He became the community's first major African-American businessman. Starting in a tiny barn, he eventually operated several livery stables including the Cottage Livery Stable on North Street (c.1886-1890), three farms, and was an original investor in the Third National Bank and owned numerous rental properties. He was the first **African-American** to run for city council in 1885, 1886 and 1887. Giles was also the driving force behind building the Cyrene A.M.E. Church (Piqua) and the Anderson-Giles Classic Theater in Dayton. The theater closed down in 1959 but not before hosting entertainment stars such as the **Mills Brothers**, Count Basie and Ella Fitzgerald. Giles was a charter member of Masonic Lodge No. 18 and a trustee of Wilberforce University. He was inducted into the **Piqua Civic Hall of Fame** in 1997.

Simon Girty (1741-1818)*

In February of 1779, Girty, under the command of the British Captain Bird, led an attack against the American forces at Fort Laurens. In 1780, Girty was living in the **Shawnee** village of Piqua on the Mad River (Clarke County) where he commanded a force of approximately 300 Indians from various tribes. He fled the village after it was attacked by General Clark in 1780. Girty was present at the death and torture of Colonel William Crawford in 1782. He received a pension from the British in Canada for his services. He served with Little Turtle when he defeated St. Clair's army in 1791 and with **Blue Jacket** when he lost to **Wayne** at the Battle of Fallen Timbers in 1794.

Christopher Gist (1706-1759) *

Gist was born in 1706 in Maryland. As a young man in 1745, he moved to North Carolina where he was first employed by the Ohio Company of Virginia. While in their employ, Gist visited **Pickawillany** in 1751 with **George Croghan** of Pennsylvania. In 1755, Gist joined General Edward Braddock and Lieutenant Colonel **George Washington** as a scout during their expedition into the Ohio country against the French. The following year Gist began his duties as an Indian Agent to the Cherokee in the Carolinas. He died in the summer of 1759 of smallpox. SEE ALSO: Trent, William.

Robert S. Graef (1916 – 1944)

He was born in Piqua, the son of Frank and Alma Graef and graduated from Piqua High School with the Class of 1935. He joined the United States Army in 1942 and became a member of the glider troops of the 101st Division. At the Normandy invasion, he was a Technical Sergeant and was quickly promoted to First Sergeant. In Holland, he successfully led three bayonet charges and won a battlefield commission to Second Lieutenant. He was killed in action in Holland in October of 1944. He was survived by his wife Betty Schneider Graef. In 1945, the Post 4874, Veterans of Foreign Wars of Piqua was named the Chaney-Graef Post in his honor.

Ulysses Simpson Grant (1822-1885) *

Numerous Piqua citizens served under General Grant during the **Civil War** but, during his years as the nation's 18th President (1869-1877), Grant had no direct contact with Piqua. His presidency was best known for the corruption of his cabinet and their various administrative departments. Locally, Grant was remembered as the great military commander. After his death on July 23, 1885, a memorial service was held in Piqua at Conover's Opera House. The service was held on August 8, with local U. S. Congressman Robert Maynard Murray as the chief speaker. SEE ALSO: Dorsey, Godwin V.

Robert Gray (c.1915 – 19__)

He left Piqua in June of 1937 to join the Abraham Lincoln Battalion of the Fifteenth International Brigade. The group was fighting on the side of the Socialist government in the Spanish Civil War against the Fascists led by Francisco Franco. He served as a medic at Albacete, Spain in 1937-1938.

Theodore M. Gray Sr. (c.1906-1962)

Gray moved to Piqua from Springfield, Ohio with his family in 1927 to teach at the Piqua High School. He taught speech, dramatics, sociology and business law. He served for three terms as an Ohio State Senator from 1941 through 1947 representing the 11th-12th Senatorial District.

Theodore "Ted" M. Gray Jr.
(c.1927-present)

Gray was born in Springfield, Ohio, the son of Theodore and Dorothy Gray. He moved to Piqua in 1927 with his parents and graduated from the Piqua High School in the Class of 1945. After graduation he served in the U.S. Navy and worked for the Frank Z. McColloch Insurance Agency. He attended Ohio State University and prior to his graduation in 1950 was elected to his first term as an Ohio State Senator from the 11th-12th Senatorial District. Gray would go on to serve forty-three years in the Ohio Senate, the longest tenure in the body's history. He served for ten years as the Senate President Pro Tempore and **Republican Party** majority leader beginning in 1965. In Piqua, Gray established the Gray Insurance Company in 1952. In the 1970's, Gray moved to the Columbus area, after his Senate District had been redefined.

Nicholas Greenham (17__ - 18__)

An Irish immigrant, he came to Piqua in 1812 and later established one of the earliest general stores in Piqua. He worked as an Indian trader with the **Shawnee** in the 1820's at the Indian Reservation at Wapakoneta. He was known to the Shawnee as *Skip-a-ge-tha*. For a brief period he partnered with **George Johnston** in his Indian trading enterprises.

Burgess R. Guy (c.1845 – 18__)

Guy served as a teacher in the segregated Colored School located on the corner of Boone and College streets. Piqua's **African-American** community petitioned the Board of Education to hire Guy in 1874. The following year, in June of 1875, Guy was hired at fifty dollars a month as the school's sole teacher and principal. He continued in that position until 1884. Guy also served as the school's janitor during the early 1880's. Beginning in 1878, Guy was assisted at the school by his sister Emma, who was paid twenty-five dollars a month. She worked at the school for several years. Guy was married to Emma J. Guy.

Mary E. Hall (c.1850 - 1905)

Hall was born in Piqua prior to the Civil War. She first served as a **teacher** in the Piqua High School from 1869 to 1877. In 1872, she briefly resigned her position as a teacher over the issue of low wages paid to women teachers. In June of 1877, she became the first women administrator in the school system, serving as **principal of the high school** until 1905. In 1896, she was one of the charter members of the Piqua Chapter of the Daughters of the American Revolution.

Frank B. Hamilton (1872 – 19__)

Hamilton was born in Urbana and moved to Piqua with his family in 1895. Before entering politics he worked in a number of different direct sales positions. He was elected in 1917 as Piqua's first **Socialist** mayor. As one of the very few elected Socialist officials in Ohio, Hamilton was asked to speak at the Socialist Convention in Canton in 1918. He was on the speakers' platform with Eugene V. Debs when Debs was arrested by federal agents. Hamilton would suffer a similar humiliation when he was arrested and taken to Dayton on charges of violating the U.S. Espionage Act by talking against the purchase of federal Liberty Bonds during **World War I**. He served one term before being defeated by a Non-Partisan Citizens Party (joint Republican-Democratic) ticket in 1919. Hamilton went on to run for Ohio Governor on the Socialist ticket in 1920. SEE ALSO: Smith, J. Harrison.

Martha Hamilton – SEE Flick

Robert M. Hance Jr.
(1914 – 2000)

Hance was born in the Piqua area the son of Robert M. and Bertha Moore Hance Sr. and graduated from the Piqua High School in 1932. During **World War II**, while serving as a chief warrant officer and band director at Fort Knox, he composed the *General Charles F. Scott March* dedicated to Major General Scott. After the service, Hance served as Piqua City Finance Director from 1946 through 1949. He served as Piqua **City Manager** from 1949 through 1972. When he was hired by the city commission in November of 1949, Hance was the youngest city manager in the city's history at age thirty-five. At his retirement in 1972, he held the Ohio record for longevity of any city manager. During his tenure, he molded the city's post-World War II image as a progressive city, promoting among other items the atomic power plant and a municipal golf course. As a life-long musician, he played cornet and served as the director of the Elks Band (Civic Band) for over fifty-four years. Hance was inducted into the Piqua **Civic Hall of Fame** in 2001. SEE ALSO: Music

Thomas C. Harbaugh
(1849 - 1924)

Born in Maryland in 1851, he moved to Casstown and later spent time in Piqua. He began writing and publishing short stories in 1867, many of which became the grist for the famous "Dime Novels" of the 1890's. Harbaugh wrote under a number of pseudonyms including, Captain Holmes, Howard Lincoln and Major Scott. *Dandy Jack or the Outlaw of the Oregon Trial* is an example of one of his dime novels. In died destitute and forgotten in the Miami County Infirmary.

Warren Gamaliel Harding
(1865-1923) *

He was born in Blooming Grove (Corsica), Ohio From the turn of the century and for the next twenty years, Harding was considered to be one of Ohio's best political orators. He was a regular participant at **Republican** rallies across the state. Harding visited Piqua twice. During his campaign for governor, Harding participated in a local Piqua parade and rally on November 3, 1910. He spoke at May's Opera House after a lengthy introduction by **Stanhope Boal**. Harding's oratory did not produce a victory. He failed to win Piqua's vote, losing by a 15% margin and never gained state-wide support. Harding campaigned in Piqua again on October 18, 1912, this time for another Republican candidate for governor, Robert Brown. Once again, Harding's appeals did little to sway Piqua voters. The Democrats won by a margin of 43.46% winning over three other gubernatorial candidates. During the 1920 presidential election between two Ohio newspapermen, Harding and **Cox**, the Republicans dominated the campaign. Harding won the election with over 60% of the total popular vote in Miami County as well as on a national level. In 1921, Harding pardoned Socialist **Eugene V. Debs**, another Piqua visitor. Warren G. Harding died in office on August 11, 1923. A memorial service was held at Fountain Park in Piqua as a final tribute to the President. Briefly in 1923, Harrison Street was renamed Harding Avenue in his honor. SEE ALSO: Presidents; Streets.

Frank A. Hardy (1819 – 1915)

He was born in Hollis, New Hampshire, the son of Amos and Mary Hardy. At the age of fourteen he entered the cooperage trade and continued in this occupation after he moved to Piqua in 1843. Hardy volunteered to serve in the Third Regiment of Ohio Volunteers in the Mexican War in 1846. He went out to make his fortune during the California Gold Rush in 1850, but returned to his wife and children in Piqua with only a modest income from working in a hardware store in Auburn, California. In 1862, he joined the 94th Ohio Volunteer Infantry Regiment as a second lieutenant. During the war he was captured and then paroled by the Confederates, wounded at the battle of Kenesaw Mountain but returned to his regiment, and finally mustered out at the end of the war with the rank of captain. Hardy was very active in the community serving as both a city clerk (1869-1871) and a Washington Township clerk. He was one of the city's first policemen in 1868, served as a township constable, a justice of the peace and a volunteer fireman for over fifty-one years. He married Elizabeth Cisco in June of 1848.

Josiah Harmar (1753-1813) *

Harmar served as a Colonel during the **Revolutionary War** and as an Indian agent for the Northwest Territory. He was a major participant in negotiating the Treaty of Fort McIntosh where he served as Commandant. Harmar was promoted to Brigadier General and, in 1790, led an army of 300 regulars and 1,100 militia from Fort Washington north to the Maumee River where he was defeated by **Miami Indians** under Chief **Little Turtle**. Harmar was court-martialed for the defeat, but the court cleared him of any wrongdoing. He retired in 1791 to Pennsylvania where he served as the State's Adjutant General from 1793 until 1799. SEE ALSO: Fort McIntosh, Treaty of; Harmar, Fort; Little Turtle.

William Murray Harris (1920-1944)

He was born in Piqua, the son of the Reverend D.E. Harris (Cyrene A.M.E. Church) and graduated from Piqua High School in 1938. He enlisted in 1942 in the Army Air Corps and attended the Tuskegee Air Force School. He was sent to Italy with the 302nd Fighter Squadron in December of 1943 as a line mechanic. Master Sergeant Harris died in plane crash in Italy in June of 1944. The first **African-American** Veterans of Foreign Wars (VFW) Post was named the **Stout-Harris Post**.

Benjamin Harrison (1833-1901) *

During the 1888 election, some of the most popular local newspaper stories were interviews with men who had voted for **William Henry Harrison** in 1840 and intended to vote for his grandson in 1888. This relationship with a well-known local figure and former president did not help Harrison in the local election. He lost Piqua by 77 votes and lost the national vote by over 90,000 votes. But like another Ohio native, Rutherford B. Hayes, Harrison won the presidency on the strength of his electoral vote total. On February 28, 1889, President-elect Harrison passed through Piqua by train. The special train paused for a few

moments, allowing Harrison to speak to the small crowd that had gathered to wish him well.

William Henry Harrison (1773-1841) *

Of all the candidates for president, Piqua's closest ties were with Harrison. During the War of 1812, General Harrison had established his headquarters at the farm of Colonel John Johnston. The two men formed a friendship that would last for the next thirty years. As a **Whig Party** candidate, Harrison was defeated in his first run for the presidency in 1836. In July of the following year, Harrison visited **Colonel Johnston** and helped Piqua celebrate the opening of the **Miami Extension Canal** from Dayton to Piqua. Harrison's last trip to Piqua came during the "Log Cabin" campaign of 1840. During the

William Henry Harrison (1773-1841)

summer of that year, he made a speech in front of the Tuttle **Hotel**, located at the north-west corner of Main and North Streets. After speaking for over an hour, Harrison slipped away to rest at Johnston's farm. Harrison defeated Martin Van Buren with almost 53% of the popular vote. The inauguration was held in March of 1841 and by April 4, 1941, William Henry Harrison had died of pneumonia. With Harrison's death, Colonel Johnston's chances at a federal appointment completely vanished. SEE ALSO: Canals; Harrison, Benjamin; Johnston, John; Parades; Piqua, Council of; Presidents; Streets; Symmes, John; Tippecanoe, Battle of; Urbana, Ohio; War of 1812.

George Washington Hartzell (1869 – 1933)

He was born in Union City, Indiana, the son of John T. Hartzell and in 1875 established a sawmill in Greeneville. The mill specialized in walnut lumber for the wagon trade. In 1900, he moved to Piqua and created the American Wagon Stock & Walnut Manufacturing Company. As trucks began replacing wagons, Hartzell began diversifying his company, creating gunstocks, propellers, automobile steering wheels, wooden Victrola cabinets, and fans. The propeller and fan divisions became the largest divisions of the New Hartzell Industries incorporated in 1927. SEE ALSO: Hartzell Industries

Robert Norris Hartzell (1896 – 1968)

Born in Greenville, he was the son of George W. and Deborah Norris Hartzell. He established the **Propeller Division of Hartzell Industries** in 1917. Propellers were sold to the Wright [Airplane] Company in Dayton. He was instrumental in establishing another company division in 1928 to manufacture ventilating fans. He became president of **Hartzell Industries** in 1933 at the death of his father. He established his primary residency in Troy, Ohio. His sons, George W. (born 1923), Thomas (born 1928) and James Richard (born 1934) would all be very active in the leadership of the various Hartzell industries He established the Hartzell-Norris Trust in 1941, which is currently one of the city's major benefactors. He was inducted into the **Piqua Civic Hall of Fame** in 1995.

Rutherford Birchard Hayes (1822-1893) *

Born in Delaware, Ohio, Hayes was a typical **Republican** candidate when he ran for the presidency in 1876. But Hayes' small town roots and Ohio connection did little to influence Piqua's vote. Hayes carried Piqua by only the slimmest of margins, 50.8% to 49.2% of the popular vote. This was reflected on the national level when Hayes lost the popular vote by 47.95% to 50.97%. He won the disputed electoral count by a single vote. After leaving the presidency in 1881, Hayes became a popular speaker at local celebrations and reunions. He visited Piqua twice in the next decade. First, he spoke at the Decoration Day celebration on May 30, 1883. Next, Hayes appeared with Governor William McKinley at the Grand Army of the Republic (Civil War veterans) encampment on May 10, 1892. Rutherford B. Hayes died at his home in Fremont, Ohio on January 17, 1893. SEE ALSO: McKinley, William.

Samuel Hudson Heitzman (1907 – 2004)

Samuel H. Heitzman (1907-2004)

He was born in Piqua, the son of Charles Emerson and Sarah Nettleship Heitzman. He graduated from Piqua High School with the Class of 1925. From 1928 to 1946 he served as the corporate assistant secretary of the Third Savings & Loan Association. In 1948, he founded the Heitzman Real Estate Service. In 1957, he returned to Third Savings as president, a position he would hold until 1978 when he became chairman of the board. He retired from Third Savings in 2001. Heitzman was very active in the community serving as president of the UVMV (**hospital**) from 1978 to 1982, the United Way and the **YMCA**. He was one of the founders and vice president of the Piqua Community Foundation. He was awarded the **Order of George** by the Chamber of Commerce in 1984.

William Emerson Heitzman (1900 – 1963)

He was born in Piqua, the son of Charles Emerson and Sarah Nettleship Heitzman. He worked as a stockboy at the F.W. Woolworth store in 1916 and several other jobs until he became a messenger boy at the Piqua National **Bank** in 1921. He worked his way up the corporate ladder, becoming cashier in 1946 and finally president of the bank in 1955. He married Helen Bernice Slagle in 1925.

Thomas Andrew Hendricks (1819-1885) *

He was **Cleveland**'s vice presidential candidate. Hendricks of Indiana visited Piqua on October 6, 1884. He gave a ten minute speech to members of the Cleveland and Hendricks Club at the Bassett House Hotel at the northeast corner of Main and Water Streets. He was introduced by **Robert M.**

Murray, Piqua's **Democratic** United States Congressman. On November 25, 1885, Hendricks died in office.

Laura C. "Lola" Hill (1888 – 1981)

Hill was born in Piqua, the daughter of Judge Walter D. Jones. She began her newspaper career in 1914 with the *Piqua Leader-Dispatch*. She wrote all of her reports in longhand without the benefit of a desk, only a tall stool against a counter. She was one of the community's earliest female reporters, in an almost exclusively male world. She served as the society editor for the *Piqua Daily Call* from 1926 through 1964. She wrote a regular column, *Piquaisms*, which ran for over forty-six years. She was inducted into the **Piqua Civic Hall of Fame** in 2005.

Leonard U. Hill (1885 – 1984)

Leonard U. Hill (1885-1984)

Hill was born on the family farm in Springcreek Township, the son of Willis Samuel and Alice A. Caven Hill. He attended the Agricultural College of Ohio in c.1904-1905. When he returned to his family farm, he plowed their one hundred acres with a walking plow and hand picked his corn. He owned his own farm by 1928 and by 1937 was plowing with a motorized tractor. He was a pioneer in rural programs including the raising of soybeans (1912), the first president of the Miami Rural Electrification Cooperative (1935), and president of the newly consolidated Springcreek Township Schools. He served as master of Miami Grange No. 1441 and a charter member of the Miami County Farm Bureau in 1919. As a historian, Hill organized both the Piqua and Miami County Historical Societies, promoted the formation of the Piqua Historical Area and authored several books including *John Johnston and the Indians* in 1957 and numerous local history articles. He married Julia Virginia Marshall in 1915. He was inducted into the Piqua **Civic Hall of Fame** in 2004.

Hilliard Family

The Piqua area's earliest pioneer family was the Hilliard clan. In 1788, **Revolutionary War** veteran John Hilliard moved to the new settlement of North Bend, Ohio with his wife Elizabeth and their children. This settlement had been established by Judge **John Cleve Symmes,** one of Ohio's largest land speculators. Two tragedies struck the Hilliards while living at North Bend. Their fifteen year old son Uriah was killed in an Indian raid. Shortly after this, Elizabeth Hilliard died of an unknown illness, leaving her husband with five children still at home. In 1797, Hilliard and five other families from North Bend area purchased land east of the Great Miami River from Judge Symmes. Hilliard and two of his sons, Charles and Joseph, moved up to the future site of Piqua and established a homestead. During their first summer, the three men planted corn in a former Shawnee Indian clearing and lived in a lean-to. By 1798, a log cabin had been built and Hilliard began laying out a small village plot along the flood plain of the river. About this same time, Hilliard was joined by his two other sons, William and Daniel, and his unmarried daughter Maria. In 1799, Judge Symmes defaulted on his payments to Congress and lost his title to the land between the Great and Little Miami Rivers. Hilliard lost a clear title to his

The original stone portion of the Hilliard family home on Staunton Street was one of the earliest permanent homes built in the area.

land and the Piqua area would be forced to wait until 1807 for the formation of a village. John Hilliard died in 1800 and it would be up to his sons to regain clear title to the Hilliard lands.

During the War of 1812, Charles raised and commanded a company of militia. After peace was secured, the Hilliards turned their energies to building. In 1816 Joseph built a stone and brick house on the top of the hill overlooking the river (415 Staunton Street). Charles followed suit with a brick house located just north and east of his brother's (306 Staunton). In 1840, Maria Hilliard married David Thomas and they built a brick house just at the top of the East Main Street hill. From their vantage points on the top of the hill, the Hilliards could look down and across the river to the community of Piqua. Only a slight slip in history prevented the Hilliards from becoming Piqua's founding family. SEE ALSO: Agriculture; Symmes, John; Town Hall; War of 1812.

John Hilliard (17__ - 1800)

A Revolutionary War veteran, Hilliard moved to Ohio from New Jersey in 1798. He worked for Judge John Cleves Symmes, one of the original founders of southeastern Ohio and the future state's largest land speculators. Hilliard purchased land west of the Great Miami River and moved his own and five other families to the future site of Piqua and Springrcreek Township in 1797

John Reed Hilliard (1817- 1901)

Hilliard was born in Springfield Township and attended local county schools. He was one of the chief civil engineers for the Columbus, Piqua and Indiana **Railroad.** In 1856, the route laid out by Hilliard reached Piqua from Columbus. He was also responsible for laying out the town of Hilliard near Columbus and for designing the City of Piqua's first **Town Hall** in 1845. In 1871, Hilliard moved to Peoria, Illinois where he served as superintendent of several regional railroad lines.

Joseph Hilliard (1784 – c.1859)

Hilliard was born in Burlington County, near Mount Holly, New Jersey, the son of John and Elizabeth Hilliard. In c.1787 he moved with his family to Wheeling, [West] Virginia

Joseph Hilliard (1784-c.1860)

and shortly after this they took a flatboat down the Ohio River to Columbia near the Little Miami River. The family then moved in the company of Judge Symmes to North Bend, Ohio below the future site of Cincinnati. During his early time in Ohio, Hilliard lost his brother Uriah to an Indian raid and his mother to illness. In 1797, Hilliard traveled with his father and brother Charles to what would become Springcreek Township in Miami County and created a small farmstead. Hilliard married Sarah Reed of North Carolina and they had seven children. He built the Piqua area's first brick and stone house (415 Staunton Street) in 1816

Charles L. Hinsch (1887 – 1967)

Charles L. Hinsch (1887-1967)

Hinsch was born in Piqua, the son of William L. and Julia M. Hinsch and attended local schools. He married Helen Scott Johnston, a faithful member of St. James Episcopal Church, in 1916. During World War I he served in the United States Army Air Service, Spruce Production Division, as a Second Lieutenant. He was president and general manager of the Champion Cutter & Fixture Company on South Downing Street as well as vice president of the **Meteor** Phonograph Company.

Lebright L. Hinsch (c. 1770 – c.1861)

A German immigrant, he served as one of the first ministers of the St. Paul's Lutheran Church. He also published the first German language **newspaper** in Piqua in 1837, *Evangelfsche Relfgfoese Zeitschrift.* His family became heavily involved in Piqua business and industry, with his son Charles Hinsch as a millwright, his grandson William Lee Hinsch a furniture manufacturer, his great-grandson Charles L. Hinsch president of the Champion Cutter & Fixture Company, and his great-great-grandson Scott Johnston Hinsch Sr. president of the Piqua National Bank.

Louis Lee Hinsch (1892 – 1957)

Hinsch was born in Piqua, the son of William L. and Julia M. Hinsch and graduated from Piqua High School in 1913. During **World War I**, he served as a private in the United States Army Air Service where he attended the School of Aerial Photography in Rochester and Ithaca, New York. He attended the Chicago Architecture School, worked as a local contractor and later became the president of the Art Plate Manufacturing Company, on South Downing Street, makers of chrome furniture. He built his home at 80 Orchard Lane in 1957. He was active with the Piqua Elks Lodge and the Knights of Columbus. His funeral was held at St. Mary's Catholic Church. SEE ALSO: Furniture

William Lee Hinsch (1856 – 1919)

Hinsch was born in Piqua and attended local schools. He worked with his father Charles L. Hinsch at his planning mill at the corner of East Greene and New Streets. He was well known as a wood carver and he established his own firm, the W.L. Hinsch Company, to manufacture chairs and other specialty **furniture** items. His sons, Charles L., and Louis Lee, became manufacturers in the city of Piqua. He was an active member of the Presbyterian Church.

Jacob Daniel Holtzerman (1808 - 1884)

He was best known for the manufacture of Holtzerman's Bitters, a type of early patent medicine. He was one of the founders and the first treasurer of the Piqua **Hydraulic** Company in 1865. Active politically, he served on the village council in the 1840's and 1850's and was elected to Piqua's first Board of Education in 1853

James Hughs (17__ - 1821)

Hughs was a missionary to Ohio Indians, but was forced to flee to Urbana, Ohio during the War of 1812. After his mission near Sandusky was destroyed by fire, he established a Presbyterian church in Urbana. He extended his ministry to Piqua by preaching part-time in the community from 1814 to 1816.

Richard E. Hunt (191_ – 2002)

Hunt was born in Troy, Ohio and served in the Pacific Theater during World War I. In 1947, he was one of the organizers of the first **radio** station in Piqua and Miami County under the call letters WPTW-AM. In the 1950's, Hunt added several Michigan radio stations to his growing media empire. Hunt partnered with several local citizens in 1965 to establish Piqua's and the area's first cable television company, Valley Antenna Systems. In 1984, he created the Miami County Foundation to provide support for county citizens. He was inducted into the Piqua **Civic Hall of Fame** in 2005.

Richard Hunt was the founder of WPTW Radio.

David Hunter (1798 – 1865)

Hunter was a man of many talents and business interests. He ran and organized a stage coach line in 1836 that held the contract for carrying mail from Piqua to Sidney three times a week. From 1836 to 1838 he ran the National Hotel and livery on the southwest corner of Main and Ash Streets. As a developer, he laid out the village of **Huntersville** in 1838 (later known as Shawnee) on the flood plain just east of the Great Miami River. He worked as a contractor for grading work for the Piqua & St. Paris Turnpike in 1847 and the Columbus, Piqua and Indiana **Railroad**. He was active in village government as constable (1843-49, 1859-60) and as the community's first street commissioner (1850-51).

Ethan E. Huntzinger (1879 - 1945)

Huntzinger was born in Pendleton, Indiana, the son of John Huntzinger. He moved to Piqua in c.1905 and setup his first **photographic** studio at 333½ North Main Street. In addition to his standard portrait work, he was best know for his early exterior shots, many of which he turned into postcards. He documented the physical environment of the city and the surrounding area from 1905 through the early 1920's. He was particularly active during the Great 1913 **Flood**, documenting the devastation of this natural disaster. Starting in 1934, Huntzinger ran the Huntzinger School Photography Service at 803 Covington Avenue. He patented a new type of camera in 1921 know as the "multiplying camera" which held a roll of film with 170 to 200 pictures. A photographer with a Huntzinger camera could take three hundred student photographs in under two hours and then sell the individual photographs to the student's families for twenty-five cents a dozen. At is height in the late 1930's, thirty local Huntzinger employees processed during the school year week over thirty thousand packets (a dozen student photographs per packet) a week for schools from California to Florida to Michigan, making it the largest such operation in the nation. Huntzinger built his own cameras out of wood and sent out over a dozen photographers to cover schools throughout the nation. After his death, the business was taken over by William R. Weber until the early 1950's.

Minabelle Abbott Hutchins (1909 – 1981)

Hutchins was born in Covington, Kentucky, the daughter of Harry D. and Bessie P. Abbott. In 1930, she began her **radio** career as the Executive Secretary to the General Manager of WLW – Radio in Cincinnati. In 1935, Hutchins won the leading role in "The Life of Mary Sothern", one of the nation's first radio soap operas. The show moved to New York in 1938, but was cancelled in July of that year. From 1938 until 1946, Hutchins broadcast for WLW a program called the WLW Mailbag Club in Cincinnati. It was oriented toward shut-ins who could mail letters to the station to be read on the air. In 1946, Hutchins and her family moved to Piqua. In 1951, she began broadcasting "Your Best Bet" for WPTW Radio in Piqua. The show would run until 1976. Hutchins married Ralph P. Hutchins in 1935, and they had two children. Hutchins other activities included promotion of the local Girl Scout program, encouraging environmental awareness through bird watching, and working with the Salvation Army, the American Red Cross, the American Cancer Society, the Fine Arts Foundation and various public school committees. She was inducted into the Piqua **Civic Hall of Fame** in 1997. SEE ALSO: Radio; Photograph p. 99

Earl T. Hydeman (c.1910 - c.1993)

He was the son of J. Earl and Lois T. Hydeman, owners of the Hydeman Printing Company in Piqua. He was a graduate of the United States Naval Academy and during **World War II** commanded the U.S.S. *Sea Dog* (SS-401), a Balao Class submarine. In 1945, Hydeman led "Hydeman's Hellcats", a nine submarine "wolf pack" into the Sea of Japan using new secret high frequency sonar equipment. Known as Operation Barney, Hydeman's mission was to find a clear path through the Japanese minefields. During the last four months of the war, Hydeman and the *Sea Dog* carried out four major war patrols in the South China Sea, the Sea of Japan and around Okinawa. The *Sea Dog* became the first United States naval warship to touch the Japanese shore during the war. During one patrol, Hydeman sank six enemy ships, placing him number eight on the list for most ships sunk in a single patrol. For his heroism during the war, Hydeman would receive the Navy Cross. He retired from the Navy as a Captain. He was married to Piqua native Helen Theora Rousseau Hydeman for over sixty-one years.

George Jaffe (1881 – 1937)

Jaffe was born in Latvia and came to the United States in 1907. Several years later he moved to Ohio with his brother Sam and opened a clothing store in Defiance, Ohio. In 1924-25, Jaffe opened a store in Piqua and settled in the city. At his death he operated stores in Piqua, Defiance, Urbana and Delaware, Ohio.

He was a member of the Anshe Emeth Temple in Piqua and was buried in Cincinnati. SEE ALSO: Jewish

W. N. Johnson (18__ - 19__)

Johnson was nominated by the **Republicans** in the Fifth Ward of Piqua in the spring of 1893 to be a candidate for city councilman from that ward. He was not elected, however he does hold the honor of being only the second **African-American** to run for political office in the city. SEE ALSO: Goodrich Giles.

Abraham Robinson Johnston (1815 – 1846)

Johnston was born at **Upper Piqua** on July 15, 1815, the second son of Colonel John and Rachel Johnston. He was a student at Miami University until 1831, when at the age of sixteen he was appointed to West Point Military Academy. He was commissioned at Second Lieutenant in the First Regiment of Dragoons in 1835. During the **Mexican War**, he served as the aide-de-camp to Brigadier General S.W. Kearney. He marched with Kearny from the capture of Santa Fe, New Mexico to San Pasqual, California. At the Battle of San Pasqual, Johnston was killed on December 6, 1846. During his time with Kearney, he kept an illustrated journal on the landscape and Native American tribes he encountered. SEE ALSO: Mexican War

Colonel John Johnston (1775-1861)

Johnston was born in Ireland and immigrated to Pennsylvania in 1786. In 1802, he was appointed factor at the Indian agency at Fort Wayne. Johnston took over as the chief Indian agent at Fort Wayne from **William Wells** in 1809. In 1811, the agency was moved to Piqua, where Johnston remained as agent until 1829. He was one of the chief agents present at the **Second Treaty of Greenville** (1814), the **Treaty of St. Mary's** (1818), and the **Treaty of Upper Sandusky** (1842). Johnston was instrumental in organizing the **Council of Piqua** during the War of 1812. From 1825 until 1836, he served as an Ohio **Canal** Commissioner and was responsible for the construction of the Miami Extension **Canal** through Piqua. Among his other activities, Johnston was one of the founders of St. James Episcopal Church (1823), one of the original trustees of Kenyon College (1824), a trustee of Miami University (1825-1849), a delegate to the **Whig** National Convention (1840), president of the Historical and Philosophical Society of Ohio (Cincinnati) (1840's), president of the Piqua Agricultural Culture Society (1845) and a member of the State Board of Agriculture (1846). He was inducted into the Piqua **Civic Hall of**

Colonel John Johnston (1775-1861)

Fame in 1995. SEE ALSO: Courthouse Wars; Dorsey, Godwin V.; Harrison, William Henry; Johnston Family; Shoemakers; War of 1812.

Francis Johnston (17__ - 18__)

An **Irish** immigrant, he came to the United States in the 1780's and settled in Kentucky. He was a brother of Colonel Johnston. He moved to **Miami County** settling as a farmer near Upper Piqua. Johnston served as one of **Washington Township**'s earliest justices of the peace serving prior to the **War Of 1812** through 1818. He also served as a Washington Township trustee from 1824 through 1826.

George C. Johnston (1793 - 1876)

George Johnston (1793-1876)

Johnston was an Irish immigrant and came to the United States and Piqua in 1817. A relative of Indian Agent Colonel **John Johnston**, he received a license to trade with the Indians and soon joined with Nicholas Greenham to form a trading post at the Wapakoneta **Reservation** with the **Shawnee Tribe**. Johnston was responsible for the local telling of the Shawnee creation myth of "man who rose from the ashes". Johnston was an active trader until the early 1830's. He built a large **Federal Style** brick home at 518-520 North Main Street in 1835. He became a successful farmer and was known for his hunting prowess. He was one of the founding members and the first Junior Warden of Warren Masonic Lodge 24 in 1841.

Rachel Johnston (1785 – 1840)

Johnston moved to Upper Piqua in 1811 with her husband, Indian Agent **Colonel John Johnston.** She was the mother of fifteen children while serving as hostess to most of Ohio's notables of the early nineteenth century at the Indian Agency. Married on July 15, 1802 at the age of sixteen, her honeymoon consisted of a thousand mile horseback ride across the Ohio country. She established one of the earliest Sunday Schools in Miami County and organized the first civic organization in the Upper Miami Valley in 1818, the Piqua Female Bible Society. She served as the business agent and farm manager during the Colonel's many absences. She was inducted into the **Piqua Civic Hall of Fame** in 2002.

Stephen Johnston (1812 – 1885)

Johnston was born at Upper Piqua (Johnston Farm), the son of Stephen and Mary Caldwell Johnston, and the nephew of **Colonel Johnston**. His father was the factor of the Fort Wayne Indian Agency, and was killed by Pottawatomi Indians in 1812 on his way to visit his wife at Upper Piqua. Johnston was a self-educated man, reading with a local attorney, before passing the Ohio Bar in 1850. He served in a number of elected positions including **Mayor** of Piqua (1837-39/1850-51), Miami County

Sheriff (1841-45), **Ohio State Representative** (1845-47) and Piqua City Solicitor (1881-83) In Piqua, Johnston organized the town's first volunteer **fire company**, the Reliance Company in 1839, drafted the 1850 City Charter, created the charter for the Columbus, Piqua and Indiana Railroad, served as the president of the Piqua **Hydraulic** Company from 1868 through 1871 and ran for Governor of Ohio under the **Greenback Party** banner in 1877. He recruited the first **Civil War** infantry company in Piqua in 1861, Company F, 11th OVI Regiment serving as its first Captain. He was one of the community's most active volunteers and promoters. His son **William C. Johnston** also practiced law in Piqua. William served as a private in his father's Company F before later accepting a promotion to Second Lieutenant with the 45th Ohio Volunteer Infantry regiment. Stephen Johnston was inducted into the Piqua **Civic Hall of Fame** in 2003. SEE ALSO: Chamber of Commerce

William Caldwell Johnston (1842-1905)

Johnston was the son of Piqua attorney **Stephen Johnston** and studied in his offices. He was admitted to the Bar in 1867. W. C. Johnston served as City Solicitor in 1869-1873 and in 1874-1879. He was a Miami County probate judge from 1879 until 1885.

Matthew H. Jones (1825-1918)

Jones studied law under **Samuel S. McKinney** and joined the Ohio Bar in 1848. He served as city recorder in 1849-1852, and as Miami County prosecutor from 1851 until 1856. He also practiced law with his son **Walter D. Jones**.

Walter Durval Jones (1857-1942)

Jones was the son of Piqua attorney **Matthew H. Jones**. He was Piqua High School's youngest graduate (in 1872) at the age of fourteen. He read law under his father and in 1878 was admitted to the State Bar. He served with M.H. Jones from 1879 until 1899 when he was appointed to the Miami County Common Pleas Court. He served on the court until 1937. Prior to his judgeship, Jones served as the first editor of the *Piqua Morning Call* in 1883, and as Piqua City Solicitor in 1879-81, 1883-91, and 1894-95. Walter D. Jones' grandson, Shirley Randolph Turner (1911-1990), graduated from Piqua High School in 1929. In 1934 he became the third generation of his family to practice law in Piqua.

Armin Jacob "A.J." Kaiser (1895-1984)

He was born in Boonville, Indiana, the son of Henry G. and Katherine Binder Kaiser. After serving in the military in **World War I**, he came to Piqua in April of 1926 to work for the **YMCA**. He first served as the youth director from 1926 through 1940 and then as general secretary through 1960. His work with the youth in Piqua was known throughout the state and culminated with his promotion and leadership of the YMCA's **Camp Wakonda** program. During World War II, Kaiser aided servicemen around the world with his constant

A.J. Kaiser (1895-1984)

stream of letters on hometown events. He worked with various post-War veterans programs, as well as serving Piqua as a local historian and civic promoter. He was inducted into the Piqua **Civic Hall of Fame** in 1996.

Joseph Martin Kastner (1889 - 1959)

Born in Potolsky, Guberne, Russia, Kastner, he immigrated to the United States in 1907. Kastner came to Piqua in 1913 from Dayton, Ohio. He established the city's largest scrap metal yard at the west end of Water Street. He served on the Piqua City Commission from 1957 to 1959. He was instrumental in starting the Piqua Fireman's Pension Board to ensure decent retirements for local firefighters. Kastner served on the board of the Salvation Army and for over twenty-five years on the Board of Directors of the Miami Valley Boy Scouts. He was very active in the B'nai B'rith.

Simon Kenton (1755 - 1836) *

Kenton was born in Virginia and began his career as an army scout for the Virginia Militia during Lord Dunmore's War in 1774. He worked as an apprentice scout under Daniel Boone during the Revolutionary War era in the west. Kenton served as a Major in General **Anthony Wayne**'s army in 1794. After Ohio became a state, Kenton was elected a Brigadier General in the Ohio Militia (1805). Kenton County, Kenton, Kentucky and Kenton, Ohio were named after him. During the **War of 1812**, he fought the British and Indians in Canada. He died in Bellefontaine, Ohio in 1836 and was buried in Urbana, Ohio. In the late 1880's, a major monument was erected in Kenton's honor. SEE ALSO: Wayne, Anthony.

Bernard S. Keyt (1901 - 1983)

Keyt was born in Piqua and graduated from the Ohio State School of Law in 1926. In 1927, he became the Piqua City Solicitor, the youngest city solicitor in the State of Ohio. He remained in this position until 1956. During his tenure he helped write the new Piqua City Charter in 1929. After the charter's passage in 1930, he wrote large portions of the city's new zoning code. Keyt was elected as a Municipal Court Judge in Miami County in 1960 and held that position until 1970.

Leopold Kiefer (1841 - 1903)

A **German** immigrant, he came to Piqua in 1852 with his family and later served in the **Civil War**. For several years after the war he operated a grocery store in the war devastated south. He returned to Piqua in 1869 and opened a grocery and later a **cigar** manufacturing operation. He organized and commanded Company D, Ohio National Guard from 1875 through 1880. Kiefer also served as the superintendent of Piqua's first Water Works. During the 1890's he managed the Piqua Driving Club on Washington Avenue. SEE ALSO: Militia; Tobacco

Robert B. Kills (c.1852 – 1907)

Kills moved to Piqua in 1868 and worked for the **L.C. & W.L. Cron Furniture Company** as the foreman of the cabinet shop. With **Andrew Jackson Cron**, Kills helped form the **Cron, Kills Company** furniture factory in 1881. The company moved to **Huntersville** in 1884 and Kills became very active in politics serving as Huntersville clerk (1875-1880, 1880-1882) and councilman (1882-1893).

Olympic medalist Kristen King is shown in the 2006 parade in her honor riding on the Fire Department's ladder truck.

Kristen King
(c.1980 - present)

She was born in Piqua and graduated from Piqua High School with the Class of 1998. She was a member of the bronze medal winning Women's Ice Hockey team during the 2006 Winter **Olympics**.

Henry Kitchen (1797 - 1883)

He moved to Piqua in 1819 and became a pioneer quarryman in the Piqua area. He was very active in the community serving as one of the founders of **Piqua Colonization Society** in 1826. As a politician and public servant, Kitchen was elected as both a Piqua and a **Washington Township** trustee. He served eight years as the township treasurer.

Ollie Klee (1900 - 1977)

Klee was a professional **baseball** player from Piqua. In 1925, while playing outfield with the Cincinnati Reds, he is recorded with one time at bat and was struck out. This was the beginning and end of his professional career in the big leagues.

E. Eugene "Gene" Kurtz
(1914 – 1964)

Kurtz was born in Missouri, the son of Earl N. and Grace Brady Kurtz. After World War II, he was the general manager of the Thyer Manufacturing Corp. of Toledo. In 1952, he was president and co-founder of **Inland Homes**, a prefabricated home manufacturer in Piqua. Kurtz would found a housing development company, First Piqua Corporation (1955) and a home financing company, Inland Mortgage Corp. (1956). Active in the community, Kurtz served as president of the Piquarea United Fund. SEE ALSO: Inland Homes; Landin Park.

Fred John Lange (1894 – 1976)

He was born in Grand Island, Nebraska, the son of Frank

(1858-1918) and Elizabeth Goeke Lange. He came to Piqua in 1898 with his family. Lange attended St. Marys Catholic High School and the Ideal Business College. His father purchased the Schneyer Brewery in 1898 and created the Lange **Brewing** Company which stayed in the family until 1938. Fred J. began work in the family brewery at age nine. In 1916, with his brother Frank N. (c.1890-1952), he purchased A.P. Klee's Piqua **Bottling** Works on Spring Street. The two brothers began distributing Coca Cola in 1917 and in 1918 bought the franchise for Miami and Shelby Counties. Their company became the Piqua Coca Cola Bottling Company with Fred J. as president. The firm moved to the old Strand Theater on the public square in 1937.

William Powell Lear Sr.
(1902 - 1978)

Lear established the **Lear Avia Company** in 1930. He moved the firm to Piqua from Vandalia in 1941. In that same year he married Moya Marie Olsen, daughter of Broadway comedian Ole Olsen. The couple moved to Piqua and lived in a small frame house on Kerns Road (Country Club Road). The company was best known for its innovative aviation radio and instrument systems. A number of the firm's products were personally patented by William Lear including the Lear-O-Scope radio direction finding system. He promoted the establishment of the city's first formal industrial training school in 1943. Lear Avia moved from Piqua to Grand Rapids, Michigan in 1945-1946.

This Christmas card photograph shows Bill and Moya Lear.

Benjamin Leavell
(1781 – 1860)

Leavell was born in Virginia and moved to what would become Piqua in 1805. He was a carpenter and is believed to have built most of the community's earliest log **houses**. His marriage to Martha McCorkle in the fall of 1807 was recorded in local folklore as the first wedding in Miami County. He served as the first treasurer of **Washington Township**. During the War of 1812 he served as a local quartermaster. Leavell left Piqua from 1825 to 1831 during which time he helped lay out the towns of Defiance and Napoleon in Williams County. Upon returning to Piqua he built and operated a small tavern on Main Street.

Ashbel Merrell Leonard
(1854 - 1940)

Born near Cincinnati, he came to Piqua with his family in 1866. He worked for the Pennsylvania Railroad and worked his way up from a telegraph operator to the Piqua Freight Agent and Cashier. In 1885, he established the Zinnia Ridge Nursery Company which by 1912 had become the A.M. Leonard & Son Company which specialized in landscaping. Leonard was involved in the formation of the Piqua Handle Company (1882) and the **French Oil Mill Machinery Company** (1900). He also served many years as a banker and as a Methodist Sunday School Superintendent.

Lewis Leonard (1825-1900)

He was born in Pennsylvania and came to Ohio after serving in the **Civil War**. In 1869, he moved to Piqua and joined with **William P. Orr** to establish the city's largest **linseed** oil mill works. He also was responsible for bringing the strawboard industry (the cardboard of the nineteenth century) to Piqua and the founding of the **Union Underwear Company.**

William Kendall Leonard (1865 - 1931)

He was born, raised and educated in Piqua and began work in the linseed oil mills with his father. He later became the president of the **Piqua Hosiery Company**. During **World War I**, he was the chief of the fanatically patriotic **American Protective League of Miami County.**

Abraham Lincoln (1809-1865) *

During his lifetime, Lincoln never visited Piqua. The closest he came was a campaign stop in Dayton. However, Lincoln had a huge impact on the city as he did on the nation as a whole. In the election of 1860, Lincoln received 59.3% of the total votes cast in Piqua and Washington Township. On a state-wide level, Lincoln gained 52.3% of the vote, and nationally only 39.8%. When president-elect Lincoln was in Cincinnati in February of 1861, the editor of Piqua's *Miami County Democrat* Joseph H. Horton traveled south to see him. Horton wrote about his experience stating that, "We are pleased to note that he [Lincoln] is not nearly so homely looking as a majority of the so-called portraits represent him". During the Civil War, Piqua responded enthusiastically to Lincoln's call for volunteers, with almost one thousand local residents serving in the Army and Navy. During the election of 1864, Lincoln received 61.5% of the total local vote. On a national level, he gained only 55% of the popular vote.

On April 15, 1865, Abraham Lincoln died from an assassin's bullet. The funeral train stopped in Piqua on April 30, 1865 at twenty minutes past midnight. A crowd estimated at ten thousand people gathered to view Lincoln's body as it lay in state in a special railroad coach. A Methodist choir sang a hymn and bands from Piqua and Troy played appropriate music. SEE ALSO: Dorsey, Godwin V.; McKinney, John F.; Moody, Granville.

Little Turtle (1752 – 1812) *

Little Turtle was a chief of the **Miami Tribe** and was also known as Me-she-kun-nogh-quoh or Michikinikwas. He led the Native American forces that defeated General Harmar in 1790 and General **St. Clair** in 1791. He came to terms with the European-American settlers and the signed the **Treaty of Greenville** in 1795. Colonel **John Johnston** was well acquainted with Chief Little Turtle during his time at the Fort Wayne Indian Agency (1802-1809). During the **Council of Piqua** held at the Johnston Farm in 1812, Little Turtle was a strong advocate for tribal neutrality during the war between the British and the Americans. SEE ALSO: Girty, Simon; Harmar, Josiah; Wells, William.

James Logan (c.1770's – 1812)

A **Shawnee** chief, known as Spemica-lawba (High Horse), was captured by General Logan in 1786. He was raised as part of Logan's family and educated in pioneer schools in Kentucky. His Native American mother was Tecumseh's sister.

He left Kentucky as a young man and moved to the Shawnee village of Wapakoneta. By 1812, he had moved to Upper Piqua with **Colonel Johnston**. In August of 1812, Logan escorted a number of women and children from Fort Wayne to the safety of Piqua. He left his home with Colonel Johnston and served as a scout for American forces during the **War of 1812** where he was killed. His two sons, Henry Clay and Martin Hardin were brought to Piqua by Johnston who fostered them to the Widney family in Piqua.

George William Lorimer (1874 - 19__)

He was born in Ontario, Canada and moved to Piqua in 1897. With his brother J. Hoyt Lormier, George Lorimer patented an automatic telephone exchange system in the 1890's. He served as the superintendent of the Callender Telephone Exchange Company which moved into the former Brendel **Furniture** factory on South Street near South Main Street in 1897 to manufacture the new Lorimer System. The company was re-organized as the American Machine Telephone Company about 1900 with Lorimer as the corporate secretary-treasurer. The firm moved its plant to southwest corner of Wayne and Sycamore Streets and stayed in Piqua until about 1909-1910 when most of the patents were transferred to the Bell Telephone Company. Another Lorimer invention, a foundry sand mixer, led to the creation of the Auto Sand Mixer Company in 1906 with Lorimer as president. In c.1913, Lorimer had established the G.W. Lorimer Company at 704 West Ash Street as an experimental laboratory for new mechanical devices. He served as Piqua's **mayor (Republican)** in 1914 and 1915. He was one of primary promoters of the rebuilding of the Shawnee Bridge after its destruction during the 1913 **Flood**. At the bridge's dedication it was named the Lorimer Bridge in his honor. Lorimer was an early tinker/inventor. He built and drove Piqua's first **automobile** in 1900. In 1905, he purchased a six-cylinder Franklin, still one the very few automobile owners in the city. Lorimer helped organize and served as the first president of the Piqua Historical Society in 1912. He moved to Troy in the early 1920's and established the Lorimer Manufacturing Company to produce phonograph motors.

Helen L. Louis (1899 – 1984)

Louis was born in Piqua and joined the staff of the **Schmidlapp** Free School **Library** in 1921. She became library director in 1946 serving through 1966. She began a number of innovative programs including providing circulating audio-visual materials to the public (one of the first five libraries in the state to provide this service), provided books to the hospital, and for the homebound. Louis was instrumental in creating new methods for adult learning in the city. She was inducted into the Piqua **Civic Hall of Fame** in 1999.

Edward "Billy" Manning (1839 - 1876)

Manning was born and raised in Piqua, the grandson of English immigrant and pioneer John Manning. At age fourteen, he had organized a traveling minstrel group with fellow Piqua boys. The show featured African-American (black-face) humor, singing and instrumental playing. He went on to individual fame and fortune in Chicago with his singing and racially oriented comedy acts performing as the Manning Minstrels.

John Manning (17__ - 18__)

An English immigrant, Manning settled in the new village of Cincinnati in 1795. He came to the future site of Piqua in 1799 and bought the cleared field and cabin of **Job Gard**. He purchased extensive land holdings west of the Miami River. He joined with Matthew Caldwell to plat out 101 lots of what would become the village of Washington (Piqua) in 1807. Manning's son Elias is often credited in local folklore as the first European-American child born in Piqua in 1800. Manning built the first industry in Piqua, a grist mill in 1804. He was one of the organizers of Piqua's first trade organization, an association of local saw mill owners.

Mahlon Dickerson Manson (1820 - 1895)

Manson was born in Piqua. He enlisted in the **Civil War** and was wounded and captured at Richmond, Virginia. He was wounded again at Resaca. He resigned on December 21, 1864 with the rank of Brigadier General. He died and was buried in Crawfordsville, Indiana.

Charles H. May (1859 - c.1920's)

May was responsible for the construction of the city's largest opera house (**May's Opera House**) in 1903. He owned and operated his own drugstore.

Luther Quinter "Lute" McCarty (1892-1913)

Born in Nebraska, the son of "Doctor" A.P. McCarty (18__-1934), he worked as a cowboy, sailor and bridge builder before moving to Piqua with his father and their medicine show in circa 1910. He started his boxing career in 1911. At six foot four inches and 205 pounds he won twenty-eight fights in his first two years. On January 01, 1913, McCarty became the heavyweight champion of the world when he defeated the Iowa Giant Al Palzer. On May 24, 1913, in a title bout in Calgary, Alberta, Canada against Arthur Pelkey, he was knocked out and a half an hour later was dead. He was buried with great fanfare in Piqua.

William McClean (1794 - 1839)

He came to Piqua prior to 1820 from Warren County, and became the village's first lawyer, setting up his office in his home on Spring Street near Ash Street. William's brother, John McClean (1785-1861), served in the United States House of Representatives from 1813 to 1816, was appointed Postmaster General from 1823 until 1829, and served as Justice of the United States Supreme Court from 1829 until 1861. William McClean became Piqua's first national level politician with his election to the **House of Representatives** in 1822 from the Miami District of Ohio serving until 1829. With his election to Congress in 1822, he sold his office and practice to General Robert Young. Politically he was a **Dem-ocratic**-Republican, and later a supporter of the **Whig** Party. He was responsible for appointing future Admiral **Stephen Rowan** to the United States Navy as a midshipman in 1826. McLean served in the Ohio **Militia** with the rank of Colonel. In 1829, he left Piqua and moved to Cincinnati.

Joseph Walker McCorkle (1819-1884)

He was born in Piqua, the son of John McCorkle, and completed his early education in local schools. He graduated from Kenyon College in Gambier, Ohio. He studied law and was admitted to the bar in 1842. He commenced the practice of law in Dayton, Ohio where he served as postmaster from 1845 until 1849. In 1849, he answered the call of the **Gold Rush** and went to California. McCorkle settled in San Francisco and went on to serve two terms in the state legislature (1850-1852), one term (1854-56) as a Democratic California Congressman and finally as a circuit court judge (1853-1857) He moved to Virginia City, Nevada in 1860 and opened up a law practice in the city. In 1870, he setup a law office in Washington, D.C. He died in Maryland and was buried in Piqua in the Forest Hill Cemetery.

William Moore McCulloch (1901-1980)

He was born on November 24, 1901, in Holmes County, the son of James H. and Ida M. McCulloch. He received a law degree from the Ohio State University and was admitted to the Ohio Bar in 1925. McCulloch and his wife, Mabel Harris, moved to Piqua in 1928 where he joined with George W. Berry to form the Berry and McCulloch law firm (later to become McCulloch, Felger, Fite, and Gutmann). In 1932, he was elected as Republican to the **Ohio House of Representatives**. By 1936, he was the House Minority Leader and, from 1939 until 1943, served as Ohio Speaker of the House. In 1943, he resigned to enter the U. S. Army, serving twenty months in Europe during **World War II**. He was elected to the United States **Congress** from the Fourth Ohio District in 1947 and stayed in the House until his retirement on January 3, 1971 (serving twelve consecutive terms). McCulloch's political triumphs include sponsorship of the Civil Rights Act of 1964, and membership on the National Advisory Commission on Civil Disorder (1967), the Commission on Causes and Prevention of Violence (1968) and the Atomic Energy Commission. At his retirement in 1971, he was the ranking Republican on the House Judiciary Committee. He died in Washington, D.C. on February 22, 1980. He was inducted into the Piqua **Civic Hall of Fame** in 1995. SEE ALSO: Civil Rights; Home Guard; Patron p. 249

William McKinley (1843-1901) *

He was born in Niles, Ohio and was a veteran of the **Civil War**, serving under **Rutherford B. Hayes**. McKinley was an active Ohio **Republican** politician, serving first as a United States congressman and them as the state governor. He visited Piqua several times during his political career. The first time occurred during the 1891 gubernatorial campaign. McKinley gave a major speech in front of the newly erected **Plaza Hotel** on September 17, 1891. The next day he visited the mills of the **Cincinnati Corrugating Company** and praised the firm for being the first in Ohio to produce purely "American tin sheeting". Despite the personal visit, McKinley carried Piqua by only nine votes, but he defeated the incumbent Democratic governor by over twenty thousand votes state-wide.

Governor McKinley visited Piqua again on May 10, 1892 to speak to the GAR encampment at Fountain Park. In 1896 and in 1900, McKinley ran for president and both times carried Piqua by solid margins (in 1896 by 53.1% of the vote and in 1900 by 52.1%). On September 6, 1901, William McKinley was shot by anarchist Leon Czolgosz. The President died of his wounds on September 14, 1901. SEE ALSO: Bryan, William J.; Rutherford, B.; Presidents.

John Franklin McKinney
(1827 - 1903)

He was born in **Springcreek Township**, the son of John P. McKinney who had settled in Miami County in 1804. He attended Ohio Wesleyan University at Delaware and in 1850 joined his brother Samuel in the practice of law. In 1853, he married Louise Wood. He was elected to the **House of Representatives** in 1862 as a **Democrat** for the Fourth Congressional District (Miami, Darke, Shelby, Logan and Champaign Counties). He had attended the inauguration of President **Abraham Lincoln** and wrote to his wife that Lincoln was one of the ugliest men he had ever seen. In 1864, McKinney was in Sidney campaigning with gubernatorial candidate C. L. Vallandingham (a peace Democrat or Copperhead). During this campaign, returning Union veterans tried to physically break-up the Democratic rally. McKinney's intervention calmed the crowds and prevented a riot. He ran for re-election in 1864 and 1866, but the coalition Union Party's (**Republicans** and War Democrats) candidates defeated him at both elections. McKinney returned to Piqua, becoming chairman of the Board of Education from 1865-67, and serving on the board of the Piqua **Hydraulic** Company from 1866 until 1874 (as President from 1871-1874). He served another term in Congress with his re-election in 1870. In 1872, McKinney chaired the Ohio State Democratic Committee and served as a delegate to the National Democratic Convention in Baltimore. McKinney supported the nomination of Horace Greeley to oppose Republican candidate U.S. Grant. By 1873, McKinney had retired from politics and devoted the next thirty years to the practice of law in Piqua and Miami County. During the late 1880's he began work as the full time secretary of the Independent Order of Odd Fellows Mutual Aid and Accident Association (**insurance**).

Samuel Scott McKinney
(1818-1894)

McKinney was born in **Springcreek Township**, the son of John P. McKinney. He began his law studies under Gordon Mott and was admitted to the Ohio Bar in 1842. He served as mayor of Piqua in 1846-1847. A member of the Ohio **Militia,** McKinney attained the rank of Major. He was joined in his practice in 1850 by his younger brother **John Franklin McKinney** (1827-1903). He was one of the original incorporators of the Piqua **Hydraulic** Company in 1865. Like his brother, McKinney was a staunch **Democrat**.

Kenneth McMaken (1911-1987)

McMaken was born in Piqua and had a long record of community service. As president of the Piqua Council of Churches, he was one of the founders of the Bassett Street Mission and he promoted inter-racial discussions among the city's churches. He was a co-founder and long time member of the Piqua Elks Band (Civic Band). His service to local youth is exemplified in over forty years as a local Boy Scout leader. He was inducted into the Piqua **Civic Hall of Fame** in 2001.

Kenneth McMaken (1911-1987)

This publicity still from the c.1940's shows the Mills Brothers and their father John Mills Sr.

Mills Brothers

This internationally known singing group began their career in 1925 as "Four Boys and a Guitar". The original group consisted of John Jr. (1911-1936), Herbert (1912-1989), Harry (1913-1982), and Donald (1915-1999). John Hutchinson "Pike" and Eathel M. Harrington Mills, parents of the Mills Brothers were married in Bellefonte, Pennsylvania in 1907 and moved to Piqua in 1908-09. John Mills Sr. went to work at the Cass Evan's Barbershop on the public square. By 1923, with seven children to support including his three daughters Margaret Mills McKinley (Mrs. Jack), Pauline Mills and Dorothea Mills Hamilton, he was working in the shop of Arthur B. Smith on the public square and rented a home on the southwest corner of Greene and Spring Streets owned by **Goodrich Giles**. The children attended Spring Street School and the family attended the Cyrene A.M.E Church. John Sr. was one of the organizers in Piqua of the Four Kings of Harmony composed of Mills, Leslie Wall, George Moss and Arthur Smith. The group was barbershop quartet made up of actual barbers. John and Ethel Mills were divorced about 1927 and for a time the four brothers boarded with Harold Beard on Spring Street. Mrs. Mills would later marry Athol Garnes.

The Mills Brothers got there first paying gig at May's Opera House where they performed during the intermission of *Rin-Tin-Tin* for four dollars a night. Local legend states that during one of the performances, one of the brothers forgot his harmonica, and that is why the brothers began imitating musical instruments, a trademark of their early musical careers. The "Four Boys" got their professional start with Piqua musician Harold Greenamyer's Orchestra, John Jr. sang bass, Herbert sang tenor, Harry sang baritone and Donald sang lead. On February 09, 1927, the Mills Brothers performed for the first time on radio on WSAI in Cincinnati. They headlined with the Greenamyer Orchestra and their listeners' most popular request was for a number entitled *Chinese Honeymoon*. They moved on to singing gigs on WLW-Radio in Cincinnati which had been established two years earlier by Powell Crosby. At WLW, the Mills Brothers performed under a variety of names including Four Boys and a Kazoo, the Tasty Yeast Jesters (Sunday night performances were sponsored by the Fleischmann Yeast Company) and the Steamboat Four.

The Mills Brothers gained national recognition since the 5,000 watt WLW station broadcast as far away as Chicago and New York City. Their first record was cut in 1927. In the next fifty years, the group cut over 1,246 records. Their first hit record was "Tiger Rag" in 1929 which, on the Brunswick Label, sold over a million copies. By this time, they were playing in New York City clubs and CBS radio signed them up for a regularly broadcast show. In January of 1936, twenty-five year old John Jr. died of pneumonia after becoming ill on a 1935 European tour. John Jr. was buried in Bellefontaine, Ohio next to his sister Margaret who had died in 1935. John Sr. (18__ - 1967) took his son's place in the group until his retirement in 1956. The Mills Brothers' biggest hits included, *Tiger Rag, Paper Doll , Cab Driver, Yellow Bird, Glow Worm* (Decca Records), *Lazy River, Till Then, You're Nobody Till Somebody Loves You, and Bye Bye Blackbird*. The Brothers biggest hit was *Paper Doll* in 1943 under the Decca record label with over six million records sold. Their last big hit was *Cab Drive* in 1968. During their very long careers, the Mills Brothers performed with Duke Ellington, Bing Crosby, Al Jolson, Louie Armstrong and Cab Calloway among others. They also have been recorded on 78's, 45's, 33LP's (all records), 8-tracks, audio and video cassettes, CD's, DVD's, sheet music, radio, movies and television.

As a group, they quit performing after Harry Mills' death in 1982. The City of Piqua dedicated a monument to the Mills Brothers on the public square in June of 1990. At that time the Mills Brothers Scholarship was formed and Matt Bogart became one the first recipients. Bogart would go on to sing on Broadway and may be currently best known for his staring role in *Miss Saigon*. In May of 1991, Donald Mills and his son John performed at the Piqua High School. The Mills Brothers were inducted into the Piqua **Civic Hall of Fame** in 2000.

John Grant Mitchell (1838 - 1894)

He was born in Piqua and graduated from Kenyon College in 1859. He opened a law office in Columbus in 1859-60. He answered Lincoln's call for volunteers as a private in 1861and quickly moved up the ranks. By 1862, he was a Lt. Colonel in the 113th Regiment and by 1865 he had become a Major General at the age of twenty-six. He would be Piqua's highest ranking army officer in the **Civil War.** He married the niece of President **Rutherford B. Hayes** and served as the Mayor of Columbus.

Moses G. Mitchell (18 – 18)

From 1828 through 1830 he served as a **Washington Township** trustee, in 1832 as the Piqua village recorder and in 1841 as township clerk. He was one of the organizers and the first president of the Columbus, Piqua and Indiana **Railroad** in 1849. As a **Militia** Colonel, Mitchell commanded the newly formed **Camp Piqua** during the **Civil War.**

Andrew Montour (c.1700-c.1780's)*

Montour was the son of Robert Hunter and Madame Montour. He was raised in various French and English trading posts and with several different clans of the Miami. During the 1740's, he worked with the Pennsylvania trader Conrad Weister as an assistant and interpreter. Montour also served as an interpreter at the Treaty of Lancaster. By 1750, he was working with another Pennsylvania trader, **George Croghan.** Montour visited **Pickawillany** with **Croghan, Gist,** and **Callender** in 1751. In August of 1753, Montour served with Captain **William Trent** in erecting a fort at the fork of the Ohio River. Montour served under **George Washington** in 1754 at the surrender of Fort Necessity.

Granville Moody (1812-18__)

Moody was born in Portland, Maine, the son of William and Harriet Brooks Moody. He moved to Ohio at the age of eigh-

teen and became a Methodist minister in 1833. He served at the Greene Street M.E. Church c.1857-1861 and c.1863-1865. In 1862, he was commissioned a colonel and took command of the 74th Ohio Volunteer Infantry Regiment which had formed in Xenia. In 1862, he also served as the commandant of Camp Chase, a prisoner of war camp located west of Columbus. While serving with his regiment in Tennessee , he participated in the Battle of Stone River. For his bravery during the battle he became known as the "Fighting Parson". He resigned his commission in May of 1863 and returned to his position of pastor at Greene Street Church. Moody would be awarded the rank of Brevet Brigadier General in March of 1865.

Never afraid of expressing his opinion, Moody was a featured speaker at a local **Republican** Union Party rally in 1863. He responded to comments about southern sympathizers having their rights trampled upon, "Rights! Rights! Let me tell you, my friends, that the only rights those people have is to be hanged in this world and damned in the next." At a convention in Philadelphia in c.1863-4, Moody met President Lincoln. Reverend Moody used his brief meeting with Lincoln to later request a political favor. Moody wrote a letter to the president in March of 1865 requesting the appointment of Joseph M. Patterson as the Piqua postmaster. Moody's letter related that First Sergeant Patterson (Company A, 110th Regiment) had lost his arm after the Battle of the Wilderness. **Lincoln** granted Moody's request and Patterson served as Piqua's postmaster from 1865 to 1879. Paterson died in 1906. In June of 1865, Rev. Moody opened the Ohio Republican Union Party Convention in Columbus with a prayer. Rev. Moody retired from the active ministry in 1883 and wrote his autobiography in 1890 entitled, *A Life's Retrospect*. SEE ALSO: Civil War; Vance, Wilson (Stone River)

Isaac Stanley Morris (1825 - 1905)

Morris grew up in the Eaton, Ohio and served as the superintendent of the Eaton Schools from 1853 to 1860. He served as the publisher of the *Eaton Register* from 1861 to 1874. He then moved to Piqua where he established Piqua's first **temperance newspaper**, the *Miami Helmet*. He also worked with his son as the editor of the *Piqua Daily Call*.

John Whittier Morris (1860 – 1906)

Morris was born in Eaton, Ohio, the son of Isaac S. and Edith T. Morris and moved to Piqua with his family in 1874. He attended the Piqua High School and graduated from Ohio Wesleyan College. He then went to work with his father on the weekly *Miami Helmet* before establishing his own **newspaper** the *Piqua Daily Call* in 1883 and later purchased his father's interest in the *Miami Helmet*. Morris was one of the city's early supporters of the new game of baseball and a member of the Piqua Glee Club. In June of 1898, Morris organized and was elected captain of Company K, 3rd Infantry, Ohio National Guard. The company was sent south during the **Spanish-American War** but the war ended before his unit was sent to Cuba. He served as a director of the Piqua National and Third National banks, and was the Piqua Postmaster from 1898 until his death in 1906. Morris served on the Ohio **Republican Party** Central Committee in 1895.

Raymond S. Mote (1892 – 1941)

Mote was born in Piqua and began his teaching career there. By 1918, he was coaching the High School students in all sports but particularly in baseball and track. Mote organized the Summer Playground Program and later created the American Legion Junior Baseball Commission as part of that program. He also served as one of Piqua's first scoutmasters and as the physical director of the **YMCA**. Mote was responsible for bringing modern organized public sports and recreation to Piqua. Mote was inducted into the Piqua **Civic Hall of Fame** in 1999.

Gordon Newell Mott (1812-1887)

Mott began practicing law in Piqua in the early 1840's, and in 1846 raised a company of **militia** to fight in the **Mexican War** obtaining the rank of Captain. Mott moved out west, and by 1863 was representing the territory of Nevada in the United States House of Representatives.

Francis Murphy (1836-1907) *

Murphy was an Irish immigrant who settled in Maine. In 1870, he was arrested for a drunken assault and while in jail he saw the light and signed a total abstinence pledge. He went on to lecture across the nation against alcohol consumption in what became known as "Gospel **Temperance**". He began handing out blue ribbons to his adherents and those pledge signers became known as the Blue Ribbon Army. Murphy spoke in Piqua in October of 1877. SEE ALSO: Temperance.

Robert Maynard Murray (1841-1913)

A lawyer by profession, Murray was admitted to the Ohio Bar in 1859 at the age of eighteen. He served as mayor of Painesville, Ohio in 1878 before moving to Piqua in 1879 as one of the founders and first president the Piqua Handle and Manufacturing Company. In 1882, he was elected to the United States **House of Representatives** from the Third Ohio Congressional District. He served until 1885 but was not re-nominated during the 1884 election, and lost to the Republican candidate in the 1886 election. Murray served as President of the Piqua Board of Education from 1885 until 1889. In 1894 Murray moved away from Piqua. SEE ALSO: Democrats; Grant, Ulysses; Knights of Labor.

Charles E. Musco (1917-1996)

He was born and died in Piqua, serving most of his adult life as an independent brick mason. During World War II, he served in the Army Corps of Engineers in the South Pacific. His civic involvement included serving on the Piqua Park Board and over twenty-five years with the Piqua Police Auxiliary. In 1985, Musco was the first **African-American** in Piqua to be elected to the Piqua City Commission.

Carrie Nation (1846-1911) *

A nationally known **temperance** and suffrage agitator, she was best known for physically destroying saloons with a hatchet. She visited Piqua on July 8, 1905.

Jacob W. Nigh (18__-19__)

Nigh was one of the founding members of the local **Knights of Labor** in 1886. He also was a successful candidate for the Piqua City Council in the fourth ward serving from 1886 until 1888 and again from 1890 to 1891. He was an unsuccessful candidate for Congress under the Labor ticket in 1886. He worked in Piqua as an independent carpenter. SEE ALSO: unions

Phoebe Anne Mosey Butler Oakley (1860-1926) *

She was born and was buried in Darke County, Ohio. She was an internationally known entertainer and sharpshooter. She traveled and performed under the stage name of Annie Oakley and was nicknamed "Little Miss Sure Shot". In 1885, Oakley and her husband, Frank Butler, joined Buffalo Bill's Wild West Show. This show appeared in Piqua on July 9, 1896. Mrs. Butler visited friends in Piqua on April 11, 1908.

Kathy Jean Antolick Oda (1948-1994)

She was born in Minnesota the daughter of Dan and Vivian Antolick. She moved to Piqua in July of 1974 and created the very first library at the newly opened Edison General and Technical **College** in the former Spring Street Elementary School. When Oda came to Edison, the library consisted of a single gray metal shelf holding a partial copy of a Webster's Dictionary. She designed the layout of the library at its first location at the Looney Road campus. Active in community events, Oda served as president and district governor of the Altrusa Club. She also worked as a freelance book and journal editor.

Harry Ronald Oda (1912-1995)

Harry R. Oda (1912-1995)

Oda was born in Piqua the son of Harry Henry and Lucretia Bruss Oda. He graduated from the Piqua High School in 1930 where he played clarinet in the High School Marching Band. He continued his musical interests with a stint in a German Polka Band and as a charter member of the Elks Band which later developed into the Piqua Civic Band. Oda was an outstanding accompanist and played the piano for numerous civic groups including the Rotary, Lions and Foreman's Clubs. He served as the organist of St. John's Lutheran Church for over fifty years beginning in 1928. He was active supporter of his community serving on the Miami County Selective Service Board, Children's Services Board, Miami County Mental Health Board, Civic Music Association, Piqua Board of Education, American **Red Cross** and the Flesh Public **Library** Board of Trustees. Oda started his work history as a young boy working in the Oda and Oda Meat Market and later as an office boy at the **Atlas Underwear Company** under **Leo M. Flesh**. As president of Citizens National **Bank**, Flesh moved Oda over to the bank as a proof clerk. Oda would later establish the Travel Department at the bank before retiring in 1977 as Vice President and trust officer. During **World War II**, Oda served in the United States Army in the Pacific Theater as a chaplain's assistant. He married Rebecca Jane Denman in 1947.

Madam Mure Elizabeth Huffman O'Fallon (1849 – 1909)

She was one the earliest *known* professional mid-wives in the city.

Dr. John O'Ferrall (1823 – 1887)

He was born in Piqua, the son of Dr. John O'Ferrall who died in c.1840. He graduated from the Louisville Medical College in 1843 and took up practice in Piqua. He served as a state senator in 1844-1845. He went out to find his fortune in the **California Gold Rush** in 1848 to 1850. He completed his military service during the **Civil War** with the rank of major. Dr. O'Ferrall was an active participant in the city's economic growth with the O'Ferrall, Daniels & Company woolen mill (1869), the O'Ferrall & Daniels' Piqua Agriculture Works (manufacturers of the Moffitts Threshing Machine) (c.1860's), and the Lock Flour Mill. He married Addie Thompson in 1874 and they had four children Dr. Robert M. O'Ferrall (1855-1926), John Jr., Mary and Katie.

Old Britain (17__ - 1752)

Old Britain was known to the French as La Demoiselle. He was the chief of the Twigtwee Division of the **Miami Tribe**. He established the village and trading post of **Pickawillany** located near Piqua in 1747. He had moved to this location to escape the influence of the French Canadians. He was killed when French troops with their Native American allies attacked and burned Pickawillany to the ground. According to local folklore, the Native Americans that had attacked Pickawillany were so impressed with Old Britain's bravery during the battle, that after his death they cut out his heart and ate it as a tribute to his courage.

Caleb W. Orr (1845-1935)

Orr was born in Covington, Ohio, the brother of **William P. Orr**. During **Civil War** he served as a sergeant major in the 124th Regiment of the Indiana Volunteer Infantry. He moved to Piqua in 1885 to manage one of his brother's **linseed** oil mills. He would later establish a dry goods store in the 400 block of North Main Street (east side).

Frances Meilly Orr (1854 - 1910)

She was born in Lima, Ohio and became **William P. Orr**'s second wife in 1884 at a marriage ceremony in Westminster Abbey, London, England. She was a founding member of the Fortnightly Club, and its President in 1903-05. In 1899 she was elected President of the Ohio Federation of Women's Clubs. Locally she was President of the Ladies Aid Society (later Associated **Charities**) from 1886 until 1901. In 1908 she was the first **woman** elected to any political office. She campaigned for School Board on a platform of new schools for the children. She served on the Piqua Board of Education (1908-1910) with one year as vice-president. Orr promoted the building of Favorite Hill School in the rather radical one story cottage style of architecture.

William Perrine Orr (1834 – 1912)

He was born in Covington, Ohio the son of Joshua Orr of Virginia. Joshua moved to Kentucky and then Covington, Ohio in c.1833. William P. Orr came to Piqua at age seventeen in 1851. He became a carriage worker's apprentice under C. W. Crozier, for a wage of forty-eight dollars a year. In 1852, he went west on a fifty yoke oxen wagon. He spent eighteen months during the **California Gold Rush** making a small fortune selling picks, shovels and other mining equipment. He returned to Covington in 1854 before moving back to Piqua in

1869. At that time, he established the Orr, Kendall and Company (**linseed** oil). This was the first of Orr's many Piqua industries. He was also President of Citizens National **Bank** (1885-1912), W. P. Orr Linseed Oil Company (1887-1898), Piqua Electric Street Railway Company (1890-1893), Miami Valley **Electric** Company (1893-1907), Piqua Strawboard and Paper Company (1890's), Orr Felt and Blanket Company (1901-1912), Piqua Savings Bank (1901-1912), and the Blaine Harrow Manufacturing Company (1904 –c1910). He was Vice-President of the Piqua Rolling Mill Company (1889-1902), Mercer Gas and Fuel Company (1888-1890's), Piqua School **Furniture** Company (1890-1903), and the **Atlas Underwear Company** (1900-1912). He was a major stockholder in the Spiker Wagon Works Company, the Piqua Lumber Company, the Piqua Edison **Electric** Illuminating Company, and the Piqua Home **Telephone** Company.

Orr served as a Piqua City councilman from 1872 until 1903, and as president of the council for over seventeen years during that period. Between 1880 and 1910, Orr headed the **Republican Party** in Piqua and in some years the Miami County organization as well. He was defeated twice in his campaigns for the United States House of Representatives (1890 and 1896). He was responsible for the erection of the **Hotel Plaza** (1890-91), and the Orr-Flesh Building (1903). Orr was named Quartermaster General of Ohio (1896-1900) by Governor Asa Bushnell. He would help organize Ohio's forces during the **Spanish-American War**.

His brothers were Joshua W., Caleb W., John W., Thomas T., and Nathan W. During the **Civil War**, his brother John was the commanding Colonel of the 124th Indiana Volunteer Infantry Regiment. Two additional brothers, Joshua and Caleb, also served with the 124th Regiment. William P. Orr served as Captain in Company C, 152nd Ohio Volunteer Infantry Regiment and later Lt. Colonel with the 28th Ohio Volunteer Infantry Regiment.

By 1890, Orr had accomplished a real life rags to riches story by becoming Piqua's most successful business and civic leader. He was inducted into the Piqua **Civic Hall of Fame** in 2004.

Vernon R. Osborn (c.1890's – c.1960's)

He served as the first **mayor** under the Piqua City charter in 1930. He was active in civic activities, serving as chairman of Miami County Boy Scouts 1930's. He was the president and founder of the Cottage Baking Company

Lucy B. Patterson (1871 – 1930)

Patterson was born near Piqua and was one of the very few women in the 1890's to receive a bachelor's degree and then continue on with graduate work in literature at Columbia University. She was an English teacher in Piqua for thirty-five years, taking charge of the upper level high school English classes in 1906. In 1919, she was the founding president of the **YWCA**, serving eight years in that position. She was also one of the founders of the local Story Teller's League. She was inducted into the Piqua **Civic Hall of Fame** in 2000.

Thomas Pierce (c.1777 – 1835)

Pierce was born in Great Britain and immigrated to the United States. He came to Piqua around 1834 and set up a physician's office. He rapidly became involved in local politics, being elected town president (**mayor**) in 1834.

William Hart Pitsenbarger
(1944 – 1966)

Pitsenbarger was born in Piqua and graduated from Piqua High School in 1962. He joined the Air Force and was sent to **Vietnam** in 1965 as a para-rescue specialist. On his day off, Pitsenbarger volunteered for a rescue mission to evacuate wounded American soldiers. He was able to aid in the evacuation of nine men before the helicopter came under heavy fire. He voluntarily stayed behind to help the wounded and as a result was killed by enemy small arms fire. Pitsenbarger was the first enlisted man in U.S. history to receive the Air Force Cross. He was awarded the **Medal of Honor** in December of 2000 in a ceremony at the Air Force Museum in Dayton, Ohio. He was inducted into the Piqua **Civic Hall of Fame** in 1998.

Hartman Ploch (18__ - 18__)

A German immigrant, he came to Piqua in the 1830's. He founded the City **Brewery** in 1835 on Spring Street. It was the city's second brewery. By 1859, the brewery had been moved to an area east of the Great Miami River and north of the Ash Street bridge, Ploch sold the brewery in 1881, but the firm would stay in operation until 1909 making it the longest running brewery in the city's history

Joseph Porquette (17__ - 18__)

A French immigrant, Poquette moved to what would become Piqua in 1804. He built a log cabin and opened a small cooperage and stayed in the **barrel** making business on South Main Street next to the Great Miami River until 1830. He also sold corn whiskey from his cabin and his home became known as the "Devil's Half Acre". He was the community's first cooper.

Albert A. Presley
(c.1842 – c.1924)

He was born the son of slave parents in Louisiana. Prior to the Civil War he came north. In 1862, Presley opened a barber shop in Piqua. Beginning in 1872, his shop was located on the northeast corner of the Public Square for thirty-five years. For a brief period in the 1880's, he partnered with George Bowles. SEE ALSO: African-American

Dr. William J. Prince Sr.
(1861 – 1919)

He was born in New Bremen, the son of Dr. William and Mary F. Redenbaugh Prince. He moved to Piqua with his family in 1864. His father practiced medicine in Piqua until his death in 1877. William J. Prince attended Piqua schools, Miami University and graduated from the Electrical Medical Institute of Cincinnati in 1883. He returned to Piqua in 1887 to set up practice as a physician and surgeon. He was active in the **Democratic Party**, serving as chairman of the Miami County Central Committee. He was instrumental in bringing Democratic presidential candidate **William Jennings Bryan** to Piqua in 1896. Prince was active locally serving as the Piqua Health Officer for two years, as a member and president of the Piqua Board of Education (1880's-1890's). He became one of the organizers and the president of the Democratic *Piqua Daily Press* in 1915. He served as Piqua's postmaster from 1914 until his death in 1919.

William J. Prince Jr.
(1889 – 1965)

He was born in Piqua, the son of Dr. William J. and Jenny Prince. He was a 1909 graduate of the Piqua High School and of the Philips Exeter Academy. He worked for his father as a reporter at the *Piqua Daily Press*. He was member of the local Company C, Third Infantry Regiment, Ohio **National Guard**. The unit was activated during the **First World War,** and Prince served as supply sergeant in France. He was cited for his bravery during the conflict. Prince would serve as temporary postmaster in Piqua after the death of this father in 1919. He worked for a time as the city editor for the *Piqua Daily Call*. The political events of the Great Depression led Prince to become one of the founders and editor of the *Progressive News* c.1934. He served as the second commander of the American Legion in Piqua in 1921.

John Randolph (c.1870 - 1918)

Randolph was born in Piqua, the son of former slaves Fountain and Sarah Randolph. He was the earliest male **African-American** graduate of the Piqua High School in 1890. He became a teacher in the Sate of Georgia. He was killed on April 10, 1918 in a railroad accident

Randolph Slaves

Three hundred Randolph slaves were manumitted (freed) in 1833 by the will of John Randolph of Virginia. After extensive legal battles, the Randolphs came to Ohio in 1847 to settle on land in Mercer County. When they arrived the former slaves were driven away by German immigrants in the area. The Randolphs settled primarily in Miami and Shelby Counties. One of the largest Randolph settlements was in **Rossville**, just north of the Great Miami River and east of Main Street. Rossville would support a church, school and cemetery. These former slaves would be some of the first **African-Americans** in the nation to fight in the **Civil War** as part of the 54th Massachusetts Infantry regiment. SEE ALSO: Rial, York.

John Allen Rayner (1864 – 1929)

Rayner was born on a farm in northern Miami County. By occupation he was a farmer and plumber, but his hobby was local history. He collected local artifacts and patiently researched the history of Piqua and the surrounding area. In 1917, he published *The First Century of Piqua* which has become the single most important history ever written about Piqua. His collection of prehistoric artifacts comprises the largest collection of its type in the city. He was inducted into the Piqua **Civic Hall of Fame** in 1998.

Ronald Wilson Reagan
(1911 - 2004) *

In 1980, Reagan was elected the nation's fortieth **president**. During his re-election bid, he turned to the old "whistle stop train campaign technique" to gain support in the Midwest. Reagan's train passed through Piqua on the CSX tracks on October 12, 1984 on its way to Sidney. The train slowed and Reagan came to the back of the train to wave to the large crowd that had gathered. Banners, farm machinery, and the high school band were also present to greet the president as he passed.

Harry Reser (1896 – 1965)

He was born in Piqua, the son of William and Bertie Wright

Reser. During his teens, he traveled the vaudeville circuit with his father as a xylophone duo. In 1920, his family moved to Buffalo, New York. He cut his first banjo music record in 1921 with the Brunswick Photograph Company. During the 1920's and 1930's he toured the country under the name Harry Reser's Jazz Pilots (among other names). From 1925 through 1935 he had a radio show on WEAF and NBC Radio. He wrote instruction books for playing both the banjo and the guitar. In 1959, he appeared with Sammy Kaye on an ABC television show.

York Rial (c.1837-1913)

Rial was born a slave on the plantation of John Randolph. At Randolph's death, his will manumitted his slaves and provided funds for them to settle in Ohio. In 1846, at the age of eight or nine, Rial traveled north to Cincinnati with the former **Randolph slaves**. They traveled up the **Miami & Erie Canal** to New Bremen where land had been purchased for them. A hostile mob met them in the village and refused to let them disembark. Rial and his family traveled back down the canal where they settled in the area east of Piqua and the Great Miami River known as Rossville. As a young boy and teenager, Rial worked in the homes of Dr. O'Ferrall and Dr. Dorsey. Rial purchased a half acre lot in **Rossville** in 1872 and resided there with his wife Nettie. SEE ALSO: African-American.

Charles Franklin Ridenour (c.1884 – 1953)

Charles F. Ridenour (1884-1953)

Ridenour moved to Piqua from Xenia, Ohio in 1919. In partnership with Joseph Parker Chew, he purchased and consolidated three Piqua **newspapers** (*Press, Leader-Dispatch* and *Piqua Daily Call)* into the Piqua Call Publishing Company. He served as president, general manager and editor of the consolidated *Piqua Daily Call*. He stayed in active management of the paper until 1951. In 1959, Mrs. Mabel Ridenour sold the family interest in the *Call* to Frank R. Myers of the *Middletown News-Journal*.

Horace J. Rollin (1845-1930)

He was born in **Springcreek Township** on the family farm, the son of Isaac T. and Eleanor H. Robbin Rollin. Delicate health prevented Rollin working on the farm and he turned to the study of art. In the 1870's, he attended McMiken University in Cincinnati studying under Thomas S. Noble. His health prevented continued study, but he did receive an honorable mention for his completed work by the faculty. Leaving Cincinnati for New York City, Rollin studied independently and met nationally known artists such as Alexander H. Wyant and George Inness. During this period his work was on exhibit at the National Academy of Design and Fine Arts.

Returning to Miami County, Rollin continued painting landscapes from around the area. In 1878, he wrote *Studio, Field, and Gallery* published by A. Appleton & Company of New York. His second book, *Yetta Segal*, left the world of art and presented the theory of racial-fusion. It was written as a novel

and published by G.W. Dillingham Company of New York in 1898. Rollin married Miss Nancy R. Bridge. There were no children born of this marriage. The public library in Piqua owns the largest collection of Rollin's oil paintings.

Theodore Roosevelt (1858-1919)*

Roosevelt succeeded to the presidency after the assassination of Ohio Republican President William McKinley in 1901. He ran for a second term in 1904 and won a major victory with 56.41% of the popular vote. After leaving the White House in 1909, Roosevelt became dissatisfied with his hand-picked successor, Ohio **Republican** president **William Howard Taft**. In the 1912 election, Roosevelt formed the Progressive "Bull Moose" Party and ran against Taft. He visited Piqua on a campaign tour on May 16, 1912 and gave a rousing talk on the square in front of the **Plaza Hotel**. The community did not respond to Roosevelt's progressive message, giving him only 18.77% of the city's total vote. He died at his home in New York State on January 6, 1919. The city honored Roosevelt after his death by renaming Chestnut Street, Roosevelt Avenue and dedicating the school park on East Ash Street as Roosevelt Park.

John W. Ross (- 1880)

He was the inventor of the Ross Turbine water wheel, a hydraulic engineer. Ross was associated with the Delphos Iron Works, the manufacturers of the turbine. He lived in Piqua for a short time.

Stephen Clegg Rowan (1808 – 1890)

Rowan was born in Ireland in 1808, and arrived in Piqua with his parents in 1818. In February of 1826, he was appointed a midshipman in the U. S. Navy by local United States Representative **William McLean**. His first cruise was on the *U.S.S. Vincennes*, which was the first United States Navy man-of-war to circumnavigate the globe. During the **Mexican War** in 1846, Rowan led a detachment of Marines and occupied San Diego. He later helped take Los Angeles. By 1855, Rowan had been promoted to the rank of Commander and, at the beginning of the **Civil War**, commanded the steam powered sloop, the *Pawnee*. In May of 1861, he directed his ships guns at Aquia Creek. These were the first shots fired from a navel vessel during the Civil War. After 1865, Rowan was promoted to Rear Admiral and, in 1870, to Vice Admiral and Commander of the New York Naval Yard. He retired from active service in February of 1889, and died in Washington, D.C. on March 31, 1890. He was Piqua's first naval admiral and, in 1909, J. G. **Schmidlapp** presented a cannon and a monument to honor Rowan (**Rowan Memorial**).

Stanislaus Roy (c.1850's - 19__)

He was born in France and immigrated to the United States. He joined the United States Army and became a sergeant in Company A, 7th United States Cavalry. At the Battle of the Little Bighorn (Custer's Last Stand) in June of 1876, Roy brought water to the wounded soldiers "at great danger to life under a most galling fire of the enemy". For his heroism was awarded the **Medal of Honor** in 1878. After serving over thirty years in the United States Army, Roy retired as a regimental Color Sergeant and moved to Piqua. He was buried in Greenlawn Cemetery in Columbus, Ohio.

Dorthea T. Rudd (18__ - 19__)

She was the first **African-American** woman to own a local industry, the Favorite Chemical & Supply Company (embalming fluid) from c.1934 through c.1942. She was also active with the **YWCA**. A variant spelling for the first name might be Dorothea. She was married to John R. Rudd

Elbert "Ruff" Ruffner
(c. 1921 – 1945)

He was born in Piqua, the son of G.F. Ruffner and graduated from Piqua High School with the Class of 1939. He joined the United Sates Army Air Force in 1942 and served in Alaska for seven months. He received his pilot's wings and commission in March of 1944 at Williams Field in Arizona. In November of 1944, he was sent overseas to the Air Transport Command in India and Burma as a P-38 fighter pilot. He completed over sixty missions before failing to return from a weather control mission in June of 1945.

Allen Garfield Rundle
(1880 – 1937)

Rundle was born and raised in Piqua and joined the family **patent medicine** business started by his father, **George H. Rundle**. He served as the City of Piqua's Treasurer, as chairman of the Board of the Piqua National **Bank**, and as president of the Board of Trustees of the Piqua Memorial **Hospital**. He organized and was the first president of the Piqua Boosters in 1912 and organized **Camp Wakonda** for the **YMCA** and Boy Scout use. Rundle was a perennial men's golf champion at the Piqua Country Club. He commissioned the only **Prairie Style** home ever built in Piqua in c.1917.

George Henry Rundle
(1847 – 1917)

Rundle moved to Piqua in 1876 to manufacture Porter's Pain King, a **patent medicine**. He took the company from

a single horse drawn cart selling door-to-door to a firm with hundreds of employees and international sales. Rundle was very active politically as a **Republican party** stalwart serving as both Miami County and Piqua City Treasurer. He was active in other local businesses as president of the Piqua National **Bank**, as one of the founders of the Piqua Home **Telephone** Company and, with his brother-in-law Allen D. Hance, as one of the founders of the **Imperial Underwear Company**. He was active in social causes including the **prohibition** movement and as the first president of the **YMCA**. He was inducted into the Piqua **Civic Hall of Fame** in 2003.

Allen G. Rundle (1880-1937)

W.E. Russ (18__ - 19__)

He was a Dayton architect responsible for designing the Su-

perior **Underwear** Factory (1909) on Riverside Drive, and the Orr **Nurse**'s Home (1911) part of the **hospital** on Park Avenue.

Arthur St. Clair (1737-1818)*

Early in his career, the Scottish born St. Clair served as a lieutenant in the British Army (1757-1762). During the American Revolution, he served as a Major General in the Regular Continental Army. He entered politics after the war and served as the President of the Continental Congress (1787). At the end of his term as President, he was appointed to the position of Governor of the newly created Northwest Territory. He would hold this position until 1802. At the time of his appointment as Governor, St. Clair was also given command of the Army of the West with the rank of Major General. In the fall of 1791, St. Clair moved his army north, building Fort Hamilton and Fort Jefferson along the way. On November 4, St. Clair's army met an Indian force led by Miami Chief **Little Turtle**. In the ensuing battle, St. Clair and his army suffered one of the worst defeats in American military history. In 1792, St. Clair resigned his military commission and was replaced as Army Commander by **Anthony Wayne**. In 1802, St. Clair opposed statehood for Ohio. This opposition led to his retirement and his return to his Pennsylvania farms. SEE ALSO: Cincinnati; Girty, Simon.

John Dale Scarbrough
(1914 – 2003)

He was born in Memphis, Tennessee, the son of Mack Dale and Margaret Parker Scarbrough. He graduated from the Michigan College of Mining & Technology and went to work for Detroit Edison Company from 1937 to 1941. During World War II, he served with the United States Army attaining the rank of major. From 1946 through 1953 he was an executive with the All Metal Products Company and brought a division of that firm, the Piqua Products Company (Wyandotte **Toys**), to Piqua in 1950. He created the Piqua Engineering Company in Piqua in 1953 and served as its president. He married Helen L. Rieckfelt in 1940.

John Scarborough (1914-2003)

Helen Schelle (1893-1984)

She was born in Piqua and became one of the original founders of Fisher-Price Toys in New York State in 1930.

Jacob Godfrey Schmidlapp
(1849 – 1919)

Schmidlapp was born in Piqua, one of six children who lived above the family grocery store. He was forced to leave school to help support his family. He went on to make his fortune, first in the tobacco warehouses of Kentucky and then to Cincinnati. It was in the Queen City that he was one of the founders of the Union Savings Bank and became a major investor in real estate. He continued to support his home town with donations that built the first public library in 1890 (Schmidlapp Free School **Library**), a monument to Admiral

Rowan and assistance in building the first community hospital. He also helped victims of the **1913 Flood** and established a number of local scholarships. He was inducted into the Piqua **Civic Hall of Fame** in 1997.

Henry Schneider
(1841 – 1903)

Henry Schneider (1841-1903)

Schneider was a **German** immigrant to the United States. He purchased the City **Brewery** on Spring Street in 1881. His massive monument in Forest Hill Cemetery, with its carved images of Schneider and his wife protected by a wing angel, is one of the most striking in the cemetery.

John L. Schneyer
(1814 – 1891)

Schneyer was born in Elsa Sachsen, Coburg, Germany and immigrated to the United States first settling in Pennsylvania c.1840. He came to Piqua in 1861 and worked as a wagon maker for several years before joining the **L.C. & W.L. Cron Furniture Company** as a partner in c.1870. He lived on East Main Street in **Huntersville** with his wife Elizabeth Roths Schneyer and their eight children.

William Scott (1801 – 1880)

He came to Piqua in 1808 and became very active in the community. He served as the village treasurer from 1832 through 1834 and city treasurer in 1876-1877. He was a member of the city's first Board of Education in 1853 and the first Water Works Board in 1872. Scott served as the first president of the Piqua Branch of the State **Bank** of Ohio in 1847. The bank would later become the Piqua National Bank (1865) which was absorbed by Fifth Third Bank. His son, John Morrow Scott (1830-1887), would serve as president of the Piqua National Bank from 1880 until his death in 1887.

Mathias Scudder
(17__ - 1827)

Scudder served in the **Revolutionary War** and then migrated to Ohio. He was one of the earliest pioneer farmers in **Springcreek Township**. Scudder Street was named in his honor.

Joseph William Sharts
(1875 – 1965) *

Sharts was born in Hamilton, Ohio and became a prominent Dayton attorney. He joined the **Socialist Party** in 1909 and edited Dayton's *Miami Valley Socialist*. He was an intimate of Eugene V. Debs, defending him in the federal trial of 1918. He retired from active politics in 1934. Sharts spoke in Piqua on a number of occasions. He defended Piqua's Socialist Mayor **Frank Hamilton** and five other local Socialists when they were arrested in October of 1918 on federal charges of violating the U.S. Espionage Act.

James Elson Sherwood
(1924 – 1945)

He was born in Piqua, the son of Elson Sherwood and attended Washington Township schools and the Piqua High School. He was employed in war work at the **Hartzell Propeller Company** before joining the United States Army in March of 1943. He was shipped to France in August of 1944 with the 41st Infantry Regiment of the Second Armored Division. He suffered shrapnel wounds in October of 1944 and was hospitalized. But he rejoined his unit and on December 27, 1944 was captured by German troops. Private First Class Sherwood died of pneumonia and malnutrition in Stalag IX-B (Prisoner of War Camp) at Bad Orb-Wegschid, Germany on March 12, 1945. The Camp was liberated by American troops in April of 1945.SEE ALSO: World War II

Winslow D. "Dick" Siedel
(1910 – 2003)

Siedel was born on Long Island, New York and obtained a degree in engineering from Northeastern University in Boston and continued with postgraduate work at Harvard University. He moved to Piqua in 1940 to work for the **Lear Avia Company**. Like several other former Lear employees, Siedel stayed in Piqua when the firm moved to Michigan and started a new business of his own. He created Siedel Communications Inc. [equipment] in 1945. He also worked as a **radio** engineer at WPTW Radio in Piqua and was one of the partners in a local housing development known as Sandel. From 1987 through the late 1990's, Siedel was known as a swimming champion, winning numerous Ohio Senior Olympic medals in the sport. He also competed in the national Senior Olympics.

Greg Simmons (c.1950 – present)

He was born in Piqua and became the first graduate of Edison General and Technical College in 1975. He would later serve in the1990's as the executive director of the West Central Juvenile Detention Facility, retiring in 2007. In 1999, he established and served as pastor of the Upper Room Faith Assembly Church in Tipp City. Simmons also served as a part-time instructor at Edison.

Cecil Melville Sims
(1891 – 1978)

Cecil Sims (1891-1978)

Sims was born in Basil, Ohio, the son of Henry and Carolyn Hensel Sims and moved to Piqua in 1919 to become the new high school principal. He later served as the **superintendent of schools** (1944-1952) and the executive director of the Chamber of Commerce (1955-1961). Sims served as the president of the Flesh Public **Library** Board, the Piqua **Chautauqua** Association (1920's), the Ohio High School Athletic Association, the Ohio Teachers Association, and a charter member of the State Board of Education (1952-1978). Sims dedicated his life to the community as a teacher, administrator, author (*Reflections*, 1978), musician and song leader, coach and civic leader. He was inducted into to the Piqua **Civic Hall of Fame** in 1998.

Harvey E. Sims (1876 - 1955)

He was born in Shelby County, Ohio, the son of William Franklin and Henrietta Snodgrass Sims. He was a graduate of the Ideal Business **College** in Piqua and worked in the offices of the **Atlas Underwear Company** from c.1900 until his death, serving as corporate secretary. From the early1920's to 1929, he was president of the Ideal Business School. Active in the local **bank**ing community, he served as vice president of the Citizens National Bank and as president of the Border City Building & Loan Association. Sims was very active in the community, serving as vice president of the **YMCA** board, and president of the Chamber of Commerce as well as of the Foreman's Club. He was the chairman of the board of trustees of Defiance College.

J. Harrison Smith (1861 - 1952)

J. Harrison Smith (1861-1952)

Smith was born in Piqua, the son of John Frederick and Mary Stoner Sullenberger Smith.

J.F. Smith was born in Baden Baden, Germany and immigrated to the United States. He served in the **Civil War** and was killed at the Battle of Stone River (1863) in Tennessee. J.H. Smith graduated from Piqua High School in 1884 and after attending several colleges, including Harvard, graduated in 1892 from George Washington School of Law in Washington, D.C. He began the practice of law in Piqua in 1895-96 as the partnership Lindsey & Smith (later became McCulloch, Felger, Fite and Gutmann) In 1896, he was elected Miami County prosecutor on the **Republican Party** ticket. He would serve in that office until 1902, when he was elected to one term as Miami County Probate Judge. Smith ran on the Non-Partisan Party (combined local Republican and Democratic Parties) ticket in 1919 to oppose Piqua's first and only **Socialist** party Mayor **Frank Hamilton**. Smith was elected and would serve one term. Smith's last political office was as the Piqua Municipal Court Judge to which he was elected in 1930. He would serve in this position until 1945. He was a charter member of the Piqua Elks Lodge 523 in 1899 and exalted Ruler in 1902. Smith lived on Staunton Street with his wife Anna Ball Smith (married in 1895). SEE ALSO: Moody, Granville (Battle of Stone River).

Robert Smith (1790- 1890)

Smith was the son of Daniel Smith a freed slave (1803) in Virginia. He came to Piqua in 1835 and established one of the community's early barber shops. This was during a period of extreme prejudice in Ohio. He would continue as an active barber until just shortly before his death in 1890. In 1867, Smith was one of the organizers of the **Colored Men's Co-Operative Association**, a retail grocery store that was the first **African-American** commercial business in the city. He married his wife Sarah (1799-1889) in Virginia in 1822.

John Perry Spiker (1871 – 1946)

John Spiker was the founder and president of the Superior Underwear Company.

Spiker was born in Piqua and became the founder of the **Superior Underwear Company**, vice president of Citizens National Bank and in 1919 president of **Cron-Kills Inc.**

Samuel Knoop Statler (1844 – 1917)

Statler was born in **Washington Township** the son and grandson of pioneer Miami County farmers. During the **Civil War**, he served as a seaman in the United States Navy. He served as the chief superintendent of the Mercer Gas Company and helped construct the first natural gas line to Piqua and Miami County to light local homes and businesses. He was a director of the Citizens National Bank and one of the co-builders of the **Plaza Hotel** on the square. Statler was also one of the county's most active and innovative farmers. He was inducted into the Piqua **Civic Hall of Fame** in 2005.

Alex Wilson Stoute (1909-1944)

Stoute was born in Piqua, the son of George W. and Carrie B. Stoute and graduated from the Piqua High School in 1931. He was the first **African-American** from the city to be killed in World War II. He joined the service as a volunteer in September of 1943 having previously been engaged in exempted war work at the **Lear-Avia Company**. He served as a medic at the D-Day invasion of Normandy Beach and died on June 10, 1944 saving the lives of others. The first African-American Veterans of Foreign Wars (VFW) Post was named the Stoute-Harris Post. He was survived by his wife Hilda Stoute.

John Cleve Symmes (1742-1814) *

Symmes served during the Revolutionary War as a Colonel of Militia, as an associate Justice of the New Jersey Supreme Court and as a member of the Continental Congress. In 1785, Symmes petitioned Congress for one million acres of land between the Great and Little Miami Rivers. The purchase was known as the Miami, or **Symmes Purchase**. In 1788, he was appointed as one of the three judges for the newly created Northwest Territory. In 1788, Symmes established the community of North Bend (now present-day Cincinnati). Symmes was unable to pay Congress for his land grant and many of the Symmes land titles were declared void. His daughter married future president **William Henry Harrison** in 1795. One of the future settlers of Piqua, **John Hilliard** worked with Symmes in his land office in North Bend.

William Howard Taft (1857-1930) *

A native of Cincinnati, Taft was elected as the nation's twenty-seventh president in 1908 and ran for re-election under the **Republican** banner in 1912. President Taft spoke at an informal rally in front of the **Hotel Plaza** on May 20, 1912. Later the same day, Taft spoke at a Republican gathering at **May's Opera House**. In 1908, Taft carried Piqua with 50.75% of the vote. He did not repeat this victory in 1912. He came in second of the four candidates with only 29.45% of the total local vote. Taft lost the national election to Wilson by over eighteen percentage points. Taft died in Washington, D.C. on March 8, 1930.

Darrell Taylor (1896 – 1967)

Taylor was a life-long resident of Piqua. He organized and ran his own auto repair business in Piqua for over twenty years.

With his wife Louise, he organized his children as the Taylor Tots to sing at local and regional church programs. He served as the first president of the local chapter of the **N.A.A.C.P.** (1942-late 1940's) and led a passive sit-in at the bus station luncheon counter in 1945 that was the beginning of the end for restaurant segregation in the city. Taylor was the first **African-American** to run for City Commission in the twentieth century. His commitment to the **Civil Rights Movement** resulted in the ruination of his business by those who resented his actions and views. He was inducted into the Piqua **Civic Hall of Fame** in 2002.

Jean Jessup Taylor (c.1920 - ____)

Taylor was born in Piqua, the daughter of Marion F. Jessup and graduated from Piqua High School in 1938. In November of 1942, she was one of the very first Piqua women to enlist in the Women's Army Corps (WAC) during **World War II**, and by July 1943 she became the first Piquad to be commissioned as a WAC officer. By 1944 she was serving in the Pacific Theater in New Guinea and the Philippines.

The Wilson Jefferson Singers were photographed before a performance in 1945.

Louise Taylor (1900 – 1996)

Taylor was active in her church and in the activities of the local chapter of the N.A.A.C.P. She organized her children into the Taylor Tots to sing at local and area church and social events. As an advisor of the **N.A.A.C.P.** youth group in the early 1940's, she helped promote the Whispering Echoes (aka Hwisperian Echoes) a singing group later led by Wilson Jefferson Sr. In 1944, she helped organize the city's first **African-American** Girl Scout Troop. She was married to Darrell Taylor.

Tecumseh (1768-1813) *

A **Shawnee** chief, also known as Tikamthi, was born in the village of Piqua on the Mad River about six miles southwest of Springfield, Ohio. With his brother the Prophet, Tecumseh organized an Indian Confederation to drive white settlers out of the Ohio Valley. During his absence, Tecumseh's forces were defeated by **William Henry Harrison** at the Battle of Tippecanoe in 1811. Tecumseh sided with the British during the **War of 1812**, and was killed at the Battle of the Thames.

Augustine Thoma (1819 – 1899)

A **German** immigrant from Baden, he settled in New York City in 1832 at the age of thirteen. He apprenticed in the watch and jewelry trade until he moved west. Thoma settled in Piqua and established a jewelry and watch stores in 1838 under the name of Thoma & Hummel. He was one of the founding members of the St. Mary's Catholic Church in 1839 and the St. Boniface Parish in 1855. Thoma served on the Piqua city council from 1860 to 1862. He was also one of the founding members of the Piqua Brass Band.

Joseph A. Thoma (1886 – 1966)

He was born in Piqua, the son of Civil War veteran Albin and Anna Weigler Thoma. He opened his own jewelry store in Bradford, Ohio which he operated from 1912 through 1918. He joined the family store in Piqua as a partner in 1918. In 1946, he became owner and took his own children into the firm, Joseph Jr., Antoinette and Eleanor. He served on the Piqua city commission from 1940 through 1947 and as **mayor** from 1943 to 1947. Active in the community, Thoma served as the president of the Piqua Rotary Club and as choir director at St. Boniface Catholic Church. SEE ALSO: Piqua Historical Area; Piqua Historical Museum.

William Trent (1715-1787) *

Trent was born in Lancaster County, Pennsylvania in 1715. He raised a company of militia in 1746 and was given the rank of Captain. At Saratoga, New York, Captain Trent's troops came under attack by French and Indian forces, but Trent was able to hold out until reinforcements arrived. From 1750 until 1756, Trent engaged in a business partnership with his brother-in-law **George Croghan** to establish Indian trading posts in the Ohio country. During this period, Trent visited a number of Indian villages in Ohio including **Pickawillany** in 1752.

Charles Butterfield Upton (1884 - 1979)

Upton was born in Piqua, the son of Matthew B. and Helen E. Davis Upton. He graduated form Piqua High School with the Class of 1902. He joined the **French Oil Mill Machinery Company** in 1905 as an office clerk. He rose through the ranks to general manager and finally to chairman of the board. Active politically, he served on the city council from 1924 through 1928. Upton helped write the original 1929 city charter and served as one of the first new city commissioners (1930-1946). He served as chairman of the board of the Piqua National **Bank**, vice president of the Third Savings & Loan Company and as the first chairman of Dettmer **Hospital**. Upton was one of the chief promoters for the creation of a state historical park at the Johnston Farm site. He was inducted into the Piqua **Civic Hall of Fame** in 2006.

Irene Hockenberry Upton (1891 – 1977)

She was born in Piqua and graduated from Piqua High School with the Class of 1911. In 1914, she graduated from the Piqua Hospital Nursing School as a registered nurse. Upton worked in Brooklyn, New York and in New Jersey before joining the United States Army in 1917. She served as a nurse until 1920 stationed at Walter Reed Hospital. Returning to Piqua, Upton became the city's public health nurse from 1921 through 1930. She was the first female member of the local American Legion. In 1938 she married Charles B. Upton.

Aaron David Urbansky (1839 - 1897)

Urbansky was born in Lautenburg, Prussia (now part of Poland) and immigrated to New York in 1857. He was a merchant tailor and when the Civil War broke out he joined Company B of the 58th Ohio Volunteer Infantry Regiment. At the Siege of Vicksburg he braved Confederate fire to save his wounded company commander. As a result of this action and for meritorious service at the Battle of Shiloh, he was awarded the Congressional **Medal of Honor**. Urbansky was one of only six **Jewish** soldiers in the Civil War to receive a Medal of Honor. Shortly after the war he moved to Piqua and established a clothing store. He was married to Rachel Henry from Schenectady, New York and the couple had twelve children. He died in Piqua and was buried in the Cedar Hill Cemetery. The family moved Urbansky to the United Jewish Cemeteries in Cincinnati, Ohio in 1914. The children legally changed their family name to Urban

Thomas B. Van Horne
(1783-1841)

Van Horne was born in New Jersey and, in 1807, moved to Warren County, Ohio, with his family. He served in the militia and later the regular army during the War of 1812. By the end of the war, he was serving as the Commander of Fort Erie with the rank of Lieutenant Colonel. Returning to Warren County, he served as an Ohio State Senator from 1812 until 1817. In 1820, he was appointed Federal Registrar for the Land Office of the northwest part of Ohio. Van Horne set up the Land Office in Piqua on the north side of Doctor Daniel Ashton's residence on the northwest corner of Main and Greene Streets. Van Horne was active in local community organizations serving on numerous Fourth of July committees and as secretary of the **Piqua Colonization Society** in 1832. Van Horne's first wife, Sophia Carmichael, had died in Warren County (c1817-1820). In 1830, he married his second wife Elizabeth Chappeze (widow of Henry). In 1835, the Federal Land Office was moved to Wapakoneta and Van Horne was replaced as the register/agent by J.P. Helfensten. The Land office moved to Lima in 1836. Van Horne returned to Warren County in 1837 and died there in 1841. Van Horne's daughter, Catharine Sophia Van Horne (1817-c1913), is remembered for a needlework piece she completed while in Piqua at age eight (1825). The framed work is today part of a private local collection.

Colonel Thomas B. Van Horne served as the federal land agent in Piqua from 1820 through 1833.

Wilson Vance (1845 – 1911)

Vance was born in Findlay, Ohio. He enlisted as a private during the **Civil War** and at the Battle of Stone River won a battle field commission and was awarded the Congressional **Medal of Honor**. He moved to Piqua in 1869 and established the city's first daily **newspaper**, the *Miami Valley News* in 1869. He later worked as a newspaper editor in Columbus and New York City and as a Washington correspondent for several western newspapers. He was a published novelist with four books published from 1880 to 1909. SEE ALSO: Moody, Granville (Stone River).

George Washington (1732-1799) *

Washington's first contact with the Ohio country came in 1753 when, as a Major in the Virginia Militia, he was sent to western Pennsylvania to order the French to stop building forts in the Upper Ohio Valley. He was ignored and, despite early military successes, Washington was forced to surrender to the superior

French military forces on July 3, 1754. Washington, now a Lieutenant Colonel, was with British General Edward Braddock when he was disastrously defeated by the French and their Indian allies in 1755. He also accompanied General John Forbes in the fall of 1758, and was present at the peaceful takeover of Fort Duquesne. Forbes renamed it Fort Pitt. Washington retained his interest in the Ohio Valley through his activities as a land speculator. His will listed over 41,000 acres of land claimed in parts of what are now Kentucky, Ohio, and West Virginia. Washington's last trip to the Ohio country occurred in 1770 when he traveled down the Ohio River from Fort Pitt to the mouth of the Great Kanawha River (West Virginia) looking for land in which to invest. SEE ALSO: Boyer, Lewis; Crawford, William; French and Indian War; Gist, Christopher; Washington Township.

"Mad" Anthony Wayne
(1745-1796) *

Wayne served as a Major General during the Revolutionary War and later campaigned against the Creek Indians in Georgia. After **St. Clair**'s defeat by **Little Turtle**, command of the Army of the West was given to Wayne in April of 1792. He gathered over twenty-five hundred troops at Pittsburgh and, by the spring of 1793, had transported them down the Ohio River to Cincinnati. He spent the next year drilling his new troops and building a series of forts. One of these supply **forts** was located at **Upper Piqua** on the Great Miami River. On August 20, 1794, Wayne's army met the Indian forces under the **Shawnee** Chief **Blue Jacket**. The battle took place at Fallen Timbers, just above the Maumee River. This major Indian defeat would lead to the signing of the **Treaty of Greenville.**

Conrad Weiser (1696-1760) *

Weiser was born in Germany in 1696 and immigrated to the Pennsylvania colony with his family in 1710. In 1731, he began working for the Pennsylvania colonial government as an interpreter and later, as an Indian agent in the Ohio country. He established a trading business at **Pickawillany** in c.1749. During the **French and Indian War**, he commanded a regiment of Pennsylvania militia with the rank of Colonel. He died on July 13, 1760.

Peter John "Johnny" Weismuller (1904-1984) *

He was born in Freidorf, Rumania and later moved with his family to Chicago. At the age of fourteen, he was already a swimming star at the YMCA. In 1924 and 1928, he was an Olympic Gold Medalist in swimming. He came to Piqua on May 29 and 30, 1924, and gave YMCA sponsored swimming demonstrations at Lange's **Pool** on Spring Street. In the early 1930's, Weismuller returned to Piqua to model swimwear produced by the **Piqua Hosiery Company**. The advertisements were photographed at Lange's Pool. **Alfred L. Flesh** released Weismuller from his modeling contract allowing him to go to Hollywood and star in "Tarzan, the Ape Man" (1932), the first of his twelve Tarzan films.

William Wells (c.1770-1812) *

Wells was born in Kentucky in circa 1770, and was captured at an early age by members of the **Miami Indian** tribe. He fought with the Miami against American forces led by General **St. Clair** and General Harmar. In 1793, he switched sides and acted as a scout for General Anthony Wayne. In 1802, he was appointed as an assistant agent for Indian affairs in the Indiana Territory at Fort Wayne. Wells was a close friend of the Miami Chief **Little Turtle**, and married into the chief's family. He served at Fort Wayne with **John Johnston** and in 1809, was replaced by Johnston as Indian agent. Wells was killed during the evacuation of the garrison of Fort Dearborn in 1812. SEE ALSO: Little Turtle; Wayne, Anthony.

Abraham M. Wendel Sr.
(1821-1894)

Wendel was born in Prussia, Germany and immigrated to the United States, first to Dayton and then in c.1852 to Piqua. He started work in Piqua as a traveling jeweler before establishing a jewelry shop on Main Street in 1856. He married Fanny Friedlich (1807-1903), the sister of local clothier Abraham Friedlich. Their son became an active partner in the shop in 1883. Wendel was one of the founders of the Ansche Emeth Congregation in 1858. He served as Cantor for the congregation for many years. The Wendels built a two story brick home on Sycamore Street and later built the house at 600 North Downing Street. He was buried in Cedar Hill Cemetery.

Harold F. Wendel (1892-1967)

Wendel was born in Piqua, the son of Jacob and Flora Wendel. He graduated from the Piqua High School in 1910. He attended the University of Michigan, graduating with the Class of 1914. He worked for the Sears Roebuck Company in Chicago before serving in the military during **World War I**. He moved to Portland, Oregon where he became president of Lipman, Wolfe & Company, one of Portland's largest department stores.

Jacob Wendel (1856-1936)

He was born in Piqua in the family homestead on Sycamore Street, the son of Abraham and Fanny Wendel. Wendell took over the family jewelry store on Main Street in 1883. He actively managed the store until his retirement in 1917.

George P. "Buck" Wertz
(1899-1969)

Wertz came to Piqua as a biology teacher and basketball/**football** coach in September of 1925. His record as a Piqua High School coach from 1925 through 1950 was 165 wins, 63 losses and 21 ties. His 1929 team won the city's first undisputed Miami Valley League championship. He served until 1968 as the Piqua Athletic Director. His outstanding accomplishments and dedication as a teacher and as a coach were recognized when Roosevelt Field was renamed Wertz Field in his honor. He was inducted into the Piqua **Civic Hall of Fame** in 2000.

John Westfall
(1926-1945)

Westfall was born in Washington Township the son of John Westfall. He graduated from Piqua High School in 1942 and joined the United States Marines in February of 1943. He was killed in action in November of 1943 in the

John C. Westfall Jr. (1924-1943)

South Pacific at the age of nineteen. Private First Class Westfall was the first Piqua High School alumni to be killed in action during **World War II**. In 1946, his name was selected to represent World War II veterans for the Piqua American Legion which became the Schnell-Westfall Post.

Isaac Johnson Whitlock
(1828 – 1892)

Whitlock was born in Butler County, Ohio, the son of Rev. Elias Whitlock. He moved to Piqua in 1853 where he took up the carpentry trade. In 1860, he purchased a planning mill on the southwest corner of Broadway and Boone Streets. He served as the carpentry contractor on the high school (1885), the skating rink at High and Downing Streets (1885) and on the **Plaza Hotel** (1890-91). In 1887, his planning mill furnished all of the interior wood for the new Miami County Courthouse in Troy including the black walnut in the court room.

Horace Eugene Whitlock
(1865 – 19__)

Whitlock was born in Piqua, the son of Isaac J. Whitlock. He attended local schools, but left school early to work in his father's planning mill. He worked with his father on the 1890-1891 on the **Plaza Hotel** project. Near the end of the project in 1891, Whitlock was elected as Piqua's city engineer, a position he would hold until 1907. He designed a number of buildings and houses in Piqua including the Manier home at 529 High Street and the Gano residence at 417 West Ash Street, and the office building at the Forest Hill Cemetery. He was an active **Republican** and member of the local Odd Fellows Lodge. SEE ALSO: Furniture Manufacturing

Lester Johnson Whitlock
(1892 – 19__)

Whitlock was born in Piqua, the son of Horace E. and Nora M. Whitlock. He graduated from the Piqua High School in 1910 and from Miami University in 1914. From 1914 to 1916 he worked for the Goodyear Tire & Rubber Company in Akron, Ohio. He went to the **Mexican border** with the **National Guard** during the Poncho Villa Expedition in 1916-1917. He was commissioned a captain in August of 1917 and went to France in World War I with the 18th Division. During Roosevelt's New Deal, he served as the Civilian Conversation Corps commander for New Mexico. In 1941, he was a Colonel serving in Australia. He became a brigadier general in June of 1942. During **World War II**, he served on General Douglas MacArthur's staff as chief of staff of the Southwest Pacific and Staff G-4. BG Whitlock would be awarded the Distinguished Service Medal by MacArthur for his service. He would serve with MacArthur after the war in occupied Japan. Whitlock was Piqua's highest ranking army officer during World War II.

George W. Wilson (1828 – 18__)

Wilson was one of the organizers of the **Colored Men's Co-Operative Trade Association** in 1867. During the **Civil War** era he served as the janitor for the town's first high school building. He organized his own huckster wagon and traveled throughout the region in the 1870's and 1880's. His daughter Maggie Wilson served as a teacher in the local school system in the 1880's. SEE ALSO: African-American

Thomas Woodrow Wilson (1856-1924) *

Wilson won the Democratic nomination for president in 1912 with the aid of William Jennings Bryan. The **Democrats** made the most of the split in the Republican Party between Roosevelt and Taft. Wilson held a "whistle stop" campaign through the Midwest and, on September 16, 1912, the candidate's private train, the "Magnet", stopped in Piqua. Wilson's train pulled up to allow the end platform car to come to a halt at Main and Sycamore Streets. Wilson shook a few hands and said a few words, but did not make a formal campaign speech. His brief appearance was all the Democratic organization needed. Wilson was the most popular of the four presidential candidates, winning 43.72% of the Piqua vote. Wilson served two full terms as President before ill health resulted in his death on February 3, 1924. SEE ALSO: Roosevelt, Theodore.

James P. Wisecup (c. 1955 – 20__)

A 1973 graduate of Piqua High School, Wisecup has attained the rank of Rear Admiral in the United States Navy. Among his many assignments, Wisecup has served as the Director of the White House Situation Room, Commander of Destroyer Squadron 21 out of San Diego, Commander of the *USS Callaghan* (1995-1997) and numerous deployments to the Persian Gulf Region. He is currently (2006) serving as the Commander of United States Naval Forces in Korea. He is a 1977 graduate of the United States Naval Academy at Annapolis. Wisecup is the second Admiral from Piqua, the first was **Stephen Rowan**.

Maurice Wolfe (1876 - 1935)

Wolfe was born in Rosewood, Indiana and moved to Piqua in December of 1913. He had organized the **Meteor Motor Car Company** in May of 1913 in Shelbyville, Indiana, but upon moving to Piqua the company was re-incorporated under Ohio law. He became known as the Henry Ford of hearses as he was the first to produce an affordable motorized hearse. He was the first in the industry to built hearses on a production line rather that individual custom construction. Wolfe was one of the first local industrialists to offer company benefits to his employees. He provided free basic medical care at the plant, reduced life and health insurance and supported various music and sports programs. He was a "self-made man" and enjoyed starting new projects such as a chain of "Low-Priced" gasoline stations in Ohio and Indiana, the production of phonograph players and records, and creating a line of wooden speed boats. He was an avid hunter and fisherman who in 1931 he built a comfortable lodge on an island in the Lake of the Woods in Ontario, Canada. He resided at 301 West Greene Street and was responsible for its massive remodeling.

Charles Amesbury Wood (c.1820 – 1905)

He was born in Hollis, New Hampshire and came to Piqua in c.1843 to establish a **cooperage** business (barrels). He was later very active in the local lumber business with his son.

Charles Leonard Wood (1841 – 19__)

He was born in Hollis, new Hampshire, the son of Charles A. and Hannah Washer Wood. He moved to Piqua with his family in the early 1840's and after reading law he went into a brief partnership with attorney W.N. Foster in 1865-1866. In 1880, he founded with his father the C.A. and C.L. Wood Planning Mill. Wood was one of the founders and president of the **Piqua Hosiery Company** in 1886. He was very active in community activities serving for twelve years on the Piqua Board of Education and as president of the YMCA. He massively remodeled the home at 600 Caldwell turning it into a **Second Empire Style** home with a new mansard roof. The first floor rooms were each decorated in a different type of wood that promoted Wood's occupation as a lumber merchant.

Britton Boal Wood (1910 – 1989)

He was born in Piqua, the son William W. and Aileen Boal Wood. He attended prep schools in Massachusetts before joining the family firm, the **Wood Shovel & Tool Company**, in 1930. Wood took control of the Geyer Manufacturing Company (produced forks, rakes, hoes and baseball bats) out of Rock Falls, Illinois after it was absorbed by Wood Shovel. In 1965, he became the executive vice president of Wood Shovel. The firm was sold to Bissell Inc. in 1965. He was the founder of the Piqua Racquet Club in 1948 and served as its president in 1961. During **World War II**, he served on active duty in the United States Naval Reserve, attaining the rank of Lt. Commander. His naval career included the command of the *U.S.S. Aquamarine* (PYc7) for two years. A former yacht built in 1926, the Aquamarine served as a naval research ship along coastal areas and major rivers from 1941 through 1946.

Harley K. Wood (1847 – 1922)

Wood was born in Piqua, the son of business pioneer William Webster Wood Sr. and Caroline Kirk Wood. He worked with his father in the **cooperage** business and later organized several local linseed oil mills (Wood **Linseed** Oil Company). He was the president and general manager of the Piqua Edison **Electric** Illuminating Company from its creation in 1885 to 1906. In 1902, he founded the **Wood Shovel and Tool Company**. He served as president of the Piqua National **Bank** and vice president of the Piqua Home **Telephone** Company (1914-1921). He served as the second president of the modern **YMCA**.

William Boal Wood (1907 – 1982)

He was born in Massachusetts, the son of William W. and Aileen Boal Wood. He graduated from Yale with the Class of 1931. Wood then joined the family firm and in 1941 became president of the **Wood Shovel & Tool Company**. During **World War II**, he served in the United States Naval Reserve. Wood was president of the firm when it was sold to Bissell Inc. in 1965.

William Webster Wood Sr. (1817 – 1905)

He was born in Hollis, New Hampshire and as a young man moved west to Ohio in the 1840's. Looking for new energy sources, he is credited with bringing the first cartload of coal into Miami County. He was an early cooper in the community and established a **linseed oil** mill to take advantage of the area's plentiful flax crop. Eager to make his fortune, he went to California by ox drawn wagon during the **California Gold Rush** in 1850-1852. He returned to Ohio by ship by way of the Panama land crossing. He was elected to Piqua's first Board of Education in 1853.

William Webster Wood III
(1878 - 1954)

He was born in Piqua, the son of Harley K. and Frances A. Wilson Wood. In 1898, he graduated from Phillips Exeter Academy, in New Hampshire. In 1896-1897, during his summer breaks from school, Wood introduced the game of **football** to Piqua for the first time. With his father, he was one of the founders of the **Wood Shovel & Tool Company** in 1902. He became

president of the firm in 1922. He was a director of the Piqua National Bank, president of the Piqua **Historical Society**, charter member of the Piqua Rotary Club and from 1908 to 1912 chairman of the Miami County **Republican** Central and Executive Committees. He was a delegate to the National Republican Conventions in 1916, 1920, 1928, 1932, 1936 and 1940. He married Aileen F. Boal Wood

William W. Wood III
(1878-1954)

Stephen C. Writer (18__ – 18__)

He was the editor of the *Piqua Register* in c.1840's -1861. At the beginning to the **Civil War**, he raised a company of the Eight Calvary Regiment in Piqua. He was transferred to the First Regiment, OVI and promoted to the rank of major. Writer came back to Piqua as a recruiter for the regiment in 1864 (opened a recruiting office over Scott's Store on Main Street). This made him one of the first semi-permanent military recruiters in Piqua.

Robert Young (17__-18__)

Young was from Warren County and became Piqua's second lawyer beginning his local practice in 1821-1822. He served as the village postmaster from 1821 to 1824. Young was elected an Ohio **State Senator** and served from 1824 to 1825. Young served in the Ohio Militia attaining the rank of General. He served as the first president of the **Piqua Colonization Society** formed in 1826. He was Piqua treasurer from 1835 to 1839. Young served on the Piqua city council as president of the council in 1852-1853. He was the father of Joseph G. and George W. Young. He passed away prior to the Civil War.

Joseph G. Young (1809 - 1875)

Young, the son of **Robert Young**, began practice as an attorney in 1832 in partnership with Moses B. Corwin. He became involved in banking as one of the organizers and the cashier of the Piqua Branch of the State **Bank** of Ohio (Piqua National Bank) in 1847. In politics, he was elected over a dozen times to the office of city treasurer in the years from 1847 to 1875 (a position held by his father) as well as serving as the treasurer for Washington Township.

Joseph Warren Yost (1842-1923)

Yost was a Columbus architect responsible for designing some of the city's most striking structures. In 1885, he designed the Miami County Courthouse in Troy. In 1889, he was selected to design the First Presbyterian Church on the corner of Ash and Caldwell Streets. In that same year, he designed the new North Street School, and the Scott-Slauson building on the northeast corner of Ash and Wayne. During the last part of 1889, Yost designed the red sandstone front for the remodeling of the Schmidlapp Free School **Library** on Main Street. Yost was best known for his use of the **Richardsonian Romanesque Style** of architecture and also for using carved human heads and animal figures in the design elements of his stone-faced structures. In 1890, Yost designed Piqua's largest structure, the **Plaza Hotel**, for **S. K. Statler** and **W. P. Orr**. In that same year, he designed South Street School. In 1891, he designed a **Queen Anne Style** frame home for Myron E. Barber at 324 West Greene Street.

The St. Mary's Church choir stands in the
choir loft in 1944.

Piqua Lists

The employees at Piqua Granite engraving
grave markers in 1948.

A young golfer practiced
his swing in 1949.

This United States Army ambulance was
built by the Meteor Motor Car Company in 1952.

Piqua Lists

ATHLETIC HALL OF FAME, PIQUA HIGH SCHOOL

1995
Craig Clemons
Dr. David Gallagher
James Ginn
Robert Heil
George Wertz
George "Tubby" Wilson

1996
Gene Bayman
Clark "Red" Gabriel
Kenny Thorpe

1997
Bernard Newman
Edward Purk
Jack W. Wagner

1998
Glenn H. Honeycutt
Richard E. Pearson Sr.
C. Richard "Dick" Sword

1999
Julie Hall
James M. Hardman
George P. "Bucky" Wertz Jr.

2000
William Kieth Cummins
Raymond S. Mote
Michael T. Ostendorf

2001
Rick Callison
Rick Grimes
Max Winans

2002
William Gray
Mike Leffel
Mike Smith

2003
Matt Finkes
Al Hackney
Meg Montgomery

2004
Chuck Asher
Tom Lyman
Peg Poling

AUTHORS

Andaloro, Michael (present) Spy novels (pen name R. W. Mykel)
Anderson, Bertha C. (1887-1971) children's fiction
Bennett, Robert (c1947-present) adventure fiction.
Best, Patricia (1924-present) local history, publicity, columnist.
Brooks, Robert C. (1874-1941) political science
Brown, Clifford (unknown) math textbooks
Davis, Arthur N. (1879-19__) Contemporary affairs (WWI)
Dorsey, Godwin V. (1812-1885) translations of Greek poetry, local history
Davis, Eileen (19__ -19__) genealogy
Fogt, Judy (19__-present) magazine articles
Gilmore, Helen (19__ -present) black history
Gross, Adeline G. (18__-19__) poetry (1884)
Harbaugh, Thomas C. (1849-1924) Dime novels, poetry
Hardesty, Corrine (c1902-1989) journalist, cookbooks
Hill, Leonard V. (1885-1984) local history
Hutchins, Ralph (19__- 2005) biography
Jenkinson, Isaac (1825-1911) history
Johnston, John (1775-1861) Indian and local history
McKinney, Louise W. (1830-1927) local history
Martin, Edwin M. (present) wildflower guidebook
May, Ralph (1892-1981) local history
Mitchell, Lynn B. (unknown) Latin textbook
Montgomery, John (1862-1917) religious
Mykel, A. W. pen name for Andaloro, M.
Oda, James C. (1951-present) local history
O'Ferrall, Kirk B. (1888-19__.) travel books
Phillis, Marilyn H. (19__-present) watercolor methods
Porcher, Connie (19__-present) local architecture
Rayner, John A. (1864-1929) local history
Rollin, Horace J. (1845-1935) painting methods, genetics
Schellhase, Nancy S. (19__-present) children's fiction
Sims, Cecil M. (1891-1978) local history, columnist
Smith, Earnest A. (1865-1926) American history
Snow, Jack (1907-19__.) Wizard of Oz books
Spengler, Joseph (1902-1980's) economics
Stevens, Carolyn B. (19__-present) long-term patient care
Trevino, Joseph J. (19__-present) mental health
Trostel, Scott D. (19__-present) railroad history
Wellmeier, Helen (present) local family history
Widney, Joseph D. (1841-1938) religion, race
Wilkenson, John (unknown) chemistry textbook
Wilson, Jack (1922-1987) poker
Wilson, Jean (19__-present) antiques
Woods, Perry D. (1881-1950) college history
Wright, Terry (19__-present) local history
*Present refers to authors living in 2007.

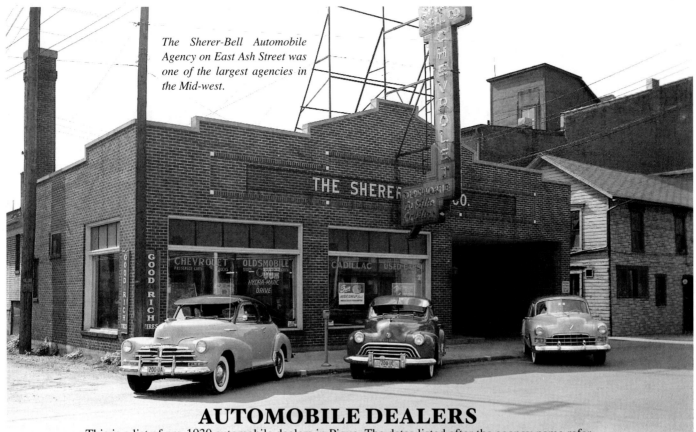

The Sherer-Bell Automobile Agency on East Ash Street was one of the largest agencies in the Mid-west.

AUTOMOBILE DEALERS

This is a list of pre-1930 automobile dealers in Piqua. The dates listed after the agency name refer to the period that the company began selling cars in general in Piqua. If the agency has three dates, the middle date refers to when they began selling that particular model. The date listed after the automobile model refers to the approximate time when the car was first sold in Piqua.

Brush (1907)   Piqua Automobile Garage (1907-1910)
Buick (1909)   Piqua Automobile Garage (1907-1910)
  Miami Automobile Company (1909-1924)
  Hemm Brothers (1913-1955)
Chalmers (1919)   Barrington Motor Car Co. (1919-1928)
Chandler (1919)   United Motor Co. (1911-1919-1920)
  Favorite Garage (123-1924)
Chevrolet (1917)   Reliance Auto Co. (1917-1920)
  Sherer-Bell Co. (1912-1966)
Chrysler (1924)   Barrington Motor Car Co.(1919-1924-1928)
  Morse Motor Car Co. (1919-1928-1940)
  N. R. Rench Motor Sales (1917-1929-1934)
Cole (1917)   Unknown
Columbia (1923)   Barringer Motor Car Co.
  (1919-1923-1928))
Crosley (1939)   Meier Appliance Store (1939)
Cutting (1912)   L. P. Marshall (1912)
Detroiter (1914)   Piqua Auto and Sales Co. (1914)
Dodge (1916)   Jones–Washburn Motor Co. (1916-1921)
  Charles Hicks Motor Co. (1921-1922)
  S. A. Bingham (1922)
  Oates Motor Co. (1922-1927)
  T. E. McCarthy (1926)
  J. C. Gardner (1927)
  Dart-Brown Motor Car Co. (1921)
  Automotive Sales Co. (1922)
  Durant-Foster & Grauser Motor Co. (1928)
Dort (1922)   Brown Motor Car Co. (1911-1922)
  Automobile Sales Co. (1922)
  Morse Motor Car (1919-1923-1940)
Durant (1928)   Foster and Grauser Motor Co. (1928)

E.M.F.(1907)   Piqua Automobile Garage (1907-1910)
Essex (1918)   Jones-Washburn Motor Co. (1916-1918-1921)
  Snyder-Lane Motor Co. (1919-1920)
Ford (1909)   Dayton & Troy Automobile Co. (1915-1917)
  Piqua Auto Sales, Piqua Motor Sales Co. (1918-1931)
Franklin1905)   S.C. Crane (1908)
Gardner (1922)   P. F. Sarver (1921-1922)
Graham-Paige (1928)   Buchanan Motor Sales Co. (1923-1928-1931)
Grant (1917)   Sexauer & Bectold Auto Services (1917)
  T.J. Wiley & Co. (1917)
  Grant Motor Sales Co. (1919)
Haines (1914)   Piqua Auto and Sales Co. (1914)
Hudson (1917)   N.R. Rench Motor sales Co. (1917-1934)
  W. T. Marshall (1919)
  Snyder-Lane Motor Co. (1919-1920)
  Jones-Washburn Motor Co. (1916-1921)
  N. R. Rench Motor Sales (1922)
  Oates Motor Co. (1922)
  Lynch Motor Co. (1929-1932)
Hupmobile (1920)   Brown Motor Car Co. (1911-1920-1922)
  J. O. Staley (1921)
  P. F. Sarver (1921-1922)
  J.O. Staley Garage (1921-1924)
  Curl & Hagelberger (1924)
Kissel (1919)   United Motor Co. (1911-1919-1920)
Lexington (1917)   N. R. Rench Motor Sales Co. (1917-1934)
  Piqua Lexington Motor Car Co. (1919)
Marmon (1928)   Marmon-Oldsmobile Sales Co. (1928)

	Maxwell-Mouch's Auto Inn (1917)
	Barringer Motor Car Co. (1919)
Maxwell (1917)	Mouch's Auto Inn (1917-1918)
	Barrington Motor Car Co. (1919-1928)
Meteor (1914)	Samuel N. Arni (1914-1915)
Nash (1919)	Morse Motor Car Co. (1919-1940)
	Coppock – Nash Co. (1928-1930)
Oakland (1918)	Oakland Auto Co. (1918)
	Hemm Brothers (1913-1955)
Oldsmobile (1920)	United Motor Co. (1911-1920)
	Marmon – Oldsmobile Sales Co. (1928)
	Charles R. Wiles (1928-1929-1938)
	Paige-Buchanan Motor Sales Co. (1923)
Overland (1911)	Miami Automobile Company (1909-1924)
Paige (1923)	Buchanan Motor Co. (1923-1931)
Peerless (1908)	Unknown
Pontiac (1926)	Amman Motor Co. (1926-1927))
	Goodwill Motor Sales (1927-1931)
	Hemm Brothers (1927)
Reo (1921)	Reo-Miller Bros. Co. (1921-1931)
Stoddard (1909)	No local dealer
Studebaker (1918)	Saul A. Bingham (1918-1924)
	Hawn-Myers Motor Co. (1924-1928)
	John K. Martin Motor Co. (1929-1930)
Thomas (1907)	Piqua Automobile Garage (1907-1910)
Willys(1924)	Miami Automobile Co. (1912)
	Overland Piqua Co. (1920)
	Howard W. Miller (1921-1924-1931)
	T. E. McCarthy Inc. (1929-1931)

CHAMBER OF COMMERCE EXECUTIVES (STAFF)

T. G. Appleyard	1917
Ralph B. Sullivan	1920 – 1921
William M. Coy	1944 – 1947 (first modern executive)
Harold Gross	1947 – 1948
George Hedger	1949 – 1951
L. Earl Murphy	1951 – 1953
Charles Manchester	1954 – 1955

Cecil M. Sims	1955 – 1963
Richard Haines	1964 – 1966
Ed Alberty	1966 – 1969
George Montgomery	1969 – 1974
Tom Besancencey	1974 – 1976
Jerry Easley	1976 – 1984
Mark Kidder	1984 – 1988
Larry Baker	1988 – 1989
David E. Vollette	1989 – 2006
Lisa Whitaker	2006 - present
	(first woman executive)

CHURCHES

Dates refer to when the church was organized or the earliest date it was listed and when the church disbanded (if known). Present refers to 2007. Accurate dates for many churches and congregations are very difficult. A group that starts meeting in a home may not be listed for several years. Congregations that merge, split or disband often do not advertise or even discuss these changes. Name and denominational changes can be difficult to follow or accurately document. SEE ALSO: Patron pp. 225, 232, 237, 239, 263, 280, 281, 282, 290.

Abiding In His Word Ministry – c.1997 - present
African Methodist Episcopal – See: Cyrene
Anshe Emeth – See: Temple Anshe Emeth
Assembly of God – See: Piqua Assembly
Associate Reformed – See: Good Shepard
Baptist Church – See: Piqua Baptist
Beech Bethel Methodist – See: Bethel United Methodist
Bethel United Methodist – 1853
Bethel Lutheran Church- c.1998 (split from St. John's Lutheran)
Bethany Church Center – c.2003
Broadway Disciple – See: Church of Christ
Calvary Baptist – 1876-1911
Calvary Baptist (Independent) – c.1980's
Campbellite Christian - c.1844
Central Baptist – c.1970's

The First Presbyterian Church on the southeast corner of Ash and Caldwell was designed by J. W. Yost.

Christ the Redeemer Full Gospel (Nazarene) – c.1990's.
Christian – See: Congregational Christian
Christian Scientist – See: First Church of Christ, Scientist
Church of Christ, Disciples – c. 1888-90 – c.1900's
Church of Christ – c.1920's
Church of God – See: First Church
Church of God – 1906 – c.1920's
Church of God Mountain Assembly (Pentecostal) – c.1930's
Church of Jesus, Pentecostal Assemblies of the World – 1971 - present
Church of Jesus Christ Latter Day Saints (Mormon) c.1960's - present
Church of the Brethren – 1927
Church of the Nazarene – 1926 – 1940's
Community Missionary – 1980's – 1990's
Congregational Christian United Church of Christ – 1890 - present
Cornerstone Assembly of God – See: Piqua Assembly of God
Cornerstone Fellowship Bible Church – c.1980's
Cornerstone Life Center – c.1993 – present
Cradle Tabernacle (WLW Radio) Nation's Auxiliary Prayer Band No. 120 of Piqua-1935
Crossroads Church of God Mountain Assembly – c. 2001
Cumberland Presbyterian – c.1838
Cumberland Presbyterian – 1902
Cyrene African Methodist Episcopal – 1853 - present
Deutsche Kirche – See: German Methodist
English Lutheran – See: St. John's
Evangelical United Methodist (Brethern) – 1893 – c.2003
Evergreen Baptist – c.1920's
Family of Grace – See: Grace United Methodist
Favorite Hill Baptist – 1970's
Favorite Hill Methodist Episcopal Mission – 1893 – 1920's
Favorite Hill Southern Baptist – c.1960's
First Baptist –See: Piqua Baptist
First Christian – See: Congregational Christian
First Church of Christ Scientist - c.1898 – c.1902 and c.1923-4
First Church of God – 1913 - present
First Evangelical & Reformed – See: First United Church of Christ
First Freewill Baptist Church of Piqua – 1980's
First Pilgrim Holiness Church – See: Pilgrim Holiness
First Presbyterian – See: Westminster
First Reformed – See: First United Church of Christ
First United Church of Christ – 1873 – c.1998
Fountain Park Baptist – 1895
Freedom Life Ministries – c.1991 - present
Friendship Baptist Church – 1990's – present
Gathering Place – c.2005
German Catholic – See: St. Boniface

German Evangelical and Reformed – See: First United Church of Christ
German Lutheran – See: St. Paul's
German Methodist – 1867
Glory Tabernacle/Temple – c.1935-1936
Goad Ministries – c.1990's (moved to Florida)
Good Shepherd United Presbyterian – 1812 - present
Grace United Methodist – 1853 - present
Greater Love Missionary Baptist Church – c.2002 (split from Park Avenue Baptist)
Greene St. United Methodist – 1807 - present
Hope Chapel Baptist Church – c.1997 – present
House of Prayer – c.1955
Irish Catholic – See: St. Mary's
Jehovah's Witness – c.1970's – present
Liberty Baptist Church – 1990's
Liberty Christian Center – See: Cornerstone Life Center
Lighthouse Pentecostal Church – c.2003
Linden Avenue Church of God (Pentecostal) – See: Church of God, Mountain Assembly
Lutheran – See: Bethel, Our Savior, St. John's, St. Paul's
Mennonite Brethren in Christ Church – 1922 – 1930's
Missionary – See: United Missionary
Mountain Assembly – See: Church of God, Mountain Assembly
New Hope Chapel, Freewill Baptist – c.1970's - 1980's
New Hope Church of God – See: Freedom Life Ministries
New Lights Presbyterian – See: Westminster
New School Presbyterian – See: Second Presbyterian
Old School Presbyterian – See: Westminster
Open Bible Church – 1991 – c.2000 See: Piqua Wesleyan
Our Savior Lutheran Church – c.1995 –present (split from St. John's)
Park Avenue Baptist – See Second Baptist Church
Pentecostal Assembly – 1920's
Pentecostal Mission – c.1914
Pilgrim's Holiness Mission – c.1930's (became Piqua Holiness Church)
Piqua Apostolic Temple – c.1970's
Piqua Assembly of God – c.1950's - present
Piqua Baptist Church– 1811 – present
Piqua Bible Temple – c.1970
Piqua Christ Temple – c.1933
Piqua Freewill Baptist – See: First Freewill Baptist
Piqua Holiness Church (1937 – 1940's)
Piqua Holiness Church – 1980's – c.1991

Piqua Missionary – See Community Missionary
Piqua Seventh Day – See: Seventh Day
Piqua Temple of Seekers of Light – 1980's – c.1997
Piqua United Pentecostal - 1980's - present
Piqua Wesleyan – c.1970's – see: Open Bible Church
St. Boniface Catholic Church – 1855 - present
St. James Episcopal Church – 1823 - present
St. John's Lutheran Church – 1890 - present
St. Mary's Catholic Church – 1839 - present
St. Paul's [Evangelical Lutheran] United Church of Christ – 1835 -2005 (see below)
St. Paul's Evangelical and Reformed Church – 2005 - present
Salem Baptist – See: Piqua Baptist – 1923
Salvation Army – 1887 and 1901 and 1905 - present
Seceder – See: Good Shepherd
Second Baptist Church – 1857 – present
Second Presbyterian – 1842 – 18__
Seventh-Day Adventist – 1940 - present
Snyder Road Church of God – c.1970's - present

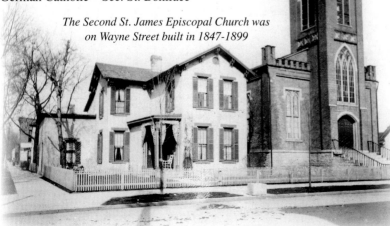

The Second St. James Episcopal Church was on Wayne Street built in 1847-1899

Springcreek Baptist – N.D. - present
Spring Street Methodist – See: Green Street
Temple Anshe Emeth (Reformed) – c.1858 - present
Tower of Truth Cathedral – c.1970's – c.1978
Trinity Church – c.2001
Trinity Southern Baptist – c.1980's – c.1989
Trinity Wesleyan Methodist – c.1930's
United Brethren – See: Evangelical United
United Brethren in Christ – c.1850's
United Brethern in Christ, Liberal – c.1900
United Missionary – See: Mennonite Brethren in Christ Church
United Pentecostal – 1978
United Presbyterian – See: Good Shepherd
Upper Valley Community Church –c.2001 - present (split from Church of the Nazarene)
Victory Heights Community Church – c.1946 – c.1948
Vision Temple Apostolic Church of God – c. 2006
Wayne Street Methodist – See: Grace Methodist
Wayne Street Methodist – See: German Methodist
Wayne Street United Brethren – See: Evangelical United Methodist
Wesleyan Methodist – c.1937 – c.1941
Wesleyan Methodist Episcopal – 1843-1853
Westminster Presbyterian – 1815 - present
Zion Reformed – See: First United Church of Christ

CITY MANAGERS

Lester G. Whitney (1930-1935)
F. R. Buechner (1935-1941)
Wilbur J. Baldwin (1941-1949)
Robert M. Hance, Jr. (1949-1972)
Wayne Barfels (1972-1978)
Frank Patrizio, Jr. (1979- 1998)
R. Mark Rohr (1998 -2004)
Frederick E. Enderle (2005 – present)

City Manager Frank Patrizio.

CIVIC HALL OF FAME INUCTEES
1995
John Johnston
William McCulloch
Robert Hartzell
1996
Scott Garbry
Don Gentile
A.J. Kaiser
1997
Goodrich Giles
Minabelle Hutchins
Jacob Schmidlapp
1998
John Rayner
C.M. Sims
William Pitsenbarger
1999
Airhart M. Fry

Helen Louis
Raymond S. Mote
2000
Mills Brothers
George Wertz
Lucy Patterson
2001
Henry Flesh
Kenneth McMaken
Robert Hance Jr.
2002
Rachel Johnston
Godwin V. Dorsey
Darrell Taylor Sr.
2003
Stephen Johnston
George Rundle
Philip Gates
2004
Matthew Caldwell Sr.
Leonard U. Hill
William P. Orr
2005
Samuel K. Statler
Lola Hill
Richard Hunt
2006
Alfred W. French Sr.
Charles B. Upton
Robert M. Davis

CIVIL WAR, AFRICAN-AMERICAN SOLDIERS

This is only a very abbreviated list of African-American men that served in the Civil War that either lived in Piqua prior to the war or moved to the city after the war.

John Anderson, Company D, 54th Massachusetts Volunteer Infantry Regiment

John Bailey, Company C, 55th Massachusetts Volunteer Infantry Regiment

Peter Boone, Company K, 16th United States Colored Troops, Infantry

James Bray, Company B, 4th Regiment, United States Colored Troops, Infantry

Thomas Brown, Company H, 5th United States Colored Heavy Artillery

Samuel Busby (aka Charles Hunter)

J.R. Cain, Company B, 27th United States Colored Troops, Infantry

Henry Clay, Company B, 27th United States Colored Troops, Infantry

Ishman Clay, Company B, 27th United States Colored Troops, Infantry

Charles Clements, Company A, 45th United States Colored Troops, Infantry

Augustus Collins, Company I, 5th United States Colored Heavy Artillery

Rose Collins, 27th Regiment, United States Colored Troops, Infantry

William Cox, Company K, 55th Massachusetts Volunteer Infantry Regiment

Paul Crowder, Corporal, Company D, 55th Massachusetts Volunteer Infantry Regiment

George W. Davis, Company B, 25th United States Colored Troops, Infantry

George Mark Ewell, Company C, 12th United States Colored Troops, Infantry

George Evans, Company H, 15th United States Colored Troops, Infantry

Goodrich Giles, unknown unit, Confederate States of America

James Gillard, Company B, 27th Regiment, United States Colored Troops, Infantry

David Hughs, Company B, 27th United States Colored Troops, Infantry

Charles Hunter, Company D, 25th United States Colored Troops, Infantry

Abel Johns[t]on, Company D, 5th United State Colored Troops, Infantry

William N. Johnson, 124th Regiment, United States Colored Troops, Infantry

S.F. Jones, Company K, 100th United States Colored Troops, Infantry

Simon Peter Jones, Company K, 100th United States Colored Troops, Infantry

William H. Kendall, Company E, 25th (21st) United States Colored Troops, Infantry

George H. Koker, 8th Pennsylvania Volunteer Infantry Regiment

Jesse Lockyear, 54th Massachusetts Volunteer Infantry Regiment

Harry [George Washington] Long, 23rd Regiment, United States Colored Troops, Infantry

John T. Marshall, Company K, 42nd, United States Colored Infantry Troops, Infantry

Samuel Price, Company F, 27th United States Colored Troops, Infantry

Wade Reece, Company F, 12th Regiment, United States Colored Troops, Infantry

W.C. Smith, Sergeant, Company D, 5th Regiment, United States Colored Troops, Infantry

Sidney Vicks, Company C, 27th Regiment, United States Colored Troops, Infantry

George Washington, Company D, 23rd Regiment, United States Colored Troops, Infantry (see Harry Long)

James Williams, Company K, 42nd Regiment, United States Colored Troops, Infantry

---

CIVIL WAR, PIQUA UNITS

These units represent units that contained significant numbers of Piqua citizens. The 94th and 110th OVI regiments were organized at **Camp Piqua.**

Company K, 1st Regiment, Ohio Volunteer Infantry
Company B, 11th Regiment, Ohio Volunteer Infantry
Company F, 11th Regiment, Ohio Volunteer Infantry (first unit organized in Piqua)
U/I Company, 20th Regiment, Ohio Volunteer Infantry
U/I Company, 50th Regiment, Ohio Volunteer Infantry
Company C, 94th Regiment, Ohio Volunteer Infantry
Company A, 110th Regiment, Ohio Volunteer Infantry
Company C, 147th Regiment, Ohio Volunteer Infantry
Company I, 8th Regiment, Ohio Volunteer Cavalry
U/I Company, 12th Regiment, Ohio Volunteer Cavalry
U/I Company, 8th Ohio Volunteer Artillery

DAIRIES

This is a list of a few of the larger Piqua area dairies. It is not a complete list of all of the small farm and dairy operations that supported Piqua's need for milk and dairy products over the years. The years usually indicate the first and last year a listing could be found for the dairy, creamery, ice cream and early retail dairy product stores.

Butterfield Creamery (A.G. and E.H. Butterfield) (c.1887 – c.1889)
Samuel Kiefer (c. 1887 – c.1890)
Guernsey Dairy (W.H. Kendall & Sons) (c. 1889)
Piqua Creamery (William E. Henderson) (c.1901-c.1910)
Henry Dorman (c.1902)
Robery F. Levering (c.1902)
Jeremiah Morrow (c.1902)
John J. Row (c.1902)
Lewis T. Shellabarger (c.1902)
George Brucker Milk Company (c.1907-1919)
Quilling – Brucker Company (1920- c.1922)
Favorite City Milk Products Company (c.1923-c.1949)
Favorite City Milk Products Company, Meadow Gold (1949-c.1953)
Meadow Gold Dairy, Division of Beatrice Foods (c.1953-c.1989)

Blaine Statler (holding the milk can) ran a home delivery dairy at the turn of the twentieth century.

Charles E. Booher (c.1910 – c. 1913)
Piqua Pure Milk Company (c.1913)
Bailey's Dairy (c.1917 –c.1918)
Lange Products Company (formerly Lange Brewery) (1919 – 1944)
Furrow's Dairy (1921 – c.1960) (see San-Fur Inc.)
Furrow Dairy Co. Div. of Miami Valley Milk Producers Assoc. (c.1962 – c.1964)
Sanitary Milk Company (Brucker & Sharp) (c.1922 - c.1924-25)
Red Wing Company (c.1923 - c.1941)
Borden's Red Wing Company (c.1942 – c. 1946)
Borden's Ice Cream & Beverage Company (c.1947 – c.1955)
Borden Company, Ice Cream and Milk Divisions (c.1956 – c.1959)
Borden Company Milk Division (c.1960 – c.1970)
Miami Valley Co-Operative Milk Producers Association (in Piqua) (c.1926- c.1931)

Farmers Co-Operative Cream Station (c.1932- c.1941)
Kiefer's Dairy (Arthur Kiefer) (c.1930-1935)
Cloverleaf Creamery Inc. (c.1930 – c.1932)
Fairmont Creamery Company (c.1930 – c.1934)
Rees Creamery (c.1936- c.1937)
White Mountain Cream Station (c.1937 –c.1938)
Clarence L. Motter (c.1930 – c.1931)
Sanders Dairy (Keller Sanders) (c.1936 – c.1959)
San-Fur Inc (Charles Sanders) (c.1960- c.1961)
Elmer's Cow (Elmer Hudson) (c.1939 – c.1944)
Black's Creamery (Forrest V. Black) (c.1941 – c.1960)
Weber W. Musser (c.1941 – c. 1943)
Isaly's Dairy Company (c.1943 – c.1945)
L. Emral Thompson (c.1946 – c.1947)
Miron M. Mills (c.1950 – c.1954)
Peltier Milk & Dairy Products (John J. Peltier) (c.1963 – c. 1975)
    SEE ALSO: Milk Bottle Cap companies

FIRE CHIEFS

Dick Manchester	1866 - 1877
Leopold Kiefer	1877 - 1882
Stephen Genslinger	1882 - 1885
Frank Hunter	1885 - 1892
Frank Dye	1892 - 1896
Jacob Shaub	1896 - 1900
William L. Miller	1900 - 1903
Peter J. Caulfield	1903 - 1939
Joseph A. Caulfield	1940 – 1941
Gilbert Grove	1941 – 1946
George Effinger	1946 – 1954
Arthur B. Russell	1954 – 1968
Louis Mikolajewski	1968 – 1973
Russell Selby	1973 – 1979
Robert Bowman	1979 – 1988
Greg Fashner	1988 – 1998
Jim Roth	1998 – 2000
Gary Connell	2000 - present

Peter J. Caulfield was Piqua's first professional fire chief.

FORTS, OHIO

Fort Adams (1794-1795)
Fort Amanda (1812-1815)
Fort Barbee (1794-1796 and 1813-1818)
Fort Black (1813-c1814)
Fort Buchanan (1812)
Fort Campus Martius (1788-1795)
Fort Defiance (1794-1797 and 1813)
Fort Finney (1785-1786)
Fort Greenville (1793-1796)
Fort Hamilton (1791-1796)
Fort Harmar (1785-1790)
Fort Industry (1794, 1805)
Fort Jefferson (1791-1796)
Fort La Demoiselle (aka Pickawillany, Fort)
Fort Laurens (1778-1779)
Fort McIntosh (1778-1791)
Fort Meigs (1813-1815)
Fort Nesbit(t) (1813)
Fort Pickawillany (1747-1752)
Fort Piqua (1794-1795)
Fort Recovery (1793-1796)
Fort Rowdy (1793-1795)

Fort St. Clair (1791-c1793)
Fort St. Marys (aka Barbee, Fort)
Fort Stanwix (1758-1781)
Fort Washington (1789-1804)
Fort Wayne (1794-1819)

MAYORS, PIQUA

TOWN GOVERNMENT

1835	John S. Johnston
1836	L. R. Brownell
1836-37	James Alexander
1837	Dr. I. T. Teller
1837-39	Stephen Johnston
1840	**Wm. R. Barrington** (only newspaper editor to be Mayor)
1841	Issac S. Clark
1842	J. P. Williamson
1843	William R. Barrington
1844	George B. Frye
1845	Joseph Horton
1846	**Samuel S. McKinney**
1847-49	Joseph C. Horton (resigned)
1849	**Stephen Johnston** (filled remainder of term)

CITY GOVERNMENT

1850-51	**Stephen Johnston**
1851-55	Wm. Elliott
1855-57	Francis Reed
1857-63	William N. Foster (resigned to join Army during CivilWar)
1863-67	John Garner
1867	Harvey Clark
1867-75	Samuel B. Garvey
1875-77	W. W. V. Buchanan (D)*
1877-81	George Dettmer (D)
1881-89	George Brooks (D)
1889-90	John C. Geyer (R)
1890-93	Edward M. Wilbee (R)
1893-97	James Ward Keyt (R)
1897-03	John E. Smith (D)
1903-05	**Lucius Cowan Cron** (D) (former Mayor of Huntersville)
1906-09	James C. Hughes (R) (two terms)
1910-13	Charles Kiser (D) (two terms)
1914-15	**G. W. Lorimer** (R) (one term)
1916-17	Elbert M. Bell (R) (one term)
1918-19	**Frank Hamilton** (S) (one term)
1920-21	**J. Harrison Smith** (I) (one term)
1922-23	Alvah DeWeese (R) (one term)
1924-27	William Crozier (R) (two terms)
1928-29	J. Harrie Stein (R) (one term)

ELECTED BY CITY COMMISSION

1930-39	**Vernon R. Osborn**** (five terms)
1940-43	Harry E. Croner (two terms)
1943-47	Joseph Thoma, Sr. (three terms)
1948-55	Wilbur Reck (four terms)
1956-57	Richard A. Goater (one term)
1958-73	Jack Wilson (eight terms)
1974-75	Joseph C. Goetz (one term)
1976-77	Jack Wilson (one term, nine terms total, the longest service of any Mayor)

1978-79   James E. Henderson (one term)
1980-83   Samuel Jackson (two terms)
1984-87   Charles E. Stevens (two terms)
1988-91   William. J. "Knobby" Cruse (two terms)
1992-95   Lucinda L. Fess (two terms) (first woman to serve as Mayor)
1996-97   William J. "Knobby" Cruse (one term, he served a total of three terms)
1998-01   Frank H. Barhorst (two terms)
2002-03   David A. Martin (one term)
2004-05   Robert L. DeBrosse (one term) (He was elected by the city commission)
2006-present   Thomas D. Hudson

*Prior to 1875 the politically affiliation of the mayor is unknown.
**Under the 1930 city charter all city elections are nonpartisan.
 D) - Democrat   (S) - Socialist
(R) - Republican   (I) - Independent
SEE ALSO: City Council; Huntersville; Individual Political Parties.

MIAMI COUNTY COMMUNITIES AND DEVELOPMENTS

The names in parentheses are alternate (usually older) names of the communities. Dates refer to the period when the community was first organized or formally laid out. The list includes communities and developments created prior to 1915. The last number in parentheses indicates the community's population in 2000.

Abe   c.1911   Newberry Township
Alcony   1850   Elizabeth Township
Bloomer   1883   Newberry Township
Bradford   1868   Newberry Township, Adams Township, Darke County (1,859)
Brandt   1839   Bethel Township
Casstown   1833   Lostcreek Township (Trimminsburg) (322)
Circle Hill   1880's   Newton Township
Clayton   1840   Newberry Township
Conover   1856   Brown Township
County Line   1903   Union Township (interurban stop)
Covington   1816   Newberry Township (Friendship, Newberry, Stillwater) (2,559)
Cowlesville,   1842   Monroe Township
Culbertson Heights   c.1910   Staunton Township
Eldean   1901   Concord Township (interurban stop)
Ellemans   1901   Newton Township (interurban stop)
Evanston   1890's   Monroe Township (interurban stop)
Fairview   c.1910   Concord Township
Farmers Nursery c.1910   Concord Township
Farrington   1890's   Washington Township
Fletcher   1830   Brown Township (510)
Frederick   1828   Monroe and Union Townships, Butler Township, Montgomery County (Fidelity)
Garland   1870's   Union Township
Ginghamsburg   1850's   Monroe Township
Grayson   1880's   Elizabeth Township (railroad stop)
Hanktown   c.1848   Union Township

(early African-American settlement)
Huntersville 1838   Springcreek Township (Shawnee)
Hyattsville   1833   Monroe Township
Jordans   c.1905 Springcreek Township (interurban stop)
Kessler   1890   Union Township
Laura   1852   Union Township (487)
Lena   1831   Brown Township (Elizabethtown, Allen)
Ludlow Falls 1882   Union Township (210)
Marshalltown 1847   Newton Township (early African-American settlement)
Nashville   1820   Union Township
New Jefferson 1828   Newberry Township
Pattytown   1850's Newton Township
Peterson   1850's Staunton Township
Phoneton   1907
Pickawillany 1747   Washington Township (Miami Tribe village, British trading post)
Piqua   1807   Washington Township (only community in county not formally part of a township) (Washington) (20,738)
Pleasant Hill   1843   Newton Township (Newton) (1,134)
Polo   1890's Newberry Township (Tidewater)
Potsdam   1845   Union Township (New Lebanon, Georgetown) (203)
Rangeville   c.1910 Newberry Township (railroad stop)
Redman   1877   Newberry Township
Rex   1880's Bethel Township (Brown) (railroad stop)
Riverside   c.1910 Washington Township
Rossville   1841   Springcreek Township (early African-American settlement)
Sodom   18__   Lostcreek Township (Pencetown)
Staunton   1798/1806   Staunton Township (Dutch Station)
Sugar Grove   c.1900 Newton Township (railroad stop)
Sunnyside   c.1910 Washington Township (subdivision)
Tipp City   1840   Monroe Township (Tippecanoe) (9,221)
Troy   1807   Concord Township (county seat) (county's largest city) (21,999)
Upper Piqua   1780   Washington Township (Johnston Farm) (Shawnee Tribe village)
Victory   1839   Location is unclear
West Charleston 1807/1815   Bethel Township (Friendtown)
West Milton   1807   Union Township (Milton) (4,645)

MILITARY DEATHS (1900-2007)

This is a list of Piqua citizens who died during active military service. The month/day/year refers to the date of death.
The following abbreviations are used:

M.O.H (Medal of Honor)
N.G. (National Guard)
P.O.W. (prisoner of war)
U.S.A.F. (United States Air Force)
U.S.A. (United States Army)
U.S.A.A.F. (United States Army Air Force)
U.S.C.G. (United States Coast Guard)
U.S.M.C. (United States Marine Corps)
U.S.N. (United States Navy)
PRE-WORLD WAR I ERA (1900 - 1916)
No known military deaths

WORLD WAR I ERA (1917 - 1920)

Downey, James E. 10/6/1918, U.S.A.
Freihofer, George J. 10/25/1918, U.S.A.
Funderburg, Cloyd D. 8/6/1918, U.S.A.
Graham, George C. 10/21/1918, U.S.A.
Kerr, Ralph M. 10/7/1918, U.S.A.
Layman, John J. 10/6/1918, U.S.A
Lurance, Walter 10/1/1918, N.G./U.S.A.
Mauchamer, Allen G. 10/2/1918, U.S.A.
Pauley, Gordon 9/29/1918, N.G./U.S.A.
Pence, Grover 10/12/1918, N.G./U.S.A.
Pequignot, Gus Joseph 11/8/1918, U.S.A.
Rousseau, Edward J. 10/13/1918, U.S.A.
Savage, Kenneth L. 12/18/1918, U.S.A.
Schmidt, Herman August 10/14/1918, U.S.A.
Schnell, Paul 10/31/1918, N.G./U.S.A.
White, Charles B. 10/15/1918, U.S.A.
White, Vernon 10/15/1918, U.S.A.
Williams, Frank 9/28/1918, U.S.A.

POST-WORLD WAR I ERA (1921 - 1939)

Chaney, Samuel N. 1/28 /1921, U.S.A.
Freshour, William McKee 8/23/1937, U.S.N.

WORLD WAR II ERA (1940 - 1950)

Asher, James N. 3/7/1945, U.S.A.
Ball, Melvin J. 2/26/1945, U.S.A.
Baumann, James Sylvester 4/6/1945, U.S.A.
Beasecker, Robert E. 5/27/1944, U.S.A.
Beaver, Frank L. 3/28/1945, U.S.A. (P.O.W.)
Benz, Robert C. 9/20/1944, U.S.A.
Berman, John 2/28/1945, Branch of service unknown
Black, Charles Harold 6/23/1944, U.S.A.A.F.
Blacke, Clifford 12/23/1944, U.S.A. (POW)
Brant, Robert Lee 4/30/1942, U.S.A.
Brewer, John H. 6/7/1944, U.S.A.
Brower, Robert F. 8/27/1943, U.S.A.A.F.
Brown, Patrick L. 12/2/1946, U.S.A.
Bryan, Norman R. date of death unknown,U.S.A.A.F.
Burkett, Willard E. 3/14/1944, U.S.A.
Coburn, Jack H. 9/13/1949, branch of service unknown
Cole, William E. 4/14/1945, U.S.A.
Cooper, Alfred Elmo 2/2/1945, U.S.A.
Couchot, Martin 5/23/1945, U.S.A.
Coyne, Virgil E. 5/30/1943, U.S.A.
Cromer, Robert J. 5/20/1944, U.S.A.A.F.
Cummins, Jack C. 12/25/1944, U.S.C.G./U.S.A.
Danford, Thomas J. 2/21/1945, U.S.A.
Dawson, Donald M. 3/1/1945, U.S.A.
Dye, Edward C. 10/4/44, U.S.A.
Eisert, Leo Carl 3/21/1945, U.S.M.C.
Ellerman, Alexander III 3/6/1944, U.S.A.A.F.
Elliott, George L. 11/19/1945, U.S.A.
Ewing, George W. 12/2/1944, U.S.A.
Faber, Frederick H. 6/19/1950, branch of service unknown
Felver, Donald M. 2/24/1945, U.S.A.
Fitzsimmons, Richard J. "Dick" 7/24 /1945, U.S.A.
Flesh, Alfred L. Jr. 1/8/1945, U.S.A.
Forsythe,William Jr. 10/14/1943, U.S.A.A.F.
Freeman, Raymond S. 5/19/1944, U.S.A.
Fry, Raymond C. Jr. 1/7/1945, U.S.A.A.F.
Gaier, Edward F. 2/19/1944, U.S.A.A.F.
Gallaway, James 8/4/1944, U.S.A.
Gearheart, Robert William 12/18/1944, U.S.A.
Graef, Robert S. 10/12/1944, U.S.A.
Gray, Zane 3/15/1944, U.S.M.C.
Groves, Floyd L. 2/7/1943, U.S.A.

Harris, William Murray 6/2/1944, U.S.A.A.F.
Heaton, Emery Wray 1/12/1945, U.S.A.
Heffner, Ralph Everett date of death unknown, U.S.N.
Hewatt, Clifford Leroy 2/28/1944, U.S.A.
Hilliard, Charles Richard 6/13/1945, U.S.A.
Huecker, Vernon Francis 12/2/1944, U.S.A.
Houdeshell, Robert E. 4/30/1945, U.S.A.
Huffman, Walter Lewis 12/18/1944, U.S.N.
Johnson, Robert 1944, U.S.A.
Keys, John 9/18/1944, U.S.A.
Kiefer, David Arthur 1/14/1946, U.S.A.
Kiesewetter, William Myrle 6 /7/1942, U.S.A.A.F.
Knight, Donovan 1945, U.S.N.
Lemmon, John B. 2/28/1945, U.S.A.
Libbee, Dick 12/20/1943, U.S.A.A.F.
Lillicrap, Fredrex George 10/11/1943, U.S.N.
Loewi, A.W. date of death unknown, branch of service unknown
Long, Maurice M. 10/13/1943, U.S.A.
Marchal, Harold date of death unknown, branch of service unknown
Meiring, Richard Frederick 1/9/1945, U.S.A.
Moniaci, James V. 7/7/1945, U.S.A.
Morlock, Edward G. Jr."Bud" "Ed" 2/25/1945, U.S.A.
Mullin, Andrew J. 7/12/1944, U.S.A.
Mullin, Vernon C. 9/15/1943, U.S.A.A.F.
Negley, Paul Lee "Doc" "Sheik" 4/8/1943, U.S.A.A.F.
Orput, James L. "Buddy" 2/23/1945, U.S.A.
Osgood, Ronald E. 5/1/1944, U.S.A.A.F.
Peters, William Warren Jr."Bill" "Pete" 1/1/1945, U.S.A.
Pitman, Glenn W. 12/21/1942, U.S.N.
Potts, Richard F. 12/25/1945, U.S.A.A.F.
Ray, Delver O. date of death unknown,U.S.A.
Rehmert, George I. 9/13/1942, U.S.N.
Ross, Jack E. 7/11/1944, U.S.A.
Rue, Robert B. 10/ /1943, U.S.A.A.F.
Ruffner, Elbert Morgan 6/24/1945, U.S.A.A.F.
Sauers, Harold J. "Pickles" 1/3/1945, U.S.A.
Scholl, David H. 5/26/1944, U.S.A.
Seipel, Richard August "Dick" 6/17/1945, U.S.M.C.
Shellabarger, John 5/3/1945, U.S.A.
Sherwood, James Elson 3/12/1945, U.S.A. (POW)
Sippel, Ollie Leo 12/13/1944, U.S.A.
Smith, Kenneth L. "Bulldog" 2/4/1945, U.S.A./U.S.A.A.F.
Smith, Robert L. Jr. 5/29/1944, U.S.A.
Snow, Robert H. "Bob" 7/27/1944, U.S.M.C.
Snyder, Sylvester J. 4/15/1945, U.S.A.
Stoute, Alex Wilson "Frag" 6/10/1944, U.S.A.
Strasser, Alfred 9/1944, U.S.N.
Stutsman, Homer date of death unknown, branch of service unknown
Thompson, Kenneth I. 12/21/1944, U.S.A.
Trydell, Martin M. 3/22/1944, U.S.A.
Wack, Robert Joseph 9/8/1943, U.S.A.
Walters, John L. Jr. 8/2/1944, U.S.A.
Westfall, John C. Jr. 11/21/1943, U.S.MC.
Wirrig, Edward date of death unknown, branch of service unknown
Woods, Clarence Harold "Hal" "Woodsie" 10/25/1944, U.S.A.
Wright, Herbert O. 1/11/1944, U.S.A.
Young, Dale B. 2/18/1945, U.S.A.
Young, James K. 1/3/1945, U.S.A.
Yount, Daniel H. 11/22/1944, U.S.A.A.F.
Ziegler, Robert L. 3/26/1945, U.S.N.
Zink, Paul date of death unknown, branch of service unknown

KOREAN CONFLICT ERA (1951 - 1960)
Berning, Maurice J. 8/6/1951, U.S.A.
Blue, Adelbert 7/31/1951, U.S.A. (POW)
Bundschuh, Dean C. 5/21/1951, U.S.A.
Ditmer, Elwood L. 11/2/1950, U.S.A.
Gentile, Dominic Salvatore "Don" 1/28/1951, U.S.A.F.
Hess, James Richard 4/20/1951, U.S.N.
Jones, Dale R. 6/30/1951, U.S.A. (POW)
Lawrence, Harry Lee 5/31/1956, U.S.A.F.
Obringer, Carl Jr. 10/7/1951, U.S.A.
O'Roark, Richard Lee 7/15/1953, U.S.A.
Pritchard, Donald Eugene 1/30/1952, U.S.A.
Smith, John H. "Jackie" 6/4/1951, U.S.A.
Tamplin, Darel Edward 09/08/1950, U.S.A.
Tamplin, Herbert Eugene Jr. 7/27/1950, U.S.A.
Zea, Donald Dale 7/25/1953, U.S.A.

VIETNAM CONFLICT ERA (1960 - 1975)
Brown, James R. "Jim" "Brownie" 3/4/1970, U.S.N.
Byrum, Donald E. / /1967, U.S.A.
Cain, Billy R. 5/1/1969, U.S.A.F.
Cotterman, Harry Andrew 5/16/1970, U.S.A.
Dix, Donald 12/19/1972, U.S.N.
Dulen, Rendle "Randy" 5/9/1968, U.S.M.C.
Durham, John A. "J.D." "Scooter" 2/4/1969, U.S.N.
Haney, Keith E. 5/ /1971, U.S.A.
Jaqua, Michael D. "Jack" 11/1/1967, U.S.M.C.
Jones, Charles Thomas "Tom" 6/ /1970, U.S.A.
Karnehm, Steven D. 9/27/1971, U.S.A.
Koon, Charles Marion "Chuck" 5/12/1970, U.S.A.
Page, John M. / /1969, U.S.A.
Pitsenbarger, William H. "Bill" "Pits" 4/11/1966, U.S.A.F.
(M.O.H.)
Rush, James T. 1/12/1969, U.S.A.
Scheeler, Victor R. 3/4/1969, U.S.A.
Siler, Dennis L. "Denny" "Si" 5/5/1976, U.S.A.F.
Staneart, Ronald K. 10/4/1966, U.S.M.C.
Wenrick, Philip 3/29/1968. U.S.A.

POST-VIETNAM ERA (1976 - 1990)
Caulfield, Joseph A. 2/25/1981, U.S.N.
Kingrey, David Scott "Tuna" "King" 7/25/1978, U.S.C.G.

GULF WARS ERA (1991 – 2007)
Pearson, Samuel Fredrick 10/10/2007, U.S.A.

Total War Deaths	
World War I	18
Post-World War I	02
World War II	103
Korean War	15
Vietnam War	19
Post-Vietnam	02
Gulf Wars	01
Total listing	160

NEWSPAPERS

The following newspapers were published in Piqua, Ohio. The list of the industrial newletters/newspapers is not intended as a complete list but only as an example of the various publications printed in the community. By the late 1990's, internets sites and blogs were replacing business and industrial newspapers.

Piqua Gazette (1820-1834) first newspaper published in Piqua
Piqua Mercury (1835)
Western Courier & Piqua Enquirer (1835-1837)
Piqua Courier & Enquirer (1837-1840)
Evangelfsche Relfgfoese Zeitschrift (1837) German language, religious
Piqua Intelligencer (1840-1841)
Piqua Register (1841-1862)
Miami Valley Register (1842-c1843)
Piqua Semi-Weekly Register (1847-1848)
Piqua Enquirer (1849-1860)
Piqua Dollar Weekly Register (1850)
Piqua Tri-Weekly Register (c1850-1854)
Piqua Weekly Register (1853-1858)
Miami County Democrat (1860-1861)
Piqua Journal (1860-1901)
Piqua Democrat (1864-1871)
Piqua Staut and Landbote (1865-1868) German language
Piqua Advertiser (1868-c1870)
Piqua Bulletin (1868)
Miami Valley News (1869-c1871)
Lilliputian (1870)
Miami Democrat (1871-1882),
Miami Helmet (1874-1911),
    Daily Bulletin (1875)
Phonetic Magazine (c1878-c1880's) educational
Der Piqua Correspondent (1878-1894) German language
Daily News (1882),
    Miami Leader (1882-1894)
Piqua Morning Call (1883)
Piqua Tribune (1883-1884)
Piqua Weekly Tribune (1883)
Piqua Daily Call (1884-present)
Piqua Daily Herald (1884)
Piqua Weekly Herald (1884)
Art Loan (1886) small entertainment
Piqua Daily Dispatch (1886-1901)
Piqua Daily Leader (1888-1901)
Piqua Evening Democrat (1888)
Der Piqua Merkur (1888) German language
Miami Observer (1888-1889)
Pythian News (1888-s1889) lodge
Buckeye Workman (1894-c1897) labor
Die Miami Post (1894-1919) German language
Miami Weekly Leader (1894-1901)
Young American (1896) small youth publication, printed on a home press by Marion Denman.
Men of Piqua (1898)
Piqua Headlight (1899)
Miami Leader-Journal (1901-1912)
Weekly Leader-Journal (1901-?)
Piqua Daily News (c1902)
Piqua Leader-Dispatch (1902-1919)
Piqua Citizen (1904)
Piqua Searchlight (1910-c1912) Socialist Party publication
Business Men's Appeal (c1912) business
Piqua News (1914-c1915)
Piqua Daily Press (1915 -1919)
May's Opera House....News (c1916) entertainment
Piqua Catholic Messenger (1917-c1918) religious
Piqua Bulletin (Dayton) (1918)
Atlas World (1919-c1920) industrial (Atlas Underwear Company)
Chatter (1919-c1920) industrial
Meteor News (1919-c1920) industrial (Meteor Motor Car Company)
Piqua Press Dispatch (1920)
Municipal Truth (1931) political
Progressive News (1934) political
Lear Log (c1943-c1945) industrial (Lear-Avia Company)
Wood Family News (c1963-c1965) industrial (Wood Shovel &

American Legion

The Memorial Day celebration was held at the Forest Hill Civil War Memorial in 1972.

The American Legion and the Piqua High School Band saluted the flag at the 1962 Veteran's Day ceremony in front of the American Legion Hall on West Water Street.

The American Legion raised the flag on Memorial Day in 1962.

Martin Bauer 1972

Order of George

Ruth Hahn 1975

Sandra Hemm 1997

Violet Das 1987

In 1978, Ray Loffer accepted the Order of George award. Clifford Alexander, the 1985 George winner, sat at Loffer's right.

Paul Gutmann 1995

Doris Perry 2002

Tool Company)
French Press (1969-1987) industrial (French Oil Mill Machinery Company)
Aero Events (1976-1990's) industrial
McDonald's McNews (c1987-1990's) business

ORDER OF GEORGE RECIPIENTS

1968	**Robert M. Hance Jr.**
1969	**Irene Ditmer** and **Robert Hartzell**
1970	**Kenneth McMaken**
1971	P.R. Thompson
1972	Martin Bauer
1973	**John D. Scarbrough** and **Charles Upton**
1974	Harold Short
1975	Ruth Hahn
1976	Samuel E. Jackson Jr.
1977	Louis W. Havenar
1978	Ray L. Loffer
1979	Beverly J. Pratt
1980	**J. Scott Garbry**
1981	**George W. Hartzell**
1982	Jean Mansfield Burner
1983	Elwood R. Penrod
1984	**Samuel H. Heitzman**
1985	Clifford R. Alexander
1986	Robert M. Davis
1987	Violet Das
1988	Thomas J. Jamieson
1989	Ralph F. Schneider
1990	Benjamin P. Scott
1991	Lucinda L. Fess
1992	Michael P. Yannucci
1993	Arthur R. Disbrow
1994	Douglas R. Murray
1995	Paul P. Gutmann
1996	James M. Robinson
1997	Sandy Hemm
1998	Tony Wendeln
1999	Henrietta Hahn
2000	Steve Staley
2001	Viola Clemens
2002	Doris Perry
2003	Karen S. Wendeln
2004	James C. Oda
2005	Cheryl Stiefel-Francis
2006	Bonnie Murray
2007	James Brown Jr.

PHOTOGRAPHERS
(1850's -1950's)

The dates are rough approximations of the time the photographers were active in Piqua.

c.1850	A. McDonald
c.1853	Isaac Davis
c.1854-1863	A. H. Rice (sold out to William McNair)
1863-1866	William McNair
1866-1867	McNair & Denman
c.1866	E. Landis
1867-1868	J. Denman (sold out to Charles Gale)
c.1867-c.1873	Robert Burge & Company
1868-1891	Charles A. Gale
1869- 1911	John R. Thorne
1884-1886	E. S. Lawson
1886-1888	Mrs. H. Lawson & Matthews
1886-c.1887	H. Meins
1888-1909	Edward W. "Dick" Matthews
c.1889-c.1890	John W. Finnell
1890	L. N. Baker
c.1897	Frank Woodmancy
c.1897	George H. Gabler
no date	_____ Owen
c.1899-c.1916	John M. Lloyd
c.1902-c.1906	William C. Rogers
c.1905-c.1943	**Ethan E. Huntzinger**
c.1907-c.1918	Ray L. Hunter
c.1907-c.1911	William K. VanDeGrift
1911-1941	Sylvester R. Beecher
c.1914-c.1932	Allen H. Middleswart (later worked for Huntzinger)
c.1920	Ralph M. Godfrey
c.1920	Violet Ray Studio (Oscar D. Berg, manager)
1923-c.1924	Lawrence C. Marble
c.1926-c.1939	George D. Crane
1931-c.1932	Lorstan Studios (Russell W. Henry, manager)
c.1936-c.1938	Norris G. Nolan
c.1939-c.1946	Adrian H. Cissna (Favorite Studio)
c.1939-c.1948	Paul Kiefer
c.1940-c.1941	Olan Mills Portrait Studio
c.1941	K. Max Smith
c.1943-c.1948	Earl R. Baker
1947-c.1954	James English, Homer English, A. Jerry Shoemaker (English Studio)
c.1947-c.1955	Raymond Step Lange
c.1948-c.1977	Roger E. Miller (Custom Photographic Service)
c.1950-c.1953	Paul R. Klasterman
c.1955-c.1981	A. Jerry Shoemaker

POLICE CHIEFS

TOWN MARSHALL (Elected)

Robert Shannon	1835-1836
John Chattam	1836-1841
Joseph Kelly	1841-1842
John Garvey	1842-1846, 1848-1849 (combined with position of marketmaster)
David Hunter	1846-1848
D.H. Freeman	1849-1850
Thomas B. Anderson	1850-1851
Samuel B. Garvey	1851-1855, 1856-1864 (1856 separated from position of Marketmaster)
John Davis	1855-1856
George Manchester	1864-1866
Christopher Klipstine	1866-1867
Isaac Clark	1867-1868
John Franz	1868-1871, 1877-1885
P.A. Steadman	1871-1877
James Livingston	1885-1891
Edward N. Mason	1891-1903

POLICE CHIEF (Appointed)

Frank Gehle	1903-1936

Frank Strickling	1937-1949
Earl McClannan	1949-1969
James Gray	1969-1975
James Huffman	1975-1980
Donald White	1981-1992
Philip Potter	1992-2004
Wayne Wilcox	2005-present

REPRESENTATIVES, STATE OF OHIO

The following Piqua citizens served in the Ohio Legislature as State Representatives for the district that included Miami County.

James Blue	1812-1813
John P. Finley	1820-1821
John McCorkle	1824-1825
David Alexander	1843-1844
Stephen Johnston	1845-1846
William Johnston	1847-1849
Mathias H. Jones	1858-1859
Samuel E. Brown	1860-1861
W. D. Alexander	1866-1867
John P. Williamson	1870-1871
William S. Garbry	1929-1932
William M. McCulloch	1933-1944
James L. Black	1945-1948
Harold L. Short	1949-1958

SCHOOL BUILDINGS

(The dates indicated the years the building was used as a school)

East School (1845-1875) 300 Block Harrison

South School (1845-1877) Wayne and Wood

North School (1845-1874) 600 block of Caldwell

Huntersville (1848-1889) 300 block of East Main

St. Boniface (1855-1890) Adams

Boone Street (1872-1885) northwest College and Boone, (segregated African-American)

Rossville (1873-1920's) Plattsville Pike

Park Avenue (1874-1925) 416 Park (also Park Avenue Annex)

Spring Street (1875-1893) northeast Spring and Ash (remodeled home)

Wayne Street (1877-1925) Wood and Wayne

North Street (1889-1981) 720 West North

Staunton Street (1889-1955) 430 Staunton (originally Huntersville School)

South Street (1890-1990's) 339 South

St. Boniface (1890-1956) northwest South Downing and Miami;

Spring Street (1894-1972) 206 East Ash

St. Mary's (1899-1970) 501 West North

Favorite Hill (c1902-c1905) 516 Cottage

Madison Avenue (1905-1925) Madison and Elm

Favorite Hill (1909-1949) 950 South

Springcreek (1922-present) 145 East U. S. Route 36 (originally township school)

Bennett (1925-present) 625 South Main

Wilder (1925-present) 1120 Nicklin

Park Avenue Annex (1925-1957) 416 Park (Piqua Catholic)

Washington (1935-present) 800 Sunset (originally Township School)

Staunton Street (1955-1980's) 430 Staunton

Favorite Hill (1955-present) 950 South Street

High Street (1956-present) 1249 High

Nicklin Avenue (1956-present) 818 Nicklin

St. Boniface (1957-present) 218 South Downing

St. Mary's Elementary (1958-present) 503 West North

Piqua Christian (1974-present) 830 Covington

Upper Valley Joint Vocational School (1975-present) 8811 Career Dr., at Looney Road

Nazarene Christian (c.1976-1980's) 400 Sunset

Seventh Day Adventist (1976-present) 4022 State Route 185

Piqua High (1981-present) 1 Indian Trail at Looney Road

Central Baptist (1983-c.1987) 500 Broadway

Piqua Holiness (1990-199_) 420 West Water

Piqua Junior High (1999-present) 1 Tomahawk Trail (next to High School)

SCHOOLS, PUBLIC, HIGH SCHOOL FOOTBALL COACHES

Edward H. Allen (attorney)	1899
John C. Crawford (dentist)	1900
C. Wallace Bassett (YMCA Physical Director)	1901-1902
LeRoy W. Hager (Piqua Ice Company)	1903-1904
Clark Libbee (occupation unknown)	1905
LeRoy W. Hager (Piqua Ice Company)	1906-1908
Otterbein A. Bailey (teacher)*	1906-1911
Walter R. Bailey	1912-1913
Merlin Ditmer	1914-1917
R.B. Patton	1918
Raymond Mote	1919-1923
Richard Hopkins	1924
George P. Wertz	1924-1950
William J. Wehr	1951
Alson Scrivner	1952-1953
Jack Bickel	1954-1957
Paul Faehl	1958-1963
Chuck Asher	1964-1977
David Cripe	1978-1979
Dave Miller	1980-1983
Steve Magoteaux	1984-1991
Bill Nees	1992-present

* All the coaches were teachers from 1906 onward.

SCHOOLS, PUBLIC, PRINCIPALS OF HIGH SCHOOL

1855 – 1879	The Superintendent also served as principal
1879 – 1901	**Mary E. Hall**
1901 – 1909	Fred E. C. Kirkendall
1909 – 1919	Daniel R. Ellabarger
1919 – 1944	**Cecil M. Sims**
1944 – 1969	Robert G. Winters
1969 – 1982	William Lester
1982 – 1997	Glen Honeycutt
1997 – present	Katherine Davisson

SEE ALSO: Superintendents of Public Schools.

SCHOOLS, PUBLIC SUPERINTENDENTS

1855 - 1855	Rev. Dr. Chauncey W. Fitch (part-time).
1856 - 1860	A. G. Chambers
1860 - 1861	Rev. Dr. C. W. Fitch.
1861 - 1862	Geo. L. Mills.
1862 - 1862	W. D. Alexander (resigned to command a Company in 110th Regt OVI)
1862 - 1866	Jonathan M. Fairbanks
1866 - 1873	William Richardson (board refused his resignation and fired him instead)
1873 - 1874	William Carter
1874 - 1907	**Charles W. Bennett** (Bennett Junior High School was named after him)
1907 - 1909	J. Reuben Beachler
1909 - 1944	**George C. Dietrich**
1944 - 1952	**Cecil M. Sims**
1952 - 1969	Wilbur Hoerner
1969 - 1975	James Wisecup
1975 - 1992	Duane Bachman
1992 - 2006	Jerry Clark
2006 - 2007	Karen Mantia (the first women superintendent)
2007 - present	Richard Hanes

Superintendents from 1855 until 1879 also served as the high school principals.

SENATORS, STATE OF OHIO

The following Piqua citizens served as Senators in the Ohio Legislature.

Robert Young	1824-1825, 1831-1832
James Johnston	1833-1834
John O'Ferrall	1844-1845
James M. Hart	1850-1851
Rankin Walkup	1852-1853
William H. Lawder	1856-1857
James M. Carson	1878-1879
Jennison Hall	1882-1883
McPherson Brown	1894-1896
Theodore Gray, Sr.	1941-1947
Theodore Gray Jr.	1951-1994
	(longest tenure in history of senate)

TOWNSHIPS, MIAMI COUNTY

	2000 Pop	Median Age	Established	Size (square miles)
Bethel	4,927	43.1	1807	34.7
Brown	1,554	36.5	1819	29.9
Concord	27,335	36.4	1807	33.0
Elizabeth	1,620	40.0	1807	29.9
Lostcreek	1,633	41.2	1818	29.9
Monroe	15,339	37.5	1818	31.2
Newberry	6,490	37.0	1819	42.2
Newton	3,354	37.6	1810	41.8
Springcreek	1,826	41.2	1814	26.3
Staunton	1,992	42.0	1819	28.3
Union	10,222	38.8	1807	48.0
Washington*	1,803	46.4	1807	29.0

*Piqua is not included as part of Washington Township.

UNDERWEAR/TEXTILE/ KNITWEAR COMPANIES

Piqua Hosiery Company (1886-1941)
Piqua Fabric Company (1894-1896)
Union Underwear Company (1895-1917)
Superior Underwear Company (1897-1951)
    BVD Inc. (1951-1967)
Piqua Underwear Company (1899-1900)
    Atlas Underwear Company (1900-1971)
    Allen-A Company (1971-1973)
    Medalist Allen-A Company (1973-1988)
    Medalist Apparel (1988-1994)
Cahill-Leonard Knitting Company (1900)
Stuart-Brown Underwear Company (1902-c1910)
    Stuart-Hance Underwear Company (c1910-1913)
Imperial Underwear Company (1909-1926)
Erlanger Knitting Mills Inc. (1928-1933)
Piqua Underwear Company (1917)
Bryan Underwear Company (1921)
Scudder Textile Company (c.1921-1935)

The Superior Underwear Company promoted its two piece men's undergarments as shown in this 1941 advertisement.

187

UNIONS

The following list of unions includes only those groups found in public listings. The dates refer to the first local listing found for a particular organization. On many of these **unions**, the date they were actually established is unknown. The 1948 *Polk City Directory* listed a number of unions for the first time.

Amalgamated Association of Iron and Steel Workers (1890)

Amalgamated Association of Steel, Tin, and Sheet Workers of North America, Piqua Lodge No. 194 (1909)

Amalgamated United Auto Workers of America, Piqua local No. 250 (1952)

American Federation of Musicians, Local No. 458 (1910) No. 576 (1948)

American Federation of Musicians, Local No. 56 (established 1918)

American Federation of State, County and Municipal Employees, Piqua Chapter

Bakers and Confectioners Local Union 142 (1948)

Barbers Local Union 971 (1948)

Bricklayers Union, Local 28 (1948)

Brotherhood of Carpenters and Joiners of American, Local No. 1920 (established 1916)

Carpenters and Joiners Union Local No. 1877 (1936)

Carpenters Local No. 190 (1911)

Central Labor Union, AFL (1930"s)

Cigar Makers Local No. 260 (1911)

Cigar Maker's International Union Local (1886)

Clerks National Protection Association No. 39 (1891)

Communication Workers of America, Local 4313 (1952)

Furniture & Upholsterers Union, Local 376 (1948)

Granite Cutters' International Association of America (1934)

International Alliance of Theatrical & Stage Employees No. 155 (1948)

International Association of Fire Fighters Union, Local 252 (1940's)

International Ladies Garment Workers, Local 172 (1948)

International Stone Cutters Union (1919)

Interurban Brotherhood of Trainmen, Local No. ___ (1917)

Iron Molders Union (1919)

Machinists Union, Lodge No. 248 (1911)

Maltsters Local No. 295 (1911)

Meat Cutters & Packing House Workers, Local 133 (established 1934)

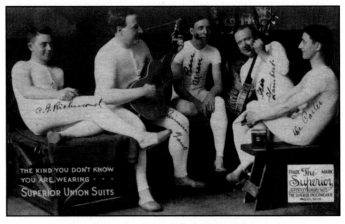

Superior Underwear Company employees and friends serving as models in this 1915 advertisement.

Metal Polishers, Buffers, Platers and Workers of North America, Local No. 4 (1906)

Miami-Shelby-Darke Counties CIO Industrial Council (1952)

Miami Valley Carpenters District Council (1947) (**May's Opera House**)

Moulders and Foudry Workers, Local 94 (1948)

National Association of Letter Carriers, Local No. 123 (established 1896)

Piqua Trade and Labor Council (1909)

Railway Trackman Local 684 (1907)

Stage Workers Local No. 155 (1911

Stationery Engineers Local No. ___ (1911)

Stove Mounters and S.P. Workers of America Local No. 23 (1898) (**Favorite Stove & Range Company**)

Teamsters, Chauffeurs & Warehousemen, Local 455 (1948)

Textile Workers of America, Local 199 (1952)

Theatrical Mechanics of America No. 61 (1907)

Toy Workers, Local 250 (1953)

Truck Drivers, Local 957, A.F.of L. (1949)

United Association of Pipe Fitters & Plumbers, Local 548 (1948)

United Automobile, Aircraft & Agricultural Implement Workers of America, Local 643, (Congress of Industrial Organizations) (1945)

United Auto Workers of America, Local 643 (1955) (**Meteor Motor Car Company**)

United Auto Workers of America, Local 827 (1952) (**Wood Shovel & Tool Company**)

United Automobile, A & A I Workers of America, Local 827, CIO (1946)

United Brotherhood of Carpenters and Joiners of America, Local 2248 (established 1919)

United Paper Workers of America, Local 195 (1952)

United Steel Workers of America, Local 6328 (1980)

United Textile Workers of America, Local No. 2251 (established 1934)

Blacksmiths are shown standing in front of their smithy in 1910.

This circa 1900 photograph shows the kitchen entrance to Johnston family home north of Piqua.

Lucy Fess, Piqua's first female city commissioner and mayor, is shown being sworn into office in 1992.

The Salvation Army tent on the Public Square was surrounded by veterans and city officials in this World War I era photograph.

The Pure Oil Service Station was located on the southwest corner of Main and North Streets in 1953. This was the former site of the O'Ferrall home.

It was great fun to cool off at the Hollow Swimming Pool in the 1950's.

Timeline

INTRODUCTION

*T*he Timeline section of this work provides a chronologically arranged listing of events relating to Piqua, Miami County and early Ohio history. The yearly and day-by-day timelines offer a wide range of events relating to local and regional history. The timeline concentrates on Piqua events and individuals (all events occurred in Piqua unless otherwise stated). A partial list of topics in the timeline includes: business, industry, religion, politics, sports, biography, military, women, population, African-Americans, charity, education, entertainment, Native Americans, immigrant groups, communication, transportation, labor and everyday events.

The Timeline is intended as a fast and brief overview pf Piqua's history. It offers an easy method of finding local anniversaries and then uniting them with national events or personalities. A more in depth review of the historical topics used in the Timeline can be found in the almanac section of this book.

Year By Year Timeline

c. 950,000 B.P.	The Nebraskan Glacier covered the entire Ohio country. (B.P. refers to Before the Present time)
c. 700,000 B.P.	The Kansan Glacier covered the entire Ohio Country.
c. 300,000 B.P.	The Illinoian Glacier covered the entire Ohio Country.
c. 100,000 B.P.	The Wisconsin Glacier covered the entire Ohio Country.
c. 12,500 B.P.	The receding Wisconsin Glacier filled in the valley created by the Teays River, which at one time had been wider than the entire state of Ohio.
10,000 B.C. – 8,000 B.C.	The Paleo-Indian Period saw the first inhabitants of the Upper Miami Valley after the Ice Age. The Paleo-Indian peoples hunted big game..
8,000 B.C. – 1,000 B.C.	During the Archaic Period agriculture began in the Ohio Valley.
5,000 B.C. – 1,000 B.C.	During the Archaic Period, the Glacial Kame People were hunting, gathering and burying their dead in Ohio.
900 B.C. – 100 B.C.	The Adena Peoples are best known for their effigy mounds in Ohio.
100 B.C. – 500 A.D.	The Hopewell Peoples developed complex trading routes and built geometric earthworks).
300 A.D. – 900 A.D.	The Late Woodland Period saw intrusive and transitional Cultures develop in the Ohio Valley.
900 A.D. – 1600 A.D.	The Fort Ancient Peoples were the last prehistoric culture in the Miami Valley. They built palisade walls around their small villages and created platform mounds.
1670	The French explorer La Salle discovered the Ohio River.
Early 1700's	The Miami Tribe began moving into the Ohio Country.
1720's	The Shawnee Tribe began moving into the Ohio Country.

1747	Old Britain and the Twightwee Band of the Miami Indians established the village of Pickawillany with the aid of English traders.
1748	George Croghan visited Pickawillany as a representative of the Colony of Pennsylvania.
1749	Celoron visited Pickawillany as a representative of New France (French Canada).
1750	Christopher Gist visited Pickawillany as a representative of the Ohio Company of Virginia.
1752	Charles Langdale and a band of Indians destroyed Pickawillany on the orders of the French commander at Fort Detroit. The Twightwee Clan dispersed into the Indiana area. Captain William Trent visited the site of Pickawillany shortly after it was destroyed.
1763	The Treaty of Paris ended the French and Indian War bringing peace to the Miami Valley.
1774	The Quebec Act extended the boundaries of British Canada south to the Ohio River.
1780	Captain Henry Bird's British Expedition marched south from Detroit to the Ohio River by way of the Miami Valley.
1780	General George Rogers Clark destroyed the Piqua Clan village on the Mad River west of Springfield. The surviving member of this Shawnee clan together with members from other Shawnee Clans moved west to the Great Miami River and established the villages of Upper and Lower Piqua.
1782	General George Rogers Clark (second Expedition) destroyed the villages of Upper and Lower Piqua and the trading post of Peter Loramie (Shelby County). The Shawnee fled into northern Ohio.
1783	The Treaty of Paris ended the American Revolutionary War. The Ohio Territory was transferred to the newly independent United States.
1785	A Land Ordinance was passed by the Articles of Confederation Congress which allowed for the first survey of the Ohio Country. The ordinance divided the area into rectangular surveying townships
1787	The Northwest Territory Ordinance was passed by the Articles of Confederation Congress giving the Ohio

	Country its first organized American government
1788	John Cleve Symmes purchased the land between the Great and Little Miami Rivers.
	The Hilliard family moved to North Bend on the Ohio River from New Jersey.
	The first permanent European-American community in Ohio was established at Marietta on the Ohio River.
1789	The Treaty of Fort Harmar was signed.
1790	General Harmar marched north from Cincinnati in a campaign against the Ohio Indians. His army passed through the future site of Piqua.
1791	A fort was established at Greene Ville.
1792	Israel Ludlow finished surveying the Symmes purchase.
	General "Mad" Anthony Wayne was appointed commander of the military in the Northwest Territory.
1793	General Wayne built and garrisoned a supply post at the site of Upper Piqua, known as Fort Piqua.
	John Johnson delivered supplies to the garrison at Fort Piqua.
1794	The Battle of Fallen Timbers resulted in the defeat of Chief Blue Jacket by General Anthony Wayne.
1795	The treaty of Greene Ville was signed.
	The village of Dayton was founded by Jonathon Dayton.
1796	Job Gard dismantled the abandoned Fort Piqua and built a cabin in the bend of the Great Miami River at the future site of Piqua.
1797	John Hilliard and his sons settled on the east side of the Great Miami River in what would become Springcreek Township.
1798	Dutch Station (Staunton Township) was established under the leadership of John Knoop.
1799	John Manning purchased the claim of Job Gard.
	John Hilliard laid out a small village east of the Great Miami River but it was never developed.
1800	Elias Manning was the first European-American settler born in Piqua.
1801	The religious "Great Revival" of the West began in Kentucky.
1802	Colonel John Johnston was appointed factor at the Fort Wayne Indian Agency.
1803	Ohio entered the union as the seventeenth state.
1804	Colonel John Johnston purchased farm land north of Piqua.
	John Manning established the county's first industry, a grist mill.
1805	Charles Manning built a distillery on the flood plain east of the Great Miami River.
	The first recorded flood in the Upper Miami Valley hit Piqua. (April).
1806	The village of Staunton was platted out.
	Alexander Ewing built the first tavern north of Dayton in what would become Piqua.
1807	Miami County was organized from the northern portion of Montgomery County.
	Washington Township was one of the original townships formed in the new county.
	Armstrong Brandon platted out the village of Washington (later Piqua) on the land of John Manning and Matthew Caldwell.
	The village of Troy was platted out to serve as the county seat.
1808	The Miami County court met for the first time at the Overfield Tavern in Troy.
1809	Piqua's first school was established.
	Charles and Joseph Hilliard planted the county's first orchard.
	Darke County was organized from the western portion of Miami County.
	Colonel John Johnston was appointed Indian Agent at Fort Wayne in the Indiana Territory.
1810	A log block house was built on south side of Water Street east of Main for protection from potential Indian attacks.
1811	A Post Office was established at "Piquatown".
1812	Colonel John Johnston was appointed as the Federal Indian Agent for Ohio and the Indiana Territory. He moved the agency moved to Johnston's Farm at Upper Piqua.
	The United States declared war on Great Britain beginning the War of 1812.
	The Council of Piqua was held at Johnston's Farm at Upper Piqua.
	General William Henry Harrison established Camp Washington at Johnston's Farm.
1813	Henry and Barbara Dilbone killed by Indians.
1814	The Treaty of Ghent ended the War of 1812.
	The Second Treaty of Greenville was signed.
1815	A Methodist Church building was erected at Johnston's Farm.
1816	Village of Washington's name was officially changed to Piqua.
1817	The Treaty of Miami Rapids was signed.
1818	The Piqua Female Bible Society was organized.
	The Treaty of St. Mary's was signed (September).
1819	Shelby County was organized from the northern portion of Miami County.
1820	The population of Piqua was 350.
	The first permanent Piqua bridge over the Great Miami River was erected.
	Piqua's first newspaper, the *Piqua Gazette* was published.
1821	The first industrial organization was established by local sawmill owners.
1822	The Route of the Piqua-Urbana Road moved northwest to connect with Ash Street.
1823	Piqua was incorporated as a town.
1824	The Spring Street Methodist Meeting House was dedicated (June).
1825	Population of Piqua was listed in the newspaper at 348.
	Work began on the Miami Canal from Cincinnati to Dayton.
1826	The Piqua Colonization Society established.
1827	The Great Squirrel Hunt was held (October).
1828	First hot air balloon ascent was held in town.
1829	The Thespian Association of Piqua was established by local amateur actors.
	John McElvain replaced John Johnston as the regional Federal Indian Agent.
1830	The population of Piqua was 488.
1831	Piqua Temperance Society was established (July).
1832	Doctor E. Taylor opened his practice as the town's first regular dentist.
1833	A Cholera Epidemic hit Piqua.
1834	David Hunter opened the town's first grocery store.
1835	The *Western Courier and Piqua Enquirer* began publication.
	John Suttle established the town's first brewery.
	Robert Smith, a barber, established the town's first

African-American business.

1836 The Piqua Land Office moved to Lima.

The Fort Wayne and Piqua Railway Company was incorporated but never constructed.

1837 The Miami Extension Canal reached Piqua from Dayton and Cincinnati.

1838 The Lock Mill was established at Lock Nine. It later became known as the Piqua Milling Company.

The Village of Huntersville was platted out.

The A. Thoma Jewelry Store was established.

1839 The Reliance [Volunteer] Fire Company No. 1 was organized.

1840 The village of Rossville was platted out. The population of Piqua was 1,480.

1841 The *Piqua Register* began publication.

1842 The Miami Extension Canal (later the Miami and Erie Canal) reached St. Marys.

1843 The first Catholic cemetery was established on North Street.

The Wesleyan Methodist Episcopal Church was incorporated (November).

1844 The Piqua and St. Mary's Turnpike Road Company was incorporated (November).

1845 Piqua's first town hall was built on the east side of the Public Square.

The Miami and Erie Canal opened from Cincinnati north to Toledo.

1846 The Piqua Cemetery Association was incorporated (January).

The State Legislature authorized the established of the Dayton, Charleston and Piqua Turnpike (February).

The manumitted Randolph Slaves from Virginia settled in Rossville.

1847 The Great Miami River overflowed its banks and washed away two bridges.

The Piqua Branch of the State Bank of Ohio, later known as the Piqua National Bank, was established.

1848 A Flour and Whiskey Inspector was appointed by the Piqua Village Council.

The First Baptist Church on High Street was erected.

1849 The Columbus, Piqua and Indiana Railroad Company was organized. It later became part of the Pennsylvania Railroad.

1850 The population of Piqua was 3,277.

The Piqua and St. Mary's Turnpike Company was organized.

Piqua reincorporated as a city of the second class.

The Market House was erected on the west side of the Public Square.

The first telegraph lines were strung between Piqua and Troy.

1851 The City Council authorized the Columbus, Piqua and Indiana Railroad to use Sycamore Street for their tracks.

1852 The Grace Methodist Episcopal Church was established.

Piqua suffered through a severe winter, with January temperatures hitting fifteen to twenty degrees below zero.

Mayor Elliott was given permission by the city council to shoot the pigeons roosting on the City Hall.

1853 The Cyrene African Methodist Church was established.

The city voted to establish a Union (High School) System.

The first Piqua Board of Managers of Public Schools was elected (later Board of Education)

Mr. Bevins was hired by the city to draw a new map of the city. He re-numbered all of the existing city lots creating a lot of confusion until the city went back to original lot numbers during the Civil War.

1854 The Dayton and Michigan Railroad began operations with tracks just east of Piqua. It would later become part of the Baltimore and Ohio Railroad system.

D.A. Silver built a stone arch bridge over the canal at Ash Street. The bridge was demolished in 1901

1855 The Piqua Artificial Gas Company was organized to provide Piqua with its first street lights.

1856 The city's first Union School (High School) opened to students.

William Schroerluke established the city's first mayor cigar factory.

The city council banned the use of fireworks and bonfires with the city limits.

1857 The Park Avenue Baptist Church was organized in Rossville.

1858 The Ladies Union Relief Society was organized (January).

College Street was extended south from High Street to what is now Covington Avenue.

1859 The Dayton and Michigan Railroad began regular runs between Dayton and Toledo.

1860 The population of Piqua was 4,643.

The Western Union Telegraph began operations in Piqua.

1861 The Miami and Erie Canal was leased to a private company.

Company F, Eleventh Regiment, Ohio Volunteer Infantry, was the first Piqua unit raised during the Civil War.

1862 Camp Piqua was officially established on the Johnston Farm. The 94th and 110th Regiments, OVI, were mustered into service at this location.

1863 A mass rally was held on the Public Square by the Union Party (October).

1864 Abraham Lincoln received sixty-one per cent of the vote in Piqua.

1865 The Citizens National Bank was organized.

The *Piqua Staut and Landbote* began publication of the city's second German language newspaper.

1866 The Sterling Club was organized as city's first baseball team.

A major flood hit the city.

1867 The Huntersville Bridge was rebuilt after it was damaged in a flood.

The Colored Men's Cooperative Trade Association was established (September).

1868 The city's first regular police force was established.

Forest Hill Cemetery was formally laid out.

1869 The Leopold Kiefer Company was organized to manufacture cigars.

1870 The population of Piqua was 5,967.

1871 The Border City Building and Loan Company was organized.

1872 The city's first and only segregated black school building was erected on College Street.

Conover's Opera House on the southeast corner of the public square opened to the public.

1873 Park Avenue Public School was opened to elementary students.

1874
The Zion German Reformed Church was organized.

The Western Ohio Fair Association was organized with a race track at Fountain Park.

The *Miami Helmet* began publication as the city's first temperance newspaper.

1875
Company D, "Kiefer Guards", Third Regiment, Ohio National Guard was organized.

1876
Piqua Board of Trade was established, the predecessor of the Chamber of Commerce.

1877
The first YMCA was organized, but it disbanded in 1881.

1878
The State of Ohio resumed active control of the Miami and Erie Canal.

1879
The Peoples' Library Association was established (July).

The Hunterville Volunteer Fire Department was organized.

H.F. Ernest is credited with setting off the first dynamite charge in Piqua.

1880
The population of Piqua was 6,031.

1881
The Cron-Kills Furniture Company was established as Huntersville's second furniture factory.

The Miami County Agricultural Society turned down Piqua's request to hold the County Fair every other year at Fountain Park.

1882
The first telephone system in the city became operational.

P.A. Becker opened an art school in Piqua.

1883
The Piqua Edison Electric Illuminating Company was organized to provide electrical power to the city.

The Great Miami River once again overflowed its banks.

The *Piqua Morning Call* began publication and later changed its name to the *Piqua Daily Call*.

1884
The Ladies Aid Society organized as a city-wide charitable group.

The Third Building and Loan Company was organized.

The city's second High School was erected on College Street on the site of the first High School.

The first electric lights were turned on in the city (May).

1885
A severe winter hit the city with March temperatures near zero degrees.

1886
The Piqua Hosiery Company, one of the city's first underwear companies, was established.

Goodrich Giles was the city's first black citizen to run for a seat on the city council.

A local Knights of Labor Lodge was organized in Piqua.

1887
Free home mail delivery began in Piqua.

The Third National Bank was organized.

1888
Natural gas was first piped to the city by the Mercer Gas and Fuel Company.

The Favorite Stove and Range Company moved to Piqua from Cincinnati.

1889
The Cincinnati Corrugating Company, manufacturers of tin ceilings and roofs moved to Piqua.

North Street Elementary School was erected.

The Huntersville School was erected on Staunton Street.

The Saint Boniface Parochial School was erected on South Downing Street.

1890
The Piqua Electric Street Railway Company began operations (January).

The population of Piqua was 9,090.

The Piqua Humane Society was organized.

The Schmidlapp Free School Library opened as a public library.

A stone jail was erected off of Wayne Street behind the Fire Station and the Plaza Hotel. It contained five iron cells.

1891
The Hotel Plaza on the public square opened for business.

The second YMCA formally organized (December)

The Australian style ballot was used for the first time in Ohio during the fall elections.

1892
Conover's Opera House was destroyed in a fire.

1893
The Miami Valley Electric Railway Company began operations from Piqua to Troy.

The Ladies Aid Society was reorganized into the Associated Charities.

Basketball was introduced in Piqua at the YMCA.

A small-pox epidemic hit Piqua and all school children were vaccinated.

1894
The Village of Huntersville was annexed by the City of Piqua.

The new YMCA building opened to the public.

Women were allowed to vote in Ohio for members of the Board of Education for the first time.

The city purchased the Manning Mill Race in East Piqua and built a brick storm sewer in its place before filling it in and calling the area Race Street.

1895
Main Street from the railroad north to the river was paved with brick by Gantz & Sullivan.

Iron hoist bridges were placed on the canal at North and Greene Streets.

The Union Underwear Company was organized.

1896
The area experienced very heavy rains all summer.

1897
The Great Miami River overflowed its banks.

The Superior Underwear Company was organized.

The Callender Telephone began manufacturing telephone exchanges in Piqua.

1898
The city suffered its worst flood to date.

1899
The first Piqua Historical Society was incorporated.

The Piqua Home Telephone Company was organized as the city's second telephone system.

1900
The population of Piqua was 12,172

Will Lorimer bought the city's first automobile.

A band stand was erected on the public square.

The Atlas Underwear Company was organized.

1901
The Piqua Savings Bank was organized.

The city's first automobile accident occurred at the corner of Main and Ash Streets.

The Dayton, Covington & Piqua Traction Company was organized (January).

1902
The Stuart-Brown Underwear Company was incorporated.

The Wood Shovel and Tool Company was organized in Piqua.

1903
The Western Ohio Traction Company began operations between Piqua and Lima.

Company C, Third Infantry Regiment, Ohio National Guard, transferred to Piqua.

May's Opera House opened to the public.

1904
The Colonial Saxony, the city's first apartment building, was completed.

1905
The Ball Memorial Hospital was officially dedicated.

1906
May's Opera House presented the city's first vaudeville act (February).

Hartzell Company

1900 was a year of economic development for Piqua with the formation of the Atlas Underwear Company, the Hartzell Company and the Orr Felt and Blanket Company.

Atlas Underwear Company

Orr Felt & Blanket Company

The city's first motion picture theater, *The Star*, opened to the public (July).

Midway Park located between Piqua and Troy was torn down.

1907 The first Piqua Retail Merchants Association was organized.

Fountain Park was purchased by the city.

1908 The German-American Alliance was formed in the city (July).

Frances Orr was the first woman to be elected to the Board of Education.

1909 The Zig's Motion Picture Theater on North Main Street opened to the public.

The first Favorite Hill School was built.

The Imperial Underwear Company was organized.

1910 Population of Piqua was 13,388.

1911 The YMCA organized a Boy Scout troop.

The Miami Granite and Marble Company was incorporated.

1912 The three major presidential candidates campaigned in Piqua, Theodore Roosevelt, William Howard Taft, and Woodrow Wilson.

The Pennsylvania Railroad began construction of the East-West railroad elevation through Piqua.

The Piqua Historical Society was re-established.

1913 The worst flood in the history of the state of Ohio swept through Piqua and the Miami Valley (March).

1914 The city's third High School was formally dedicated.

The Rotary Club of Piqua organized.

1915 A new Federal Building (Post Office) was completed.

1916 The first Piqua Chamber of Commerce was organized.

Company C, Ohio National Guard was activated and sent to the Mexican-U.S. border (June).

1917 The Police Department obtains its first motorized patrol cars.

The city's first and only socialist mayor, Frank Hamilton, was elected.

The Meteor Motor Car Company began production of phonographs.

The Piqua Chapter of the American Red Cross was organized at the beginning of America's involvement in World War I.

The Piqua Underwear Company was incorporated (July).

1918 Boy Scouts were reintroduced in Piqua (February).

Anti-German hysteria led to German language textbooks being stolen from the High School and publicly burned on the playground of Spring Street Elementary School.

The national Influenza Epidemic hit the city.

A Mausoleum at Forest Hill Cemetery was erected.

1919 The YWCA was organized.

With the end of World War I a local American Legion Post was formed (October).

The Miami Conservancy District completed the earthen Lockington Dam.

1920 The population of Piqua was 15,044.

National Prohibition took effect in Piqua.

Women voted for the first time in a presidential election.

The Atlas Underwear Company opened a new plant in Urbana and the Superior Underwear Company opened one in Bradford.

1921 The Piqua Municipal Court was created by the Ohio Legislature (April).

The Miami Conservancy District finished the flood control levees in Piqua.

1922 The Meteor Motor Car Company began manufacturing radios.

1923 The Piqua Planning Commission was organized.

Lange's Swimming Pool on Water Street at Spring Street was opened to the public

1924 The Piqua Dance Hall War began.

The second Piqua Community Players Club, a local theater group, was organized (July).

The Red Top Cab Company of Lima began operations in Piqua.

1925 Bennett and Wilder Junior High Schools were erected.

The Church of the Brethren was established on Boal Aveneue.

1926 The Miami and Erie Canal was filled in from Water Street north to the Great Miami River.

The City Water Treatment Plant was formally dedicated (October).

The East Ash Street Bridge was formally dedicated (October).

1927 A new Fire Station on Water Street was completed.

The remodeled old Fire Station on Water street become the new City Building.

1928 A brick City Market House was erected on South Downing Street.

The Meteor Car Company began building motor speed boats.

1929 The Ohio Theater was dedicated on the corner of Main and Greene Streets (September).

1930 The population of Piqua was 16,009.

The City Council/Mayor changed to the City Commission/City Manager form of government.

The Citizens National Bank was robbed.

1931 The remodeled Piqua Club opened as the Flesh Public Library.

The local Ohio National Guard Armory was formally dedicated.

1932 The Miami County Non-Partisan Taxpayers' League was organized (November).

1933 The Municipal Power Plant began operations.

The last independent movie theater, The Favorite, closed.

1934 The Central Labor Union of Piqua, American Federation of Labor, organized fourteen new unions.

1935 The Pioneer Rural Electric Co-Operative was organized (June).

The Piqua Hosiery Company began production of the *La Bourrasque* woman's bathing suit using the new elastic Lastex yarn.

1936 The Piqua Kiwanis Club was chartered.

The American Pullmatch Company was organized (June).

The city's first steel house was erected at 518 Vine Street (September).

1937 Battery E, 135th Field Artillery, Ohio National Guard was organized.

1938 Piqua celebrated the Sesqui-Centennial of the Northwest Territory.

1939 The Works Progress Administration (WPA) approves $35,000 for the Roosevelt Stadium Project on Ash Street (May).

1940 The population of Piqua was 16,049

The Miami County Selective Service Board #1 was established in Piqua.

Piqua Boy Scout Maynard Cherington contemplates the flood damage in East Piqua.

1913
A Year of Disaster

Below:
The devastation of Shawnee is evident in this photograph showing damage on First Street.

The Willow Cottage in Rossville was destroyed in the flood.

The local Ohio National Guard units were activated for one year of training.

1941 Lear Avia Inc. moved to Piqua.

1941 The Tyke Toy Company was organized to manufacture plastic baby toys.

The Atlas Underwear Company purchased the Allen-A Company of Wisconsin.

1942 Air raid and blackout drills were begun by the Piqua Civilian Defense Council.

Captain Don Gentile shot down his first German plane (August).

1943 The Victory Heights Federal Housing Project begun on the west edge of the city.

1944 Captain Don Gentile became the highest scoring fighter pilot in America history.

1945 The Meteor Motor Car Company began manufacturing bodies for Reo busses.

Lear Inc. closed down its Piqua plant and moved to Michigan (August).

1946 The Piqua Machine and Manufacturing Company was incorporated by former Lear Avia Company employees to produced small electric motors.

The Piqua Sesquicentennial (1796-1946) celebrations were held.

1947 The first Piqua Community Chest Drive was held (May).

Radio Station WPTW went on the air.

The Veterans Administration Contact Office opened in Piqua.

1948 Thoma & Sons Jewelry Store began selling the city's first television sets.

The House of Lowell moved to Piqua and began manufacturing cosmetics.

1949 Work began on the construction of a new Favorite Hill School.

1950 The population of Piqua was 17,447.

All Metal Products Company moved to Piqua and began producing metal toys.

A major snow storm hit Piqua dumping over fourteen and a half inches of snow.

1951 The Superior Underwear Company purchased the B.V.D. underwear franchise.

WPTW Radio opened a Greenville remote broadcasting studio.

Sefton Fibre Company began operations in the city producing cardboard containers

1952 Inland Homes was incorporated and began producing prefabricated houses.

Battery C, 136th Field Artillery, Ohio National Guard was activated during the Korean War.

1953 The Schines Miami Theater (formerly May's Opera House) closed.

Mote Park Community Center was dedicated (July).

The Dettmer Convalescent Hospital opened halfway between Piqua and Troy.

1954 The local National Guard units were released from active service.

1955 A new District Five, Ohio State Highway Patrol Headquarters was opened east of Piqua.

1956 Miami and Ohio Universities began jointly offering off-campus college classes at the Piqua High School.

1957 The Rose-Derry Ohio Company moved to Piqua to produce baby mattresses.

1958 The Piqua Academic Center was established by Miami University.

1959 The Champion Paper Specialties Inc. began operations.

1960 The population of Piqua was 19,219.

The Pennsylvania Railroad passenger station was closed.

1961 The Piqua telephone system changed from PR-3 prefix to 773 (March).

1962 Dixie Highway was officially renamed County Road 25-A (July).

1963 The nuclear reactor first produced steam for the City Power Plant (November).

The new YMCA building dedicated.

The Post Office introduced the zip code 45356 for Piqua (July).

1964 The Blue Magic Company of Ohio Inc. moved to city.

1965 The Valley Antenna Systems brought cable television to city.

1966 The nuclear reactor closed down (January).

1967 The Superior Mills, B.V.D. Inc. on North Downing Street closed down.

The Piqua Airport was expanded to handle small business jets (October).

1968 Wright State University took over the administration of the Piqua Academic Center.

Washington and Springcreek Township Schools merged with the Piqua School District.

1969 Construction begun on the expansion of the Sunset Shopping Center.

Construction begun on the new Piqua East Mall.

1970 The population of Piqua was 20,741.

The Union Fork and Hoe Company, Uniwood Division, closed down its local plants (formerly Wood Shovel & Tool Co.).

1971 The Atlas Underwear Company became the Allen-A Company.

1972 A new YWCA building was dedicated (April).

The Piqua Historical Area on the Johnston Farm was formally dedicated (September).

The Crayex Corporation was founded to produce plastic wrap.

1973 The Edison State General and Technical College was chartered by the State of Ohio.

1974 The Piqua Ohio Development Corporation (PODC) organized to promote change in Piqua.

1975 The Upper Valley Joint Vocational School was opened to students from the surrounding area.

1976 Piqua celebrated the Bicentennial of the Declaration of Independence.

The third Piqua Historical Society was established.

1977 Natural gas (D. P. & L.) shortages and extremely cold temperatures caused school, business and industry closings (January-February).

1978 A blizzard hits city with heavy snow and winds in excess of seventy miles per hour.

1979 The Miller-Meteor Company closed down its operations in Piqua.

1980 The population of Piqua was 20,150.

The Val Decker Packing Company closed down all its operations.

A Grand Opening was held for the Piqua Office of Winters National Bank (December).

1981 The fourth Piqua High School was dedicated on the east edge of the city.

1982 The first Piqua Heritage Festival held on the grounds of the Piqua Historical Area.

This is the east side of North Main Street showing the 400 block.

Piqua's Downtown in 1946

Despite the economic hardships that hit the city after the war, Piqua's downtown in 1946 was active and thriving.

This is the east side of North Wayne Street showing the 100 block.

This is the west side of North Main Street showing the 400 block.

This is the east side of North Main Street showing the 200 block.

1983   The Rossville Historical Museum and Cultural Center was opened.

The first Piqua Historical Preservation Committee was organized (February).

Joanna Hill became the first woman to hold the office of president of the Piqua Chamber of Commerce.

1984   President Ronald Reagan passed through Piqua on the CSX Railroad (formerly B&O Railroad).

Centel Cable Television Company of Ohio was assigned the city's C.A.T.V. franchise.

1985   The Conrail tracks (east-west) were removed from the railroad elevation.

1986   Company B, 12th Military Police Battalion, Ohio Military Reserve was organized (January).

The Community Swimming Pool at Eisenhower Park was dedicated

A dedication of Don Gentile Statue was held on the square (July).

Piqua's first Claude Dupin Crusade was held at the football stadium on East Ash Street (August).

Miami Citizens and Heritage National Banks merged and became The Citizens Heritage Bank (November).

1987   A groundbreaking was held for a new Technical Education building on the campus of Edison State Community College.

1988   Heritage National Bank merged with Fifth Third Bancorp of Cincinnati.

The Piqua and Troy Red Cross Chapters merged to form the Miami County, Ohio Chapter.

The Miami Valley Center Mall opened.

1989   The Flesh Public Library took over the management of the Piqua Historical Museum on North Main Street.

The Nippon Food Store, the city's first retail Japanese business, opened on East Ash Street.

1990   The population of Piqua was 20,612

Dawn Blake became the city's first female police officer.

Over three thousand residents were evacuated from their homes in response to a bomb scare on Vine Street.

1991   The 1487th Transportation Detachment, Ohio National Guard was federalized during the First Persian Gulf War and sent to Saudi Arabia.

The city began tearing down the east-west railroad elevation.

1992   Lucy Fess took office as the city's first female city commissioner and mayor.

Battalion Headquarters, 12th MP Battalion, Ohio Military Reserve, was transferred to Dayton. The 122nd MP Support Company was established and remained in Piqua. (September).

The Great Outdoor Underwear Festival sold autographed boxer shorts from Republican President George Bush and Democratic Candidate Bill Clinton (October).

1993   The Aerovent Fan Company closed down.

Medalist Apparel closed their Piqua plant and moved to Sidney. The Sidney plant closed in 1995.

1994   The Medalist (Atlas) plant was torn down (May).

1995   The Piqua Civic Hall of Fame inducted its first three honorees, Robert Hartzell, William McCulloch, and John Johnston (January)

The Junior World Barefoot Waterskiing Championship was held on the Great Miami River east of the Bennett School Building (August).

Washington Township was formally separated from the City of Piqua. This left Piqua the only community in the county not to be situated within the boundaries of a township.

1996   People's Bank of Troy announces the opening of a Piqua office at 124 West High Street (November)

Piqua's telephone area code changed from 513 to 937 (September).

1997   Linda S. Gheen became the city's first female fire fighter and paramedic.

1998   Lock Nine Park on Water Street at Spring Street was formally dedicated.

1999   The new Junior High School was dedicated.

2000   The population of Piqua was 20,738

Vietnam War hero William Pitsenbarger was awarded the Medal of Honor. (December).

2001   The Linear Park bike trail on the abandoned Pennsylvania Railroad tracks and French Park on West Water Street, were dedicated (May).

The new High School Alexander Stadium and Purke Field were dedicated (August).

The new Municipal Complex (City Hall) on Water Street was dedicated (November).

The second Claude Dupin Crusade was held at the old football stadium on Ash Street.

2002   Downtown Piqua began a major revitalization program using a $400,000 Community Development Block Grant.

2003   Kathy Rank of Piqua was named as the Ohio Teacher of the Year.

2004   Police Chief Phil Potter and City Manager Mark Rohr left Piqua for out-of-state jobs.

The Readmore Hallmark store massively remodeled the old theater on the southwest corner of Main and Greene Streets.

A new Kroger Super Store (grocery) was opened at 1923 Covington Avenue.

2005   For the first time in the city's political history a team of candidates ran for openings on the Piqua Board of Education. Mimi Crawford, Andy Hite and Bob Luby ran and were elected as representatives of a community group known as Learning Can Happen.

Fred Enderle was selected as Piqua's new City Manager.

2006   The 1850's Farrington Grain Elevator at 101 South Main Street was completely destroyed by fire (May).

Lisa Whitaker became the first women to become president (staff) of the Piqua Area Chamber of Commerce (July).

2007   Piqua celebrated the Bicentennial (1807-2007) of its founding.

Work began on the restoration of the Plaza Hotel on the public square. (January)

Edison Community College dedicated a new library and nursing education complex known as the Emerson Center (May).

Judith Bardo

Travis Boose

Joseph W. Brown

Maggie Clark

Representative Citizens in the 1990's

Stanley Harrison

Matthew Smith

Colombe Nicholas

Dr. Jack Steinhilber

Dr. Kenneth Yowell

Matthew Williams

This Baltimore & Ohio steam locomotive came through the Piqua during the World War I era.

This gentleman is attempting to play tennis during the second decade of the twentieth century.

Piqua's Chautauqua in 1918 was held in Fountain Park.

Day By Day Timeline

The Elk's band traveled to Denver, Colorado in 1937. Director Phil Gates is pictured on the right.

ELKS BAND

NATIONAL CHAMPIONS 1935

An advertisement for the Elgin Tractor Company in 1917.

01　1784　Pioneer settler Joseph Hilliard was born in New Jersey.

　　　1838　The Volunteer German Engine Company (fire fighters) was formally organized.

　　　1884　The first issue of the *Piqua Daily Call* was published.

02　1916　William King Boal, owner and founder of the Favorite Stove & Range Company died in Piqua.

03　1883　A meteor was sighted at 8:00 P.M. over Piqua.

　　　1890　This was the first day of operation for the Piqua Street Railway Company.

04　1915　The motorization of the city Fire Department was authorized.

05　1823　Saint James Episcopal Church was organized.

　　1909　Mrs. Frances M. Orr was elected vice president of the Board of Education.

　　1942　The Piqua Civil Defense Council was organized.

06　1930　Lester G. Whitney was appointed as the city's first City Manager.

07　1819　Shelby County was formed from the northern portions of Miami County.

　　1886　The city was officially divided into six wards.

　　1952　The announcement was made of the formation of the Piqua Heavier-Than-Air-Society.

08　1860　Airhart Marion Fry, a prominent local builder and contractor was born.

09　1820　George S. Clark, a local machinist, grocer and bridge tender was born in Dayton, Ohio.

10　1887　The Kitts Low Water Alarm Company was organized.

11　1883　The Piqua Reading Room Association was established.

12　1935　Miller & Fry received the contract to build the Washington Township School.

13　1899　The Piqua Underwear Company, later know as the Atlas Underwear Company was incorporated.

14　1928　Maurice Wolfe became the president of both Meteor Motor Car Co. and the Favorite Stove & Range Company.

15　1883　The *Piqua Tribune* was established.

　　1952　Battery C, 136th Field Artillery, ONG was federalized during Korean War.

16　1882　T. H. Foley opened the Business Night School.

17　1827　The *Piqua Gazette* ran an advertisement for a one cent reward for the return of a runaway apprentice.

18　1849　James D. Keyt, an early Piqua brick mason, died on this date.

19　1882　Company F of the Ohio National Guard, better known as the Wikoff Guards, held a masquerade ball in Piqua.

　　1905　A mini-smallpox epidemic broke out at the Per Diue Boarding House.

20　1901　The Wayne Street United Brethren Church was dedicated.

　　1913　Mrs. Rachel Johnston Davies, an early Piqua pioneer died at the age of one hundred.

21　1908　The Piqua Club, on the northeast corner of Greene and Wayne Streets held a Grand Opening of its new home.

　　1967　Air Force Major William Baugh was shot down and captured by the North Vietnamese.

22　1902　The Stuart-Brown Underwear Company was incorporated.

23　1918　The Elgin Tractor Company moved to Piqua.

24　1952　Horace Lilley, a local attorney and the city's solicitor died on this date.

25　1886　The Art Loan Exhibit opened to the public in a private home on West Ash Street.

26　1898　David M. Fleming, the editor of the *Piqua Journal* died on this date.

27　1877　Cummings Scudder, a local contractor died on this date.

　　1886　Henry Flesh was elected president of the Miami & Erie Canal Association.

28　1887　The Grand Army of the Republic, a Civil War veterans organization, opened a public reading room.

29　1899　Lodge No. 152, BPOE (Elks) was established.

30　1888　Nationally known poet, James Whitcomb Riley read his own poetry at the Presbyterian Church.

31　1942　The Church of God was the first church in the city to offer a free Sunday bus service for its congregational members.

The Piqua Club shown in this 1910 postcard was located on the northeast corner of West Greene and North Wayne Streets.

01	1930	The Piqua City Bus service began operations.
02	1926	Lieutenant Jimmy Doolittle, while serving at McCook Field in Dayton spoke to the Piqua Rotary Club. He would become one of heroes of World War II.
03	1893	A meeting of the [Ladies] Amusement Club was held
	1905	Isaac Morris, publisher and editor of the *Miami Helmet* died on this date.
04	1930	The Dayton and Troy traction line ended local electric street car service.
	1952	The Ohio State Highway Patrol Post 55 moved from Troy to Piqua.
	1963	Fire destroyed the upper floors of Buecker Building, on the northeast corner of Ash and Wayne Streets.
05	1883	The Great Miami River overflowed its banks and more than 200 homes were damaged.
06	1855	A contract was awarded to the Piqua Gas & Coke Company for city street lights.
	1899	The Piqua Home Telephone Company was organized.
07	1825	Isaac S. Morris, a temperance advocate and newspaper publisher was born on this date.
08	1897	An announcement was published for the first rehearsal of the new Piqua Mandolin Club.
09	1882	The Odd Fellows Mutual Aid Association, a life and accident insurance company, was formed.
10	1836	Benjamin B. Beall leased water power rights at the new canal lock number nine for use with a flour mill.
11	1846	The Piqua Bridge Company was incorporated.
12	1903	Piqua Aerie 614, Fraternal Order of Eagles, was organized.
13	1836	A meeting was held for the community's first choral group, known as Piqua's Singing Society.
	1906	The city's first vaudeville performance was held at May's Opera House.
14	1905	The new yellow brick Central Fire Station opened on West Water Street.
15	1905	The City Council formally approved the abandonment of the Miami & Erie Canal.
16	1905	An announcement was published that Dr. Arthur N. Davis had been appointed as the court dentist to the Emperor of Germany, Wilhelm II.
17	1903	A special Grand Opening was held for the new May's Opera House on North Wayne.
	1942	The city leased the former Orr home on the northeast corner of Greene and Downing for emergency hospital during World War II.
18	1861	Colonel John Johnston, a Federal Indian Agent farmer, author and canal commissioner died on this date in Washington, D.C.
	1874	The local chapter of the Women's Christian Temperance Union (WCTU) was established.
	1914	The Health Department reported ten homes had been quarantined due to scarlet fever.
19	1835	The Methodist Episcopal Church was incorporated.
	1918	The Piqua Board of Health condemned the Piqua City Jail as dangerous and unhealthy.
20	1939	An open house was held for newly remodeled Spring Street School.
21	1901	The Piqua Artificial Ice and Cold Storage Company was incorporated.
22	1877	Piqua's first iron bridge at Bridge Street was opened.
23	1849	The Columbus, Piqua, and Indiana Railroad Company was chartered.
24	1834	The Presbyterian Church of Piqua was incorporated.
25	1846	The State of Ohio authorized the laying out of the Dayton, Charleston & Piqua Turnpike.
	1884	The Ladies Aid Society of Piqua was organized.
	1889	The Favorite Stove & Range Company opened for business in Piqua.
26	1838	A meeting was held in Piqua to discuss the question "Ought Slavery … be immediately abolished?"
27	1838	A meeting of the Piqua Temperance Society was held at "first candlelight".
	1908	Wayne Wheeler of the Ohio Anti-Saloon League gave a talk to local leaders.
28	1939	The School Superintendent reported nearly two thirds of all local students had joined the Junior Red Cross.
29	1904	The Piqua Humane Society was organized.

Annette Kellerman was a favorite at May's Opera House.

Many of the Favorite Stove & Range Company cooking stoves were highly ornate.

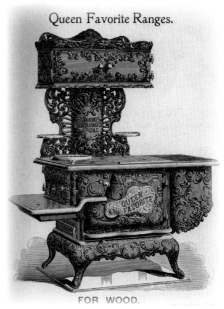

Queen Favorite Ranges.

FOR WOOD.

MARCH

01   1887   The city stopped using signal flags to notify citizens of weather predictions.

      1939   The first issue of the *Peoples Friend*, an advertising journal, hit the newsstands.

02   1952   John Boylan, a steam shovel engineer during building of the Panama Canal, died on this date.

03   1845   The first council meeting was held in the new Town Hall.

04   1914   A meeting of the Miami County Anti-Reservoir Committee was held.

05   1851   The Dayton and Michigan Railroad Company was chartered.

06   1903   The Miami County Anti-Saloon League was organized.

07   1934   A strike by the Meat Cutters and Packing House Workers, Local No. 133, took place at the Val Decker Packing Company on East Ash Street.

08   1845   The dedication of an early one story Presbyterian Church was held on the on the corner of Ash and Wayne Streets.

      1845   The Ohio State Legislature authorized the appointment of a flour and whiskey inspector in Piqua.

      1894   The Women's Auxiliary of the YMCA was established.

09   1876   A short-lived Piqua Board of Trade was organized.

10   1908   W. E. Simpkinson conducted the Piqua Symphony Orchestra at May's Opera House.

11   1895   The first women's political convention was held in Piqua.

      1908   The Wood Shovel and Tool Company was awarded a contract to make 85,000 entrenching tools [shovels] for the Army.

12   1897   The "Commerce" was advertised as the best ten cent cigar manufactured in Piqua.

13   1932   The Aerovent Fan Company was established.

14   1835   The first issue of the *Western Courier and Piqua Enquirer* was published.

      1899   Frank C. Davis was appointed Canal Collector at Piqua.

15   1849   The Cincinnati, Hamilton, and Dayton Railroad Company was chartered.

      1886   A city ordinance was passed that prohibited excessively speedy horses within the city limits

16   1908   A former Randolph Slave, William Rial, died on this date.

17   1924   A city ordinance was passed prohibiting liquor in all forms within the city limits.

The Rowan Memorial was located in the northwest corner of the Public Square.

      1934   The first regular meeting of the Textile Workers of America, Local No. 2141 was held in Piqua.

      1942   Construction began on the Victory Heights Housing Project on the west edge of town.

18   1887   General Lew Wallace, author of Ben Hur, spoke at the Greene Street Methodist Episcopal Church on the corner of Green and Wayne Streets.

19   1850   An act was passed by the state legislature to incorporate Piqua as a city.

      1890   The Piqua Castle No. 27, Knights of the Golden Eagle, was organized.

20   1801   John Johnston was appointed as a clerk in the United States War Department.

21   1927   The Great Miami River reached a height of 14.7 feet, the highest since the 1913 flood.

22   1919   The Young Women's Christian Association of Piqua, Ohio was incorporated.

23   1884   Co. F, 3rd Regiment, Ohio National Guard was sent south to aid in suppressing the crowds during the Cincinnati Courthouse Riots.

      1898   This was the worst flood to date of the Great Miami River.

      1939   The Junior Chamber of Commerce (JC's) was established.

24   1884   The Piqua Milling Company was established.

25   1775   Colonel John Johnston was born in Ireland, later becoming the local Federal Indian Agent.

      1913   The Great Miami River overflowed its banks and caused the worst flood in the city's history..

      1976   A Homecoming Celebration was held for Vietnam Conflict Prisoner of War, Major William Baugh.

26   1841   Colonel John Johnston was brought out of retirement and appointed as the Indian Commissioner to negotiate the removal of the Wyandot, Ohio's last organized tribe.

27   1877   The first YMCA was established.

      1922   The Meteor Motor Car Co. announced it would begin manufacturing phonographs.

28   1886   Stephen Widney, an early pioneer, died on this date.

29   1868   Frederick Douglas, an African-American politician, abolitionist and orator stopped in Piqua staying at the City Hotel.

      1882   The Piqua Chair Manufacturing Company was incorporated.

30   1876   Company F, Third Regiment, Ohio National Guard, known as the Wikoff Centennial Guards, was organized.

31   1890   Piqua's first Admiral, Stephen Clegg Rowan died on this date.

The original town hall stood on the east side of Main Street at the Public Square.

01	1807	Miami County was established.
	1811	The first Post Office was established at Piqua-town.
02	1903	An announcement was made of the formation of the Piqua Automobile Station, the city's first service garage.
	1903	The Piqua Electric Company was purchased by the Miami Light, Heat, and Power Company.
03	1912	The Piqua "Spots", a semi-pro baseball team, was organized.
04	1797	John Hilliard settled on top of the hill east of the Great Miami River in what is now know as Shawnee.
05	1886	The Sons of Veterans [Civil War], Camp No. 104, was organized.
	1903	The first regular run of the Western Ohio Traction line between Piqua and Lima was held on this date.
06	1850	Stephen Johnston was elected as the newly incorporated City of Piqua's first mayor.
	1918	The Princess Theater showed its last film on this date.
07	1933	The first 3.2 beer was sold on this date in Piqua with the ending of Prohibition.
	1947	Ohio Bell Telephone workers went out on strike.
08	1861	The McClarn Working Men's Institute of Piqua was formally incorporated.
09	1884	A heavy winter storm hit the city dumping over four inches of snow.
	1893	Huntersville was annexed into the City of Piqua.
10	1939	The opening of the Miami Foundry was announced.
11	1906	The Woodman of the World, Willow Camp No. 145, was established.
	1908	Annie Oakley visited friends in Piqua.
	1930	The Citizens National Bank was robbed and one man was killed.
	1966	William H. Pitsenbarger, an Air Force para-rescue specialist, was killed in action in Vietnam. He would later be awarded the Medal of Honor.
12	1871	The Border City Savings & Loan Company was incorporated.
	1883	Doctor Belle C. Buchanan advertised the opening of her office on Park Avenue.
13	1865	The Piqua National Bank was issued its charter.
	1939	A Piqua Policeman's Benefit Ball was held at the Winter Garden.
14	1903	The semi-pro Piqua Baseball Association was organized.
	1952	The week-long Ohio Bell Telephone strike ended.
15	1888	The Miami County Women's Christian Temperance Union was established in Piqua.
16	1972	The new YWCA building was dedicated.
17	1887	The first Salvation Army meeting was held in the city.
18	1919	The last issue of the German language newspaper, *Die Miami Post* was published.
	1897	Easter services were held at seventeen Piqua churches.
19	1897	Bernhardt Pietz, owner of the Pietz Bottling Works died on this date.
20	1829	John McElvain replaced Colonel John Johnston as the Federal Indian Agent in western Ohio.
	1908	The city's African-American baseball team was re-organized as the Rossville Stars.
21	1924	The city passed an ordinance providing for the implementation of Daylight Savings Time.
	1936	The Pioneer Rural Electric Co-operative was incorporated.
22	1879	The Doctor Bosanko Medicine Company was organized.
	1920	Piqua Press Publishing Company was formally dissolved.
23	1875	Robert Muchmore, a pioneer furniture maker and undertaker died on this date.
24	1875	Local newspapers carried an advertisement for the Leopold Kiefer Havana Cigar Factory, promoting the five cent "Havana" cigar.
	1917	The first modern Central High School Band Concert was held on this date.
	1946	Union Local 827, United Automobile Workers, C.I.O., ended a 107-day strike at the Wood Shovel & Tool Company plant.
25	1897	Dr. C. W. Bennett, school superintendent, addressed the YMCA Men's Club on the evils of cigarette smoking.
	1918	German language textbooks were burned at a public bonfire as part of the anti-German hysteria of World War I.
26	1861	The city's first Civil War unit, Company F, 11th Regiment, was mustered into service.
	1865	A charter was issued to the Citizens National Bank.
	1866	The city's first baseball team, the Sterling Baseball Club, was organized.
27	1887	William P. Bennett, a furniture maker and undertaker died on this date.
28	1839	Lodge No. 8, Improved Order of Odd Fellows, was organized.
	1929	The First Christian Church was formally dedicated.
29	1865	Doctor Godwin V. Dorsey laid a wreath on the breast of Abraham Lincoln when he was lying in state in Columbus, Ohio.
30	1865	Lincoln's funeral train stopped for a brief period in Piqua.
	1884	The Edison Electric Illuminating Company of Piqua turned on the city's first electric lights.
	1970	Battery C, Ohio National Guard, was sent to the Ohio State University riots.

MAY

01 1866 The Piqua Hydraulic Company was organized to bring water power to Piqua.
Sam Lee established the first Chinese laundry in the city.

02 1887 A cyclone hit the city, taking off roof of St. Boniface Church.

1918 Henry Ford stopped in Piqua to visit H. C. Waite.

1923 A joint YMCA/YWCA clothing drive was held as part of the Student Friendship Fund of Russia.

03 1834 A local newspaper advertisement stated, "Wanted immediately one hundred laboring men for work on Miami Canal."

1909 A strike was held by members of the Carpenter's Local No. 1908, United Brotherhood of Carpenters, demanding twenty-eight cents an hour.

04 1903 The new state mandated Municipal Code went into effect.

05 1812 Captain George Buchanan mustered in a company of local militia as protection against the potential of hostile Native Americans.

06 1906 The Grand Opening of the Bijou Family Theater on West Ash Street was held.

2001 The Linear Park (P.A.T.H) and French Park were formally dedicated.

07 1908 The Amokee Tribe of the Independent Order of Red Men was established.

1928 The Piqua Council House on the public square was demolished.

08 1915 The Campaign for "Miss Piqua" was held at the Princess Theater.

09 1835 An advertisement appeared for a new stage coach line from Piqua to Dayton.

10 1892 William McKinley and Rutherford B. Hayes spoke at the Grand Army of the Republic (Civil War Veterans) encampment at Piqua.

11 1897 Work commenced on the St. Mary's School on North Street.

1915 The city's dog catcher Ivan Brush resigned, complaining of excessive abuse from dog owners.

12 1836 A fire ordinance was passed requiring every building owner to have a ladder and two leather buckets.

1877 The Piqua National Temperance Union adopted a constitution.

13 1915 A local cleanliness campaign used the slogan, "Help to Make Piqua a Flyless Town".

14 1919 The Lange Brewing Company (beer) became the Lange Products Company (milk).

15 1839 Billy Manning, a musician in racially oriented minstrel shows, was born and died (1876) on this date.

1885 Godwin Volney Dorsey, physician, industrialist, state and local politician, historian and author died on this date.

16 1887 An ordinance was passed providing for the re-numbering of buildings in the city.

1911 The Western Ohio Music Festival preformed on the public square with a five hundred voice chorus.

1912 Former President Theodore Roosevelt spoke on the public square during his Bull Moose Campaign

17 1895 The Y.M.C.A. Orchestra played for the Anna Station School commencement exercise.

18 1868 The attempted murder of Dr. and Mrs. W.P. Hall on this date led to the creation of the city's first police force.

1942 The local scrap drive committee ran an advertisement to "Conserve the Rubber in your Girdles and Help Win the War".

1973 The Edison State General and Technical College was granted a charter by the State of Ohio.

19 1909 A newspaper article discussed fashion for young men that consisted of a narrow, solid-color tie that matched your socks.

20 1912 President William Howard Taft spoke at the May's Opera House.

21 1823 An ordinance was passed requiring Main Street lot owners to pave their sidewalks with brick, stone or gravel.

22 1919 A new Y.W.C.A. Club, The Swastika Smiles, was established by women working at the Imperial Underwear Co.

1926 The Piqua Electric Service Company, later incorporated as the Aerovent Fan Company, announced the production of the "Airway" exhaust fan.

1939 The Schines Theatrical Co. took over the operations of Piqua's two motion picture theaters.

23 1835 An ordinance was passed prohibiting the shooting of muskets, rifles, or pistols within the village limits.

1908 The Grand Opening of the Calomiris Candy Kitchen was held on this date.

24 1975 The groundbreaking for the first new building of the Edison State General & Technical College was held on this date.

1986 The new community swimming pool on the west edge of the city was formally dedicated.

25 1882 Miles Orton's New Mastodon Shows & Royal German Menagerie appeared in the city.

26 1910 The Ball Memorial Hospital Training School for Nurses held its first graduation commencement ceremony.

27 1879 The Jones home on West High exploded killing four people. The disaster was caused by a leaking barrel of gasoline in the basement.

28 1883 The Border City Base Ball Team played the Mechanicsburg Nine at the baseball field in Huntersville.

29 1917 An Anti-Conservancy District (flood control) meeting was held at May's Opera House.

30 1832 The local newspaper ran an advertisement of a "Six Cent Reward but No Thanks" for the return of an eighteen year-old apprentice who had run away.

1883 Ex-President Rutherford B. Hayes spoke at the Decoration Day celebration.

31 1900 The French Oil Mill Machinery Company was formally incorporated.

01	1933	The Lange Brewery Co. began production of 3.2 beer, "Golden Lager" after the end of national prohibition.
	1937	Battery C, 136th Field Artillery, Ohio National Guard, was organized.
02	1902	The Wood Shovel & Tool Company was incorporated on this date.
03	1878	A city ordinance was passed to suppress vice, immorality, brothels or houses of ill fame.
04	1923	A Fountain Park Revival was held by the Evangelistic Prayer League of Piqua.
05	1917	The Piqua Chapter of the American Red Cross was organized at the beginning of World War I.
	1942	An air raid and blackout drill was held by the Civil Defense Committee during World War II.
06	1927	A Hartzell Propeller was used on the record-breaking air flight of Chamberlain and Levine.
07	1900	The Piqua Historical Society was organized.
	1918	The Jones-Washburn Motor Company was incorporated.
08	1881	The Miami Boating Company for Pleasure and Recreation was incorporated.
	1909	The City Police began enforcing the downtown speed limit of 8 mph.
09	1942	William Edwards Simpkinson, a violinist and conductor of the May's Opera House Orchestra, died on this date.
10	1960	Hartzell Industries assumed control of the Piqua Aircraft Company and the Piqua Airport on State Route 185, west of the city.
11	1891	Piqua men attended the Ohio Prohibition Party Convention in Springfield and endorsed banning the liquor trade, women's suffrage and the strict observation of the Sabbath.
12	1884	The Clark House, at 628 North Main, became the first private home in the city to have electric lights.
	1890	A contract was awarded to Brotherton & Scudder to build South Street School.
13	1903	John Franklin McKinney, a Democratic Congressman and attorney from Piqua, died on this date.
14	1896	A local chapter of the Daughters of the American Revolution (DAR) was organized.
15	1882	The Hamlin's Wizard Oil Company (patent medicine) gave a free band concert from their wagon on the square.
	1885	The Miami County Prohibition Party held their convention held in the City Hall.

16	1876	The formal opening of the Piqua Hydraulic Canal was held on this date.
	1908	Buffalo Bill's Wild West Show with William Cody and Annie Oakley opened on Favorite Hill.
	1923	The Lange's Natatorium (swimming pool) opened to the public.
17	1898	The East India Manufacturing Co. came to the city from Brooklyn, New York.
18	1828	The *Piqua Gazette* ran an advertisement for hot air balloon rides at twenty-five cents.
	1882	Jeweled garters were discussed as the fashion rage for young ladies in Piqua.
	1888	Natural gas was officially turned in on the city.
19	1884	An ordinance was passed prohibiting the playing of baseball on city streets or alleys.
	1982	The North Street School was torn down.
20	1915	A formal opening of Airdome at Stein's Park in Rossville was held on this date.
21	1837	The first canal boat to reach Piqua on the Miami Extension Canal tied up at a temporary dock in the city.
22	1961	The Border City Savings and Loan Association formally dedicated their new building.
23	1927	The State Fish Hatchery at Fountain Park was dedicated.
24	1831	A "Menagerie of Living Animals" consisting of a lion, camels, hyenas, a kangaroo, a leopard, and a zebra visited the city.
25	1915	The formal dedication of the Lorimer Bridge from Piqua to Shawnee across the Great Miami River was held.
26	1923	The Citizen's Military Training Corps recruiting office was opened.
27	1915	The Grace Methodist Episcopal Church dedicated their new church on West Ash Street.
28	1909	George C. Dietrich was hired as the Superintendent of Schools with a salary of two thousand dollars a year.
29	1807	The village of Washington (Piqua) was surveyed and platted by Armstrong Brandon.
	1925	The Ideal Business School was incorporated.
30	1886	The cigar workers at John Laug's shop went out on strike.
	1887	A meeting of Assembly 5417, Knights of Labor of Piqua was held on this date.
	1919	The Piqua Home Telephone Company was dissolved.

Young men cleaned up the baseball diamond on East Ash Street in about 1900.

140. The Lange Swimming Pool was located on Water Street at the dead-end of Spring Street.

01	1802	Colonel John Johnston was appointed as the Indian Agent at the Fort Wayne Agency.
	1887	The first free home mail delivery in city began on this date.
	1909	The fire station on the corner of Virginia and Park Streets was officially opened.
	1963	The 45356 Zip Code became the official postal designation for Piqua.
02	1888	The Piqua Board of Health was established.
03	1879	An organizational meeting of the People's Library Association was held on this date.
	1926	The city's first Zoning Ordinance was passed.
04	1896	The Buffalo Bill's Wild West Show with Annie Oakley performed in town.
05	1837	General William Henry Harrison spoke in Piqua at the opening of the canal.
	1918	The 148th Infantry Regiment, 37th Infantry Division landed at Brest, France during World War I.
06	1820	The first issue of the *Piqua Gazette* was published.
	1837	The first canal boat to traveled north from Dayton docked at Piqua.
	1919	Heavyweight boxing champion Jack Dempsey stopped in Piqua for gas on his way to Cincinnati.
	1986	A bronze statue of Don Gentile was dedicated on the east side of the public square.
07	1939	The first band concert of the newly formed Elks Band was held in Fountain Park.
08	1884	Piqua's African-American voters formed a Republican Blaine and Logan Club.
	1905	Prohibitionist Carrie A. Nation visited the city.
09	1883	The Young Women's Christian Temperance Union was organized.
	1918	Local No. 576 of the American Federation of Musicians was formed.
10	1862	During the Civil War, Camp Piqua at Johnston's Farm was established by the Ohio Adjutant General's Office.
	1890	The Second Baptist Church on Park Avenue was formally dedicated.
11	1960	Von Ellis of Piqua captured the cup at the Pro-Amateur Golf Tournament at the Piqua County Club.
12	1900	The Cahill–Leonard Knitting Company was incorporated.
13	1897	The City Health Board appointed Peter Jones as the city's sanitary policeman.
	1935	A Curtis Condor biplane landed at the Piqua Airport and offered rides to local citizens for fifty cents an hour. At the time, it was the largest commercial passenger plane in the United States.
	1916	Company C, Third Regiment of the Ohio National Guard was activated and sent to Texas to guard against Pancho Villa along the Texas-Mexican border.
14	1892	The First Regiment of the Ohio National Guard camped at Fountain Park, temporarily renamed "Camp McKinley".
	1903	Frank Gehle was appointed as the city's first police chief.
15	1802	Colonel John Johnston married Rachel Robinson in Lancaster, Pennsylvania.
	1908	The local German-American Alliance was organized.
	1975	Piqua National Bank announced the appointment of Mary Rebecca Upton Allen as its first woman director in 128 years.
16	1952	A UFO was reported flying in skies southeast of the city.
17	1897	Mayor G. E. Smith issued warning against playing baseball on Sundays.
18	1887	John Morrow Scott, a merchant and banker died on this date.
19	1834	An ordinance was passed prohibiting swine from running at large in the town.
	1882	The Great Forepaugh Show with twenty-two trained elephants was in the city.
20	1903	An ordinance was passed prohibiting spitting on paved sidewalks within the city.
	1962	The former Dixie Highway was officially designated County Road 25-A.
21	1908	A Republican Campaign Glee Club was organized.
22	1814	The Second Treaty of Greenville was signed.
23	1912	Piqua Lodge No. 1067 of the Loyal Order of Moose was organized with fifty men led by Dictator Ed Crampton.
24	1840	Rachel Robinson Johnston (Mrs. John), the founder of the Piqua Female Bible Society died on this date at Upper Piqua.
25	1934	A meeting was held by the Young Negro Voters' League of Miami County.
	1950	Private First Class Herbert E. Tamplin, Jr. was the first Piquad killed in action in Korea.
26	1883	The Border City Baseball Team beat the Troy Eagles by a score of fifteen to twelve in ten innings.
27	1899	George Curtis announced that he had sold the Piqua Broom Company to Harry M. McCurdy.
28	1887	Harry S. Frye began publication of the *Pythian News*, a lodge newspaper.
29	1831	A canal meeting was held to promote the extension of the canal north from Dayton to Piqua and beyond.
	1879	The Huntersville Water Works were formally opened.
	1933	"Der Rathskeller" opened in the basement of the Hotel Favorite on the square, the first bar in Piqua after the end of Prohibition.
30	1909	The Aeronautics Club was formed.
	1929	The Piqua City Charter was formally adopted.
31	1944	George C. Detrich resigned as Superintendent of Schools after thirty-five years of service.

AUGUST

01	1887	The W. P. Orr Linseed Oil Company was incorporated.
	1887	The Third National Bank opened to the public.
02	1894	The first issue of *Die Miami Post*, a German language newspaper, hit the stands.
	1900	The first public band concert was held in the new bandstand on the public square.
03	1795	The Treaty of Greenville was signed.
04	1846	The Piqua Division No. 19 of the Sons of Temperance of Ohio was incorporated.
	1946	This was the beginning of the Piqua Sesquicentennial Celebration, 1796-1946 which was held in Piqua from August 4 to August 8. This celebrated the arrival of Job Gard on the future site of Piqua.
05	1891	A formal notice was printed announcing the formation of a three man city police department appointed by the Mayor with compensation set at fifty dollars a month.
06	1874	The first issue of the temperance newspaper, the *Miami Helmet* was published.
	1889	An ordinance was passed granting the Miami Valley Railway Company the right to use the city streets for a new electric street railway.
07	1908	The Piqua Automobile Club was first organized.
08	1935	A new automatic elevator was installed at the Memorial Hospital on Park Avenue.
09	1905	An announcement was made of the election of former Piqua citizen Charles H. Genslinger to the Western Committee of the Fourth International Olympic Games.
10	1923	Memorial service were held at Fountain Park for President Warren G. Harding.
11	1904	A local newspaper reported that there were now four electric carriages (automobiles) in city.
12	1952	Irene Ditmer was appointed as the Executive Secretary of the Community Chest.
13	1812	Captain George Buchanan's War of 1812 Militia Company was disbanded.
	1885	The Board of Education closed the segregated African-American school on the corner of Boone and College Streets.
14	1905	An ordinance was passed establishing free public band concerts on the square.
15	1829	An advertisement was published that offered a reward of one cent and a chew of tobacco for the return of runaway apprentice Jesse Claig.
	1888	The first issue of the *Piqua Daily Leader* was printed.
16	1901	The Orr Felt & Blanket Company was incorporated.
	1912	Piqua's first Chautauqua opened at Fountain Park.
17	1812	The Council of Piqua was held on the farm of Colonel Johnston, with over nine hundred Native Americans attending.
	1935	A dance ordinance went into effect in the city that created the new position of "dance inspector" for restaurants and beer halls that provided live music. The inspectors were appointed by the police department and paid four dollars a night.
18	1813	Henry and Barbara Dilbone were killed by renegade Indians.
	1829	The Thespian Association of Piqua performed "Fortune's Frolic", with tickets selling at 12 1/2 cents.
19	1837	A new stage line was advertised with a route from Piqua to St. Marys.
	1869	The Piqua Grove of the United and Ancient Order of Druids was formally incorporated.
	1942	Captain Don Gentile shot down his first German plane during World War II.
20	1794	In the Battle of Fallen Timbers, Anthony Wayne defeated the Indian Confederation in northwestern Ohio.
21	1813	Captain Charles Hilliard's Militia Company disbanded after serving since 1812.
	1837	The first issue of the *Evangelfsche Relfgfoese Zeitschrift*, the community's first German language newspaper was published by Lebriend L.Hinsch.
	1876	A city wide fire department was authorized to replace the semi-private fire companies.
22	1887	Mrs. A. R. Thompson opened a private kindergarten school in Piqua.
23	1862	The Ninety-Fourth Regiment, Ohio Volunteer Infantry, was mustered in at Camp Piqua during the Civil War.
	1884	The city's first building permit was issued.
24	2001	Alexander Stadium and Purk Field at the High School on Looney Road were formally dedicated.
25	1904	The United Spanish-American War Veterans changed the name of the local camp from the Henry W. Lawton Camp to the Edgar F. Wallace Camp.
26	1828	A caravan of live animals including lions, a zebra, and an African leopard visited Piqua.
	1915	The Federal Post Office building on Wayne Street was completed.
27	1940	Battery C, 136th Field Artillery was federalized for training.
28	1812	Stephen Johnston, brother of Colonel Johnston, was killed by Native Americans between Ft. Wayne and Upper Piqua.
	1884	The Piqua Base Ball Club was disbanded after only one season.
29	1812	General William Henry Harrison established his headquarters at Camp Washington (Johnston's Farm) at the beginning of the War of 1812.
30	1811	The Salem Baptist Church, later known as the First Baptist, was established.
	1837	A new stage line was advertised with a route between Piqua and Urbana.
31	1886	Earthquake shocks were felt in city at 9:20 P.M.

SEPTEMBER

01 1862 The Ninety-Fourth Regiment from Piqua participated in the Battle of Tate's Ferry during the Civil War.

1900 The Coachman Harness Soap Company of Piqua was incorporated.

02 1875 The "Piqua Light Guard," Company D, Third Regiment of the Ohio National Guard was organized.

03 1972 The official dedication of the Piqua Historical Area (Johnston Farm) was held on this date.

04 1908 The YMCA's bowling alley was opened to the public.

05 1885 An open house was held for the New High School on College Street.

1935 The grand opening of the LoRa Hamburger Shop at 119 West Ash Street was formally announced. The shop specialized in "Five Cent Hamburgers, "Buy'Em By The Sack".

1936 An open house for the city's first steel residence at 518 Vine Street was held on this date.

06 1886 An ordinance was passed to suppress ten pin bowling alleys in city.

07 1874 Texas Street was renamed Park Avenue because it connected the city to the Western Ohio Fair Grounds on Forest Street.

08 1935 The new Washington Township Centralized School on Park Avenue was formally dedicated.

1939 The Cole Brothers Circus was held in Piqua at the Meteor Field on South Main Street.

09 1961 Contracts were awarded for a two story brick addition to the YWCA.

10 1885 A concert was held by the Ideal Band and cornetist Harry Hardy at the Ideal Skating Rink on High Street.

1912 The Piqua Historical Society was organized again.

11 1905 The Madison Avenue School was formally opened.

1934 Workers at the Orr Felt & Blanket Co. began a thirty-two day strike.

12 1956 Warren S. Gravett was elected as President of Citizens National Bank & Trust Co.

1998 The Lock Nine Park on East Water Street was dedicated.

13 1749 Celeron de Blainville, a French Canadian explorer and soldier, visited Pickawillany.

1883 The Edison Electrical Illuminating Company of Piqua, Ohio was incorporated.

14 1857 William H. Hayner was born in Piqua. He would later establish a mail order liquor business in Troy.

15 1960 A. J. Kaiser retired after thirty-four years with the YMCA.

16 1842 Colonel John Johnston concluded a treaty with the Wyandot Tribe forcing them to move to land west of the Mississippi River. This was the last organized tribe living in Ohio.

1912 Democratic presidential candidate Woodrow Wilson spoke in Piqua from the back of his train as part of his "whistle stop campaign".

17 1812 While he was camped at Upper Piqua, William Henry Harrison was commissioned a Brigadier General and given command of the Army of the Northwest.

1908 The Independent Civic League of Miami County was organized with James Pettiford as its first President. This was one of the earliest nonpartisan African-American political groups in the county.

1910 Eugene V. Debs, the leader and one of the founders of the Socialist Party of America, spoke in Piqua.

18 1952 The price for city bus tokens increased from ten for a dollar to eight for a dollar.

19 1863 The Ninety-fourth Regiment, organized at Camp Piqua, was engaged in the Battle of Chickamauga in Georgia.

20 1863 Leo M. Flesh was born on this date in Piqua. He would later become a leading industrialist, banker and art collector.

21 1908 The rival Piqua Commercial College and the Ideal Business College merged to form one local business school.

1912 John Philip Sousa and his military style band performed at May's Opera House.

22 1911 Frank H. Miller, formerly of Dayton, was killed in an airplane crash at the Miami County Fairgrounds.

23 1884 The Third Savings and Loan Company was established.

24 1891 Lodge No. 103, of the Ancient Order of United Workman was organized in Piqua.

1973 The first classes were held by Edison State General and Technical College in the former Spring Street Elementary School building.

25 1867 The Colored Men's Co-operative Trade Association was established. It was the city's first African-American retail business.

1886 J. W. Nigh of Piqua was nominated as the Knights of Labor's candidate for Congress.

26 1812 Lieutenant Gardner Bobo's Militia Company was mustered into service during the War of 1812.

1846 The Miami County Agricultural Society was established.

27 1890 The Piqua Humane Society was organized.

28 1939 Mrs. Mae Hetherington, the Civilian Conservation Corps (CCC) enlistment officer, announced that Miami County's quota would be twenty young men.

29 1917 Jonathan Fairbanks, superintendent of the Piqua Schools during the Civil War passed away on this date.

30 1891 The first guests registered at the newly opened Hotel Plaza on the public square.

OCTOBER

01 1856   This was the first day of school for the city's first High School.

      1887   Grover Cleveland passed through Piqua on a train.

      1947   Parking meters were first put into operation in the downtown area.

02 1845   Artist and author Horace J. Rollin was born in Springcreek Township.

03 1862   The One Hundred Tenth Regiment mustered into service at Camp Piqua during the Civil War.

      1907   The local group of the National Union of Railway Trackmen was organized.

04 1887   The first train left Piqua for Troy on the Piqua and Troy Railroad Line.

05 1918   The Piqua Board of Health closed schools, churches, lodges, and theaters to help slow the spread of the Spanish influenza. This epidemic was spreading across the nation.

06 1863   General John C. Fremont spoke on the public square at a Union Party mass political meeting during the Civil War.

      1893   The Associated Charities of Piqua was organized.

07 1939   The Annual Fall Festival was held in the American Legion Hall by the Piqua Aid Society for the Deaf.

08 1921   The Sherer-Bell Automobile Agency was established. It would become one of the largest car dealerships in the Midwest.

09 1914   The Piqua Rotary Club was chartered.

10 1929   The Piqua National Bank moved into its new building on the southeast corner of Wayne and Market Streets.

11 1853   A proposition to establish a Union School System or High School was passed by a vote of 289 to 13.

      1912   The Miami Light, Heat & Power Company was purchased by the Dayton Power & Light Company.

      1925   The Piqua Eagles Lodge building on Wayne Street was dedicated.

12 1927   The Piqua Fire Department moved into the current fire station on the corner of Water and Downing Streets.

      1984   President Ronald Reagan passed through Piqua on the former Baltimore & Ohio Railroad Line (CSX). He waved to the gathered crowd.

13 1895   The Christian Church on the southeast corner of Broadway and Greene was formally dedicated.

      1933   The Piqua Municipal Electric Light Plant began operations.

14 1886   James Keyt, one of Piqua's earliest brick masons, died on this date.

15 1788   John Cleve Symmes signed a contract with Congress to purchase all of the land between the Great Miami and Little Miami Rivers.

      1908   The Ball Memorial Hospital's Nurse's Training School opened to students.

      1982   Rick Callison of Piqua won the Athens Open International Marathon in Greece.

16 1908   An advertisement ran in the local newspapers for the opening of the Dream Moving Picture Show.

17 1918   Socialist Mayor Frank B. Hamilton was arrested by Federal Marshals and charged with sedition. The charges were later dropped due to the lack of any credible evidence.

      1952   A formal groundbreaking was held for the Mote Park Community Center.

18 1883   The first issue of the *Piqua Morning Call* was published.

      1890   The Schmidlapp Free School Library opened to the public.

19 1896   Democratic and Populist presidential candidate William Jennings Bryan spoke on the public square.

20 1920   F Troop, First Ohio Cavalry of the Ohio National Guard was organized.

21 1883   The Piqua Baseball Club was organized.

      1889   Border City Tent No. 72 of the Order of Maccabees was established.

22 1826   The Piqua Colonization Society was organized to promote sending freed slaves back to Africa.

      1891   The grand opening of the Plaza Hotel was held on this date.

      1967   The Piqua Airport was formally rededicated.

23 1887   James Noland, a carpenter, builder, and politician died on this date.

24 1841   The Masonic Warren Lodge No. 24 was established in Piqua.

      1900   The Elk's Fair and Corn Festival's Flower Parade was held.

25 1887   The first iron canal boats docked in Piqua.

26 1901   The Piqua Savings Bank opened to the public.

      1933   The Municipal Light Plant held its formal dedication.

27 1908   May's Opera House hosted Harry Hasting's Boston Belles Burlesque.

      1915   Williams Jennings Bryan spoke for Prohibition at May's Opera House.

      1926   The formal dedication of the city Water Works plant was held on this date.

28 1919   It was announced that the Paul Schnell Post No. 184 of the American Legion had been organized.

      1919   William Jennings Bryan spoke for Prohibition at the First Presbyterian Church. This was Bryan's third appearance in Piqua.

      1926   The East Ash Street Bridge was formally dedicated.

29 1841   Leopold Kiefer was born in Germany. He came to Piqua and became a cigar manufacturer and Democratic politician.

30 1887   A rally was held by the Union Labor Party at Border Hall.

31 1928   The Buchanan Motor Sales Company, agents for the Graham-Paige automobile, moved into new headquarters on the east side of the public square.

NOVEMBER

01 1874 The congregation of the Anshe Emeth Temple of Piqua was incorporated.

1887 The Border City Wheelman, an athletic club, was organized.

1939 The Third Savings & Loan Co. was robbed by four bandits.

02 1883 Louisa Timmons Bennett (Mrs. Charles.W.) died on this date. She was the first woman to receive a Masters of Music Degree from Ohio Wesleyan College.

03 1874 The Western Ohio Fair and Driving Park Association located at Fountain Park was incorporated.

1933 The Atlas Underwear Company received a contract for one hundred thousand suits of heavy underwear for the U. S. Army.

04 1910 Future President and Ohio native Warren G. Harding, spoke at May's Opera House.

1963 The Piqua Atomic Power Plant generated steam for the first time for use in generating electricity for the city.

05 1929 Elections were held for the five newly created City Commission seats.

06 1915 A wrestling match was held at the Bijou Theater. Admission to the event was twenty-five cents with ladies being admitted free.

1955 The new District Five, Ohio State Highway Patrol Headquarters opened on U. S. Route 36.

07 1889 The Piqua Malt Company was incorporated.

1894 John G. Mitchell died on this date. He was Piqua's only Civil War General.

08 1864 It was reported that Abraham Lincoln received sixty-one per cent of the vote in Piqua.

09 1881 The Alexander Post of the Grand Army of the Republic (Civil War Veterans) was established.

10 1905 A meeting of the Miami County Good Roads Association was held at the Hotel Plaza.

1935 Army Captain Albert W. Stevens piloted the Explorer II balloon that set the world altitude record of 72,395 feet. For warmth, he wore a suit of underwear presented to him by J.L. Black of the Superior Underwear Company.

11 1873 Conover's Opera House opened to the public with a production of *Rip Van Winkle*.

12 1927 A special May's Opera House performance was held for children with an admittance charge of a single potato it be used for the city's poor.

13 1812 Captain Reuben Westfall's Militia Company was disbanded.

14 1912 The Bijou Theater had a special showing of a moving picture about Piqua.

1935 The first pole for the rural electrification was set outside the Piqua Municipal Power Plant.

2001 The new Municipal Government Complex on Water Street was formally dedicated.

15 1886 The Piqua Hosiery Company began operations on Spring Street.

1915 The French Oil Mill Machinery Company became the first large industry in Piqua to run its industrial machinery with electricity.

16 1885 The Piqua Choral Society was organized.

17 1812 Godwin Volney Dorsey was born in Oxford, Ohio. He would be elected Treasurer of the State of Ohio during the Civil War.

18 1915 The United States Marine Band performed at May's Opera House in a benefit for Piqua Boy Scouts.

1939 The Fall Festival and Corn Show began on the public square.

19 1863 John F. McKinney, a Congressman from Piqua, attended Lincoln's "Gettysburg Address" speech in Pennsylvania.

1935 Piqua Unit 3417 of the Veterans of Foreign Wars was organized with eighteen charter members and Frank Kyle as the first post commander. The following month, the unit adopted the name Samuel Chaney Post 3417.

20 1908 An advertisement ran in the local newspapers for the Piqua Automobile Garage (Bertling's), the city's first auto garage and rental business.

21 1829 A one-cent reward was offered in an advertisement for the return of a thirteen year old indentured servant.

1986 Former rivals, the Miami Citizens and Heritage National (Piqua National) Banks merged to became the Citizens Heritage Bank (later a Fifth Third Bank).

22 1891 Miss Boal played the Mozart "Te Deum" on the new St. James Episcopal Church organ.

24 1901 William McCulloch was born on this date in Holmes County, Ohio. He would become an attorney and congressman.

25 1876 The consolidation of the First and Second Presbyterian Churches occurred on this date.

1915 Piqua High School beat Troy High School 27 to 0 to win the state High School Football Championship.

26 1904 It was announcement that a new independent political group was being formed, to be known as the Municipal Voter's League.

27 1962 Mrs. Guinivere T. Armstrong was named Executive Secretary of the Piqua Chapter of the American Red Cross.

28 1841 Robert Maynard Murray, a Democratic Congressman from Piqua was born on this date.

29 1932 The Retail Merchants Division of the Piqua Civic Association passed a resolution against having Christmas trees on downtown sidewalks.

30 1905 The Ball Memorial Hospital on Park Avenue was formally dedicated.

DECEMBER

01	1887	The Mercer Gas & Fuel Company, with its headquarters in Piqua, was incorporated.
	1901	The Piqua Club, a private men's group was organized.
02	1837	James Hanks officially surveyed the plat of Huntersville east of the Great Miami River.
	1939	The Hartzell Propeller Company won a U. S. Navy contract for propeller blades.
03	1924	Piqua city officials announced a crackdown on the city's "jaywalkers".
04	1932	The Associated Charities of Piqua announced an "Adopt a Family for Christmas" plan.
05	1833	The *Piqua Gazette* published a letter from former Piqua Federal Land Agent Thomas B. Van Horne defending himself against charges of illegal land speculation.
06	1980	The grand opening of the Piqua office of Winters National Bank on the northwest corner of Ash and Spring Streets was held on this date.
07	1947	WPTW Radio Station began broadcasting.
08	1884	Joseph Chambers was hired as special Merchant's Night Policeman.
	2000	Vietnam hero William Pitsenbarger posthumously received the Medal of Honor at a ceremony at the Air Force Museum in Dayton.
09	1907	The Piqua Retail Merchants Associated was organized.
10	1835	Pioneer farmer Isaac Statler died in Washington Township.
11	1939	A new obstetric wing and laboratory was opened at the Piqua Memorial Hospital.
12	1883	The Invincible Lodge No. 176 of the Knights of Pythias was organized.
13	1977	Mary C. Quirk, a pioneer in the field of speech and hearing therapy, died on this date.
14	1918	The Western Ohio and the Dayton & Troy Traction Companies moved into their new joint office on the corner of Main and Ash Streets.
15	1875	The city's public market moved to the east side of Main Street on the south side of the City Hall.
16	1811	Severe earthquake were felt in this area.
	1884	The Piqua Society of Clinical Medicine was organized.
17	1939	Finland Day was declared in Piqua by mayoral proclamation in protest of Russia's invasion of Finland.

18	1904	The first local production of Handel's "Messiah" was held at May's Opera House.
	1939	A one-hundred-thousand-dollar fire destroyed the Holland Mills on South Wayne Street. Fire Chief P. J. Caulfield died of a heart attack while fighting the fire.
19	1927	The Piqua Fire Department added flashing red lights to all of their vehicles.
20	1960	Seven inches of snow fell on the city.
21	1891	The City Council passed an ordinance prohibiting dance halls in connection with saloons.
	1935	The first known public concert using an "electric guitar" was held at the Winter Garden dance hall on South Wayne Street.
22	1939	St. Paul's Evangelical Church choir presented a concert in the lobby of the Piqua National Bank.
23	1901	James B. Hicks, President of Cincinnati Corrugating Company, died on this date.
24	1832	The Piqua Land Office offered land for sale at the former Hogs Creek, Wapoghkonnetta and Lewistown Indian Reservations.
	1891	The YMCA Constitution was formally adopted.
25	1935	This year was the coldest Christmas in fifty years with temperatures hitting six degrees below zero. The temperature was matched by a near blizzard with eight to ten inches of snow and forty mile-an-hour winds leaving three foot drifts.
26	1930	May's Opera House reopened as a motion picture theater.
27	1828	John Webb was elected Brigadier General of the Second Brigade of the Ohio Militia.
28	1917	George H. Rundle, founder of Rundle [Patent Medicine] Company, died on this date.
29	1930	The Piqua Club on West Greene Street was donated to the Schmidlapp Free School Library for use as a new and larger public library.
30	1935	Firemen pump a layer of water over the ice-covered Echo Lake to provide a smooth skating surface for local citizens.
31	1862	The Ninety-fourth Regiment, Ohio Volunteer Infantry was engaged in the Battle of Stone River, Tennessee during the Civil War.
	1927	An open house was held for the new City Hall located in the former Central Fire Station on Water Street.

Left: Piqua Fire Chief Paul Caulfield is seen here in his full dress uniform in 1939.

Right: Radio announcer Bob Bupp is shown conducting WPTW's "Man on the Street" interviews in front of the Fort Piqua Hotel in 1948.

Paul Treon shelving books in the 1990's at the Flesh Public Library.

Bibliography

Bibliography

ORIGINAL SOURCE MATERIAL

The Flesh Public Library & Museum at 124 West Greene Street in Piqua, Ohio contains a wealth of manuscript (MS) and small collection (SC) materials on Piqua's history. The Library also contains an extensive clipping files/vertical files (VF) and microfilm collections of local newspapers. The following list contains only a rough smattering of the more extensive collections that were used for the *Encyclopedia*.

MANUSCRIPT COLLECTIONS
(Flesh Public Library)

MS-01, Piqua Female Bible Collection
MS-02, Leonard U. Hill Collection
MS-03, Ralph May Collection
MS-06, Piqua Chamber of Commerce Collection
MS-07, Piqua Chapter of the American Red Cross Collection
MS-09, Piqua Area United Fund Collection
MS-15, City Federation of Women's Clubs Collection
MS-16, Lange Photograph Collection
MS-19, Home Town Bugle (World War II) Collection
MS-48, *Piqua Daily Call* Photograph Collection
MS-79, Rayner Glass Plate Negative Collection
MS-89, Piqua Police Department Record of Arrests (1905-1985)
MS-94, Aerovent Fan Collection
MS-96, Piqua School Board Minutes Collection (1853-1898)
MS-97, McVety Real Estate Photographic Collection
MS 105, Dick Dunkle Photograph Collection
MS-119, Eleventh Regiment, Ohio Volunteer Infantry (Civil War) Collection
MS-133, Citizens National Bank Collection

PIQUA CITY DIRECTORIES
(Flesh Public Library)

The library's collection of city and business directories covers the period from the 1850's to the present. The earliest name directory covers 1870-71 and the complete run of Polk City Directories begins in 1920. The first city directory with an address listing begins in 1906-07.

VERTICAL FILES
(Flesh Public Library)

The Library's vertical files contain over four thousand files comprised of clippings and other secondary material on Piqua area people, events, companies and miscellaneous topics.

NEWSPAPERS

The Library collections contain microfilm editions of Piqua newspapers published from 1820 to the present. The earlier newspapers have only scattered editions remaining, while the *Piqua Daily Call* has an almost complete run on microfilm. While newspapers from almost every year have been used to document this work, the most intense use was made of newspapers from 1820 to 1850, the 1880's, the 1930's and the 1940's. The newspaper portion of the List section of the *Encyclopedia* provides an extensive listing of Piqua's newspapers.

ORAL HISTORY

The below listed oral histories were compiled in both a formal interview context and in more informal public meetings, panel discussions and group discussion format.

Bertling, Don
A Piqua native, Mr. Bertling graduated from the Piqua High School in 1943. He provided information on Piqua's cable television, family history and local individuals and structures.

Burton, Dorothea F.
A Piqua native, Ms Burton graduated from the Piqua High School in 1959. She provided information of African-American –white relations from the 1950's through the 1970's.

Clemons, Viola
A native of Mechanicsburg, Ohio, Ms. Clemons moved to Piqua in the 1920's with her husband Emerson. She provided information on African-American working conditions from the 1920's through 1960's, on the NAACP and the Piqua Altrusa Club.

Cron, Robert
A native of Piqua, Cron graduated from the Piqua High school in 1930. He was active in the Cron Funeral Homes and the grandson of L.C. Cron. He provided material on Piqua in the 1930's through the 1960's, on death rituals and customs in the area, and on the history of the Cron furniture companies and on Huntersville.

Hance, Robert M.
A native of the Piqua area, Mr. Hance served as the Piqua City Manager and the director of the Piqua Civic Band. He provided information on Piqua in the post-World War II era, the nuclear power plant, Victory Heights, city government and the Piqua Civic Band.

Havenar, Louis
A Springfield Township resident, Mr. Havenar is long time community activist since the 1950's. He provide information on post-World War II banking practices, Piqua businesses, Promise Keepers, local individuals, Democratic Party activities, the Piqua Heritage Festival and the Piqua Bicentennial Event (1776-1976).

Heitzman, Samuel
A native of Piqua, Mr. Heitzman graduated for the Piqua High School in 1926. He discussed local issues including, banking, family, World War II Homefront and local artists.

Johnson, Beatrice
A Piqua native, Ms. Johnson graduated from the Piqua High school in 1945. She provided material on the African-American churches in Piqua, segregation and racial inequality issues from the 1930's through the 1960's.

Jones, Imogene Freels Hall
Ms. Jones came to Piqua with her family as an infant and graduated from the Piqua High school in 1944. She provided information on the YWCA, the NAACP, and African-American-white relations from the 1930's through the 1960's.

Mitchell, Mary

A native of Piqua, Miss Mitchell graduated from the Piqua High School in 1914. She provided material on late nineteenth century Piqua (her father was a Piqua resident and Civil War veteran), Piqua school system, Victory Heights, Frank Hamilton, and the Hilliard Family.

Oda, Harry R.

A native of Piqua, Mr. Oda graduated from the Piqua High School in 1930. He provided information on local banking, the United Way, the Red Cross, community musical events, the Board of Education, local individuals and the Piqua Rotary Club.

Scarborough, John

He came to Piqua in the 1950's and established the Piqua Engineering Company. He provided material on economic development from the 1950's through the 1990's.

Thomas, Art

A Piqua native, Mr. Thomas graduated from the Piqua High School in 1952. He provided material on local school activities and African-American-white relations from the 1940's through the 1960's.

PUBLISHED SOURCE MATERIAL

Art Work of Miami County. Chicago; W.H. Parish Publishing Co., 1897.

Blumenson, John J.-G., *Identifying American Architecture, A Pictorial Guide to Styles and Terms, 1600-1945.* Nashville: American Association for State and Local History, 1978.

Clayton, Andrew R.L. *Ohio, The History of A People.* Columbus, Ohio: The Ohio State University Press, 2002.

The County of Miami, Ohio, An Imperial Atlas and Art Folio, 1894. Richmond, Indiana: Rerick Brothers, 1894.

Douglas, Rev. F.A. *History and Origin of First Baptist Church, Piqua, Ohio.* N.P., October 05, 1870.

Edgar, John F. *Pioneer Life in Dayton and Vicinity, 1796-1840.* Dayton, Ohio: United Brethern Publishing House, 1896.

Frary, L.T. *Early Homes of Ohio.* New York: Dover Publications, 1970.

Goodman, Rebecca and Barrett J. Brunsman. *This Day in Ohio History.* Cincinnati: Emmis Books, 2005.

Gordon, Stephen C. *How to Complete the Ohio Historic Inventory.* Columbus, Ohio: Ohio Historic Preservation Office, Ohio Historical Society, 1992.

Harbaugh, Thomas C. *Centennial History Troy, Piqua and Miami County, Ohio and Representative Citizens.* Chicago: Richmond-Arnold Publishing Company, 1909.

Hill, Leonard U. editor. *A History of Miami County, Ohio (1807-1953).* Columbus, Ohio: F.J. Heer Printing Company, 1953.

History of Miami County, Ohio. Chicago: W.H. Beers & Co., 1880.

Hoover, John C. M*emoirs of the Miami Valley.* 3 volumes. Chicago: Robert O. Law, 1919.

Howe, Henry. *Historical Collections of Ohio in Two Volumes.* Cincinnati, Ohio: State of Ohio, 1908.

Illustrated Historical Atlas of Miami County, Ohio. Philadelphis: L.H. Everts & Co., 1875.

Kaiser, A.J. *The Piqua, Ohio YMCA, 1877-1970.* Piqua, Ohio: Hammer Graphics Inc., 1971.

Knepper, George W. *Ohio and Its People.* Kent, Ohio: The Kent State University Press, 1989.

McAlester, Virginia and Lee. *A Field Guide to American Houses.* New York: Alfred K. Knopf, 1985.

Oda, James C. *A Diversity of Piqua Industry, 1800-1900.* Piqua, Ohio: Piqua Historical Society/ Quality Quick Printing, 1985.

Oda, James C. *Col. John Johnston, The Piqua Years.* Piqua, Ohio: Piqua Historical Society/Quality Quick Printing, 1984.

Oda, James C. *From Buggy Whips to Steering Wheels, The Impact of the Automobile on Piqua, Ohio, 1890 – 1930.* Piqua, Ohio: Piqua Historical Society/Miami Printery, 1990.

Oda, James C. *A History of Piqua, The Impact of Transportation.* Piqua, Ohio: Flesh Public Library & Museum and the Piqua Area Chamber of Commerce/Hammer Graphics, 1998.

Oda, James C. *Hotel Plaza, A Poem in Stone, 1891 – 1991.* Piqua, Ohio: Piqua Historical Society/Miami Printery, 1991.

Oda, James C. *Hustle and Bustle, 1861 – 1920, A History of Women in Piqua, Ohio.* Piqua, Ohio: Piqua Historical Society/Quality Quick Printing, 1988.

Oda, James C. *Piqua and the Miami and Erie Canal.* Piqua, Ohio: Piqua Historical Society/Quality Quick Printing, 1987.

Oda, James C. *Service Above Self, Piqua Rotary Club, 1915-1990.* Piqua, Ohio: Rotary Club No. 135/Quality Quick Printing, 1990.

Piqua, Miami County, Ohio [Insurance Map]. New York: Sanborn Map Company, August 1887 and January 1931 with update paste-overs to January 1949. (also microfilm editions for June 1892, August 1898, November 1905, February 1911, November 1920, January 1931 with no updates)

Plat Book of Miami County, Ohio. Des Moines, Iowa: Northwest Publishing Company, 1911.

Porcher, Connie M. *Heritage Preserved, Piqua-Caldwell National Register Historic District, Piqua, Ohio.* Piqua, Ohio: Piqua Historical Society, 1985.

Powell, Thomas E. Ed. *The Democratic Party of the State of Ohio.* Ohio Publishing Company, 1913.

Quadrennial Appraisement of Lots, lands, Buildings and Structures Belonging to "Realty" in Piqua, Ohio, made by...Board of Appraisers in 1910. Piqua: [Magee Brothers], 1910.

Rayner, John A. *The First Century of Piqua, Ohio.* Piqua, Ohio: Magee Brothers Company, 1916 (reprinted 1967).

Roseboom, Eugene H. and Francis P. Weisenburger. *A History of Ohio.* Columbus, Ohio, Ohio Historical Society, 1973.

Roster of Ohio Soldiers in the War of 1812. Columbus, Ohio: Edward T. Miller Company, 1916.

Schlesinger Jr., Arthur M. general editor. *The Almanac of American History.* New York: Barnes & Noble Books, 1993.

Selders, A. and J.P. Bradway. *General Business Review of Miami County.* Newark, Ohio: American Publishing Co., 1890.

Shriver, Phillip R. *The Documentary Heritage of Ohio.* Athens, Ohio: Ohio University Press, 2000.

Smith, Joseph P. ed. *History of the Republican Party in Ohio and Memoirs of Its Representative Supporters.* two volumes, Chicago: The Lewis Publishing Company, 1898.

Smith, William E. *History of Southwestern Ohio The Miami Valleys.* New York: Lewis Historical Publishing Company, 1964.

Sterrett, Frank M. *A History of Miami County.* Troy, Ohio: Montgomery Printing Company, 1917.

Wagner, Dean R. ed. *Historic Piqua, An Architectural Survey.* Piqua, Ohio: Piqua Branch, American Association of University Women/Hammer Graphics, 1976.

Wright, Terry. *Echoes of the Miami Valley.* Apollo, PA: Clossen Press, 1991.

Wright, Terry. *An Unusual Time on the Home Front, Life in Piqua, Ohio 1916-1918.* Wooster, Ohio: Wooster Book Company, 2003.

The band stand on the Public Square in 1909 was a favorite place to relax and learn what was happening in and around town.

This is a view of the foundry of the Favorite Stove & Range Company in 1905.

Patrons

A congregational photograph was taken by the Grace Methodist Episcopal Church on West Ash Street in 1918. The street car waited until the photograph had been taken.

Benjamin Franklin Reed, Brick Manufacturer

The need for bricks to build one of Piqua's grandest buildings brought Benjamin Franklin Reed to Piqua in the early 1890s, when Piqua entered a golden age as a prosperous and progressive community. Ben and his brothers Horace ("Haul") and Charles ("Charlie") moved their brickyard and family to Piqua after winning a contract to supply bricks for the Plaza Hotel, later known as the Hotel Fort Piqua.

The brickyard was located on Rossville Hill, on the west side of what is now County Road 25-A, north of Hetzler Road. Bricks from the yard were also used in the construction of Spring Street School (1893-4).

The Reeds emigrated from Scotland to Northern Ireland about 1680, to near Gettysburg, Pennsylvania circa 1728, and to Paris, Bourbon County, Kentucky in 1780. They were pioneer settlers of Dayton, moving there in 1806.

Ben and his brothers were born in Union, Randolph Township, Montgomery County. Their parents were Martin M. and Sarah J. Reed. Martin operated a cooperage on the Stillwater River near Little York. He died at age 41 in 1864 when Horace was 6, Charles 10, and Ben 12. Their mother Sarah later moved to Piqua and was a strong presence until she died at age 88 in 1916. Their grandparents, William and Sallie Reed, were prominent early Methodists and farmers in the Northridge area of Dayton. Their farm was south of present day Needmore Road and east of Frederick Pike. It was sold in 1871.

The Reed brothers started in brick manufacturing while in Montgomery County. They operated a brickyard and a sideline timber business in Greenville from the 1870s until moving to Piqua. Their bricks were used to construct the Darke County Infirmary. Two of their siblings died in their early 20s while living in Greenville: brother Bart and sister Marcella.

Initially known as "H.E. Reed & Bro., Manufacturers of Brick," the name changed to "B.F. Reed, Manufacturer of Brick," although all three brothers were involved. Horace was the "brain" and Charles the "brawn," a "gentle giant." Ben was the entrepreneur and driving force.

Horace and Charles never married. Ben married Barbara Lucy Ann Wills in Greenville in 1880. She died at age 47 in 1905. Their children included Maude O. (1884-1970), Versel E. (1886-1980), Hazel M. (1889-1973) and Charles Forrest (1896-1974). Maude was a long-time teacher at Park Avenue and Wilder public schools. Versel was a principal of Stelzer & Reed Insurance (see Reed Mote Staley patron page in this book).

H. E. Reed & Bro.,

Manufacturers of Brick,

Yard: North Main St., on the Wm. Miller Farm.

B. F. REED,

Manufacturer ... of **BRICK** ...

PHONE: 2 on 281.

N. Main St.   PIQUA, OHIO.

Reed brickyard in active operation c. 1890s, known as "H.E. Reed & Bro." and "B.F. Reed". Inset (close-up from main photo): man on right is either Benjamin or Horace Reed. Note wheelbarrow full of wet clay.

Ben was very gregarious. He could stand for hours talking with people. He usually wore a Stetson hat, often with coat and tie, and chewed on a cigar. After retirement he devoted his time to social and community activities. He went downtown every night and was active in lodge work, including the I.O.O.F (Independent Order of Odd Fellows). For years, Ben was the paid secretary of the Knights of Pythias (K of P). Their lodge rooms were on the second floor of May's Opera House.

In summer, Ben would spend an entire week at the Miami County Fair, riding from Piqua to Troy on the interurban train (traction line). This was fun for him because he could talk to scores of people he knew, and enjoy the exhibits and harness racing.

On Sunday night, May 7, 1933, Ben was walking home from a visit to the Dunkle Brothers store downtown. He was on the east side of Broadway between Park Avenue and Camp Street – just a few yards from his home. He was struck by a car and died an hour later. He was 81. The front page banner headline and story in the *Piqua Daily Call* the next day was a testament to this well-known and well-liked maker of bricks.

Written by: Richard K. Reed,
fourth generation, son of Robert

Top: Benjamin, mother Sarah, and brothers Horace and Charles, c. 1915.
Lower Right: Benjamin F. Reed in Stetson hat, at his home, 820 Broadway c. 1915.
Lower Left: Benjamin F. Reed c. 1890

Benjamin and Lucy Reed's children:
Versel, Maude, Forrest, and Hazel, 1897

Hazel was married to T. Rey Wiley. His family owned a tanning business on South Main Street for many years. Forrest was an executive with Hartzell Industries.

The third and most of the fourth generation following Ben are Piqua natives: third generation children of Versel and Stella Reed are Virginia, Lucille, Robert B. and William G. Forrest and Margaret Reed's children are James B. and Dorothy J. The fourth generation collectively comprises eleven sons and five daughters.

The brickyard closed about 1913, when brick making became more mechanized. Ben razed most of the buildings, but retained the land and a small barn. Several acres were left to grow wild. He farmed the balance, hiring people to plant and harvest. He grew potatoes, corn, barley, and planted timothy between crop rotations. His grandchildren picked wild raspberries on the property they knew as "the brickyard." However, Ben called it "the place." It may have been his way of acknowledging that the brick business was no more. As late as 1920, he would visit the site by horse and buggy.

After the brickyard closed, Horace and Charles worked at the Piqua Hosiery Company on Spring Street. They lived in East Piqua (on North and Harrison Streets) and survived the flood of 1913. They died in 1927 and 1932.

Second and third generation 1938:
Forrest, Robert B., Versel, William G., Rey Wiley, Stella Stelzer Reed, Hazel Reed Wiley, Maude, Lucille, Margaret Poince Reed, James B., Dorothy J.

A.M. Leonard Inc.

In 1885, Ashbel Merrel Leonard started a nursery as a hobby in his backyard at 607 Wood Street, Piqua, Ohio. By 1912 he and his sons Parker and Stanley established A.M. Leonard & Sons as a nursery/landscaping service. The business was further developed in 1928 when A.M. and his son John started a wholesale horticultural tool company at 512 Walker Street. In 1941, following the death of A.M. Leonard, John became the President of the company and moved it to 1714 West High Street. John's forte was customer service. He mailed out 7,500 pocket-sized catalogs per year and monitored the purchases of each customer. John kept impeccable notes. When an order was not received from a customer within a year, John would contact the customer personally to ask how his organization might be of better service. The call usually resulted in product sales. Since only the finest quality tools were offered, customers always knew that when they chose something from the Piqua based company, they would receive the best money could buy.

Howard Kyle became a partner with John Leonard in February 1964. Like the Leonards, Howard had a strong background in the nursery and mail order businesses. His family owned Springhill Nursery in Tipp City, Ohio. Howard quickly learned the A.M. Leonard operation. Ill health caused John Leonard to retire early, and Howard took over as sole owner inheriting a staff of 8. Howard and the staff expanded the catalog and merchandising operations emphasizing customer service, product dependability, and fast order response. Continuous growth caused the company to move to 6665 Spiker Road where by 1979 about 15 employees were kept busy in an area totaling 30,000 square feet. In November 1993, the company made a major commitment to its customers and the community by constructing a new 50,000 square foot facility at 241 Fox Drive.

In 1996, A.M. Leonard produced its first Retail Catalog to reach the serious home gardener. In 2005, as this segment of the business continued to grow, A.M. Leonard re-introduced the Retail publication as A.M. Leonard's *Gardeners Edge*. This move proved to further distinguish this market and to address its unique needs. Meanwhile, attention was also being focused on how to better serve and support the loyal Professional customers who were the foundation of the business' success. To that end, in 1999 the Account Manger Program was born. The philosophy here was to partner a knowledgeable and responsive A.M. Leonard salesperson with an assigned group of professional customers and have them work together to meet the needs of the customer's business on an ongoing basis. This relationship building process has built a dynamic partnership between A.M. Leonard and their Professional customers and contributed greatly to customer satisfaction and success.

In recent years, A.M. Leonard has continued to grow its ever expanding Private Label line of tools. The skilled Merchandising and Product Support Technicians hand-pick the features and benefits of other similar tools and design a product that more exactly meets the demands and specifications of their customers. The Internet had added another exciting dimension to the daily business activity at A.M. Leonard as their presence there continues to grow with two company websites and sales through amazon.com.

A.M. Leonard keeps in close touch with local customers through their Counter Sales in the company showroom. Here city employees, park department workers and area residents enjoy picking up their product on the spot and getting right back to the job. Plans are underway now for an expansion project for both the office and Distribution Center to even better serve customers close to home and across the country.

Today, under the leadership of Gregory Stephens, grandson of Howard Kyle, over 90 people meet the needs of an ever-expanding list of customers. A.M. Leonard, Inc. is a leader in the horticultural tool implement business with emphasis on customer satisfaction. A selection of over 7,000 first class tools for nursery workers, landscapers, foresters, arborists, contractors and gardeners is readily available at competitive prices. The company's success is a function of the fine, dedicated employees who carefully assist each customer, treat one another with respect, and work together to maintain a safe, enjoyable, productive business environment.

Access Piqua Television Association

The Access Piqua Television Association (APTA) was one outcome of the first Future Piqua study. Citizens express their desire to promote the City's positive image. Two ideas were proposed to accomplish the wishes of the citizens. The City of Piqua and Piqua Area Chamber of Commerce formed a partnership to make these a reality. The first, a quarterly, community-wide newsletter entitled *Pro Piqua Focus,* chaired by Ruth Koon to develop a more traditional communication project. The second to broadcast programs on Time Warner cable television. *APTA* was chaired by longtime WPTW Radio Manager Joanna Hill-Heitzman. Both boards were comprised of volunteers appointed by the City of Piqua, the Chamber of Commerce and the Pro-Focus and APTA committees.

Funding for equipment and supplies came from the City's franchise fees received from Time Warner. APTA started with one camera, a handheld microphone and tri-pod with the stipulation equipment was to be loaned out to anyone wanting to tape and air a program.

APTA aired its first program, *Focus on Piqua,* in May of 1995, hosted and narrated by Dale Robbins and James Oda, on Time Warner cable channel 13. This program featured the Piqua Arts Council's community art show held at the Piqua Historical Museum on Main Street.

Volunteers did it all: directors, videographers, editors, narrators, and researchers pushed APTA programming onto the next level. One new show a week (broadcast on Tuesdays and Thursdays) expanded into dozens of shows ranging from historical documentaries and sporting events to school presentations and how-to shows. Initial editing was done in a closet at St. Paul's United Church of Christ. As APTA production grew, editing was moved into the backroom at the offices of Time Warner Cable Company on Main Street?

In 1998, APTA expanded and moved to the Chamber of Commerce building on the southwest corner of Main and Ash Streets. The facility featured a studio, production department and an office for the new executive director. Jan Koon came on board in January of 1998 as APTA's first staff person. Ms Koon's salary, the video equipment and supplies came from the City of Piqua's cable franchise fees. Under Koon's strong direction, APTA began producing regular monthly programming.

One of the first programs, *What's Happening in Piqua,* began in 1998 and continues to the present (2007). Other early programs included *Mainstreet Piqua Presents, Focus on Industry (Spotlighting Business), Flesh Public Library Storytime, Church Net, Piqua Police Department, Report of the Superintendent, The Mayor's Report* and many others. Bonnie Murray and

Doug Fosnight with APTA cameras on their shoulders became a common sight at school graduations, community events, parades and recitals as volunteers taped literally hundreds of hours of Piqua events for later broadcast. A major increase in programming led to the next big step in APTA's history.

In February of 1999, APTA expanded to twenty-four hour a day programming on Time Warner Cable's Piqua Access Channel 10. APTA also took over the live broadcasts of the Piqua City Commission meetings which had formerly been broadcast by the cable company for several decades. Various churches submitted their Sunday services and were broadcast on Sundays. Added to the regular schedule are programs sponsored by groups as diverse as the Chamber of Commerce, the United Way, the Piqua Parks Department, Edison State College and the Upper Valley Medical Center. Today, local citizens groups continue to submit dozens of videos on topics ranging from Piqua High School boys and girls soccer games to dance recitals and from Christmas programs to fishing shows.

Currently, APTA broadcasts close to 30 monthly programs, quarterly, bi-monthly, and 160 submitted programs. 2007 the Piqua Board of Education started broadcasting live their monthly meetings. Between airing of programs the message board provides viewers with the weekly program schedule, schedule of city meetings and local obituaries and notices keeping the citizens informed of City projects.

The purpose of APTA from its formative years through today is summed up in the association's mission statement.

APTA volunteers Andy Hite & Ron Kloecker editing a program to air on Piqua Channel 10

APTA MISSION STATEMENT

The goal of the ACCESS PIQUA TELEVISION ASSOCIATION is to present a wide diversity of local programming on the community's access channel, providing a means of communication to promote and improve the quality of life within our community. To that end, individuals and organizations are encouraged to contribute their own message to the viewing community. It is the policy of the Association to promote freedom of speech and artistic expression on the community access channel....

In August of 2007 Time Warner moved APTA to Piqua access cable channel 5.

A number of original programs aired on Piqua Channel 10 have been preserved as an archive of Piqua's history and tapes are available at the Piqua Library.

Long time program contributors Lloyd & Virginia Smith taping an Out & About program

American Legion/VFW

The American Legion

The American Legion was founded at the historic Paris Caucus in March of 1919. The name "The American Legion" was finally adopted and the framework of the new organization was established at the St. Louis Caucus on May 8-10, 1919.

Charters were granted to 189 Posts in 78 Ohio counties prior to the first convention. The convention was held in Columbus, on October 8 and 9, 1919, with a paid-up membership of 11,604. Today the Department of Ohio has over 150,000 members in 618 Posts. The American Legion in Piqua received its charter as Paul Schnell Post 184 on October 10, 1919. It was later renamed as Schnell-Westfall Post 184 on February 5, 1947.

Paul Schnell, enlisted June 3, 1917, with Company C, 3rd Infantry, Ohio National Guard, later organized as Company C, 148th Infantry. He arrived overseas on June 22, 1918, as a Supply Sergeant. He saw action in the Ypres-Lys and Meuse-Argonne sectors. Paul Schnell was killed in action in France on October 31, 1918, and was buried at Flanders Field.

John Westfall enlisted in the Marines on February 26, 1943. The following July he was sent to the Pacific Theater as a machine gunner in an infantry outfit. John Westfall was killed in action during the landing at Tarawa on November 21, 1943. Mr. Westfall was chosen from the names of the 44 Piquads killed in action in World War II.

Schnell-Westfall Post 184 has provided assistance to many non-profit organizations in Piqua. The Piqua Ambulance Fund has enabled the city to purchase new emergency squads and emergency medical equipment. Many youth activities are also funded to provide a positive influence for our children. On the National level Post 184 supports the Gifts for Yanks program, USO, American Red Cross, and the Salvation Army.

VFW Post

VFW

In 1899, the American Veterans of Foreign Service (Columbus, Ohio) and the National Society of the Army of the Philippines (Denver, Colorado) were organized to secure rights and benefits for veterans of the Spanish-American War (1898) and the Philippines War (1899-1902). These two organizations merged in 1914, creating the Veterans of Foreign Wars of the United States.

Piqua Post 4874 was chartered on November 18th, 1945 with 145 charter members under Commander Richard Chronerberry. The membership elected to call the post Chaney-Graef in honor of Samuel Chaney and Robert Graef.

Samuel Chaney, a sergeant serving with the 148th Infantry in France during World War I, was gassed during the Argonne Forest battle. Mr. Chaney died in 1921 from the effects of the gassing. Sergeant Chaney had an outstanding record with his outfit, was considered the best of the non-commissioned officers, and was sometimes placed in command of his platoon.

Robert Graef, a Lieutenant with the famous 101st Airborne Division, was killed in action in Holland in 1944. Mr. Graef trained for service in the glider infantry and went overseas as a staff sergeant. He earned a battlefield promotion to Lieutenant from his superior officers for his heroic leading of his command.

The name Pitsenbarger was added to the Post in 2002 in honor of William Pitsenbarger, a Piqua native, who was awarded the Congressional Medal of Honor for his actions on the battlefield in Vietnam. Mr. Pitsenbarger volunteered to stay behind and help treat and defend wounded soldiers, giving his life in the process.

Chaney-Graef-Pitsenbarger Post 4874 is one of more than 9,000 Posts across the world. The VFW is an organization of war veterans committed to ensuring rights, remembering sacrifices, promoting patriotism, performing community services, and advocating for a strong national defense.

Post 4874 has made donations to many organizations on the national, state and local levels over the years. A partial list on the national and state level would include the VFW National Home, American Red Cross, The March of Dimes, USO, Robert Combs Cancer Fund, VFW Voice of Democracy, Department of Ohio Military Assistance Fund, and the National VFW for Hurricane Katrina relief.

On the local level, Post 4874 has donated to various groups including Clear Creek Farms, Rehab Center for Neurological Development, The Bethany Center, Piqua Police Department Honor Guard, Piqua Veterans Association, Veterans Elite Tribute Squad, Piqua Youth Baseball & Softball, Piqua High School All Night Party, Piqua Junior High School Olympiad, Dayton VA Service Officer, and others too numerous to mention.

American Legion

Bayman Auto Sales

Bayman Auto Sales was founded in 1958 by Robert W. Bayman. Robert originally hailed from the Versailles area. He was always interested in cars and loved to sell so he decided to open a used car business. His first location was the corner of Water and Wayne Streets. He began with a $3,000 loan from the bank and $3,000 in cash. The average price of a car was between $300 and $1,200. You could buy a year old car for only $1,200. Robert retailed between four and five vehicles a month. He traveled all over Ohio and several other states buying and selling cars. In those days cars did not have seatbelts and he would take along his wife Phyllis and their baby daughter Krysta. His business grew and since he was on the road so much he hired several retired individuals to sell cars for him while he was gone. Bayman Auto Sales remained in this location until 1969.

In 1969 Carl Zimmerman purchased 201 Spring Street, tore down the ice plant and made it into a car lot. Robert rented this location from Carl. Little did he know at the time that 30 years later he would purchase the whole corner from Carl and relocate the business to its current home. Robert kept the business at 201 Spring Street until 1981. At that time Bob purchased a property on Co. Rd 25A and started another business, Interstate Auction Service. He maintained his dealers license and mostly wholesaled from this location while running a consignment auction house. Mr. Bayman, along with being a car dealer, has always been an auctioneer. The two go hand in hand as he also held jobs at dealer wholesale auctions most of his adult working life. In fact, to date, he continues to work at two auctions every week. In 1981, son Tony and son-in-law Chuck joined the family business. Wife Phyllis operated Avenue and Alley antiques from 1971 until 2004.

Robert purchased the old Sohio property on South Street. It is an entire city block. After months of EPA cleanup, Robert began a very successful repo car auction that continues to this day. The auction sells vehicles for banks, local dealers, and the US Bankruptcy court. He opened his car lot and remained at that location until 1999.

Carl Zimmerman approached Bob in 1999 to buy the entire corner showroom property at 219 Spring Street. Robert remodeled the showroom and expanded his car business. In 2001, daughter Julie and her husband Joe returned from Florida and joined the family business. We now sell over $2.5 million in vehicles per year and those numbers go up every year. The exposure we experience on this corner cannot be bought. Being on a busy State Route is the best advertising a business could want.

Robert Bayman continues to work 70 hours a week. His hard work and dedication and the sacrifices made by Phyllis and his children enabled Bayman Auto Sales to succeed in a business where many fail. For 50 years, Robert Bayman and his business have had the reputation of honesty and fairness. No amount of money can buy that kind of reputation.

Buecker's Interiors

*L*eonard J. Buecker opened the original Buecker's Interiors in March 1946, at 128 West Ash Street. He had worked, starting in high school, at Benkert's Department Store on the third floor where he managed the furniture and flooring departments until they closed. It was at that time that he started his own business based on the tradition of "fine" furniture and custom-made draperies. The business occupied the first floor of the four-story building with the drapery department on the third floor. Mr. Buecker employed a full-time carpet installer, Rufus Harmony, and a full-time drapery department with employees Stella Libby and later Pearl Krampe. A full-time salesperson, Kyle Haynes, assisted with sales and installations while Chuck Brubaker helped with carpentry, flooring and installations. Leonard's wife Margaret was a valuable member of the store team, attending semi-annual furniture markets and adding her personal touch.

In February 1962, a devastating fire leveled the building. Mr. Buecker did not hesitate to rebuild his business on the same site as his oldest Richard J. Buecker, was attending the Kendall School of Design in Grand Rapids, Michigan, with the intention of joining his father in the family business. In 1965 Richard became certified by the American Society of Interior Design (ASID) and added a design element to the business. Over the next 35 years he developed a reputation as a very personable, knowledgeable, and creative designer.

The third generation was added to the family business when Eric J. Buecker, Richard's oldest son, joined them. Eric remembers that he had "been helping Dad and Grandpa deliver and move furniture forever." Eric studied interior design at the University of Dayton and Sinclair Community College. He became a full time employee in 1992, after realizing that he was able to learn much more about furniture and interior design by working side-by-side with his father and grandfather.

It was a three-man team for over five years when Eric's wife, Beth A. Buecker joined them in the fall of 1997. The four of them worked together until the sudden death of Richard in April 1999 and unfortunately, shortly after that, Leonard passed away in June 2000. Eric and Beth were left to carry on the tradition of the family business. They were committed to Buecker's Interiors and took on the challenge of continuing as a Third Generation Family Owned and Operated Business.

After growing the Piqua business for seven years, Eric and Beth expanded by opening a second store in Bellbrook, Ohio. Buecker's Fine Furniture and Interiors at 4389 St. Rt. 725 opened its doors in February 2006. In a newly renovated building they found an opportunity to bring higher end furniture and experienced interior design service to Dayton and the surrounding areas.

Buecker's Interiors has served Piqua and the surrounding communities for over 61 years with fine furniture, interior design, flooring, window treatments, wall coverings, accessories, oriental rugs, and oil paintings. With companies like Henredon, Century, Hickory White, Stanley & Lexington and many more the Buecker tradition of "fine" furnishings and interior design continues.

History

The Church of Jesus first was established in 1971 when the Reverend Howard Collier began having cabin meetings in the home of the late Mr. and Mrs. Joseph Creath on Bassett Avenue. Those meetings were the open door to the beginning of great accomplishments.

In May of 1971, with the financial assistance from the Ohio District Council of the Pentecostal Assemblies of the World, a tent was erected to hold meetings for the duration of 21 days. Near the conclusion of the gatherings and seeing a desperate need to reach those that seemed hopeless, Reverend Collier searched until he found a vacant building – not necessarily a favorable location – but visionary Collier had much insight as to what it could become! This vacant building was known throughout the state as the *"Log Cabin"* or *"Barney's Tavern."*

Pastor Collier applied for his first loan at a local bank to purchase the property on Bassett Avenue and was rejected because the loan officer simply felt that he would be another "fly by night preacher." However, after securing funds for the property, Pastor Collier and his family moved into the property in June of 1971. With dedication and sacrifices of the pastor and his family the membership flourished to where the current facility became inadequate. The pastor began to explore all the avenues to having an adequate facility. He even felt at one time that he would upgrade the Bassett Avenue property and even went as far as having blueprints drawn and approved by the state. However during the process of the model being constructed and the gathering of materials, he was informed that a church building on the corner of Broadway and Boone was on the market. Pastor Collier believed this facility was a perfect location and suitable for the needs of his dedicated parishioners. Consequently in October of 1977 the congregation moved into that edifice.

After an approximate sixteen years, once again the congregation outgrew its facility; and realizing this, the pastor again was faced with the task of upgrading to meet the congregational needs.

The possibility of expanding the facilities on Broadway was researched and after much consideration, Pastor Collier and the congregation realized it just wasn't feasible, due to a number of circumstances. The pastor began to look for property within the city limits for the convenience of its membership; and after approximately two years of research, the property on the corner of Wood and Commercial was selected to be the sight of the new "Church of Jesus." The new church was built with a seating capacity of approximately five hundred with additional facilities for Christian education, etc.

For many years Pastor Collier and The Church of Jesus produced and aired a television broadcast, "Because He Lives" which covered the State of Ohio, and Jackson, Michigan.

W. Howard Collier PhD., DD, and his wife are the owners of Ohio Ministries; a Christian based publishing company that reaches worldwide. Bishop Collier also holds numerous offices in the Ohio District Council of the Pentecostal Assemblies of the World Inc.

In 2004, after thirty-three years of tending to the spiritual well-being of his dedicated parishioners, Bishop Collier passed the mantle to Assistant Pastor Brian Hamilton.

Under the watchful eyes of Pastor Hamilton the church continued to expand its presence in the community. In 2007 the Church completed the renovation of yet another old bar located at 428 Wood Street. The transformed facility is the gathering place of many community activities housing Wood Street Community Development Corporation.

The "Church of Jesus" has touched many lives during its reign in the "City of Opportunity" Piqua, Ohio; and is highly recognized across the country.

Visit the Church of Jesus
421 Wood Street
Piqua, Ohio 45356
937-773-4004
http://www.churchofjesuspiqua.com

Service hours are as follows:
Sunday
9:30 am - Sunday School
11:00 am - Morning Worship
Wednesday
6:30 – Prayer
7 pm - Bible Class

City Of Piqua Bicentennial History

The City of Piqua is a city rich with history from years gone by, as well as a city that has a history of citizens that have left their mark on this wonderful community. Together as a community, we celebrate our heritage and history during this 2007 Bicentennial celebration.

The City of Piqua was incorporated in 1823 and reincorporated in 1835 with the election of John S. Johnston as its first Mayor. In 1929, the City of Piqua changed its form of government with the adoption of a Charter City with Commission/Manager form of government beginning in January of 1930.

Lester G. Whitney was appointed the first City Manager with 7 City Managers appointed since that time. Mr. Robert Hance was the longest serving City Manager from 1949 to 1972.

The City Manager for Piqua is Mr. Frederick E. Enderle. The Mayor of Piqua is Mr. Thomas Hudson, 3rd Ward; along with City Commissioners: Frank H. Barhorst, 1st Ward, William D. Vogt, 2nd Ward, Julia (Judy) Terry, 4th Ward and Frank J. Patrizio, 5th Ward.

The mission of the City of Piqua is to promote the health, safety and welfare of the community through the efficient and effective delivery of services based on addressing the needs of, and making continuing improvements in the City, in partnership with the community.

The City started a full-time Fire Department in 1876 and in 1973 the department began offering paramedic services. Today, the Fire Department has 29 professional firefighter/paramedics that are also trained in a variety of special skills such as rope rescue, water rescue and hazardous material handling.

The Police Department traces its roots back to the late 1800's. In 1903 the Police Department became a full-time department with one employee, and that was Chief Gehle. Later in 1903, Chief Gehle inherited several part-time employees, however most of them were laid-off in 1904. That left the Department with Chief Gehle and one part-time night officer. Today, the Police Department has 34 sworn officers and is accredited by CALEA.

The City of Piqua began an Electric Power System in 1933. Today the City maintains over 200 miles of distribution lines and serves over 10,000 customers. The City also began its' own Wastewater Treatment system in 1939. Today the Wastewater Plant treats over 4 million gallons of wastewater per day. Also, the City began its own water supply and distribution system in 1876. Today they produce over 1 billion gallons of finished water per year.

The City of Piqua has 20 parks totaling over 260 acres. The oldest park is in the City of Piqua is Fountain Park on Forest Avenue. The City also maintains 12 miles of bike path titled "The Loop" which project construction began in 2001.

The City of Piqua has many Boards and Committees which have been established for many years as follows: Access Piqua Television Association (APTA), Board of Zoning Appeals, Charter Review Committee, Civil Service Commission, Community Diversity Committee, Downtown District Design Review Board, Energy Board, Forest Hill Union Cemetery Board, Golf Advisory Board, Housing Council Committee, Income Tax Board of Review, Miami County Council, Miami Valley Regional Planning Commission, Park Board, Piqua Improvement Corporation Board of Trustees, Planning Commission, Records Board, Salary Review Committee, Tax Incentive Review Council, Tree Committee which encompasses 112 members to these Boards. These Committee members have dedicated time and energy to help guide the City into the future, which in turn helps the City Manager, City Staff and City Commission make the necessary decisions for the betterment of the community.

In 2006-2007 the City of Piqua worked to develop a list of goals to help ensure that the quality of life for all citizens continuously improves. The steps put in place to do this are to improve the city's visual appeal, develop the economic vitality of the downtown and community, support our local educational opportunities, expand recreational opportunities, strengthen the city's infrastructure, enhance the historical and cultural character of the city and embrace the diversity of the community. With putting these goals at the forefront, this will enable the City of Piqua to serve our citizens well into the future.

The City of Piqua looks forward to the future, yet looks back at the last 200 years of history with great appreciation and thanks to the leaders from the past.

Craycon Homes

Changing The Face Of Piqua

*A*long the North West end of Piqua, a productive farm known as the "Lambert Farm" shaped Piqua's land-scape for many years. The farm was owned and operated by Ora Lambert and transferred to Dorthea Lambert, his niece, upon his passing.

Dorthea continued the farm along with her husband Robert M. Davis, a successful banker and significant leader in the City of Piqua. Mr. Davis was always planning for the future, envisioning Piqua as it would someday be. The farm was part of his "vision". Mr. Davis recognized Piqua's need for adequate housing in order to lure new businesses to town and ultimately see the city grow.

In 1989, Mr. Davis contacted Dave and Mimi Crawford to share his plan for Piqua's future. The Crawford's founded Craycon Homes, Inc. and began building custom homes in Piqua.

In October of 1990 sadly Mr. Davis passed away. The Crawford's took Mr. Davis' vision one step farther and hired an architect and land planner. They spent the next three years working on the design plan for a unique and different neighborhood. They didn't want just an ordinary neighborhood with straight streets. After much surveying and many market researches they were then ready to turn this vision into a reality.

"For the last (50) years the use of the automobile has been a major factor in the design of homes and subdivisions," stated Mrs. Crawford, "but now in the 90's, families are again asking for the many features that were part of the "old" neighborhood." The "old" neighborhood was more "pedestrian friendly", typically with a mix of age groups. The neighborhoods were safe and friendly with people walking and bicycling. Children would gather in the street to play a game of kickball. Neighbors would gather to chat over a cup of coffee and people would look after each other. Often these neighborhoods featured narrower streets designed for low volume, low-speed movement, occasional curvilinear streets and strong visual elements. Dave and Mimi Crawford knew that this is what Deerfield needed to be.

By this time many similar residential neighborhoods began springing up all over the country. In October of 1994, the new Deerfield Community was founded by Craycon Homes, Inc. and has since "changed the face of Piqua."

The development would be new in its design, architecture and amenities for the Piqua area. In keeping with the variation of housing types found in these new development communities, Deerfield consists of three distinct neighborhoods offering something for everyone. Deerfield Trace features paired patio homes offering a maintenance free lifestyle. Deerfield Crossing offers upscale apartment living, while Deerfield Trails comprises one and two story single family homes for all ages. Craycon Homes utilizes all of the latest technology and energy efficiencies in their homes.

On June 9, 1996, Craycon Homes held their Grand Opening for the Deerfield Subdivision. They offered walking tours

through their furnished model home located in the heart of Deerfield Trails and tours of the Deerfield Crossing apartment buildings. Lemonade stands were set up at every block corner. McGruff the Crime Dog and the McDonald's characters made a special appearance to support this extraordinary day.

That same year, Craycon Homes created the R.M. Davis Park at the front entrance of Deerfield. The park features beautiful landscaping, state-of-the art playground equipment, park benches, a picnic shelter and a black-granite memorial of Robert M. Davis. Craycon Homes dedicated this new park to the City of Piqua with a formal dedication honoring Mr. Davis for his countless contributions to our city. U.S. Representative John Boehner, state and local government officials, fellow business leaders, friends and family were all in attendance.

Lifestyle is the key theme encompassing all of Deerfield. Lifestyle is addressed first with Deerfield's location. Just off High Street at the extreme west end of town, you are within five minutes of the public swimming pool, 18 hole public golf course, soccer fields, baseball, tennis, schools, grocery stores, drug stores, banks, and medical offices. Within the Deerfield Community, lifestyle continues to be the key theme with the brick entrance, tree lined streets and boulevards to welcome you home. Parks and open green spaces were created for playing or relaxing while taking in the beautiful sunsets. Children and adults alike enjoy fishing in the many ponds throughout the Deerfield Subdivision. Social activities are coordinated throughout the year for all ages to enjoy. Annual Christmas decorating contests, Easter Egg hunts and block parties are just to name a few. It's an opportunity to get to know each other. A sound, well managed association exists providing restrictive covenants to protect each homeowner's long-term investment.

Now in the year 2007 our vision for a unique, progressive neighborhood based on old time values and aesthetics has become a reality. The Deerfield Community has nearly 200 homes and continues to "Change the face of Piqua".

Dan's BP

Dan's BP is a convenience store located at the corner of North Main and North Streets. Owned by Dan Poast, this retail store is open long hours and carries a limited selection of goods including BP gasoline, Ohio Lottery, beer and wine, tobacco products, and various food and convenience items.

This location has been a gasoline service station since the early 1900's when The Standard Oil Company purchased the location. For years this was the busiest spot between Dayton and Lima on Old Route 25, long before I-75 was constructed. The store was open 24 hours a day and employees from this time would talk of spending all night repairing tires for the traffic on Route 25.

Before 1950 David Whitmore sold Packard automobiles, and provided a full line of auto repair along with Standard Oil gasoline.

Soon after that there was a gasoline problem in the basement and the old building had to be razed. The lot was expanded by taking another house and the current building was constructed.

I first operated the site in 1977. I had operated several stores in the Dayton area and was anxious to move to a smaller, slower paced area. I can still remember the first six months in Piqua - every day was like vacation. I operated several store sites between Dayton and Miami County including Covington Avenue and Sunset, Looney Road and I-75 and

25-A and I-75 in the Piqua area. The Total Automotive repair facility on Covington Avenue was also mine. In 1991, I bought the store at 600 N. Main Street from BP Oil. The store was operated as a full service gasoline service station until 1998. At that time it was converted to a convenience store as it is today.

Gasoline sales and auto service has changed so much over the 30-years I have been in Piqua. No more 'points & plugs' every 10,000 miles. No more snow tires. It used to be that it was too dangerous for customers to handle the gasoline. Full service was the law. Then came self-service, I was one of the last in Piqua to give up full service gas. All gas used to be leaded to reduce valve wear. Our premium gas was called Boron. It had the element Boron in it instead of lead. Now all is unleaded to work better with pollution controls on the cars of today. Recently we began selling gasoline with 10% ethanol added. Vapor recovery was added. This captures the fuel vapors that are formed from the tank as you are filling. All the vapors from the store tanks are captured to lower pollution.

The atmosphere around a filling station has greatly improved over the past 30 years. Who knows what we will use to fuel our cars and how it will be dispensed in another 50 years. This gasoline service station was the first business location for me in Piqua and it will be the last.

Dan Poast – May 2007

Decker Family

Valentine Decker was born in Baden, Germany on April 7, 1847. As a young man he apprenticed as a butcher in his homeland.

He came to America in 1868, working in a butcher shop in Troy for 6 months. In 1869 he came to Piqua, working for P.J. Muellan who owned a slaughter house on East Main St. Then he spent a short time in Union City, Indiana. Returning to Piqua and married Johanna Schafer on February 20, 1873.

To this union were born five sons and two daughters. They were Louis F., George H., Carl F., Walter J., Caroline (Schwable), Johanna (Yenney), and William J. All the sons later joined their father in the operation of the plant. Carl F. died in 1915 before the birth of his son Carl who joined the company in 1930.

In 1877 he opened his own retail butcher shop at 512-514 West High St. A few years later he started slaughtering animals in a small building on a lot he had purchased in the 600 block of West Water St. This proved to be prosperous.

The land in the bend of the river was purchased in the early 1880's. In the mid-1880's Decker purchased a lot at 513 West High where he built a two story Italianate home. This structure still stands.

By the late 1890's Louis F. was in charge of the meat shop and Valentine took over the wholesale end of the business, selling to the 20 other butcher shops in town.

Decker owned an ice house near Echo Lake to provide ice for his packing operations. Operations were moved in 1903 to the new location at 727 East Ash St. As the packing business prospered the retail market was sold to B.F. Julian around 1906.

After damages to the earlier building by the 1913 flood an addition was built. At that time the company had 42 employees and annual sales of $500,000. This is the same year that Walter O. Decker (no relation) joined the company as its only office employee- he later became president in 1960.

In 1927 government inspection was instituted and the company, having inspection #95, changed its logo from "Our Pride" to "Piquality". The next major expansion was in 1928 and there were more than 200 employees. In 1931, Val Decker spent a quarter of a million dollars on a new addition and new equipment and another third of a million in 1933.

Although his banker friends advised him not to spend the money from his capitol reserves his answer was- "Why not? I have the money. We need the plant. Now is the time to buy, besides look at the additional employment it will give."

At the dedication on April 30, 1933 an estimated 6,500 people some coming from Chicago, New York, and Kansas City toured the facility. Population of Piqua was estimated to be 18,000. With a payroll of $7000.00 about 275 people were employed a Decker's. The new facility went into operation of May 1, 1933. At that time it was the third largest employer in Piqua.

Products were delivered by truck to locations within a 200 mile radius to customers in Ohio and portions of West Virginia, Indiana, Kentucky and Michigan. Although there was a staff of salesmen the truck drivers also acted as salesmen since daily delivery was guaranteed.

Louis F. was VP/Assistant Sales Manager, George H. was Treasurer/Sales Manager and Walter J. was Secretary/Plant Manager.

After the death of Valentine in 1937, Louis F. assumed leadership as Chairman of the Board and William J. became President.

In the early years the livestock was delivered by train from Missouri and walked down Water St. from the station to Decker's. Livestock ordinarily was delivered by truck. The maintenance of the plant and fleet were the responsibility of John (Jack) Jordan, son-in-law of George H.

During World War II 40,000 lbs. of lard was sold to Russia however the product didn't reach its destination as the boat was sunk by the Japanese. At that time most of the meat processed was shipped to our military camps along the Eastern seaboard and the naval base in Chicago.

In 1953 officers of the company were George H. Chairman of the Board; Walter O. Executive VP/Secretary, Louis V. Treasurer/Sales Manager. Additional VP's were Carl F. Decker, William B. Decker, Donald L. Decker and Robert W. Schwable.

Although there was a union in the 1930's (a strike in 1934 and a major strike in 1935) the plant didn't become a closed shop until about 1952. There was a strike in 1964.

Carloads of meat were shipped to New Jersey, New York, Georgia, Florida, Virginia, Oregon, Massachusetts, Washington State and California by outside trucking companies.

Everything but the "squeal" was sold. By-products were sold to pharmaceutical companies such as Eli-Llily and Parke Davis. Hides and skins were sold to shoe companies such as Edmonson and Hush Puppy. Other by-products were sold to Alpo for dog food, meat to Campbell soup and tallow to Proctor & Gamble.

At this time Decker was the largest employer in Piqua; also the largest user of electricity and water in Piqua. In the 1960's officers were Louis V. Chairman of the Board; Walter O. President; William B. Executive VP; Carl F. VP/Secretary; Donald L. VP/Treasurer; R. Patrick VP of livestock and Robert Schwable VP in charge of operations.

Decker's stock was family owned until the 1970's when it was sold to "outsiders". Many third, fourth and fifth generation descendants and in-laws have worked in the plant.

In 1978 Jim Ruppell assumed control of the plant via stock purchases. Many factors were involved in the closing of the Val Decker Packing Company on June 27, 1980.

It was a sad day for over 350 employees. Decker had an annual sales figure of over $45 million.

Tom Jordan, Traffic Manager and Bob Jordan, Head of Maintenance and Sally Jordan Barker, Sales – all descendants of George H. Decker were the last of the family employed there on Jun 27, 1980.

When no buyers came forth the building was sold to Lloyd Fry and the equipment was auctioned off.

DeWeese Family

The DeWeese Boys
Dick, Bob, Alvah Sr., Alvah Jr., Jim

The name DeWeese, apparently of Dutch origin, first came into use about the twelfth century. It means "the orphan". The earliest DeWees settlers in America were Gerrard Hendricks DeWees, his wife Zytian, and their children. They came about 1688 and first settled at New Amsterdam. Their son Lewis was a weaver in Philadelphia. In 1727 he moved to Delaware with his family including son Samuel. Samuel's son Joshua was with General Washington's Army at Valley Forge and lost a portion of his foot due to the cold. Joshua's family moved to West Virginia and he became a minister. His son Samuel also became a minister and traveled on the Ohio River and up the Miami River to Fort Staunton near Troy. He was the organizing minister of the Fort Staunton Baptist Church near Troy. His son Joshua, also a minister at that church, served in the War of 1812 and later married Mary Gerard who is claimed to be the first white female born in Miami County. Their son Henry had eleven children, the youngest of whom was Alvah. He was the only one of the eleven children to go to college. He became a lawyer, married Grace Doren, and had four sons-Alvah Jr., James, Robert, and Richard. Grace's mother's maiden name was DeWeese. She was also a descendant of Joshua DeWeese- but through his second wife.

Alvah and Grace took up housekeeping in the house to the north of the YWCA on North Wayne Street. A few days before the flood of 1913, they moved to a brick house at the bottom of Covington Avenue. About seven years later Alvah purchased and moved into the house next door so there would be enough signatures on a petition to get Covington Avenue paved.

Alvah ran for Mayor in 1903. His platform was "a good clean city government with a rigid enforcement of the Sunday closing law." Although he lost, he ran again in 1921 and won by a mere 28 votes. True to his word, he shut down all the bars in town on Sundays which caused a lot of controversy in town. Alvah also became a State Senator. In 1921 he and Grace attended President Harding's inauguration as members of the official Ohio delegation. Alvah is considered responsible for the establishment of the municipal court in Piqua and served as Judge.

The DeWeese boys had a lot of work to do. There was the laundry every Monday before school, vegetable and flower gardens, mowing the grass on that huge hill, beating the carpets, paper routes, tending to the outhouse, and working at the quarry across the street Alvah owned. There was lots of fun though too. They had a slide and teeter-totter. They built a roller coaster and a tennis court. The family belonged to the Country Club, but in the winter it was closed so they went to the Piqua Club at Greene and Wayne. There was a bowling alley in the basement and a restaurant and barber shop on the first floor. The boys took dance lessons there and learned to waltz and fox trot.

Son Jim did not originally want to go into law, but his father wanted a son to join his law practice. So Jim attended San Diego State University (where he played varsity basketball) and then the University of Cincinnati for law school, graduating in 1933. In those days it was a good week if he made $20. He practiced law with Alvah until 1946 when he was elected Judge of municipal court and was sworn in by his father. In 1948 he ran for county prosecuting attorney and served in that capacity for the next 16 years. He had a reputation as being "a tiger in the courtroom." From 1956 until 1966 he was also senior partner in the law firm of DeWeese and Wilson with Richard Wilson. He went on to serve as president of the Ohio and National Prosecuting Attorneys Associations and was elected Judge of Miami County Common Pleas Court from 1966-1973. He practiced law in private practice until his retirement in 1998 after serving 65 years in the legal profession. Jim was instrumental, with cooperation of the Miami County Bar Association, in getting Miami County's new courthouse. He established the Bureau of Support in 1967 before it was required by state law. He also had the first female bailiff in the county.

Jim married his neighbor on Covington Avenue, Lucille Frigge, in 1934. During World War II Jim worked full time at WACO and Lear Avia during the days and practiced law nights and weekends. They had three children-James Jr., David, and Denise. In 1977 he married Shirley Tewart Harris, and they were married until his death in 2006. Jim Jr. had Debbie, Lori, and Jim III. David's children are April and Scott. Denise has one son Jonathan. Other DeWeese descendants include Chad, Isaiah, Anna, Amy, McKenzie, Noah, Jennifer, Josh, Toni, Luke, Brooke, and Dani.

Jim DeWeese, Sr with his three children at the 90th birthday party.
Left to Right. Jim Jr., Denise, Jim Sr., and David.

The Draving Family Heritage

A gentleman, Hitius Schmidt and his wife Johanna lived on a 40 acre farm on Rakestraw Road (in the 1800's). They requested farm help from Germany during the "Civil War." Several persons came from Merien Stein, close to Hanover, Germany. Their passage was on a steamship called the "New York" that sailed from Bremen. Also Caroline Zimmerle was on the ship and she later married another passenger, August Drewing.

The Drewings were told the correct pronunciation for Drewing was Draving. The graves of Schmidt, Drewing, and Draving are left of the main gate entrance to Forest Hill Cemetery.

The original small farm home on Rakestraw Road was replaced by a two story brick. When Mr. Schmidt deceased, the farm was given to August and Caroline Draving. This couple had five children: John, Louis, August E., Albert, and Gustave. Three of these brothers are also buried in Forest Hill Cemetery. In recent years the original house has been refurbished and has a new caring family.

August E. Draving's main interest was steam engines (not farming.) He helped many farms run steam engines from threshing machines. August met his wife, Clara Haller, at a threshing dinner. They lived at 515 east Greene Street, where Clarence E. was born. August worked for a time at the Piqua Plaza Hotel. Then the family moved to Dayton and worked for Callahan Power Plant, Beckel Hotel, etc. They came back to Piqua because of the 1913 flood. He resumed the position at Piqua Favorite Hotel, which later was named Fort Piqua Hotel.

Several family members spoke German until entering Piqua Public Schools. All brothers attended St. Paul's Church where German services were offered.

The family settled at 1401 & 1403 Broadway. A daughter, Irma Pauline (Deeter) was born in Dayton and Lester W. in Piqua, completing their family of three.

Clarence E. Draving's main interest was electricity. His hobbies included creating and designing new things. He built one of the first radio sets in Piqua using vacuum tubes. His first new car was a 1924 four-door Chevrolet Touring Car—Cost $550—top speed 35 mph. His working days included Hosiery Co. – Superior Co. During the depression his father hired him part time at Fort Piqua Hotel. His favorite memory is climbing in the clock tower (with his dad) twice a week to check and wind the three round faced clocks. Clarence retired from Hobart Mfg. Co. During WWII he assembled M3 Telescope Mounts for 75MM guns—then went to electric motor testing. He worked there 29 years and then retired to Bradenton, Florida. He continued creating many electrical games in Florida and kept in touch with friends and family via letter writing and fax machine messages. He read the *Piqua Daily Call* on a regular basis. Clarence E. and Gladys I. (McClannan) Draving were married in 1926 by Rev. Paul Gehm (St. Paul's Church). They have three children: Belva Jean, Alva Duane, and Karen Elaine.

Charles and Belva Black have resided in Piqua their entire lives. They maintain an almost daily communication with brother and sister who now live elsewhere. Duane and Glenna (Lutes) Draving live in Wichita, KS. And John and Karen (Draving) Robinson live in Tennessee.

The male members who continue the Draving name are: Duane Draving, Wichita; Steven, Colorado Springs; and his son Austin, age 12.

The above information was originally written by Clarence E. Draving in a booklet he entitled the **DRAVING DYNASTY**, which he gave to his children and grandchildren when he was 93 years old. The condensation above was compiled by Belva J. (Draving) Black at age 80 years. Duane Draving maintains a complete family history of all the Draving decendents.

It is interesting to observe that many of the traits, skills, and abilities have continued to exist through the generations. Examples include; belief in **GOD**, a sense of humor, and the joy of daily living. Skills include engineers, electrical inventions and patents, building techniques, and an ability to create. However, most of all, the entire family – past and present – agree that **Piqua, Ohio is a very grand place to live.**

Clarence Draving's Children
Left to right: Karen, Duane, Belva

August Draving Family
Left to right: Lester, Clara, August,
Pauline, Clarence

Favorite Hill Baptist Church

Favorite Hill Baptist Church began as a mission in 1958 with the first services being held in the National Guard Armory. In July 1958, summer student workers from the Dayton Baptist Association and the associational missionary held Vacation Bible School in the National Guard Armory. By the fall of 1958, there were five faithful women attending the mission and supporting this work which grew out of the Vacation Bible School.

In May, 1959, the First Baptist Church of Fairborn provided financial support for the mission to call Earl Burnside from Kentucky as the full time pastor for the mission. In July, 1959, the new pastor and his wife Ethel moved to Piqua. Also, the Fairborn church sent three families to the mission for Sunday mornings to help organize and lead the Piqua mission.

The chapel started growing while continuing to hold services in the Armory until they moved to the current location on Brown Road. On October 10, 1959, the land was purchased on Brown Road for the purpose of building a new church building. The ground breaking took place on December 13, 1960. In May, 1961, the congregation moved into the 36' by 104' new building which comprised one-third of the overall church project. The name became Favorite Hill Baptist Church when it moved from the Armory to the Brown Road address which later became South Street.

The Favorite Hill Baptist Church organized on January 5, 1964, with 91 charter members as the 300th Southern Baptist Church in the state of Ohio. According to information in the church records by the late Hazel Mumford (one of the five women), "the church was built a lot on faith." Also, in the church records is information that the favorite scripture in those early years was Matthew 18:20, "For where two or three are gathered together in My name, there am I in the midst of them." This church was started through outreach because of the concern for the spiritual needs of people.

The second phase of the building program was started with the addition of a new sanctuary which is still in use today. The first service was held November 16, 1969, in the new sanctuary. On May 24, 1970, the dedication service was held for this part of the building program. The theme scripture for the service was Psalm 127:1, "Except the Lord build the house, they labour in vain that build it."

The church continued to grow during the 70's with a vision to complete the third phase of the overall church project. In 1977 the new 5,000 square feet education unit was started for the growing Sunday School. In May 1979, the dedication service was held for the new educational unit.

The church over the last several years has added many upgrades to the buildings. The original baptistry was replaced in the late 1980's. The original seats in the sanctuary were replaced with pews in 2001. There have been many other changes in the 30 and 40 year old buildings during the last several years, with a continued vision of the future.

There have been 13 men who have served as pastor of Favorite Hill Baptist Church from the beginning until the present time. These ordained ministers are Earl Burnside (1959-1966), David Cochran (1967-1971), Eugene Broome (1971-1972), Dewie Schell (1972-1975), (1994-1995), Ronald Stewart (1975-1979), Bobby Petrey (1979-1980), Barry Lovett (1980-1983), Ernie Jones (1984-1991), Michael Ellis (1991-1993), Allen Sanders (1996-2001), Dennis Nickel (2001-2004), and Larry Haynes (2005-present). Also, there have been other ministers who have served as interim pastor during the life of the church.

The church continues to be mission-minded, with a desire for people to find salvation by accepting Christ, by believing in the heart that Christ died for their sins, and confessing Christ as their Lord and Savior. It is the congregation's desire for the church to have an impact on the lives of people in the community through the Lord Jesus Christ. The church gives to mission efforts for local, state, and foreign missions through the Cooperative Program of the Southern Baptist Convention.

The church has affiliation with the West Central Baptist Association, State Convention of Baptists in Ohio, and the Southern Baptist Convention. However, the church is a local autonomous church with decisions relating to the church being made by the local body. The church supports the Baptist faith and the message of the Southern Baptist Convention. The church has various programs for all ages, groups and families. This church has been blessed by the Lord over almost 50 years of ministry as a mission and church. The church, located at 1601 South Street in Piqua will continue to be a loving, caring, and friendly instrument of the Lord. Also, the church can be contacted at (937) 773-6469 and by email at *favoritehillbc@yahoo.com*.

F.C. Skinner Painting Service

F.C. Skinner Painting Service was established by Francis Cecil Skinner in 1944. He began painting at the young age of 15 with his Uncle Orville. After years of working with his uncle, he decided to go out on his own. He purchased a Dodge Stake Rack Truck and one pick up truck. His grandpa and uncle helped him from time-to-time as he developed his company.

With a wife and two daughters at home to support, he worked nights at Dodge Taxi Service as a taxi cab driver and during the day he ran his business. When Dodge Taxi Service went out of business he worked for Calland Taxi Service. Eventually, his business was doing well enough that he didn't work a second job.

In 1946 Cecil was the first in the area to have spray equipment. With a paint sprayer which consisted of a paint pump, compressor, one paint pot, and one hose, he was able to paint buildings and roofs much quicker than brush application. With this new technology he was able to save time on the job and the customer money. After hiring a couple more employees, and with him working on some of the jobs, his business began to grow.

While Cecil was working on jobs and cold calling on potential customers, his wife Doris was home taking calls from customers, typing estimates, invoicing, and running the household when she wasn't working as swimming instructor. She would take messages for Cecil and he would call the customers back in the evening to schedule appointments.

Most of his customers were farmers. Cecil and his men would paint barns, roofs, silos, and other farm buildings. They used triple extension ladders to clean and paint the silos until the mid 1950's when bucket trucks became available. Cecil bought his first 20' bed truck in 1955 and took it to a company in Indiana to have a folding knuckle boom installed in 1958. F.C. Skinner Painting Service began doing industrial cleaning and painting in 1955 due to companies in the surrounding areas showing an interest in having their buildings painted.

With the continual growth of his company he found the need for a telescopic boom truck. In 1967 he purchased a 40' telescopic boom truck which enabled his employees to reach areas without having to use the knuckle boom. In 1968 Cecil bought his first sandblast truck. Sand blasting allowed them to clean rust and other hard to remove substances at a quicker pace with better results; however, hand scraping always remained a part of the job.

By the early 1970's Cecil had eight to ten employees and at times he had up to 12 employees. Business was good and he stayed busy. Some employees would come and go although; he had seasoned employees that are still with the company today. In 1974 he bought his first 55' complete bucket truck which consisted of hydraulic paint pumps mounted onto the side of the truck. This truck was designed just for painting. In 1976 he purchased his second complete bucket truck.

Cecil hired his 14 year old grandson, David Middleton in 1976. David worked part-time during the school year and full time in the summers. In 1980 after he graduated from high school he became a full time employee. Recognizing David's interest in working for the painting company, Cecil mentored him ensuring that he learned how to do every service they had to offer. Over the years David became a strong leader for the company.

In the early 1980's water blasting technology began to increase. Cecil purchased the needed equipment for his crews. With the additional water blast and pressure wash equipment they were able to clean structures that may have required sand

blasting in the past. Business was good and everyone worked hard. Cecil had a lot of returning customers that needed other buildings on their property painted. Even though he had a solid customer base he was always looking for more work. He worked long hours and expected his men to have the same work ethic.

In the late 1990's Cecil had begun to sell part of his company to David. He had groomed him so that one day he would continue his legacy as owner and president of F.C. Skinner Painting Service. In June of 1999 Cecil passed away leaving his wife Doris and his grandson David as co-owners of the company. David became his successor as president and began running the crews and selling the jobs.

Today in 2007, F.C. Skinner Painting Service continues to thrive in the City of Piqua and remains family owned and operated since 1944. David continues to grow the company with employees and types of services available, therefore keeping up with the changing times.

Fifth Third Bank

Two banks become one. . . .

Fifth Third Bank has provided banking, lending, and investment services for individuals and businesses in Piqua tracing its origins back to 1847.

In the 1800s, two banks were prominent in Piqua. One was the Piqua branch of the State Bank of Ohio which was established on March 26, 1847. This bank became known as The Piqua National Bank on March 23, 1865. The other prominent bank in Piqua was The Citizens National Bank which was established on April 26, 1865. Many mergers and acquisitions occurred over the years, however, these two banks continued to operate independently until the 1980s.

On December 31, 1986, the two prominent banks in Piqua became one, known as Citizens Heritage Bank, National Association.

Fifth Third Bank then purchased Citizens Heritage Bank in 1988 and has continued to be a major contributor to Piqua's economic vitality.

The buildings and locations. . . .

In 1847, the Piqua branch of the State Bank of Ohio was established. The original location was in an old storeroom on the west side of Main Street just south of what is now Ash Street. In 1865, the bank became known as The Piqua National Bank and moved into a new site just north of Ash Street. In 1900, The Piqua National Bank moved into new and larger quarters providing two teller windows and a large vault. This site is currently owned by Joe Thoma & Sons Jewelers and they still use the vault today. Piqua was growing and The Piqua National Bank began plans for a beautiful new bank building and on December 1, 1928 the cornerstone for its current location was laid. Inside this cornerstone is a box containing letterheads and catalogues of every product made in Piqua, a brief history of the community, schools, churches, city officials, lodges, clubs and organizations. There is also a bible, a $5 bill of the bank's own currency, and pictures of all bank Directors, Officers and employees.

Miami Citizens' location history is a unique story in the fact that it changed buildings over the years but remained at the same site for the entirety of its existence. The bank began in a room on the northeast corner of Main & Ash Streets inside the Johnston building, which was owned by a nephew of the memorable Col-

onel John Johnston. The bank remained in the Johnston building until 1882 when it erected a three story building on the same location and served as its headquarters until 1920. The bank then decided to erect a modern banking house of Bedford limestone, which is still an impressive structure in downtown Piqua. In 1950 a modernization effort was completed adding such amenities as an auto Drive-In Window, air conditioning, carpeted lobbies, and beautiful walnut paneling provided by Hartzell Industries, Inc. It was believed to be from a huge tree, estimated age 300 years, and once owned by George Washington.

As a result of these two fine institutions merging together in 1987, Fifth Third Bank owned and operated eight different banking locations in Piqua over the years. Only two offices remain today, our High Street office, and our Market Street office in addition to the drive-thru facility on Greene Street.

The people who make a difference. . . .

Especially important are the people to which our success can be attributed. Our employees are involved with their own families, and at the same time they reach out to help others. They are members of school boards, PTA, YMCA, YWCA, hospitals, Chamber of Commerce, United Way, Kiwanis, Rotary, Optimist, VFW, Moose, Eagles, and other organizations. They volunteer in scouting, coach little league baseball, soccer, football, basketball, and provide many services for our youth. They help raise funds to fight against heart disease, cancer, and other diseases. They help to provide a better quality of life to our senior citizens. They do all of these things right here in Piqua.

Many citizens have contributed to this organization over the years. Prominent names like William Megrue, William Scott, Alfred Flesh, William Orr, George Rundle, H.K. Wood, William Kadel, and Robert Davis to name a few. These are some of the names who have helped to create a company which led to much of the wealth in the city of Piqua.

Fifth Third Bank today . . . .

Today, Fifth Third Bank operates 18 affiliates with over 1,100 full-service locations serving in Ohio, Kentucky, Indiana, Michigan, Illinois, Florida, Tennessee, West Virginia, Pennsylvania, and Missouri. Known as a super regional, Fifth Third Bank's affiliate structure allows for local decision making in all of our markets. Piqua is in the Western Ohio affiliate and is unique to other financial markets with a complete sales team.

CItizens National Bank

Piqua National Bank

The French Oil Mill Machinery Company

The French Oil Mill Machinery Company was founded May 25, 1900 by Alfred Willard French, an M.I.T. graduate. He moved to Piqua and incorporated the Company with local investors who put in $5,000 and French put in his patents and himself. They hired two assemblers and people to work in the foundry, and shop areas, as well as the office and Engineering Department. French believed engineering creativity and research would produce superior vegetable oil mill machinery, and set the company's mission as "Makers of Improved Oil Mill Machinery".

Piqua provided a number of positive features for the new company. It was a regional center for the growing of flax and the production of linseed oil, with 11 linseed oil mills, and was also a regional railroad hub. It also had available factory sites tied to electric streetcar routes, a trained labor force, and cheap power sources in gas and electricity.

The first few years in his new venture were difficult, and French was quoted: "We can not afford a decent funeral for this business so we have to go ahead ... but I think I ought to have my head examined for leaving the good job I had with an assured salary and only ten hours a day of work, for this 24 hours a day of worry, and darn near as much work."

The Company survived because the superior new machinery was important to the vegetable oil industries that were pressing oil from linseed, cottonseed, peanuts, castor beans, copra, sesame seeds, and others.

A. W. French had a vision for the future of the company. By 1905, he was exporting to markets outside of the USA, building equipment for use in Great Britain, Germany, and Norway. Alfred and Grace French went around the world in 1920-21, to sell French machinery. This strong tradition of partnering across the seas continues today with installations in major countries on every continent, except Antarctica.

French and his team transitioned their expertise in vegetable oil hydraulic press technology to other processes, such as metal forming and rubber curing. He was granted 55 patents while doing so.

Mrs. Alfred W. French took over as President, ably assisted by General Manager Charles B. Upton, after her husband's untimely death in 1925. The company remained dedicated to the same principles of creative engineering, research and quality manufacturing.

Alfred W. French, Jr. joined the company in 1926, rising to Vice President in 1931 and President in 1962. Under his direction, the company expanded offerings to vegetable oil mills with mechanical screw presses and other products. He also pioneered the use of screw presses in the synthetic and natural rubber, the wood pulp and the cane sugar industries. He was Chairman of the Board until his death in 1992.

Daniel P. French, the younger son of Alfred W. French, Jr., joined the company in 1971, was promoted to President in 1982, and is now also Chairman of the Board. He has continued the company's innovations and market expansion.

Today, the company has three main market groups:

French's Oilseed Group is one of the world's leading suppliers and innovators of oilseed preparation and extraction equipment and systems, with customers in more than 80 countries. French supplies equipment and custom engineered systems for oilseed preparation and mechanical screw pressing.

French's Polymer Group designs and manufactures mechanical screw presses for dewatering and drying all types of synthetic rubber and other polymers, such as ABS plastic. French

mechanical dewatering presses have long been recognized as the leader in the industry, with customers in more than 23 countries. This group also provides screw presses for removing water from wood pulp fiber for the pulping industry and the paper recycling industry.

French's Hydraulic Group supplies equipment for use in molding rubber, thermoset plastic and composite materials, with an installed base of more than 20,000 presses worldwide. Some presses are supplied with very sophisticated computer control systems and process automation, to help our customers be more profitable.

French's Manufacturing Facility produces critical parts for oilseed, polymer, and hydraulic machinery, manufactured to exacting quality standards, and is ISO-9001 certified. French does contract machining for area companies, and responds to customer needs by applying continuous improvement concepts in quality, prompt delivery, and supplier relationships.

The leaders, families and friends of French Oil have always been active in the Piqua community. French parade floats can be seen in pictures through the years. The company sponsors local children's community teams in baseball, softball and soccer, and contributes to many other community organizations and projects. French employees tutor and support activities at Wilder Intermediate School through the "School-Business Partnership". The company and its people believe in "giving back to the community", and wish Piqua well, as we move into Piqua's third century.

1997. Four generations of the French Family: Alfred W. French, Jr. (portrait), Peter Loomis French, Katherine Taylor French, Daniel Phelps French, and Alfred W. French, Sr. (portrait).

GeNell's Flowers

*I*n the early 1950's, GeNell's Flowers was located at 166 East Ash in downtown Piqua, Ohio. GeNell Hewey Horner, the owner of the shop, remained at this site until she relocated the shop in 1970. On the northeast corner of Harrison and Ash, Horner had the current site of the shop constructed. The new, two-story building consisted of the store and an apartment, which Horner and her husband occupied. Horner purchased the site from the First Piqua Corporation's Quality House Furniture Division.

After owning and operating the flower shop for thirty-two years, Horner decided to retire. She sold the business to Mark Casto on December 1, 1982.

Casto's background included years of experience with flowers and plants. His first job was at Gerhart's Greenhouses Inc., where he learned about flower arranging. Casto also worked for Gerlach's Florist and Andy's Garden. He shared his skills and knowledge by teaching students at the Upper Valley JVS and speaking with people at the YWCA.

On December 1, 1984, Casto married Kim Hampshire. The two worked side-by-side in the flower shop until Casto began landscaping full-time. His new venture, Casto Landscaping, has thrived since.

Ms. Casto now runs the daily operations of GeNell's Flowers. With the development of the east side of Piqua, the shop's location at 300 East Ash has provided the store with many opportunities for growth.

Good Shepherd United Church

This church built its first church, which was a log church, in 1815. It was on the east side of Downing Street between Sycamore and Wood Streets. On March 29, 1815, John Campbell gave a tract of land for the church. Prior to 1815, services began in 1812-1813 by four Wiley families and the families of John Campbell and Joseph Hunter, who came from Milton County, Pa. Being impressed with the necessity of a preaching Gospel, they met in homes of these families and then held their services in the home of Samuel Wiley, whose house stood on a hill in Rossville. In 1815, this church was known as the Associated Reformed Presbyterian Church and was connected with the Presbytery of Kentucky, which was at that time under the care of the Synod of Scioto. The first regular pastor was called to the church on Oct. 9, 1934. His salary was $330.00 for three-fourths time.

In 1838, a neat brick church was erected on the same site. On the 20th of May, 1858, the Associated Reformed Church and the Reformed Church united and formed the United Presbyterian Church of North America. In the same year, the church at 415 N. Downing Street was completed and on the third day of October 1858 it was dedicated. This was the third church for this congregation. This building was damaged by the flood of 1913. This church was sold to the Church of Christ Scientist.

In 1922, plans were made for the present building and land had been purchased at 524 Park Ave. Services were held for several years in a wooden building in the rear of the lot. Dedication services were held on the Sabbath, Feb. 3rd, 1924. In 1958 was the merger of the United Presbyterian Church of North America and the Presbyterian Church in the U.S.A. On Jan. 7, 1959, the congregation selected the name of Good Shepherd United Presbyterian Church. Roger Toon, an ordained minister from the Church of Christ has served this congregation since June 1996.

Gover Harley-Davidson / Buell

The Gover family came to be an authorized, full-service Harley-Davidson Dealer in September of 1999. We purchased Ludy's Harley-Davidson in Painter Creek, Ohio from Bob, Esther and Steve Ludy. From the beginning, it was our intention to move the business to Piqua and we immediately began looking for the perfect location. We were very fortunate to find and purchase 12.4 acres from Miss Emily Garbry and John Garbry. Construction commenced immediately and we moved from Painter Creek to our new facility on the east side of Piqua in April of 2001.

Initially, the Piqua store was 17,500 sq ft. An addition completed in 2006 brought us to our current 28,000 sq ft facility. The new facility allows us to provide our customers with many more services and benefits than ever before, including winter storage and a high tech tuning center for engine performance. It also gave us a more convenient location and afforded us the opportunity to host more events and rides. We experienced tremendous sales growth with the relocation and, as a result, in eight short years we have gone from five employees to thirty employees. We sincerely believe that we have the best employees anywhere and we consider them to be part of our family. In 2006, with much help from our staff, the dealership's performance earned us a Bronze Bar & Shield Award from Harley-Davidson Motor Company.

Our business has been accepted and welcomed by the people of Piqua and the surrounding area. Being an integral part of small town America is a special and rewarding experience for our family. We love Piqua and the Miami Valley and look forward to attending to the needs of Harley-Davidson, Buell and all motorcycling enthusiasts for years to come. We have, without a doubt, most loyal and supportive customers a business could ever want. We appreciate our customers and we work hard every day to continue earning their business. Customer service was the foundation of our business and continues to be a priority.

The business and the family members are involved in several local charities and enjoy giving back to the community. We also sponsor the Miami-Shawnee Chapter of H.O.G. (Harley Owners Group), which took it's name from the Native American tribes that once lived in the Piqua area. The H.O.G. Chapter, in conjunction with the dealership, holds a Poker Run each August. We typically have over 500 registered riders and participants. What a beautiful sight it is to see several hundred motorcycles, mostly Harleys, gathered to support a worthy cause. Currently the recipient of the proceeds from our H.O.G. Chapter's Poker Run is the Rehabilitation Center for Neurological Development. In 2006 we proudly presented them with nearly $6400. We have also partnered with Koester Pavilion and Heartland of Piqua. Several of their residents have taken "Hearts Desire" rides on Harley and/or in sidecars. They were most appreciative and really enjoyed the experience.

Owners: James D. Gover, Tracy N. Gover, Ella Anne Gover, Shirley Gover & James M. Gover at 1501 East Ash St. (U.S. Rte. 36), Piqua, Ohio 45356

Gover Harley-Davidson holds six or seven large events per year. Beginning in February with Beat the Winter Blues, we host events regularly right up to Christmas. Some of our activities have included Blood Drives, Need for Speed Day, Dog Days of Summer, our Annual Anniversary and National Open House Day, and a Christmas Open House (complete with visits from Santa Claus). We possess a great respect for law enforcement and we have partnered with local the Police, Sheriff and Highway Patrol for Safety Awareness events. We also plan to host a Military/Veterans appreciation event for the first time this year.

To commemorate Piqua's bicentennial celebration, we commissioned artwork for our T-Shirts that captures the heritage of Piqua. We now have three custom back prints. One was inspired by the legend of the "Otath-he-wagh-Pe-qua" and the others depict elements of the Native American history of the Piqua area and Johnston Farm.

Somewhere down the road, Miss Ella Anne Gover (age four, daughter of Jim and Tracy, pride and joy of Nana and Papa) may own and run the family business. For now, Ella is much more interested in being a ballet dancer or visiting the recently improved play ground at Fountain Park than she is becoming a Harley-Davidson dealer! Whether business owner, Harley passenger, ballet dancer, student or fun-loving kid, she will be raised in the Piqua community and benefit from all the area has to offer.

We are very proud to be a part of Piqua's heritage and we look forward with great enthusiasm to continuing to be an integral part of the Piqua community for years to come.

Congratulations Piqua on your Two Hundredth Birthday!

The Gover Family

Greene Street United Methodist Church
1807-2007

Methodism in Ohio had its beginning in 1797 when Francis McCormick crossed the Ohio river from Kentucky and organized a Methodist Class near Milford, Ohio. John Kobler joined him in 1798 and they journeyed north along the Miami River and Mad River Valleys. This circuit was known as the Mad River Circuit, of which Piqua was a part.

The Methodist Church in Piqua was born in the fall of 1807 on what is now Broadway, near the junction of River Street and Broadway. Here, in the home of Casper Hendershott, thirteen devout pioneers met to organize the first Methodist class in Piqua.

After eight years of meeting in members' homes the group grew in numbers and strength, and began to search for a permanent church home. In 1815 they constructed, by subscriptions, a log structure on two acres of ground donated by John Johnston and Richard Winans. The first church was near what is now known as Johnston's Cemetery. Any denomination was permitted to use it for religious services and it was also used for school purposes.

In 1818 two years after Piqua was disconnected from the Mad River Circuit, the original log structure was replaced by a brick building on the same ground.

In 1823 the members, in their Quarterly Conference, began planning for a new church home. For $30 they bought half of Lot No. 24 in the original plot of Piqua, which was on the west side of Spring Street between Ash & High Streets. Contractor and builder John B. Davis built the 36' by 40' structure at a cost of $650. The date of completion was June 1, 1824.

The name Greene Street originated in 1835 when the first steps were taken to erect a building at the corner of Greene and Wayne Streets.

This church served the Methodists until the present structure was built in 1925. Lot No. 57 in the original plot of Piqua was purchased from General Young and on it John Keyt built a church for the sum of $4,167. The dedication took place in October, 1837.

During the winter of 1852-1853, the Rev. M. P. Gaddis conducted a most fruitful revival, with about four hundred members being added. As a result, a mission, known as Wayne Street was established and it soon became a self-supporting congregation. Today it is the Family of Grace Church.

Rev. Granville Moody was appointed to Greene Street from 1863-1866. During his pastorate the building was raised, steeples added and a first floor placed beneath the existing Sanctuary. In 1893 large stained glass windows were put in the church and the pipe organ was installed.

Greene Street Church suffered no irreparable loss during the destructive flood of 1913 though about three feet of water covered the entire first floor. Extensive repairs were made, but the incident, together with the growth of the church, pointed out the need for a modern church with expanded facilities.

In 1923 the present site was purchased from A.C. Wilson and John Anderson and the church membership organized for the erecting of a new and modern temple of worship.

J. C. Fulton & Sons, church architects, designed the building and the contract for construction was awarded to A. M. Fry. Cornerstone-laying services were held Sunday, June 7, 1925.

Early in the morning of December 17, 1927, a disastrous fire broke out in the new church. The flames were quickly extinguished but there was extensive smoke damage in the entire building. It was necessary to refinish the interior and to replace much of the equipment.

In 1966 an educational wing was added to the present building which was later dedicated to the life of Mildred B. Groves, long time Christian educator. An elevator was added in 1994. In 1980, Greene Street Day Care & Pre-School opened and continues to serve area families.

The community and Greene Street benefitted greatly in 1980 with the gift of money from William and Ruth Wall. The Wall Trust has provided education, music, scholarships and programs.

In 1987 West Ohio Chrysalis was formed and over 3,000 young adults have attended In 1996 a Food Pantry was opened and continues to serve Piqua area residents.

Green Street Church provides facilities and programs for the families in Piqua. The mission of Green Street Church is "Making Disciples by serving God's Family through Christ's Love." Children's Ministries, scouts, exercise classes, VBS, Church School, worship services and a caring outreach ministry touch countless lives. All of these things are the heart of Greene Street Church.

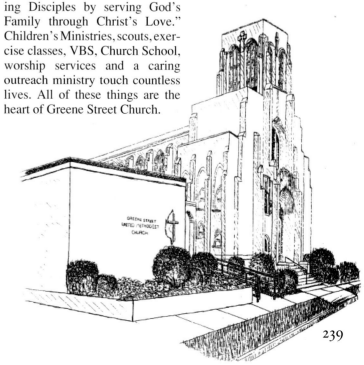

Hartzell Companies

In the late1860's John T. Hartzell made the decision that he did not want to work on his father's farm so he borrowed $25 from his family to purchase a horse and huckster wagon to start a business. He went from farm to farm selling items from his wagon including lighting rods. This developed into a decent business.

In 1875 John started a sawmill in Greenville, Ohio cutting general hardwoods. From the sawmill they produced a variety of lumber items for buildings and fences. Later he began to manufacture and repair farm wagons. There was the shipment of lumber to Europe as early as 1889. This business was the largest employer in Darke County.

John's son George began working in the business at an early age and in 1900 his father's ill health required George to buy out his father from the business. George moved the business to Piqua that year. Here the business specialized in manufacture of Walnut and Oak lumber. The market for Walnut was almost entirely in England and Germany.

The company expanded into the manufacture of hardwood veneers in 1915. The veneer operation provided hardwood veneer both for domestic markets in the United States and to export markets in several countries. A variety of species such as walnut, red oak, white oak, cherry, maple, and pecan were manufactured at this facility. A decision was made in 1992 to expand the hardwood lumber facility and to close the veneer slicing facility in Piqua.

Currently, Hartzell Hardwoods Inc. purchases green lumber and processes it through dry kilns to supply dry Walnut and Oak lumber to distributors throughout the world. Long recognized as a worldwide leader in walnut and top quality thick lumber, Hartzell Hardwood's philosophy continues to be characterized by innovation, quality, and integrity.

At the outbreak of World War I, the company was selling 100% of its product abroad. A war embargo stopped these shipments overnight. The company quickly responded by developing walnut gunstocks and walnut airplane propellers. George's son Robert N. Hartzell started the propeller division in 1917. The company supplied wood fixed pitch propellers for the war. This business continued to grow until the close of World War II. During the war metal propeller blades were produced for military aircraft. After the war this business stopped and a new controllable pitch propeller for small general aviation aircraft was developed. The propeller business developed into a major supplier to aircraft manufacturers throughout the world. The business was sold in 1981 and continues to operate in Piqua.

From experiments conducted on propeller airfoils the industrial fan division was started in 1927 known as Hartzell Fan, Inc.

The use of a propeller type fan with a ring increased airflow by more than 20% compared to flat blade type fans. The fan division has a broad product line to service a wide variety of ventilation requirements. These fan products may be manufactured from steel, aluminum, stainless steel, or fiberglass depending on the operating environment. Hartzell Fan currently has manufacturing operations in Piqua and Portland, Indiana. Hartzell fans can be found in a variety of industrial processes and manufacturing facilities. Today, Hartzell Fan continues with the traditions of the past – changing with our markets to always be a leader in the marketplace for high quality, industrial fans.

As an expansion in the marketing of hardwood veneer Hartzell purchased Arkansas Face Veneer located in Benton, Arkansas in 1971. At this facility hardwood veneer is purchased and cut to size for architectural doors, plywood, and furniture products. After the material is sized the components are spliced into a product that will be applied to the surface of the finished product. The majority of the veneer faces are applied to architectural doors and plywood. More than 100 species of veneer maybe used to manufacture the faces sold to Arkansas's customers.

Over the years there have been numerous products that the Hartzell Companies have manufactured that as the markets changed they have been replaced by new ventures. The Lumber operation manufactured gunstocks, steering wheels, battery cases, and the Propeller Division even built an airplane.

Hartzell Industries' business activities include real estate rentals in both Ohio and North Carolina and farming in Ohio. The company has corporate services, human resources, a maintenance department, and is the Administrator of various company retirement programs and employee benefits for the benefit of both itself and the three affiliated operating companies (Hartzell Hardwoods, Inc., Hartzell Fan, Inc., and Arkansas Face Veneer Co., Inc.).

The current Hartzell Companies are being managed by the fifth generation of the family. This generation is participating in the management of the company as members of the board of directors. Members of the Hartzell family continue to manage the Hartzell-Norris Charitable Trust. This trust provides funding for both local and worldwide charitable causes.

Hartzell Propeller Inc.

Hartzell Propeller Inc. is a privately held, non-union company with four facilities located in Piqua and employing over 300 people. The company designs and manufacturers constant-speed aircraft propellers and accessories. The propellers are installed on both piston-engine and turboprop aircraft. Aircraft propellers are highly engineered, flight-critical components tailored to individual aircraft. Hence, engineering and quality assurance skills are crucial to the business, as are best-in-class manufacturing capabilities.

As a teenager, George Hartzell's son, Robert N. Hartzell, had a burning desire to be involved in aviation. In 1914, fate brought Robert the encouragement he needed when Orville Wright moved into the newly built Hawthorn Hill mansion the Wright brothers designed, one block from the Hartzell residence in Oakwood. Robert spoke to Orville often about his interest in aviation, and Orville, knowing that the George W. Hartzell Company was already supplying high quality walnut lumber to others for production of aircraft propellers, encouraged young Robert to begin manufacture of their own propellers.

From walnut propellers on early aircraft to six-bladed propellers on modern regional airliners, Hartzell has continued to be a pioneering aviation company for 90 years.

Prior to 1917, though, Hartzell wasn't yet an aviation leader. The fledgling company was one of several businesses launched by the Hartzell family. John T. Hartzell started a small circle sawmill in Greenville, Ohio, in 1875. His son, George W. Hartzell, joined the business as a partner around 1890. In 1900, George bought his father's interest in the company and moved operations to Piqua. There the company specialized in wood products like gunstocks and veneer.

It was 17 years later that Robert Hartzell, the grandson of the founder, entered the business and steered the company toward a future in building propellers. Since then Hartzell has manufactured propellers "Built on Honor" through two world wars, 16 presidents, and into the space age.

The Hartzell family sold its propeller business in 1981 to TRW Inc. of Cleveland. In 1987, Cleveland-based Horsburgh & Scott Co. teamed with Jim Brown, a former naval aviator, to buy the propeller company. In 1988, Brown bought out H&S and owns the business today, along with his two sons, Jim III and Joe.

Included among Hartzell's credits are many industry firsts. Hartzell was the first to introduce a full-feathering, low-cost, reversible propeller for turboprops that encouraged the development of business and commuter aircraft. Hartzell also developed the first composite structural aircraft propeller blades. In 1986, Hartzell provided propellers for the Voyager and its non-stop around-the-world flight.

Today, Hartzell Propeller serves the general aviation and commuter aviation communities as a leader in propeller manufacturing and service.

Recently, Hartzell took another technological step forward with the introduction of its second generation of composite propellers, the ASC-II. This cost-reducing technology is making composite propellers viable for general aviation aircraft.

Along with building the best in propeller systems, Hartzell is dedicated to providing the finest service for its customers. The Hartzell Service Center is a factory-affiliated facility that provides complete overhaul and repair service for Hartzell propeller owners and operators. The service center, along with an internal product support organization and worldwide support network, provides immediate service for Hartzell customers. Located at the Piqua airport, just a few miles from the Hartzell factory, the advanced facility services all Hartzell products from the smallest two-blade to the largest six-blade propeller, including composite blades, spinners, governors, and synchrophasers.

Hartzell propellers are widely known and respected. The company sells its products in U.S. and foreign markets. The sales mix of two-thirds U.S. and one-third foreign mirrors worldwide aircraft activity. The company enjoys a happy mix of OEM and aftermarket sales.

The company has earned a sole-supplier position with many customers, including Beech Aircraft (Hawker Beechcraft), Cirrus, Piaggio (Italy), Pilatus (Switzerland), and Socata (France).

Havenar Sampson Auctioneers

"**H**ave gavel will travel" is the well-known slogan associated with Havenar and Sampson Auctioneers. Two father and son teams comprise the business - Lou Havenar and his son Mike and Bruce Sampson and his son Joe.

Lou Havenar started the whole thing back in 1961. He was an International Harvester dealer then, but business was bad and an auction sale was in order. "After the two-day sale was over, I realized how much commission the auctioneer got from it," Havenar explained. "I told my wife Mary Lou auctioneering was my next line of business."

A Piqua native, Havenar attended Piqua schools and then went to work at a service station on South and Garnsey Streets. He bought the Woodland Trailer Court in 1949 and operated a restaurant and service station in conjunction with it until 1958.

Havenar began operating earthmoving equipment for the construction of I-75 in 1956. After two years of that work, he joined the Piqua National Bank. When he left the institution 18 years later, he was vice president in charge of consumer lending.

"The auctioneering began as a hobby, really," said Havenar, "and that's still the way I think of it."

Havenar started the auction business with just himself and two clerks. He soon realized he needed help. Louis called a sale at Vosler Auction House on Saturday night. Bob Bayman came to Vosler and he and Louie became friends and then partners in 1969. Bob's wife Phyllis also worked in the business for several years.

Bruce Sampson joined Havenar in 1974. A licensed real estate salesman with Galbreath Realty, Sampson added that dimension to the auctioneering service.

Mike Havenar joined the business in 1979. After a year's apprenticeship, he became a licensed auctioneer.

Joe Sampson joined the business in 1989. He was employed at Shepard Grain Company, Fletcher.

The Havenars and Sampsons do "a lot of benefit sales," according to Lou Havenar, who named annual auctions at Upper Valley Joint Vocational School, golf tournament auctions at the Piqua Country Club, Ducks Unlimited Day and Kings Island sales, sales for the Congregational Christian United Church of Christ, Kiwanis Club and Lions Club. They also conduct the livestock auctions at the Miami County Fair each year at no charge.

The majority of their auctions take place in Miami and Shelby Counties, Havenar said, but they are licensed to sell anywhere in Ohio.

In 1991 Brad Havenar, a nephew, joined the auction business. Through the years Jean Sampson, Phyllis McVety and Mary Lou Havenar have been clerks for the company.

Joe Sampson attended the Missouri Auction School, Kansas City, Mo., in February of 1983. He served a six-month apprenticeship under the Havenar-Sampson Auction Service and later became a certified auctioneer.

Lou Havenar, a member of the Ohio Auctioneers Association, resides with his wife Mary Lou on Snodgrass Road. They are parents of Mrs. Thomas Baker (Marsha), Judy King, Mrs. Rick Snyder (Beverly), and Mike who married Tammi Meyers. They all reside in the Piqua area.

Havenar likes to keep busy. He was a Springcreek Twp. Trustee for 29 years and served on the Miami County Commission for one four year term. He was also a member of the Warren Lodge 24, F & AM, which also includes membership in the Masonic chapter, council and Order of Eastern Star, the Ancient and Accepted Scottish Rite of Dayton, Antioch Shrine of Dayton and Piqua Kiwanis Club.

Havenar chaired two school bond issue campaigns. He was chairman of the Piqua Bicentennial Celebration for two years and as a member of the Piqua Chamber of Commerce Board of Directors and a charter member of its Ambassador Club and tourist committee, he was natural for the Chamber's community affairs committee as well.

That latter position is how he became instrumental in establishing Piqua's Heritage Festival in 1982. Havenar was its first chairman and, since the festival become an incorporated effort, he has served as chairman of the board.

Mike Havenar, a 1975 graduate of Piqua Central High School, lives with his wife and three children - Zachary, Abby, and Ryan and they live on E. Statler Road. Further education was obtained through real estate courses at Edison Community College and appraisal school at Ohio State University. He also served on the Miami County Fair's board of directors.

Bruce Sampson had been a member of the Masonic Lodge in Lena since 1950 and the Scottish Rite and Shrine in Dayton since 1955. A member of the Fletcher United Methodist Church, he has served on the church board. He also is past member of the Fletcher Village Council. Bruce died in 1984 at the age of 57.

Joe Sampson, who graduated from Piqua Central High School in 1974, lives with his wife Missy and sons on Casstown-Fletcher Rd., Fletcher.

He was a member of the Fletcher volunteer Fire Department and Fletcher Emergency Squad, of which he is a past president. Besides working at Shepard Grain Elevator, he also managed and was part-owner of a crossbred herd of cattle for the B and J Farms.

Hemmert Plumbing

Fred Hemmert Sr. went to work in a factory in Botkins, Ohio, at the young age of 12 years old. His father died at the early age of 46, leaving his widow with seven young children to raise. The entire family eventually moved to Piqua, Ohio. In about 1908, Fred Hemmert, Sr. apprenticed to a local plumber. Meanwhile, his brother Alex had become skilled in electrical work. At this time, having plumbing and electric in a house was a new thing. Your choice for plumbing fixtures was white. Fred and Alex formed a new plumbing and electrical business in 1913 in a rented building at 111 S. Main Street. Hemmert Bros. was born. In the early 1920's Fred and Alex split up. Alex and later his son Marion worked at the large French Oil Mill Machinery Company for many years. Fred Sr. carried on the plumbing side of the business with assistance from another Hemmert brother and his name was Urban Hemmert. Irma Meyer came to work for Fred Sr. in 1917 as a bookkeeper, and they later married in 1921. In 1925, Fred Hemmert, Jr. was born and he became well known as Fritz. In that same year, Fred Sr. had a new plumbing shop erected at 221 Wood Street, and just around the corner had a new home built at 216 S. Wayne Street. For many years they had a doorbell at the shop that would ring into their house so they could conduct business at the shop after hours.

Fritz grew up and joined the Air Force during World War II, he was a bombardier in the South Pacific. He returned home from the service in 1945, and went into the plumbing business with his father, Fred Sr. In 1953, Fred Sr. passed away. In just a couple of weeks after that, Bill was born to Fritz and Betty Hemmert, the future third generation of Hemmert Bros. Irma Hemmert continued to be the bookkeeper until 1960 when she moved to Kettering, Ohio. Irma passed away in 1969. Betty Hemmert, Fritz's wife took over the bookkeeping.

Bill Hemmert spent two years in college, ran out of money and decided to try the plumbing business. He went to work as an apprentice for Fritz in 1973. He eventually got his journeymen license, and then later got his master plumbing license. Fritz and Bill worked together as a team until Fritz fell ill in the late 1980's. Bill took over the business in 1990, becoming the

third generation. Fritz Hemmert passed away in 1993. Betty Hemmert moved to a retirement home in Cincinnati in the mid 1990's. Joe Barhorst came to work for Bill as an apprentice in 1990, and he got his journeymen license a few years later. Sue Staley took over the bookkeeping duties in 1993. Sue and Joe are still with the business to this day.

Bill takes great pride in working with some of the tools that his grandfather used. Fritz taught Bill the value of honest and good work. There are some families in Piqua that have had no one else but a Hemmert doing their plumbing work. It's hard to believe that there has been a Hemmert doing plumbing in Piqua for the past century.

Fritz, Betty & Bill Hemmert

Fred Hemmert Senior is on far right

Right: Joe Barhorst, Sue Staley, Bill Hemmert - May '07

Hemm's Glass Shops, Inc.

In 1946, R.C. Hemm returned home from his Air Force duties in World War II as the pilot of a B-24 bomber. R.C. began his career working as a purchasing agent for a local company called Miller Meteor. At that time R.C. was purchasing glass for Miller Meteor from a local glass shop which was owned by the Britton family. The glass shop's roots began in 1921 at 514 S Main St. in Piqua. By July of 1948, R.C. and his wife Doris had reached an agreement with the Britton's to purchase the glass shop and thus began their journey as owners of Hemm's Glass Shops, Inc.

In the beginning, R.C., along with two other men, did all the physical cutting and installing of the glass. Most of the work was glass for automobiles, buses and hearse type vehicles along with tabletops, mirrors and glasswork in homes. Doris did all the bookwork and record keeping.

As the business began to grow, R.C. and Doris opened a second shop in Troy in 1952 and a third shop in Sidney in 1957. In the 1960's they began doing small storefront frames and continued to become more involved in commercial work and new construction.

Throughout the 1950's and 1960's, the company was truly a family business. R.C. and Doris' son, R.C. "Chuck" Hemm Jr., spent a lot of time at the glass shop, learning the business from the ground up. While attending Ohio University, Chuck Jr. met his future wife Sandy Oberschlake. In 1967 Chuck Jr. and Sandy were married. In the early 1970's, after a brief teaching career in the Pleasant Hill School District, Chuck Jr. joined the family glass business full time. Sandy joined the office team in 1986 part time while raising their 2 sons Jeff and Rich. In 1992 she began working full time and worked until 2005. Chuck Jr. successfully ran the company until the early 2000's. Currently Jeff, as the third generation, is running the company.

Since 1948 Hemm's Glass Shops, Inc has continuously been the complete, full service glass company for the entire Miami Valley. Hemm's Glass Shops, Inc. currently provides and installs auto glass, window glass, table tops, mirrors, shower doors, screens, commercial storefronts, building entrances, aluminum doors, aluminum, wood and vinyl windows as well as the service and maintenance for these products.

Hemm's Glass Shops, Inc. is prepared to perform any type of glass service. There is no job too big or too small. From replacing a window in your home or business, to auto glass replacement, to retail, factory or industrial maintenance to multi-story commercial buildings, Hemm's Glass Shop's, Inc. will serve all your glass needs.

As a result of committed team members and loyal customers, Hemm's Glass Shops, Inc. has continued to grow and expand; however Hemm's Glass Shop's Inc. will never outgrow our complete dedication to providing the highest quality glass service that is available in the industry.

Jackson Tube Service

Jackson Tube Service was the brainchild of Sam Jackson, Jr., a native of Brooklyn, New York, and the third generation of the Jackson family to be involved in the tubing industry. His family was in the tubing business in England, Connecticut, and New York prior to bringing tubing operations to Piqua in the 1940's. That operation, known as the Piqua branch of The Jackson Steel Tube Co. of Brooklyn, New York, was located on Weber Street. There are several families currently living in Piqua who also have their roots tied to the New York tubing operation. After being sold, Miami Industries was born. That business was bought and sold several times with Sam Jackson Jr. becoming the president of MSL Industries, the corporate parent in Chicago. After tiring of the weekly commutes to Chicago, Sam Jackson, Jr. left MSL and put the wheels in motion to start another tubing operation in his beloved Piqua.

The idea began with the purchase of farmland along the Miami River, which was accessible through Rossville. The initial project, named Riverside Products, began in March of 1972. Along with the development of the future site of Jackson Tube Service was the development of Industry Park Drive with access from North CR 25-A, within a mile of the relatively new Interstate 75. The company's name was changed to Jackson Tube Service, and the first piece of steel tubing was produced in 1974. Mr. Jackson added "Service" to the name of the company as a permanent reminder to its employees and customers as to why they are there.

Jackson Tube Service manufactures electric welded steel tubing in a variety of shapes, sizes, and densities. In addition to the production of steel tubing, the company also performs cutting to length, chamfering, brush deburring, slitting, annealing, straightening, insertion, fabrication, identification, inventory management, engineering and computer

Above: Aerial photo of Jackson Tube Service

Left: Employees of Jackson Steel Tube Company

software services, and customized bundling for its customers. Jackson Tube's steel tubing can be found in a wide variety of products including automobiles, motorcycles, ATVs, recreational vehicles, refrigeration, fabrication, store fixtures, furniture, agriculture, hospital equipment, etc. Tubing is produced for customers across the United States as well as in Canada and Mexico. Jackson Tube Service takes great pride in the high quality steel tubing that it provides to its customers. The company's motto is *"Quality Tubing by Quality People"*.

Jackson Tube Service currently employs 330 between its original plant in Piqua and its facility in Charlotte, North Carolina. The Piqua facility has grown tremendously over its existence to its present 450,000 square feet of factory and office space. The 60,000 square foot Charlotte facility began production in August of 2000. The two plants manufacture over 200 million feet of steel tubing each year.

Sam Jackson, Jr. served Jackson Tube Service as its first president followed by Don Massa, T. Gordon Ralph, and Bob Jackson (Sam's son), current company president. The company takes great pride in its past and present employees who have made and continue to make significant contributions to its tremendous growth and success over its 35-year history.

Jackson Tube Service has been an active participant in the promotion and improvement of the Piqua community. In addition to his responsibilities as company president, Sam Jackson, Jr. also served the City of Piqua as city commissioner and mayor. The company is a promoter of numerous local charitable organizations and currently enjoys school-business partnership relationships with both High Street Primary and Washington Intermediate schools.

Jackson Tube Service proudly displays two distinctive landmarks at its Piqua facility. The globe, located at the company's entrance, was erected in 1998 and is made almost exclusively from tubing produced in the plant. It revolves and rotates on a regular basis. The globe signifies the company's position in the marketplace as a worldwide, world-class company. In the spring of 2005, the company and the Jackson family erected a 170-foot flagpole in honor and memory of the significant contributions of its founder, Sam Jackson, Jr. The flag can be seen for miles away, and is brilliantly illuminated at night. Mr. Jackson's great love of Piqua and the United States of America make this a most appropriate tribute.

Bob Jackson, along with his sisters, is the fourth generation of the Jackson family to be involved in the tubing business. It is the desire of the Jackson family to keep Jackson Tube Service a privately owned family business proudly supporting its employees and the Piqua community for many generations to come.

The Jamieson & Yannucci Funeral Home

The Jamieson & Yannucci Funeral Home has evolved as a result of a family commitment to serve the Piqua area as funeral service professionals. Thomas J. Jamieson, Sr. founded the Jamieson Funeral Home in 1940 with his wife Erma. The business was located at 512 N. Main Street and was the seventh funeral home in Piqua at the time. The funeral home was relocated to its present location, 333 W. High Street, the former Marion Freshour residence, in 1941. Tom and Erma resided in the home and their kitchen is still a gathering place for friends today. Tom is remembered for his genuine caring and his humor. In addition to helping her husband, Erma was a Registered Nurse at the former Piqua Memorial Hospital.

The original building was significantly expanded in 1958, 1964, and in 1989. In 1958 a large addition was added to the back of the original residence. In 1964 the residence was expanded to the front and to the east side. During the sixties and seventies, several Piqua funeral homes ceased operations, which placed additional burdens on the staff and facilities at the Funeral Home. In 1989 the expansion on the west side nearly doubled the useable public space. To accommodate requests for higher confidence with cremations, we brought that actual process into our funeral home in 2001. We have the trained staff to ensure no one leaves our personal care when cremation services are selected. The early expansion accommodated the trend away from funeral services being held in private family residences to a central funeral home. The later expansions resulted from society wanting additional conveniences and services from funerals.

Following college and a period of service to his country, Thomas J. Jamieson Jr. returned to Piqua in 1958 with his wife Charlyne to join in the family business. One of their challenges was successfully adjusting to the increased workload while maintaining the personal attention they felt bereaved families required. Tom Sr. and Erma continued to work at the funeral home until their deaths in 1973 and 1974 respectively. Tom Jr. and Charlyne had been extremely active in Piqua assuming many volunteer positions and serving on numerous boards and committees to help the community prosper. They enjoyed a more normal lifestyle spending more time with their ten grandchildren, while day-to-day operations were handled by the current staff. During this Bicentennial year, the community felt a personal loss of one of its own as Tom Jr., became ill and succumbed on August 22, 2007.

Michael P. Yannucci, originally a Funeral Director in Springfield, joined the Funeral Home and moved to Piqua in 1976. He became a partner in 1980, which precipitated the expansion of the name to Jamieson & Yannucci Funeral Home. Susan K. Jamieson married Yannucci in 1981, obtained her Funeral Directors License in 1985 and they now represent the third generation to continue the family business. They also continue to be integral in increasing the quality of life in Piqua through their service to numerous charitable and civic organizations. The Yannucci's have four children. While maintaining the high level of activity at home, Susan tends to administrative responsibilities at the funeral home. The Yannucci's state that while it is "too soon" to determine if there is an interest by any of their children to become the fourth generation that "it would be a natural progression."

Thomas and Charlyne comment often that Tom and Erma would be quite proud of how their humble beginnings of personal service to the Piqua area continues today.

The personnel has increased and become better educated over the years to both the facilitate the increase in the number of families served and to provide the comprehensive service expected of funeral directors today including our unique Follow Through Services program. Yannucci states, "Our Funeral Home enjoys the best combination of personnel necessary to continue to provide a premiere comprehensive service to the Piqua area."

Tom and Emma Jamieson

Michael and Susan Yannucci

Tom and Charlyne Jamieson

Dick Lumpkin's Auto Body

Dick Lumpkin, owner of Dick Lumpkin's Auto Body, started his career in the automotive business in the late 1950's when he was just a young teenager. Dick was raised and went to school in Piqua and he was about twelve or thirteen when he began working around cars. He began his career working and learning from a neighbor when they worked on the neighbor's 1940 Ford. From that experience he caught the automotive repair bug.

When he was about fifteen or sixteen, he worked for Adrian Roul in his Body Shop. He would help him work on cars after school and sometimes in place of school.

In the early 1960's, he started his own auto repair business and it was located on North 25A close to where Paul Sherry is now located in Piqua. After a few years, he later worked with Paul Sherry when he was located on Wood Street in Piqua. He later purchased that building from Paul Sherry and started another auto repair business. And from there he bought the old Bordon's building on Roosevelt Street and started a repair shop.

He later sold that shop and ran a couple salvage yards but was eventually drawn back into the repair business. His next location of auto repair business was at 517 North Main Street and he operated out of that facility for several years. Due to the increase in business and the need for a larger facility, Dick purchased land on R.M. Davis Parkway and was the first business built on that road. In 2000, he built an 8,000 square foot state-of-the-art, full-service auto body repair facility with equipment and personnel to accommodate all of ones auto body needs. But, there was still a need for expansion and Dick added another 12,000 square foot addition in 2002.

Dick has sixteen employees and still works daily in the auto body business located at 150 R.M. Davis Parkway.

Mainstreet Piqua, Inc.

2008 will mark the fifteenth year of the Mainstreet Piqua organization. Through the community visioning process known as "Future Piqua" the citizens identified that the downtown needed to be a community priority. Vacant storefronts, empty buildings and a general state of disrepair resulted in a Piqua Area Chamber of Commerce committee investigating the "Main Street approach." The Chamber visited various downtown organizations across the state to see how other communities were bringing life back to their downtowns. It was eventually decided, in early 1993, that downtown Piqua needed the attention of a new organization, which was incorporated in March of 1993 as Mainstreet Piqua, Inc.

The first Mainstreet Piqua office was at 102 W. Ash Street. A dedicated group of volunteers raised money for the organization from the downtown building and business owners as well as the banks and industries throughout the Piqua community. Key supporters in the early years of the Main Street program included Ruth A. Koon, Ray Loffer, Dave Vollette, Doug Murray, Ed Pierce, Stanley Harrison, Joe Brown, Tom Zechman, Ron Johnson and James Oda.

The organization's first director was Cynthia Louis followed that same year by Doug Pessefall as the second director. An early accomplishment of the Mainstreet Piqua program was the creation of the Christmas on the Green event through the generous support of Dan & Margaret French. Also, with the leadership of downtown restaurant owner Phil Schnippel, the Taste of the Arts event was created to showcase restaurants, arts and the downtown in an early spring event.

Later events that were added to the Mainstreet Piqua event calendar included the downtown Brown Bag series and Victorian Christmas.

Through the generous support of the City of Piqua the Mainstreet Piqua program guided a comprehensive downtown market study and strategic planning process. In March of 1997, Mainstreet Piqua played a role in the creation of the Downtown District Design Review Board and early that summer Mainstreet Piqua partnered with the City of Piqua to allow downtown building and business owners to use the City of Piqua's Federal Formula funds to make exterior improvements to their buildings. The program went on for three years and was replaced by the Community Development Block Grant (CDBG) Downtown Revitalization Funds in 2001.

The third director to lead Mainstreet Piqua is Lorna Swisher. She was hired in May of 1997. Later that year the Downtown Piqua Association officially came under the Mainstreet Piqua umbrella, allowing the entire downtown to speak with one voice. Also in 1997 Mainstreet Piqua moved into the Piqua Area Chamber of Commerce building at 326 N. Main Street (the former Kresge Store).

In 1998, with the assistance of a federal grant, Lock 9 Park was created on the southeast corner of the downtown – giving Piqua residents the opportunity to enjoy an unobscured view of the great Miami River for the first time.

In 1999 Mainstreet Piqua applied for the designation of an Ohio Main Street Program through Downtown Ohio, Inc. This designation was awarded and has resulted in Mainstreet Piqua staff and volunteers being able to attend trainings and participate in networking sessions with Main Street programs across the state. Mainstreet Piqua was also able to attain the benchmarks needed to be certified as a National Main Street program.

The 2000 CDBG Downtown Revitalization grant application was funded in the amount of $400,000 and during the grant period over sixteen projects were completed. As a result of the flurry of activity Mainstreet Piqua assisted the City in making application for a second downtown revitalization grant and in December of 2002 the city received word that they had been granted an additional $340,000 to be used to assist downtown property owners in rehabilitating their buildings. During this period streetscape improvements were also made on Ash Street as well as the area around the Municipal Government Complex and the Bike Path. As a result of the investment by the property owners and the streetscaping the appearance of downtown Piqua was transformed and resulted in a boost in community pride.

The Mainstreet Piqua board has always had a strong desire to see the redevelopment of the Fort Piqua Hotel come to fruition and has worked hard to that end. Mainstreet has also partnered with the Piqua Improvement Corporation and the Piqua Area Chamber of Commerce to help promote the Piqua community.

In 2005 Mainstreet Piqua developed the niche to make available keepsake and collectible items bearing Piqua's name. Mainstreet Piqua has had coffee mugs, ornaments, playing cards, postcards and note cards produced to pay tribute to Piqua's rich heritage.

In 2007 Mainstreet Piqua played a major role in the planning of activities for the Piqua Bicentennial Celebration.

Mainstreet Piqua is committed to fulfilling the Mission of continuing economic development efforts in the downtown area, historically preserving and aesthetically enhancing the downtown area, promoting and marketing the unique features of the downtown area and helping to unite the community in achieving these goals.

McCulloch, Felger, Fite & Gutmann Co., L.P.A.

Attorneys at Law

History of the Firm

The law firm of McCulloch, Felger, Fite & Gutmann Co., L.P.A. traces its origin to 1895, when local attorneys **David S. Lindsey** and **J. Harrison Smith** united their law practices. Mr. Lindsey served as the Piqua city attorney for many years. J. Harrison Smith was elected as the Miami County Prosecuting Attorney, then Probate Judge and later served as Mayor of the city (1920-21). In 1907, **Horace N. Lilley** partnered with David Lindsey to form Lindsey and Lilley. **George W. Berry**, a native of Piqua, joined the partnership in 1915 and their association extended until Mr. Lindsey's death in 1928.

Bill McCulloch

In 1929, **William M. McCulloch** joined the firm which still bears his name. McCulloch served as Speaker of the Ohio House of Representatives from 1939 to 1944. He was elected to the United States Congress in a special election in 1947 and was re-elected to twelve succeeding terms. As the senior Republican on the House Judiciary Committee, McCulloch was instrumental in the passage the Civil Rights Act of 1964. In 1995, Congressman McCulloch was elected to the inaugural class of the Piqua Civic Hall of Fame.

With Mr. McCulloch busy in Washington, D.C., George Berry enlisted the aid of **Carl B. Felger**, a native Covington, Ohio. Felger had been elected Miami County Probate and Juvenile Judge in 1941 and served in that capacity until he joined the firm on January 1, 1948. In addition to a distinguished career in his legal profession, Judge Felger was known throughout the county for his public and community service.

In 1949, the firm added **Robert P. Fite**, who was born in Georgetown, Ohio and graduated from the Ohio State University College of Law. Fite was a skilled trial attorney and equally adept at corporate and tax law. He also contributed countless hours to his community serving on the Piqua Board of Education for 20 years, the YMCA Board of Trustees, the American Red Cross and Edison State Community College.

In 1958, **Paul P. Gutmann**, a native of Columbus, Ohio joined the firm. He had graduated from St. Vincent College in Pennsylvania and received his law degree from Ohio State University. Gutmann continued in the practice of law for 43 years and was honored with the "Order of George" award in 1996, the highest award that the City of Piqua can bestow upon one of its citizens.

Today, the firm conducts a full service general practice of law, representing many of the area's leading businesses, financial institutions and individuals in banking, commerce, real estate, estate and trust planning and administration and litigation. Its broad base of experience and expertise enables the firm to provide legal services effectively and economically.

The present members of the firm include:

William B. McNeil (*Penn State University; Harvard University, J.D.*) joined the firm in 1964.

Jack L. Neuenschwander (*Harvard University; University of Michigan, J.D.*) joined the firm in 1967, served in the U.S. Army 1967-69 and returned to the firm in 1969.

Dale G. Davis (*Duke University; Georgetown University, J.D.*) joined the firm in 1976.

Michael E. Gutmann (*Miami University; University of Cincinnati, J.D.*) joined the firm in 1984

Daniel E. Ramer (*University of Miami; Ohio State University, J.D.*) joined the firm in 1990.

Frank J. Patrizio (*University of Dayton; Ohio State University, J.D.*) joined the firm in 1991.

Laura Hornish-Schlosser (*Adrian College; University of Toledo, J.D.*) joined the firm in 2001.

McCulloch plays leading role in passage of Civil Rights Act.

As the senior Republican on the House Judiciary Committee, William M. McCulloch was instrumental in the passage the **Civil Rights Act of 1964**. The comprehensive bill would extend voting rights to minorities, prohibit discrimination in public places and begin to desegregate public schools. President John F. Kennedy needed the assistance of Congressman McCulloch to steer the bill through the committee and to obtain the votes necessary for passage by the full House. In July 1963, Robert Kennedy, the Attorney General, sent his Deputy, Burke Marshall, to Piqua to meet McCulloch in person and to seek his assurance that he would support the bill. Finally, the measure was signed into law by President Lyndon Johnson. McCulloch is shown in the photograph (second from left), along with other national leaders, including Martin Luther King, Jr., at the signing of the bill.

McVety
REALTY

*William F. McVety,
owner 1945-1978*

*Charles I. Sanders,
owner 1978-2004*

*Jeanie Jordan-Bates,
owner 2004-current*

William F. McVety was a hard-working and ambitious man with an eye toward the future. In 1945 he founded Bill McVety Realty, which is the oldest real estate firm in Piqua and in Miami County. McVety was an owner and developer of Park Ridge subdivision and a primary builder of the new homes there and around the Piqua area. He also was the first builder for Inland Homes in Piqua with over 100 homes built in Philbrook Park, most of which had full basements.

His son in-law, Charles Sanders, joined the company as a licensed agent in 1963, became a Broker in 1965 and became owner of the company in 1978 when Mr. McVety retired. Charles worked with his wife as office manager, the former Shirley McVety who retired in 2004.

McVety and Sanders joined forces as Premier Investment Corporation, a construction company, having built approximately 200 homes in Piqua and Troy consisting of 2 bedroom brick homes featuring quality, low maintenance and easy living. These homes line Westview and Parkway Drive and various streets bordering Park Ridge and Deerfield subdivisions. Charles has also developed Sandel Subdivision, focusing on 4-unit apartment buildings, double and single-family homes. Sandel is located between County Road 25A and Looney Rd.

Jeanie Jordan-Bates, who started as a sales associate with the company in 1992, purchased the company in January 2004 and became Broker of the company in 2005.

The company has been located in the Piqua Business District having opened its doors at 212 West Ash St before moving to its current location at 222 West Ash St in 1950 and received a facelift in 2004. 2007 brought a new image to Bill McVety Realty as the name was shortened to McVety Realty and a new logo and motto, "Experience Counts," was put in place.

Current licensed agents include Jeanie Jordan-Bates, Laura Bates, Anthony Bayman, Julie Howell, Roger Motter, and Charles Sanders.

McVety Realty continues to be a family owned and operated business with seven professionals offering over 125 years of combined experience to serve you. Our Company has always worked diligently to meet the needs of our customers by providing the best possible real estate services and properties, and by observing the highest standards of business conduct, ethics and integrity.

This long-standing tradition has allowed us to develop a service unparallel to any other brokerage. Still to this day we continue to receive calls asking for "Bill". These calls come from young and old alike saying things like "My grandparents purchased their home from Bill McVety Realty and we need to sell it" or "We left Piqua several years ago and are ready to move back home". These loyal customers, though it has been several years or perhaps several generations later, remember one thing, the second-to-none customer service and personal attention.

McVety Realty specializes in single-family residential sales, multi-family, investments and small to medium sized commercial properties. In addition, we handle individual building lots, farms, vacant land and land development. To date we have developed communities such as Park Ridge, Sandel, Brook Park North (Troy), Ron Aire Drive and Philbrook Park, built over 800 homes and helped thousands of individuals and families buying and selling homes.

Since its inception, McVety Realty has been a leader in the Real Estate industry. For this we owe one group of people: Our loyal customers. We thank you for your continued support over the years. We feel that by providing you with exemplary personalized service, you will then refer us to your family and friends.

212 West Ash St, first office 1945-1950

222 West Ash St., Current office.

MIAMI COUNTY'S OLDEST REAL ESTATE FIRM

EXPERIENCE COUNTS

The Medicine Shoppe Pharmacy

During the early 1900's a new Drug Store (Kiefer's Broadway Pharmacy) was started at 428-430 West High Street, also known as the corner of Broadway and High. It was started by George C. Kiefer Sr. who was a Pharmacist and also a musician, who also owned a music store on Main Street where he gave music lessons to many of his instrument purchasers. During the 1920's two of his sons, Charles W. and George C. Jr. became Pharmacists and joined him. The Kiefer's were also local promoters and in the late 20's sponsored a semi-professional football team known as Kiefer's Drugs. Comprised of a collection of High School and College players a number of who played under assumed names so they could collect money and still qualify to play college ball. The teams of 1928 and 1929 went undefeated playing teams from central and west-central Ohio. Games were played in the old Rossville Park along the river.

In 1962 the Kiefer brothers looking to retire employed Ernest (Ernie) E. Smith as a pharmacist who happened to be looking for a similar position as an owner. By 1970 Ernie had become the new owner and business prospered. Ernie met and married Roni Timmons, daughter of Harry, a barber and owner of the oldest family held barber shop in the State located in Potsdam, and Mildred Millbourn Timmons one of the areas finest Avonladies, residents of Boone Street. The Smiths have 3 sons, John, Mike and Brian who is also a Pharmacist and presently lives in Kernersville, NC.

In the earlier days pharmacies relied upon prescriptions from Physicians who had practices in their homes or in offices converted from neighborhood homes. Within two blocks of the corner of High and Broadway we had Dr. John Gallagher, Dr. Jack Steinhilber, Dr. Robert Neth, Dr. Larry Bunnell, two dentists, two chiropractors and an optometrist. Eventually Physicians moved into buildings owned by the Hospital or into new buildings with better parking for customers.

Having changed the Business name to Ernie's Prescription Center we also moved to 1722 West High Street where the business was downsized from a full line pharmacy to primarily a prescription only pharmacy where it remained until 1986 when we decided to become a Medicine Shoppe franchise and moved to 124 N Sunset across the street from what was known at that time as The Doctors Building. At that location we started the first heath care screenings in Piqua. Screenings for blood pressure, blood glucose and eventually cholesterol were offered, some on a monthly basis. Home health care supplies and equipment for sale and rental was added and then we entered compounding medications from scratch and all of this helped grow the business.

Running out of space and parking we purchased the now empty Spot Restaurant building and remodeled it into a Pharmacy with a drive thru window, again something new, an added convenience for our customers. Five years later in 1998 we purchased the corner of High and College and built our present building, opening in May of 1999. We continue to offer medical screenings, home health care equipment and diabetes counseling and supplies, but we are most widely known for our compounding. We specialize in bio-identical hormone compounding in very minute exact dosing, giving relief presently to over 3000 area women suffering from hormone deficiencies. We presently make over 600 formulas and constantly need more. This Medicine Shoppe is one of only 15 compounding pharmacies in the country listed in Suzanne Somers latest book written about hormones titled Ageless. The Medicine Shoppe Pharmacy plans to be a big part of Piqua for many years to come.

Submitted by Ernie Smith

Kiefer Drug Football Team

Melcher-Sowers Funeral Home

Melcher-Sowers Funeral Home was founded in 1898 by Bernard Groven and his son, Bernard Groven, Jr. A combination furniture store and undertaking establishment known as the Groven Funeral Home, it was located at the site of the present Elks building on the corner of Ash and Wayne streets. In 1930 the funeral home was moved to 126 N. Wayne Street; where Murray, Wells, Wendeln and Robinson is now located.

In 1952 Louis and Lorraine Melcher joined the Groven Funeral Home and in 1956, purchased the business. The move to the present location at 646 W. High Street was made in 1957, when the name was changed to Melcher Funeral Home. In 1984, Jerry and Pam Sowers bought the business and two years later changed the name to Melcher-Sowers Funeral Home. Jerry, a graduate of Greenville High School attended Wright State University and graduated and received his degree in mortuary science from the Cincinnati College of Mortuary Science in 1973. He has been a Licensed Funeral Director and Embalmer since 1974. Pamela graduated from Greenville High School. She is the founder and coordinator of the funeral home's Aftercare Program. Pam is the funeral home's Grief Recovery Facilitator. Jerry and Pamela have been married for 35 years and have two children and seven grandchildren.

In 1991 construction began on a 10,000 square foot addition, which included a new chapel, coffee lounge, restrooms, and new offices. This addition made the building handicapped accessible including the original building. This addition was created to better serve families in a large more comfortable environment. Melcher-Sowers is now celebrating over 100 years of service to the families of Piqua.

Recently, in order to serve customers better, Jerry and Pam Sowers purchased 5.5 acres on W. High Street, located across from Deerfield sub-division. Construction will soon begin on a new 25,000 square foot state-of-the-art facility. The new single story funeral home will have a 200 space parking area (with ample handicapped spaces and overhead carport area), a family center for families to return for meals and fellowship, a children's center, a foyer with fireplace for warm gatherings, an Arrangement Center for At-need and Pre-need consultations.

Brian A. Sowers is now a member of the firm. A graduate of Edison Community College and the Cincinnati College of Mortuary Science, with a Bachelors Degree in Mortuary Science, Brian is married to Laura A. Freisthler and they have four daughters and a son. In 2006, Brian received his certification as a Certified Funeral Service Practitioner (CFSP) from the Academy of Professional Funeral Service Practice.

Others employed at Melcher-Sowers are Loverna Dilbone and Wanda Wahl. As office manager, Loverna explains her job in her own words, "I look at my job as an outreach. It's an opportunity for me to help families and make sure everything goes smoothly for them." Loverna lives in Sidney with her husband Mitch. They have four children and ten grandchildren.

As Family Service Advisor, Wanda meets with families when they have lost a loved one. She also meets with families for pre-arranging services. She has been married for 37 years to Frank and lives east of Troy. They have two sons and four granddaughters.

Melcher-Sowers Funeral Home, serving the Community for over 100 years.

Jerry and Pam Sowers

Melcher-Sowers Funeral Home Staff
Pam Sowers, Loverna Dilbone, Wanda Wahl, Jerry Sowers, Brian Sowers

Louis and Lorraine Melcher

Miami County Auto Club AAA

On Monday, February 22, 1915 a group of people met at the Wagner Groven Furniture Store to create an automobile owners club in order to maintain and defend the rights and privileges of automobile ownership and encourage the construction of good roads. Two weeks later, on March 1, a second meeting was held and officers were elected to the Piqua Auto Club. The first officers were L. E. Chamberlin, president; A. C. Wilson, vice president and A. L. Richey, secretary-treasurer. By the end of this meeting, 91 individuals had paid their $1 membership fee and joined the club. The club applied and was accepted into the American Automobile Association (AAA). The activities of the club during its first years included securing accurate maps of routes from Cincinnati to Toledo and from Columbus to Indianapolis, placing signs on roads leading into Piqua and signs welcoming motorists to the city. By 1918 the club had 111 members and had established offices on the second floor of the Piqua National Bank Building at 310 N. Main St.

In 1919 the club expanded its outreach and reconstituted itself as the Miami County Auto Club. In the next decade the club standardized road emergency services, donated four traffic lights to Piqua, paid for special policemen to direct traffic around areas of road construction in the county, and organized the elementary school "patrol boy" program. The club continued to sponsor the "patrol boy" program for many years. The club was also active in sponsoring and supported the enforcement of safe driving laws and regulations.

In the 1920's the Miami County Auto Club began to branch out into the travel business, marketing train tickets, hotel and steam ship reservations, tour packages and admissions to various attractions such as Coney Island, Cedar Point, and later, Kings Island. The club was also the license bureau for both automobile and driver's licenses until 1998. The AAA maps, tour books, TripTiks, travel insurance and roadside assistance are still vital services enjoyed by club members. In 2002 the purchase of the club by AAA Cincinnati was finalized and the club became a part of AAA Allied Group.

The club has benefited from stable leadership over its many years of existence. Among the presidents of the club were the following: L. E. Chamberlin (1915-1920), G. F. Fryling (1920-1930), David M. Whitmore (1930-1980) and Frank Neff (1980-2003). One of the first travel agents was Virginia L. Ross who worked for the club for 54 years.

As the Miami County Auto Club approaches its 100th anniversary the club looks forward to continuing to serve your travel and motoring needs.

Left:
David Whitmore receiving a 1966 Membership Achievement Award from Roger McCloskey of AAA.

Right:
Office at 308 N. Main St. in the Favorite Hotel Building, 1937-1961

Below:
School Safety Patrol Boys in front of Shines Piqua Theater, 1948

253

Miami County Foundation

Residents of Miami County have been the grateful recipients, since 1986, of over $2.8 million from a quiet benefactor with a lasting love for this county.

Richard E. Hunt established, what now is the MIAMI COUNTY FOUNDATION, in 1985, in honor of his mother, wife and two children, with the express purpose of *"People Helping People"*.

Those serving on the Board of Directors are charged with the mission statement: *"To effectively assist, encourage and promote the health, education and welfare of the citizens of Miami County by soliciting, receiving and administering assets exclusively for their charitable needs."*

This private foundation serves to provide grant support for programs in the arts, community development, education, health and human services. From the beginning scholarship funding was provided for residents of the county wishing to pursue post-high school education in any accredited college, trade/vocational, nursing or health related facility.

Mr. Hunt's broadcasting career began on December 7, 1947 when WPTW-AM first went on the air. Several years later he was involved with WPTW-FM, and other stations in Ohio and Michigan as well as the construction of Valley Antenna Systems. Interesting to note the call letters represented Piqua, Troy, and West Milton!

With the sale of the Piqua radio stations in 1997, Mr. Hunt transferred one million dollars to the Foundation. Upon his death, April 1, 2002, his entire estate came to the Foundation.

The Miami County Foundation has been chosen through the years by other Miami County benefactors.

In 1992 Mary Deeter of Troy honored her husband by creating the *DON FAVORITE DEETER, M.D.MEMORIAL SCHOLARSHIP FUND*. Newton High School graduates wishing to pursue a degree in the science/math field in a four year college are eligible to apply for this annual, renewable for three years, and up to $2,500 scholarship. A new scholarship is awarded each year. The Advisory Committee for these funds includes the Newton School Superintendent, Principal and Science Instructor.

The *THELMA ROSS DALTON MEMORIAL SCHOLARSHIP FUND* was established in 2000. Her $1 million dollar bequest provides scholarships for Miami County residents wishing to further their post-high school education in any accredited college, trade/vocation, nursing or health related facility. Grant applications must be received annually by November 1st.

The Dalton Agency created industrial and commercial advertising for many years in Troy. They were responsible for the development and production of the instruction manuals for WACO aircraft as well as the Hobart generators used extensively in World War II. The agency also produced and placed commercial advertising for many other area manufacturers.

The Foundation also manages the *BRADFORD, OHIO RAILROAD MUSEUM ENDOWMENT FUND* which was created in 2004. Donations to this fund supports the creation and maintenance of railroad museum artifacts and history, funds the acquisition, construction and maintenance of the museum and supports educational events to promote and preserve the rich Bradford, Ohio railroad history.

The Miami County Foundation also serves as the fiscal charitable agent for funds received on behalf of special fund raising events.

Distributions have increased from $15,000 in 1986 when the first grants were awarded to the $193,806 awarded on April 26, 2007. To date more than $2.8 million has been distributed in grants and scholarships and Miami County Fund assets total more than $12,000,000.

The Miami County Foundation stands ready to help individuals and organizations establish funds with the Foundation. You can:

- Designate your own fund to be managed as you specify
- Name one or more organizations to receive grants
- Establish a scholarship fund in your name
- Honor family members or friends

Located at 317 North Wayne Street, Piqua, Ohio 45356
www.miamicountyfoundation.org
937-773-9012

Mr. Richard Hunt, Founder

Miami County Foundation

Miami Valley Centre Mall

The *Miami Valley Centre Mall* was brought to the upper Miami Valley in Piqua, Ohio by The Mall Company in 1988. The mall is located at exit 82 off of Interstate 75.

Construction of the 5-story Comfort Inn was built on the south side of the mall incorporating the food court (known as the Café Court)/Cinema entrance to the mall and gave interior access from the hotel to the mall. The hotel officially opened October 20, 1988. The mall is the largest shopping, food, and entertainment facility in the area being a focus point for those from Troy, Tipp, Sidney, Greenville, Urbana, and all towns in between.

The mall opened with anchor stores: Elder Beerman, JCPenny, and Hills Department Store. The mall at that time consisted of 322,000 square feet, which also included (and still does) a 6-screen cinema. Some "early" stores to open in the mall included The Canary & The Elephant, El-Bee Shoes, Rogers Jewelers, Jolly Time Arcade (now Pocket Change), Afterthoughts (now Claire's), Gold Star Chili & Great Steak & Fry, Kinney Shoe and Lemstone Books among a few.

The 45,000 square foot strip center known as "Riverside Place" was constructed a few months following the enclosed mall. Bob Evans was the first restaurant to be built in front of the center. McDonald's followed in 1993 and Red Lobster in 1994.

Events early in the years of the mall included Edison State Community College Information Days, Dave Morgan and The Melody Music Makers, United Way Information Day, Elvis Presley Impersonator Ray Maas and the first mall Trick or Treat night which continues to this day.

In 1994, the mall was sold to The Mid-America Management Corporation out of Cleveland, Ohio. To this day, the company still owns and manages the mall. The mall was expanded in 1999 to accommodate a 100,381 square foot Sears store.

As the real estate industry changed, so did the *Miami Valley Centre Mall*. Stores came and went and the addition of Steve & Barry's University Sportswear in 2004 stabilized the "four anchor" requirement for additional retailers. Over the years, both regional and national retailers have joined the wide selection of stores.

In past years, the *Miami Valley Centre Mall* played host to the World's Largest Cruise-In featuring over 1500 show cars and over 15,000 people. With the entertainment of Chubby Checker and seven other bands, the event became a big success and the talk of the town along with being published in "Retail Ad Week" magazine published out of New York City.

The mall participates in supporting different charities and organizations such as United Way, Young Life, The Salvation Army, Hospice of Miami County, Boy Scouts, Girl Scouts, Piqua Community Foundation, Community Blood Center, Darke County Fair, Mainstreet Piqua, Miami County Visitors and Convention Bureau, Piqua and Troy Chamber of Commerce, American Red Cross, American Heart Association, Home Builders Association of Miami County, and area schools.

With an attached hotel, you never know who you might see shopping in the mall such as Travis Tritt, The Stadtler Brothers, Gary Puckett, Ohio State football players, former Cincinnati Reds' Sean Casey and Hal Morris, former Cincinnati Bengal's Ickey Woods and Justin Smith, WWF Wrestlers, the Easter Bunny, Santa, Ronald McDonald, Jared from the Subway commercials, Indianapolis Colts' Mike Doss and Ben Hartsock (to name a few).

The *Miami Valley Centre Mall* received the Piqua Improvement Corporation Economic Development Appearance Award in 1999 for contribution to the economic growth of the City of Piqua.

The *Miami Valley Centre Mall* offers customers what they want with Shopping, Dining, Cinemas and Lodging…all under **one** roof!

Midwest Maintenance, Inc.

William R. Meyer and Ervin R. Conley founded Conley Meyer Construction in Piqua, Ohio in 1979. What began as a small, family-run commercial contractor would eventually grow into one of the top general contractors in building restoration specializing in historically significant structures.

Due to the untimely death of Ervin R. Conley in 1982, the name of the company was changed to **Midwest Maintenance, Inc.** The company started with just two trucks and some very basic equipment. From this starting point, Midwest Maintenance, Inc. has added equipment and manpower to successfully complete any job, anywhere, no matter how large or complex.

From the beginning, our founders' goals were to establish a company that would specialize in the renovation and restoration of historic structures that could leverage our eighteen years of experience in building restoration and working in masonry and concrete into a dynamic new company. Through this exceptional leadership this company became what it is today, the leader in building restoration.

The foundation of our business has a more intrinsic value than just dollars and cents. It's based more on the idea that a community's history does not have to pass into oblivion. That the emotional ties created by a community's structures are very strong.

To see a church where three generations of a family's children were baptized, or a courthouse where the marriage license for a couple celebrating their sixtieth wedding anniversary was issued…to see these structures being razed in the name of progress is actually not progress at all.

We feel strongly that at Midwest Maintenance, Inc. we become part of the communities we serve by offering twenty-eight years of expert services to retain the emotional ties of the people of that community, and to allow future generations to remain tied to their past. Can an economic value be tied to this belief? Probably not. But we know that what we see in the eyes of a community when an important part of their history has been preserved is priceless.

In creating our company, we established a set of exacting standards for the work we would do. And, because the kind of expert professional that would be needed to meet those standards were rare, we did the majority of the work on this project ourselves. Over time, the company has attracted and trained a number of skilled craftsmen who share their dedication to quality work. These people form the cornerstone of a company that's gained a reputation for total client satisfaction in the work they do.

To accommodate the increasing volume of projects in the southern states, in 2002, Midwest Maintenance, Inc. opened a regional office in Augusta, Georgia.

Midwest Maintenance, Inc. has been preserving a part of history through Complete Building Restoration for over a quarter of a century and is proud to have gained wide spread recognition for its work. From their peers, to architects and engineers, to the building owners they serve, Midwest Maintenance, Inc. has received a number of regional and national awards for project excellence and has established itself as a leader in professional building renovation and restoration. Fort Sumter National Monument, Charleston, South Carolina; Grove Park Inn, Asheville, North Carolina; Twin Stone Arches, Troy, Ohio and Captain Roland Roberts House, Green Turtle Cay, Abaco, Bahamas are just a few of our award winning projects.

Midwest Maintenance, Inc. has entered the new millennium prepared to pursue a wide range of projects in Ohio, Indiana, Kentucky, North Carolina, South Carolina, Georgia, Louisiana, Illinois, West Virginia, and Pennsylvania. We've grown over the past twenty-eight years, but one thing has remained a constant.... we still share our founders dedication of providing the best quality work that can be done today.

We are very proud and grateful for the opportunity to be a part of such a successful entrepreneurial family that has established a company that has become a leader in the construction industry for building restoration. We have had the opportunity to take control of our own destiny and experience an immeasurable satisfaction of knowing that what is being achieved and accomplished we did as a family.

It's difficult to sum up a legacy of over twenty-eight years. It may rest in the restoration of a historic building in downtown Piqua, or in other communities across the Midwest and southern states where Midwest Maintenance, Inc.'s crane now reaches skyward. Maybe it's in the ability to survive and grow as a family-owned business in an era of corporations, or in the way Midwest Maintenance, Inc. has fostered loyalty among generations of employees. One this is certain: The Midwest Maintenance, Inc. legacy can be found in its spirit of excellence, of giving and growing into the 21st century, and its continued commitment to core values.

William R. Meyer – President

M J Koon & Sons Insurance Agency

M. J. Koon and Sons

The M. J. Koon and Sons Insurance Agency had it's beginnings after WWII with George Weadock selling Property and Casualty insurance from his home on Broadway.

Also after the war, Marion J. Koon left his wartime employment at Robbins & Myers and became a life insurance agent for The Prudential. Many life insurers were represented in Piqua at that time; Prudential alone had 16 full time agents employed.

On January 1, 1959 Marion Koon and George Weadock joined forces to start the Weadock-Koon Insurance Service combining both casualty and life products. The business moved to new offices above the Third Savings and Loan (now Unity Bank). The agency grew rapidly but, unfortunately, George Weadock contracted cancer and passed away in 1963.

After a period of time Bob Arbogast, formerly of the Bradford Adjustment Service, joined the firm which became Koon-Arbogast Insurance and the offices moved to the Orr Flesh Building.

1977 saw the addition of Richard W. Koon and M. James Koon to the firm as well as the retirement of Robert Arbogast. Shortly thereafter the name changed once again to M. J. Koon and Sons and the offices moved to the DASK building. Marion retired in the early 80s and the firm made it's final move to 421 N. Downing St. in the early 90s.

M. J. Koon and Sons evolved from a small agency in the founder's living room to a full service Property and Casualty and Life agency serving a significant number of residents in Piqua and the surrounding area.

M.J. Koon
circa 1952

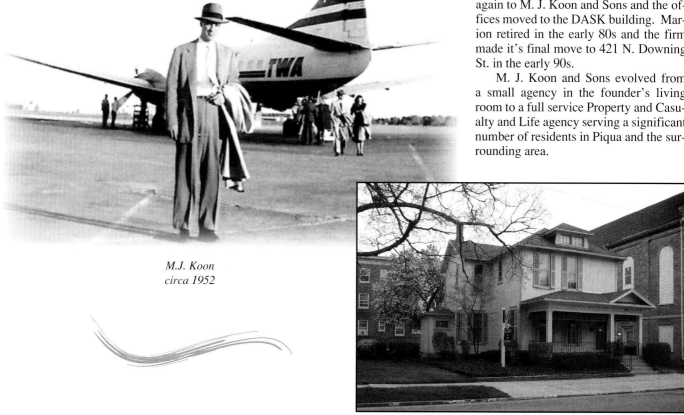

M. J. Koon and Sons Insurance Agency office.

Mullenbrock & Associates

-A financial advisory
practice of Ameriprise Financial Services, Inc.
228 West Ash Street

Craig Mullenbrock

*I*n 1984, a young resident of Piqua began looking at careers that showed growing potential. Researching at the Flesh Public Library, Craig W. Mullenbrock found several articles highlighting the recent acquisition by American Express of the Minneapolis based IDS Financial Services (IDS). In fact the same Pittsburgh family that owned IDS, for a time owned Miami Industries, a tubing manufacturer located in Piqua. What Mullenbrock found intriguing about this company that traced its roots back to 1894 (Investor's Syndicate), was the mid-western values its field force were trained in combined with a new mission of making the fledgling field of financial planning the centerpiece of a company culture.

On July 31, 1985 Mullenbrock left his supervisory position with Hartzell Hardwoods and started his financial planning career. Original offices were located on the third floor of the Orr Flesh Building, sharing an office suite for a time with the then semi-retired Ralph Gunter, CPA.

In 1986 the personal computer (PC) became available and showed promising potential for a financial planning business prompting Mullenbrock to purchase the most advanced IBM XT unit at the time. Shortly thereafter, Mullenbrock outgrew the Orr Flesh suite and leased much larger offices at 117 West Ash Street. During this time staff was added and he also began training and managing other IDS independent contractors in the Dayton area.

After completing three years in the business, Mullenbrock sat for the Certified Financial Planner ™ exam. Mullenbrock was one of the earliest CFP® designees in west-central Ohio. As the field of financial planning grew, more space was needed to house other IDS/American Express advisors and he opened a second office at 117 South Market Street in Troy. During this time Mullenbrock managed both a growing personal practice, trained new financial advisors and provided support to established advisors from Springfield to Greenville.

By 1994, the firm was re-branded American Express Financial Advisors (AEFA). However, the landscape of financial services was changing. Mullenbrock chose to leave management duties to become a franchise owner of AEFA, thus allowing the building of equity in his practice. With a solid personal practice now established in the northern Miami Valley, Mullenbrock returned to Piqua, purchasing a two-story office building at 228 West Ash Street (this property was well-known for over 80 years as the offices/home of physicians Dr. John Beachler, Sr. and Dr. John Beachler, Jr.).

During these years Mullenbrock focused on building an advisory-focused practice, where a majority of clients paid an ongoing fee for comprehensive and/or need-specific advice. Over time a high level of trust was forged with clients who appreciate a firm run with mid-western values and impeccable service. Also, during this time investment management became an integral part of business focus.

Mullenbrock added a second professional designation in 1997—Certified Divorce Financial Analyst (CDFA™), in response to the need in west-central Ohio to be well-qualified to provide advice to both attorneys and individuals of higher-income/net worth divorces.

In cooperation with Main Street Piqua, significant renovation was done to the circa 1853 office building during the years 2002-2005. In 2006, office signage was changed to reflect the decision of American Express to "spin off" AEFA as the newest member of the S&P 500—Ameriprise Financial Services, Inc.

In 2007, Mullenbrock and Associates-A financial advisory practice of Ameriprise Financial, had staff consisting of two full time and two part-time employees. To handle increasing volume, expansion and eventual succession planning, a junior associate with a B.S. degree in financial services joined the firm. Clients no longer are just located in west-central Ohio—as they move away from Piqua they desire to maintain the firm's guidance. Clients now reside from Hawaii to Florida and California to Michigan.

Over the years, Mullenbrock has received many awards including Mercury, Career Development conferences, numerous national conference qualifications, silver, gold and platinum office designations and induction into the Diamond Ring club, reserved for Ameriprise franchisees that consistently are in the top 5% nationally for more than 13 years running.

As Piqua celebrates its bicentennial, Mullenbrock & Associates is proud to be an integral part of a community that once was the border of the fledgling United States. Now as a community where vision is becoming reality, Mullenbrock & Associates will be the firm that west-central Ohio will engage to help them achieve their dreams, incorporating solid mid-west values to shape financial solutions for their lifetimes.

Murray Wells Wendeln & Robinson CPAs

***T**he roots of Murray Wells Wendeln & Robinson CPAs (MWWR)* go back to the late 1940s. In July of 1972, Covington, Ohio natives Doug Murray and Steve Wells purchased the certified public accounting practice of Ralph Gunter, which dated back to 1948. Steve and Doug opened their new practice, *Murray Wells and Co. CPAs* in the Piqua National Bank Building in downtown Piqua. Their services included bookkeeping, accounting and auditing, business and personal taxation planning and compliance, and management advisory services. As the business grew, Tony Wendeln of Fort Loramie joined the firm as a staff accountant in 1975. In 1977 the business moved to the newly remodeled DASK Building at the corner of Ash and Wayne Streets in Piqua where it remains today.

Tony was named partner in 1982 and the name changed to *Murray Wells & Wendeln CPAs* shortly thereafter. The 1980s continued to see growth for the firm. Sam Robinson of Piqua joined the firm in 1985 and was named partner in 1989. Karen Benanzer, who was named partner in 2003, became part of the enterprise in 1988. A second office on Main Street in Troy was established in 1989.

Growth and progress continued through the 1990s and into the new millennium. In 1999 the firm name was changed to Murray Wells Wendeln & Robinson CPAs and the Troy office moved to 212 W. Franklin Street to better serve clients in southern Miami County. Present partner Mike Hulme joined the firm in 1994. In 2000, *MWWR* acquired the practice formerly owned by Marion Fessler. In 2005, *MWWR* further enhanced its capabilities by merging with Thomas R. Murray Jr. CPA & Associates. An experienced and talented staff has made *MWWR* not only one of the largest but also one of the most respected CPA firms in the region.

As time has progressed, *MWWR* has seen changes in leadership with the retirements of Doug Murray in 1999 and Steve Wells in 2006. Partners Tony Wendeln, Sam Robinson, Karen Benanzer, Mike Hulme and Tom Murray ably lead the firm today with products and services that reach far beyond those offered in the early days of the firm. The desire to provide clients with a full array of financial services led to the formation of the *MWWR Group* in 2003.

The *MWWR Group* offers a broad base of services to both individual and business clients from two convenient locations: 326 N. Wayne Street in Piqua and 121 W. Franklin Street in Troy. The *MWWR Group* is anchored by the certified public accounting firm of *Murray Wells Wendeln & Robinson CPAs* providing tax, audit, accounting and management advisory services. In 2003 *MWWR Financial Services** and *Preferred Payroll Services* were born.

The investment professionals of *MWWR Financial Services** work with all aspects of business retirement plans including 401(k) plans, non-profit endowment plans and individual accounts including IRAs with a focus on investment asset allocation. *MWWR Financial Services** is a local, independent investment advisor that teams its clients with experienced money managers and asset allocation specialists to accomplish investment objectives.

Rounding out the family of services is *Preferred Payroll Services (PPS)*. In-house professionals use state of the art systems to deliver the highest level of payroll processing services. *PPS* offers the ease and flexibility of working with a local provider for payroll processing and complete payroll tax filing services at prices that are competitive with those charged by the national companies.

When you work with the team from the *MWWR Group* you are engaging a group of professionals with diversity and depth of experience in business, industry and personal account management. *MWWR Group* is positioned to continue to offer the area exceptional service well into the future.

121 W. Franklin St., Troy

326 N. Wayne St., Piqua

*MWWR Financial Services offers securities and investment advisory services through H. Beck, Inc. Member NASD, SIPC. 11140 Rockville Pike, 4th Floor, Rockville, MD 20852, (301) 468-0100. H. Beck Inc. and MWWR are not affiliated.

The Orr Felt Company

In 1848, the seed from which The Orr Felt Company would blossom was planted. Young and Yager, one of the first textile companies in the Midwest, began producing woolen fabrics in Piqua that year. Custom carding of fleeces for comforts and homespuns was carried on, and some coarse materials, such as "jeans" and flannels, were manufactured.

By 1869, U.S. Grant had become the 18th U.S. President, the Suez Canal was opened, the Cincinnati Red Stockings became baseball's first professional team and the ownership of Young and Yager changed to O'Ferrall, Daniels & Company, and a considerably larger plant had been built. A few years later it became the property of Mr. F. Gray, who came to Piqua from Cynthiana, Kentucky, and the name of the mill was changed to The F. Gray Company. This company at first manufactured blankets, yarns for home knitting and weaving, flannels and jeans.

During that same year, The Akron Woolen Company in Akron, Ohio, went out of business and The F. Gray Company purchased the machinery and moved it to Piqua. The manufacturing of papermaker's wet felts in Piqua began at that date and Mr. Gray continued to manufacture the other products listed.

The F. Gray Company went into receivership in 1900 and Mr. A.M. Orr of Piqua and G.L. Marble, of Van Wert, became the receivers. A year later, Colonel W.P. Orr, a prominent Piqua businessman in linseed oil manufacturing and banking, together with his son, A.M. Orr, bought the woolen mill property and organized The Orr Felt & Blanket Company with the following officers: Colonel W.P. Orr, President; A.M. Orr, Vice President; Louis O. Koester, Secretary and Treasurer. At this time, the mill was located between Water Street and the Pennsylvania Railroad, adjacent to the Miami and Erie Canal. The new company, under the leadership of W.P. and A.M. Orr, continued to manufacture woolen bed blankets and papermaker's felts. These products gained wide acceptance throughout the country and the company experienced steady growth. A complete worsted mill unit was added for the production of serges and other worsted cloths for the men's wear trade.

In 1909, additional machinery and manufacturing space necessitated the building at the present location on South Main Street. The felt and blanket manufacturing operations were moved to the new mill, with the worsted manufacturing continuing at the old location.

In 1912, Colonel Orr died and was succeeded as president by his son, A.M. Orr.

The following year, a flood caused extensive damage to the plant and equipment of the worsted mill. The damage was repaired after many weeks of work and the plant was scheduled to open on a Monday morning. On the day before production was to resume, the plant was destroyed by fire and the company decided to discontinue the manufacture of worsteds and confine it's activities to the operations at the new mill on South Main Street.

The untimely death of A.M. Orr followed in December and his wife, Mrs. Eliza Boal Orr, was made President, with M.C. Burrell as Vice-President and General Manager, and L.O. Koester continuing as Secretary and Treasurer. Under the leadership of the new officers, the company continued to experience a steady growth and by the onset of the "Roaring 20's" further expansion of the plant and manufacturing facilities was necessary. New cards, looms, and spinning mules were purchased and a large addition added to the north end of the present building. This increased the capacity of the plant approximately forty percent. The business maintained a slow, but steady growth during the depression of 1929. In 1933, the volume was curtailed somewhat, but unlike most industries, the plant was never entirely closed.

In 1937, Japanese planes sank the U.S. gunboat "Panay" in Chinese waters, Steinbeck introduced "Of Mice and Men" and "Babes in Arms" was the toast of Broadway. Orr toasted its success by adding a large warehouse for raw wool and finished blankets.

During the period of World War II, The Orr Felt & Blanket Company produced approximately a quarter of a million blankets for the army and navy, plus many thousands of yards of olive drab woolen lining cloth which was used in sleeping bags for the armed forces. During the war, Mrs. A.M. Orr, who served as President of the company for thirty years, died. William Casparis, grandson of Mrs. Orr, became President and General Manager, and served in this capacity until March, 1948, when he resigned and moved to California. At this time, Morrison B. Orr, son of A.M. and Mrs. Eliza Boal Orr, was elected to the office of President. Under his leadership, a program of diversification of products, a broadening of sales outlets was established, and the growth of the company continued.

1964 also became a pivotal year in the history of The Orr Felt Company. The company was reorganized under the direction of Dimitri Nicholas. The old machinery was replaced with modern production equipment, but traditional craftsmanship was maintained.

Today, The Orr Felt Company is the largest independently held manufacturer of papermaker wet felts in the industry and a well-known supplier to every major papermaker in the United States. Well into its second century, The Orr Felt Company celebrated its 25th Anniversary (as of 1989) under the leadership of Mr. Dimitri P. Nicholas. In 1990, Mr. Nicholas sold The Orr Felt Company to his family and Mr. Nicholas' daughter, Colombe Nicholas, was in control of the company for a period of two years. At the end of her term, Mr. Nicholas' son, Mr. Dimitri M. Nicholas, became acting President and C.E.O. of the company.

Now having entered the new millennium, the objectives of The Orr Felt Company remain committed to the quality of their products, state of the art machinery, and respect and dedication to their customers. The Orr Felt Company looks toward greater development in the future. Our continued progress has made Orr as "up to date" as tomorrow's paper.

ORR...

THE WET FELTS OF TOMORROW...
TODAY !

The Piqua Chamber of Commerce

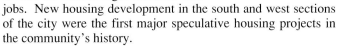

The first formal business association in Piqua was organized in March of 1876 under the leadership of Dr. Godwin Dorsey. Known as the Board of Trade of Piqua, Ohio, the group promoted the revitalization of the Miami and Erie Canal and the promotion of local industries. A second group was organized eight years later in February 1884, after a citizen's meeting demanded that Piqua's interests be promoted throughout the county. Chaired by Stephen Johnston, the new Citizen's Association of Piqua encouraged industrial development for the city. Unfortunately, the Citizen's Association got bogged down in the Piqua-Troy courthouse controversy and quickly lost its economic focus. The last group of the 1880's came into being in April of 1886. It became the most successful organization to date. Bringing back the name of the Piqua Board of Trade, the group actively sought new industries and new housing for the community. The Board brought in the Favorite Stove and Range Company in 1888 and the Cincinnati Corrugating Company/Piqua Rolling Mill Company in 1889 for a total in the next decade of almost eight hundred new jobs. New housing development in the south and west sections of the city were the first major speculative housing projects in the community's history.

The 1890's saw numerous new developments in Piqua such as the Miami Valley Railway Company and the Miami Valley Gas and Fuel Company and the Piqua School Furniture Company among many others. But most of these additions were privately promoted and the Board of Trade met only periodically.

The most active group in Piqua after the turn of the century was the downtown merchants. They formally organized themselves in December of 1907 as the Piqua Retail Merchants Association led by Albin L. Thoma. This group gradually broadened its activities and by 1909 had become the Piqua Business Men's Association. Looking towards the community as a whole, the group reorganized again in December of 1913 as the Piqua Chamber of Commerce. The first meeting of this new group was chaired by John T. Nelson who led discussion on the need of a paved road from Piqua to Urbana and hitching posts on Main Street. Typical of the period, the new Chamber ended their meeting with an informal session of coffee and cigars. The Chamber (formally incorporated in 1914) lasted until the early 1920's when a decline in membership led to its demise.

Near the beginning of the Great Depression, the Piqua Civic Association (1930) was organized to help the community and its businesses deal with the problems of the nations devastating economic upheaval. Under the management of Executive Secretary, Joseph M. Dine, the association was active for over two-and-a-half years. The group revived in 1939 in response to the Lion Club's "Good Neighbor Week". The most successful venture of the group was the bringing of Jackson Tube Company to Piqua in 1940. The organization became inactive after the beginning of World War II in 1941. War brought economic prosperity to Piqua as well as new industries including Robbins and Myers Company and the Lear Avia Incorporated. By 1944,

the nation knew that the war was coming to a close and post-war planning had to begin.

The city commission organized a city-wide meeting in February of 1944 to plan for Piqua's future and to deal with the closings of local wartime industries. Out of this meeting came the formation of the modern Piqua Chamber of Commerce on March 3, 1944. The new group elected Armotte Boyer (Meteor Motor Car Company) as its first president and began a systematic program for promoting the City of Piqua. During that first year, the Chamber worked to establish an official Piqua Park Board, a new municipal golf course, an airport, a music series, a sesquicentennial celebration (1796-1946) and a state historical park at Johnston Farm.

Since that time, the Piqua Area Chamber of Commerce has promoted a new community swimming pool, improved parks, new industries; better parking, new school structures, city-wide cultural events and the renovation of the Fort Piqua Hotel.

Today's Chamber mission is basically the same as it was in 1876. It is a voluntary organization of the business community. The Chamber is a private, non-profit taxpaying organization. It unites hundreds of business and professional firms, therefore creating a unique central organization working to improve and promote business and build even a stronger community. Fourteen individuals have shared the Presidency of the Chamber and none more noteworthy than David Vollette who served seventeen years.

The organization is recognized and respected locally and nationally. This active Chamber, lead by Lisa K. Whitaker, its first women President enables our community to stay in step with current issues and projects while working to promote economic vitality and enhance the quality of life of our citizens.

Piqua Area Chamber of Commerce Ambassadors
Formed August 4, 1968

The Piqua Baptist Church

The Piqua Baptist Church will celebrate 200 years of service to our Lord Jesus Christ and the Piqua community in 2011. "The church on the hill with Piqua on its heart" is located at 1402 West High Street. Its current pastors are Donald Wells, senior pastor, and Daniel Helms, Director of Family Ministries. Services are held on Sunday mornings, with Sunday School beginning at 9:15 am, and worship at 10:30 am. Prayer and Bible Study are held on Wednesdays at 7 pm. Everyone is welcome!

Hilliard House

Masonic Temple

Milestones Along the Way at Piqua Baptist Church

- **August 30, 1811** – 13 men and 13 women met at 415 Staunton Street, in Shawnee, at the home of Charles B. Hilliard, to organize the Salem Baptist Church.
- **July 8, 1820** – a 26 x 30 -foot long log church was constructed on the east bank of Spring Creek, three fourths of a mile north of U.S. Route 36.
- **1834** – The first area Baptist Sunday School was organized and services were conducted in a frame church built at the southwest corner of Ash and Harrison Streets.
- **November 4, 1948** – The First Baptist Church built a brick structure on the south side of West High Street, currently occupied by the Masonic Lodge.
- **1911** – Piqua Baptist Church was organized when members of First Baptist and Calvary Baptist united to form one church at 500 Broadway.
- **1913** – The Great Miami River Flood of 1913 halted construction of the church and members turned their energy to helping those in need.
- **March 19, 1916** – Piqua Baptist Church at 500 Broadway was dedicated.
- **November 6, 1976** – After 60 years on Broadway, the Piqua Baptist Church celebrated its first service at 1402 W. High St.
  (**Phase 1**: Sunday School and Fellowship Hall wing)
- **April 13, 1980** – The first service was held in the Sanctuary.
  (**Phase 2**: Completion of the Sanctuary)
- **October 16, 2005** – Twenty-five year Homecoming Celebration of worshiping in the Sanctuary.
- **2011 – Piqua Baptist's 200th Anniversary!** May God continue to bless!

Piqua Baptist Church

Piqua Baptist Church

Piqua Concrete Company

Piqua Concrete Company started operating in September 1972. The Piqua plant and office, located at 8395 N. Piqua-Lockington Road still remain at the same location, with several additions and changes to the facility.

In 1972 Piqua Concrete Co. employed five drivers, an office assistant and a dispatcher. Maintenance on the trucks was performed in a small garage located in the original building.

In 1979 a subsidiary company named Piqua Transport Co was established to handle transporting of the aggregate and cement needed in the manufacturing of ready mixed concrete. Today a fleet of six tractors, six trailers and five dump trucks keep our plants supplied with the raw materials needed daily.

In 1982 Piqua Concrete Company began to grow, increasing the fleet of trucks. The office staff had outgrown the original building so the large garage and second office area were added to the Piqua plant.

In an effort to meet our customers needs for ready mix concrete in an ever-expanding market area, additional plants were added. In May 1987 a second plant started operation on Old Springfield Road near Englewood. In May 1992 a third plant opened on Haddix Road near Fairborn. On April 18, 2004 the fourth plant began operations on Central Avenue in Carlisle. Today Piqua Concrete Company employs approximately 80 individuals with 26 in Piqua, 14 in Englewood, 18 in Fairborn, 18 in Carlisle and office staff of four.

In June 2005 an additional subsidiary company named Piqua Transport Co Pump Division began pumping operations for customers. Two pump trucks, 34 meters and 39 meters, were added to our fleet. With capabilities of reaching to 127 feet vertical and 105 feet horizontal our pump trucks can place the concrete right where the customer needs it. These pump trucks cover an area as far north as Auglaize, Mercer and Logan counties and as far south as Hamilton and Clermont counties.

Today each of our four plans is capable of producing 125 to 150 yards of read mix concrete per hour. We have approximately 15 front loader trucks at each plant. Our fleet consists of 2005, 2006 and 2007 Advance Mixer trucks.

Company success is based on the commitment to provide the highest quality products and service to Piqua Concrete Co customers.

Piqua Daily Call

By Tom Millhouse, Piqua Daily Call News Editor

Much has changed since the first edition of the *Piqua Daily Call* hit the streets Oct. 18, 1883. One thing that hasn't changed in the past 124 years is the Daily Call's commitment to providing its readers with the information they need in their lives.

The brainchild of John Morris, the *Daily Call* (initially called the *Piqua Morning Call*) was born during time of keen competition among several newspapers vying for the public's attention.

In a day of primitive printing technology, the bundle of papers that carrier H.F. Keyt toted around town was so small that he could carry them under his arm as he made his rounds.

The first of many changes for the *Call* came Jan. 1, 1884, when Morris switched the paper to an evening print time. Thus, the *Piqua Daily Call* debuted that day. The *Call* remained an afternoon paper until 2003, when it returned to an early morning edition.

In addition to the *Daily Call*, Morris also published the *Miami Helmet*, a weekly paper. He continued in the newspaper business until his death in 1906.

With the passing of Morris, the *Daily Call* underwent the first of several changes in ownership. The new owners went under the name of the *Piqua Daily Call Publishing Co.* with H.R. Snyder as manager. Snyder gave way to Merritt C. Spiegel in 1909, when the company reorganized.

The *Daily Call* faced a major challenge in March 1913, when a deadly flood swept through the Miami Valley. A story written by Judge W.D. Jones later in 1913 recounted the bravery of the *Daily Call's* staff in turning out a newspaper.

"With the water at their door and under their feet, the whole staff stood at their posts" to make sure the paper was published, Jones wrote. A major change in the local newspaper business would take place in 1919.

Through that year, three separately owned and operated daily newspapers — *The Daily Call*, *The Piqua Press* and the *Piqua Leader-Dispatch* — served the community.

In November 1919, as World War I was grinding to a halt in Europe, C. Frank Ridenour and J.A. Chew purchased the *Piqua Press* and *Piqua Leader-Dispatch*. A short time later, they bought the common stock of *The Piqua Daily Call* and merged all three papers into the *Daily Call* in December 1919.

The Daily Call then was the lone newspaper in town after years of publications that included foreign-language and political party-affiliated newspapers.

Following Ridenour's death in 1953, Chew purchased complete control of the *Daily Call*, making it part of Chew Newspapers Inc. Chew retained ownership of the *Daily Call* until 1978, when the newspapers were acquired by Thomson Newspapers Inc.

The Daily Call was acquired by its present owner, Brown Publishing Co., in September 1998.

For nearly 50 years, the *Daily Call* operated out of a building at 316 N. Wayne St. The *Daily Call* name still is etched in the front of the building.

With a need for additional space, the *Daily Call* moved to the former Piqua Hosiery building at 121 E. Ash St. in 1952. In addition to having new quarters, the *Daily Call* installed a new press

in 1952. That press would serve the *Daily Call* until 1970, when the newspaper would move from the old hot-lead type to offset printing. An addition to the building was constructed to house the new press, which still is being used today. The *Daily Call* was the third newspaper in Ohio to switch to offset printing.

A new building was constructed for the *Daily Call* offices in 1990. The *Daily Call* continues to operate out of the building, located at 310 Spring St.

Through the years, the *Daily Call* has provided an opportunity for Piqua High School and Lehman Catholic High School (and Piqua Catholic before it merged with Holy Angels in Sidney) students to develop journalism skills by working on the staff of *Smoke Signals* and the *Cavalier Crier*.

The *Daily Call* also broke ground in the hiring of women to the newspaper staff. In a 1990 *Daily Call* story, local historian Jim Oda noted the *Daily Call* hired Frances H. Fleming as society editor in 1911. Lola Hill assumed the society editor's position in 1920 and wrote for the *Daily Call* for about 40 years.

In addition to the new printing process, the *Daily Call* has undergone many other changes in technology through the years. Special electric IBM typewriters replaced the old manual typewriters in the early 1980s. The new machines produced copy on paper, which would be scanned by an optical reader to produce type that was pasted onto pages. Later that same decade the switch was made to computer terminals used by reporters and editors to produce the news.

In the 1990s, the *Daily Call* saw another advance in technology with the introduction of pagination, which involves the complete design of pages on a computer screen.

Also in keeping with modern technology, the *Daily Call's* Web site, *www.dailycall.com*, is a work in progress, with changes currently in the works for online subscribers.

While technology has changed, the *Daily Call's* employees remain the key to the newspaper's success.

Among the editorial employees who served *Daily Call* readers for many years were Kenny Shofstall, Jack Murray, Lola Hill, Ella May Purdy, Ray Heater, Ruth Reed, Dave Fogt and Gloria Minnich. Some other longtime *Daily Call* employees included Clete Klosterman, Howard Griffith, Dick Sullenberger, Bob Carothers, Jim "Moose" McMaken, Glenn Murphy, Carol Devers, Charles Householder and Eldon Shepard. The current leadership of the *Daily Call* includes: Kimberly Kiehl-Oen, group publisher; Susan Hartley, executive editor; Jeffrey Billiel, regional group editor; Leiann Stewart, advertising manager; John Carnahan, classified and major accounts manager; Cheryl Hall, circulation manager; Betty Brownlee, business manager; Greta Silvers, graphics manager; and Don King, production manager.

Joining Hartley on the editorial staff are: News Editor Tom Millhouse, Sports Editor Rob Kiser, staff writers Will E Sanders, Becca Manning and Jennifer Runyon; News Clerk/Writer Brenda Clement; Photographer Mike Ullery; and Internet editor Scot Trisel.

Commitment to Community remains the *Call's* motto — commitment to providing up-to-date information to the Piqua community and commitment to serving the community.

This past year, the *Call* has printed a popular weekly Bicentennial Page, highlighting the city's 200-year history. Call staffers participated in the city's Bicentennial Parade and volunteered in the city's beautification project Renew Piqua by painting a home. The employees also participate in a variety of community service projects, for example, collecting school supplies for Miami County Children's Services.

Piqua Emery Foundry

From the Finest Grains of Sand

Start with grains of sand so fine it feels like powder. Add a little bit of water and clay, and you've got the ingredients for the perfect mold. From those molds, Piqua Emery Foundry has been making quality aluminum castings for more than 87 years.

Founded by Charlie Sheaf and Frank Mikolajewski in 1920, the foundry remains a tight knit family operation, owned by life-long Piqua residents Helen, Stephen, and Beverly Mikolajewski. Piqua Emery now encompasses a full city block, and continues to pride itself in producing quality parts for customers all across the Eastern half of the United States. Over the decades, some processes have been automated, but the roots are still in the time-tested art of the master craft molder. The molder works his magic with the sand to make the mold; aluminum ingot is heated to a temperature in excess of 1300^0, then the molten metal is poured into the mold to form the part. Additional finishing (sawing, grinding, heat-treating, and machining) is done to the casting prior to shipment, all done by dedicated employees who take tremendous pride in producing quality parts.

Piqua Emery has been a long trusted name in the aluminum casting business due to the keen business acumen of the Mikolajewski brothers (Frank, Richard, and Louis), and the tradition continues today. Growth was never a major concern for them, rather the ability to provide the customer what they wanted...Quality Parts---On Time. Their vision was if they could consistently do that, growth would naturally occur. Whether it is one fan blade made for Hartzell Fan, or five hundred valves made for Crane Pumps, the ability to make a wide variety of parts in small or large quantities is what sets Piqua Emery apart from much larger foundries, and also enables them to withstand the onslaught of foreign competition.

The average citizen does not truly understand what a foundry is, or what they really do inside the walls of the factory. Foundry's make many items for the home that people just naturally take for granted, such as silverware, pots and pans, faucets, lighting fixtures, electrical fixtures, parts for washers and dryers, refrigerators, ranges, ovens, etc. In the automotive world, engines for cars and trucks, engine components, brake parts, wheels, etc. are made in foundries.

Piqua Emery's legacy of producing aluminum parts can be found in the parts they make for the Aston Martin automobile, car of choice for Ian Fleming's *James Bond*. You can also find parts such as *Kentucky Fried Chicken* fryer lids, *Whirlpool* and *KitchenAid* appliances, and *Buell* motorcycles. One of the foundry's proudest moments, however, was watching the 1984 United States Olympic Cycling Team win the Gold Medal at the Los Angeles games. Members of the team rode *Huffy* bicycles with uniquely designed aerodynamic parts manufactured at Piqua Emery Foundry, Inc.

Today the tradition continues. The owners and employees of Piqua Emery Foundry, Inc. look back proudly on their rich and storied history and tradition, and keep their eyes on the future as the next generation of manufacturing unfolds. Hopefully, that future holds chapters dedicated to the foundry, and the quality people who sacrifice their energy and efforts daily to produce some of the finest aluminum parts found anywhere in the world.

Grinding a smooth finish on a casting

Pouring metal into a mold.

Piqua Granite & Marble Company

Piqua Granite and Marble Company is celebrating its 125th anniversary during Piqua's Bicentennial year. On May 1, 1882 at High and Wayne Piqua Granite and Marble Works, Inc. was born.

Flatz and Eby, who had operated earlier in business on East Water Street from 1869, established the company. In 1904 the company was reorganized and purchased property owned by the American Tin Plate Corporation at 900 S. Main Street. The first contract written at this location is framed and still hangs on the wall at Piqua Granite. It is for a 3 piece 5' tall Barre Gray Granite Memorial for the Licklider family. Total cost was $150.00.

Later, Paul and Catherine Hank, and Jasper Comolli purchased the company. Addison Elston became a stockholder and started working for the firm in 1926, his employment continued well into the 1980's.

In October of 1972, a chemical engineer by profession, Z.J. Obara, bought Piqua Granite. In Mr. Obara's first fifteen years of ownership he managed to quadruple the business. He added several more employees, built a new building, and expanded to another building where Piqua Granite currently resides at 123 N. Main Street. In 1982, for the 100th anniversary of Piqua Granite, 100 memorials, approximately 90,000 pounds of granite, were moved in to the current location on North Main Street in celebration. Piqua Granite still boasts as having one of the largest indoor displays in the Miami Valley.

Monuments once were manufactured in Piqua, originally along the canal for easy transport of granite to the plant. Later, the railroad was the vital link between material sources and the plant. Manufacturing in Piqua ceased due to the halt of the rail service and in response to growing environmental regulations involving disposal of waste granite. Most manufacturing plants now are based at a quarry site.

Piqua Granite was one of the first companies in the city to have a fax machine. The fax machine was added because of the difficulty involved in describing an unusual memorial over the phone to the quarry.

Another first for Piqua Granite is being the first monument company in the entire Miami Valley to use the Monu-Cad system for designing and cutting of granite memorials. This system enabled Piqua Granite to expand its design collection, with the current collection of designs topping 10,000.

The current president of Piqua Granite is Pat Obara, who took over after her husband passed away in 2000. Currently the company has 5 showrooms, the largest is in Piqua and the others are in Shelbyville, Lebanon, and Indianapolis, Indiana with the last being in Lansing, Michigan.

Piqua Granite & Marble Co. Inc. is proud to have been a part of so many memorials. Some well-known examples of the company's work include:

- The Carillon Bell Tower in Dayton.
- The statue of Hippocrates at Wright State University.
- The Piqua Veterans Memorial.
- The Miami County FOP Memorial in Troy.
- The water fountain at the public square in downtown Piqua.
- Forest Hill Cemetery's entrance.
- The Don Gentile memorial in downtown Piqua.
- The Mills brothers memorial on the square in Piqua, near the gazebo.
- Construction of the Tipp City Veterans Memorial is planned for the summer of 2007.

Piqua Granite has placed thousands of cemetery memorials as well as numerous Civic Monuments and signage throughout the Eastern Midwest. The company has maintained one of the most enviable histories in the monument industry.

Left: Piqua Granite 1950s

Piqua Heritage Festival

OHIO WILDERNESS FRONTIER

Since 1982 Piqua has been celebrating its past at the Johnston Farm on the Labor Day Weekend. In 2007 while Piqua is marking its bicentennial, the Piqua Heritage Festival is commemorating its 25th anniversary. What began as an event to provide the citizens a reason to remain in Piqua over the holiday weekend has become a destination as thousands of people now make this an annual event and come to Piqua to enjoy all the Heritage Festival has to offer. Often times families use this weekend as a reason to host a family reunion as people return for one more ear of corn, or another edition of the old fashion melodrama.

Visitors are able to walk the ground on which many early events that shaped Ohio had taken place. Today, these visitors can watch as demonstrators bring back to life many of the skills needed to make a life for themselves in early 19th century Ohio. The Piqua Heritage Festival also highlights some of the best crafters in the Midwest, as they bring many handmade items that reflect the time of the Ohio frontier. Another highlight of the weekend is the pre-1870's encampment area. Here families and individuals gather, and for the weekend, live, dress, and demonstrate for the visitors how our ancestors lived, worked, and played at the time that Ohio was a new state.

Throughout the three days of the weekend, entertainment reminiscent of the time period abounds on the festival grounds. There is something for everyone as performers share some amazing talents that also help to carry visitors back to an earlier Ohio.

No festival would be complete without food, and the best food east of the Mississippi River can be enjoyed at the Piqua Heritage Festival. Local groups provide a menu of food that can satisfy even the most discriminating festival-goer. The aromas of these menus all blend together to make the mouths of those walking the grounds water in anticipation of mealtime.

The Ohio Historical Society is proud to be a partner of the Piqua Heritage Festival. Since 1982 the Festival has been held on the land that once belonged to Col. John Johnston, and where much early Ohio history unfolded. During the three day celebration the Johnston home, the Historic Woodland Indian and Canal Museum, as well as the *General Harrison* canal boat are all open, staffed, and operating as a part of the festival.

The Piqua Heritage Festival combines many elements that come together in one place and gives the visitor a small taste of a much earlier Ohio and how families coped with what that life was like. By strolling among the big tents, small camps, and open-air vendors, those who attend the festival will enjoy a brief glimpse into Ohio in its infancy.

The Piqua Heritage Festival is truly a community event, and the result of a strong partnership between many different groups and individuals. The Festival itself is governed and planned annually by an all volunteer Board of Directors, who in turn create a committee structure that is responsible for the planning and implementation of all of the segments that come together to make the Piqua Heritage Festival what it has become. Each year people from many of the organizations throughout the city become involved as they help with the Festival set-up, man demonstration booths, or provide the food for Festival-goers to enjoy. The Festival also enjoys a particularly valuable relationship with many of the departments of the City of Piqua. This is truly a community event that affords Piqua the opportunity to put its best foot forward each year over the Labor Day Weekend.

Lou Havenar, known as Mr. Heritage Festival to most people, chairs the Piqua Heritage Festival Board of Directors; Vice Chairmen are Bill Havenar and Tom Hildebrand. Secretary to the Board and Committees is Marlene Reid and Becky Campbell is the Heritage Festival Treasurer. Each year the Board selects an individual to serve as the Chairman, the 2007 Chairman is Andy Hite. Other Heritage Festival Board members are Lynn Bierly, Duaine Campbell, Pat Campbell, Connie Dembski, Scott Helman, Judy King, Tony Lyons, Chuck McGlaughlin, Frank Patrizio, Jr., Russ Reid, and Wayne Willcox. Two more important individuals are Director Emeritus Jim Schulz and Honorary Director Dorothy Tyler. Many of these Board members have been a part of the Festival since its beginning, and along with the Piqua community as a whole look toward the Labor Day Weekend as one of the highpoints of each year.

Past Heritage Festival Chairs

1982	Lou Havenar	1995	Mike Havenar
1983	Charles Householder	1996	Jim Schulz
1984	Bruce Hogston	1997	Steve Koon
1985	Jan Koon	1998	Tom Hildebrand
1986	Bill Havenar	1999	Lynn Bierly
1987	Tony White	2000	Jill Lyons
1988	Brian Caserta	2001	Jim Shepard
1989	Brian Caserta	2002	Frank Patrizio, Jr.
1990	Bob Von Aschen	2003	Russ & Marlene Reid
1991	Ron Ventura	2004	Wayne Willcox
1992	Rick Snyder	2005	Carol Hogston
1993	Dave Powell	2006	Duaine Campbell
1994	Steve Sowry	2007	Andy Hite

Piqua Historical Area

In September of 1972 the Ohio Historical Society officially opened the Piqua Historical Area. This was a culmination of work by many individuals in the Piqua community, the Ohio Historical Society, and many levels of government. Since its opening, people from around Ohio, across the United States, and foreign visitors have come here to visit the site that literally has seen human occupation from the time that people first ventured into what is called Ohio today. The Johnston Farm, as it is known locally, has been the site of many of the events that played a major role in the shaping of today's Buckeye State.

Visitors to the Piqua Historical Area are immersed in many stories at once. The story begins with the prehistoric cultures that began the human saga here. The Adena Culture, the first to construct mounds and earthworks, is manifest with a small burial mound and donut shaped earthwork found nestled in one corner of the site. The Pickawillany village further evidences the Native American presence. This was a Miami Indian village that became home of the first large English trading post in the west. This village site was added to the Johnston Farm in 1999, and was a part of the worldwide struggle between England and France for world domination. The events here were a forerunner of what we know as the French and Indian War. The destruction of the Miami village in 1752 gave way to the establishment of Shawnee villages in the latter part of the 1700's.

Our ancestors arrived here in greater numbers in the mid 1790's with the march of "Mad Anthony" Wayne's forces as they made their way north to the Battle of Fallen Timbers and the signing of the Greenville Treaty in 1795. This also marked the first time a young John Johnston set foot on the land that would eventually become his Upper Piqua Farm in 1804. By 1808, the then federally employed Johnston began to develop his Piqua holdings, and in 1811 moved his growing family here permanently from the Indian Agency in Fort Wayne wishing to become a "gentleman farmer." From that time on, a parade of dignitaries from all walks of life came to Piqua to visit the Colonel, a true politician, and a man who could be counted on to get things done. Local, state, and national issues were all standard fare for those who came here to conduct business in Johnston's impressive brick home that still stands among the other restored buildings of the family's farmstead.

During Johnston's time here he served as a U.S. Indian Agent, charged with gaining Native neutrality in the War of 1812. He continued in that post until 1829, when Democratic President Jackson requested that the Whig Johnston step down from that assignment. In 1825 when Ohio began building canals he was appointed an Ohio Canal Commissioner and worked to bring the canals to Piqua and eventually north to Lake Erie. He, along with his wife Rachel worked tirelessly to bring both education and religion to the frontier, and succeeded at both.

Today this site tells the story of all of these, and more events that have gone on here. A modern museum relates the story of the interaction of Ohio's Woodland Indians with the European settlers that journeyed here. There are also exhibits in the museum that tell the story of the construction, use, and eventual decline of Ohio's nearly 1,000 miles of canals. Visiting the restored home and buildings that comprised John Johnston's farm helps visitors gain understanding of life on the Ohio frontier, and how the family made a life for themselves in a much earlier Ohio. No visit to the area would be complete without boarding the *General Harrison of Piqua*, a replica of the mule-drawn canal boats that once passed through Miami County, for a ride on a one-mile restored stretch of the Miami and Erie Canal.

While Native history, the story of life on Ohio's frontier, and canals do not seem related to each other; it is John Johnston and his life that ties all of this together. Through the efforts of the staff and volunteers who make the Johnston Farm function, visitors are able to take a step back to a much different Ohio than we are familiar with today and learn where we have come from, and perhaps gain some insight into where we may be going in the future.

Piqua Kiwanis Club

A Brief History

*I*n 2006 The Piqua Kiwanis Club held its 70th Anniversary celebration. The club has seen many changes in Piqua, has helped to implement some of these changes and has honored many citizens who brought about these changes. The club is best known for the Kiwanis Pancake Day and the Annual Piqua Kiwanis Halloween Parade. The following are some of the highlights of Kiwanis involvement in the Piqua Community.

In January of 1936 the Piqua Kiwanis Club had their first meeting at Retter's Tea Room which was located in the building that housed Ed Liette Realty. That building was raised in 2007 and now the property is owned by St. James Episcopal Church. The cost of the lunch was $ 0.41. 1937 brought about the Piqua Kiwanis Club's sponsorship of the first Dental Clinic for all Piqua school children. In 1948 Kiwanis road signs were erected at all city entrances and Piqua Kiwanis Club was ranked as an Outstanding Kiwanis club in Kiwanis International. The Club sponsored "Kids Train Ride to Troy" in 1952; over 2,000 children were treated to popcorn and ice cream cones. At an opening football game in 1954 Piqua Kiwanis Club hosted over 1,500 children with refreshments; on November 3 the Key Club was organized with 14 charter members. October 29, 1955 marked the first Pancake Day at Greene Street UM Church. Food was furnished by local businesses, pancake mix by Quaker Oats Co., and were served by Aunt Jemima. The chairman was Dr. Kenneth Lyon and a profit of $162.33 was realized. Today over $5,000 is netted.

The Annual Halloween Parade was started in 1956 by Joe Thoma, Jr. Joe saw a parade such as this on a visit to Celina and brought the idea to Piqua. Joe was also installed as club president in this year by his brother Louis, who was Lt. Governor in Zanesville. Joe's father was president of the Piqua Rotary Club at the time.

Anuual Halloween Parade

In 1957 over 2,800 eggs were purchased for the very first Easter Egg Hunt. The Club's 25th Anniversary was celebrated in March 11, 1961 at the Elks Club. In 1962 the first Kiwanis Pancake day at the Piqua Armory was held. The carousel pancake grills were manufactured in 1963 and are still in use today. They are also rented out for use by other organizations.

On to 1969, the club purchased and planted 83 flowering crab trees in the boulevard on Nicklin Avenue. That same year the club treated all new teachers to a free luncheon. This practice continues today. The chairmanship of the restoration of Hance Pavilion was taken on by Em Shear in 1979 due to snow storm damage. He was awarded "honorary member" of the Piqua Civic Band. In 1983 the development was started for Kiwanis Park at the site of the old North Street School. The park serves many children and has two shelters along with playground equipment.

The first Church Worker of the Year Jim Wheeler was honored in 1985. The first recipient of the Hugh O'Brien Award was given to a high school sophomore. The club's 50th Anniversary was celebrated in 1986 at Husmann's Restaurant. In 1988 interest in the Key Club was at an all time low and sponsorship was given up. Paul Mehling established an all-time high of $2,500 for an individual in pancake ticket sales in 1991. In 1994 Mark Reedy, rejuvenated the Key Club; Patti Jenkins, first female to be elected president, took office.

Joe Thoma, Jr. received his 44 year Perfect Attendance tab in 1995. In 1996 The Flesh Public Library received clocks for each United States time zones. The 60th Anniversary of the club was held at Upper Valley JVS. A donation to the Salvation Army Summer Lunch Program marked the beginning of a yearly tradition in 1997. Don Smith and Dot Leininger were the first father daughter members in 1998.

The weekly meeting place moved from Terry's Cafeteria to the Piqua Eagle's in 1999 and Warren Parker's dog Reba was made an "honorary member". Paul Mehling was presented with the George F. Hixon Award in which a $1,000 donation was made in his name. Congressman John Boehner made a visit and purchased the first Pancake Day ticket in 2000. Past International President Walter Sellers presented the charter to the new Builders Club of the Piqua Junior High School. In 2003 Joe Thoma was named Kiwanian of the year. This honor also includes the distinction of Grand Marshall of the Halloween Parade.

Pancakes at the Armory

Joe Thoma was recognized with the Legion of Honor for 55 years of service along with Jerry Fiessinger and Dr. Conrad Booher for 45 years in 2006 at the 70th Anniversary celebration of the club on May 23, 2006. The club hosted a visit from 2006 Olympic Women's Hockey Bronze Medalist, Kristin King at one of our weekly meetings. In 2007 Pancake Day was moved to the Upper Valley JVS. The club lost beloved member Joe Thoma but he left us with a legacy that will benefit children for many years to come.

2007 Piqua Police Department

The Piqua Police Department

The Piqua Police Department can trace its roots back to 1835, when the first City Marshal, Robert Shannon, was sworn in to uphold the law and to protect the citizens of Piqua. Between 1835 and 1903, part-time City Marshals and night watchmen protected the city. In 1903, Piqua started its full-time police department.

The city hired Frank Gehle, a former wrestler and bar owner, as the first police chief. Chief Gehle was known as a no nonsense police officer throughout his 34 years with the department.

In the 104 year history of the full-time Piqua Police Department, three officers have lost their lives in the line of duty.

The first officer to die in the line of duty was Lt. Noah Daniel Studebaker, who joined the Piqua Police Department on February 13, 1929. On May 29, 1949, Lt. Studebaker and Patrolman Ed Henderson were dispatched to a burglary in progress at the Hemm Brothers Garage at 119 N. Main Street. As the officers approached the business, men armed with shotguns ambushed both officers. Lt. Studebaker and Patrolman Henderson suffered shotgun wounds. Lt. Studebaker never recovered from his wounds and died on October 17, 1957 from chronic complications of the shotgun wounds.

The second Piqua Police Officer to give his life in the line of duty was Patrolman Jan Mulder II, who was appointed as a Piqua Police officer on May 23, 1966. Jan was born in the Netherlands. Shortly after World War II, his family immigrated to the United States.

On August 11, 1970, Patrolman Mulder was on foot patrol in the downtown area. He saw a suspicious person, and stopped him in the lobby of the Fort Piqua Hotel. Patrolman Mulder suspected the man of selling stolen property and was going to search the suspect and the bag he was carrying, when the man pulled a .32 caliber pistol and shot Jan three times, mortally wounding him. Jan died a short time later at Piqua Memorial Hospital.

The most recent Piqua Officer to die in the line of duty was Detective Robert C. Taylor, who joined the police department on September 9, 1956. Bob was the first official police department photographer, he was the first patrolman appointed to the detective assignment, and he started the first modern evidence room for the department. He was the senior officer of the department and wore the coveted badge #1. Detective Taylor was also the Piqua Police Officer of the year for 1979.

On November 2, 1982, after more than 26 years of service, Detective Taylor was participating in a department training exercise. The exercise consisted of strenuous physical activity that included running and shooting multiple firearms on a timed course.

Within a minute of completing the course, Detective Robert C. Taylor, suffered a fatal heart attack. His fellow officers performed CPR, however, Detective Taylor passed away later that night at Piqua Memorial Hospital.

In 2006, the Piqua Police Department Honor Guard participated in ceremonies in Washington D.C., where the memories of our fallen officers were honored. The names of all three officers are inscribed on the National Police Officers Memorial Wall of Honor, along with the rest of the Police Heroes, who have died serving their communities.

1935 Piqua Police Department

Piqua Rotary: A History of Service

By Daniel E. Ramer

*T*he Piqua Rotary Club was chartered in 1915 as Rotary's 135th chapter. The club was started by William Kendall Leonard, president of the Piqua Hosiery Company. Piqua's club was a notable addition to Rotary, being the first Rotary club established in a city with a population of under 25,000.

What is Rotary?

Rotary itself was founded in 1905, just 10 years prior to the formation of the Piqua club, at a time when the newspapers were rife with stories of corruption in the business world. Paul Harris and three other Chicago businessmen formed Rotary to show the good that business people of sound character can do, in the community and internationally, when acting together.

Having been in existence for the most recent 92 of Piqua's first 200 years, the Piqua club in 2007 is one of more than 32,000 Rotary clubs around the world. The club's purpose is to unite service-minded individuals to provide *humanitarian service*, to *promote high ethical standards in business and the professions*, and to help *build goodwill and peace internationally.*

Weekly Piqua Rotary Meetings

The Piqua club pursues these objectives to this day, meeting each Tuesday at 11:45 A.M. at the Piqua Country Club. Through the years, many of the leading citizens of Piqua have been members and leaders of the Rotary Club.

The weekly Piqua Rotary meeting features a program with guest speaker, often a person or group promoting a worthy cause or program. The club remains apolitical, focusing instead on education and information. Among program speakers over the years have been three-time presidential candidate William Jennings Bryan; TV talk show host Phil Donahue; James O'Grady, an engineer with RCA Corporation who was the first person to discuss in Piqua the newfangled invention called a "television;" and local Congressman William McCulloch, who spoke to the club some 21 times. In 2006, the Piqua Rotary Club was the first local group to host Piqua Olympian Kristen King following her return from the XX Winter Olympiad in Torino, Italy, and the first to offer her a chance to speak publicly to the people of her home town. Her appearance was televised live on Dayton TV.

Piqua Rotary in the Community

The Piqua Rotary Club is an enthusiastic supporter of local education. The Piqua Rotary Scholarship Fund has awarded hundreds of scholarships through the years to graduating Piqua area high school seniors. In addition, the club regularly hosts student guests from Piqua High School, Lehman Catholic High School, and the Upper Valley JVS at club meetings.

The Piqua Rotary Club enjoys a strong partnership with Nicklin Learning Center, Piqua's public kindergarten school. The many facets of the club's involvement with Nicklin include providing Rotarians as volunteer readers, reading age-appropriate books aloud to small groups in a relaxed setting; attending monthly school assemblies, distributing books and ribbons to each month's birthday children; providing volunteers and material support for quarterly *Family Literacy Nights* and family literacy "Take-Home Kits"; sponsoring cultural activities such as the Piqua Arts Council's art enrichment program and the *Artist in Residence* program; partnering with Nicklin parents and staff for worthy fund raisers; and furnishing financial support for Nicklin's *100th Day of School* celebration.

The club also provides funding assistance for a host of community activities and projects. It assists with the Protect Our Water Ways (P.O.W.W.) organization in its annual Great Miami River clean-up, helps with local park clean-up days, and sponsors the always-popular Rotary Corn Booth at the annual Piqua Heritage Festival. Each November on Election Day, the club hosts a fish dinner at the Upper Valley JVS, offering local citizens an opportunity to gather together and support the community after they have voted.

Piqua Rotary Internationally

Piqua Rotary also is active in Rotary International's efforts, including its International Youth Exchange program. The Piqua club has hosted a number of students from other countries over the years and recently has renewed its involvement in sending Piqua students abroad, to foster goodwill and understanding among nations and cultures.

The Rotary Foundation is one of the largest charitable foundations in the world. Among its successful efforts has been the *Polio Plus* polio-eradication program, a $600 million effort, supported by Piqua Rotarians, that has overseen a dramatic reduction in the number of polio cases reported worldwide, from 350,000 in 1988 to only 500 in 2005.

Piqua Rotary Today

As Piqua celebrates its bicentennial, the Piqua Rotary Club is in the midst of considerable growth and rededication to its founding purposes, having inducted more than 30 new members since June of 2005. The club currently has 103 members.

More information on Piqua Rotary is available at the club's Web site, *www.clubrunner.ca/piqua*. In addition, the Club presents a monthly program, *Piqua Rotary Report*, on Piqua's public-access channel, Piqua Channel 5.

Piqua Steel Company

About Seventy Five Years Ago...

In 1933, Earl F. Sever Sr., had the foresight to create a business that would withstand the turbulent times of the depression. Through hard work and determination, Earl took the initiative to found Piqua Steel Company. He along with his personnel traveled throughout Ohio, Michigan, Pennsylvania, Kentucky and Indiana focusing primarily on demolition and plant dismantling. As the country entered W.W.II, Bill Lear of Lear Avia Corp. moved his company to Piqua. Piqua Steel Company was the prime contractor to rig all the equipment out of the existing plant, which was then unloaded and installed in Piqua. In turn, this allowed Piqua Steel Company to enter the Machinery Moving, Rigging and Crane Rental Industry. Due to exceptional growth, Earl Sr. brought Earl Jr. onboard and instilled in him the many high quality standards he had developed through the years. Earl F. Sever Sr. proved he was a man of determination, learning many new trades and aspiring to be a success. He was a 'working mans' man" and built long term relations on the foundations of: Trust, Honesty, and Hard Work. Every employee was his friend and considered family.

In the late 1940's and early fifties Earl Jr. started a steel fabrication, steel erection, and steel sales shop located on Steele Ave. He sold steel to individuals, contractors, farmers, and small businesses. He sold fabricated steel for new buildings and erected the steel for general contractors. Earl Jr. also performed a lot of steel fabrication for industrial plants, stone and gravel plants, and asphalt plants. When the business out grew the building on Steele Ave. in Piqua, Earl Jr. built a new building on West US 36 for fabrication, steel erection and steel sales. That building is presently utilized by the machinery moving, crane rental, and rigging business, today. At the same time, the company provided crane service throughout the area and moving machinery for several of the local businesses.

In the late sixties Earl Jr. brought on Earl III (Lynn Sever). Lynn as well expanded the company into purely a Crane Rental and Rigging Business performing machinery moving, rigging and crane rental for many area mechanical and electrical contractors and major manufactures including Honda of America, Crown Equipment and Emerson Climate Control. Lynn developed PSC's motto... **"If we don't take care of our customers, someone else will."** He also developed PSC's advertising slogan... **"Committed to dependable service with qualified personnel."**

Lynn now serves as President and is still involved with estimating, business development and long range planning. During the 80's Lynn hired his wife Nancy to manage the office and has since brought on board his two sons Earl IV (Randy Sever) and Jim Sever. Nancy Sever now serves as Treasurer. Both Randy and Jim joined the company after college and serve as Vice President of Operations and Vice President / Controller respectively.

Since the mid 90's the company has grown to provide its services nationwide and into Canada and Mexico. The company developed its mission statement as follows: **'As a company, we are striving to provide our customers with the highest quality service possible in the machinery moving – erecting, rigging and crane rental industry. Our concerted efforts to become the safest service provider in our industry will allow us to become superior to competition. By building relationships with customers, employees and the external environment our businesses will succeed together.'**

In 2004, the company changed its name to PSC Crane & Rigging to better identify the services it provides today. The company has added to its fleet several state of the art rigging assets, tooling, and cranes that has awarded them several prestigious jobs – most notably Rigging Job of the Year in 2005. Their largest equipment includes a 120 Ton Truck Crane, (3) 30 Ton Forklifts and a 500 Ton Gantry System. The company has also recently received industry-wide awards for safety including the Zero Accident Award in 2005. Lynn and Earl Jr. continue to support and educate Randy and Jim on the core values of Trust, Honesty and Hard Work and hope to see the four grandsons (Brandyn, Devon, Dylon and Hayden) take the company into its fifth generation.

Machinery Erectors ❢ Riggers ❢ Crane Rental

Piqua Area United Way

The Piqua Area United Way has its roots in the Soldiers Aid Society that was established in 1862 to provide support to Civil War soldiers and their families. Piqua's history of taking care of its citizens through various aid societies did not take on the semblance of today's United Way until after World War II. H.W. Sims, The Piqua Chamber of Commerce president and Managing Director William Cory thought that Piqua was ready to establish a Community Chest organization and did the necessary research in the eastern half of the country to learn how to administer a Community Chest. The first campaign was held in 1947 under the name of Community Welfare Federation of Piquarea with a goal of $42, 235. The funds were divided between the Boy Scouts, Girl Scouts, YMCA, YWCA and the Salvation Army.

The 50th campaign will be held in 2007 with a goal of $565,000, which will be divided among 22 member agencies: American Red Cross, Big Brothers/Big Sisters, Boy Scouts, Child and Family Health Services, Family Abuse Shelter of Miami County, Family Service Association, Girl Scouts, Greene Street Child Care Center, Health Partners of Miami Co., Hospice of Miami Co., Meals on Wheels of Piqua, Mental Health Association of Miami Co., Miami County Recovery Council, Miami County YMCA, Parents as Teachers, Rehabilitation Center, SafeHaven, Inc., Sunrise Center for Adults, The Arc of Miami Co., Salvation Army, YWCA of Piqua and the U.S.O.

The first 145 years of societal support began as aid going directly to individuals or families in need of a helping hand. Today, the community's desire to help has been harnessed into one large campaign under the auspices of the Piqua Area United Way. The responsibility of the Campaign Cabinet is to raise funds and the Allocations Committee is charged with distributing those funds.

A change in the criteria used to determine how the funds are distributed is on the horizon. In the past the member agencies were funded if the agency served a need in the community. Then the move was to fund programs within those agencies. Now the current criteria is how well a program impacts a community's critical need. The Piqua Area United Way did a Community Needs Assessment in 2005. From this survey, four Impact Areas were crystallized: Meeting Basic Needs, Improving Health and Well Being, Helping Youth Succeed and Strengthening Families and Individuals. Member agency programs should impact one or more of these four areas. Impact funding will insure that our donors' contributions are actually changing the human services landscape in Piqua.

For example: An Impact Program- Job Training. The objective is to reduce the unemployment rate in Piqua and improve the economic status of the Piqua area. 1) 2000 people learn of the job training program. 2) 400 enroll and 300 attend the session 3) 200 retain information/skills from the session. 4) 80 start a job, 60 perform satisfactorily. 5) 17% of the program attendees (50) stay on the job for at least 6 months. 6) Unemployment decreased by 2% and the economic status of this group increased. The job training program had a measurable impact on individuals and on the community. Impact Funding supports those programs that actually make a difference. This type of funding will help agencies to reevaluate current programming and to discard those programs that have not performed well. This will focus the agency's resources on those programs that do make a difference and will insure the donating public that their monies are working hard in those programs that will demonstrably change the Piqua community for the better.

Over the past 50 years, the Piqua Area United Way has raised over $13.2 million that has been invested in Piqua to support our residents in need. The Piqua Area United Way has been especially lucky to have the creative and dynamic leadership of six women in the past 60 years: Irene Ditmer 1949-1974; Joanne Harmon 1975 to 1976; Dorie Perry 1976-1992; Cheryl Stiefel-Francis 1992-1999; Lisa Whitaker, 1999-2006; and then Ginny Koon succeeded Lisa in 2007. Under these leaders, the Piqua Area United Way has grown to be a force for good in the community and is laying plans to continue in this tradition for a strong future.

Rayner Electric Inc.

Rayner Electric Inc. as it is known today had its beginning in 1941 at 124 West Water St. and at that time was called the Favorite City Electric. George Rayner had been an electrician there since 1920 and decided to purchase the business and re-name it Rayner Electric Shop.

During World War II the business had to be closed for a brief time due to material shortages. George stored his tools and existing supplies and re-opened immediately after the war. In 1946 Rayner Electric Shop moved to 118 East Ash St. and remained at that location until 1970 when they moved to 112 West Ash Street. In 1969 George retired and sold his business to his son-in-law Norbert (Nub Lyons) who ran the business until his retirement in 1982. At that time Nub sold the business to his son Robert Lyons and long time friend and employee Richard Wenrick. Bob and Rick remained partners until Rick retired on December 31, 1999. At that time Dave Hall, a long time employee became a partner. Rayner Electric Inc. had grown from one man working on pumps and windmills in the early 1900's into a small electrical contracting business. Three generations have owned the business and it continues to grow each year, meeting the electrical needs of the community.

Reed Mote Staley Insurance Inc.

Reed Mote Staley Insurance has served Piqua for 132 of its first 200 years – the oldest insurance agency in the Upper Miami Valley. From humble beginnings, the firm has prospered through hard work, innovation and planned growth.

George Stelzer made and sold cigars. He did not like to drink beer or whiskey. Saloons were plentiful in 1870s Piqua and were a primary market of cigar sellers. Selling included sharing drinks with saloonkeepers. So George considered a new line of work.

George's brother-in-law Joseph Schlosser began selling fire insurance about 1875. George took over insurance sales in 1888 as a sideline to his family cigar business. Schlosser and Stelzer grew their business serving Piqua's large German immigrant community.

In the 1890s, George devoted full time to insurance, paralleling Piqua's rise as a thriving industrial community. He was joined in 1910 by his son-in-law Versel E. Reed, son of Piqua brick manufacturer Benjamin Franklin Reed (see Benjamin Franklin Reed patron page in this book).

Stelzer & Reed, the firm's new name, competed by introducing new forms of insurance and tailoring coverage to customer's specific needs. They served individual and commercial accounts, including Piqua's industrial heavyweights and growing service economy. Government, school and church accounts were shared among several firms. Versel earned a reputation for generosity and integrity working with other firms to service these public accounts. With extensive knowledge of insurance and the Piqua market, Versel was a frequent and reliable source of advice, even to competitors.

Stelzer & Reed were great diplomats. Some customers fiercely competed with each other, particularly Piqua's great banks – Piqua National and Citizens. Piqua's commercial sector and their local family owners divided their business fairly evenly between the two banks. George, Versel, and the generations that followed earned the community's trust by treating everyone with the utmost fairness, respect and propriety.

George and Versel mastered the balance between business and family life – a challenge for many family-run firms. They had a terrific business partnership, but when the work day ended, family life and service to community took priority.

George Stelzer retired in 1925 and Versel single-handedly rode the wave of prosperity through the Roaring 20s. During the Great Depression of the 1930s, the firm survived by helping customers cope with extraordinary economic and personal difficulties.

In 1936 and 1941, Versel's sons Robert B. Reed and William G. Reed joined the firm. World War II took them off to serve in the Navy and Army. Versel again took the helm and worked day and night to service accounts and absorb new business from a booming war economy.

Versel E. Reed, Stelzer & Reed offices, Orr-Flesh Building, 1915

To keep up with the postwar boom, Bob and Bill returned to the firm. In 1957 Stelzer & Reed acquired the J. Ben Wilkinson Company, a prominent firm with roots in Piqua back to 1878. Early founders were Henry Grafflin and John E. Mendenhall.

In 1969 the firm was transformed by the merger of Stelzer & Reed with Miles Mote Agency to form Reed Mote Reed Insurance Inc., ("RMR Insurance"). Versel Reed retired and Thomas R. Mote joined as partner. Miles Mote was founded in 1902 by J.R. Miles. His son Chidsey soon assumed ownership followed by his nephew Tom Mote.

On June 21, 1980 RMR became RMS – Reed Mote Staley Insurance Inc. – with the merger of Reed Mote Reed and Staley-Zimmerlin Insurance. Charles E. Staley joined as partner. Ralph Zimmerlin had retired several years earlier. Mr. Staley had owned the Staley-Zimmerlin firm since 1963. Its predecessor was a firm founded by Lue Recker in the 1930s.

The hand-off to the fourth generation followed the sudden loss of Chuck Staley in 1982. His son, Piqua native Steven K. Staley, had joined RMS with his dad and soon rose to become a partner in the firm. In 1984, Steve was joined by Greenville native J. Frederick Wright. Fred had 15 years experience in insurance sales and claims with firms including the Central Insurance Companies of Van Wert. Later, Steve and Fred became sole owners followed by the retirement of Bob Reed, Bill Reed and Tom Mote.

Steve Staley and Fred Wright retained the firm's name and rich heritage. They have extended its reputation for quality insurance products and exceptional customer service to a third century. Reed Mote Staley continues a long tradition of innovation and meeting customer's insurance needs.

Since 1961 Reed Mote Staley has maintained their offices in the historic Greek Revival building at 500 N. Wayne Street; constructed in 1847 for Samuel Davies, builder of locks on the Miami & Erie Canal, and his wife Rachel, niece of Piqua's Col. John Johnston. (Rachel's son Frank was a prominent local businessman who employed Versel Reed prior to his joining the firm in 1910). RMS is only the building's third owner. Earlier offices were on the SE corner of Public Square and in the Orr Flesh Building.

Written by: Richard K. Reed

500 N. Wayne Street offices of Reed Mote Staley Insurance, 1968

Remembering 1976

With all the excitement over the celebration of Piqua's bi-centennial, we are reminded of all the festivities that took place during our nation's bi-centennial in 1976.

Lou Havenar was chairman of the committee who planned all of the events that took place during that memorable year, but he had plenty of help. Many people who were part of the committee are now deceased, but it is good to remember their service. The following men and women helped in some way with the festivities: Bruce Hogston, William Tyler, William Higgins, Gerald McAfee, James Puterbaugh, Rev. Terry McKenzie, Richard Cron, Rick Missy, Charles Householder, Glen Rohr, Robert Shriver, Donald J. Smith, Nancy Ford, Beatrice Johnson, Mr. and Mrs. Lloyd Beach, Charles Popham, James Swarts, Tom Brown, William Grissom, Henry Johnson, Wallace White, Jerry Zimmerman, Mike, Jack, Bill, Richard and Brad Havenar, Joe Sampson, Lynn, Scott and Tod Bierly, Wayne and Terry Wones, Doug Heater, Rick Snyder, Tom Baker and others.

During most of the summer of that year a replica of a fort stood in the public square of Piqua. A group of men including Lou went out into the woods and chopped down trees which they used to build the fort which was adjacent to the old Coke Hall and next to the present Zender's. It was similar to the one which originally stood at Fort Pickawillany near the Johnston Farm and contained a log cabin on the inside and a catwalk around the edge. Mary Lou Havenar told of the night they held a candlelight walk when many Piquads walked to the fort carrying lighted candles while those inside sang appropriate songs. A wedding even took place inside the fort during that year. After the bi-centennial the fort was put up for auction and Mr. Havenar bought it himself and had it reconstructed on his property.

Some of the special events that were planned for this celebration were snowmobile races, dog sled races, farmers' markets that were held weekly during the summer, ice cream socials, and several special dinners. The Piqua Players also put on the musical "1776" during the year. A costume ball was planned but had to be cancelled due to lack of interest. There was even a demonstration of methods of harvesting used 200 years ago.

A special memorial of this bi-centennial can still be seen in the yard next to the fire station in Piqua. The old bell which used to hang in the City Hall on Water Street was installed in a specially-constructed frame by the brick and masonry department of the Upper Valley Joint Vocational School. It was dedicated by Bill Baugh, a Piqua hero who returned home safely after being a prisoner-of-war during the Viet Nam War. He was also the Grand Marshall of the parade that was the culmination of the celebration.

The spectacular parade held on September 18, which was organized by Bruce Hogston, lasted about two hours, and was made up of at least 12 bands from area high schools as well as the Piqua Civic Band and the Alumni Band. Elaborate floats prepared by many organizations, various clowns including an Uncle Sam on stilts, classic cars and fire equipment from all over the area were just some of the participants.

Another reminder of this local celebration is the Tourist Information Center that was established in front of the old Scot's Inn Motel on Route 36. It has since been moved to Troy but still provided information for those touring our area.

A special bicentennial flag hung on the public square throughout the year, and a time capsule was buried which contained money and other items typical of the time. Unfortunately no one can remember where it was buried.

Lou Havenar went on to organize the first Heritage Festival in 1982 and continues to be very involved with this yearly event as well as many other civic activities. His wife Mary Lou has assisted with many of these endeavors. They are to be commended for their great service to Piqua and the surrounding community.

1976 was a memorable year all over the country, and it serves as a prelude to the bi-centennial of our town and county which we are celebrating in 2007.

Jean Wilson Reed
Sponsored by Mary Lou Havenar

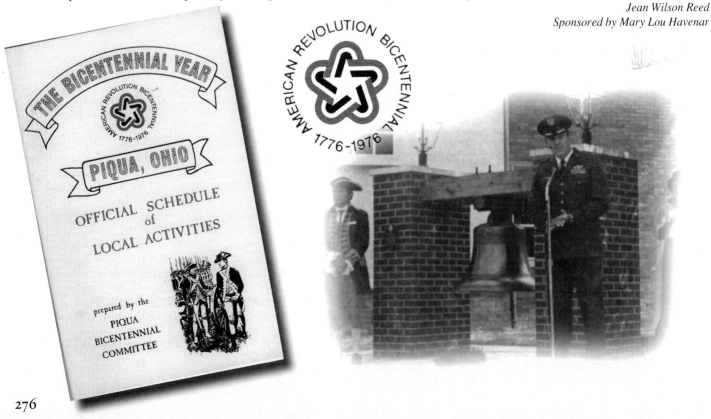

R.W. Fry Company

In May of 1995 Ralph and Lloyd Fry, father and son, formed the R.W. Fry Company. The company would do blacktop paving and general construction work. They operated this company until Ralph's retirement in 1958. Lloyd then started the L.B. Fry Tar & Asphalt Company to carry on the work of the previous company.

After a few years of hard work and success in 1960, Lloyd and his new partner Lyle Mitchell teamed up to purchased the Trojan Asphalt Company. Trojan Asphalt was also in the road construction and asphalt paving business. Three years later in 1963, in an effort to vertically integrate Lloyd & Lyle purchased the G.A. Smally Company. This company manufactured asphalt hot mix and had two plants. The main asphalt plant was on Union Street in Troy, Ohio and the second asphalt plant was near West Milton. Lloyd and Lyle renamed this company the Miami Asphalt Company.

In 1965, Lloyd bought out his partner Lyle Mitchell and became sole owner of Trojan Asphalt and Miami Asphalt companies. Lloyd continued to bid commercial, private, township, county and State of Ohio road construction and paving contracts.

In 1974 Lloyd's son-in-law Dave Vosler came into the family business to learn to operate and manage the manufacturing operations. Dave became an expert in asphalt production as well as the manufacturing of various types of aggregates. Dave was also instrumental in the transition from Ohio DOT testing and production control to contractor end result material production and testing.

In 1976, Lloyd began further integration in the construction industry with the purchase of Middleboro Stone, a stone quarry, in Richmond, IN. Immediately upon taking ownership of Middleboro Stone, Lloyd purchased another asphalt plant from Michigan and moved it to Middleboro Stone.

In 1977, Lloyd purchased another stone quarry, Ludlow Stone, Corp. This quarry was located on Davis Road near West Milton, Ohio.

The following year in 1978, Lloyd started another road construction company, Stone Valley Paving and based it out of the Middleboro Stone quarry. Stone Valley Paving began with small private projects but quickly grew to became a dominate construction company in eastern Indiana. Ultimately Stove Valley Paving was the prime contractor on many large State of Indiana highway projects as well as numerous commercial and private projects from as far south as Batesville, Indiana to as far north as Portland and west to Indianapolis, Indiana.

In 1980, Lloyd purchased his first portable asphalt plant. This plant was the first highly portable asphalt plant in the industry designed by Lloyd and his long time friend Don Brock, of Astec Industries located in Chattanooga, TN.

In 1983 Lloyd purchased the former Decker's building from the Small Business Administration and hired the Upper Valley JVS students to remodel the building. For two years the junior and senior carpentry students got hand on experience gutting and then rebuilding the interior of the building.

In the early 80's, Lloyd started to experiment with a granular "crumb" rubber mixed together with liquid asphalt and other ingredients. This product was ground breaking technology in the area of filling cracks in asphalt paved surfaces. This product was also used in an experimental paving process called "Sami mix". One such paving job was located at St. Rt. 36, west of Greenville, Ohio and another job on St. Rt. 50 near Athens, Ohio. This product led to the creation of yet another company name Dura Sports Surfacing, Inc. which constructed state of the art running track surfaces from Pennsylvania to as far west as Long View, TX and as far south as Pensacola, Florida and to Duluth Minnesota. Dura Sports also provided the surface on the new running tracks at the Piqua High School's Alexander Stadium and the Troy High School's running track.

In 1985, Lloyd purchased B & G Bituminous Co. in Sidney, Ohio. This company also owned a 50% share of Miami River Stone located along the Miami River, halfway between Sidney and Piqua.

In 1986, Lloyd purchased 51% of Republic Asphalt Materials an asphalt manufacturing company in Dayton, Ohio.

During the period between 1955 and 1990, Lloyd had assembled a group of over eight companies. In order to effectively manage and finance the operations of those companies a holding company called The Northwood Group, Inc. was formed

In January, 1990 the assets of the eight construction companies were sold to Barrett Paving.

In 1991, Lloyd and three partners purchased a stone quarry in Hugo, OK near the Texas, Oklahoma border. Their market was Oklahoma, Texas and Arkansas. They called this company Amrock, which stood for American Rock Products. They ran this company for 22 months and sold it to an Irish company called Old Castle, the second largest corporation in Ireland.

In May 1993 the Fry family purchased a company in Tucson, AZ called Tucson Rock and Sand. This company made sand, gravel, concrete and hot mix. The main office and gravel pit were located at the I-10 and Orange Grove exit, just north of downtown Tucson. A second gravel pit, ready mix plant and hot mix plant was located on the southeast side of Tucson. With 55 ready mix trucks, 2 gravel plants, 5 redi mix plants and 2 hot mix plants Tucson Rock was a major supplier of construction materials to the Tucson market. Lloyd and his son Ed ran Tucson Rock & Sand for until June of 1997when it was sold to the RMC Company headquartered in England.

The same year the Fry family sold Tucson Rock and Sand, Lloyd started another small paving company in Piqua, and named it Ticon Construction and Paving. This company ran for three years doing local paving. The managers of this company were Joe Adams and Matt Lowe. In January, 2004 the company was turned over to Joe Adams and Matt Lowe. Lloyd tried to retire one more time. But that did not work.

In 2004 Lloyd along with Ron and Chris Howell formed a company called F & H Development. F & H Development purchased a 25 acre tract of land south of Piqua on Washington Road and designed a development for 87 homes.

Currently Lloyd is in the initial stages of a new development in partnership with Bob Jackson. This new development will be called Swift Run Lakes. Swift Run Lakes is located on the north side of Piqua and consists of 275 acres that will be developed for high end executive housing.

Scott Family McDonald's

*I*t was 1973, when Ben Scott, a local bar owner from Toledo, Ohio decided it was time to make a change. With wife Louise and two young children, Caryn and Benny, he made a career change that would shape his future and his children's. In his search for "a stable and family oriented business" he contacted McDonald's. At the age of 32, in January of 1974 McDonald's approved Ben and he bought his 1st McDonald's, on 1239 East Ash Street, across from the old Piqua Mall.

From there his hard work grew the business rapidly over the next few years. At a time when McDonald's was growing and expanding in small towns all over America, Ben added 6 new restaurants in the local market. In addition to working hard in the restaurants he built, Troy (1976), Sidney (1978), Tipp City (1979), Piqua West (1981),. Ben also bought Greenville North in (1986) and relocated it in (1988), rebuilt and relocated the Piqua East store in 1993. Ben Scott built his final store in Greenville in 1994.

It was at this time his son, Benny Scott, Jr., completed his training with McDonald's corporation and decided to work for his father. In 1995 Benny managed his first restaurant at the newly opened Greenville South McDonald's. In January of 2001, Benny bought the business from his father and has since added 3 additional restaurants in Fairborn, Ohio.

In 1982 the Scott Family McDonald's management office moved to their current location after completely restoring a historical home originally built in 1869. The office is located at 218 West Ash Street in Piqua, Ohio. The business now has over 650 employees, and restaurants in 6 local communities. They pride themselves on being an active part of the community, creating a positive work environment and delivering fast, fresh, quality food. The Scott organization has great employees and managers, many of whom have worked for the family for over 25 years. The Scott organization cares about this community and that is why we are dedicated and proud to be serving you.

St. James Church

Col. John Johnston, Indian Agent, transferred from Ft. Wayne, Indiana to Upper Piqua in June, 1811, and moved his family into a log house which stood about 100 feet northwest of this present house, which was finished in 1814.

To the left of this house and barn is the Johnston Cemetery and it was there where the Episcopalians held their first services in a log Church building.

About 6 months after Col. Johnston moved to this farm, he and his adjoining neighbor, Richard Winans, donated adjoining tracts of land, amounting to 2 acres, to the Methodist congregation for a Church, a burying ground and a schoolhouse. The deed was dated January 12, 1812. A log Church was built in 1815 and three years later, Johnston donated one half the costs toward a brick Church building and loaned the Church organization enough money to pay for the other half. By 1824 the Methodists built a Church in Lower Piqua and the tract was deeded back to Col. Johnston. It became a meeting place for the Episcopalians who had been coming together in homes.

On Sept. 29, 1825, John and Rachel Johnston donated and deeded this ground to the Trustees of St. James Episcopal Church.

Col. Johnston was one of the few present in 1818 when the first Episcopal Diocese was organized in Ohio. A few years later he was a member of the first Board of Trustees of Kenyon College. He is credited with being responsible for the organization of St. James Parish in 1819. Bishop Chase visited in this home in 1822 and appointed the Col. as a Lay Reader.

At the 1822 Episcopal convention, Bishop Philander Chase's first account of Piqua services was mentioned. "The Rev. Spencer Wall in his report dated March 27, 1822, says of his labors from Oct. 19, 1821, to March 24, 1822: At Piqua the prospects are such as to justify sanguine expectation of the permanent establishment and regular growth of a Church. Her friends have already raised a subscription amounting to about $600 for the purpose of erecting a Church." The Bishop prepared for circulation Articles of Association. On the 5th day of January, 1823, a Parish was duly organized by The Rev. Intrepid Morse of Steubenville, Ohio. This followed some days of preaching and baptizing in December. Col. Johnston, who had been appointed Lay Reader by Bishop Chase, commenced at once holding the regular services of the Church.

In 1825 the Vestry of St. James Church called The Rev. Gideon McMillen who accepted and became the first Minister. At the present time, St. James Parish is being served by its 30th Rector.

Until 1828 no Episcopal Church building was erected either in Piqua proper or Upper Piqua. Services were held in the

St. James 1885

schoolhouse in the Cemetery, the brick schoolhouse and in Piqua proper, both regular services and Sunday School were held in a log school house at the corner of Wayne and Ash Streets. In 1828 St. James Church was built at the corner of North And Spring Streets, costing around $1,411. and was consecrated by The Rt. Rev. C.P. McIllvaine on November 11, 1833.

The Church was built on a lot given by Charles Manning.

The bell, which is rung every Sunday, was given to this Church to honor the Greenham family, by friends in Liverpool, England.

The next Church was built at the corner of Wayne and High Streets, facing Wayne St., on a lot donated by John H.D. Johnston, the son of Col. John Johnston.

The Church was consecrated December 1, 1847.

Many items found in the present Church were given as gifts or memorials, the Pulpit, Lectern, the Altar, the Font, The Bishop's and Priest's chairs just to name a few. The lovely rose window above the Reredos was given to this Church in memory of James Starrett, by his wife, Elizabeth.

The present Church was built on the same site, but facing High St. The Dedication and Consecration were on October 1, 1899. The officiant was The Rev. Abdiel Ramsey who served the Church from 1884 to 1904.

In 1923, the Aeolean pipe organ was built and installed by Ernest M. Skinner, a memorial gift by the Boal family.

In 1961 a major renovation of the Nave and Chancel was carried out. The present Reredos was designed and built by Leslie Hobbs, a New York based liturgical architect. The light oak pews were installed, replacing the original dark stained high back pews.

In 1999 the interior was completely redecorated, kindly and generously advised by Ruth Koon of Piqua.

The stained glass windows were cleaned and renovated and all structural signs of wear and tear were repaired.

A formal Memorial Garden has been blessed and dedicated for the interment of ashes of those parishioners who wish to be buried on the Church grounds.

From 1994 to 2000, St. James, Piqua, together with St. Marks, Sidney and St. Pauls of Greenville formed the Western Ohio Episcopal Cluster. This organization was discontinued in 2000 and in 2002 The Rev. Robert E. Baldwin became the 30th Rector of St. James.

On the land to the west of the building an addition is planned to meet the needs of a growing congregation and an ever expanding Outreach Program.

St. James Episcopal Church looks forward to a bright future of worship and service, living up to its motto: "Nurturing the faith of every generation"

St. James 2007

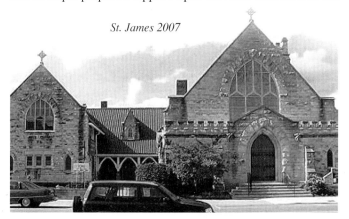

St. John's Lutheran Church

248 Wood Street
Piqua, Ohio

St. John's was founded by a group of first and second generation German immigrants in 1888. Since that time, the church has worshipped in four buildings and has been served by eleven ministers.

Every Sunday the congregation gathers in their 1913 Gothic-Romanesque Church on the northeast corner of Wood and Downing Streets to worship God and enjoy Christian fellowship.

The church is very active in mission work both internationally (supporting Jeffrey Truscott's mission in Japan) and locally with volunteers and contributions to the Bethany Center in Piqua on South Street. Christian education is fostered on all levels with classes from tots to teens to adults.

Music has always been an important part of Lutheran wor-

ship and St. John's continues that tradition with an active adult choir and music presented on both the piano and pipe organ. One of the church's enduring fundraisers continues today as the Spring Rummage and Bake Sale bringing together people from the church and the neighborhood.

The congregation supports a Christian Library on the first floor of the church with books and audio visuals for study and entertainment. St. John's massively remodeled the sanctuary of the church in 1999, creating for the first time a center aisle between the pews. This was followed by an elevator and air conditioning. In the twenty-first century, the church has gone electronic with a website and constantly changing digital pictures of church events.

Pastor Shannon Vogelezng received the call to St. John's in 2004 and became the church's eleventh full time minister.

St Paul's Evangelical & Reformed Church

*I*n 1835 the Rev. C. Hinsch gathered a small group of German families to worship in his home and sometimes in nearby fields. By 1840 they had gathered $400 and purchased the site at 500 North Downing Street where the present-day church now stands. In 1845 a log building that had been the Cumberland Presbyterian Church was purchased and moved to the lot for $300. The first constitution was adopted on October 18, 1846 and the church was named St. Paul's Evangelical Protestant Church of Piqua, Ohio.

In 1853 a school building and parsonage were erected and the first organ was imported from Bavaria, Germany. The Ladies Aid Society met in 1855 and Sunday school met for the first time on Christmas 1855. The first Choir sang on Palm Sunday 1856.

The congregation outgrew the original log building and on June 28, 1868 a cornerstone was laid and a new church constructed. The dedication took place April 24, 1870. Members felt the need for a finishing touch so a tower was built for $2,300. Three bells, weighing almost two tons were hung at a cost of $891. On dedication Sunday the Rev. A. Klein named the bells, Faith, Hope & Charity and they still ring each Sunday morning. The first time they rang was for a joyful occasion, a wedding.

In 1889 the Young People's League was formed which became the Youth Fellowship.

The 1853 German organ was replaced in 1870. In 1890 it was moved from the fellowship hall into the Chancel and replaced again in 1910. In 1926 it was rebuilt and enlarged and underwent major work in 1965.

In 1875 St. Paul's consisted of 165 families. Today the congregation consists of 300 families and is continually growing.

The Missions Society was organized in 1912. Its last action was, as it disbanded in 1964, to present the large lectern Bible that is still in use today.

In 1912 the Rev. Paul J. Gehm began a 39-year pastorate.

March 25, 1913 the flood struck Piqua. Ten of the congregation's adults and children lost their lives and 57 members lost all of their worldly possessions. The parsonage was also ruined.

Our 75th Birthday was in 1921. Classrooms on the south were added, circular stairways were replaced, the exterior was given a stone look, two front entrances were added, the chancel rearranged and the art glass windows installed.

In World War II at least 57 of our sons & daughters answered their country's call.

In 1944 there were many upgrades to prepare for our 100th Birthday, which we celebrated in October 1946.

In 1952 property to the north was purchased and an educational building consisting of offices, a parlor and classrooms were built. This was dedicated in 1960. In 1965 another renovation program was completed.

The original ceilings were patterned tin and made by Cincinnati Corrugated. Most are still in place and visible.

In 1914 St. Paul's joined the Evangelical Synod of North America, which became the Evangelical and Reformed Church in 1934.

In 1957 we became St. Paul's United Church of Christ. In January 2006 we went back to our German heritage and became St. Paul's Evangelical & Reformed Church.

The story of St. Paul's is a story of persons:
>   persons of vision and courage
>   persons of fears and hopes
>   persons who knew suffering and
>   sorrow, sacrifice and hard work
>   persons who found joy in their faith
>   persons who believe in Christ and his church.

Early ministers were Lutherans or Free Protestant. Our present ministers are the Rev. Frank Sapp, Sr. and his daughter the Rev. Meg Carnahan.

The Tapestry Angel

Ginny Koon, having been an avid stitcher for 20 plus years, decided in 1984 that this was the time to implement a dream she had had for a number of years. The dream was to own a needlework shop that would serve those women and men who appreciated good design and materials in needlework, especially needlepoint.

With the support of her husband, Richard and their children, Christy and Rob, the search began for a retail space to house this dream. After several weeks of looking with real estate agent Dick Miller, she settled on a little house at 516 Spring St. Being built circa 1839 along the Miami Erie Canal, in its first life it had housed the canal workers and then been converted to a single family dwelling. The location was good, just off Main St. and easily found from I-75, and it was configured well for retail flow. So the dotted line was signed and the adventure began in earnest with cleaning, scraping wallpaper, painting, sewing curtains, purchasing stock, having shelves built, advertising and all the myriad things that go into opening a new business.

One day, while Ginny was scraping wallpaper, Marilyn Jacomet walked in. She was a basket maker and wondered if she could set up her own shop in one of the rooms. Since there was not enough needlework stock to fill all the rooms, this seemed like a good way to make The Tapestry Angel more appealing as a destination. So the bargain was struck and Marilyn opened her own business called Heart of the Country. This was an agreeable arrangement that lasted for 2 1/2 years, until Ginny's business grew enough to need the space.

The Chamber of Commerce Ambassadors opened Piqua's newest business in November of 1984. Before long, the inventory expanded to include all things needlepoint and cross stitch—patterns and fibers and beads and fabric and accessories. Services included beginning, intermediate and advanced classes in cross stitch and needlepoint, finishing (making pillows, ornaments, tea cozies, etc. out of the completed piece), color consultation and design. Ginny saw an opportunity to expand these services by offering framing to her customers. This turned out to be an especially satisfying and lucrative piece of the business.

Ginny also started a chapter of the Embroiderers Guild of America in the area. This group is still going strong and continues to meet monthly.

In the 10 years that Ginny owned The Tapestry Angel, it became a gathering place for women who loved to talk and stitch. Many of them made models for the shop and would help out during sale time. Some even taught classes.

In August of 1994, Mary Teach bought The Tapestry Angel. Mary was one of the women who helped from time to time and had often mentioned that if Ginny ever wanted to sell… And so it came to pass that Mary became the proud owner of The Tapestry Angel. She expanded the cross stitch line and has added all the new fibers, buttons, embellishments and fabrics that the marketplace brings out while continuing all the other services.

With the advent of the internet, stitchers have a virtual shop in their homes, but there is just something about being able to see and touch the product. The shop is a delight to enter, since Mary, her sister-in-law, Linda Hemmert, and her sister, Donna Schlegel have filled the walls with examples of the needle arts.

As the guest book attests, stitchers come from far and wide, coast to coast, north to south and some from abroad. It is still being discovered by a new generation of stitchers. In 2009, The Tapestry Angel will turn 25.

The Ulbrich Family Business

The growth of Ulbrich's I.G.A. from a small 20- by 100-foot corner meat market 90 plus years ago, to a full line supermarket, was the result of hard work and love of people. When Ulbrich's first opened its doors shoppers in Piqua could buy the equivalent of a gallon of milk for a quarter, a dozen eggs for 24 cents, and a loaf of bread for a dime or less. Total cost: 59 cents. Needless to say in 2007 that would cost at least seven times that amount.

Ulbrich's began in 1913 when German immigrant Michael Ulbrich and his wife, Mary, purchased Remelmeyer's Meat Market at 407 South Wayne. The old neighborhood store, with horse drawn delivery wagon, specialized in meats slaughtered on the Ulbrich farm on Hetzler Road. Only meat, bread and milk were handled then, and money transactions were conducted out of the elder Ulbrich's pocket.

The second generation, William Carl, joined the business. He made deliveries on his Harley Davidson motorcycle and, in 1928, became a partner with his father, Mike. In 1932, the two razed the old wooden building and built the first brick store, which is the basis of today's Ulbrich's.

The early days of business were not without hardship and humor. Old Mike bought lard cans with advertising on them from a saleswoman who charmed him into buying a supply that lasted many years.

Most businessmen have a little bit of gambler in them. Three times a year Mike sold tanned hides to a particular customer. After one transaction they began to throw dice. Mike lost the entire store at one point. Desperate, he kept playing the man all night and won it back, plus the cash paid for the hides. The second remodeling of Ulbrich's was completed in 1935.

After World War II, William Carl took over the reins in 1946. A father-son relationship began, with a keen feel for customer satisfaction and service to set the stage for greater accomplishments.

Boyd Ulbrich of the third generation entered the business as a 10-year-old. He often helped deliver, stock and unload empty cases from beer trucks. In addition to groceries, Ulbrich's owned a beer distributorship and sold appliances with Bill Christian in the rear of the store. "The store was almost as much home as our house," Boyd often said as his mother Onnolee also worked many hours. Following college in 1957, Boyd became a full time employee.

The building then had a single front entrance with wooden screen door, green painted wooden produce bins and one cash register. In the office, Grandma Mary Ulbrich sat behind a small wooden table with paper money arranged in cigar boxes and coins in a grocery sack.

In 1958 more property was purchased and expansion continued into 1970. The largest remodeling and growth took place in 1977, when the 14th and 15th properties were purchased and demolished. The small, one-room meat market is now a 30,000 square foot, full line supermarket with in-store bakery and deli. Groceries are still delivered to the elderly and shut-ins. Meat continues to be a main attraction as beef and pork are cut on site. Family recipes of barbeque ribs, baked beans, sausage and cheese spread are homemade, as are all the hot deli items. Often, former Piquads home for a visit, have sausage and cheese spread frozen to take with them when they leave.

With the sudden death of Boyd Ulbrich in 2003, the operation continues with Boyd's wife Barbara and fourth generation sons Brad, Bill and daughter-in-law Nancy. They are carrying on a family relationship that started in 1928.

Ulbrich's market is proud to be a locally owned grocery that can credit its success to strong family tradition, competitive prices, revolutionary customer savings programs and "personal touches" of being friendly to customers both new and old. The Ulbrich's continue to be "hometown proud" and are totally dedicated to their customers and community!

Unity National Bank

For 123 years, Unity National Bank has been strong, secure and growing from its humble beginnings as Third Piqua Building & Loan with L.C. Cron as President in 1884. The first office with assets of only $20,000 was located above the George Brooks Law Offices in the 400 block of North Main Street. In 1892, a move was made to the southeast corner of Ash and Wayne Streets, where Z's is currently located. 1908 brought a relocation to the rear of the Piqua National Bank building approximately where Thoma & Sons Jewelry is in business today, followed closely in 1909 by a name change to The Third Savings & Loan Co. 1916 found Third Savings on the move again, this time to its present downtown Piqua location, 215 North Wayne Street, sharing the building with Lape's Home Appliance Store. During the 1920's, assets surpassed the $2 million mark, and in 1925 A.M. Leonard was named President.

In 1936, membership in the Federal Home Loan Bank System was approved with Federal Savings & Loan Insurance. The November 1, 1939 lunch hour brought a little excitement to the then bookkeeper Sam Heitzman as he looked down the barrel of a revolver. $1,726 was taken by three men thought to be a part of the Dillinger gang. No shots were fired, and no one was injured. Ironically, the 1930's also saw the removal of grillwork and cages for tellers, replaced by shoulder-high counters partitioning the workspace from the patron's lobby.

The 1940's brought prosperity to Third Savings and also a new President, Louis G. Peffer (1940). Assets grew from $3 million in 1943 to $5 million in 1947. With the decade of the 50's, assets surpassed the $15 million mark and extensive remodeling of the 215 N. Wayne Street location began. In 1953, artist Michael Chomyk completed his wall mural depicting the Indian legend from which Piqua derives its name. Sam Heitzman returned to Third Savings in 1957 to become its fourth President. Third Savings celebrated its 75th anniversary by occupying all of the completely renovated 215 North Wayne Street building. Enhancements included state of the art banking equipment and the latest in banking design features, including Third Savings' first drive-in window facility on the south side of the building.

The 1960's and 70's saw assets growing to over $50 million and the first branch office in 1970 at the Piqua East Mall. In 1977, the original clock downtown was changed to digital in keeping with the times. Carl Newbright was elected President in 1978, and the Sunset branch was opened. The 1980's brought even further growth and expansion with assets topping the $100 million level and de-regulation allowing checking accounts to be authorized. 1983 saw the opening of the first out of town branch in Troy followed in 1989 by a branch in Tipp City. In 1984, Third Savings moved its administrative staff to the renovated former Benkert's department store, most recently the Orr Toy Store. By retaining the flavor of the nearly 100 year old building, Third Savings had added to the general appearance of downtown Piqua.

The original East Mall office was closed in 1990, while the Sunset branch remodeled and expanded in 1991. Kenneth Rupp was elected to President in 1991 and assets grew to the $121 million mark. In 1993, Third Savings converted from a mutual savings and loan company to a stock savings and loan company, and concurrently became the wholly owned subsidiary of Third Financial Corporation. In October of 1996, Third Financial Corporation merged with Security National Bank in Springfield, Ohio, and Scott Gabriel was elected President in 1997.

In March of 2001, Security National Bank merged with Park National Corporation of Newark, Ohio. That same year, Third Savings received approval to convert from a thrift charter to a national bank charter, which necessitated a name change to Unity National Bank, Division of Security National Bank. John Brown joined Unity National Bank in October of 2003 as President, after 15 years with Park National Bank. Today, with $198 million in assets, Unity National Bank has six full-service offices, 5 ATMs, and more extended-hour offices than any other financial institution in Miami County. Unity's associates provide a full array of personal and commercial banking and lending services, trust and investment services, online banking, courier service, Freedom Years, and more.

Unity serves Miami and contiguous county communities with dedication and commitment. Customers develop lasting relationships and work with the same local, experienced professionals they've known for years. Unity National Bank proudly accepts their responsibility as a community leader and partner and is repeatedly ranked among the top organizations in Miami County for community involvement and philanthropy.

Upper Valley JVS

Community effort brought career-technical training to Piqua

The Upper Valley Joint Vocational School District formally began in 1972 and in 1975 opened the doors to adult students, high school juniors and in subsequent years juniors and seniors. The high school students came from Troy, Newton, Covington, Bradford, Piqua, Sidney, Fairlawn, Hardin-Houston, Fort Loramie, Anna, Lehman and eventually Botkins, Jackson Center and Russia.

In November 1972 these communities demonstrated their support for career-technical education by approving a 2.9 mill multi-purpose levy. Passage of the levy which built, equipped, and provided means for initial operation of the school paved the way for over 30 years of continued excellence and outstanding collaboration with local individuals, civic and business leaders, and educators.

Community support has been further evidenced by land acquisitions thanks to the generosity of John Garbry, Mr. and Mrs. J. Scott Garbry, Ralph Garbry, and the Hartzell-Norris Trust. Countless volunteer hours have been contributed by a cross-section of professionals, who each year share their expertise to assure that program curriculum and equipment remain current and in alignment with local industry needs.

The school has expanded services to reach underclassmen through satellite programs operated in many local schools. In the most recent school year over 3,000 Shelby and Miami County high school students were enrolled in career-technical programming provided by the Upper Valley JVS. While 835 of the students were enrolled in programs offered at the main campus, another 2,240 students attended satellite programs provided in eleven participating school districts. The ISO certified UVJVS Adult Division served 260 businesses and 3000 individual participants during that same time frame.

A 1992 expansion of the adult programming was facilitated with construction of the Applied Technology

1975

Center just north of the main campus building. Adult training programs currently operate at the main campus, Applied Technology Center, Stouder Center, and Garbry Conference and Learning Center. Adult Basic and Literacy Education operates in a variety of churches and community centers throughout the service area. A more recent expansion at the main campus added over 40,000 square feet of classroom, lab, dining commons, student services, and office space to the original 1975 structure. The contemporary addition reflects staff and administrations' intent to look forward as they address the educational needs of future generations.

"Community support is what made Upper Valley JVS possible way back in 1972, and community support is what keeps the UVJVS career-technical training programs viable and relevant today. The JVS has helped thousands of high school and adult students become productive members of the local work force. Having a prepared workforce is key to the continued economic well being of the Greater Miami Valley."

Karl Wilson, Superintendent
UVJVS High School – 937.778.1980
Applied Technology Center – 937.778.8419
Garbry Conference and Learning Center – 937.778.1078
Stouder Center LPN Program – 937.440.0550
Stouder Center ABLE – 937.440.1692

Upper Valley Medical Center
The Evolution of Local Health Care

UVMC is a not-for-profit health care system serving Miami County and the surrounding area. The UVMC health system was founded in 1986 as the umbrella corporation for the merger of Miami County's three hospitals: Piqua Memorial in Piqua, Stouder Memorial in Troy and Dettmer Hospital located midway between Piqua and Troy. A new hospital -- the Upper Valley Medical Center -- opened in 1998, consolidating acute care services to a central location within the county. The Upper Valley Medical Center is located just off I-75, between Piqua and Troy.

BACKGROUND

Prior to the formation of UVMC, the three hospitals in Miami County operated as independent and competitive entities located within a 10-mile radius. In 1979, Piqua Memorial, Dettmer and Stouder formed the Miami County Health Care Coordinating Committee to investigate ways to cooperate, control health care costs and avoid duplication of services. The underlying goal of this initiative was to preserve local access to comprehensive, quality health care by maintaining an economically viable health care system in Miami County.

In 1981, a group of Miami County physicians outlined the need for a consolidation of inpatient acute care services of the three hospitals into a single hospital. Formal discussions occurred, guiding subsequent efforts to unite the three hospitals to serve area residents in the most cost-effective and appropriate manner possible.

Within a few years, continuing discussions culminated in the consolidation of Piqua Memorial and Dettmer in 1986, joined shortly after by Stouder, forming UVMC. The 1986 consolidation was a significant milestone in that it opened the door toward eliminating duplication of services, enhancing purchasing power and combining resources of the local hospitals.

The next phase of UVMC's evolution involved construction of the new Upper Valley Medical Center to consolidate acute care services into one centrally located facility. The new hospital opened in 1998 on the 100-acre Dettmer campus. Piqua Memorial and Stouder subsequently were closed, and Dettmer remained housing behavioral medicine programs and a variety of non-clinical services.

The Upper Valley Medical Center was intentionally designed with maximum flexibility to accommodate expansion to keep up with the community's ever-growing health care needs. Increases in patient volumes led to an expansion in 2004 which added 11 inpatient beds and other enhancements in maternity, med/surg and the emergency department.

As a result of an ongoing strategic planning process and resulting actions, throughout its first two decades, UVMC experienced growth and diversification evolving into a comprehensive health care system to better serve the needs of area residents and to maintain economic viability.

SERVICES AND PROGRAMS

The UVMC health care continuum today provides comprehensive inpatient and outpatient care with a full complement of diagnostic services and behavioral health care programs. Along with emergency care, women's services, pediatrics, inpatient/outpatient surgery/orthopedics, gastroenterology, intensive care/progressive care, neurology, cardiac catheterization and cardiopulmonary rehabilitation, UVMC offers the latest in medical technologies, therapies, medical laboratory, pharmacy, and advanced imaging services.

The health system also includes comprehensive multidisciplinary cancer care, regional renal dialysis services, a sleep disorders center, extensive rehabilitation services, sports medicine, after hours care and occupational health services. In addition, UVMC has long term care centers with designated Alzheimer's units and residential living options, home health care services (the first home health agency in Ohio) and more.

Dettmer Behavioral Health is one of Ohio's most comprehensive providers of behavioral medicine programs. Highly individualized chemical dependency and psychiatric treatment programs are provided for all ages. Dettmer also provides tailored Employee Assistance Programs for area employers.

OUTPATIENT FACILITIES

UVMC's conveniently located satellite facilities and physician office complexes serve the area communities with outpatient services such as:

• Outpatient Care Center/North in Piqua provides offices for medical specialists and primary care physicians, diagnostic laboratory, radiology and physical therapy.

• Outpatient Care Center/South in Troy features occupational health and industrial rehabilitation, laboratory and radiology services, physical and occupational therapies and physician offices.

• Hyatt Center in Tipp City houses the region's first free-standing outpatient surgery center as well as Sports Medicine, After Hours Family Care, physician offices, diagnostic lab and radiology.

• Stanfield Place in Troy houses physician offices, diagnostic laboratory and radiology services.

LONG TERM CARE FACILITIES

• Koester Pavilion is located adjacent to the UVMC campus between Piqua and Troy.

• Spring Meade Health Center and Residence Complex is located in Tipp City.

CAREGIVER PHILOSOPHY

UVMC today employs 1,800+ employees and has 219 physicians on medical staff. The health care professionals of UVMC are proud to be part of a patient-centered, quality-oriented care team recognized for excellence at the national and regional levels. For example, UVMC was:

• Recipient of numerous VHA awards, including the President's Award of Honor and Leadership Awards for Clinical Excellence.

• The first hospital in southwest Ohio (third in the state) to achieve national Magnet status.

• Named by the *Dayton Business Journal* among the "Best Places to Work" in the Dayton region for 2005, 2006 and 2007.

Urban Elsass & Son, Inc.

Murray Elsass has been celebrating the scrap metal industry since his present business began with his father Urban H. Elsass in the early forties! "Find a need and fill it" was their work-ethic motto. The rest of the story… is history, for this well-organized and personal company.

It all started during World War II when father and young son began their partnership by the disassembling of obsolete farm machinery, junk autos, and antiquated manufacturing equipment…by hand. This disassembly was absolutely essential because all lifting, sorting and loaded of scrap onto the trucks was done also… by hand. That was then.

Today, Urban Elsass and Son, Inc. is a modern, clean and efficient company boasting a new state-of-the-art environmentally designed sheltered storage facility having technological innovations to more than meet EPA (Environmental Protection Agency) regulations into the next century! "We provide leadership and equipment designed to foster environmentally responsible scrap metal operations. With over 50-years of professional experience in the science & safety of industrial recycling, our company is able to skillfully control the sequential processes of reclaiming and up-grading industrial scrap, thus marketing a product that will generate more profit for our clients," comments Mr, Elsass.

From a historical viewpoint, Urban Elsass & Sons, Inc, as it is now known, was started back in the late 20's or 30's. It was used to fill the gap between a small farm income from approximately 40 acres and the need to provide a living for a family of seven; two parents and five children. One of the children was Urban H. Elsass, the father of the current owner.

Industrial plants as we know them today were in their infancy, and Urban Elsass, living near the small village of Botkins, Ohio, did not have access to any industrial clients until the forties when he met a man named Robert E. Bertch, president of Slusser McClean, a factory that made earth moving equipment.

This relationship led to the introduction to several industrial business heads including William Goode, the owner of Goodes Scraper Shop, which manufactured wheelbarrows; Frank Fields, President and General Manager of the Sidney Machine Tool Co. of Sidney; Lee Harmony, President of Stamco, manufacturer of Steel Mill Equipment.

Out of these humble beginnings has grown what is today a thriving business reclaiming and recycling. The company has a staff of 18 full time employees with over 101 combined years of experience. Urban Elsass and Son, Inc. relocated to the Piqua area from Botkins in 1982 when they bought the operating business of Sussman, Inc. located at 600 E. Statler Road. The business consists of buying, processing and selling of industrial scrap and metals to foundries, steel mills and smelters.

The scrap metal industry is specialized requiring different equipment for each customer. The company has different size containers that they provide so the various metals can be kept separate, generating a higher price for the customer. The company also has different trucks required to pick up, haul and dump the containers. Magnet cranes are used in the yard to reload the scrap on to dump trailers and train cars, depending on the destination. If the material needs to be processed, Urban Elsass has a metal baler that will turn loose scrap into cubes measuring 16 x 16", weighing up to 400 or 500 pounds per cube. The whole operating is completely in compliance with EPA (Environmental Protection Agency) regulations.

Right: The office staff at Urban Elsass consists of (Front Row) Evelyn Keller (18 years), Molly Emmel (6 years) (Back Row) Pete Thompson, Vice President (33 years), Mark Gallagher, Maintenance (19 years), Daryl Tubb, Non Ferrous (18 years) Murray Elsass, Owner (60 years)

Below: Aerial Photo of Statler Road Location

Westminster Presbyterian Church

A Brief History of the Presbyterian Church in Piqua, 1812-2007

Piqua's rich history is closely intertwined with the account of local Presbyterianism. The April 1812 minutes of the Miami Presbytery shows a request by the church at Washington for occasional supplies (visiting ministers). Another request in 1816 came from Piqua after residents of Washington had petitioned the State Legislature to restore its old Indian name.

In 1816 members of the Associated Reformed Church, later known as the United Presbyterian Church, built a log structure on a plot of ground by the cemetery laid out in 1809 by Matthew Caldwell, Sr. That church was the cause of the jog in Downing Street where Water and Wood streets intersect. In 1816 another group of Presbyterians organized to form the Presbyterian Church of Piqua.

In 1825 this church built its first building at the northeast corner of the Wood Street Cemetery on the west side of Wayne Street between the railroad and Wood Street. Parishioners worshiped here until a new church was built at the southeast corner of Ash and Wayne Streets. It was dedicated March 8, 1845, as the First Presbyterian Church.

Probably because of a controversy in the General Assembly causing Presbyterians to divide across the region and the nation, sixteen members, including such notables as Matthew Caldwell, Jr. and Abner Keyt, left to form The Second Presbyterian Church of Piqua. They built and dedicated their church on the west side of Wayne Street at the second lot north of Ash Street in 1847. This church was known as The New School Church, while the First Church was known as The Old School Church.

For almost forty years there were two Presbyterian churches in Piqua, located fewer than one hundred yards of one another. In 1866 the churches cooperated to form Piqua's first baseball team, called the Sterling Nine, which defeated a team from Dayton.

As the two churches began to discuss the possibility of sharing a minister, talks led to their consolidation in 1867. From 1867 to 1890, the merged churches met in the First Presbyterian Church facility at the corner of Ash and Downing and began to flourish.

The Consolidated Church grew from 454 in 1884 to 601 in 1887. In 1888 a committee determined that for $36,500 a building could be erected to house over a thousand people in its sanctuary and 400 in an adjoining lecture room. The old building at Ash and Downing was sold for more than $11,000, $9000 of which was used to buy the lot at the corner of Ash and Caldwell. The house of Matthew Caldwell, Jr., which had been built in 1841, occupied the lot.

Construction of the new church began in April of 1889. The foundation was laid by Joseph Geiger with local stone furnished by D.C. Statler and Company. Cleveland sandstone was purchased for the front of the building and Miami Valley blue limestone for the back walls. This accounts for the difference between two colors of stone at the southeast part of the circular chapel in the back of the church.

The cornerstone was laid on September 12, 1889. In his remarks at that ceremony, Dr. A.N. Carson told his congregation that shortly before Mrs. Caldwell's death in 1887, she had said she would die contented if she could be sure that at some future day, her beloved church would erect a new building on the lot where her life had been passed. The membership at that time was 495; by 1962 it was more than 1100.

During the first half of the 1900's, the First Presbyterian Church thrived as its many programs focused on youth, missions, education, and music. Long-time member Elinor Gattshall can recall the church at its largest. She remembers the Men's Good Fellowship class, which had a membership of 500 men from all over the city and county. One of the teachers of this class was Emanuel Kahn, a Piqua clothier, whose business was located at today's Barclay's. Mr. Kahn was a Rabbi who occasionally served the Anshe Emeth Temple on Caldwell, across the street from Westminster. Mrs. Gattshall also remembers the active Women's Programs and large Sunday School that sometimes had an attendance of over 500 during the 1960's. Among its ministries, the church supported several missionaries, mission projects, and a refugee family from Hungary.

The original church parsonage, which now houses the administration offices of the church was vacated in 1917, following the death of pastor Dr. John Montgomery. A short time later, the church purchased the house at 714 North Wayne Street, which served as the church parsonage until it was sold in 1958.

Westminster Presbyterian Church has been known by several names over the years due to the reuniting of various Presbyterian groups. In 1959 the First Presbyterian Church became Westminster United Presbyterian and later its present designation: Westminster Presbyterian Church (PCUSA).

In 1965 the church dedicated a new educational wing to house the large Sunday school. The facility has also been used by many community groups as well as the YMCA for part of its preschool program. Today's congregation of Westminster continues to do the Lord's work at its location on the corner of Ash and Caldwell Streets by sponsoring a monthly free lunch among other mission programs and providing excellent educational and music programs. The congregation is looking forward to continuing the Lord's work in Piqua for another two hundred years.

Sources

Hill, Leonard U. et al. *A Sesquicentennial History of the Westminster United Presbyterian Church of Piqua, Ohio, 1812-1962*. Magee Bros., Piqua Ohio, 1962.

Gattshall, Elinor. Interview. Saturday, June 2, 2007.

Rayner, John A. *The First Century of Piqua, Ohio.* Magee Bros. Company, Piqua Ohio, 1967. Revised Edition.

Wellmeier, Helen. *Westminster Presbyterian Church of Piqua, Ohio: The 175th Anniversary Supplement to a History of Our Church from 1812 to 1962.*

Westminster Presbyterian Church, Piqua, Ohio, 1987

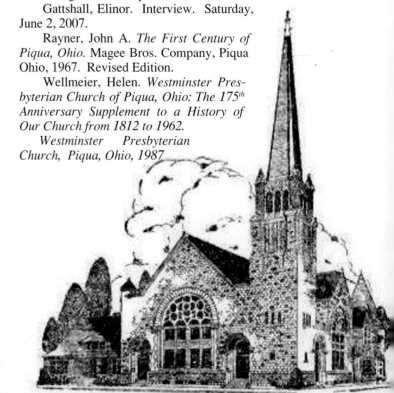

YWCA

For almost 90 years the YWCA Piqua has been a constant force in the community by advocating and meeting the changing needs of women, girls and their families.

In 1919, the women in Piqua spearheaded a highly organized campaign to create a Young Women's Christian Association. Over 300 women, many of them workers from the local mills, attended the initial meeting on February 2. The following week charter memberships could be purchased for $1, and by the following month(,) 900 women from throughout the city had joined.

Meeting space over the *Piqua Daily Call* office on Wayne Street was rented for the YWCA's use. To cover expenses for rent and staff for the first two years, a financial goal of $10,000 was established. The women organized teams and over a 3-day period in March, solicited donations throughout the community. A total of $17,807 was raised, thus assuring financial stability for the new YWCA. On March 22, 1919 a formal organizational meeting was held at the Piqua High School auditorium. Miss Lucy Patterson, a teacher at the high school, was elected as YWCA president and Mrs. Leo Flesh, wife of the owner of Atlas Underwear, was elected vice-president. Leo Flesh, James L. Black, Logan Frazier, Mrs. Rebecca Ludlow and Mrs. W.C. Kerns were selected as trustees.

The women from various factories began that April to form clubs, with each club comprised of women from an individual business. The clubs established included: Fiwelco Club, composed of women from Superior Underwear; Pickawillany Club from the Piqua Hosiery; Twightwee, from Atlas Underwear; Swastika Smiles from Imperial Underwear; and the High Times Club (Hiticlu) from Orr Felt and Blanket.

In the first month of organization, over 400 women were members of these YWCA groups, referred to as the Blue Triangle Clubs. The groups met weekly at the YWCA and once each month a joint dinner was held. Songs, cheers, speakers, and outings were enjoyed, and welfare work in the community was undertaken together. Leadership skills were developed and the YWCA provided a registry of housing and job tips. By the summer of 1919, the YWCA was well entrenched in the Piqua community, and it has remained so ever since.

In the 21st century the YWCA Piqua unveiled the new national logo/brand to the community. Long dedicated to empowering women, the lesser known and equally important goal – the elimination of racism – is being brought to the forefront of the organization.

With this brand revitalization which states "eliminating racism, empowering women – YWCA", the YWCA Piqua placed its commitment before the public with several new initiatives. The Racial Justice Reading Circle meets quarterly to discuss books about racism in the safe and open environment of the YWCA. "The color of a person's skin reveals only one thing…the color of a person's skin" was the theme for the Racial Justice Awareness campaign where special United Way funds provided billboards throughout the community and posters for display in the schools. Commenting on the posters a Piqua High School faculty member stated "Racism harms everyone. It is our responsibility as parents and teachers to do everything in our power to make our children more respectful and eliminate discrimination."

Special advocacy initiatives have been developed with the Family Abuse Shelter of Miami County, Inc. in an attempt to increase awareness of the signs of domestic violence. A long-standing, annual, comprehensive, women's financial workshop features understanding family and personal finances, investing for the future and organizing documents and records. Women of all ages are empowered by these programs.

To recognize women who distinguished themselves in their careers and/or in civic and community activities, the YWCA annually presents the Women of Excellence award. The Young Woman of Tomorrow award honors young women under age 25 for their volunteer service and activities.

Continuing a tradition, the YWCA Piqua provides opportunities through which women and their families find fulfillment and gain self-assurance. Pre-school aged programs, health and fitness, senior citizen activities, and enrichment classes for all age groups are offered.

"Whether assisting voters with new electronic equipment, providing self defense training to ease fears or empowering women to take charge of their own health, the YWCA is a constant," states Board President, Catherine J. Oda. "The YWCA continues a tradition of advocacy for women, girls and their families to fulfill our mission of eliminating racism and empowering woman."

The sidewalk is repaired in front of the Fort Piqua Hotel in 1962.

T. Rey Wiley is shown playing the organ at St. James Church in about 1900.

A Pennsylvania Railroad freight train jumped the tracks in 1958 onto Sycamore Street west of South Downing Street.

Index

297

1888 Bird's-eye view of Piqua

MANUFACTURERS.

Bowdle Bros., Founders and Machinists, North end of Downing St.

Bowman & Brendel, Mfrs. of Book Cases and Secretaries, corner of Main and South Streets.

Brendel, C., Furniture, &c., cor. Main and South sts.

Bohlander, Wm. F., Saw Mill and Lumber Dealer, E. of River, S. of Main

Consolidated Tank Line Co., C. D. Healy, Mgr. cor. South & Commercial

Cofield, L., Prop. Kirkwood & Piqua Lime Kilns, W. O. Cofield, Manager 630 South Main street.

Cron, Kills & Co., Mfrs. of Furniture, Second st. E. of the River.

Cron & Son, W. L., Furniture, 321 Main st.

Curtis & Reed, Mfrs. of Carriages, Buggies, &c., S. E. cor. Wayne & Water.

Crozier & Wither, Mfrs. of Carriages, Buggies, &c., Downing St.

Conover's Opera House, W. G. Conover, Prop., S. E. cor. Main & High sts.

City Brewery, Hy Schneider, Prop. S. Spring st.

Clark, J. H., Stone Quarry, South of city on Main st.

Dubois, Reynolds & Co., Dealers in Agricultural Implements and Farm machinery, cor. of Broadway and Water sts.

Emmett, E., Mfr of Cigars and Tobacco, 118 Sycamore st.

Farrington & Co., Distillers, South of city, on Main st.

Farrington, Slawson & Nelson, Shippers of Western Grain, Offices and Warehouses by the Canal on High st. and on Sycamore st.

Fillebrown & Son, Mfrs. of D Shovel handle Machinery, &c. West Water st., next to the Hydraulic Canal.

Holtzermann & Co., J. D Wholesale Wine & Liquor Dealers, cor Main & Water

Kaiser's Brewery, Karl Kaiser, Prop., Ash st., E of the Canal.

Kitts, C. A., Wholesale & Retail Dealer in Pianos & Organs, 413 Caldwell.

Kloeb, Jos. A., Gas Fittings, &c. Mfr. and Patentee of Kloeb's Cook and Heating Burners, 117 Wood st.

Kunta & Fralich, Dealers in all kinds of Lumber, &c. N. E. corner of Commercial and South sts

Kershner, L. N., Saw Mill & Lumber Dealer, 614 N. Main st.

Loog, John, Mfr. of Cigars & Tobacco, 118 N. Main st.

Mercer Gas Light Co., Offices cor Green & Main sts. R. G. Cochran, supt.

Nagleisen, W. F., Mfr of Cigars & Tobacco, 158 N. Main st.

Piqua Straw Board & Paper Co. Mills No. 1 & 2, South end of Main st.

" " " 3, North st. & Washington ave.

Piqua Oat Meal Co., by South Bridge, East of River.

Piqua Planing Mills & Lumber Yards, C. A. & C L. Woods, props ,W. Water

Piqua Gas Light & Coke Co., North end of Spring st

Piqua Broom Factory, G. E. Curtis & Co., props., North Downing st.

Rankin & Co., C. F., Malsters, cor. Downing and Sycamore sts.

Rundle, C. H., prop. & Mfr. of Porters Pain King, 527 N. Main st.

Snyder & Son, Mfr. of Shafts, Poles, Whiffletrees, &c. South end of Main street on the east side.

Schneyers Brewery, J. L. Schneyer, prop, cor. Spring and Water sts.

Schnell, Math Boat Building and Repairing Dry Docks, by South Bridge

The Favorite Stove & Range Co. bet. Young and South sts., E. of Hydraulic

The Piqua Manufacturing Co., Mattresses, Bedding, &c H. S. Sternberger, Prop. West end of Water st.

The Piqua Milling Co. Main st, bet Sycamore and Water sts.

The F. Gray Co., Woolen and Felt Mills, Water st., South end of Spring st.